People on the Edge
in the Horn

People on the Edge in the Horn

Displacement, Land Use & the Environment in the Gedaref Region, Sudan

GAIM KIBREAB
Department of Economic History
Uppsala University

JAMES CURREY
OXFORD

THE RED SEA PRESS, INC.
LAWRENCEVILLE, NJ

James Currey
www.jamescurrey.com
is an imprint of Boydell & Brewer Ltd
PO Box 9, Woodbridge, Suffolk IP12 3DF, UK
and of Boydell & Brewer Inc.
668 Mt Hope Avenue, Rochester, NY 14620, USA
www.boydellandbrewer.com

The Red Sea Press, Inc.
11 D Princess Road
Lawrence, NJ 08648

First published 1996
Transferred to digital printing

A catalogue record is available from the British Library

ISBN 978-0-85255-235-3 (James Currey cased)
ISBN 978-0-85255-233-9 (James Currey paper)

ISBN 978-1-56902-038-8 (The Red Sea Press, Inc. cloth)
ISBN 978-1-56902-039-5 (The Red Sea Press, Inc. paper)

Typeset in 10.5/11 Bembo and Optima display by
Exe Valley Dataset Ltd, Exeter, England

To my mother, my brothers, my sister
& to the memory of my father
for their unfailing guidance and love

Acknowledgements

I am grateful to Jan Wallander and Tom Hedelius' Foundation for Social Science Research (Jan Wallanders och Tom Hedelius' Stiftelse for Samhallsveternskaplig Forskning), Stockholm, and the Faculty of Social Science and Law, Uppsala University, for funding the research project generously.

The debt of gratitude I owe to individuals and groups among the refugee and the Sudanese farmers on and around the Qala en Nahal refugee settlement scheme defy accounting, but I would not have been in a position to write this volume had it not been for their cooperation and willingness to share their wealth of knowledge with me.

I wish to thank Dr Adem Saleh for making his unpublished data on vegetation available and for his help in the collection and processing of the data for Chapter 3. I express my gratitude to Dr M. Gamal Ahmed Younis, Director of the Department of Soil Conservation, Land Use and Water Programming (Khartoum), and his team for their help in the collection and analysis of the data in Chapter 2.

Friends among the refugee communities to whom I feel a special gratitude include Mohamed Berhan Omer, Habte Kesete (Wodi Bashai), Kidane Gebremedhim (Qui'itu), Ramedan Osman, Mehari Awate and Omer Mensur. I have gained enormously from their intimate knowledge of the refugees and the local communities in the study area. I am also grateful to ACORD and their local staff, especially to Hamed Ahmed, El Hadi Abdella, Asim El Haj, Mohamed Said Sufaf and Meriem. A debt of gratitude is also due to the staff of the Commissioner's Office for Refugees (COR), especially to Mohamed Ahmed Abdel Alim, El Tayib, Mohamed Hasen El Tijani and the Agricultural Officer at Umsagata, Nejmedin Abdelrazak.

Bo Gustafsson has, since my undergraduate days, been a source of encouragement and inspiration; special debts of gratitude are due to him. Fatah el Rahman Babikir Ahmed and Abdel Karim Sabir Ali (University of Khartoum) have read Chapters 2 and 3. Borge Petterson (Uppsala University) also read Chapter 3. Without their help I would undoubtedly have fallen into more errors of facts and analysis than I have done. A special debt of gratitude is due to M.A. Abu Sin for his constructive criticism of early drafts of some of the chapters, as well as for his advice and generous hospitality. A debt of gratitude is acknowledged to Sidney Waldron, Robert Walker, Alan Nicol, Tim Allen, JoAnn McGregor, John Markakis and Richard Black for their comments and constructive suggestions. I would like also to thank Kemal Ibrahim Neberay for his invaluable help in processing the data. Thanks are also due to Iyasu Gebre-Sellasse for his generous hospitality and encouragement.

I wish to acknowledge a special gratitude to my forbearing friend and wife, Teblez, who not only put up with my long periods of absence from home, but also took the responsibility of caring for our children with great kindness and good humour in spite of her own demanding profession. I wish also to state that my children, Showhat, Nahom and Reem, had virtually nothing to do with this work. They were hardly understanding when it came to my absence on their birthdays, Christmas and New Year, and, during the little time I had at home, the interruptions which took me away from writing to the pleasures of our family life were countless. I hope it will always remain so.

Contents

Maps
Figures
& Tables

Maps

Figures

Tables

1 Introduction and Overview

The position of a person on the edge can be described as that of a man standing permanently up to the neck in water so that even a ripple might drown him.[1]
(R.H. Tawney, 1966)

Untamed nature drew narrow limits within which people in the Horn devised ways to sustain themselves. Essentially it was a process of adaptation to, rather than of, the environment. (J. Markakis, 1990)

Rationale of the study

In Africa, a large proportion of internally displaced persons or refugees are resettled in transit centres or organized settlements within the countries of origin or reception. Large-scale movements of returnees (former refugees) have also occurred and hundreds of thousands are resettled in their countries of origin. These countries include Sudan, Guinea-Bissau, Angola, Mozambique, Zimbabwe, Zaïre, Uganda, Namibia, Eritrea and Ethiopia. Large-scale mass distress movements within or between countries, whatever their cause, have a tendency to result in heavy concentrations of populations in limited geographical areas such as camps, reception centres, villages and settlements. Destitute people are forced to congregate around emergency relief centres, settlements and watering-points because of poverty or lack of water or because migration from such sites of heavy concentrations is restricted by government decision or ongoing conflict and insecurity. Various African governments have been embarking on large-scale resettlement programmes for nomads, peasants, returnees and refugees during the last decades. Such heavy population concentrations may create heavy pressures on natural resources and may consequently weaken or eliminate the traditional resource-management systems. In the absence of restorative measures, this may lead to land degradation resulting from overcultivation, overgrazing and vegetation destruction for fuel wood and timber consumption required for building houses and fencing. This outcome is not, however, inevitable. Communities usually have their own resource-regulating institutional arrangements designed to keep resource use to a sustainable level unless these institutions are rendered inoperative due to internal and external pressures.

Governments argue that settlement of scattered populations, refugees, victims of natural disasters, nomads and peasants facilitates the provision of basic social services such as health, water, education, veterinary services, emergency relief in adverse seasons, etc. In reality, however, it is generally not concern for the well-being of such communities that prompts most governments to establish settlement schemes, but rather the desire to gain access to resources which were previously controlled by the subsistence producers concerned so that they (the governments) can allocate such resources, mainly land, to alternative economic activities such as commercial agriculture where returns are believed to be higher. Allocation of land formerly

1

utilized by nomadic and small sedentary farming populations to cash–crop and/or commercialized livestock production is considered by many governments as an imperative, dictated by the need of optimal resource allocation. Settlement also facilitates governments' ability to levy taxes and to control refugees, peasants and nomads politically. One important factor which governments do not seem to realize is that nomadic pastoralism, peasant homestead settlement patterns and self-settlement of refugees are not 'random', but are governed by purposeful and well-calculated considerations, taking into account the reality of the local physical environment, particularly the unpredictability and variability of rainfall in both space and time.

The decision of governments to place refugees in camps, reception centres and settlements is determined by a whole range of political, economic and security concerns. In general, the policies of the governments are designed to minimize short-term costs and to maximize short-term gains to themselves and sometimes their citizens (Kibreab, 1990c). The potential long-term environmental impacts are overlooked. Policies concerning the settlement of nomads, peasants, refugees, internally displaced persons and returnees are often characterized by lack of environmental consideration. There is a need to study, therefore, the impact of such population concentrations on the environment and to document the technical, economic and social adaptational changes made by the populations concerned in the process of eking out their living from resources under pressure. While this is essentially a study of a limited area in the Gedaref district of Sudan, most of the points and problems raised and discussed may have relevance to many of the African and other Third World countries affected by the problem of refugees and internally displaced persons.[2]

Objectives of the study

The central objective of this study is to analyse the social causes and consequences of land degradation on the Qala en Nahal refugee settlement scheme and in the surrounding Sudanese villages. The study is divided into two parts. The first part establishes the current level of land degradation in the central rain-lands of Sudan, specifically in the Qala en Nahal area. Land degradation is measured in terms of soil erosion (loss of minerals, organic matter and nutrients) and changes in soil structure, texture and fertility as well as changes in vegetation cover, reductions in palatable and nutritious plant species, increases in unpalatable and non–nutritious species, decreases in perennial grasses and increases in annuals (Abel and Blaikie, 1989).

The aims of the second part are, first, to unravel the economic, political, social, institutional and motivational factors underlying the process of land degradation; second, to assess the consequences of resource degradation on the living conditions of the resource users concerned; and, third, to examine the responses of the resource users to land degradation.

The first part of the study was undertaken to provide a point of departure for the central concern of the research project. The purpose was to establish empirically whether or not there was a real problem of land degradation on and around the scheme resulting from intensive human and livestock interferences. Often, despite apparent physical indicators, there is a degree of uncertainty as to whether there is land degradation caused by human interference.

Even though degradation can be measured in physical and social terms, for a social scientist, whether changes in terms of soil and vegetation deterioration constitute degradation, *inter alia*, depends on the consequences of such changes on the incomes and livelihoods of the resource users concerned. Thus, the changes that have occurred are evaluated socially in terms of decline in crop yields per unit of land, depletion of sources of fuel wood and timber for construction as well as deterioration in grazing and browse resources for livestock. (Trees have also aesthetic values which are not measured in income terms.) Even when the changes result in reduction of crop and biomass productivity, the consequence on the welfare of resource users can be mitigated by opportunities for off-farm income-generating activities, the possibility of bringing new land into the production process, migration, resorting to alternative sources of energy, etc.

Once the problem of land degradation measured in physical and social terms has been established according to the above stated criteria, an attempt is made to explain the cause/s of land degradation. The explanations are sought in the land-use practices such as overcultivation (lack of fallow periods, crop rotation or manure and/or fertilizer application designed to replenish depleted soil nutrients), deforestation manifested in excessive tree felling (for firewood, charcoal, timber and clearance for cultivation), overgrazing resulting from overstocking and shrinkage of previously available grazing areas due to expansion of commercial agricultural production or increased subsistence cultivation and unfavourable physical environment.

After identifying why land degradation has been taking place, an attempt is made to tackle the complex question: why the resource users in question make land-use decisions which deplete the scarce resources or use such resources in a non-sustainable manner, not only undermining their own well-being but also threatening the future of their own offspring. Since the conditions in which subsistence producers eke out their living, among other things, depend on decisions taken by others, including by the state, the explanations are sought both at the local level and in the wider society in which the land users in question live. The study also explores the effects of misguided government land and other policies, lack of secure communal property rights, lack of environmental awareness, high population density, refugee status, poverty and inapplicability of previous traditional resource-management systems.

The next question the study tries to come to grips with is the impact of the environmental changes on the livelihoods of the resource users and their responses (both at a household and at a community level) to the problem of land degradation. How do they respond to land degradation or to the loss of income precipitated by the process of land degradation? Do they become more innovative and more responsive to changes in agricultural techniques? Or do their land-use practices become ever more exploitative of the natural environment, causing further degradation of the available land-resource base?

These are the main areas covered in the study. For a study like this, a historical perspective is indispensable. The ever-changing land-use practices which cause degradation, the traditional natural resource-management regimes designed to halt the processes of land degradation, the institutional rules designed to regulate allocation and use of scarce resources, the enforcement mechanisms and the forces of change that weaken them or render them inoperative, the institutions of property rights (common, state and private), changes in agricultural techniques of production – leading to intensification and disintensification – resource users' responses to population pressures on natural resources or to land shortages, etc. are all easier to understand if conceptualized, described and explained in a historical perspective.

The resource users covered here are Eritreans and Sudanese. The former came to Sudan as refugees about three decades ago. An attempt is therefore made to document the traditional resource-management systems that were operative before they fled to Sudan. The degree of change that has occurred and the causes of the changes are also discussed. A major part of the study also deals with the role of the Sudanese state in the management of natural resources (government land laws, ability of the government to enforce its own laws and the consequences of failure to enforce such laws) and in the disruption of previous resource-management systems.

Methods and data sources

The data for this study were collected between July 1991 and July 1994. The methods used for data gathering, the difficulties encountered and the measures undertaken to overcome the difficulties are discussed in detail in the relevant chapters. Here the diverse sources of the data used are discussed briefly.

Land degradation is caused by natural processes and human interferences; hence an interdisciplinary methodological approach is adopted. In order to document empirically the level of degradation that has occurred as a result of inappropriate land-use practices, soil samples were taken from pits dug on farms with diverse land-use histories varying from 0 to 20 years of continuous cultivation. A vegetation survey was also carried out within and outside the scheme in order to assess the effect of intensive human interference. The interdisciplinary nature of the study necessitated collaboration with people from other disciplines. The tests of the soil samples and the interpretation of the results of the experiments (concerning physical and chemical properties of soils) were carried out in collaboration with a team of soil scientists from the Soil Conservation, Land Use and Water Programming Administration, Khartoum. The team was led by Dr M.G.A. Younis (soil conservationist, Director). The survey of vegetation on sites defined in terms of relative distance ranges from population concentration centres were carried out in collaboration with two consultants – one botanist who specializes in range management[3] and an ecologist.[4] The third research instrument used for data collection was a structured-interview schedule (questionnaire). The interview schedule was administered to 306 randomly selected heads of families, comprising 215 who were refugees in three villages (Umsagata, Salmin and Umbrush) and 91 who were Sudanese heads of families in four villages (Salmin, Dehema, Shangiya and Umsagata) in the surrounding area. Data from the sample family heads were elicited on: resource-base availability; rules governing use of and access to such resources; tenurial rights; the communities' future intentions and how these affect investment of labour and capital in conservation works; customary indigenous technical knowledge and its relevance in the new environment; demography; ethnicity; environmental perception; the methods used to conserve soil, water and vegetation and the effect of resource depletion, including fuel wood, on women, children, division of labour, household budget, patterns of energy (fuel wood) consumption, etc. In order to examine whether refugee status or being a refugee engenders unsustainable land-use practices, Sudanese farmers from the surrounding villages were included in the study as a control group.

One of the major problems faced by social scientists who use survey methods in rural Africa is the lack of a sample frame from which to draw a representative sample. In most cases sample study units (households) are drawn from an unknown population, which may preclude generalization. There are even social scientists who question whether the application in rural developing societies of social research methods and techniques developed and refined in the developed Western world can generate meaningful knowledge, since the social values and conditions of existence are entirely different (Pausewang, 1973; Chambers, 1983).

No such problem existed on the scheme. In this study, since there was a sample frame from which to draw a representative sample, the survey method of data gathering was found to be a useful research instrument because: (i) it was one of the several methods used to gather data; (ii) the respondents were drawn from a sample frame in which all household heads had an equal chance of being included in the sample; (iii) questions in which respondents might have had potential or actual interest in withholding information were avoided; (iv) the interview was conducted by competent interviewers, conversant with the language and culture of the population studied; (v) the researcher understood the language and culture of the population; (vi) the population, instead of being objectified, was involved in an active social interaction in the research process; (vii) qualitative methods were combined with quantitative methods; and (viii) in view of the fact that the survey research method was developed to be used in the industrialized countries, an attempt was made to be sensitive to the specificity of the sociocultural situation of the population studied.

During previous fieldwork in the Qala en Nahal scheme in 1982–1983, the sample family heads were drawn from the records of the Sudan Council of Churches tuberculosis (TB) clinic, where there were detailed data on the population (Kibreab, 1987). The procedures for identifying the sample were arduous and time-consuming. In the present research project, however, since the focus of the study is on natural-resource management and its impact on society and environment, the 10,700 *hawashas* (holdings) within the 107 *meshruas* were used as a sample frame (see Map 1.3). The *meshruas* are numbered and each is divided into 100 *hawashas* (holdings). The sample farms were drawn from the *meshruas* by the use of a random table. The *hawashas* within the selected *meshruas* were listed and numbered and a sample drawn from the list on a simple random basis. The households that cultivated the selected *hawashas* constituted the sample. The selection was made on the basis of the records of the tractor hire service (THS) on the scheme.

The draft of the research instrument was pretested in the settlements before the final interview schedule was developed. The purpose of the pretest was to determine the validity of the approach; to see if the questions were formulated in a way that could be understood by the respondents; to evaluate the performance and competence of the interviewers; to identify redundant questions and gaps in information, etc. After processing the results of the pretest, the final research instrument was developed. A modified research instrument was administered to the randomly selected sample household heads between October 1991 and March 1992. As far as possible the questions relating to fuel-wood consumption were administered to women unless the households were headed by single males. (This was because men did not participate in cooking and had no idea about how much fuel wood was consumed.) Other data sources included the records of the Commissioner's Office for Refugees (COR) in Umsagata, Gedaref and Khartoum and ACORD's records in Umsagata and London. Semistructured open-ended interview schedules were also used for discussions with key informants such as elders, agricultural extension workers, village officers and government officials in Khartoum and in the Eastern Region (Gedaref district).

Primary source materials were also collected from the National Record Office, Khartoum, and various ministries, departments, agencies and corporations which were directly or indirectly involved in the management and/or study of the natural resources in the Eastern Region of Sudan. These included: the Ministry of Agriculture; the Soil Conservation, Land Use and Water Programming Administration; the National Forestry Corporation; the Range and Pasture Administration; the National Committee for Environment; and the National Energy Administration and Mechanized Farming Corporation. Data on the backgrounds of the refugees and their previous resource-management systems were also gathered from the Public Record Office, London, the various codes of customary laws in Eritrea and reports of the British Military Administration in Eritrea.

Background data on the communities' traditional resource-management systems and the changes that have taken place over time were gathered in in-depth interviews with 35 refugee elders and eight Sudanese elders, all systematically selected. The study of land degradation in rural Africa is fraught with considerable methodological, interpretational and source problems due to a lack of historical baseline data against which changes in vegetation and soils resulting from land-use practices could be measured over time. Ibrahim, for example, states that before any 'intervention, it is important to know the level of degradation of both plant and soil which is difficult, because the starting point is merely conjunctural' (Ibrahim, 1984: 25). An attempt has been made to capture the change through building information from scattered sources at village level through interviews with knowledgeable elders and focus groups who had survived the changes both in their country of origin and in their present location.

Data from the archives of the agencies that have been operating on the scheme and from the records of the scheme administration's office have been pieced together to measure quantitatively and qualitatively the changes that have occurred over time. Interviews with Sudanese and refugee elders who have seen and survived the consequences of changes in natural resources, traditional farming systems (indigenous technical knowledge), social control mechanisms, production relations, etc. in their lifetime constituted an important data source.

In this respect, the refugee settlement scheme at Qala en Nahal provides several distinct advantages for the study of the process of land degradation and human adaptation. For example, the size of the populations and their ethnic compositions are known. The area of the scheme is clearly defined in a detailed map (see Map 1.3). All this is easily traceable on the map. The land within the scheme is classified in detail, according to land-forms. The period when the area was inhabited is easy to establish. The history of land use of the mapped *meshruas* can also be established from the records of COR and ACORD. There were also records of tests of comparative tillage and productivity which served as a source of data.

The results of the land-use surveys conducted in 1981 and 1990 were used to see whether or not the population pressure on the scheme had led to expansion of cultivation on to less productive areas formerly used as browse, grazing and wood-fuel sources. This was supplemented with data obtained from interviews with key informants, scheme administration staff and the staff of the non-governmental organizations (NGOs) operating on the scheme.

The reason for using diverse data sources was to compensate partially for the inadequacy of the historical records regarding some of the important issues which would have contributed to the re-creation of the past in order to understand the present. Within the existing source constraints, an attempt has been made to capture the change through building information from scattered sources.

Land degradation defined

Land degradation is caused by a combination of natural and human processes. In the study, the criteria by which physical land degradation will be judged include: soil erosion, change in soil texture, change in soil structure, change in soil fertility, change in vegetation density and composition, such as reduction in palatable plant species and increase in unpalatable plant species, reduction in perennial grasses and increase in annuals and deterioration in forage resources. The term degradation is defined contextually, i.e. on the one hand, in terms of a specific form of use of the land in question and, on the other, in terms of existing management practices and technology in use. In some of the literature, the term land degradation refers to irreversible environmental damage. In the study here, degradation refers to reduction of productive capability under a given land-use practice and management regime without necessarily implying that the damage is irreversible. The term degradation is perceptual (Blaikie and Brookfield, 1987), suggesting the absence of a universally valid definition. It can be defined in various ways depending on the particular use of the resource in question.

For example, a piece of land which could be used sustainably for grazing could be unsustainable if cleared for cultivation. A hunter or a herder may not perceive the replacement of woodland by savanna as degradation because this would enhance the availability of forage resources to wild animals or livestock. To commercial farmers in the clay plains of the Sudan, the destruction of forest resources may not in the short term constitute degradation, while to herders the stripping of the vast tracts of land of vegetation (grasses, forbs, shrubs and trees) for cultivation may indirectly represent degradation of forage resources because of increased grazing, browsing and trampling pressures on the remaining forage resources. In a farm community where advanced technology, such as chemical fertilizers, improved seeds, pesticides and herbicides, are used to maintain and restore soil fertility and to minimize the effects of insects and weeds on productivity, continuous cropping may not lead to degradation of the arable land. However, in a farm community where there is scarcity of land-resource base to allow fallowing, rotational cropping or grazing or where the use of modern productivity-boosting inputs or organic manure is unknown, continuous cropping depletes soil nutrients and thus may contribute to land degradation.

The problem of degradation is inextricably linked with sustainability, and a sustainable land use is one which can continue indefinitely (Warren and Agnew, 1988: 1). Sustainability is determined both by the qualities or properties of the resource in question and by the way it is managed. A resource is sustainable or susceptible to degradation depending on its resilience or sensitivity to degradation. Sensitivity refers to the 'degree to which a given land system undergoes changes due to natural forces, following human interference' (Blaikie and Brookfield, 1987: 10), while resilience refers to the ability of a resource to recover to its previous or similar condition after it has been subjected to conditions that affect its intrinsic properties, e.g. human interference.

The term degradation in this study refers to reduction in the quantitative and qualitative productive capability of the land. 'When land is degraded, it suffers a loss of intrinsic qualities or a decline in capability' (Blaikie and Brookfield, 1987: 6). Here degradation is defined socially, i.e. in relation to the particular use of land at a given time and in a specific space. For the change in physical and chemical properties to result in degradation, there has to be a reduction in the capability of land to satisfy a particular use or need.

As stated earlier, land degradation is caused by natural processes and human interference. The phenomena of natural processes and human interference contribute not only to the impoverishment of the capability of land, but also to its restoration.[5] In view of this, Blaikie and Brookfield make the definition:

Net degradation = (natural degrading processes + human interference) −
(natural reproduction + restorative management)

(Blaikie and Brookfield, 1987: 7)

This definition indicates that, on the one hand, loss of capability is a result of natural processes and human interference and, on the other, restoration of capability is a result of natural processes and human interference in the form of restorative or conservation measures.

For example, the fertility of land that remains fallow may be replenished by natural processes (replenishment of soil nutrients during fallow periods, gullies filled by the formation of new soils and grass growth) and/or human interference such as undertaking conservation measures (crop/grazing rotation, fertilization, manuring, terracing, water harvesting, making contour bunds, stone diversion structures across slopes, tree planting, construction of stone barriers to accumulate debris in gullies, etc.). Thus, degradation occurs when the degree of loss of capability is greater than the rate of regeneration. The two key elements in land degradation are, therefore, as pointed out earlier, the property of the resource and the way it is utilized by humans and/or ruminants.

In the study here, some of the changes that are taken as possible indicators of land degradation are: (i) change in soil texture; (ii) change in soil structure; (iii) change in fertility; (iv) soil erosion; and (v) change in vegetation (trees, shrubs, forbs and grasses) species composition. Whether these changes constitute degradation, among other things, depends on the consequence of these changes on the incomes and livelihoods of the resource users. Thus, the changes that have occurred are evaluated socially in terms of decline in yields per unit of land cropped and depletion of sources of fuel wood and timber for construction as well as deterioration of grazing and browse resources for livestock and their productivity. Even when the changes result in reduction of crop and biomass yields, the consequences for the welfare of resource users cannot be taken for granted. This is due to the existence of some factors which palliate the effects of such changes on their incomes and their livelihoods. These mitigating factors include opportunities for non-farm income-generating activities, availability of employment which can cause rural–rural or rural–urban migration, the possibility of clearing new arable land without detrimentally affecting the available forage resources and finding alternative sources of energy. These opportunities may be available around settlements or in distant places requiring seasonal or permanent migration of humans and livestock. The existence of such opportunities not only offsets the detrimental effects of the changes that occur as a result of physical processes and human interference on the incomes of the resource users in question, but also provides the resources concerned with a temporary respite and hence contributes to restoration of capability.

If there is no opportunity for earning an income from non-farm economic activities, the community in question is unwilling to change the basis of its customary livelihood or there are no alternative sources of energy, even a slight change in the productive capability of the land may have a far-reaching consequence on the welfare of resource users.

The community, its composition and origins

The majority of the refugees in the Qala en Nahal refugee settlement came to Sudan between February and March 1967, as the then Commissioner of Kassala Province put it, to escape 'the looting and destruction caused by Ethiopian army' (quoted in Karadawi, 1977: 98). These were mainly nomadic pastoralists and agropastoralists from the western and eastern lowlands. Until 1991, when the factors that prompted the Eritreans to abandon their homes in search of international protection were eliminated, there were uninterrupted flows of refugees into Kassala Province.

In May 1967, six temporary camps were set up south of Kassala town to accommodate a total of 25,503 refugees (Karadawi, 1977: 100). They were subsequently relocated to the Qala en Nahal refugee settlement scheme. Relocations took place during two periods, namely 1969–1972 and 1978–1979. The first group was relocated in 1969. According to government statistics, the total population on the scheme was estimated at over 40,000 (COR, 1993). About 85% of the scheme population were refugees and the remaining were Sudanese.

The refugees in Qala en Nahal represent a microcosm of Eritrean society in terms of their geographical, ethnic and religious origins. Except a few who originated from the nothern Ethiopian province of Tigray, all the settlers were Eritreans, coming from all parts of the country. Prior to their displacement, even though there were intermittent interactions between the various ethnic groups inhabiting the different geographical regions, each group occupied distinctively defined territory where there was common ownership or usufruct and control of the means of production and common property resources as well as common leadership, culture and a traditional resource-management system. Not only did exile separate the former subsistence producers from their means of livelihoods, but also for the first time it brought together a wide mixture of people with different socio-economic and cultural backgrounds and traditional resource-management systems.

The aims of the settlement scheme were, firstly, to remove the refugees to 'safer' areas in accordance with the stipulations of the Organization of African Unity (OAU) Convention, in which it is stated that countries of asylum should relocate refugees at least 50 km from the border of their country of origin; secondly, to enable the refugees to become self-supporting and consequently ease the burden on the host country and the international donor community; and, thirdly, to avoid ethnic imbalance in the border areas, which the government feared might be the cause of political instability. On the part of the host government, relocation of the self-settled refugees to organized settlements was perceived partly as a means of offsetting the burden on the economic and social infrastructures of the urban areas and partly as a means of shifting the responsibility of catering to the needs of the refugees to the international community. In the government's view, this required the need to place the refugees in spatially segregated sites where their needs could be met by the international donor community until the factors that prompted their flight ceased to exist.

The first settlers that were relocated to the scheme included different ethnic groups. The largest group, about 35% of the total number of the settlers, was the Saho-speaking ethnic group, who originated from the eastern and southeastern parts (Semhar and Akele-Guzai) of Eritrea, but some of whom, prior to their displacement, lived in different parts of the country such as Serae and the western lowlands of Eritrea (Kibreab, 1987, 1995). Even though the Saho had been undergoing dramatic changes in their lifestyles since the 1850s (Nadel, 1946b: 3), until the 1940s the majority were still said to be predominantly nomadic (Longrigg, 1945: Appendix C; Trevaskis, 1960: 15). On the scheme, the Saho-speaking groups were dominant in the villages of Dehema, Adingrar and Umzurzur. They also occupied a separate section of the Umsagata village.

The Beni Amer from the western Eritrean lowlands represented the second largest group among the settlers on the scheme. The Beni Amer were dissected into two by the administrative boundary agreed upon by Italy after it colonized Eritrea and by the Anglo-Egyptian forces subsequent to their reoccupation of Sudan. According to this boundary agreement, two-thirds of the Beni Amer were left in Eritrea and a third in Sudan (Paul, 1950: 226–227). The Beni Amer were predominantly nomadic pastoralists prior to their displacement (Nadel, 1945: 52). They represent about 30% of the settlers in the six villages of the Qala en Nahal refugee settlement scheme (see Table 7.2). They were dominant in the villages of Salmin and Umbrush.

The third largest group is the Maria (12%) from Senhit Province. Prior to their flight, the majority of the Maria lived in the Gash Setit, where pasture and arable land in comparison to their areas of origin were abundant. Most of the Maria migrated to the Gash Setit during the 1930s and 1940s in response to deteriorating environmental conditions in their areas of origin. The Maria are a Tigre-speaking group who were agropastoralists prior to their displacement. On the scheme, they were mainly in Umsagata, Salmin and Umbrush.

The fourth largest group comprised the Nara, who lived in the south-western Eritrean lowlands known as Gash Setit. The Nara had their own language and, unlike their neighbours, the Beni Amer, were settled agriculturalists (Nadel, 1945; Trevaskis, 1960; Kibreab, 1987). The Nara represent about 10% of the total number of settlers in the scheme. The Nara were in Umsagata, Salmin and Umbrush.

The fifth largest group among the refugees were the Bilen (3%) who were predominantly from Senhit in the vicinity of Keren. Prior to their flight, they were settled agriculturalists who derived the bulk of their livelihoods from rain-fed cultivation. On the scheme, the Bilen were mainly concentrated in Dehema, Umsagata and Umbrush.

The second major relocation to the settlement scheme took place between 1978 and 1979 in response to the large influx of refugees that had taken place towards the end of 1974 and throughout 1975, when the struggle for national independence was escalated to an unprecedented scale. New waves of refugee influxes also occurred in 1978 in connection with the withdrawal of the national liberation movements from most of the urban centres throughout the country after the involvement of the former Soviet Union on the side of the Ethiopian military dictators, the Dergue. In 1978–1979, a considerable proportion of the self-settled refugees in Wad Heleu were forcibly relocated to the four villages of Dehema, Adingrar, Umzurzur and Umbrush in Qala en Nahal. Others were relocated to the three wage-earning settlements of Fatah el Rahman, Awad es Sid and Kilo 7 in Es Suki (Kibreab, 1990b). Some of the refugees that were relocated during this period included groups who had strong urban and sedentary backgrounds. Among the total number of settlers, over 20% were former urban dwellers, mainly in western Eritrea, such as Agordat, Barantu, Tessenei, Um Hajer, etc. They included the Tigrinya, Beit Juk, Ad Shuma, etc. (see Table 7.2). Before the arrival of the new settlers (1978–1979), the refugees on the scheme were predominantly former pastoralists originating from the eastern and western lowlands.

These data clearly show that the refugee settlers in the six villages of Qala en Nahal refugee settlement comprised a wide variety of ethnic, language, religious and socio-economic backgrounds. As we shall see later, this diversity produced a series of complications in the management of the resources located within and outside the scheme area. This is because of the fact that traditional resource-management systems are often more effective among socio-economically and culturally homogeneous communities.

This is exacerbated by the fact that the Sudanese villagers on the scheme area are immigrants, mostly coming from the western provinces of the Sudan and from some West African countries, such as Chad, northern Nigeria and Senegal. Not only did these groups lack any form of linguistic or cultural relationship with the refugees, who were relocated to a distant area from the border (about 180 miles south-west of Kassala), but they also lacked any form of commonality of language or culture with each other. Interviews with ninety-one randomly selected heads of households showed that the Sudanese villagers originated from twelve distinct, unrelated, ethnic groups.

Before the Anglo-Egyptian government launched the regional and national programmes of water provision at the end of the 1940s, the area was devoid of any permanent settlements. The absence of permanent water-supply in combination with the presence of biting flies discouraged the nomadic tribesmen from crossing the railway into what is now the scheme area (Barbour, 1961: 194). It was only after the digging of boreholes and excavation of water *hafirs* in the 1940s and 1950s by the Anglo-Egyptian government that the first migrants settled in the area. Since the 1950s, a steady stream of settlers continued arriving into what is now the scheme area. These migrations were induced by deteriorating conditions of living in the sending areas (ILO, 1976: ch. 7) and by the demand for seasonal agricultural labour in the mechanized rain-fed agricultural schemes which were initiated by the Anglo-Egyptian government during the Second World War in the eastern and central regions of the country (Tully, 1983: 17). Another important pulling factor during the 1960s and early 1970s was availability of unoccupied arable land in the southern part of the Gedaref district.

Among the ninety-one randomly selected sample of household heads interviewed in 1991, 13.2, 25.3, 34.00 and 27.5% came to the area in 1950–1960, 1961–1970, 1971–1980 and 1981–1989, respectively. The number of immigrants peaked during the Sahel drought in the 1970s and 1980s. By the end of the 1980s, the land pressure exerted by the refugee settlements and by the expansion of mechanized rain-fed cultivation, led to a decline in the number of Sudanese settlers in the area.

Prior to the establishment of the refugee settlements, the Sudanese villagers used to abandon their villages to migrate to the Rahad River during the dry season in search of water. They lived along the banks of the Rahad until they returned to their villages during the rains. The establishment of the refugee settlements and the subsequent tapping of water from the Rahad River to the settlements and the Sudanese villages throughout the year brought to an end the seasonal migrations of the Sudanese villagers to the Rahad River.

The Qala en Nahal refugee settlement scheme

The Qala en Nahal refugee settlement scheme was established by the government of Sudan in collaboration with the United Nations High Commissioner for Refugees (UNHCR) in 1969 with a view to creating a self-sufficient agricultural population. The scheme is situated in Gedaref district in the Eastern State of Sudan.

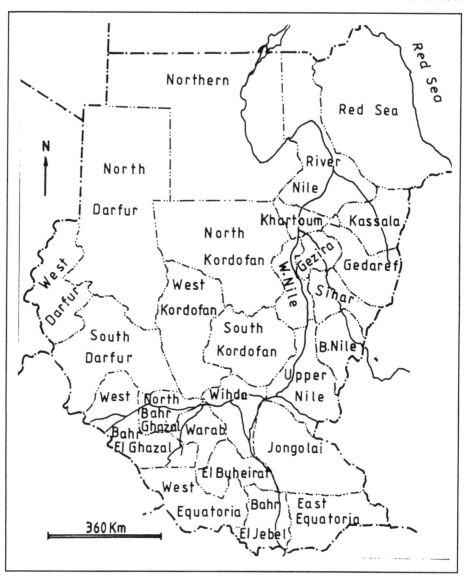

Map 1.1 The new states of Sudan

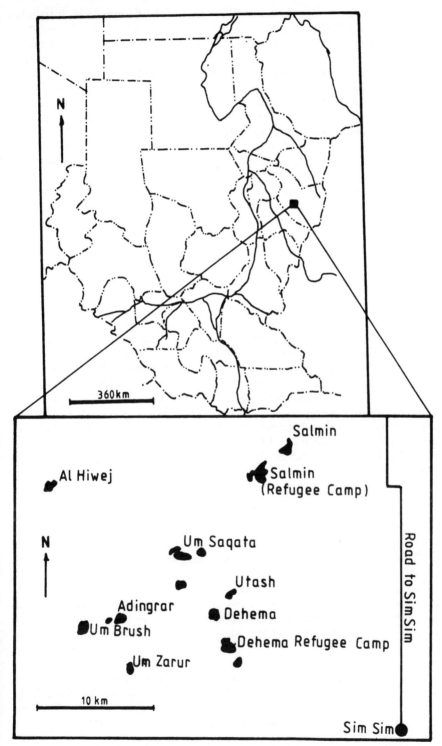

Map 1.2 Location of the Qala en Nahal refugee settlement scheme

The Gedaref district is located in the southern part of the Eastern State. It stretches between 34° and 36°30'E longitudes, and 12°30'N and 14°30'N latitudes (Map 1.1). It lies between the two major tributaries of the Nile, the Rahad and Atbara.

The scheme covers some 480 km² of land (latitude 13°23'N and longitude 34°58'E). It is situated about 30 km south of the town of Qala en Nahal and 80 km south-west of Gedaref (Map 1.2). It lies in the semiarid zone between the dry monsoon to the south and the semidesert climatic zone to the north. Temperatures are high: the monthly mean of daily means varies from 30°C in April to 26°C in January and maximum and minimum daily temperatures of 40 and 17°C occur in April and January, respectively. Rainfall is unimodal occurring mainly between June and early September, and is connected with the northward movemement of the intertropical convergence zone.

Occasional showers occur in May. July and August have the highest monthly rainfall and there is little or no rainfall between October and May (see Tables 4.9 and 4.10). The dates at which the first rains occur can vary by several weeks and sometimes months, not only from season to season but even between short distances in the same season. Total rainfall is also variable. Variability in the distribution of rainfall is, therefore, one of the most critical influences on agricultural production in the area. During the dry period evapotranspiration is high.

The central plain of Sudan where the Qala en Nahal refugee settlement scheme is situated is considered by the country's standards as fertile (Agabawi, 1968, 1969). The dominant physical feature of the area is its clay plain. The clays are alkaline and montmorillonitic. They comprise the major part of the scheme's soil, but are interspersed with a few rocky hills (*jebels*) and pediment areas, which were in the past important sources of pasture, fuel wood and timber. Agriculture is the major economic activity in the area. Sorghum (*Sorghum bicolor*) and sesame (*Sesamum indicum*) are the main crops grown by the farmers on and around the scheme area.

Sudan has been receiving refugees from its neighbouring countries (Uganda, Eritrea, Ethiopia, Chad and Zaïre) since the mid-1960s. The total number of refugees in the whole country is 1,084,031, of which 824,371 are in the Eastern State (COR, 1993). Even though the government's ambition, at policy level, has been to place all refugees in organized settlements (NCAR, 1980), among the 824,371 refugees in the Eastern State of the country only 178,034 are in organized settlements. Among the remaining refugees, 193,337 are in reception centres and 453,000 are self-settled (COR, 1993). There are twenty-nine refugee settlements in the country. Of these, twenty-five (nineteen agricultural, three wage-earning and three semi-urban) are in the Eastern State with a total population of 179,361 (COR, 1993). The six refugee villages in Qala en Nahal settlement (Umsagata, Salmin, Umbrush, Dehema, Adingrar and Umzurzur) are the largest and the oldest of the twenty-nine settlements assisted by UNHCR and by a few NGOs through COR.

Beside the six refugee villages mentioned earlier, there are seven Sudanese villages on the Qala en Nahal refugee settlement scheme. These are Salmin, Dehema, Umsagata, Umbrush, Shangiya and Huweig. There are also other Sudanese villages, such as Bia, Balos and Utash, bordering the scheme (Map 1.3). There are four distinct groups who use the scheme resources. These are, first, the pastoralists, who still exercise their historical rights of passage and grazing during their north–south movements at the beginning and end of every season. Second, the Sudanese Arabs consider themselves as having historical rights to the resources in and off the scheme areas. From the turn of the twentieth century, a large number of Arabs immigrated into Kassala Province – some temporarily, for grazing, which was the great attraction, while others settled more or less permanently (Reports 2/2/5,

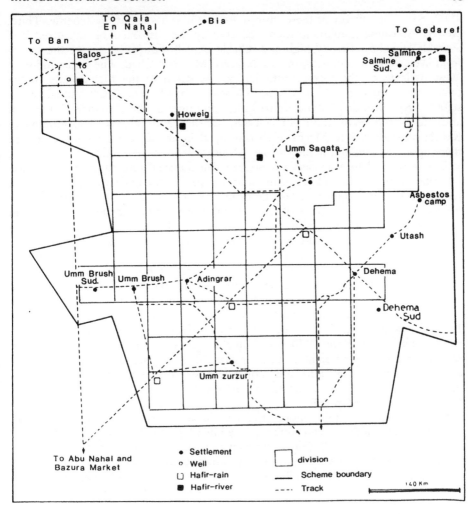

Map 1.3   The Qala en Nahal refugee settlement scheme layout showing divisions into
meshruas *(land blocks) (for explanation see page 5)*

1902: 85). The villages of these groups are in the outskirts of the scheme. Third, western Sudanese immigrants were attracted by the vast tracts of unutilized land available and the relatively high and reliable rainfall. Fourth, there are the Fellata from West African countries, mainly Nigeria, Mali and Chad. The initial influx of West Africans to the Gedaref district can be dated to the first decade of the twentieth century. For example, the Consul General in his 1909 annual report stated, '[A] testimony to the flourishing condition of the province [Kassala] is afforded by the yearly influx of Haussas, Takruris and Fellatas, who coming to Kassala on their way to Mecca often take up their abode in it for good or return there upon completing the pilgrimage' (Reports 2/4/12, 1909: 77).

Even though there is evidence to suggest that the area prior to the Mahdiya was inhabited, many of the villages in the southern part of the district of Gedaref are of recent origin (Mackinnon, 1948; Graham, 1962). The stories recounted by the original Sudanese Arab settlers of the area, the Fellata and the refugees also confirm these facts. Before the establishment of the refugee settlements, not only was the area underpopulated, but it was also unconducive for human and animal habitation during the wet season, being heavily infested with sandflies and mosquitoes. This was because the high vegetation cover provided a favourable habitat for sandflies and mosquitoes (see Chapter 9). The early settlers, including the refugees, saw a strong association between the prevalence of diseases, biting flies and dense vegetation cover.

The scheme is nearly rectangular in shape, measuring about 24 km×20 km (Map 1.3). The land was divided, according to land-demarcation survey maps, which were published in June 1970, into square blocks of land known as *meshrua*, measuring 2 km^2, equivalent to 952.9 *feddans*. The *meshruas* are identified on the ground by 2-metre-high numbered concrete posts situated on the corners of each of the blocks. The *meshruas* are further subdivided into 100 family farming units known as *hawasha* (Map 1.3).

Each refugee household among the first allocatees received 9.5 *feddans* of land. However, many of those who were relocated in 1978 and 1979 only received 5.0 or 2.4 *feddans* (Kibreab, 1987). Since the establishment of the scheme, there has been no land redistribution and young families have been unable to acquire a land-holding. Most of them are landless or are sharing their parents' holdings. Prior to being designated for resettlement, the land was inhabited seasonally by a few families. The land was donated by the government of Sudan without consultation or consent of the local residents, while the basic infrastructure for the settlement – roads, health care, primary education, tractors, etc. – was provided by UNHCR. Cultivation is mechanized (tractorized) while all other agricultural activities are carried out manually. Until 1973, all initial investment and recurrent costs were met by UNHCR and its implementing partner, Sudan's COR. UNHCR's financial involvement was phased out in 1974 and responsibility for the scheme was handed over to the local government at Qala en Nahal town. The running of the scheme proved beyond the financial means of the local government and the scheme nearly collapsed. Consequently UNHCR assumed partial responsibility in 1978 in order to salvage the scheme from collapse.

A few NGOs were involved in delivery of services to the refugees and the local population on the Qala en Nahal scheme. The most important NGOs were the Sudan Council of Churches (mainly involved in health care, education and assistance to vulnerable groups) and ACORD (then Euro Action-Acord), which at the end of the 1970s, implemented small projects at Qala en Nahal. In 1981 ACORD took the responsibility of refurbishing and managing the THS and the workshop at Umsagata by utilizing Overseas Development Administration (ODA)

Plate 1.1   Water supply for the settlements and the surrounding Sudanese villages is provided from a pump station at Abu Nahl and a pipeline about 34 km long is laid between the storage hafirs and the settlements. Water is the most scarce and valuable resource in the refugee settlements. Fetching water is one of the daily tasks of young unmarried women. (Photo: UNHCR/14016/W. Wallace)

funds pledged at the 1980 Khartoum International Conference on Refugees. Since then, ACORD's programmes have diversified to include tractors, workshops, conservation and development of natural resources, forestry and community development (ACORD, 1989a). Most of the components of ACORD's projects are critically discussed in relation to their contribution to conservation or depletion of the natural resources on and around the scheme (see Chapters 11–13).

Initially, the basis of livelihood on the scheme was designed to be crop production and no allowance was made for other economic activities, such as livestock production. However, over time the refugee communities have made their own adjustments and other activities such as livestock rearing, agricultural wage employment and small-scale trading activities have become some of the important diverse income-generating activities on the scheme. Since the mid-1980s, activities such as livestock production and wage labour have been increasing, but crop production still remains the dominant basis of livelihood for the majority of the families. Livestock – cattle, sheep, goats, camels and donkeys – are kept by the refugee and Sudanese farmers on the scheme.

Since the establishment of the scheme, the population has increased drastically. The population increase has not been accompanied by the allocation of additional land. The per capita share of arable and grazing lands has been progressively decreasing over time. The population, which has grown over twofold in the last two decades, is eking out a living from the same resource base which was initially designed for a smaller population. This is because, when the refugee settlement in Qala en Nahal was established in 1969–1971, the government of Sudan saw the problem of the refugees within its territories as a transient phenomenon. It was anticipated that the problem prompting their flight would be resolved within a short time and that refugees would return to their country of origin. The long-term resource-base needs of the refugee communities for arable and grazing lands were not, therefore, taken into account when the settlement was initially planned. Most refugee settlements in Africa are faced with similar problems because host governments perceive the refugee problem as transient (Kibreab, 1989).

The Qala en Nahal refugee settlement provides a unique opportunity to study the effects of confinement because of: (i) the relative availability of baseline data against which to measure some of the environmental changes that have occurred over time; (ii) the heavy population density, one of the heaviest in all planned settlements in Africa; (iii) its location in a semiarid region, where the combined effects of natural and human interference may cause degradation in the absence of countering intervention; (iv) the technology in use – tractors – which is said to contribute to the adoption of inappropriate land-use practices and consequently to land degradation; and (v) its age.

The Qala en Nahal refugee settlement scheme is among the oldest refugee settlements in the world and one of the factors which influences the likelihood of accelerated environmental changes is the length of time over which refugees have been displaced to an area. The scheme also provides an opportunity for critical assessment of the role of international NGOs in building or undermining the resource-management capacities of refugees and their local hosts.

Environment, insecurity and involuntary migration

In recent decades involuntary mass migration has become a common feature over much of sub-Saharan Africa. The reasons that prompt such movements are varied, but they often include interacting causes, such as persecution, international or civil war, economic hardship, environmental degradation, famine, expulsion and forcible resettlement of refugees, nomads and peasants. These movements occur within and between countries. Mass movements between countries have occurred during the last three decades in countries such as Sudan, Somalia, Zambia, Zaïre, Angola, Eritrea, Ethiopia, Burundi, Rwanda, Tanzania, Uganda, Algeria, Cameroon, Chad, Liberia, Sierra Leone, Mozambique, South Africa and Ivory Coast. As of 31 December 1993, the total number of refugees and asylum seekers in need of international protection and/or assistance in Africa was 5,825,000 (US Committee for Refugees, 1994). Another 472,000 had left their countries of origin and were living in refugee-like situations in neighbouring countries without being recognized as refugees or as asylum seekers by the receiving governments (US Committee for Refugees, 1994). The number of displaced persons is growing all the time. Since the first half of 1994, hundreds of thousands of Rwandans have been displaced and killed. The problem of large-scale internal displacement is also widespread in various African countries, such as Sudan, South Africa, Mozambique, Somalia, Ethiopia, Angola, Liberia, Rwanda, Sierra Leone and Zaïre. As of 31 December 1993, there were about 15.7 million internally displaced persons in the continent (US Committee for Refugees, 1994).

Since the mid-1980s, there has been a surge of interest in the role of environmental factors in security issues and forced migration (El-Hinnawi, 1985; Tamondong-Helin and Helin, 1990–1991; RPG, 1992). The major assumption underlying the plethora of recent publications and reports is that environmental changes make conditions in certain areas temporarily or permanently life-threatening or hazardous for human habitation and as a result large population displacements occur. With the staggering rise in the number of people who flee their homelands for a combination of political, economic and environmental reasons, the attempts of analysts to disentangle specific factor/s that generate refugee movements from the multicausality of the crises which provoke such movements has proved methodologically daunting and analytically sterile (Kibreab, 1994a). Instead of acknowledging the multicausality of the crises or the inextricability of the political, economic and environmental factors which generate refugee movements, the tendency has been to confuse relationships, to invert causality and to resort to seductive explanations, introducing worthless concepts which further bewilder the already confused research field. For example, there are those who conceptualize environmental impoverishment as being the major cause of political conflicts (Myers, 1986, 1989; Lazarus, 1990; Molvaer, 1991; Homer-Dixon, 1992) which allegedly provoke population movements, when the available empirical evidence unmistakably points in the opposite direction.

Westing argues, '[S]ince the assaults on the human environment are particularly severe in the Third World, and since the developing countries are ill-equipped to deal with these threats to their sustainable development, it becomes easy to understand why their numbers of environmental refugees keep growing' (Westing, 1992). Some even interpret the large-scale displacement that occured in Ethiopia during the period of the military dictatorship as environment-induced. Myers, among others, argues, '[W]e have already noted the situation in Ethiopia, where some 5 million people are believed to have become displaced since 1970, and at least half a million have crossed into neighbouring countries, many if not most, for reasons of environmental decline' (Myers, 1986: 253). The available evidence shows that it was the scorched-earth policy of the Ethiopian government which led to the breakdown of traditional resource-management systems, strategies for coping with spatial and temporal environmental variabilities and the resilience of the physical environment in the sending areas. Yet most of the literature on environmental and security issues seems to reverse the sequence of cause and effect (e.g. Hjort and Mohamed Ali, 1989). In the Horn of Africa, what we have been witnessing is not environmental change engendering political conflict or insecurity. Rather, the escalating levels of insecurity and conflict have themselves forced people to congregate in safer zones, intensifying degradation of the available local resources, while the unsafe areas remain underutilized.

In these arid and semiarid areas, both small farmers and pastoralists are aware of the constraints inherent in their environments and have developed farming and grazing systems to minimize problems associated with variable soil fertility and low and unpredictable rainfall. The underpinning principle in these farming and grazing systems is mobility, which is manifest in seasonal and permanent migration and is designed to take advantage of environmental variability in different zones during different seasons. The escalating levels of conflict and insecurity have rendered these long-standing traditional resource-management systems inoperative. When the levels of degradation in these safer areas become life-threatening because war has made the insecure areas inaccessible, for some people flight to a neighbouring country becomes the only viable option. To see these involuntary migrations as environment-induced when it is clear that it is insecurity and conflict that are the fundamental causes of confinement and consequently of flight is to mistake correlations for causes. In the Horn of Africa, insecurity and conflict are the ultimate causes of environmental degradation and consequently of involuntary migration, and not vice versa. That is where the recent literature on the so-called environmentally induced conflicts is awry.

The political roots of environmental problems are well documented, especially in areas of drought and famine. For example, Sen's understanding of famine focuses on socio-economic processes which result in a failure of 'exchange entitlements', not on a departure from a climatic norm (Sen, 1981; Dreze and Sen, 1989). There is also evidence to show that famine often occurs in countries affected by war (Duffield, 1991). The causes of the famine of the 1980s that afflicted the Horn of Africa and the large-scale population displacements are well documented and the evidence indisputably shows that war and misguided government policies were at the heart of the problem of livelihood crises which prompted the displacement of hundreds of thousands of people within and outside the countries concerned. This is illustrated by the following evidence.

> Interviews conducted with famine victims from Tigray in eastern Sudan indicate that insects, drought and Ethiopian military policies were the three leading causes of declines in agricultural production. Most of those interviewed stated that armyworms were the main reason for crop failure in 1984–85. Armyworms can destroy a crop overnight, but the long-term stripping of the region's productive assets by the Ethiopian military was no less debilitating. Ninety-five per cent of the famine victims who fled to the Sudan before the end of 1984 reported that in their villages the Ethiopian army had destroyed crops in the fields and grain they had harvested. . . The army routinely attacks during planting and harvesting; attacks that delay planting increase the destruction by insect and weed pests. (Clay and Holcombe, 1985)

In a different study, Clay et al. also found a clear correlation between the famine-affected areas in 1987–1988 and specific government policies in the different regions of Ethiopia (Clay, Steingraber and Niggli, 1988).

Among the consequences of the large-scale displacements that occurred in the 1980s were not only the failure to appreciate the multicausality of the crises that engendered refugee movements and the intricacies of the interrelationships between causes and effects (e.g. between conflict and environmental change as well as between environment and forced migration), but also the introduction of new but ill-defined and vague concepts such as 'environmental refugees' (Kibreab, 1994a). The term 'environmental refugee' was used for the first time in 1984 in an Earthscan document, which stated: '[T]hird World environmental refugees are increasingly fleeing worn out lands for the industrialized countries in the North' (cited in Kibreab, 1994a). In 1985, El-Hinnawi defined 'environmental refugees' as referring to 'those people who have been forced to leave their traditional habitat, temporarily or permanently, because of marked environmental disruption (natural and/or triggered by people) that jeopardized their existence and/or seriously affected the quality of their life' (El-Hinnawi, 1985). The concept was further popularized in various publications and since then has become a catch-all (Myers, 1986; Jacobson, 1988; Lazarus, 1990; Islam, 1991; Westing, 1992).

It is worth noting that the introduction of the concept into the study of forced migration serves no other purpose than to confuse and misinterpret the inter-relations between environment and forced migration (McGregor, 1993; Kibreab, 1994a). This is because the concept lacks legal and conceptual foundation. It is important to state, however, that, even though most of the available literature on the relationship between refugee migration and environmental change is characterized by lack of methodological vigour and analytical clarity, there has been an increasing academic interest in the issue in the past few years. However, the issue of environmental impacts of refugee flows to host countries has been neglected almost entirely by academics.

Environmental impacts of refugees

Until recently, the issue of the environmental impact of refugee camps, reception centres and settlements was neglected by UNHCR and other refugee-orientated international organizations. UNHCR's refugee assistance programmes have been devoid of environmental considerations. It was only after the General Assembly passed resolution 44/228 in September 1989 to hold a conference in Brazil on environment and development that UNHCR for the first time devoted a pamphlet to the question of the environmental impact of refugee flows to poor Third World countries (UNHCR, 1991). In May 1992, one month before the United Nations Conference on Environment and Development (UNCED) held at Rio, UNHCR devoted part of its monthly magazine, *Refugees*, to the examination of environ-mental considerations and to presentation of a few conservation projects in refugee-affected areas (UNHCR, 1992a). The absence of concern with environmental conservation matters in their assistance programmes was admitted by the UNHCR: '[I]n emergency situations, the immediate focus of relief agencies always has been the urgent needs for food, water and shelter. As long as there were bushes within sight, no one ever asked where starving refugees would get the three tons of firewood needed to cook each ton of wheat and beans supplied by humanitarian agencies' (UNHCR, 1992b: 5). It has to be pointed out, however, that it is not only in emergency situations that UNHCR and other agencies failed to ask themselves where refugees would get the firewood needed for cooking and warming their houses as well as the timber to construct their houses, but even post-emergency situations have been devoid of any environmental considerations. Between 1962 and 1987, over 155 refugee settlements have been established in

Africa and in no single case did environmental-impact assessment precede the establishment of such settlements. In the aftermath of the Rio summit, i.e. 35 years after provision of assistance to African refugees began, UNHCR have, at least in theory, begun to see the importance of environmental conservation and they have consequently decided to take into account environmental considerations in the planning of assistance programmes for refugees. They have also appointed a senior environmental coordinator at their headquarters (Black, 1993).

In the past few years, it is not only UNHCR which has become vocal about environmental impacts of refugee camps and settlements and about the need to undertake measures to alleviate the damage, but other agencies such as the World Food Programme (WFP, 1992), the German Agency for Technical Cooperation (GTZ) and the International Federation of Red Cross and Red Crescent Societies. All these agencies have advocated the need for increased attention to be given to environmental impacts in refugee-affected areas (von Buchwald, 1992). The European Economic Community (EEC) also provides funds to mitigate refugees' negative environmental impact on areas of resettlement through development-funding arrangements with African, Caribbean and Pacific countries (art. 204 of Lome III and art. 255 of Lome IV). According to Lome IV, which came into force in 1991, environmental impacts should be considered before rather than after the approval of development projects. In the aftermath of the Rio Summit on the Environment and Development (June 1992), most agencies have suddenly discovered the importance of the environment and are promising to include environmental conservation as an important element in their agenda. There is no doubt that this shift represents a positive step forward, but it remains to be seen how much it reflects the environmental euphoria generated by the Rio Summit and how much it is a genuine pledge translatable into concrete action. These statements cannot be taken for granted. For example, in the immediate post International Conference on Assistance to African Refugees (ICARA) II period, the international donor community, including the UNHCR, was seized with a development euphoria, but a decade later the phrase 'refugee aid and development' has almost fallen into oblivion.

It is worth noting, however, that not only were UNHCR's and other agencies' agendas characterized by lack of environmental consideration, but research on refugee studies has also hitherto been environment-blind. A review of the literature on the impact of refugees on national, regional and local levels reveals that the environment has been either totally neglected or has been touched upon in passing, not only in government settlement policies and international assistance pro-grammes, but also in scientific research. The available literature, however, abounds with a myriad of impressionistic and unsubstantiated assumptions, such as 'refugees damage the environment in the countries of reception' (Report of Meeting of Experts, 1983; UN, 1983, 1984a,b; ICVA/UNHCR, 1985). This can be illustrated by the following example.

> UNHCR and other agencies are becoming increasingly concerned about the negative environmental impacts of large influxes of refugees and displaced persons. UNHCR estimates that refugees . . . have deforested about 36,000 ha to meet basic shelter needs. In addition, refugees consume an estimated 13 million metric tons of fuelwood annually for settlements worldwide . . . Asylum and host countries, particularly those in degraded or fragile areas, cannot continue to bear these ecological costs. Some countries already refuse to accept refugees and displaced people, fearing negative environmental and social impacts. (Lind and Peniston, 1991)

If the source of such gross generalization is the UNHCR, this may backfire and undermine their own future efforts in promoting protection because host countries may respond to these alarming statements by closing their doors to asylum seekers for fear of damage to their environment. The World Food Programme also describes the impacts refugees have on the environment as 'staggering' and based on government estimates they state that the refugees in Pakistan 'consume 2.8 million tons of firewood each month' and in Malawi 'about 680,000 cubic metres of forest' is cleared every year, which amounts 'to clear cutting 28.7 hectares of natural forest land every day' (WFP, 1992). According to Helin, UNHCR estimates the total fuel-wood consumption by the 15 million world refugees at 13 million m^3 per annum (Helin, 1990). On the impact of refugees on the environment in western Ethiopia, Fikre Mariam honestly states: '[I] must confess that much of what I try to show in this paper is not backed by quantitative data,' but nevertheless goes on to give quantitative data based on inductive assumptions (Fikre Mariam, 1991).

These generalizations are not based on empirical studies and hence not only is their validity questionable, but they may also prove detrimental to the refugees' cause. The major flaws of these generalizations are, first, that they equate the area of deforested land with the amount of fuel wood consumed with no regard taken of the ability of the coppiced trees to regenerate. Sometimes the rate of regeneration of coppiced trees can be higher than that of non-coppiced ones. Second, the total amount of fuel wood consumed by the world refugee population and hence the area deforested is derived from per capita fuel-wood requirements of refugees on a global scale. The per capita fuel-wood requirements of refugees cannot be generalized because requirements vary with climate, the types of food consumed and the way the fire is managed. Actual amounts of fuel wood consumed are seldom equivalent to the theoretical amounts required. Calculations which equate actual fuel-wood consumption with fuel-wood requirements are wrong because they imply that refugees' fuel-wood needs are fully met when available evidence suggests that, in many countries, refugees are faced with severe shortages.

Many refugee camps, reception centres and settlements are located in areas almost completely devoid of vegetation so refugees cannot have a negative impact on non-existent resources. For example, most of the Afghan refugees in Pakistan were resettled in the North-West Frontier Province, where 'there is very little cultivated land, forest, or pasture . . . these camps have virtually no impact on the environment' (Allan, 1987: 202). But negative environmental impacts did occur in situations where refugee officials placed camps in prime forest areas (Allan, 1987: 202). In eastern Sudan the wage-earning settlements and some of the camps and settlements, such as Wad Sherifey, Kashm el Girba, Kilo 26, Fatah el Rahman and Kilo 7, are located in areas completely devoid of vegetation. The refugees purchase fuel wood brought from distant places to the local market. Some of the refugee camps in Hararghe province, Ethiopia, are also located in areas where there is no vegetation. In such situations, it does not make sense to talk about negative impacts of refugees on vegetation resources.

A third flaw in the generalizations is that deforestation in refugee-affected areas is often attributed to refugees, disregarding the degrading forces that might have been operative long before the arrival of refugees. In Somalia, even though there was evidence of environmental degradation, reflected in depleted vegetation resources, caused by the need of the refugees for fuel wood and construction materials around the refugee camps (Young, 1985; Kibreab, 1990a), '[m]an's role in transforming the environment through the process of overstocking the range lands and the deforestation of large tracts of territory were in operation long before the burden of hundreds of thousands of refugees descended on Somalia' (Young, 1985: 123). In Pakistan, contrary to the widely held view, the severe deforestation on the southern slopes of the Hindu Raj and western Himalaya is not attributable to the arrival of the refugees. The degrading social forces were at play long before their arrival. The confusion with regard to land rights created by the arrival of the refugees also provided favourable conditions for local Pakistanis to overexploit the pasture and forest resources in the refugee-affected regions (Allan, 1987: 202). Fourth, no distinction is made in the available literature between the consumption of live and dead-wood, although it is common knowledge that harvesting dead-wood does not have a negative impact on forest stock or productivity. Dead-wood is preferred to live trees by rural communities, including refugees, because the former is easier to harvest, lighter to carry and readily usable.

Therefore, the extent of deforestation on and around refugee camps and settlements cannot be extrapolated from total amounts of fuel wood consumed by refugees unless it can be shown that the fuel wood consumed comprised live trees and that the rate of regeneration of the coppiced trees is zero. When there is heavy human and animal pressure on vegetation resources, the rate of regeneration may not match the offtake rate, but, unless it can be shown that the extent of the damage caused to the environment is irreversible, derivations of deforested areas from consumption figures are misleading and provide an exaggerated picture. Not only do the available data err in method, but some of them border on sheer stereotype. Von Buchwald from the International Federation of the Red Cross and Red Crescent Societies, Geneva, for example, stated:

> [U]sually, neighbouring host countries are already facing . . . additional environmental degradation. The new arrivals, moreover, lack the resources to contribute to a sustainable use of the environment. At the same time the threat of environmental deterioration raises the potential for conflict with the affected population. In the worst event, an environmentally provoked extinction of survival means can lead to wars, vandalism, violent expulsions and a breakdown of order. (von Buchwald, 1992)

Not only do such generalizations lack empirical base and consequently have little to do with the reality prevailing in most refugee-hosting Third World countries, but wherever there have been incidents of violence and vandalism against refugee communities they have occurred in Western Europe where the presence of refugees is not remotely linked to the environmental decay suffered by these societies.[6] Unfortunately, this assumption of environmental damage associated with hosting refugees in the Third World countries is reported consistently; as a result, the fiction has through repetition become the 'truth' and it may be only a question of time before some host countries become influenced by such inaccuracies and decide to pursue restrictive refugee policies. There are already two countries who have refused to accept refugees on these grounds (Ferris, 1993). The recent growth in concern for environmental problems associated with hosting large number of refugees is a welcome development. However, this concern has not been accompanied by a proper understanding of the complexities of the issues involved.

Whether refugees contribute to environmental degradation or not is an empirical question. The danger of alarming generalizations which lack empirical support is that environmental damage which has other causes may conveniently be blamed on refugees and an opportunity to prescribe appropriate measures to alleviate the alleged damage may be missed. Wrong diagnoses more often than not lead to wrong prescriptions and as a result both the environment and refugees may continue to suffer – the former due to misdirected 'corrective measures' which may be undertaken without understanding the real cause of the problem and the latter due to xenophobic attitudes of governments and local populations because of the belief that refugees are the cause of environmental degradation suffered by the host countries.

This is not to deny that, under some circumstances, hosting refugees may constitute a burden on the environment, but one needs to go beyond appearances and correlations and establish the real causes of environmental degradation in refugee-affected regions. The factors that induce inappropriate land-use practices at the local level, including in refugee camps, reception centres and settlements, are sometimes the result of misguided government settlement and agricultural policies as well as ill-conceived assistance programmes over which refugees and local people have no control.

The available literature on the question of the environmental impact of refugees is based on impressionistic and visual evidence and is invariably presented along the following predictable lines: 'the environs of refugee camps and settlements are stripped of trees, bushes, grasses and deadwood reflected in the formation of concentric circles of bare land' (UNHCR, 1992b; see also Young, 1985; Allan, 1987; Long et al., 1990; WFP, 1992). The factors that induce such unsustainable resource use are rarely unearthed. The central question which is overlooked in the literature is whether non-displaced populations (nationals) forced to operate under similar circumstances, i.e. inadequate resource base and high population density with severe restriction on freedom of movement and residence, which creates a condition of confinement, behave differently from refugees. As long as this cannot be established empirically, there is little or nothing which suggests that refugee status and not the conditions under which they eke out their living is a factor which induces unsustainable resource use.

The conditions under which refugees eke out their living are invariably defined by authorities and organizations outside refugee communities. One of the major theoretical issues addressed in this study is the question of whether there is anything in refugee status or in being a refugee which engenders a predisposition to adopt ravenous or unsustainable land-use practices. If this cannot be established, the explanations for the 'concentric circles around refugee camps and settlements' have to be sought, in the deprivations and powerlessness attending refugee status, which are results of misguided host government/s' settlement policies and ill-conceived international assistance programmes which invariably tend to exclude refugee communities from the processes of designing, planning and implementing such programmes. If there is a relationship between refugee status (being a refugee) and adoption of land-use practices which lead to degradation of the environment, there is a need to unravel the changes that refugees undergo as a result of involuntary displacement and the conditions under which they are settled, which may, on the one hand, predispose them to adopt unsustainable land-use practices and, on the other, prevent them from taking environmental-conservation measures to replenish the resources on which their well-being depends.

This is not achievable through generalizations, as is the case at present, but through careful case-studies which draw methodological insights from both the natural and the social sciences. As Black in a review of the literature observes,

> [A]lthough the studies mentioned above provide an indication of concern for environmental degradation in refugee-affected areas, relatively little quantitative evidence exists either of the scale of environmental degradation in such areas, or whether such degradation that has been identified is of a long-term nature. In addition, it is difficult at present to link directly the presence of refugees in an area with long-term environmental change. (Black, 1993: 7)

In the literature, environmental degradation is measured in terms of deforestation. The question of how this affects the productive capability of the resource base and consequently the livelihoods of the people concerned is rarely mentioned when in fact these issues should constitute the *raison d'être* of any meaningful environmental assessment. As long as it cannot be shown that the reduction in density of forest stock has resulted in diminished productive capability of the resources in question (arable land, forest, pasture, water, etc.), affecting the livelihood of people and animals in a detrimental way, deforestation may not necessarily constitute environmental degradation. The reason why environmental degradation is measured solely in terms of deforestation in refugee-affected areas to the complete neglect of the other measures of degradation, such as soil erosion, changes in soil structure, texture and fertility, reduction in palatable and nutritious plant species and reduction in perennial grasses and increase in unpalatable and non-nutritious ones as well as increase in annuals is because the other measures of degradation are more difficult to establish and require more sophisticated methodology than visual observation.

Thus, case-studies or comparative studies are lacking to enable host governments and aid agencies to understand the degree of damage and the causes underlying the damage as well as to assess the consequences of such damage on local communities and on the ecological sustainability of the areas concerned. Such knowledge is indispensable for planning and undertaking degradation-countering and restorative measures. Similarly, little or no attention has been devoted to how refugee communities and their poor hosts in the affected areas cope with environmental stress. In light of this paucity of data, the question of potential environmental impacts of refugee flows and refugee settlement schemes should constitute an important element in the research agenda. Some useful insights could also be drawn from such studies which may have an implication for the formulation of policies on resettlement of internally displaced populations and others. The environmental impacts of refugee camps, reception centres and settlements are potentially considerable, but, as pointed out earlier, this is an empirical question.

Demographic consequences of environmental change

Generally, the causes of environmental degradation in Third World countries are varied, but the bulk of the literature attributes it to high population density. A negative relationship between demographic pressure and the environment was hypothesized as early as the end of the eighteenth century by Malthus, who stated that the potential increase in food supply could not keep pace with that of population and theorized that, if humans did not exercise preventive checks (moral restraint and responsible attitudes to marriage), population growth would be brought to a halt by welfare checks (poverty, disease, famine and war) (Malthus, 1798). The reverse was postulated by Boserup who considered population pressure to be an essential precondition for technological innovation in agricultural production (Boserup, 1965, 1981). The risk of collapse in livelihood resulting from diminishing agricultural returns in a situation of rising population densities can provide an opportunity for change and progress rather than a threat to subsistence. As we shall see below, it is this principle which underpins the Boserupian theory of agricultural intensification.

Even though the recent debate on the relationship between demographic pressures and the environment has been to some extent coloured by the two lines of thinking (Malthusian and Boserupian), neither Malthus nor Boserup was concerned with the environment *per se* except as a resource base for agricultural livelihoods. The debate on the relationship between population growth and resource degradation is one of the most sustained controversies in the social sciences. Even though the subject has received substantial attention in the various social science disciplines, not many have succeeded in showing a direct causal relationship between rates of growth of population and environmental degradation (Kibreab, 1994a). Indeed, there is a growing body of literature which argues that it is an indirect relationship mediated by culture, social institutions and broader political and economic processes. Yet an inverse relationship between natural-resource depletion and population pressure is often taken for granted. It is assumed that the cause of the environmental degradation experienced by many countries in the developing world is the high rate of population growth, which is presumed to place a heavy demand on the natural environment (Hardin, 1968; Prothero, 1972; Curry-Lindahl, 1974; Eckholm, 1975b). In the mainstream literature, it is argued that, as the per capita area of arable and grazing lands shrinks under the pressure of growing population, the sheer necessity of making ends meet forces farmers and pastoralists to use land in total disregard of long-term consequence (Curry-Lindahl, 1974). McNamara, for example, states that arable land per capita in sub-Saharan Africa declined from 0.5 ha in 1965 to 0.3 ha in 1987 (McNamara, 1990: 36). The consequence of this has been a reduction in the productive capacity of the land due to the pressure of growing numbers of people who 'do not have the wherewithal to put back into the land what they are forced to take from it' (McNamara, 1990: 36). Eckholm also argues, '[W]hatever the root causes of suicidal land treatment and rapid population growth . . . in nearly every instance the rise in human numbers is the immediate catalyst of deteriorating food-production systems' (Eckholm, 1976: 18). Sadik also states: '[I]increasing human demands are damaging the natural resource base' (Sadik cited in Shaw, 1989: 199). The implication of these assumptions is that there would be no serious problem of natural resource depletion if the rate of population growth were not as high as it is at present.

The empirical studies that have been carried out in different parts of the Third World in recent years, however, show that population pressure *per se* does not under all circumstances cause natural-resource depletion (Blaikie and Brookfield, 1987; Vivian, 1991; Tiffen *et al.*, 1994). It is often in the presence of other underlying or ultimate factors that population pressure contributes to natural-resource depletion. Some argue that most of the underlying factors of environmental degradation are not directly related to population growth. Commoner, among many others, states, '[E]nvironmental impact is not correlated with the rate of population growth. The theory that environmental degradation is largely due to population growth is not supported by the data' (Commoner cited in Shaw, 1989: 199). In his view, environmental quality is largely governed, not by population growth, but by the nature of the technologies of production. His findings show that the major causes of environmental degradation are polluting technologies, affluent consumption and wastes.

However, Harrison argues that Commoner's findings underestimate the role of population growth on environmental degradation. He states that, during earlier stages of development, population growth is the sole cause of deforestation (Harrison, 1990: 14). The implication of this is that pollutants do not cause environmental degradation in preindustrial societies. In his view, in such societies environmental problems are not caused by pollution or by adding something hazardous to the environment, but rather by 'taking something away: deforestation;

loss of species; soil erosion; loss of land to urbanization' (Harrison, 1990: 17). These four causes of environmental degradation, he argues, are directly related to rapid population growth. He takes the example of a rapidly growing population where shifting cultivation is the major agricultural technique in use. When population increases, new land is cleared for cultivation. This causes deforestation, with the result of loss of plant species (biological diversity) and soil erosion due to loss of vegetation cover and reduction of organic content of soil (Harrison, 1990: 17). Harrison admits that in the 1980s commercial logging increased as a result of increased indebtedness and the need to repay or service such debts, but in his view 'only conversion to farmland, pasture, transport and settlements can cause permanent deforestation' (Harrison, 1990: 20). The major culprit responsible for the environmental problem in the developing world, according to this view, is population growth and the consequent increased subsistence demand on the natural environment.

The literature abounds with contradictory statements. Harrison's findings are contradicted by many others. Hurtado, for example, argues that in countries such as Costa Rica and Paraguay[7] deforestation is not caused by increased susbsistence demand, but by clearance of forests for 'cattle-ranching and commercial agriculture', which have nothing to do with population growth (Hurtado, 1991: 20). According to Bilsborrow and Geores, the deforestation or clearance of land in Brazil has little to do with population factors. In fact, in the 1970s there was a great increase in 'new agricultural land but an actual decline in the rural population' (Bilsborrow and Geores cited in Hurtado, 1991: 20).

Shaw argues that it is important to distinguish between ultimate and proximate causes of natural resource depletion. He considers rapid population growth as a proximate and not an ultimate cause of resource depletion (Shaw, 1989). The implication of this distinction is that tackling the problem of rapid population growth alone would not be effective unless 'implemented jointly with measures to tackle more ultimate "deeper" causes' (Shaw, 1989). Of the major causes of global environmental degradation, Shaw identifies the following factors, ranked in order of importance. He attributes more than three-quarters of global environmental degradation to polluting technologies, affluent consumption and related wastes. Distortionary government policies, poverty and humanity's warfare account equally for almost the remaining quarter of the global environmental degradation. Only a very small fraction is ascribed to rapid population growth (Shaw, 1989: 203). Barraclough and Ghimire also reject the hypothesis that natural-resource depletion is caused by poverty and rapid population growth as 'facile' and 'tautological' (Barraclough and Ghimire, 1990: 13). There are also others who see no relationship between population growth and environmental degradation. Hurtado, for example, argues that regions like Latin America and the Caribbean are facing unprecedented problems of environmental decline at a time when there is a demographic transition towards lower fertility rates. 'In the 1960s, the continental average was six children per woman; now it is a little over three' (Hurtado, 1991: 19).

Under some circumstances, other writers argue, high population density, instead of being a cause of land degradation, can represent an important resource for construction and the maintenance of conservation works. In this view, a decline in population density due to out-migration, decrease in fertility,[8] increase in mortality or any other reason would result in resource degradation (Lockwood, 1991: Vivian, 1991). A deterioration in the maintenance of terraces in hill systems of cultivation, leading to soil erosion, may be caused by reduced population densities (Mortimore, 1989). Tree planting, which can be essential for maintaining the fertility of the soil and countering erosion, is labour-intensive and lower population densities could mean lower tree densities or vice versa (Mortimore *et al.* referred to in Lockwood, 1991). In the densely populated area of Jebel (Mount) Mara in Sudan, carefully managed agroforestry systems have been a part of the traditional resource-management regimes in the region and have contributed to sustainable land-use practices for centuries (Meihe, 1989). In recent years the area has suffered loss of population due to out-migration and this has substantially affected the traditional resource-management system, reflected among other things in a decline of tree cover. The existing mature trees were planted 60 years ago, suggesting loss not only of trees but also of an important indigenous skill (Vivian, 1991: 12). An interesting example of a situation where high population density has represented an indispensable resource for conservation and maintenance is in Nepal. Population densities reach up to 1,500 per km^2 of cultivated land and the country is highly mountainous. In the middle range of hills, all arable land is terraced. High population density (to ensure labour supply) and the skill of the Nepalese farmers, acquired over time through processes of trial and error, are the two key factors in the viable traditional environmental-management systems (Caplan, 1970; Bajracharya, 1983).

The complex farming systems on the Eritrean plateau were developed during the last centuries to accommodate a growing population in limited areas of arable land and in a highly varied environment. These farming systems incorporated diverse conservation methods that were carried from generation to generation. Most of these methods were labour-intensive. Even though the impact of warfare on the natural environment remains unquantified, interviews with farmers suggest that thetraditional environmental-management systems have suffered a great deal during the 30 years of war because of the withdrawal of labour. A considerable proportion of the Eritrean peasants left their farms to participate in the war of national liberation; others were either forced to flee the country in search of safety or were forcibly recruited into the Ethiopian army or the 'people's militia'. The remaining peasants were unable to maintain and repair the conservation structures because of conflicting demands for their labour time and the military conflict, which disrupted the fabric of rural social, economic and political life.

This brief review of the literature shows that the inverse causal relationship between population growth and environmental degradation cannot be taken for granted. The problem is an empirical one and the impact of population pressures on resources varies from one situation to another depending on the level of agricultural development of the society in question and the existence of opportunities for earning non-agricultural income to offset the burden of population pressure on resources other than by resource overuse. To illustrate this, the population-based theory of agricultural change will be discussed.

Population-based theory of agricultural change

Boserup, reversing Malthusian and neo-Malthusian hypotheses, argues that, when production cannot be increased by extending cultivation into new areas, population growth in peasant societies has historically led to an intensification of production by making more productive use of underemployed labour, by introducing new crops, fertilizers or leguminous fodder crops on a crop rotation scheme and by intensifying production in other ways (Boserup, 1965, 1981). Geertz's principle of 'agricultural involution' is also based on the intensification of labour inputs to increase production from the same arable plot (Geertz, 1963). When population pressure causes land shortage, Boserup states, 'to preserve the land's "carrying capacity" the society may then switch over to a new technique that can offer the possibility of maintaining or improving the quality of land to be cultivated despite the general reduction in fallow time' (Boserup cited in Darity, 1980: 138).

Boserup not only rejects indirectly the inverse relationship between population growth and environmental degradation, but also sees population pressure as the major cause of change in land-use practices (intensification), farm technology and land tenure systems. She sees population pressure in preindustrial societies as a vehicle to progress and development (Boserup, 1965, 1975). The thrust of her thesis is that population pressure intensifies land use, in contrast to the arguments of the classical economists, Malthus and Ricardo, who argued that environmental constraints (climate and soil conditions) placed an upper 'threshold level' on population growth. She treats population growth as an independent variable and agricultural technology as a dependent variable (Boserup, 1965: 11–12). Unlike the classical economists, who argued that population growth was a result of increased agricultural output, she argues that population growth is independent of food supply. The concept of intensification occupies a central position in her model. However, the meaning of intensification she uses is different from that of the classical economists. In the Boserupian sense intensification refers to the frequency with which the available land is cropped, while for the classical economists intensification meant increased application of capital and labour per unit of cropped land. There are also contemporary researchers for whom intensification implies nothing but greater input of labour, capital and skill (Brookfield, 1972: 31).

Although widely commented on, there have been only a few empirical tests of Boserup's theory. Some findings, however, tally with the fundamental principles of her theoretical construct. For example, Gleave and White in their study of the relationship between population density and agricultural systems in West Africa have, independently of Boserup's theory, arrived at almost identical conclusions (Gleave and White, 1969: 297). Their findings show that intensive land-use practices reflected in the reduction in length of fallow period, institutional changes reflected in the emergence of a land market in previously communally owned land and the restructuring of crops sown and manure applications were more evident in the areas where there were higher population densities (Gleave and White, 1969: 284). The authors state, '[T]here is evidence to suggest a connection between population density and agricultural practice, and that the practice becomes modified as density changes' (Gleave and White, 1969: 275). In India, a study on the relationship between population density and agricultural growth based on interregional variations shows a positive correlation between the two variables (Krishnaji and Satya Sekhar, 1991: A-65).

In northern Zambia, where the *chitemene*[9] shifting cultivation is practised, population pressure on the land has led to intensification, which is reflected in a reduction in the length of the fallow period from 25 years to 12 years (Chidumayo, 1987). This land use, being wood-dependent, has caused deforestation, but the farmers have not yet developed alternative and less wood-dependent agricultural practices (Chidumayo, 1987). Even though the necessity to make ends meet has led to shorter fallow periods and increased labour expended on cutting and transporting wood from 'outfields' to be piled and burnt in the garden where crops are grown, population pressure has not induced the farmers to innovate. Why farmers fail to innovate, despite the threat *chitemene* shifting cultivation poses to the long-term sustainability of the agricultural system, can be explained by looking at the variables disregarded by Boserup, namely the constraints posed by the physical environment and, in particular, soil types and climatic conditions. The *chitemene* land-use practice was developed in response to the 'inherently infertile, leached and acid soils of northern Zambia' (Chidumayo, 1987: 18). The farmers who might have succeeded in innovating the sophisticated system of *chitemene* land use would probably have devised a land-use practice that does not undermine the sustainability of their farming system, but the constraint posed by the physical environment seems to have been overwhelming.

The central question that springs to mind is that, if Boserup's theory of agricultural change is generally plausible, why is it that some societies when faced with population pressure on resources 'choose' to starve rather than to embark on innovative changes in agricultural techniques and intensive land-use practices in order to increase the absorptive capacity of their environments? In this study, it is assumed that, in certain climatic and soil conditions and certain politico-economic contexts, population pressure on resources can lead to degradation of land capability and human dignity. One of the weaknesses of Boserup's theory emanates from her assumption that spatial variations in natural conditions can be disregarded. In her view, spatial variations reflect only variations in population pressures (Grigg, 1979: 69). However, in arid and semiarid environments such as this particular case-study area, natural environmental constraints constitute an important influence on farmers' responses and behaviour. The way the farmers respond to population pressure on land, for example, is not determined solely by their adaptive capacity or by whether they are predisposed to innovative changes. Within the given range of techniques of agricultural production, their capabilities to make adaptational changes are also limited by climatic and soil conditions. Although the farmers' adaptive responses to the changing land/population ratio are to a large extent likely to be affected by the characteristics of the soil, they are, above all, inclined to be conditioned by climatic conditions, over which they have little or no control.

In the Gedaref district, where the scheme is located, rainfall is erratic, to the point of not coming at all, and most of the year is dry. The highest form of intensive agricultural practice in traditional farming in the Boserupian sequence of land-use changes is multiple cropping, in which two or more crops are grown and harvested successively. This, in her view, would necessitate a shift from dependence on rainfall to irrigation. But whether farmers would use irrigation is not solely determined by construction and farming knowledge, but also by the natural endowments of the area of habitation. This does not suggest, however, that environmental constraints are insurmountable for ever.

In order for population pressure on resources to lead to technological change in the form of irrigation requires the availability, or at least potential availability, of surface water or groundwater. Thus, in arid and semiarid regions such as Qala in Nahal, where there are no streams or rich groundwater supplies, multiple cropping as a strategy for maintaining overall production is not feasible.[10] Also, if the area in question enjoys adequate rainfall throughout the year, population pressure cannot be expected to lead to technological change in the form of irrigation. For Boserup, however, variations in land-use intensity reflect differences in population pressure rather than differences in the natural environment. As far as the area covered in this study is concerned, this aspect of her theory may appear to be divorced from reality.

The types of crops grown on the scheme area are also very few in number, which severely limits the farmers' opportunity on the one hand, to diversify production and restructure the crops grown in order to minimize the risk of crop failure due to lack of moisture availability, and, on the other, to spread labour requirements between the different crops grown. In some parts of the refugees' country of origin, one way in which farmers responded to the diminishing land/population ratio and to depletion of soil nutrients was by restructuring the crops grown. Unlike on the Qala en Nahal scheme, where only two crops (sorghum and sesame) are grown, the farmers in their country of origin planted many varieties of crops, such as cereals (barley, maize, millet (*Pennisetum typhoideum*), teff (*Eragrostis abyssinica*), *dagusa* (*Eleusine coracana*) and wheat), oil-seeds (*Linum usitatissimum, Guizotia abyssinica, Carthamus tinctorius*) and, in the lowlands, sesame (*Sesamum* sp.) and earth-nuts (*Arachys hypogea*), legumes, tobacco, coffee, cotton and vegetables (FO 1015/43, 1947: 18).

The varieties of nitrogen-fixing or leguminous crops grown on the Eritrean plateau included *Cicer arietinum, Pisum sativum, Phaseolus, Dolichos, Tathyrus sativus, Vicia faba* and *Lens esculenta* (FO 1015/43, 1947: 18). For example, in 1946 over 30,500 acres of land were sown with legumes. This would not have been possible if it were not for the climatic and soil conditions of the area. It is assumed here that the farmers in the Gedaref region, including the refugees, are constrained by the physical conditions, which prevent them from adopting a flexible farming system.

Geertz's findings were based on an empirical study of small farmers in Java, where there was not only a labour surplus but also a favourable climate, which allowed multiple cropping, intercropping and diversification in terms of the growing of different types of crops successively or simultaneously. In Geertz's case-study, the farmers' response to population pressure on resources included use of labour-intensive methods and a gradual shift from other crops to rice, partly because of that particular crop's ability to absorb additional labour inputs and partly because of its high calorific value (Geertz, 1963). In such climatic conditions, it was, of course, possible to raise total production to a certain level by continuously increasing the labour input, even in the face of the declining marginal productivity of labour. The types of crops grown in the semiarid regions such as eastern Sudan are mainly sorghum, sesame and millet. They are not as labour-intensive, for example, as wet rice, on which Geertz based his theoretical construct of 'agricultural involution'.

Another important conceivable response to population pressure, but one which was overlooked in the Boserupian theory of agricultural change, is out-migration. One of the assumptions underlying this study is that, even though the refugees on the scheme are not legally free to relocate themselves or to bring new arable land into the production process outside the designated area, the limitation on freedom of movement and residence notwithstanding, out-migration to other areas where the actual or perceived opportunities for income-earning or pasturage are better is likely to constitute one of the means by which pressure on the scheme's resources is relieved.

The above discussion suggests that there is no easy answer to whether rapid population growth is a major cause of natural-resource depletion or a prerequisite for technological innovation in agriculture. In some circumstances, high population density may represent an asset for undertaking and maintaining labour-intensive conservation works, while in other circumstances, such as on the Qala en Nahal scheme, where the refugees are kept in a state of confinement, rapid population growth may contribute directly or indirectly to adverse changes in land use, with far-reaching consequences for sustainability of resources, fragmentation of holdings (Kibreab, 1987), landlessness, unemployment and out-migration. The problems of overgrazing, soil erosion and overcultivation are liable to be exacerbated by high population density. This may not necessarily imply that the problem of resource depletion on the scheme is caused only by high population density.

That the inverse relationship between ecological degradation and population pressure is not as straightforward as many take it to be can be further illustrated by the following example. In the Sahelian countries, one of the consequences of drought has been declining food production. However, the rate of population growth in the countries most affected by the Sahel drought, namely Senegal, Burkina Faso, Mauritania, Mali, Niger, Chad, Sudan and Somalia, has been remarkably low compared with the rest of the continent (2.75% per annum as opposed to 3.3% for all sub-Saharan African countries (World Bank cited in Sinclair and Wells (1989): 457–458).[11]

In this study, it is expected that non-demographic factors play an important role or even a more important role than rapid population growth, in causing environmental degradation. It is assumed that, wherever the non-demographic factors are operative, population pressure on resources is expected to exacerbate the problem of land degradation. The point of departure here is that population growth is a problem only in certain given political, historical, socio-economic and institutional frameworks. The multicausality of the problem that may induce the refugees and the Sudanese farmers to use the environment in a non-sustainable manner requires an approach which seeks the explanations for environmental degradation not only in the user community itself but also outside it.

Notes

1. Tawney uses this metaphor to describe the position of the rural poor in some districts in China.
2. This study, *inter alia*, aims to make a modest contribution to fill part of the lacunae in the existing knowledge by generating knowledge which may lead to corrective measures in existing schemes and to informed policy formulation in the future in countries where there are heavy population concentrations, be it as a result of government decisions or due to natural disasters.
3. Dr Adem Saleh, who was for many years ACORD's Livestock Officer in Umsagata.
4. Mr Abdella Haj Nasser, a postgraduate student from Khartoum.
5. Land can repair itself. New soil can be formed, grass can grow in gullies and soil nutrients can be restored in fallow periods. Conservation work can also have similar effects.
6. In recent years, there have been numerous attacks on refugee homes and reception centres in Germany, Sweden and Denmark. In Sweden shops owned by refugees are vandalized. There have also been a few attacks on Third World refugee camps by host populations, but again for reasons unrelated to environmental degradation or resource scarcity. Whenever these incidents took place in the refugee-hosting Third World countries, they occurred in response to governments' failure to consult with the local population before such camps were set up.
7. Paraguay is one of the most sparsely populated countries in the western hemisphere.
8. Decrease in fertility may result from nuptiality (postponement of marriage and/or increased celibacy) and/or a decline in marital fertility due to the increased use of contraceptives or abstinence and increased abortions of undesired pregnancies.
9. The *chitemene* shifting cultivation is a land-use system in which trees are cut, the wood is piled and burnt and crops are planted in the ash-covered area.
10. There might be a possibility, but sophisticated technologies are required to locate and tap groundwater.
11. To my knowledge, there are no studies which look at the relationship between population growth and drought. The low rate of growth experienced by the Sahel countries may be due to drought itself.

2 Overcultivation and Land Degradation on the Qala en Nahal Scheme

The climate had stayed the same (with its normal variations) since the close of the final wet phase of Pleistocene time ... the soil deterioration that has occurred, and which is still occurring, may, therefore, be safely attributed to the work of mankind and to his domesticated animals, rather than to any change in basic climate. (Report of the Soil Conservation Committee, 1944)

Land degradation is caused by a combination of natural and human processes. The human processes that cause soil and vegetation degradation are a result of inappropriate land-use practices, namely overcultivation, overgrazing and deforestation. Overcultivation is caused by excessive cultivation, too frequent cropping without fallowing, rotation or use of fertilizers, or baring the soil through grazing or removal of crop residues (Eckholm, 1975b, 1979, 1982; UNCOD, 1977; Hunter and Ntiri, 1978; Grainger, 1982; Timberlake, 1985; IFAD, 1986; Dixon et al., 1989; Munslow et al., 1989; Mann, 1990). Excessive cultivation often breaks down soil structure, compacts the soil below the plough layer and, depending on the type of soil, can cause crusting and result in moisture reduction and increased run-off and erosion. This may hinder seedling emergence, crop establishment and hence lower yields. In the central rain-lands of Sudan, where tractors are used for cultivation, El Khalil showed that the use of the wide level disc at constant depth resulted in the creation of hardpan at the depth of the plough layer. The consequence of the hardpan formation was reduced infiltration following the first rains when the cracks in the vertisols are closed and this results in increased run-off and in decreased infiltration below the hardpan layer (El Khalil, 1981: 75). In the absence of fertilizer application, too frequent cropping also depletes soil nutrients, resulting in poor plant cover and poor yields. Rosswall, for example, showed that the nitrogen content in soils increases under pasture ecosystems and decreases during cropping (Rosswall, 1976).

Why does overcultivation lead to land degradation? Intensive land use leads to a progressive shortening or disappearance of the fallow period from the farming system. In the ecosystem where the scheme is located, there is ample empirical evidence to show that continuous cultivation, in the absence of yield-boosting inputs, leads to depletion of soil nutrients, resulting in poor plant cover, poor yields and weed infestation (Agabawi, 1968, 1969; Simpson and Khalifa, 1976a, b; O'Brien, 1983; Ibrahim, 1984). Simpson and Khalifa, for example, state, '[O]n the large mechanized farms ... crop yields tended to fall below economic levels in about 9 to 10 years after initial cultivation. Farmers then applied for new land and moved further south and west' (Simpson and Khalifa, 1976b). It is an established fact that the lack of a fallow period in the absence of restorative measures reduces the organic-matter content, leading to lower fertility and to a less stable surface soil structure (Timberlake, 1985; Grainger, 1990). Continuous cultivation leaves the soil devoid of vegetation, which in turn leads to a decline in fertility and a deterioration of surface soil structure. It also leads to increased run-off erosion and sub-surface flow, which remove nutrients and organic matter with the consequence of reduced annual replenishment of soil moisture (Grainger, 1990).

The available evidence shows that expansion of cultivation on to less productive areas, coupled with diminishing returns from lands under shorter fallows, results in a decrease of average crop yields per unit of land (Timberlake, 1985; Grainger, 1990). Continuous cultivation results in shorter fallows and thus in poorer regrowth. There are increasing leaching, deflocculation and breakdown of humus. Soil moisture relationships change and there is an overall decline in the nutrient status of the soil. With elimination of fallows and diversified cropping patterns, the natural ecosystem's control of agricultural disease becomes greatly weakened and devastating imbalances can occur in areas of monoculture (Hunter and Ntiri, 1978: 194; Ignatief cited in Mann, 1990).

In the semiarid zone of Sudan, Ibrahim argues that it has been proved that excessive rain-fed cultivation is one of the major causes of land degradation because of the high rainfall variability, fragile soil and unsuitable land-use methods (Ibrahim, 1984: 106–107). Overcultivation occurs 'when farmers try to crop the land more intensively than permitted by its natural fertility, and fail to compensate for the export of nutrients in the crop by using artificial [or natural] fertilizers or fallowing the land so that its fertility can regenerate naturally' (Grainger, 1990: 65). Fallowing as a technique of soil fertility conservation and restoration was common in the refugees' country of origin (Chapter 7) and shifting cultivation has always been a common practice in the central rainlands of Sudan; it entailed the reallotment of land every three to five years in order to give the used land time to rest and regain its fertility. This made it possible for every member of the tribe to get at one time or another a plot in the better lands of the tribe (Awad, 1975: 217).

In the Gedaref district, even though the reasons are not clearly established, there is indisputable evidence to show that, under continuous cultivation, crop yields decline rapidly over time, all other factors such as rainfall being equal (Agabawi, 1968, 1969; Simpson and Khalifa, 1976a; El-Moula, 1985; Gedaref District Study Area, 1985). For example, a 17-year time-series analysis on data for the Gedaref area shows that yields over time are falling, even when rainfall is kept constant.[1] This rapid loss of soil fertility resulting from continuous cropping is one reason why farmers in the past practised shifting agriculture in the area. The same method is now also used by commercial farmers to counter soil fertility decline (Simpson and Khalifa, 1976b).

The problem of fertility decline resulting from several seasons of continuous cropping was recognized by the Ministry of Agriculture as early as 1959. During that year, the Land Allotment Board in the Ministry of Agriculture discovered that private investors were faced with the problem of yield decline after their holdings were cropped for four or more seasons continuously. After 4 years of cropping, yields fell 'to unremunerative level' (Agabawi, 1968: 79). Consequently the Land Allotment Board decided to introduce an eight-course rotation of 4 years' cropping, followed by 4 years' bush fallow. In order to facilitate the enforcement of this land-use practice, it allocated an additional land allotment to the commercial farmers.

It is interesting to observe that the decision of the Land Allotment Board to introduce rotation was in some respects similar to reverting to the traditional system of shifting cultivation because its eight-course rotation neither specified crop sequence during the 4 years of cropping nor recommended the introduction of legumes, fertilizers and manures to replenish soil fertility. Even though the decision of the Land Allotment Board to introduce eight-course rotation was not preceded by experiments, it was clear that, even without experiments, after 4 years of natural vegetation, the productivity of the land was much improved (Agabawi, 1969: 107; Simpson and Khalifa, 1976a: 99).

It is important to point out, however, that any correlation between the extent of soil erosion, decline in soil fertility, deterioration of soil texture and structure and changes in vegetation species which accompanied the process of agricultural development of the study area and the decreasing crop yields cannot be established quantitatively. This is due either to lack of time-series and reliable data or due to the complex interrelationships between many potential contributing factors. The issues pertaining to vegetation changes are presented in Chapter 3. The aim of this chapter is, therefore, to investigate and to assess empirically the changes in some soil properties that have occurred under conditions of continuous mechanized rain-fed cultivation with inadequate rotations, fertilizer applications or fallow periods. This is done in order to measure the level of change in the properties of the soil, if any, on the Qala en Nahal scheme.

In this section, whether or not there is a problem of overcultivation on the scheme will be discussed. One way in which farmers generally respond to an increased demand for arable land in the context of limited land supply and population growth is by shortening or eliminating the fallow period. It is interesting to see, therefore, if such is the case among the farmers on the scheme area. The data in Table 2.1 clearly show that fallowing as a technique of conserving and restoring soil nutrients, especially among the refugee farmers, is insignificant. Less than 5% leave part of their *hawashas* to lie in fallow.

As can be observed from Table 2.1, there is a significant relationship between nationality and the practice of fallow periods for countering soil-nutrient depletion.[2] The proportion of farmers practising fallow periods as a means of restoring soil fertility was much higher among the Sudanese. This difference reflects nothing more than a differentiated access to the land resource by the two groups living on the scheme. The Sudanese farmers are faced with the problem of land shortage, but the level of scarcity is not as extreme as among the refugees. This is reflected in the fact that a considerable proportion of the Sudanese farmers (47%) allow their plots to rest. Among the refugees, an insignificant proportion resort to fallow periods to counter fertility depletion (Table 2.1).

The refugee families have been cultivating the *hawashas* continuously for a mean period of 16.5 years (standard deviation (SD) 6.6). The corresponding figure for the Sudanese farmers is 9.7 years (SD 6.5). The refugee farmers have been cropping their plots continuously since the establishment of the settlement, with no fallow periods. The majority of the refugee families were settled in 1970–1971, but a considerable number of families were also relocated to the scheme in 1978–1979

Table 2.1 Distribution of respondents by the practice of fallow periods as a technique for conserving and restoring soil fertility (%)

	Refugees	Sudanese
Fallow periods	4.6	47.0
No fallow periods	95.4	53.0

$\chi^2 = 79$, 2 d.f., $P < 0.01$.
χ^2, chi-square tests; d.f., degrees of freedom; P, probability.

(COR Files, 1978–1979). The results are, therefore, influenced by the impact of the late settlers. The data show that the overwhelming majority of the early settlers have been cultivating their plots for 21 years without any fallow periods.

Among the refugees, 36% have been cultivating their holdings continuously between 16 and 20 years and 28% between 21 and 22 years. The corresponding figures for the Sudanese farmers are 7% and 7% respectively.[3] Of the Sudanese farmers, 60% have been cultivating their holdings continuously for less than 9 years. The communities are aware of the necessity of fallow periods as a means of reversing productivity decline resulting from land overcultivation. The refugee respondents stated that a *hawasha* can be cultivated continuously without yield decline, other things being equal, if sesame and sorghum are rotated, for about 6 years (mean 5.8, SD 1.6) and only about 3 years (mean 2.9, SD 0.98) if only sorghum is grown, without rotation. The corresponding figures for the Sudanese farmers were almost identical (mean 5.9, SD 1.6) with rotation (sorghum following sesame or sesame following sorghum) and without rotation (mean 2.8, SD 0.76). The dominant crops grown in the area are sorghum and sesame and neither of them is leguminous or nitrogen-fixing, but, within the climatic and soil constraints in the area, rotation of the two crops is helpful, or is at least better than nothing, in countering yield decline. The fact that the data elicited from both the refugees and the Sudanese farmers matched exactly in terms of their perceptions of the number of years a farm could be cultivated without suffering from fertility loss, with and without rotation, indicates the relative accuracy of their agronomic knowledge regarding the relationship between productivity and intensity of land use and the relationship between farm age and productivity. It is also important to point out that in the whole district of Gedaref, including the scheme and its environs, neither organic manure nor fertilizers are used to restore soil fertility. This is in spite of the refugees' long-established cultural practice, which included intensive organic-manure application in their country of origin (Chapter 7). The major reason why farmers do not use manure is for fear of spreading weeds, especially *Sorghum sudanense* (Arabic, *adar*), through animal droppings. In fact, it is quite common to come across both subsistence and commercial farmers sweeping animal waste from their *hawashas* or *meshruas*.

What is the consequence of this system of intensive land use on the sustainability of the farming system? Here intensification refers to the increased frequency with which the available land is cropped without such a change necessarily being accompanied by change in techniques of production. The objective of any sustainable land-use plan is to counter both environmental degradation and declining productivity. In most cases, the two are inextricably linked. Loss of soil productivity is often a result of land degradation, which may have a detrimental consequence on the incomes and livelihoods of resource users.

The extent of soil erosion on the scheme

The soils on the scheme area vary with the types of land-form but the most extensive soil types belong to the vertisol order (see Table 3.1) (Soil Survey Administration, 1973). Dickinson identifies five major land-form and three soil types on the scheme area (Dickinson, 1983; Dickinson and Howard, 1983). The vertisols are part of the central clay plain stretching from the Ethiopian border in the east to Darfur in the west, occupying the area between isohyets 450 and 800 mm (Agabawi, 1968). The vertisol soils are deep (in excess of 3 m), dark-coloured and heavy, with extensively cracking clays during the dry seasons (Knibbe, 1964). The clay fraction of the soil varies from 61% to 73% (Laing, 1953). The clay content of the soil in a site near the scheme area was measured to be as high as 85% (Dickinson, 1983: 25). The clays are alkaline and montmorillonitic (Graham, 1969), montmorillonite being a clay mineral which allows the soil to expand and absorb water. It is the shrinking characteristic upon drying which produces cracks 2–6 cm wide and 40–120 cm deep (Knibbe, 1964). When wet, the vertisol soil swells and when dry it shrinks, producing cracks. On becoming wet, the surface tends to swell and lose its discrete structure, while at the same time the impact of raindrops physically breaks down the soil to form a crust, which rapidly reduces its infiltration rate. The cracks tend to become choked in the upper 20–50 cm, but remain open below well into the rains, allowing rapid movement of water and subsurface erosion. This swelling and shrinking characteristic is the most important feature of vertisols, which directly and indirectly has an enormous bearing on their erodibility, structure and fertility. In sites stripped of trees, bushes and grasses, the first intensive storms have an erosive effect, but this is reduced by the open cracks, which absorb most of the run-off and leave little surface run-off to cause erosion. Run-off occurs during the later stage of the rainy season, when all the cracks are filled. This is to a limited extent again mitigated by regeneration of grasses. However, the more intense the rainfall, the greater is its power to dislodge soil particles from the binding effects of their neighbours. On moderately sloping land, splash erosion is considered 'to be the primary component of soil erosion in many areas' (Dickinson, 1983: 49).

The second type of soil is found in the jebels. The jebels are steep-sided rocky or stony hills with sharp crests or ridges, with a slope angle greater than 5° and a height of 10–280 m. They are separated by wide low-angled expanses of clay plains and are composed of resistant rock material. The soils of the jebels are discontinuous, shallow, stony and highly eroded (Dickinson, 1983). The third type of soil on the scheme is situated in the pediments. The pediments are formed by the deposition of material eroded from the jebels. They are stony or non-stony foot-slopes to the jebels, extending up to 50 m from the foot of the jebel. They are lower-angled than the jebels, varying from 1 to 5°, with a concave or rectilinear slope profile. The pediment soils are reddish brown sandy loams to clays and are highly eroded with a poor surface structure, leading to capping and low infiltration rates. The low infiltration rate is, however, not due to a high sand content as such, but probably the rocky structures down the soil profile form a barrier to water infiltration.

Generally, the rate of erosion is a function of four main physical factors, namely the erosivity of the rainfall, the erodibility of the soil, the topography and the amount of vegetation cover. The extent of soil erosion on the scheme, therefore, varies with the land-form, surrounding land-form, slope, soil type, vegetation cover, agricultural practices and position of tracks and roads. Erosion is a function of natural processes and the intensity of human interference. The impact of the latter varies not only with the intensity of such interference, but also with the ability of the particular land-form to absorb intensified change in land-use practices. The soils of the jebels and pediments are characterized by low resilience and high sensitivity. A land-form with such characteristics is easily degraded and does not easily respond to land management once degradation occurs. Owing to the removal of the natural vegetation (due to expansion of cultivation, grazing and browsing of livestock, tree-lopping for fodder, firewood collection, charcoal making, burning for improvement of grass regrowth, etc.), their steep slopes, stony surface and thin and erodible soils,

Plate 2.1   When gullies cut across farmers' hawashas, many abandon their farms and seek seasonal employment in the mechanized rain-fed crop production schemes. (Photo: Gaim Kibreab)

the jebels are subjected to severe wash and gully erosion during the rains. This is manifested in the increasing number of V-shaped gullies, which cut from the top to the bottom of the jebels.

During field research in 1982 by the author only a few V-shaped gullies were witnessed cutting across the jebels and pediments, but 10 years later many more gullies had formed and cut across several *meshruas* (Plate 2.1). This implies that the extent of soil erosion is being aggravated by the increased intensity of human interference and particularly by biomass removal from the erosion-prone sites. The fact that the extent of erosion is accelerated over time is also clear from the amount of soil deposited on the farms situated at the foot of the pediments or on sites neighbouring the jebels. In some areas up to 50–75% of the area of the fields was covered with sediments removed from upstream. The low-lying plots, especially those at the foot of the jebels, are subjected to extensive flooding and waterlogging.

Flooding is also becoming a major problem for an increasing number of farmers. The cause of flooding is clearly the removal of vegetation upstream in the jebels and pediments, manifested, among other things, in heavy soil loss and the formation of numerous V-shaped gullies. The pediments are also subjected to severe erosion, due partly to their steep slope and partly to the high sand content of the soil. Neither the jebels nor the pediments are cultivable, but the fact that they are subjected to severe erosion has considerably affected the availability of forage resources for livestock. This is also having detrimental consequences downstream. The problem of sediment deposition and waterlogging in the *hawashas* situated beneath the jebels and pediments is due to destruction of the vegetation on the jebels and pediments, which has accelerated the problem of soil erosion.

Generally, the cultivable areas are not as badly eroded, due to the relatively flat landscape. The extent of surface-flow erosion in the clay soils is not, therefore, considerable. However, farms located on the upper valley sides are eroded by the khors (streams), which flow from the north to the south and often create broad valleys. There are also sites which receive mud flow from the jebels and other water shedding sites. Much of the soil eroded upslope is also deposited on the flood plain. Even though it is difficult to estimate the extent of cultivable area affected by erosion (this depends on rainfall), the farmers whose *hawashas* are located on the upper valley slopes suffer lower crop yields and increased problems of floods. In 1983, over 55% of the total scheme area had a low or negligible erosion hazard and 25% of the cultivable land had a high or moderate erosion hazard and 10.5% was subject to flooding (Dickinson, 1983: 54). By 1993 it was clear that the intensification of cultivation, excessive wood cutting, intensive grazing and browsing had clearly aggravated the problem of soil erosion since 1983. The areas affected by run-off, rill and gully erosion were much larger than they were in 1983.

The amount of soil lost to the scheme may not be drastic as such, because what is lost may be compensated by what comes in from sites outside the scheme area, but, at the level of individual farms, there are families who are faced with loss of productivity due to loss of soils and nutrients or due to deposition of sandy and nutrient-poor soils transported from the jebels and pediments. Generally, the vertisol soils on the scheme are characterized by relatively high resilience and low sensitivity to degradation in terms of soil erosion, but their resilience is undermined by lack of appropriate land-management practices being designed to make immediate ends meet at the expense of long-term sustainability. The land-management practices on the scheme do not include fallowing, manuring, fertilization or the growing of nitrogen-fixing crops such as legumes. In the absence of such management practices, continuous cropping taxes the soil heavily and the previously resilient and stable land becomes vulnerable to the degrading forces of nature as exacerbated by intensified human interference.

Crop residues are removed to be used as building material and fodder for animals and to facilitate the smooth operation of tractors. This has a detrimental effect not only on soil fertility, but also on the structural stability of the soil. Crop residues not only enrich the organic matter of the soil, but also bind the soil and protect it against wind erosion. According to existing practice, the use of tractors for cultivation is said to require clearance of the field of crop residues. A report prepared for ACORD, for example, recommends that sorghum straw should not be left on the field because it sticks to the disc plough and causes a lot of unnecessary stoppage and waste of time to clean the discs. It is also argued that sorghum straw hinders disc land penetration leading to poor weed control (ACORD, 1987a). The report states that sorghum straw had to be cleared for good land cultivation. Farmers are urged by extension officers to clear their plots of sorghum stalk in order to allow smooth tractor operation so as to increase efficiency measured in the amount of land cultivated, disregarding the issues of soil fertility and the problem of erosion. The sorghum stalks are used as animal feed and the remains are not used for composting. The standard agricultural practice on the scheme is therefore to clear the fields of crop residues and to leave the soil open for wind erosion. The soil surface is left bare during the first rains and this often leads to splash erosion, crusting by raindrop impact, reduced infiltration and increased run-off. This is one of the negative consequences of tractor use in the area. Crop residue reduces wind velocity at the soil surface when it is incorporated into the soil, increases soil moisture storage capacity and promotes a more stable granular structure. Under high solar radiation it may also encourage micro-biological activities (Young, 1985). Another factor which contributes to the problem of run-off is the technique of concentric cultivation by disc harrows, which results in a proportion of the field being cultivated up and down the slope (interview with Asim El Haj, 1991).

Other causes of erosion on the scheme are deforestation of the non-cultivable areas, namely the jebels and the pediments. In the clay plains of Sudan where tractors are used for cultivation all natural vegetation is removed from arable land. This is done partly to allow effective tractor cultivation, to remove the risk of destructive birds and insects and due to some farmers' belief that trees compete with crops for scarce moisture and space. The beneficial effects of some tree species are overlooked.[4] Natural vegetation reduces run-off by:

> intercepting rainfall before it reaches the ground surface, converting a proportion from high energy raindrops to low energy stem-flow, storing some water on leaves or in depressions between branches and trunks ... Leaf litter from trees plays a part in maintaining the organic matter content and thus structural stability of the soil, allowing it to absorb more rainfall, and increasing its resistance to erosion. (Dickinson, 1983: 59)

In view of the livestock build-up that has been taking place on the scheme, there are increasing grazing and browsing pressures on the jebels and pediments. The removal of the perennial grass cover under wet-season heavy grazing and its replacement either by bare ground or by annuals is also contributing to erosion. Grasses, especially herbaceous grasses, are effective in reducing run-off velocities. The situation is exacerbated by the burning of grasses during the dry seasons by herders. One consequence of the livestock build-up in the context of shrinking grazing areas has been the collection of crop residues for animal fodder. With the increased pressure of population on the scarce land resource, erosion-prone areas are brought under cultivation, exacerbating the problem of soil erosion. Grassed field boundaries also have an erosion-countering effect, but the problem of land shortage has led many farmers to cultivate every inch of their *hawashas*, including field boundaries. This has clearly exacerbated the problem of soil erosion.

It is worthwhile pointing out that, on the scheme, there are certain conditions which mitigate the degrading impact of the natural processes and human interference. First, rainfall is limited to only 3 months of the year. The vertisol soils are deep and their nutrients and organic matter are evenly spread throughout rather than being concentrated in a shallow surface horizon. The slope angles of the cultivated areas are always less than 1°.

The experimental results of the effects of continuous cultivation on the chemical and physical properties of the vertisols on the scheme area show that continuous cultivation constitutes one of the major factors that cause reduction in the capability of the land to grow crops. The level of land degradation in terms of deforestation, change in plant species composition, decreases in perennial grasses and increases in annuals will be discussed in Chapter 3.

Effects of continuous cultivation on the physical and chemical properties of vertisol soils on the scheme

As pointed out before, in the central clay plains of Sudan where the Qala en Nahal refugee settlement scheme is located, it is widely believed that continuous monocropping constitutes one of the major causes of land degradation. If this is true, the scheme at Qala en Nahal represents a unique opportunity to test this hypothesis. Over 95% of the refugee farmers have been cropping their *hawashas* continuously since the establishment of the scheme without fallowing. This land-use practice is expected to result in changes in the physical and chemical properties of the soils, leading to a decline in productive capability (degradation) of the basic resource – land. It is assumed that increased frequency of cropping of the arable land, if unaccompanied by adequate crop rotation or application of productivity-boosting inputs, will lead to deterioration in the quality of the land.

Methodology

In order to determine the level of change in productive capability of land on the scheme and on the surrounding Sudanese villages, soil samples from 0–20 and 20–40 cm layers were taken from systematically selected different subplots with different land-use histories on the same day simultaneously. The history of land use of every plot from which the samples were taken was compiled from the documents of the tractor hire service (THS) in consultation with the extension officers and the farmers. The sites where the pits were dug are given in Table 2.2. Twenty soil samples were collected from five different *meshruas*, whose land-use histories are summarized in Table 2.2. Two pits were dug in each site, except in *meshrua 83* where four pits were dug.[5]

All but two of the pits from where the soil samples were drawn were dug in cultivated sites. The two pits were dug in an undisturbed bush/savannah site. Thus, the main type of human interference considered was continuous cultivation and postharvest grazing. Since one of the points of departure of the study was to establish a relationship between continuous cropping (without improvement) and reduction in the productive capability of the land in question, measured in terms of the factors stated earlier, the sites for digging the pits were carefully selected by establishing the particular land-use history of every site (*hawasha*). Since the occurrence of adverse changes was expected to be highest in the sites where human interference was most intensive (measured in terms of cropping without fallow, rotation[6] and fertilization), five categories were selected. The first site was a bush/savannah area where human interference was limited to grazing and tapping of fuel wood, timber and gum arabic (from the *Acacia* trees).[7] It is important to note, however, that the trees on the site were young and sparse. The level of intensity of vegetation use is so high that most trees are cut before they reach maturity. The consequence of this is that the impact of the woody vegetation on soil fertility, manifest in rising nitrogen and phosphorus contents, is limited because the trees are not mature enough to produce leaf litter, which is crucial for enriching fertility.

Table 2.2   Sites for the vertisol soil samples

Farm no.	Forest 0–20	20–40	5 years 0–20	20–40	10 years 0–20	20–40	15 years 0–20	20–40	20 years 0–20	20–40
Forest	1	1								
102			1	1						
36					1	1				
97							1	1		
62									1	1
36									1	1
40							1	1		
62					1	1				
83	1	1	1	1						
Total samples	2	2	2	2	2	2	2	2	2	2

Relatively, however, the site was not stripped of all natural vegetation and hence human interference was least intensive. The second, third, fourth and fifth sites were cultivated and sown with sorghum and sesame for 5, 10, 15 and 20 years continuously without fallowing or the use of any form of fertilization or crop rotation, except sorghum following sesame or sesame following sorghum.

This is not considered an effective form of crop rotation because neither of the two crops is leguminous – leguminous crops help restore soil fertility. The main advantage of alternating the two crops, namely sorghum and sesame, is to combat weed infestation, especially by the parasite species *Striga*, not to counter soil-nutrient depletion resulting from continuous cultivation. Sesame is not affected by *Striga*. (In the following chapters the social impacts of these changes will be assessed by looking at crop, livestock, fuel-wood and timber production.) The results of the soil tests would have been more effective had separate yield figures existed for each of the sites (*hawashas*) from which the soil samples were drawn. This gap was filled partly by using the average crop yields over time for the whole scheme and partly by data elicited from farmers and extension officers. The samples were analysed in a laboratory for certain chemical and physical properties. The soil survey and the laboratory analysis were conducted in cooperation with the Soil Conservation, Land Use and Water Programming Administration in Khartoum.[8]

We were aware from the outset that the results of soil analysis should be interpreted with the utmost prudence. For example, the nitrogen plant use may not be the same as the one extracted in a laboratory and, since chemical properties of soils can vary even over a short distance and at different times of the year, it is difficult to determine the representativeness of the samples taken. The representativeness of the results may also be affected by the small number of pits dug. The results are therefore taken as indicative rather than conclusive.

Firstly, the soil samples were tested to see if there was a change in texture as a result of increased cropping time. The results of the different samples were also compared with each other to see if soil texture change was a function of continuous cropping. This was expected to be manifested in reduction in clay content of the soil due to downward movement of clay, lower saturation percentage and increase in sand particles on the top soil. Secondly, in order to assess the change in soil structure, a test of soil resistance to penetration was done. If change in soil structure was, among other things, due to increased time of cropping, a difference was expected to be observed between the results of the different sites, depending on the land-use history of the particular site. Thirdly, tests were carried out to determine the chemical composition of the soil. The samples were analysed for pH, total nitrogen (N), total phosphorus (P) and organic carbon content. The particle size distribution was determined by hydrometer for silt and clay fractions (Day, 1965) after removal of organic matter (OM) (Anderson, 1963), and the carbonate content by using a minimum amount of $0.1\,\text{N}$ hydrochloric acid (HCl) (Younis, 1983). The results are expressed as weight percentage on an oven-dry basis (except for pH). Aggregate stability was determined by dry sieving with rotary sieve equipment (Chapil, 1962), bulk density by the core method (Black, 1965) and organic carbon by the modified Walkley–Black method (Black, 1965).

Discussion of results
In the following sections the results of the tests on the physical and chemical properties of the soil are presented and discussed.

Changes in soil texture

The results of particle-size distribution are presented in Table 2.3. The data show a reduction in clay content or increase in sand particles with the increased time of cropping. It is believed that soils usually become degraded when sand particles increase in the top layer, because of removal of fine particles either by wind or water, by downward movement of clay or by the addition of sand particles from adjacent areas. Thus, continuous cropping for longer periods leads to reduction of clay content and hence to soil degradation. It is the clay content, composed mainly of montmorillonite, a clay mineral, that allows the soil to expand and absorb water. A reduction in clay content of the top soil caused by its downward movement to the sub-soil blocks the pores and hence results in a considerably reduced infiltration rate. Generally, in the absence of cracks or in the sites away from cracks, infiltration rates are extremely low, but there is also a marked reduction in the infiltration rate in areas cropped continuously.

The process is further accentuated by the removal of vegetative cover, as the latter prevents transportation of finer particles by wind or water. This is because vegetative cover holds the fine soil particles in an aggregate form and so hinders its removal. The clay content of the soil is an important factor in moisture availability, especially in areas of limited rainfall. According to Brady, the capacity of the soil to hold moisture increases with the increasing silt and clay content (Brady, 1974). From Table 2.3, it is clear that a lower moisture content was found in the analysis of soil samples representing the old cultivated areas (10, 15 and 20 years). So, there is a decrease in saturation percentage (SP) with longer periods of cropping. This decrease in SP coincides with the decrease in the clay content of the soil (Table 2.3). It is believed that reduction of clay content and SP of a soil are important measures of soil degradation. Generally, reduction in clay content or increase of sand particles, together with reduction in SP, in the old cultivated areas indicates a reduction in soil productive capability.

Table 2.3 Some chemical and physical properties of the vertisol soil on sites with different land-use histories

Cultivation period (years)	Depth (cm)	Particle size distribution			Bulk density g/cm^3	SP	OM	Total N (%)	P (p.p.m.)	SAR
		Clay <0.002 mm (%)	Silt 0.06–0.002 mm (%)	Sand 2–0.06 mm (%)						
0	0–20	70	24	6	51	1.20	0.81	0.10	5	2
	20–40	70	25	5	50	1.19	0.70	0.08	5	4
5	0–20	69	25	6	55	1.25	0.79	0.08	4	2
	20–40	70	25	5	54	1.25	0.62	0.06	5	5
10	0–20	64	28	8	58	1.31	0.60	0.06	3	5
	20–40	68	27	5	56	1.28	0.58	0.05	4	6
15	0–20	61	29	10	63	1.40	0.54	0.03	3	6
	20–40	69	25	6	60	1.35	0.56	0.03	4	8
20	0–20	61	27	12	66	1.44	0.55	0.04	3	6
	20–40	67	26	7	64	1.40	0.50	0.03	3	7

SP, saturation percentage; OM, organic matter; N, nitrogen; P, phosphorus; p.p.m., parts per million; SAR, sodium absorption ratio.

Therefore, our working hypothesis, namely 'land management practices of farmers on the scheme result in soil degradation', is upheld since continuous cropping of the same holding resulted in change in soil texture.

Changes in soil structure

To evaluate the change in soil structure, size distribution of aggregates and bulk-density studies were carried out. Soil structure describes the degree of binding of individual particles of soil, its strength, the size and shape of the resulting discrete units (peds) and the number, size and continuity of pores and fissures (Dickinson, 1983: 37).

From Table 2.4 and Fig. 2.1, it is clear that a significant change has occurred in the content of <2.0 mm and 2.0–1.0 mm aggregates in the soil. Both sizes decreased by almost 50% after 20 years of continuous cultivation. However, Mitchell showed that the aggregates of vertisols in Malawi declined from 2.0 mm to 0.6–1.0 mm after 4 or 5 years of continuous cropping, with no further reduction thereafter (Mitchell, 1987). He also suggested that, under good grass cover, soil aggregates might be restored to their original size in about 3 years. It is possible that yield decline is somehow related to aggregate size. Both Mitchell (1987) and Coughlan *et al.* (1987) stress that the breakdown of soil aggregate influences infiltration, run-off and erosion in wet soil, and crusting, clodding and ease of tillage in dry soil. The net effect of these processes is to reduce the moisture available to plants, so yield reductions due to water shortage in areas of low, variable or erratic rainfall are quite likely.

The data on bulk density indicate that there is a significant reduction in bulk density in the 20–40 cm layer after 10 years of continuous cultivation, with no further reduction thereafter, indicating a subsoil pan. However, considerable care must be exercised if one interprets bulk density as an indicator of pans, because the

Table 2.4   Size distribution of aggregates on sites with different land-use histories

Cultivation period (years)	Depth (cm)	<2.0 mm (%)	2.0–1.0 mm (%)	1.0–0.5 mm (%)	0.5–0.35 mm (%)	0.35–0.25 mm (%)	0.25–0.12 mm (%)	0.12–0.06 mm (%)	>0.06 mm (%)
0	0–20	50.40	9.10	19.65	11.10	2.80	4.20	0.45	2.10
	20–40	40.90	7.90	20.40	15.70	4.55	6.95	0.85	2.75
5	0–20	41.40	8.05	21.50	15.70	4.15	6.05	0.60	2.55
	20–40	80.20	5.80	8.60	3.05	0.75	1.05	0.15	0.40
10	0–20	39.90	7.75	24.05	13.85	3.20	6.15	1.35	3.75
	20–40	64.00	10.30	15.40	5.00	2.15	1.40	0.25	1.50
15	0–20	29.70	7.10	19.50	15.60	14.90	7.75	1.00	4.35
	20–40	28.20	7.65	22.35	18.08	6.55	9.15	1.30	6.75
20	0–20	29.10	4.90	14.25	12.05	13.80	16.35	2.15	7.40
	20–40	33.55	6.40	18.30	15.65	4.80	11.50	1.45	8.35

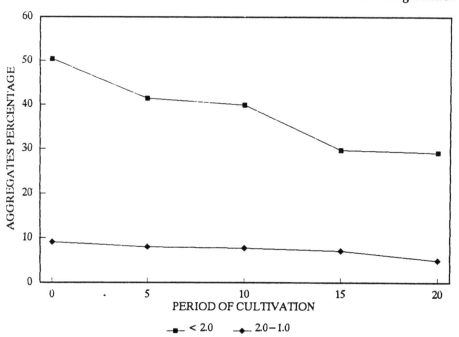

Fig. 2.1   Distribution <2.00 and 2.0−1.0 mm size aggregates with cultivation period

density of clods in vertisols varies significantly according to moisture content, generally from around 1.1 g/cm³ when soil is wet to 1.9 g/cm³ as the soil dries.

Although there are no data for the scheme, in a nearby agricultural project El Khalil found significant variations between bulk density of vertisols and number of discings in the 0–10 and 10–20 cm horizons, with a 14% increase between undisturbed soils and those that had been cultivated for at least 10 years (El Khalil, 1981). This finding is supported by a similar earlier study, which concluded that wide-level discing causes changes in size and amount of air voids (Hassan and Osman, 1972). The pan inhibits root and water penetration and thereby increases the risks of drought to the crop and erosion by running water as a result of increased run-off. On flat land, pounding will become more acute. On vertisols at the Gadambalyia mechanized crop-production scheme (MCPS) with a longer history of cropping, a cultivation pan comprising a massive soil horizon 10–15 cm thick just below the surface has been claimed by Van Deweg to be an outstanding example of compaction caused by the use of heavy machinery for a period of over 40 years (Van Deweg, 1987). On the Qala en Nahal scheme, the clearance of the natural vegetation for cultivation and fuel wood, as well as the problem of overgrazing with the consequent reduction in organic matter and root densities, also has a clear detrimental effect on surface structure. The results of the soil tests show that the soils of the natural woodland vegetation (zero years' cropping) have a better structure than those which have been under continuous cropping.

Changes in soil fertility
One measure of land degradation is reduction in fertility. This was tested by the analysis of soils for all the nutrient elements and components affecting plant growth.

Agabawi states that the vertisol clay soils are among the most fertile soils in Africa and are capable of producing a wide variety of crops (Agabawi, 1968: 72). Dudal, however, argues that the fertility level of the dark clay soils is not particularly high. He states:

> Absolute amounts of essential nutrients may be limited or, when certain elements are more plentiful, the ratio between the different nutrients may become unbalanced ... In general, dark clays are relatively low or even deficient in phosphorus and nitrogen ... Potassium may be present at a moderate level but is sometimes unavailable owing to potassium fixation. Calcium and magnesium are present in high amounts. Sodium may form a substantial percentage of the absorbed bases, especially in the lower layers. Secondary elements, such as sulphur, and the trace elements such as iron and molybdenum are often lacking. The content of organic matter is relatively low. (Dudal quoted in Dickinson, 1983: 34)

The available literature on the subject indicates that the soils in the Gedaref district can be exploited for 9 to 10 years continuously, after which yields decline below economic levels and those farmers with a choice abandon such schemes and open up virgin sites (Agabawi, 1968, 1969; Simpson and Khalifa, 1976a, b; Simpson and Simpson, 1991). In the area, yield potential on cleared land declines from over 1,000 kg/*feddan* to 100–200 kg/*feddan* after 6–10 years of continuous cropping (World Bank cited in Dickinson, 1983). Most of the land on the scheme has been under continuous cropping for over 15 years and the consequence of this intensification for soil fertility is expected to be considerable.

In order to determine whether continuous cropping without rotation and fertilizer application leads to loss of soil fertility, tests of the chemical composition of the soil were carried out in sites with different land use histories. OM, N and P contents were found to be slightly higher in the sites where there had been 0 or 5 years of cropping compared with the sites where there had been 10 or 20 years of continuous monocropping.

A test was carried out to determine the level of sodium absorption ratio (SAR). The results indicate that there is a slight increase in the SAR in the older plots that have been under continuous cultivation for 15 or 20 years compared with the younger plots or with the undisturbed site. This increase is expected to result in a collapse of soil structure, leading to poor water infiltration, poor soil aeration and an increase in osmotic pressure.

The results of the various tests clearly show that there is a general decrease in some of the nutrients essential for crops with increased duration of cropping, indicating a decline in soil fertility. A similar study conducted by Mutasim (El-Moula, 1985) in the Gadambalyia also shows similar results. His analysis of variance tests showed a significant variation in OM, N and P with years of cropping. He concluded that the natural fertility of the soils generally decreases with increased periods of cropping (El Moula, 1985). These findings are supported by the information elicited from farmers and key informants, who claimed with conviction that, if sorghum is grown for long periods without any regular fertiliz-ation, rotation or fallowing, degradation, reflected in a dramatic increase in weed infestation and in fertility loss, resulting in lower crop yields, is inevitable. Sorghum is known to impoverish the soil to an extent that yields of following crops are reduced. A grain yield of 5 bags/*feddan* removes about 4 kg N, 15 kg P and 45 kg potassium (K) (Iiaco, 1981). Alternating sorghum and sesame minimizes the problem of weed infestation, but the farmers believe it is not effective in combating depletion of soil nutrients. Experimental results in western Nigeria also showed that in the absence of treatments, including crop residue and rotation, continuous cropping led to considerable crop-yield decline (Juo and Lal, 1977). It is important to state, however, that continuous cropping without rotation, fallowing, manuring or fertilization is one of the numerous interacting factors that affect fertility. In traditional agriculture where application of modern inputs designed to boost soil fertility is unknown, crop residues play a key role in enriching the soil.

Removal of crop residues deprives the soil of important organic matter. As we shall see later, on the scheme all crop residues are collected for animal fodder and the consequence of this mismanagement on fertility cannot be underestimated. Although there are no data on the amount of crop yields foregone because of crop-residue removal on the scheme or in the district of Gedaref, in western Nigeria experimental results showed that plots where crop residues were returned as surface mulch yielded higher crops than unmulched plots (Juo and Lal, 1977: 579). Crop residues alone accounted for about 2 metric ton/ha of maize grain. This may suggest that a considerable amount of grain yield is foregone as a result of removal of crop residues. In light of the recurrent droughts and the key role livestock play in the economic life of the scheme, however, it is not clear whether the farmers would be better off leaving the crop residues on the farms rather than removing the entire sorghum plants for animal fodder.

Conclusion

In view of the severe land scarcity, the farmers have responded to increased demand for arable land by eliminating fallow periods from their farming systems. Fallowing as a technique of conserving and restoring soil nutrients has almost disappeared among the refugee farmers and is shortened among the local Sudanese population.

One of the major consequences of continuous cropping has been overcultivation. The results of the soil analysis regarding the effects of continuous cultivation on the physical and chemical properties of the vertisols (the cultivable soils on the scheme) show that there is a difference in the extent of change that has occurred in terms of structure, texture and fertility depending on the particular history of land use of the sites concerned. In other words, there was a correlation between continuous cultivation and change in soil structure, texture and fertility. The areas affected by water erosion are also increasing considerably as degradation-prone sites are brought under cultivation in response to increasing demand for arable and grazing land.

Notes

1. Simple correlation between:

time and rainfall	$r = -0.53$
crop yield and time	$r = -0.68$
rainfall and crop yield	$r = +0.37$

Partial correlation between time and crop yield, with rainfall constant $r = -0.61$ Quoted in Simpson and Khalifa (1976a). See also O'Brien (1985: footnote 14).

2. This was tested by means of a chi-square test (χ^2) and a figure of 79 was obtained for χ^2. With 2 degrees of freedom (d.f.) and a level of significance of $P < 0.01$, a statistically significant relationship was established between nationality and use of fallow periods to replenish soil fertility.

3. Distribution of the respondents by number of years of cultivation (%)

Years	Refugees (n = 212)	Sudanese (n = 90)
1–9	17.0	60.0
10–15	19.0	26.0
16–20	36.0	7.0
21–22	28.0	7.0
Total	100.00	100.00

4. Even though no distinction is made in most of the literature, it has to be pointed out that some tree species compete for moisture and nutrients with crops, while others do not.
5. The *hawashas* in meshrua 83 had different land-use histories and that was the reason why more than two pits were dug.
6. The only rotation practised was alternating sorghum and sesame. Since neither of these crops is leguminous, this does not constitute effective rotation.
7. The pit was dug away from the tree canopy.
8. The soil study team was led by Dr M. Gamal Ahmed Younis (BSc, MSc, Water and Soil Science, PhD, Soil Science, and Diploma, Environmental Management).

3
Change in Vegetation Resources on and around the Qala en Nahal Refugee Settlement Scheme

> The survival of small-scale peasant farming systems is largely dependent on the continued existence of natural forest vegetation, woodlands and trees. (L. Roche, 1989)

The available literature abounds with statements to the effect that removal of natural vegetation constitutes one of the most important direct or indirect causes of the environmental problems faced by the arid and semiarid regions in Africa and elsewhere (Eckholm, 1975b, 1979, 1982; USAID, 1980; Ibrahaim, 1984; Dixon *et al.*, 1989; Grainger, 1982, 1990). Generally, the loss of vegetation cover resulting from clearance for cultivation, overgrazing and excessive tree felling for fuel and building houses is well documented (Digernes, 1977, 1979; Hunter and Ntiri, 1978; Repetto and Holmes, 1984; Mann, 1987, 1990; Roche, 1989; Grainger, 1990; Rees, 1990). Mann, among others, states that the removal of vegetation results in daytime air and soil surface temperature increase, rising wind speeds, soil-structure deterioration, soil-moisture increase, greater reflection of solar radiation back into the troposphere from the denuded ground and accelerated erosion of the top soil (Mann, 1990; 48–49). By the same token, high vegetation cover means lower soil temperature, low daytime temperature, high water-storage capacity, rainfall infiltration and groundwater table, low run-off, low levels of water erosion, good soil structure, virtually non-existent wind erosion and high soil fertility (IFAD, 1986; Dixon *et al.*, 1989; Grainger, 1990; Mann, 1990). For example, Mann conducted field experiments in The Gambia in 1984–1985 and significant differences in readings were found between soil temperatures taken in the shade, on mulch around trees and on bare ground below 30 m (Mann, 1987).

As mentioned, vegetation cover is also important in preventing soil erosion. For example, in Ethiopia, a grass-covered plot next to the plot with the highest loss of vegetation lost only 0.15 tons of soil per hectare per year (Hurni, 1982, 1988). Experiments conducted in Nigeria also showed that deforestation drastically altered the water balance. 'While there was none or only slight surface run-off in a forested watershed, the total water yield was 30 to 40% of the rainfall after forest removal' (Lal, 1985: 139). In addition, Christiansson's study in Tanzania showed that run-off and soil loss after deforestation increased about 100-fold (Christiansson, 1981). There are also researchers who identify a clear relationship between soil fertility and vegetation cover. Under fallow periods, trees, shrubs, forbs and grasses regenerate on abandoned farms. The roots of the trees penetrate deep into the soil and bring up nutrients from below that are released into the soil from decaying leaves (Digernes, 1977; Coppock, 1993). Billè and Corra's findings also show that leaf litter from woody plants improves nitrogen and phosphorus content of the soil (Billè and Corra cited in Coppock, 1993). As pointed out above, when vegetation cover is removed, soil temperature rises, which in turn affects the organic matter in the top soil associated with the essential biological processes crucial for determining soil fertility and structure (Young, 1985). Trees are not only important for environmental protection as sources of fuel wood, timber and fodder, but also as a source of food. During seasons when there is crop failure, certain types of trees represent an important source of food. In western Sudan in 1985 the fruits of the naturally growing tree species, *Balanites aegyptiaca* and *Boscia senegalensis*, may have accounted for the same calorific intake as all the food aid delivered to the area during the same period (cited in Roche, 1989: 18). In eastern Sudan, where gum arabic, frankincense and various herbal medicines are tapped from trees, deforestation has exacerbated the plight of the poor rural people, who in the past supplemented their incomes from forest products.

One of the indirect consequences of deforestation is shortage of the fuel-wood resource, which induces farmers to substitute crop residues as fuel, which is to the detriment of soil structure and fertility. Fuel-wood scarcity also induces farmers to substitute animal dung for fuel wood. Again, this not only leads to loss of agricultural nutrients, but it also causes indirect damage to soil structure due to the lack of humus contribution. A chain of causation can be set in motion in which, as Eckholm puts it, fuel-wood scarcity leads to the burning of more dung, which reduces the application of manure to farms; this in turn causes output to decline, thereby inducing farmers to clear on steeper forest gradients, resulting in intensified erosion and degradation (Eckholm, 1975a, b).

One of the major aims of this chapter is to measure the level of vegetation change that has occurred over time on and around the scheme area and to assess the implication of the change for the sustainability of the farming systems. Generally, the causes of change may be ascribed to natural processes, such as climatic changes or even seasonal fluctuations of rainfall (see Table 4.9). Although the method adopted here may enable us to measure roughly the level of human interference with regard to the vegetation resources on and around the scheme area, in view of the difficulty involved in the distinction between drought-induced fluctuations and human-induced changes, the results are taken as indicative rather than conclusive.

Assessment of vegetation change on the scheme

It is easy to see the vegetational changes that have occurred in the last 20–30 years, as a result not only of the enormous increase of permanent settlements, but also of the expansion in mechanized agriculture and commercial charcoal production. Unfortunately, there is a dearth of data relating not only to the changes that have occurred in a given period, but also to vegetation productivity, cover and species composition before the intensification of human activities in the area. In order to assess the changes that have occurred over time in terms of vegetation productivity, vegetation cover and plant-species composition of use to humans and animals, we carried out a vegetation survey in 1991. One of the most critical problems faced by researchers who try to assess environmental changes resulting from natural processes and human interference in most African situations is the lack of time-series data which would enable the researchers concerned to set standards against which to measure changes. The landscape of the area has no doubt changed drastically in the last two and half decades, but, since there are no records which show how things were before the enormous change in the pattern of settlement and external pressure, it is very difficult to state with certainty the level of vegetation decline that has taken place during this period.

The results of our survey are compared with the baseline data based on a similar survey conducted five years earlier. The question, however, is whether a period of

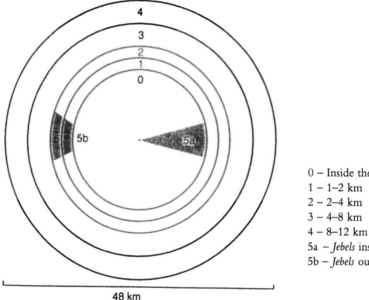

0 – Inside the Scheme
1 – 1–2 km
2 – 2–4 km
3 – 4–8 km
4 – 8–12 km
5a – *Jebels* inside the Scheme
5b – *Jebels* outside the Scheme

Figure 3.1 Sample frame of the vegetation survey

five years is long enough to measure vegetation changes in a meaningful way. In sparsely populated areas, a five-year period is not long enough to measure changes, but, in situations where the pressure on the natural environment is severe, changes that affect immediate demands can occur over a short span of time. This is not to suggest, however, that the long-term consequences of these vegetation changes can be established with an acceptable degree of certainty from such studies. Our method of selection of the sample sites, which included different distance ranges from the villages or sites of high population density, highlights the role of human interference in the process of the vegetation change (Fig. 3.1). The reason we did this was to see whether vegetation change was more pronounced in the areas where human activities were more intensive. The rationale of our assumption was based on the fact that the intensity of resource use by both humans and animals is likely to be more concentrated in the areas closer to the centres of settlements. If this assumption were true, we would expect to find differences in the level of changes that have occurred between the different sites depending on their location *vis-à-vis* the settlement sites.

One of the weaknesses of this method was that the pressure on land was not only coming from one direction, namely from the refugee settlements or the local Sudanese villages included in our study, but also from other directions, including charcoal producers from as far away as Sennar, Wad Madeni, Gedaref and Khartoum. However, since nowhere was the level of population concentration so high and consequently the pressure on the land so severe as on the scheme, we still expected to discover variations in the level of vegetation changes between the different locations. It is important to bear in mind, though, that, as we shall see in the following chapters, the common resources on the scheme area are open access resources and are consequently virtually exploitable at will by anybody. The refugees do not enjoy exclusive rights to the common resources available within the confines of the scheme (see Chapter 8). It is beyond doubt that there has been visible change in vegetation resources since the establishment of the refugee settlement scheme. But one cannot put the blame on the refugees as the sole cause of this change because their mere arrival attracted neighbouring Sudanese on to the settlement area to benefit from the services and facilities provided for the refugees. The shortcomings of our method notwithstanding, the most important contribution of this kind of research is the opportunity it provides for future researchers to measure changes over time.

The methodology of the vegetation survey

Within the given natural processes operative in the environment of the area, vegetation change was hypothesized to be a function of intensity of human interference and the level of interference was expected to be higher in the settlement area itself and in its immediate vicinity. As we moved away from the locations of population concentrations, we expected to discover higher vegetation productivity, denser vegetation cover, less pronounced change in vegetation species composition reflected in increases in palatable and nutritious plant species, increases in perennial grasses and increases in quality and quantity of forage. The opposite outcome was expected as we moved closer to the centres of population concentration. In light of the fact that human interference is in all directions, we also expected a diffuse pattern of change. Thus, the surveyed areas included (Fig. 3.1): (i) the settlement area itself; (ii) the immediate 1–2 km from the settlement boundaries; (iii) a further 2–4 km from (ii); (iv) a further 4–8 km from (iii); and (v) the area lying 8–12 km from (iv).

Random samples of 1 km² each in four directions along two perpendicular transects were surveyed in each of the five distance categories at various levels (Greig-Smith, 1964). Throughout the survey, a random sampling method was used. Although it is difficult to fully randomize sampling in such a study, the combination of various methods and careful counterchecking of the information gathered enabled us to minimize the risk of gathering inaccurate data. Most of the sites were revisited for further rechecking and, in every case, the next km² to the selected site was used for comparison/counterchecking. Smaller quadrats or sampling units of 20 m × 20 m or 30 m × 30 m sizes were closely surveyed within the same km². This means that each km² was surveyed at least twice, namely once using a whole km² and the second time using smaller plots (subsampling) within the same area. From each sample, the following data were gathered: (i) site location; (ii) number and species of trees, including seedlings per km²; (iii) distance to closest neighbour tree in metres; (iv) height of each tree in metres; (v) diameter at breast height (d.b.h.) in metres; and (vi) vegetation other than trees by species, number and weight using a m² quadrat – grasses and forbs. The woody vegetation was mapped by using transects, analysis of tree communities was carried out by use of plotless sampling techniques and profile diagrams were drawn to show the structure and the general physiognomy at different strata (ecological zones).

All the species of trees, grasses or forbs found on the same site were recorded to allow testing for their association with a particular land-form. Measurement of the heights and d.b.h. in metres is important in indicating the stage of growth and the volume of wood contained in each species. The d.b.h. was measured using a tape-measure while the heights for taller trees were estimated by means of actual measurement of the shorter trees. The grass biomass contents of 1 km² – a quadrat

– were weighed, using a balance with 0.1 g precision. After drying in the hot sun, these weights were used to estimate the total above-ground biomass per unit area and hence the total plant production of various species of grass. The samples were, as stated earlier, systematically selected along two perpendicular transects.

The data generated in our survey were compared with the results of a similar survey which was carried out in 1987 using the same methods.[1] As pointed out earlier, normally the time between the two surveys would not be enough to measure changes in vegetation species or cover, but in special situations, such as when the pressure on the resource base is high either because of high population density or due to a state of confinement resulting from a government policy, a measurable level of degradation may occur even in short periods.[2]

The fieldwork information was collected during October–November 1991, a time when sesame was harvested and other early-planted and/or early-maturing sorghum and millet[3] crop varieties were being harvested. Much of the grass cover, especially on the boundaries of the individual holdings, some of the hills and other closed areas, was still intact. Many rain-fed water reservoirs (*hafirs*) for livestock were not accessible to animals because of the surrounding standing crops.

Vegetation species distribution

Despite intensive human activities in the area over the last two decades, it is still possible to identify the origins of the dominant communities described by earlier studies (Harrison and Jackson, 1958). The findings show that the distribution of the tree species broadly conforms to the land-form. In 1983 Howard (Howard, 1983) and Dickinson and Howard (Dickinson and Howard, 1983) identified seven land-forms and vegetation types which occurred on each land-form, together with the area each land-form occupied (Table 3.1). The findings of the present study reveal that much change has taken place since 1983 (Table 3.2). What is interesting about the data in Table 3.2 is that, despite the fact that the surveys were conducted only 5 years apart, a measurable change in the frequencies of the dominant tree species on and around the scheme area seems to have occurred.

Table 3.1. Vegetation types, land-forms and areas covered

Vegetation types	Land-form	Area (ha)	Area (*feddan*)
Boswellia–Combretum woodland on hills	Steep-sided rocky hills	2,635	6,271
Combretum shrub savannah on hills	Steep-sided rocky hills	724	1,723
Combretum tree savannah	Pediments and low stony	1,720	4,094
Grazing area around villages		3,065	7,295
Acacia low woodland	Clay plains	2,732	6,502
Permanent cultivation divided into 200 m × 200 m *hawasha*	Clay plains	23,081	54,933
Cultivated land with bush fallow system	Clay plains	10,641	25,326
Total area		44,598	106,144

Sources: Dickinson and Howard, 1983; Howard, 1983.

Table 3.2 Average frequencies of common tree species per km^2 for 1987 and 1991 (%)

Local name	Botanical name	0		1–2		2–4		4–8		8–12	
		1987	1991	1987	1991	1987	1991	1987	1991	1987	1991
Hijlij	Balanites aegyptiaca	63	60	0	0	33	30	44	42	25	27
Talih	Acacia seyal	49	48	51	50	51	46	61	57	57	54
Hashab	Acacia senegal	27	28	49	50	41	46	65	71	23	27
Kitir	Acacia mellifera	23	28	63	50	37	30	70	71	31	36
Nabag	Zizyphus spina-christi	12	12	0	0	25	23	12	14	42	54
Luban	Combretum hartmannianum	26	24	75	50	30	23	33	28	29	27
Luban	Boswellia papyrifera	6	4	0	0	0	0	0	0	11	1
Kudad	Dichrostachys glomerata	9	8	0	0	0	0	0	0	0	0
Shedra beida	Lannea kerstignii	1	4	0	0	0	0	0	0	0	0

0, Scheme area; 1–2, 2–4, 4–8, 8–12, distances in kilometres outside the scheme.
Source: for 1987 A. Saleh's unpublished data, 1991, and for 1991 Survey results.

It is also noteworthy that the frequency of the occurrence of *Acacia senegal* (gum arabic tree) increased between 1987 and 1991. This was also stated by the farmers in the area. There were very few *A. senegal* when they first came into the area, but, as more trees were cut to clear land for cultivation and for other purposes, more *A. senegal* trees began to emerge, especially on cultivable land that was left to remain fallow for over 3 years (Key informants, 1991, 1994). The greater prevalence of *A. senegal* is an indication of a certain degree of depletion of soil nutrients because, on top of being drought resistant, *A. senegal* is a leguminous plant and can easily survive in very poor soils, even on a site which cannot support the growth of other trees. It has very deep roots which reach deep groundwater easily (Nar El Din Sid Ahmed, producer of TV programme *Field and Science*, Forestry Corporation, Khartoum, pers. comm., 6 December 1991). Studies elsewhere also show similar results. Coppock, for example, states that, in areas where there is a problem of nutrient depletion in top soils, woody seedlings with their deep roots establish and 'tolerate nutrient-depleted top soils to a higher degree than shallower-rooted grasses' (Coppock, 1993: 56).

The present study places more emphasis on average relative frequencies of dominant species rather than numbers. It could be concluded from the comparison that there has been some change in the frequencies of the dominant species, i.e. while some species have declined, others have increased.

The *Balanites aegyptiaca* population seems to be less disturbed than other species because of its site location. Most of the trees are conserved with *hawashas* (plots) of the individual farmers. Outside the scheme, they are less dominant and are, in most instances, vulnerable to felling by charcoal makers or herdsmen. *B. aegyptiaca* is dominant in the flat clay plains of the settlement, in the villages and, to a lesser extent, towards the River Rahad. It can attain a height of up to 10 m. Due to excessive cutting of its branches for browse, the canopy is markedly reduced, to less than 30%. More than 95% of the trees are mature. *B. aegyptiaca* has long been used traditionally as a medicinal tree. The soft bark is a strong detergent and is used for washing clothes. The fleshy fruits are used as a laxative, the kernel as fuel and the seed for cooking-oil production. The kernel is made into an edible cake. The leaves, especially those of the fruitless trees, are used as antidiabetics, anti-hypertensives and anti-icteric. This may explain why many farmers have left several *B. aegyptiaca* trees standing on their *hawashas*. There is, however, a slight decrease (6%) between 1987 and 1991 in all sites.

Acacia seyal dominates on the stony clay plains and along the water courses, usually mixed with other acacias and *Combretum*. Pure stands of mature *A. seyal* species are a rarity, but shrubs are very frequent. They are most abundant outside the settlement area. *A. seyal* is the favourite species for charcoal makers. It produces top-quality charcoal with minimum waste on burning. According to the colour of the bark, one can distinguish three types: red-barked (*talih ahmer*), brown-barked (*talih aswad*) and white-barked (*talih abyad*). *A. seyal* is seldom used as building poles, as it is quickly attacked by pests. The tree is a good browse for goats and camels. It is also used for gum production, although the quality is inferior to that produced from *A. senegal*. Due to its thin leaves and canopy, the tree provides poor shade. Mature trees reach a height of up to 11 m. The data in Table 3.2 show that there is a decrease (14%) in the frequency of the plant species between 1987 and 1991. An additional factor that might have contributed to its depletion is that the thorny nature of *A. seyal* provides a protective habitat for nesting by *Quelea quelea* (Arab. *zarzour*, Eng. red-billed quelea).

Quelea quelea is considered by the farmers in the area to be the most destructive bird pest of grains. Although the extent of cereal loss suffered by *Quelea quelea* attack is unknown on the scheme, in 1976 and 1980 about 150 hectares and 600 tonnes of sorghum, respectively, were completely destroyed in a nearby site – Jebel Sim Sim (Bruggers *et al.*, 1984). In 1978, 98% of sorghum was destroyed in 44 hectares of land in Hawata, which is only a few miles away from the scheme area (DWRC cited in Elliott, 1989). In 1974–1975, the estimated value of grain loss due to *Quelea quelea* attack was US $6.3 million nationwide in Sudan (FAO cited in Elliott, 1989). It was because of this that the farmers on the scheme disliked *A. seyal* on and around their *hawashas*. *Quelea quelea* is considered the most serious of all agricultural pest birds in Africa and elsewhere in the world (De Grazio in Bruggers *et al.*, 1984).

Acacia mellifera dominates on the clay plains, alternating with *A. senegal* and *B. aegyptiaca* mainly outside the scheme. At maturity the canopy, which is formed of several branches spreading from the base slightly horizontal to the ground, may cover, above ground, a circumference of up to 30 m. The height rarely exceeds 4 m. Apart from its uses as fencing (live) and fuel wood, *A. mellifera* is browsed by goats and camels. Clearing for cultivation would be an extremely hard task as the stems are very difficult to uproot. The data in Table 3.2 show a decrease (9%) of this tree over the 5-year period.

A. senegal or the gum arabic tree is of high economic importance countrywide. Sudan is the largest single producer of gum arabic in the world. The tree, like any other crop, is protected by law. However, large areas of *A. senegal* were cleared for settling refugees and preparing land for crop production. The remaining trees are exclusively owned by the Sudanese. *A. senegal* dominates on the clay plains. Pure stands can be seen, but usually they are found in association with other acacias, mainly *A. seyal*. Old forests of the tree are visible between Qala el Bagar and the River Rahad and in the Ban–Balos–Umburush triangle. Like *A. seyal*, the canopy can be very poor and the tree height rarely exceeds 5 m in a mature forest. The girths are from 0.2 to 0.7 m.

A. senegal, like other acacias on and around the scheme, are frequently attacked by grasshoppers and other insects causing severe damage to the foliage. This results in a complete cessation of, or marked reduction in, gum production. Gum arabic tree orchards do not exist within the scheme area, although it is common to see such gum orchards in the neighbouring Sudanese villages of Balos and Ban. These gardens are owned by individual families known locally as 'card holders'. Introduced in 1924 (S.O. Ibrahim Mohamed, Director of Mechanized Farming Corporation, Gedaref, pers. comm., 1991), the cards refer to a sort of certificate of ownership of the trees issued by the local authorities in Qala en Nahal town or Hawata. The card holder pays an annual fee to the government. Cards are exclusively issued to the Sudanese Arabs in the area. Neither the refugees nor the migrant settlers from the western part of the country or West Africa are entitled to own gum arabic trees. Gum arabic is tapped from *A. senegal* trees by cutting in the bark and tearing off a strip of bark 2–3 cm wide and 300–100 cm long. After 20 days, gum drops form along the damaged cambium and these globules are collected. Normally tapping takes place between September and November on trees that are 5 or more years of age.

With the decline in the living conditions of the resource users concerned, it is becoming more common to see ever-younger trees being severely overexploited with no possibility for regeneration. There are no figures available from the scheme on yields and on the importance of gum arabic in the economics of the scheme. We did not come across any refugee family which reported having earned any income from gum arabic. In fact as we shall see later, it is not clear if refugees have the right to own gum arabic trees even when such trees grow on their own farms. The immigrants from West Africa and western Sudan not only lack ownership rights of gum arabic trees, but the growth of such trees on their farms leads to loss of possession of the land where the *A. senegal* trees grow. Unlike the other trees, there has been an increase in the frequency (17%) of this tree species between 1987 and 1991 (Table 3.2). In view of the heavy browsing pressure and continuous cultivation without fallow periods, this is a remarkable increase.

Zizyphus spina-christi is another thorny tree, most abundant along water courses, in waterlogged areas and along the River Rahad. The tree is of medium height (1 m) and size (d.b.h. 0.2–0.65 m). As a tree it is mainly found in the compounds, and in bush form along the river and scattered in *hawashas* on the clay plains. *Z. spina-christi* is traditionally used as vermifuge, stomachic and hair toner. The fleshy fruits and seeds are edible. The seeds are boiled to produce an edible honey-like juice. *Z. spina-christi* is a good browse for camels and goats. It is rarely used for charcoal making but can be used as fuel wood. Table 3.2 shows that the frequency of this plant has slightly increased (12%) over the 5-year period.

Combretum hartmannianum dominates many land-forms. Together with *Boswellia papyrifera*, it is a key species of the mountain and low-hill vegetation. In addition to these sites, it is to be found on low stony clay, on clay plains and along water courses. It is by far the most abundant tree species in the settlement area and some 70–80% is found in shrub form. The mature trees are confined to mountain peaks or are scattered in the *hawashas*. Mature trees can reach a height of up to 6 m, while the shrubs range between 0.2 and 2 m high.

The tree is the second best for charcoal making because, despite the massive destruction, the rate of regeneration of this species is enormous. This is probably because the shrubs shed their leaves during the dry season, thus becoming less vulnerable to browsing by animals. In the wet season, other tree species, grasses and forbs are more attractive and more palatable to animals; so, in both cases, this species can avoid livestock browse. In folk medicine, the bark and leaves are used as skin tonic in general, and against post-partum uterine involution in particular. Like *Zizyphus* bark, the fleshy fruits and seeds are used as a vermifuge. None the less, as the data in Table 3.2 show, *C. hartmannianum* shows the highest decrease (37%) in the district in a matter of just 5 years.

B. papyrifera is on the verge of extinction. Of high economic value for its gum, this species was once second to *Combretum* as the dominant species in the mountain flora. It is a tall (up to 12 m), smooth, brown-barked tree with an average d.b.h. of 1.70 m. The tree sheds leaves soon after the rains and flowers in May. Tapping of the tree produces a pleasant aromatic gum of high commercial value, known as frankincense. The refugees are quite familiar with the species and excessive tapping seems to have taken place in the early days of the settlement. Whether because of old age, storms, drought, excessive tapping or the location of the trees, it was observed that most individuals of the species have begun to fall down. Of course, one cannot exclude human intervention in one way or another, but the fact is that there are no new shoots coming up. Even if it is coppiced, this species rarely regenerates, probably because of its nature or because of ecological zonation. However, over the 5-year period, the frequency of this tree species has declined by 12% (Table 3.2).

Dichrostachys glomerata was probably once the numerically dominant species. During the survey, it was encountered in only two localities, associated with acacias: on stony clay and clay plains in cultivated fields. As a thorny shrub, it is used for fencing. As shown in Table 3.2, a slight decrease (1%) in the frequency is noticeable between 1987 and 1991.

Lannea kerstignii is found on clay plains close to water courses associated with *A. mellifera* and *B. aegyptiaca*. It is a tall, 5 m, white-barked tree with thin leaves. Branches are sometimes used as browse for livestock. Between 1987 and 1991, this tree species has shown a slight increase (3%) (Table 3.2). The average changes that have occurred between the different site locations are summarized in Table 3.3.

The data in Table 3.3 show that the impact of human and animal interference on the different tree species in the different site locations has not been uniform. Different tree species are affected differently, depending on their economic value, social use and resistance/resilience to disturbance of different types, including fluctuations in rainfall. The influence of human interference on trees of economic value is twofold.

In some instances trees are preserved because of their economic value, e.g. *A. senegal*, and others are depleted for the same reason, e.g. *A. seyal*. The former is preserved for the production of gum arabic and the latter is excessively cut for charcoal production. In the scheme area there has been no change in the frequencies of the common tree species over the period of 5 years. In zones 1–2 km, 2–4 km and 4–8 km, there has been a general decrease in the frequency of the dominant tree species. The decrease is most prominent in zone 2–4 km, with a decrease of about 19%, followed by 1–2 km, where the decrease is about 12%. The smallest decrease is recorded, as expected, in zone 4–8 km (2%), while in zone

Table 3.3   Average frequencies of change of common trees over five-year period 1987–1991 (%)

	0	1–2	2–4	4–8	8–12	Average change in sites 5 years
Balanites aegyptiaca	−3	0	−3	−2	2	−6
Acacia seyal	−1	−1	−5	−4	3	−14
Acacia senegal	1	1	5	6	4	17
Acacia mellifera	5	−13	−7	1	5	−9
Zizyphus spina-christi	0	0	2	2	12	12
Combretum hartmannianum	−2	25	−7	−5	−2	−37
Boswellia papyrifera	−2	0	0	0	−10	−12
Dichrostachys glomerata	−1	0	0	0	0	−1
Lannea kerstignii	3	0	0	0	0	3
Average change all trees	0	−12	−19	−2	26	

0, Scheme area; 1–2, 2–4, 4–8, 8–12, distance in kilometres outside the scheme.

8–12 km there has been, on average, a remarkable increase (26%) in trees. The results show that there is an overall decrease of about 7% in all locations (zones). Figure 3.2 draws the general conclusions of the data contained in Table 3.2. The reason why there is no change in the scheme area is because the plant species were already depleted. The few remaining ones are protected by the owners of the *hawashas* either because of their economic value or because they provide firewood (by cutting the twigs) or shade against the heat of the sun.

The sites which are located between 0 and 4 km bear the brunt of the burden because of pressures of trampling, fuel-wood harvests, gum tapping, browsing and grazing. In these locations, trees are also lopped for animal fodder. Lopping does not *per se* decrease their frequency. In fact, if given enough respite, lopping may even stimulate growth, but this depends on the extent of browsing pressure. Zone 4–8 km is also affected because of the same factors, but, because of greater distance, the impact is less. The least affected site, as expected, was the area located furthest from the scheme.

As can be seen from the data in Table 3.3, the average frequency of *B. aegyptiaca*

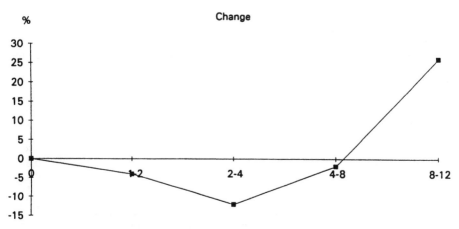

Fig. 3.2   Change in common plant species in the various distance ranges 1987–1991

has decreased by 6% throughout all the locations over the 5-year period. *A. seyal* has also decreased by 14% in all the locations, while *A. senegal* has on average increased by 17% over all the locations. *A. mellifera* has on average decreased by 9% over the same period while *Z. spina-christi*, like *A. senegal*, has on average increased by 12% in all the locations over the period under study. The most threatened tree species is *C. hartmannianum*, in which the average decline in a period of 5 years in all sites has been dramatic – in the range of 37%. *B. papyrifera* has also decreased by 12% in all the locations in the same period. *D. glomerata* has decreased by 1%. *L. kerstignii* has on average shown a slight increase, of 3%. The frequencies of some species were even found to be higher within the scheme area than outside the scheme. One of these trees is *B. aegyptiaca*. This tree does not exist in the area between 1 and 2 km outside the scheme.

Vegetation cover

A measure of vegetation cover was obtained by estimating the degree of canopy cover of each individual species in each quadrat. Each canopy was classified into one of six size classes. The mean percentages are below the 1987 findings in all the different distance locations surveyed, except for *Z. spina-christi* and *A. senegal* (Table 3.4). This confirms the findings in Table 3.2. This is obvious from the observed fact that all tree species are affected by either complete felling, coppicing or cropping of branches for browse or other use. Within the holdings, apart from facilitating the smooth running of tractors, much of the clearing was practised to avoid harbouring birds and other pests which many farmers thought would cause crop damage.

The second piece of evidence that emerges from the data in Table 3.4 is that, while there has indeed been considerable loss of vegetation cover in just 5 years in the different locations, some of the areas outside the scheme are also subject to excessive tree removal.

The results show that a certain degree of change in vegetation cover has taken place in and outside the settlement area between 1987 and 1991 (Fig. 3.2). Vegetation cover is lower on the scheme than in the areas outside it. Except for *A. senegal* the mean vegetation cover is sparser in 1991 than in 1987. In 1987 the mean

Table 3.4   The mean percentage cover of common plant species in the different distance ranges 1987–1991

Species	Mean % for species 1987	0	1–2	2–4	4–8	8–12	Mean % for species 1991
Balanites aegyptiaca	0.5	0.0	0.5	0.5	0.5	0.5	0.4
Acacia seyal	5.0	0.5	0.5	17.5	0.5	5.0	3.9
Acacia senegal	5.0	5.0	5.0	17.5	37.5	17.5	16.5
Acacia mellifera	62.5	0.5	17.5	17.5	62.5	17.5	23.1
Zizyphus spina-christi	5.0	0.5	37.5	5.0	0.5	17.5	12.2
Combretum hartmannianum	5.0	0.5	0.0	17.5	0.5	0.5	3.8
Boswellia papyrifera	0.5	0.5	0.0	0.0	0.0	0.5	0.2
Dichrostachys glomerata	0.5	0.5	0.0	0.0	0.0	0.0	0.1
Lannea kerstignii	0.5	0.5	0.0	0.0	0.0	0.0	0.1
Average Mean	9.4	0.94	6.78	8.39	11.33	6.56	6.7

0, Settlement area, 1–2, 2–4, 4–8, 8–12, distances in km outside the settlement area.
Source: for 1987 A. Saleh's unpublished data; for 1991 our survey results.

vegetation cover in the scheme was 9.4% but in 1991 only 6.7%. The data in Table 3.4 show that the level of deforestation on and around the scheme is severe. This gives serious cause for concern. If this trend in the process of decline in vegetation cover continues in the next 10 years, the whole vegetation may disappear.

However, since the rate of regeneration of coppiced plants is dependent on so many factors, prediction about the future state of the vegetation is impossible. Whether this trend will continue is dependent on many factors, such as rainfall and the extent of pressure on vegetation resources. The extent of pressure on the available resources may ease as resources become scarce, because people may seek other sources of forage, fuel wood, etc., in which case the decline may not continue at the same rate.

Plant density

The density of a species is measured in terms of the number of individuals of that species per unit area. From the plotless data collected, the densities per hectare of each of the more dominant species was calculated (Table 3.5).

B. aegyptiaca is the most dominant and conspicuous species in the clay plains in the permanent cultivation area, most other species having been cleared for cultivation. In this area, it is almost entirely mature in form, with more than 50% of the branches cut down for fodder and in order not to provide a habitat for bird pests. Outside the area a few shrubs can be seen in widely scattered zones. The only mature trees are found in the vicinity of the Sudanese villages. This tree has been extensively used in charcoal making.

More than 95% of the *A. seyal* is found in shrub form, with a d.b.h. far less than 0.17 m which renders it unsuitable for charcoal production. However, these shrubs are still used for fencing compounds. It is interesting to observe that, due to the scarcity of *A. seyal* for charcoal production and due to the high demand for charcoal in the urban areas, such as Khartoum, Umdurman, Gedaref, etc., the prices of charcoal have increased more than threefold on the scheme (see Table 5.12). Charcoal prices also fluctuate seasonally. During the rainy season, production is reduced and consequently prices increase because of declining supply.

The most affected area is the location 1–2 km from the scheme. This is because of the proximity of the site to the settlement centres and because of the 'open access' nature of the common resources, including trees (with the exception of *A. senegal* orchards). On the scheme area, even though the farmers complain about people who cut trees inside their farms, the data in Table 3.5 suggest that trees

Table 3.5   Density per hectare of the more common species 1991

Species	0	1–2	2–4	4–8	8–12
Balanites aegyptiaca	90	0	109	204	0
Acacia seyal	219	0	17,313	25	292
Acacia senegal	493	0	0	164	1,750
Acacia mellifera	114	0	0	657	625
Zizyphus spina-christi	277	0	0	4.444	0
Combretum hartmannianum	229	2,770	3,718	2,500	1,479

0, Scheme area; 1–2, 2–4, 4–8, 8–12, distance in km from the scheme.
Source: Our field survey, 1991.

growing on the farms seem to stand a better chance of survival than trees growing in non-cultivated sites. Charcoal makers, especially if they are resident in the area, are restrained by moral pressure from cutting trees standing inside *hawashas* belonging to farmers on the scheme. The areas located between 8 and 12 km from the scheme are also devoid of *B. aegyptiaca*, but it is less probable that the depletion has anything to do with the scheme. Generally, the data in Table 3.5 clearly show that the trees in the whole area are overexploited.

A. mellifera is much less used. Because of the difficulty of clearing, it is mostly left untouched. It also has a high rate of regeneration. Another factor that may contribute to its presence in the farms is that it rarely harbours birds that cause crop damage.

Z. spina-christi occurs mostly as bushes. Because of its root system, it is one of the most troublesome trees to clear off the land. The roots can persist for years, producing sprouts whenever soil moisture rises. Even in holdings which are cleared annually, this species is still a major cause of inconvenience to farmers.

C. hartmannianum, although it is intensively used for charcoal making and as fuel wood, is the most abundant species, especially outside the scheme area. As mentioned earlier, 70–80% is in shrub form covering some of the hills, the foothills and the lowland plains. It has a very high seeding rate. No easily discernible trend is shown in the data except that the 2–4 km distance range is most affected by excessive tree cutting, followed by the scheme area.

Forage value

Analysis of the crude chemical composition of some of the important trees and shrubs shows that, apart from the content of basic food constituents and some minerals, all the dominant species are also rich in vitamins, especially the precursors of vitamin A. The green leaves have been used in reversing avitaminosis A among livestock on the scheme. All animals recovered from night blindness 3–4 days after feeding on green leaves of *B. aegyptiaca* (interview with A. Saleh, 1991).

There is seasonal variation in the productivity of the nine species. Only *Balanites* and *Zizyphus* are evergreen; the others shed their leaves for the greater part of the dry season. All species except *Combretum* are highly palatable for goats and camels. These species are also under severe threat from grasshoppers and desert locusts.

Distribution of grasses and forbs

Like the tree species, the distribution of the grasses and herbs (forbs) follows the same land-form. We have identified five groups of grasses and forbs which are considered as key species (Table 3.6). Harrison and Jackson (1958) report that the major grasses on the clay plains are *Sorghum purpureosericeum*, *Hyparrheina pseudo-cymbara* and *Cymbopogon nervatus* (Harrison and Jackson, 1958). When they conducted their survey in 1958, these species occurred as pure stands in patchy pockets. Today, however, these pure stands are very rare except in *Ischaemum*, *Cymbopogon* and *Schima*, which are confined to a few land-forms.

All over the scheme, a high degree of mixing has taken place, most probably as a result of increased human and animal pressures. The more palatable species, such as *Brachiaria* and *Schima*, have been largely replaced by unpalatable species, such as *Cassia tora*, *Acanthospermum*, *Calotropis* and *Ocimum*. *Blepharis ciliaris* (siha), the most

Table 3.6   Distribution of major groups of grasses and forbs according to land-form and locality

Group	Species		Local names	Land-form/locality
I	Ischaemum brachyantherum	A	Tubas	Clay plain, waterlogged water
	Brachiaria xantholeuca	A	Gangar	courses
	Acanthospermum hispidum	A	Hurab hausa	
II	Cassia tora (invader)	A	Kawal	Village surroundings, jebels, hills, azazas (shallow soils), clay plains, water catchment areas, water courses, cultivation fields
III	Cymbopogon nervatus	P	Mahreib	Jebels, low hills, azazas
	Schima ischaemoides	A	Dumbulab	
	Andropogon distachyos	A	Dander	
	Cassia tora (invader)	A	Kawal	
	Aristida adsconsionis	A	Danabel bashom	
	Calatropis procera	A	Usher	
IV	Sorghum purpureosericeum	A	Anis	Stony, clay plains, azazas
	Cymbopogon nervatus	P	Mahreib	
	Elytrophorus spicatus	A	Luseik	
	Tribulus terrestris	A	Direisa	
	Calotropis procera	A	Usher	
	Cassia tora	A	Kawal	
V	Eragrostis aspera	A	Humeira	Permanent cultivation, bush
	Schmidtia pappophoroides	A	Mileiha	fallow, continuously cultivated
	Cassia tora	A	Kawal	hawashas
	Leptadenia hastata	P	Direi'a	
	Dinebra arabica	A	Moleta	
	Sorghum sudanense	A	Abu sabein	
	Striga hermontheca	A	Buda	
	Setaria incrassata	A	Luseik	
	Ocimum americanum	P	Rihan	

A, Annual, P, Perennial.
Source: Our field survey, 1991.

palatable and nutritious herb, has totally disappeared. In the study area, there was no trace of B. ciliaris. B. ciliaris is the best dry-season grazing plant for sheep and camels (Harrison, 1958: 8). Harrison states, '[I]f they [livestock] get enough of it they want little else and will thrive well. In order to reach it they are prepared to walk across many miles.' One feature of Blepharis is its susceptibility to overgrazing because it does not shed its seeds in the dry season (Harrison, 1958: 8).

C. tora (kawal) now represents the greatest danger to all grazing lands, including the hilltops in the area. This species is an unpalatable annual broad-leaved weed, unknown to the area until very recently. It appeared more than a decade following the establishment of the refugee settlement scheme and the immigration of many Sudanese from the western part of the country into the area. Most of the farmers say that C. tora has become a major problem only since the 1984 drought. It is the most unpalatable species and now covers the entire village environs and is to be found in abundance in all land-forms, including the tops of the hills. The dehiscent characteristics are the main factor in the accelerated spread of the plant. The broad leaves form a dense canopy which deters the growth of vegetation underneath. Animals grazing on the sparse grasses in the vicinity may pick up some *Cassia* seeds and, since these are indigestible, they are easily spread through their faeces.

Cassia leaves, however, can be fermented anaerobically in earthen pots; after full decomposition, the contents are removed, turned into small balls, dried in the sun, then ground into fine flour and used with soup as porridge spice and appetizer. This is only consumed by the Sudanese immigrants in the area. The refugees do not utilize the *Cassia* leaves for any useful purpose.

All the members of group V (Table 3.6) except *Ocimum* are secondary invaders. They are most abundant in the old deserted *hawashas*. In the cultivated fields, they create a major weed problem. *Leptadenia* is a creeping weed which can spread in vast areas. Its removal is extremely time-consuming and energy-intensive. It is, however, highly palatable to all types of stock. *Striga* is a sorghum parasite that deprives the crop of all soil nutrients, resulting in a complete cessation of plant growth and eventual wilting and death (Bebawi, El-Hag and Khogali, 1985). This species is now the main cause of partial or total crop failure in the settlement area (see Chapter 4). Its effects get relatively more severe as soil fertility declines.

Dinebra is a prostrate broad-leaved species normally found in marshy fields. As it quickly germinates following the early showers, the plant forms a canopy over the newly germinating crops. This results in crop growth failure. Although a noxious weed, *Dinebra* can be used as food for humans (green salad) and as fodder for animals; also the vigour and growth rate are so high that it is not practicable or desirable to weed it out completely.

Sorghum sudanense (Sudan grass or, in Arabic, *adar*) resembles the sorghum crop in shape, colour and growth form. When weeding, unskilled farmers, and especially the refugees, often get confused and, instead, remove individual sorghum crop plants, leaving behind the 'false sorghum', as it is sometimes called. The distinction between the two, for most farmers, can only be made at heading time. The heads of 'false sorghum' are thin, compact and spicular, while the 'true sorghum' has less compact heads. The difference becomes more obvious as seeds are gradually found after flowering. This weed is considered a major problem by many of the refugee farmers in the area. The Sudanese farmers seem to have no difficulty identifying it at an early stage. Both Sudanese and refugee farmers state that one of the reasons for not using organic manure to replenish soil nutrients is because animal dung contains seeds of *S. sudanense*.

Although they share nutrients with the crops, the other weeds are less problematic in terms of clearing or differentiation from crops, but the major problem of their rapid numerical increase remains. Many of the farmers in the area see a relationship between the emergence of such noxious weeds and vegetation change resulting from fluctuations in rainfall, overcultivation and grazing pressures. The frequency of occurrence of the dominant species of grasses within and outside the settlement areas is given in Table 3.7.

Adem Saleh, the former Livestock Officer in the scheme, has, since 1987, been closely observing the growth, vigour and abundance of the grasses and forbs in the scheme. It is now well established that all species have a relative period of growth dormancy consistent with soil moisture content. For example, *C. tora* and *Hibiscus micranthus* exhibit massive growth and abundance once every 2 years. This usually follows a high soil moisture content, but it is so cyclical that, however satisfactory the soil moisture might be, the growth rate and abundance do not break the cycle (interview with A. Saleh, 1991). This is why yearly surveys give different results. It

Table 3.7 Frequencies of some common species of grasses and forbs in 1987 and 1991 per m^2 quadrat

Species	% 1987	0	1–2	2–4	4–8	8–12	% 1991
Brachiaria xantholeuca	40.0	8	50	0	57	0	23.0
Ischaemum brachyantherum	51.0	56	50	23	57	45	46.2
Acanthospermum hispidum	27.4	0	0	0	0	0	31.0
Cassia tora	18.2	75	50	30	28	18	40.2
Cymbopogon nervatus	31.0	24	50	15	28	36	30.6
Schima ischaemoides	34.0	24	50	7	14	9	20.8
Andropogon distachyos	9.8	20	0	7	14	18	11.8
Dinebra arabica	1.2	12	0	7	0	0	3.8
Aristida adsconsionis	7.0	16	0	7	0	27	10.0
Calatropis procera	8.0	12	0	0	0	0	14.0
Sorghum purpureosericeum	35.0	16	0	7	71	72	33.2
Elytrophorus spicatus	23.0	28	0	23	57	9	23.4
Tribulus terrestris	5.7	0	0	0	14	0	6.0
Eragrostis aspera	23.7	16	50	0	57	18	28.2
Schmidtia pappophoroides	39.2	56	50	7	57	45	43.0
Leptadenia hastata	23.4	36	50	7	28	9	26.0
Sorghum sudanense	11.0	8	0	0	42	9	11.8
Striga hermontheca	22.8	8	0	0	14	0	30.3
Setaria incrassata	21.9	28	0	23	57	9	23.4
Ocimum americanum	16.0	20	50	7	14	0	18.2

0, Scheme area; 1–2, 2–4, 4–8, 8–12, distance in km from scheme.

is desirable, therefore, when undertaking a vegetation survey to take such cyclical variations into consideration.

From Table 3.7, it is evident that, while the frequency of some species has substantially declined, other species have attained high frequencies, meaning that species with reduced frequencies are the more palatable, the remainder being either less palatable or completely unpalatable. For example, the species of *C. tora*, the invader, not only increased drastically between 1987 and 1991, but is also considerably higher within the scheme area, where human and livestock influence was greater, than outside it. The data in Table 3.7, as expected, show that annual grasses have become dominant and perennial grasses drastically reduced. Of the eighteen common grasses identified in the study area, fifteen were annuals and only four species were perennials.

Grass cover

This has been extremely difficult to estimate because most of the area was grazed. The remnants of the grasses were so trampled and mixed that the identification of the species was impracticable. Only a few species, some whole and some partially grazed, could be identified and their mean percentage cover estimated.

Grass cover is also temporarily variable. Table 3.8 shows the results for some species. It is evident from the table that grasses of economic value, i.e., used either as fodder for livestock or as thatching material for huts, are being continuously used. The demand for thatching grass is even higher outside the scheme. It is

Table 3.8   The mean percentage cover of some dominant grass and forb species in the different distance ranges

Species	Species mean % 1987	0	1–2	2–4	4–8	8–12	Species mean % 1991
Ischaemum brachyantherum	38.4	0.60	5.60	5.30	0.55	0.58	2.50
Brachiaria xantholeuca	32.5	0.70	18.50	5.10	0.50	0.60	5.08
Acanthospermum hispidum	4.0	17.00	0.60	3.50	0.52	0.54	4.40
Cassia tora	43.4	62.50	62.50	67.50	37.50	37.50	53.50
Cymbopogon nervatus	34.5	18.20	31.70	49.00	17.30	60.00	29.90
Schima ischaemoides	16.4	0.30	7.90	9.40	4.00	0.60	4.40
Andropogon distachyos	17.0	3.00	2.40	0.90	11.90	29.20	9.48
Aristida adsconsionis	0.0	0.0	0.0	0.0	0.0	0.0	0.0
Calatropis procera	0.5	0.50	0.50	0.50	0.50	0.50	0.50
Sorghum purpureosericeum	30.9	16.70	34.00	36.00	44.00	0.30	26.70
Elytrophorus spicatus	18.7	25.00	35.00	37.20	11.20	8.30	23.30
Tribulus terrestris	3.0	0.00	0.00	0.00	0.00	5.00	0.00
Eragrostis aspera	14.5	38.00	25.00	17.20	0.00	3.70	16.78
Schmidtia pappophoroides	32.0	61.00	45.20	28.00	27.00	18.00	35.80
Leptadenia hastata	11.5	81.50	27.30	15.40	0.00	0.00	24.80
Dinebra arabica	11.2	62.00	0.00	3.40	1.10	0.00	13.30
Sorghum sudanense	12.0	44.50	0.00	0.00	0	36.00	16.10
Striga hermontheca	16.3	89.00	0.00	0.00	0.00	0.00	17.80
Setaria incrassata	29.4	67.00	45.70	27.20	11.20	7.00	31.60
Ocimum americanum	9.8	7.90	11.20	13.00	8.70	12.70	10.70

0, Scheme area; 1–2, 2–4, 4–8, 8–12, distance ranges outside the scheme area in km.
Source: 1987 A. Saleh's unpublished data; 1991 our survey results.

common to see lorries from and around the scheme leaving for as far as Gedaref (109 km north-west of the scheme) packed with thatching grass. In 1987, the price of a bundle of thatching grass (about 10 kg) was £S5.00. The same amount in 1991 cost £S30.00. Similarly, the price of mats made from the same grass and used for fencing compounds (*hosh*) or for making shades (*rakuba*) rose from £S15.00 a mat in 1987 to £S60.00 in mid-1991. Grass collected for animal feed was in 1991 sold at £S30.00 per sack (15–20 kg); this was available for less than £S1.00 in 1987. These drastic price increases were not due solely to declining sources of supply, but also to an upsurge in demand and the high rate of inflation.[4]

The abundance and availability of grasses for grazing or construction purposes, assuming favourable physical conditions exist, is largely determined by the incidence of bush fires. Charcoal makers deliberately set fire to grasses to clear paths and expose trees prior to cutting them down. Before the domestic water-supply system was refurbished, the neighbouring Sudanese would normally move towards the River Rahad (30 km to the south-west) in search of water. Before setting out, they would set fire to all the village environs lest stray fires destroyed the village in their absence. Other fires were the direct consequence of herdsmen leaving behind unextinguished fires when they moved to a new camp.[5] Some herders also deliberately set fire to grasses in the jebel to encourage grass regrowth in the next season. With the depletion of vegetation resources on and around the scheme area, fire outbreaks are no longer common.

Density of grasses and forbs

The numbers of each individual species per m^2 quadrat of the dominant grasses and forbs are given in Table 3.9 for 1987 and 1991. It is clear from the table that the grass and forb species of greater economic value have invariably decreased while those of lesser value, for example, *C. tora*, have increased sharply. It is also noteworthy to observe that the density of most species is quite considerable in the settlement area as compared with other distance ranges.

It seems that frequency of weeding coupled with animal movements (when allowed to graze on *hawashas* after harvest) enhances the spread and growth of less desirable species. Some species that were of no significance in 1987 are now gaining importance, mainly in the cropped areas. *Striga hermontheca* now covers a considerable part of the *hawashas* in the settlement area. It is the main factor in the declining yields of sorghum, the staple crop among the refugee communities. Holdings which are heavily infested normally end in total crop failure, leading to their abandonment.

The problem of abandonment of plots cannot, however, be looked at in isolation from the economic positions and demographic compositions of the households. Those families with an adequate supply of family labour and those who can afford to hire labourers are in a better position to combat weed infestation. This does not, however, apply to *S. hermontheca* because, according to the farmers, the latter cannot be controlled by weeding. In the past few years, wage rates have increased drastically. Weeding costs were £S50.00 per *hawasha* (10 *feddans*) in the 1970s. It

Table 3.9   Density of the more dominant grasses and forbs (numbers per m^2 quadrat) in different distance ranges (in km) 1987 and 1991

Species	1987 (mean)	0	1–2	2–4	4–8	8–12	1991 (mean)
Ischaemum brachyantherum	23	11	14	20	31	33	22
Calotropis procera	0	0	0	0	0	0	0
Brachiaria xantholeuca	9	0	5	4	0	0	2
Sorghum purpureosericeum	11	0	10	9	7	25	10
Acanthospermum hispidum	0	2	5	0	0	0	1
Elytrophorus spicatus	0	9	11	8	6	0	7
Cassia tora	2	41	34	32	20	15	28
Tribulus terrestris	0	0	0	0	2	1	1
Cymbopogon nervatus	8	4	5	3	2	10	5
Eragrostis aspera	10	18	14	0	7	0	8
Schima ischaemoides	5	0	0	2	2	1	1
Schmidtia pappophoroides	6	13	11	6	4	1	7
Andropogon distachyos	0	1	0	3	4	1	2
Leptadenia hastata	1	19	9	4	5	0	7
Aristida adsconsionis	0	0	0	0	0	0	0
Dinebra arabica	0	18	2	0	0	0	4
Sorghum sudanense	0	15	7	0	0	0	4
Striga hermontheca	2	16	7	0	0	0	5
Setaria incrassata	0	8	8	5	4	0	5
Ocimum americanum	0	3	0	0	2	4	2

0, Scheme area; 1–2, 2–4, 4–8, 8–12, distance ranges outside the scheme area in km.
Source: 1987 A. Saleh's unpublished data; 1991 our survey results.

was normal in 1991 to pay £S2,000–3,000 for the first weeding depending on the level of weed infestation and about half that amount for the second and third weeding. Some of this dramatic increase was due to inflation. This has led many farmers to abandon their *hawashas* and clearly suggests that there is a correlation between land degradation and weed infestation.

Biomass of grasses and forbs

A comparison between the net weight – biomass – of some species would indicate the extent of depletion of some types of grasses. As can be seen from Table 3.10, the growth of all species studied has decreased considerably, except for the most undesired species, such as *C. tora*, whose occurrence almost doubled from 1987 to 1991. Even though these results show the extent of depletion of range resources between the two periods, they do not provide us with conclusive evidence about potential future productivity. This is because seasonal fluctuations are influenced by a host of factors, such as seasonal variation in rainfall.

The most critical and complex question is whether the decline in biomass production between the two periods is attributable to variation in rainfall or is due to grazing pressure. The total amounts of rainfall in 1987 and 1991, when the data on vegetation were collected, were 581 and 549 mm, respectively (see Table 4.10). The difference between the two years is about 6%. The question, therefore, is whether the decline in biomass production observed between the two years is due to this difference. This is unlikely. In the study area, vegetation growth is not only dependent on the amount of annual rainfall, but also on distribution. Rainfall was poorly distributed in 1987 as opposed to 1991. In 1987 there were 47 days with rain as against 23 in 1991 (see Table 4.10). There can be little doubt about the impact of this on vegetation growth. It is not clear, however, how much of this can be ascribed to fluctuation in rainfall as opposed to other non–rainfall-related interferences, such as grazing pressure.

Most of the data in this chapter suggest that the causes of the vegetation changes observed are difficult to attribute to one factor to the exclusion of other variables. The changes are the result of multiple interacting forces. It is extremely difficult to measure with an acceptable degree of precision the role of the specific relevant factors in the dynamic process of change. The shrinkage of forage resources is

Table 3.10   Biomass of the more common species in g/m² 1987 and 1991

Species	Biomass	
	1987	1991
Ischaemum brachyantherum	390.7	70.0
Eragrostis aspera	300.0	68.5
Brachiaria xantholeuca	416.6	125.0
Schmidtia pappophoroides	168.0	48.9
Sorghum purpureosericeum	353.8	92.0
Schima ischaemoides	323.8	102.0
Ocimum americanum	250.0	75.0
Cassia tora	316.0	600.0
Cymbopogon nervatus	250.0	52.0

Plate 3.1 The areas in the immediate vicinity of the settlements are covered with non-palatable species such as Cassia tora *reflecting the extent of the pressure on the environment. (Photo: Gaim Kibreab)*

precipitated by expansion of cultivation and by grazing and browsing pressures as well as by rainfall fluctuations, but it is impossible to single out a sole factor as responsible.

Discussion of the findings

The area, which was once described geographically as a woodland savannah, has by and large turned into a scattered, patchy wooded territory. Over the years, owing to high population density and an inadequate resource base, the pressure on natural resources has greatly increased. Building materials, firewood and pasture have been considerably reduced. From the data collected, it is worthwhile to consider the features discussed below. Trees, the most dominant species, are discussed in terms of occurrence, frequency, mean cover, density and forage value; grasses and forbs are discussed likewise.

Distribution of tree species

From Table 3.1 it can be observed that the main feature more or less typifies the areas occupied by the same plant species. The results of our survey show that most of the tree cover has greatly changed since Howard undertook his survey in 1983. Not only has the number of trees decreased quantitively, but there has also been a considerable qualitative change in vegetation resources. Most of the change has occurred in favour of less commonly utilized or unpalatable annual plant species. *Balanites* and *A. seyal* have been extensively used as fuel wood and animal fodder. The few species that could be found on the scheme are mainly confined to the *hawashas* or villages. These sites are normally protected from further removal because they are located on plots belonging to individual farmers. The fact that these trees stand within the *hawashas* is not on its own a guarantee against exploitation by outsiders, because illegal felling of trees standing on individual farms is common. The mean percentage cover is very low for most of the species, which again implies that trees have been chopped for grazing or fuel wood, and regeneration of the coppiced trees and new seedlings is also hampered by browsing animals such as goats. Relatively more vegetation cover is to be found as one moves away from the scheme, i.e. from 2 km outwards. The reason for this is that pressure on the land seems to decrease slightly with distance from the scheme. Some of the areas adjacent to the Sudanese villages also have gum arabic trees mixed with other species and this provides a certain degree of protection against exploitation. Gum arabic trees (*A. senegal*) are protected by law. The real protection, however, does not emanate from formal statutory protection, but rather from individual ownership of gum-arabic-producing trees.

Outside the settlement area, tree cover is more evident. This is due to several interacting and interrelated factors. Firstly, compared with the refugee farmers, who are in a state of confinement, the Sudanese farmers' access to natural resources, namely arable, grazing and woodland, is greater than that of the refugees. Hence the pressure on wood and other resources is not as severe as it is on the scheme. Secondly, the higher frequency of trees indicates a reasonable degree of awareness among the Sudanese small farmers of the need for natural-resource conservation. Thirdly, this may also be a reflection of variation in perception regarding tenurial security or insecurity among the refugees and the Sudanese in the surrounding areas.[6] Despite this difference, however, there is clear evidence that, even in the neighbourhood of the Sudanese villages, some species of trees were largely overexploited as sources of energy, fuel wood and charcoal by villagers and outsiders who come into the area to cut trees for charcoal making for sale in the regional towns or the capital, Khartoum. The drastic increase of charcoal prices may, among other things, indicate the extent of depletion of woodland resources. This is not, however, always true because local fuel-wood prices can rise in response to increased urban demands for fuel wood. On the scheme, the drastic increase in prices is not only due to physical scarcity, but also due to increased urban demands and the increased costs, in terms of labour input, of making charcoal. The amount of charcoal consumed locally is inconsiderable and could easily be met from the local vegetation resources.

It could also be argued that densities of trees on the settlement area are higher than expected. The explanation lies in the fact that most of these trees are standing on the plots of individual farmers. As stated earlier, this inhibits outsiders from cutting such trees. Normally villagers do not cut trees standing on other farmers' *hawashas*. Such is not the case, however, with charcoal makers who come from distant areas. They have a tendency to cut trees indiscriminately as long as they can escape detection. Since 1983, a lot of tree removal has taken place. The areas that were occupied by the different species in 1983 are no longer the same. Their frequency has been drastically reduced. For example, the *Combretum* tree savannah on *azaza* (reddish shallow soil) that was reported by Dickinson and Howard in 1983 no longer exists. This means that 4,094 *feddans* now consist of bare land without tree cover. The reason for the severe devegetation of these sites is that, compared with the hills, they are easily accessible to grazing and trampling by livestock and humans.

Except for *B. aegyptiaca*, which are generally mature trees, all the other species are extremely small with an average d.b.h. of only 0.34 m. This suggests that other mature trees are cut for either construction timber, charcoal making, firewood, clearing of land for cultivation or for animal fodder. The relative 'high' density of some species, for example, *A. seyal*, *A. senegal*, *Z. spina-christi* and *C. hartmannianum*, can be explained in light of the fact that all the old trees were used up for various purposes: construction of huts, fencing, charcoal and fuel wood. Species that show abundance are almost invariably newly emerging young shoots from coppiced stock or from seeds.

Basic information on the amount of charcoal produced on the scheme for export to the cities is completely lacking but it may be said that the total amount was more than 15,000 sacks per month during the 1980s. This has dropped to less than 5,000 sacks during the early 1990s. The reason for the decline in the production figures is because the wood resource on the scheme is exhausted and the remaining trees are too young to be used for charcoal making. The average d.b.h. for the trees used in charcoal production (*Combretum*) within the scheme is 0.34 m. Refugees were not involved in charcoal production in the early years, but, with the shortage of cultivable land and lack of other sources of livelihood, refugees have begun to engage in charcoal making. This activity was unknown to them previously. Before the pressure on natural resources had become severe on the scheme, the trade of charcoal making was mainly monopolized by the Sudanese farmers and migrants from the western part of the country. Dire poverty seems to have forced some of the refugees to engage in charcoal production, exerting more pressure on woodland resources. As will be shown later, continuous cultivation of plots without fallowing or use of yield-boosting inputs has led to a drastic decline of yields (Chapter 4). As a result, many farmers, both Sudanese and refugees, are searching for an alternative means of survival, and charcoal making seems to offer the easiest outlet, requiring no investment except labour power and a simple axe. Despite the high level of poverty that abounds in the refugee villages, the activity is still mainly dominated by the non-refugees, both within and outside the scheme.

Distribution of grasses and forbs
Many grass species of high nutritive value have virtually disappeared from the settlement. The combined effect of the shrinkage of the grazing areas, the growing livestock population and the frequent movements to and from the scheme area in the context of erratic and low rainfall has led to reduction of grass cover. The abundance of previously rare species was enhanced by the effect of agriculture and livestock on the reproductive ecology. Most of the species are noxious and unpalatable. The original species – *S. purpureosericeum*, *H. pseudo-cymbara* and *C. nervatus* – are now confined to very few pockets on the scheme. Instead species peculiar to the area are now a common feature. Their productivity has also greatly changed. It is very difficult to find pure stands of grasses nowadays. It is also quite obvious that the spread of the more unpalatable species, for example, *C. tora*, and *Acanthospermum hispidum*, is becoming more common. *C. tora*, in particular, could be found almost everywhere, from the holdings up to the tops of the hills. The entire village sites and the surroundings, which once provided very good grazing for livestock, are now dominated by this species.

The results of the study suggest that selective grazing and trampling over the ever-decreasing residual land constitute one of the causes of disappearance or reduced frequency of the more grazable plant species. Some animals are selective, but others such as goats and sheep, are less selective. In the context of choice, animals graze selectively; as a consequence the most palatable species are most affected by the pressure of intensive grazing. With the drastic shrinkage of the wet grazing areas, precipitated by expansion of cultivation on to previous pastures and increased animal population, the most preferred species are grazed at an early stage of their development or when they are most vulnerable. Grazing year after year at this stage of growth may eventually lead to their disappearance from the grassland community. In this manner they give way to less palatable grasses, because the latter risk no destruction through selective grazing. The data show that, as the intensity of wet season grazing increased, the more palatable grasses were succeeded by less palatable species.

More and more vigorous weeds could also be seen in all the *hawashas*. The dominance of these weeds poses great problems for farmers. Another factor contributing to the widespread existence of these grasses (annuals) is their ability to grow very vigorously on very poor soils. For example, in south Turkana (Kenya), where annuals are dominant, Coppock argues that annuals have special features which contribute to the severity of drought impacts and the resilience of an arid ecosystem (Coppock, 1993: 59). First, even a 2-year drought period can result in almost no standing herbaceous biomass. Second, annuals have a tendency to persist in seed banks and standing biomass is lost by weathering or grazing. This suggests that, in areas where annuals are dominant such as in south Turkana, drought can have a 'devastating impact on cattle, irrespective of their pre-drought densities' (Coppock, 1993: 59). Third, upon receiving sufficient rainfall, annual grasses mature and set seed within 6 weeks. Therefore, the number of grazers required to compromise this seed production within the given 6-week period is very high, and in most years probably higher than the existing number of grazers. In such areas, Coppock argues, herbaceous production and cattle population are relatively uncoupled to a significant degree. Rainfall, not consumers, largely dictates the composition of vegetation from year to year (Coppock, 1993: 59–60). The opposite patterns were observed in Borana (southern Ethiopia), where perennial herbs and not annuals were dominant (Coppock, 1993: 59–60). This suggests the complexity and difficulty of differentiating between human/livestock-induced changes and fluctuations caused by variations in rainfall. It is on a given soil type, landscape and vegetation that these forces of change become operative and it seems that the impacts of human and livestock population as well as rainfall cannot be established independent of the features of the dominant vegetation species in the study area concerned.

What is not clear in Coppock's comparative analysis of the impacts of stocking rates on rangelands in south Turkana and southern Ethiopia is whether the dominance of annuals in south Turkana was a result of overgrazing in the past or whether they have always been dominant, independent of livestock densities. In the present study area, studies conducted at the end of the 1950s show that perennial grasses were dominant (Harrison and Jackson, 1958). Annuals were relatively unknown until the mid-1980s on and around the scheme (interview with herders and former ACORD LO, 1991). There was a severe drought in the mid-1980s and, according to the farmers in the area, it is since then that annuals have become a problem. The question is, therefore, whether the appearance of the annual grasses and the reduction of perennials are precipitated by drought or by human/livestock interference. Behnke and Scoones, for example, state: '[U]nder very dry conditions, annuals are dominant' (Behnke and Scoones, 1993: 27). However, if the advent of annuals is solely due to moisture availability, why is it that all the areas are not equally affected? The annuals are dominant on the sites where grazing and trampling are highest. In the study area, the vegetation changes observed seem to be due to an interplay between natural processes and human interference. However, at this stage, it has to be admitted that it has not been possible to measure satisfactorily the role of each in the process of change. Future research may accomplish this complex task. The question of whether the vegetation changes are reversible cannot be determined either. This is because the results do not warrant any conclusion on this subject. This is, however, generally the case, because current knowledge does not allow a distinction to be made between drought-induced fluctuations and permanent changes in vegetation states (Laykock, 1991). The consequence of this is that it is very difficult to distinguish between permanent human-induced degradation and temporary rainfall-induced vegetation change.

Conclusion

Before the establishment of the refugee settlement scheme, the area was covered with dense savannah vegetation. There was very little human interference, among other things due to heavy sandfly infestation. One of the most evident impacts of the refugee settlement scheme is on the vegetation resources of the area. Large numbers of trees were felled for construction of dwellings. Vast areas of land were also cleared for cultivation and establishment of villages. Over time, fuel-wood requirements have also increased the pressure on the forest resources of the area. The removal of vegetation has reduced the problem of sandfly infestation and the area has become hospitable. However, if the extent of deterioration of the vegetation resources continues unabated, the area may suffer more grievous vegetation changes and consequently become inhospitable. At present this outcome is remote, but, in the absence of corrective measures, the areas that are stripped of vegetation may increase in the future. At present the areas which are devoid of vegetation are limited to the immediate vicinity of the villages, watering-points and human/animal tracks. There are, however, some areas which are covered with non-palatable invading annual weeds that are of no value to humans or animals. The occurrence of these types of vegetation is clearly limited to the areas where there is intensive human and animal pressures. Until the early 1980s, the jebels and pediments were covered with diverse species of trees and perennial grasses. At present most of these sites are reduced to bare ground and have become the major cause of enhanced run-off.

The results show that there has been a negative impact on the vegetation resources, reflected in the changes in vegetation cover, reduction in palatable and nutritious grasses, increases in unpalatable and non-nutritious species, decreases in perennial grasses and increases in annuals. It is important to point out, however, that, even though it was after the establishment of the scheme that the area began to be inhabited continuously, it is wrong to attribute the change in the vegetation resources solely to the presence of the refugees. The provision of a perennial water-supply and social services by the international refugee regime has, since the establishment of the settlement, been 'pulling' settlers from as far as West Africa and western Sudan. This was exacerbated by the non-exclusive nature of the woodland and grazing resources. The refugees are not entitled to prevent outsiders from using the vegetation resources. As a result, charcoal wholesalers from as far as Khartoum amd Omdurman come with contractual workers to cut trees for charcoal production. Livestock herders also come from distant areas to take advantage of the water-supply systems during the dry season. Hence, the changes in vegetation resources that have occurred cannot be attributed solely to the refugees and their animals.

Although the results show that the vegetation resources have deteriorated considerably, in the case of trees not all is doom and gloom. Some tree species are protected, while others have resisted the pressure, either because of their resilience, manifested in high regenerative capability, or because of their remarkable ability to withstand human and animal interference. There is a considerable change in grasses, forbs and weeds. The question is whether the trend toward unpalatability and dominance of annuals can be reversed.

Notes

1. I am grateful to Dr Adem Saleh for making these unpublished primary raw data available for my use.
2. Equipment used for the survey included : (i) one m^2 quadrat; (ii) a 30m-long chain for transects and quadrats; (iii) A 2m tape for measuring d.b.h.; (iv) iron poles for measuring tree heights; (v) an electronic scale for weighing contents of quadrats. A total of fifty-four trips were made to collect the necessary data initially, but further trips became inevitable to countercheck some of the data gathered.
3. Millet is planted by a few farmers only.
4. The precise effect of inflation on this price hike is not easy to establish because of the lack of a consumer-price index for the rural areas.
5. Historically, fire destroyed a major proportion of the grazing resources throughout northern Sudan. For example, M.N. Harrison observed that, in southern Kordofan and southern Darfur, 'every year over 80 per cent of the potential grazing is lost by fire' (Harrison, 1958: Part III, pp. 28–29).
6. As we shall see, all land that was unregistered at the time of the Unregistered Land Act (1970) belongs to the government. However, the Sudanese consider the land in their possession as their own, but this is not so for the refugees. This difference of perception may influence the sense of security or insecurity experienced by the two groups.

4

Decline in Crop Yields

The economy of the rural poor is measured in the fertility and productivity of their environment. (A.B. Durning, 1989b)

The results of the soil tests (Chapter 2) show that some negative changes have occurred in the physical and chemical properties of the vertisol soils of the plots that had been under continuous cultivation without fallow periods, application of fertilizers or other fertility-boosting inputs or improvements in the techniques of production. The question is whether or not these changes constitute land degradation. Land degradation is defined here in economic terms (Chapter 1), i.e. the changes are interesting inasmuch as they cause changes in productivity, measured, in this particular case, in deteriorating crop yields. Thus, whether the changes that have occurred in terms of soil and vegetation deterioration constitute degradation *inter alia* depends on the consequences of such changes for livestock and crop productivity. The changes are evaluated socially, in this chapter, in terms of decline in crop yields per unit of land cropped. Once this is established, the causes underlying the decline in crop yields will be explained.

In subsistence economies, one of the key indicators of a reduction in the capability of land is crop-yield decline. Three methods were used to establish whether there has been a decline in crop yields. First, various meetings were held with systematically selected groups of villagers, comprising Sudanese and refugee farmers. Second, data were elicited from randomly selected heads of households. Third, data were gathered from the records of the Commissioner's Office for Refugees (COR) and ACORD at Umsagata. The participants in the various meetings agreed unanimously that there has been a progressive decline in crop yields on the scheme over time. Of the randomly selected refugee groups, 98% said that yields have declined drastically over time. The corresponding figure for the Sudanese farmers was 93.4%.

The average yields for the two crops, namely sorghum and sesame, for the period 1971–1992 are given in Table 4.1. The gaps in the data were not possible to fill because there were no records at all for the missing years. The settlement was handed over to the local people's government at Qala en Nahal town by the United Nations High Commissioner for Refugees in 1974. Between 1974 and 1980, the Qala en Nahal scheme was under the responsibility of local people's government. During these years, the scheme was on the verge of total collapse (Kibreab, 1987). Data collection was one of the many casualties of the period. It was only with ACORD's involvement in 1981 that the performance of the scheme improved and proper data collection began.

As can be seen from Table 4.1, there is a progressive trend of yield decline over time, with some fluctuations, attributable to exceptionally good or bad rains in some seasons. In 1971 when the land in the settlement was virgin, as expected the sorghum yield was 3.9 times more than it was in 1989 and about 27 times more

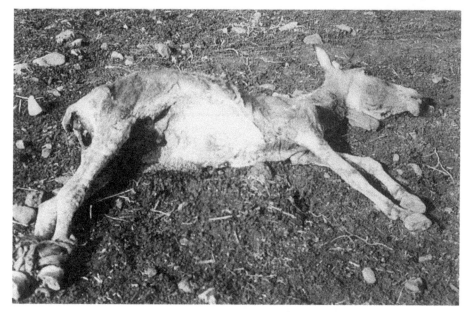

Plate 4.1   This animal like many others did not make it to the next wet season. Drought is part of life in the areas where the refugee settlements are located. (Photo: Gaim Kibreab)

than in 1990. After the 1982 season, sorghum yields never exceeded the 22-year average. It is worthwhile pointing out, however, that 1990 was a drought season and the extremely low yield for that particular season is attributable to low rainfall.

The trend of progressive yield decline is less obvious in sesame than in sorghum. This is mainly explained by distribution of rainfall and by the fact that sesame is less vulnerable to *Striga hermontheca*. Sesame is planted earlier than sorghum and is highly sensitive to fluctuations in rainfall. An early planting means higher sesame yields and late planting, irrespective of the total amount of rainfall throughout the season, often entails lower yields. The sensitivity of sesame to rainfall fluctuations notwithstanding, however, the data in Table 4.1 show higher sesame yields for the early periods.

The trend in productivity decline over time is not limited to the scheme. A similar trend is discernible in the mechanized rain-fed agricultural schemes in the Gedaref district, where the Qala en Nahal scheme is located and where crops are grown under similar conditions (Tables 4.2 and 4.3). The average yield for every 5 years in Table 4.2 clearly shows that yield per unit area cultivated has been declining over time. The average yields of sorghum for the periods 1968/69–1972/73, 1973/74–1977/78, 1978/79–1982/83 and 1983/84–1989/90 were 309, 303, 294 and 257 kg/*feddan* respectively. The progressively declining trend in sorghum yields is clear.

The data in Table 4.3 also show similar trends of productivity decline for sesame. The years 1983/84 and 1984/85 were bad years, in which the amounts of rainfall were comparatively very low, but even the remaining years show a discernible declining trend. The only exception is the 1978/79–1982/83 period, in which the five years' average yield was higher than in the preceding season.

Table 4.1   Average yields of sorghum and sesame and rainfall in the Qala en Nahal
Refugee Settlement 1971–1993 (in sacks per *feddan*)

Season	Sorghum (sacks/fd)	Sesame (sacks/fd)	Average rainfall (mm)	Average starting date of sowing
1971	7.0	3.0	240.6	
1972	6.0	2.5	233.0	
1973	7.0	2.5	330.4	
1974	n.a.	n.a.	456.0	
1975	n.a.	n.a.	696.0	
1976	n.a.	n.a.	551.0	
1977	n.a.	n.a.	658.0	
1978	n.a.	n.a.	614.0	
1979	n.a.	n.a.	543.0	
1980	n.a.	n.a.	n.a.	
1981	3.0	1.5	n.a.	1 July
1982	2.9	1.6	n.a.	18 July
1983	1.1	1.0	n.a	30 July
1984	0.3	0.0	400.0	6 July
1985	2.1	0.35	629.0	2 July
1986	2.1	0.50	614.0	6 July
1987	1.7	0.70	581.0	25 July
1988	n.a.	n.a.	645.0	
1989	1.8	0.83	722.0	
1990	0.26	0.39	471.0	
1991	1.35	0.55	547.0	
1992	1.57	1.48	610.0	
1993	0.56[1]	1.05	891.0	

fd, *feddan*; n.a., not available
Sources: Yields: for the years 1971–1973, COR Administration Records (1971–1994); for
1981, Flint, Natural Resources and Farming systems at Qala en Nahal Refugee
Resettlement, (1988); for 1982–1990, Crop Yield Survey, ACORD, Qala en Nahal.
Rainfall: 1970–1979 (40 km north of the scheme at the Sudanese village of Qala en Nahal),
Sudan Meteorological Department, Khartoum, File no. 0185; 1984–1993, ACORD's
Annual Reports Files, Umsagata. The data on starting date of sowing are compiled from
ACORD Tractor Hire Service Records (1981–1993).

Causes of crop-yield decline

The data presented above show that crop yields have been progressively declining
over time. It is, therefore, important to examine the factors underlying such
changes. Agricultural productivity is influenced by a myriad of interrelated multiple
variables and, as a result, it is extremely difficult to measure with certainty the role
of specific factors in the process of productivity change. The problem emanates
from the difficulty of ascertaining how much of the change is in reality attributable,
on the one hand, to degradation of soil nutrients and, on the other, to low and
erratic rainfall. However, a description of the most important relevant variables
influencing crop yields can shed light on the relative roles of the different factors.

The most important causes of crop-yield decline, as understood by the sample
households, in order of priority are land exhaustion (depletion of soil nutrients,
deterioration of texture and structure), weed infestation, inadequate rainfall,

Table 4.2   Average yields of sorghum in mechanized rain-fed agriculture in the Gedaref
district 1968/69–1989/90

Season	Yield (kg/fd)	5 years' average yield (kg/fd)	Annual average rainfall (mm)
1968/69	305		530.5
1969/70	263		451.2
1970/71	477		518.0
1971/72	309		473.7
1972/73	191	309	618.0
1973/74	320		633.8
1974/75	245		705.5
1975/76	399		605.5
1976/77	299		627.7
1977/78	250	303	578.0
1978/79	252		574.5
1979/80	279		682.4
1980/81	348		637.1
1981/82	390		646.5
1982/83	200	294	711.1
1983/84	n.a.		481.6
1984/85	97		320.5
1985/86	290		725.4
1986/87	318		604.0
1987/88	n.a.		527.0
1988/89	426		584.1
1989/90	152	257	758.9

fd, *feddan*; n.a., not available.
Sources: 1968/69–1976/77, Mechanized Farming Corporation (1979) *Agricultural Statistics
Bulletin 2*; 1977/78–1982/83, Mechanized Farming Corporation (1984) *Agricultural Statistics
Bulletin 3*. Rainfall data for 1968/69–1982/83 are adapted from Galal El Din El Tayeb (ed.)
(1985) *Gedaref District Study Area*, Khartoum: Institute of Environmental Studies, University
of Khartoum. The data for 1983/84–1989/90, including the rainfall data, are compiled from
the archives of the Mechanized Farming Corporation, Khartoum and Gedaref.

insect-pest infestation, soil erosion, flooding and waterlogging (Table 4.4).
Although these are the most important factors underlying the progressively declining crop yields, it is important to point out that crop-yield decline is also a function
of other complex and interacting factors, including poor management manifested in
untimely sowing, improper cultivation methods, inefficient weed control, poor
varieties and poor seed quality, lack of rotation, reduced moisture availability
because of increased run-off, scarcity or high cost of labour, which delays agricultural operations, lack of extension services and fluctuation in producer prices.

For example, one of the factors which affect productivity per unit of cropped
land in semiarid regions such as the Gedaref district is the date of sowing. This is
obvious from Table 4.9, where rainfall is concentrated in the three months of June,
July and August only. This makes agricultural production a risky activity. Timeliness
of sowing is, therefore, critically important. Data on the starting date of sowing are
not available except for the period since 1981 when ACORD has been involved in

Table 4.3   Average yields of sesame 1968/69–1989/90 in the Gedaref district

Season	Average yield (kg/fd)	5 years' average yield (kg/fd)
1968/69	124	
1969/70	160	
1970/71	149	
1971/72	188	
1972/73	219	168
1973/74	162	
1974/75	67	
1975/76	88	
1976/77	135	
1977/78	135	117.4
1978/79	135	
1979/80	157	
1980/81	149	
1981/82	180	
1982/83	113	147.0
1983/84	n.a.	
1984/85	70	
1985/86	85	
1986/87	134	
1987/88	n.a.	
1988/89	88	
1989/90	168	109.0

fd, *feddan*; n.a., not available.
Sources: 1968/69–1976/77, Mechanized Farming Corporation (1979) *Agricultural Statistics Bulletin* 2; 1977/78–1982/83, Mechanized Farming Corporation (1984) *Agricultural Statistics Bulletin* 3; the data for 1983/84–1989/90 are compiled from the archives of the Mechanized Farming Corporation, Khartoum and Gedaref.

Table 4.4   Reported causes of yield decline

	Number of times causes mentioned	
	Refugees ($n = 215$)	Sudanese ($n = 91$)
Land exhaustion	209	70
Weed infestation	172	68
Inadequate rainfall	130	69
Soil erosion	35	34
Waterlogging and flooding	31	47
Insect-pest infestations	49	28
Total	626	264

Table 4.5   Starting date of cultivation by village in Qala en Nahal 1981–1987

	1981	1982	1983	1984	1985	1986	1987
Salmin	8/7	20/7	1/7	4/7	2/7	6/7	24/6
Umsagata	4/7	17/7	29/7	6/7	1/7	6/7	24/6
Dehema	28/6	14/7	29/6	5/7	2/7	6/7	25/7
Adingrar	29/6	16/7	1/7	5/7	2/7	6/7	26/6
Umbrush	30/6	15/7	1/7	6/7	2/7	6/7	24/6
Umzurzur	28/6	15/7	30/6	3/7	3/7	6/7	24/6
Sud A	–	19/7	1/7	7/7	1/7	7/7	26/7
Sud B	–	19/7	1/7	7/7	1/7	8/7	24/6
Average	1/7	18/7	30/7	6/7	2/7	6/7	25/6

Source: Compiled from ACORD Tractor Hire Service Records (1981–1993).

the scheme. As can be seen from Tables 4.1 and 4.5, there seems to be a positive correlation between crop yields and date of sowing, whereby an early starting date of sowing meant higher yields, except for 1984, when there was inadequate rainfall to support any kind of crop growth.

Soil exhaustion

In order to gain an insight into the causes of yield decline on the scheme, a series of meetings was held with groups of key informants in the various refugee and Sudanese villages. The most critical cause of agricultural productivity decline in their view was loss of fertility caused by soil exhaustion. The sample household-based surveys also show similar results (Table 4.4). Both the key informants and the respondents see a direct causal relationship between continuous cropping and soil fertility depletion.

The dominant view among the farmers (Sudanese and refugees) was that land should never be cultivated continuously for more than 5 years without being left to rest for at least 6 years. A similar conclusion was also reached at villagers' meetings held in November 1985 with ACORD's Project Coordinator, where they stated that land should be left to rest for 5–7 years after each 5 years of continuous cropping (ACORD, 1985a: 9). The main reason why such land use is not practised is due to scarcity of arable land. As we shall see later, the land allocated to the scheme was inadequate to meet the growing needs of the communities. At the planning stage, no consideration was taken of the communities' future needs arising from natural population growth and immigration. Nor was the central question of maintenance of soil fertility taken into account. The land-use survey conducted by COR in 1990 showed that all land within the scheme was either cropped continuously without fallow periods or was abandoned because of fertility decline. It is common practice among commercial farmers in the region to exploit a farm continuously until yields decline below remunerative levels, without using any form of fertilizer. After the exhaustion of the soil nutrients, they abandon their farms and open up new land illegally in the undemarcated areas. This often happens after 6–8 years of continuous cropping. None of these options is open to the refugee farmers, however. They cannot practise shifting cultivation or rotational fallow periods because all the land within the scheme is already allocated. Also, they cannot bring land outside the scheme under cultivation because they are forbidden by law from doing so. They cannot join the ranks of those who are illegally opening up new land because of their politically vulnerable position. Owing to the small size of the holdings, continuous cultivation without fallow periods has reduced the productive capability and the value of their land, reflected in crop-yield decline over time. Most of the refugee farmers lack enough land to be able to leave part or all their *hawasha* in fallow.

Although the possibility for the Sudanese small farmers in the area to resort to shifting cultivation is being undermined by the horizontal expansion of commercial mechanized farming, there are still some farmers who leave part of their holdings in fallow when yields start to decline due to continuous cultivation. Compared with the mean amount of land possessed by the refugee families on the scheme, the Sudanese farmers are far better off, but, despite this difference, land shortage is considered by both communities as one of the major constraints on agricultural production.[2] However, the problem of land exhaustion is more severely experienced by the refugees than by the Sudanese farmers.

The mean land size of the Sudanese farmers is 25.4 *feddans*, but, in their view, this was no longer enough for a family of average size to earn sufficient income to enable it to meet its annual needs for consumption and its social obligations and to make good payment of taxes to the government. In the early days, when the supply of virgin arable land was abundant, a family did not need to cultivate more than 3 *feddans* to earn an income to match its needs. Yields per unit of land were then much higher, as a result of many centuries of soil-nutrient accumulation. The reason why 25 *feddans* are no longer enough is because most of the land within the scheme has been under continuous cropping and the consequence has been lower yields per unit of land cropped. The longer a holding is cropped, the less the yield and, with declining yield, the farmer concerned needs to bring more areas under cultivation in order to maintain overall production. In the context of a limited land supply, this leads to continuous cultivation of the available arable land and the consequence is depletion of soil nutrients. Over time, this leads to land degradation, reflected in yield decline and a higher density of noxious weeds (Affan, 1984; El-Moula, 1985; Gedaref District Study Area, 1985; Mohamed, 1990). Because continuous cultivation of staple crops, such as sorghum, mines important soil nutrients (El-Ashry, 1987)[3] beyond a certain threshold level, farmers find it no longer economic to cultivate the ageing *hawashas*. This forces some farmers to abandon their holdings. The available evidence in the area also shows that yield potential on cleared land declines from about 1,000 kg per *feddan* to about 100–200 kg per *feddan* after 6–10 years of continuous cropping (World Bank cited in Dickinson, 1983).

It is worthwhile pointing out that, although there are a myriad of factors that may affect yield per unit of land cultivated, there was no doubt among the farmers – both Sudanese and refugees – that continuous cultivation without fallow periods was one of the key causes of yield decline. On average, the refugees have been cultivating their *hawashas* continuously for over 16 years and the estimated level of yield decline suffered by the farmers due to continuous cropping without fallow periods is about 66% (mean = 65.8, SD = 18.3). The corresponding figure for the Sudanese farmers is about 39% (mean = 39, SD = 19.1). The difference in the level of yield decline reported by the Sudanese and refugee farmers is a reflection of the number of years their plots have been under continuous cultivation. However, as stated earlier, the accepted view among the farmers is that land should never be cultivated continuously for more than 6 years; otherwise there is drastic loss of soil fertility, resulting in low yields or complete crop failure. This view is supported by field experiments conducted by ACORD on the scheme showing yields in old sites to be lower (all other inputs being equal) than in newly opened sites. The results of the trial plots show that continuous cultivation and weed infestation are some of the major problems influencing yields (ACORD, 1987c). This was also confirmed by the results of our own soil fertility tests.

Soil exhaustion, for example, is reported by the farmers as the cause of land abandonment on the scheme. The results show that 14%, 22%, 6% and 8% of the refugee respondents have abandoned all, half, a third or a quarter of their original allocations, respectively. The corresponding figures for the Sudanese farmers are 2%, 25%, 5% and 8%, respectively. As expected, the proportion of refugee families that have abandoned their whole farms due to soil exhaustion and weed infestation is higher. The fact that a considerable proportion of the refugee families have abandoned their holdings despite the difficulties of obtaining alternative holdings is a reflection of the severity of the problem of land degradation. The consequences of the abandonment of land on the living conditions of the two communities is not the same, because the refugees who abandon their plots end up being landless while their Sudanese counterparts often succeed in opening up new cultivable land.

Among non-displaced stable communities, abandoned land is returned to cultivation after the regrowth of natural vegetation for 7–10 years. This option does not exist for the refugees because land which is left uncultivated for more than one season is automatically repossessed by COR. This policy was for the first time loosened in 1993. For example, the 1993 ACORD annual report stated, '[T]his year COR relaxed their ruling that those who did not cultivate might have their rights to use the land rescinded' (ACORD, 1993). The land-tenure system on the scheme is one of the obstacles constraining appropriate land-use practice (see Chapter 8). A few of the farmers, for example, do not practise fallow periods for fear of losing possession of their holdings. The majority were Sudanese, but there were also a few refugee families who reported that fear of losing their *hawasha* discouraged them from practising fallow periods. As we shall see later, over 18,000 *feddans* of land was either abandoned or was left uncultivated in the scheme when the land-use survey was conducted in 1990. Most of the land was abandoned because of soil exhaustion.

Weed infestation

The second major cause of yield decline on the scheme is weed infestation. There is a relationship between weed build-up and continuous cultivation, especially the occurrence of the sorghum parasite weed, *S. hermontheca* (Arabic: *buda*, English: purple witchweed). *S. hermontheca* is a parasitic herb which attacks sorghum and millet in Sudan (Parker and Reid, 1979). The effect of an attack by *Striga* on sorghum yields can be devastating. It is a problem on land continuously cropped for several years with sorghum. For example, Ivens stated: '[I]n the Sudan *S. hermontheca* is worst on poor soils exhausted by continuous cropping' (Ivens, 1989: 245). This is not to suggest, however, that only poor soils are affected. Crops on fertile soils can also be badly affected by *S. hermontheca* (Ivens, 1989: 245). Bebawi and Farah's findings show that an attack by *S. hermontheca* on a sorghum crop can reduce yields by up to 65% (Bebawi and Farah, 1981). On the scheme, the farmers' estimate of the loss is much higher. *Striga* infestation is often allied to other factors, such as soil exhaustion and rainfall fluctuations (Bebawi *et al.*, 1985: 1). As all land on the scheme is under constant sorghum or sesame cultivation, and land pressure makes fallowing an unacceptable option, *Striga* infestation remains a major problem for many farmers on the scheme. One of the causes of *buda* infestation is soil exhaustion resulting from continuous cultivation without fallowing. Bebawi *et al.'s*

Plate 4.2   Two farmers displaying the noxious parasitic weed Striga hermontheca *dreaded by all farmers, especially by those who are on the edge of survival. (Photo: Gaim Kibreab)*

study for example, showed a positive correlation between increased *buda* infestation and intensification of cultivation (Bebawi *et al.*, 1985: 6). According to farmers on the scheme, one of the factors that saved the situation in the past was the practice of crop rotation and fallowing. *Buda* infestation is more severe in agricultural systems that do not include regular fallowing and crop rotation. In Sudan, especially in the east, the problem is becoming more severe with the increased pressure of population on resources 'as buda appears to thrive best on heavily used soils of less fertility' (Bebawi *et al.*, 1985: 6).

On the scheme all the farmers, both Sudanese and refugees, attribute the drastic decline of yields to *buda* infestation. In the refugee villages, 100% of the respondents reported severe *buda* infestation as being the major cause of loss of productivity. The corresponding figure for the Sudanese villages was 89%. Bebawi, El-Hag and Khogali's findings in the Gedaref district also show the same result: 100% of the farmers they interviewed reported severe *buda* infestation as the most important cause of lower yields or crop failures (Bebawi *et al.*, 1985: 8).

When there was no shortage of land supply in the Gedaref district, the appearance of *S. hermontheca* indicated soil exhaustion. The farmers then left the plots concerned to rest for a certain period of time. This method of restoring soil fertility was practised not only in the Gedaref district, but also in most parts of northern Sudan. For example, the farmers in Darfur took the appearance of the same weed as an indication of exhausted soil (Mohamed, 1990). This was also true in other parts of rural Africa. Benneh, for example, observed the same thing in northern Ghana, where the appearance of a flowering plant *Supubia ramosa* on cultivated land was regarded by the farmers as indicative of exhausted soil and as a signal to move to new sites (Benneh, 1972: 246). On the Qala en Nahal scheme, the appearance of *Striga* was equally indicative of exhausted soil, but, this notwithstanding, the farmers continued cropping their plots due to land shortage. Herein lies one of the key problems of resource depletion resulting in yield decline. As pointed out earlier, there is a linkage between age of *hawasha* and density of weed population. This is confirmed by the results in Table 4.6, where the overwhelming majority of the respondents attribute the cause of weed infestation to soil exhaustion. The older the *hawasha*, the denser the weed population. In old *hawashas*, not only is the weed population denser, but the species of the weeds also change. For example, older plots are often invaded by the parasitic weed, *Striga*, which in many cases leads to crop failure. The farmers dread this type of weed. Unlike other weeds, *S. hermontheca* cannot be weeded out, even with a massive application of labour. According to the farmers, uprooting stimulates others to grow. Application of nitrogenous fertilizer increases yields but does not control the parasite (Ivens, 1989: 245). One of the most effective ways of controlling *S. hermontheca* is by the use of trap crops, i.e. by growing sorghum species, or other grasses, such as *Sorghum sudanense*, parasitized by *Striga* to stimulate germination of the seed and then ploughing in before the weed reaches maturity. By repeating this process several times in a season the number of seeds in the soil can be greatly reduced (Ivens, 1989: 245). In view of the land-resource constraints under which the farmers on the scheme are operating, this method of control is beyond their reach. *S. sudanense* is also considered by the farmers to be a major problem because of the difficulty of distinguishing it from sorghum grain until flowering time. Its occurrence is also higher among older farms than among newly opened farms. It is not only *Striga* and *S. sudanense* which have become a problem on the scheme in recent years. Many other noxious weeds, which were uncommon prior to the change in plant species composition in the area, are now considered by the farmers to have a negative effect on crop yields. These include *Cassia tora*, *Leptedina hastata* and *Dinebra arabica*.

In the past, farmers responded to weed infestation by shifting to another site, leaving the old plot to rest. In light of the massive expansion of commercial agricultural production in the area, this traditional land-management system is considerably undermined, but it is not yet totally eliminated among the Sudanese farmers. Among the refugees this traditional method (fallowing) of restoring soil fertility is not practised. This is not because their indigenous knowledge did not include fallowing as a method of conserving and restoring soil fertility, but, instead, due to lack of access to adequate land which could support such land-use practice.[4] Thus, the incidence of noxious weeds and drastic yield decline notwithstanding, the

Table 4.6   Reported causes of weed build-up on the scheme

	Refugees ($n=215$)	Sudanese ($n=87$)
Soil exhaustion	83.7	48.3
Improper weeding in previous seasons	6.5	3.4
Livestock build-up	7.9	47.2
Late cultivation	1.9	1.1
Total	100.0	100.0

$\chi^2=65$, d.f. $=4$, $P<0.001$.

refugee farmers continue to cultivate their farms for lack of an alternative land resource until the crops are either totally overtaken by weeds or until yields decline to near zero level.

It is important to realize, however, that the level of crop-yield decline tolerated by farmers is a function of the opportunity cost of their families' labour time. Weed infestation is, among other things, a function of the type of husbandry practised in the preceding seasons. If a *hawasha* was not properly weeded in the previous seasons, the density of weed population increases in the following seasons and the risk of crop failure increases. In a previous study among these populations, the findings of the author showed that, in order to tide themselves over a crisis during the hungry seasons, the poor households hired themselves and their families out to other farmers, thereby neglecting the proper weeding of their own *hawashas*. They were consequently faced not only with lower yields or crop failures during that season, but with massive weed build-up in the following seasons. Often the density of the weed population was so high that the families were forced to abandon their plots to join the ranks of the landless or sharecroppers (Kibreab, 1987).

According to the farmers, especially the Sudanese, there is also a relationship between livestock and weed-population build-up. This may sound anomalous because it contradicts the corpus of knowledge that exists on mixed peasant agricultural production. Historically, in peasant societies, livestock ownership not only supplemented the owners' food supply, but also contributed to higher productivity per unit of land cultivated by providing a source of draught power and access to manure, which was indispensable for the replenishment of depleted soil nutrients. In societies where there was limited land supply, manure application was one way in which yield per unit of land was raised. The history of small farming has always been inextricably linked with the use of manure supplied by a small stock of animals kept in the homestead. Sudan, at least the district of Gedaref, seems to be an exception in this regard. Not only do farmers in the district use no manure at all, but they sweep animal dung from their farms for fear of spreading *adar* weed seeds.[5] Among the refugees, 89% stated that the reason for not using organic manure on their farms was the fear of spreading weed seeds through animal droppings. The corresponding figure among the Sudanese was 82%. In many other Third World countries, animal dung is used as a fuel. In view of the acute fuel-wood shortage on the scheme, it was contrary to expectation to find only 7.9% of the refugee families using animal dung as fuel. Among the Sudanese the corresponding figure is 2.3% (Table 5.7). In the view of the Sudanese farmers in the area, one of the negative impacts of the presence of the refugee settlements in the area was livestock build-up, which has in turn led to weed (*adar*) build-up through the spreading of animal droppings.

Although this was not mentioned by the farmers, grazing pressure, besides depleting the soil of nutrients in arable lands, is one of the multiple forces that contributes to changes in plant species composition. It is, *inter alia*, as a result of the changes in plant-species composition that previously rare weeds (invaders) such as *S. hermontheca, S. sudanense, C. tora, D. arabica, L. hastata*, etc. have become a major problem. All the species in group V (see Table 3.6) have caused weeding costs to soar. The result for those families who are unable to hire additional labour to weed their plots is often crop failure.

Climatic fluctuation

The third major cause of crop-yield decline stated by the sample household heads is inadequate rainfall. The role of climatic fluctuations in determining crop yield and vegetation productivity levels in arid and semiarid regions is a highly complex matter. By the same token, whether the decline in crop yields in rain-fed agriculture in Sudan is caused by climatic changes or by a man-made land-degradation process is a moot point. The two variables are inseparably interactive. There are researchers who explain the decline in crop yields and vegetation productivity experienced by Sudan as being a result of man-made changes (degradation) induced by improper land-use practices. One of the most important findings of the Soil Conservation Committee, which was established by the colonial government in the early 1940s, was:

> [T]he climate has stayed the same (with its normal variations) since the close of the final wet phase of Pleistocene time . . . the soil deterioration that has occurred, and which is still occurring, may, therefore, be safely attributed to the work of mankind and to his domesticated animals, rather than to any change in basic climate. (Government of Sudan, 1944)

The Soil Conservation Committee did not directly address the problem of declining crop yields, but, since there is an unquestionable link between soil deterioration and crop-yield decline and since climatic factors had not allegedly played a role in the deterioration of the soil, it can be inferred from this that in the Committee's view, human interference and not climate was the cause of decline in soil fertility. Ibrahim also attributes the decline – close to 50% – in crop yields in northern Darfur (western Sudan) between 1960 and 1975 to the consequences of human interference (Ibrahim, 1978). His later study also shows the same findings (Ibrahim, 1984). El Hassan's study of the causes of range-productivity decline in Butana shows that the 'high variability of rainfall, typical of the semiarid zone, does not cause degradation' (El Hassan, 1981: 21). In the Gedaref district, the pattern of deviation of annual precipitation from the median and the mean for the period between 1922 and 1979 had not changed considerably. He does not deny the relevance of rainfall variability for range productivity, but stresses 'the importance of human practice in explaining the degradation in Central Butana' (El Hassan, 1981: 21). Ibrahim attributes the land degradation in the south Kassala district to improper land-use practices precipitated by uncontrolled expansion of mechanized rain-fed agriculture (Ibrahim, 1989). Abu Sin explains the degradation that has occurred in central and eastern Sudan as being the result of human interference, exacerbated by institutional changes (Abu Sin, 1989a, b, 1992).

A study commissioned by USAID in the Gedaref district in the mid-1980s thoroughly analysed the rainfall data for the district between 1950 and 1979 and concluded that climate in the Gedaref district had not changed for the last 30 years. The 10-year coefficients of variance were very small, ranging between 12 and 15% only (Table 4.7). As can be seen from the data in Tables 4.7 and 4.8, not only is there little variation between the 10-year averages, but even the total rainfall was almost evenly distributed. The data show that annual distribution remained fairly

Table 4.7   Rainfall data for the Gedaref district 1950–1979

Year	10–year average (mm)	S.D. (mm)	Coefficient of variance (%)
1950–1959	583.8	71.85	12.31
1960–1969	582.4	87.47	15.02
1970–1979	615.5	81.12	12.28

Source: Gedaref District Study Area (1985).

Table 4.8 Average rainfall in July, August and September 1950–1979

Year	10–year monthly average (mm)			Annual average (mm)	% of annual total
	July	August	September		
1950–1959	155.6	188.4	107.4	583.4	77
1960–1969	177.9	179.7	65.4	582.4	73
1970–1979	187.4	167.0	110.6	615.5	75

Source: Gedaref District Study Area (1985).

stable during the period, with about 75% of the rainfall occurring in the months of July, August and September. Temperatures in the Gedaref district also remained fairly stable during the 1950–1980 period (Gedaref District Study, 1985).

All these studies ascribe the problem of land degradation to human interference occurring within the given political, economic and social policy environment. Fluctuations in either the total amount or distribution of rainfall are not considered important in the explanation of yield decline over time.

A converse view is espoused by a group of geographers from Lund University, Sweden, who have studied the problem of desertification in western Sudan. Even though soils, landscapes, vegetation and the degree of human and livestock pressure on available resources may not be the same in the study area (Gedaref district) and western Sudan, the discussion may shed light on the central question of the cause of crop-yield decline experienced by farmers in the Gedaref district and particularly in the Qala en Nahal scheme. Establishing causation of crop-yield decline in semiarid areas is as complex and difficult as establishing the causes of changes in primary productivity (Chapters 3 and 6). As in vegetation changes, the most daunting question is how to distinguish between crop-yield decline caused by human interference (degradation) and rainfall-induced crop-yield fluctuations.

For the Lund geographers, climatic variation, not human interference, was the key explanatory variable for the major changes in crop yields or negative vegetation productivity observed in western Sudan between 1965 and 1974. Helldèn, for example, summarizes the findings of the various studies conducted by his colleagues: '[N]o major change in the vegetation cover and crop productivity was identified, which could not be explained by varying rainfall characteristics. There was a severe drought impact on crop yield during the Sahelian drought 1965–1974 in the Sudan followed by a significant recovery as soon as the rains returned' (Helldèn, 1991: 380). He argues that most of the negative and positive annual deviations from the mean annual production of major natural and rain-fed agricultural production systems of Sudan could be explained by climatic variations rather than the adverse effects of human interference. Olsson, in his study of Kordofan, also argued that 'the decrease in crop yield experienced since the early 1960s is due to pure natural factors beyond the control of man' (cited in Olsson and Rapp, 1988: 11). Ahlcrona, in her study of the White Nile, found a close relationship between crop-yield and rainfall variables, but she argued that the variation in crop yield could not be entirely attributed to climatic fluctuations. At most, about 56% ($r = 0.74$) of the variation could be explained by fluctuation in rainfall variables (Ahlcrona, 1988: 39). Although Ahlcrona disagrees with authors, such as Ibrahim, who attribute crop-yield decline to land degradation resulting entirely from human interference, she argues that, although droughts may cause a 'quantitative decrease of the biological productivity, droughts alone are not responsible for land degradation. In situations of mismanagement of land, droughts may increase the rate of land degradation' (Ahlcrona, 1988: 13).

Suliman, using long-term records from transects located in open rangelands and livestock exclosures in the Kordofan region, studied empirically the dynamics and changes of forage resources in relation to grazing. He selected three sites, namely El Nahud, where the annual average rainfall was 400 mm, El Khuwie (375 mm) and El Mazrub (280 mm) (Suliman, 1988). The latter site was the most northerly and driest of the three sites selected. If climate and not human activity were the decisive factor in determining vegetation density and species diversity, one would expect El Mazrub to be more affected by desertification than the other two sites. The results of the study, however, show the opposite. Suliman's findings showed that the 'rate of man-induced desertification and general environmental degradation were higher at El Nahud and El Khuwie than at El Mazrub' (Suliman, 1988: 29). He further stated:

> [F]rom changes in plant composition, plant cover, litter and bare soil at the three sites, some conclusions can be drawn. As indicated by species diversity, the reduction of plant cover, and the increase in bare soil at the three sites, the most northerly site at El Mazrub was least affected by desertification. This suggests that aridity was not the major cause of desertification at the three sites during the study period and that the degradation was largely anthropogenic. (Suliman, 1988: 29)

This may suggest that in some situations, in the absence of human interference, natural phenomena on their own may not cause deterioration in vegetation resources. In others, human interference causes degradation in vegetation resources, no matter how favourable climatic conditions may be.

On the scheme, the Sudanese and refugee farmers rank inadequate rainfall as a second and third major cause of yield decline, respectively (see Table 4.4). The reason why the farmers did not give low rainfall as the single most critical constraint on agricultural production probably has to do with their perception of what is considered to be within the realm of human control. For the farmers, rainfall is a gift from God and hence beyond human control, while other factors, such as scarcity of arable and grazing lands, which prevent proper land-use practices, are considered to be due to misguided government policy. Had there been an adequate land-resource base allocated to the scheme, the farmers would have been able to counter the constraint of fertility loss and the deterioration in soil structures and textures by utilizing some of the key elements in their traditional resource-management systems. In the farmers' view, if it were not for the wrong government policy of confinement, such constraints would not have been experienced. Hence, the fact that rainfall was ranked second and third by the refugee and the Sudanese farmers, respectively, is not to suggest that fluctuation in rainfall is less important in causing crop-yield decline than human-induced degradation. In savannah ecosystems, rainfall is the life artery of subsistence economic life. In such environments (without irrigation), no crops or animals can be produced without rainfall. However, in view of the wide variation in the environment, the subsistence producers (small farmers, agropastoralists and pastoralists) in these areas have developed resource-management systems which enable them to cope with such physical constraints. These management systems are undermined, among other things, by a government policy which limits their adaptational capability. It is within this context that the farmers ranked soil exhaustion and weed infestation as the two most critical causes of yield decline.

How important is rainfall in the explanation of crop-yield decline? Generally, in rain-fed agriculture, the relationship between rainfall and productivity is not a moot point. This relationship is even more evident in low-rainfall areas such as the refugee settlements in the Eastern State of Sudan, where agricultural output varies from year to year, depending on the amount and distribution of rainfall (Kibreab, 1994b). Before 1984, there were no rainfall-gauging stations on the scheme. The nearest rainfall-recording station was in Qala en Nahal town about 30 km north of the scheme. The data in Table 4.9 are taken from the Sudan Meteorological Department in Khartoum.

There are two significant points that should be mentioned in connection with the data in Table 4.9. Firstly, in the arid and semiarid ecosystems, rainfall fluctuates not only interannually, but also between short distances. In the study area, rainfall decreases from south to north. Thus, the amount of rainfall on the scheme for the period between 1971 and 1979 was probably higher than that given in Table 4.9. Secondly, the data in Table 4.9 are very probably less reliable than those given in Table 4.10. The data in Table 4.10 were carefully collected by the ACORD staff on six sites within the scheme. With this caveat in mind, it can safely be stated that, except in drought years, crop productivity was not solely a function of rainfall availability.

As can be seen from Table 4.1 yields were highest in the early 1970s, when the land was freshly cultivated, and the high yield levels were independent of the amount and distribution of rainfall. The average rainfall in 1971 was only 240.6 mm and it was 722 mm in 1989. Although the low amount of rainfall for the first three years could be a reflection of the Sahel drought, there must have been inaccurate recording because the amount for the first three years does not seem to be enough to support crop growth, no matter how fertile and stable the soils were. However, even though the figures represent an underestimation, there can be little doubt that the amount of rainfall during the 1971–1973 period was below average. The amount of rainfall was higher in the post-Sahel drought period, at least until the trend was brought to a temporary halt by the 1984 drought (Tables 4.9 and 4.10). In spite of this, however, the crop yield for 1971 was much higher than for most of the following years. In semiarid regions, temporal distribution of rainfall throughout the growing season is as important as total annual rainfall. The data in Table 4.9 show the monthly averages for the period 1971–1979, but the monthly average number of days with rain is not clear from the data. Despite this limitation, however, the available evidence shows that rainfall was less erratic between 1989

Table 4.9 Average and monthly distribution of rainfall in Qala en Nahal 1971–1979 (in mm)

Year	Apr.	May	June	July	Aug.	Sept.	Oct.	Total
1971	0.0	9.0	0.0	71.6	133.5	25.0	1.5	240.6
1972	0.0	0.0	72.5	44.0	59.0	44.5	13.0	233.0
1973	0.0	8.0	29.0	71.0	82.7	121.0	18.7	330.4
1974	0.0	0.0	117.0	142.0	103.0	94.0	0.0	456.0
1975	0.0	TR	151.0	167.0	245.0	123.0	10.0	696.0
1976	0.0	12.0	137.0	163.0	125.0	107.0	7.0	551.0
1977	0.0	27.0	157.0	220.0	115.0	84.0	55.0	658.0
1978	14.0	0.0	58.0	277.0	198.0	63.0	4.0	614.0
1979	TR	7.0	43.0	140.0	282.0	59.0	12.0	543.0

Source: Sudan Meteorological Department, File no. 0185, Khartoum.

Table 4.10   Rainfall data 1984–1993

	1984	1985	1986	1987	1988	1989	1990	1991	1992	1993	Grand average
Average all stations (mm)	400	629	614	581	645	722	471	549	610	892	611
No. of stations	6	6	6	6	6	6	1	6	2	5	
Average number of days with rain											
Apr.	0	0	0	0	0	0	0	0	0	1	0
May	0	2	0	5	2	6	0	4	3	5	3
June	4	7	8	10	12	8	2	2	6	6	7
July	11	12	10	16	12	10	10	7	14	10	11
Aug.	7	11	12	12	11	12	8	7	12	12	10
Sept.	5	8	6	3	7	8	5	6	5	6	6
Oct.	0	0	1	1	6	0	2	1	0	0	1
Total	27	38	39	47	50	44	27	23	40	40	38
Maximum recorded in 24 hours (in mm)											
Apr.	0	0	0	0	0	0	0	0	0	2	
May	0	26	0	36	23	38	0	34	18	67	
June	42	29	53	67	68	72	10	64	14	51	
July	42	60	74	47	42	101	76	62	66	68	
Aug.	57	60	50	59	68	50	30	54	46	60	
Sep.	45	35	90	22	35	51	36	30	32	50	
Oct.	0	0	13	5	96	0	0	7	10	0	

Source: ACORD Documents, Umsagata.

and 1993 than in 1971 and 1973. This difference in total amount of rainfall and distribution notwithstanding, yield per *feddan* was highest in 1971 and 1972. The change in yield per unit of land cultivated cannot, therefore, be explained solely by difference in amount or distribution of rainfall.

The data in Tables 4.1, 4.9 and 4.10 show that rainfall is the most critical of all the relevant factors, but the fact that there was a tendency for crop-yield decline even in good years suggests that fertility is declining as a result of factors other than rainfall. For example, in 1989, the total amount was above the 10 years' average (722 mm) and there were 44 days with rain. In spite of this ideal rainfall condition, however, sorghum yields were lower than in 1985 and 1986. In 1993, in spite of the unprecedented amounts of rainfall (in terms of amount and distribution), sorghum yields were the lowest ever recorded except for the drought years of 1984 and 1990. In that particular year, however, crop failure is, among other things, attributable to flooding, insect-pest infestation and heavy weed infestation. The fact that the soil could easily be washed away is an indication of reduction of resilience and rising sensitivity. This may suggest that, in areas subjected to intensive levels of human interference, it is not only shortage, but also abundance of rainfall that causes yield decline.

The available evidence indicates that the progressively diminishing crop yield is not only due to fluctuations in rainfall, but also influenced by the depletion of soil

Table 4.11   Sorghum and sesame yields for the Simsim scheme 1973–1980

Year	Sorghum Sack/fd	Sesame Sack/fd	Rainfall mm
1973	5.9	1.9	530
1974	3.7	0.5	999
1975	2.1	0.3	747
1976	2.7	n.a.	890
1977	2.0	0.4	709
1978	1.4	n.a.	710

fd, *feddan*; n.a., not available
Source: El Khalil, 1981.

nutrients and weed infestation resulting from 20–22 years of continuous cultivation. The data on crop yields in Table 4.11 for the Simsim scheme outside the Qala en Nahal refugee settlement also show the same trend, yields having been on the decline independent of the amount of rainfall. The establishment of the Simsim rain-fed mechanized scheme was preceded by a preinvestment feasibility study in the mid-1960s. It was stated in the report that a complete mineralogical analysis showed the absence of 'comparatively well-weatherable minerals releasing plant nutrients' (NEDEC and ILACO, N.V., 1966: 100). It was further stated, that the absence of a noticeable mineralogical nutrient reserve, the comparatively low level of total available plant nutrients and the annual rainfall of about 730 mm gave rise to the question of how long sustainable yields will be maintained.

The declining crop-yield figures given in Table 4.11 may therefore be a reflection of loss of the meagre minerals inherent in the soil after the land was cropped with non-leguminous annual crops for a few seasons rather than fluctuating climatic conditions. The data show that yield levels have declined progressively with the age of the scheme, independent of rainfall.

In the Qala en Nahal scheme, the same trend is discernible in sesame production where yield per unit of land cultivated was considerably higher during the early history of the settlement than in the second half of the 1980s. The only exception is the 1992 season, in which sesame yields were higher than for the previous nine seasons. The rainfall data suggest that, beyond a certain threshold level, there does not seem to be an obvious linkage between rainfall and yield. In the period under consideration, there has not been a marked change in the amount or distribution of rainfall on the scheme area, except in the drought years of 1984–1985 and 1990. The level of rainfall threshold is important because poor rainfall or its bad distribution is invariably followed by crop failure. For example, the crop failures experienced in the country in both 1984 and 1990 can be explained by the drought, which hit the whole region. The data for rainfall were the lowest for those particular years since ACORD began to collect data on rainfall in 1984 at the scheme site. The progressively declining trend in crop yields is also discernible in Tables 4.2 and 4.3, and this often happened in conditions of unchanged rainfall in terms of amount and distribution. This suggests that, within the given physical constraints, declining fertility on the scheme is to a greater extent a function of soil exhaustion, which is a result of continuous cropping without fallow periods or application of manure or fertilizers. As we saw earlier, land degradation has also contributed directly or indirectly to the outbreak of insect pests and weed infestation.

The location of the scheme being a semiarid area, shortage or uneven distribution of rainfall constitutes a major problem. It is interesting to see, however, that, within this given constraint, soil-nutrient depletion resulting from continuous cultivation as experienced by refugee and Sudanese farmers is the major cause of yield decline over time. In fact the majority of farmers consider this problem to be more serious than the risk of rainfall failure. As expected, there is a significant difference between the refugee and the Sudanese farmers' views in this regard. Crop yields are influenced by amounts of rainfall, distribution, evapotranspiration, cultural practices such as farm age, date of sowing, weeding, pest infestations, diseases, availability of fertilizers, cultivation methods and crop and soil characteristics. However, the level of yield decline as reflected in Table 4.1 and as reported by the farmers may not only be due to soil exhaustion or ageing of the farms. On the Qala en Nahal scheme, within the given climatic conditions, improper land use induced by misguided government policies and external and internal pressures is the major cause of yield decline.

The climate/anthropogenic divide in the explanation of crop-yield decline is not helpful in a situation like this. This is not only because of the formidable methodological problems involved in terms of determining with precision how much of the productivity decline is actually due to climatic variation, improper land use (human activity), wrong time of planting, poor seed quality, soil characteristics, method of cultivation, pest infestations, etc., but also due to the inextricable linkages between bad land management and the negative impact of drought on productivity. In this study, even though rainfall is regarded as the major limiting factor in crop production and this is true in any semiarid area, the decline of vegetation and crop productivity observed on and around the scheme area is due to a combination of man-made and natural phenomena. In the plots where there has been no depletion of soil nutrients, crop yields improved with higher rainfall, but, in the plots where there has been soil-nutrient depletion due to overuse, crop yields did not respond to higher amounts and better distribution of rainfall, at least in the short term. Crop failures were common occurrences in drought years, irrespective of the quality of the soil, but even in good years, measured in terms of the total amount and distribution of rainfall, there were plots whose yields were either small or zero. These were plots whose soil-nutrient status was completely exhausted and where high amounts or a good distribution of rainfall had little or no impact on crop yield. In the semiarid areas where the Qala en Nahal scheme is located, it cannot be denied that moisture is one of the pivotal factors which influences crop yields, but it is equally important to take cognizance of the fact that, under the existing local resource-management systems, rainfall (moisture) tends to have little or no impact on soils whose nutrients are exhausted due to overuse.

Insect-pest infestation

Insect-pest infestation is another factor seriously limiting grain production. During the establishment season, grasshoppers and crickets cause damage to seeds and the problem is escalating over time. *Contarinia sorghicola* (midge) infestation of sorghum crops is considered a major problem. The larvae of the sorghum midge feed on the developing seeds within the sorghum flower. The wide infestation within the scheme is exacerbated by the outbreak of *S. sudanense*, which functions as reservoir host to the midge from its emergence from diapause up to the time of its infestation of the main crop (ACORD, 1993). The whole scheme was affected by midge damage in 1993. ACORD's estimates suggest that about 50% of the failure of sorghum was attributable to midge damage in 1993 (ACORD, 1993). The red-bundled blister beetle and the American bollworm are also a major problem limiting the success of leguminous crops on the trial plots (ACORD, 1993).

It was clear from the meetings the author had with the scheme residents that the farmers see a causal relationship between the occurrence of diseases, insect-pest infestations and farm age. The older the farm the higher the risk of pest infestation. The number of farmers that saw such a relationship were not, however, as many as those who saw a causal relationship, on the one hand, between soil exhaustion and yield decline, and, on the other, between soil exhaustion and weed infestation. These relationships were obvious to all those who attended the meetings. The existence of these relationships was also confirmed by the findings of the sample household-based study on the scheme as well as by many other studies in the region (see, for example, Simpson and Khalifa, 1976a, b). On the refugee farms, pest infestation is ranked as the fourth factor accounting for crop-yield decline. The fact that the problem of pest infestation is more severe on the refugee farms, where no fallow periods are used, may suggest that there is a link between farm age and pest infestation. On the scheme, soil-fertility decline, *Striga* attack and the outbreak of insect pests are inextricably interrelated.

Flooding and waterlogging

Waterlogging is a cause of yield decline or crop failure in the plots located at the foot of hills. The effect of this, however, is dependent on the amount of rainfall in a given season, and it is the same with flooding. In some seasons, flooding precipitated by heavy rainfall can be the single major cause of crop failure. The amount of rainfall in 1993 was excessive – nearly 900 mm – with the highest flooding occurring in August and September (ACORD, 1993). The excessive rain caused 'extensive sheet and gulley erosion, and this, together with the flooding, caused tremendous damage to crops . . . A large area required replanting, but even so, crop yields were practically nil' (ACORD, 1993). This suggests that, in such environments, it is not only lack of rainfall, but also high amounts of rainfall that cause crop failure.

Conclusion

Fertility was measured by analysis of soil for the elements and compounds affecting plant growth. The results show that negative changes have occurred in the soil characteristics of sites which were subjected to continuous cropping without fallow periods, application of fertilizers or other fertility-boosting inputs. This was supplemented by data on crop yields. Data on crop yields were pieced together and the results show that there has been a decline over time. The relationship between soil-fertility decline and the decline in crop yields is complicated by the presence of a myriad of interacting factors that directly or indirectly influence crop yields. It is only in controlled trials in which all other factors are held constant that declines in fertility can be assessed by decline in crop yields. It is with this in mind that the soil analysis results are interpreted.

Bearing this caveat in mind, the major causes of crop-yield decline on the scheme were inadequate and variable rainfall, land exhaustion, manifested in depletion of soil nutrients and weed and insect-pest infestation. There are several other studies which show that continuous cultivation leads to loss of soil fertility and productivity. The central question which needs to be addressed is whether there is a threshold beyond which crop productivity, irrespective of the amount of labour input, is reduced to zero. On the scheme, there is no evidence which lends support to such a scenario. The fact that some farmers abandon their plots does not suggest that the loss of fertility has reached 100%. Overcultivated holdings are invariably infested by heavy noxious weeds and that is the immediate cause of farm abandonment. It is important to note, however, that the threshold beyond which cultivation is considered uneconomic is mediated by the particular family's economic status. Not only are the consequences of lower crop yields varied depending on the individual farmer's economic position, but there is also a clear difference in the perception of the well-off and the poor with regard to what constitutes exhausted soil. While the well-off families hired additional labourers to maximize soil nutrients and moisture availability to crops by removing the weeds effectively, those who lacked an adequate supply of family labour and/or cash to hire labourers were left with no alternative but to abandon their *hawashas* and join the ranks of the landless agricultural labourers.

Notes

1. This result is based on a crop-yield survey conducted in Umbrush village, but it was stated in the 1993 ACORD Annual Report that yields in other villages were much lower than this (ACORD, 1993).
2. This was measured by means of the chi-square test, and no significant difference was observed between the answers given by members of the two communities.
3. M.T. El-Ashry (1987) 'Degradation of Natural Resources in the Horn of Africa: Causes, Effects and Prevention'. Paper presented at the Conference on 'Crisis in the Horn of Africa: Causes and Prospects', Woodrow Wilson International Centre, Washington, DC, 17–20 June.
4. As we shall see later, the background characteristics of the refugee communities are diverse. So are their traditional natural resource-management regimes.
5. The reasons reported by the farmers for not using manure are:

	Refugees	Sudanese
Fear of spread of weed seeds	89.0	82.0
Have no livestock	1.0	10.0
Animal droppings used for fuel	1.0	5.0
Organic manure does not boost productivity	5.0	1.0
Don't know the benefit of organic manure	4.0	2.0
Total	100.0	100.0

5 The Impact of Wood-fuel Use on Environmental Degradation

> If one were to ask for an expression, in a single sentence, of the main accomplishment and direction of the social sciences to date, a fair answer would be the progressive substitution of sociocultural explanations for those stressing the determinative influence of physical nature. It is thus ironic that so much of the explicit discussion of scarcity should still rest on the physical notion of natural resource deficiencies. (M. Stanley, 1968)

Nowhere is this more true than in the phenomenon of the so-called wood-fuel crisis. It is often taken for granted that physical changes in forest-resource availability invariably engender a wood-fuel crisis. It is argued here that a wood-fuel crisis is by no means a function solely of scarcity in forest resources. This is not to suggest, however, that the demands for wood fuel and timber for construction do not cause deforestation. Sometimes, the link between wood-fuel consumption and deforestation is evident, but not the link between deterioration in woody resources and a wood-fuel crisis.

A major cause of deforestation in the Gedaref district is land clearance for mechanized rain-fed agriculture. This is exacerbated by excessive felling of trees for charcoal production. A report of the National Energy Administration (NEA) Ministry of Energy and Mining, for example, attributes the problem of desertification to the destruction of vegetation for the purpose of mechanized agriculture and wood-fuel production (NEA, 1991). Wood-fuel production does not, however, cause deforestation because, unlike land clearance for mechanized agriculture, tree felling for wood fuel use involves no uprooting of whole trees. Under favourable conditions, felled trees can be replaced by coppice regrowth. In this particular case, however, climatic conditions and livestock pressure coalesce to limit the regenerative capacity of the coppiced trees. Since the 1940s, not only has the Eastern State, especially the Gedaref district, been the centre of expansion of rain-fed agricultural production, but it has also been the major supplier of wood fuel for the urban centres such as Khartoum and Omdurman. More than 98% of the recorded charcoal production and more than 81% of the recorded firewood production come from the Central and Eastern Regions of the country (Abdalla, 1987).

In this study, the causes of deforestation in the Gedaref district are directly related to expansion of mechanized rain-fed cultivation. Removal of trees for wood fuel and animal pressure contribute to deforestation, but they are considered to be aggravating, not ultimate, causes. The forest resources in the district have been shrinking in proportion to the amount of land cleared for cultivation. As more land was cleared for cultivation, the forest resources declined drastically. As a result, firewood and charcoal production as well as grazing and browsing over the remaining vegetation resources intensified and the result was deforestation. It is in this sense that tree felling for wood-fuel production contributes to deforestation in the area.

Sudan is heavily dependent on biomass products for its energy consumption. Wood-based energy, animal waste and agricultural residues utilized as fuel resources constitute about 80% of the country's total energy consumption (NEA, 1991). Generally, poor countries like Sudan have little choice but to mine their forest resources for fuel rather than spend their scarce foreign-exchange earnings on financing the import of fossil fuels. This economic rationale does not, however, justify the continued mining of forest resources regardless of the social and environmental costs involved. Environmental degradation resulting from excessive removal of vegetation cover (trees, agricultural residues and grasslands) has a direct negative consequence on the livelihoods of subsistence producers, who, in order to secure forage for their animals and wood fuel, construction timber and thatch grass for themselves, have to travel longer distances, foregoing income that would have been earned had not their labour time been allocated to such activities. Although the social costs of environmental degradation will not be considered directly, we shall see later that subsistence producers see a close association between erosion of social well-being and depletion of forest resources. The prevention of forest-resource mining on a non-sustainable basis and the consequences of the depletion of forest resources for the social and economic welfare of the rural population (peasants, nomads, women and children) are often not prioritized by the various state governments in the country. The overwhelming concern seems to be to save hard-currency earnings, disregarding environmental sustainability and the short- and long-term interests of subsistence producers.

What gives cause for concern from the point of view of environmental protection and efficient allocation of scarce resources is that the trees removed for the purpose of mechanized agriculture are often wasted without being utilized for charcoal production. There is little coordination between the two activities. Paddon, Food and Agriculture Organization (FAO) Biomass Officer in Sudan, for instance, states that, even though large mechanized agricultural schemes are cleared every year for production of sorghum, only a fraction of this timber is converted to charcoal, as large quantities are windrowed and burnt to ashes. This practice stems 'from the reluctance of the agriculturalist to become involved in charcoal production and is sometimes due to the delay in his obtaining the necessary land use permits, leaving little time for charcoal-making before the planting season begins' (Paddon, 1989a: 7).

Reliable data on total annual production and consumption are lacking and the forestry authorities are constrained in their planning efforts by this scarcity. According to a study by the Forestry Administration, the recorded quantity of charcoal produced over the period 1979 to 1985 fluctuated between 3,793,000 and 6,344,000 sacks (114,000 and 190,000 tonnes, respectively). Average output of charcoal per year between 1979/80 and 1984/85 was 5,525,000 sacks and the amount of wood fuel for the same period varied between 141,000 and 225,000 steres or about 178,140 stacked m^3 per annum (Abdalla, 1987: 4). These figures were based on the royalty and revenue returns from individual forest units of the Central and the Eastern Regions. The author of the report estimates that the total amount actually produced was 15 to 20% higher. This was because, firstly, the amounts consumed at the local level did not require removal permits and thus were not reflected in the records of the royalty and revenue returns and, secondly, there were illegal production and evasion of royalty payments (Abella, 1987: 3). Other authors, however, suggest an additional 90% of the recorded output reflects actual production (Earl, 1984). Paddon argues that 'with the inconsistencies and logistical difficulties throughout the regional offices regarding their royalty and revenue recording facilities, even a 100% addition to the recorded production figures would be totally inadequate' (Paddon, 1989b: 4). In fact according to the survey con-ducted by the National Energy Administration, Khartoum alone consumes more charcoal than the total recorded output for the whole country (NEA, 1987). According to Paddon the recorded statistics account for only 4% of the estimated consumption of wood-based fuels in the country (Paddon, 1989b).

This suggests that over 95% of the total firewood and charcoal consumed in the country are not recorded. This is despite the fact that, formally, no person or firm is allowed to make charcoal or to collect firewood for commercial purposes without a permit from the Forestry Corporation. Removal permits are also required to move firewood or charcoal from the production sites. There is also formal monitoring carried out at the major checkpoints throughout the highways entering the urban centres. Nevertheless, apparently over 95% of the total firewood and charcoal brought to the urban centres are not recorded in the royalty and revenue returns. Since no firewood or charcoal can come into the urban centres without having a removal permit, it is not clear how the merchants beat the system. Section 16 (1) of the Forest Act (1989) states:

> [N]o person shall transport or attempt to transport any forest produce by any means of transport without obtaining a permit from the competent authority; provided that such forest produce transported or about to be transported shall conform with that included in the permit as regards, kind, quantity, date, place transported thereto and any other information contained in such permit in the form specified by the regulations.

The driver of the means of transport is required to carry the permit with him throughout the time he is transporting the forest produce and should present it whenever asked (Forest Act (1989): Art. 16(3)). Purchase or obtaining of forest produce is prohibited unless it is accompanied by a removal pass from the competent authority (Art. 16(4)). These restrictions also apply outside the reserve areas. Section 18(1) states: '[N]o person shall cut, take, consume or utilise for any purpose any growing or fallen tree in any land under the disposal of the government outside the reserved areas.' As we shall see later, following the promulgation of the Unregistered Land Act (1970) all unregistered land, and this includes over 90% of all rural land (Abu Sin, 1989a), fell under the disposal of the government.

As stated earlier, charcoal and wood fuel produced for local consumption require no removal permits and are not reflected in the records, but the difference cannot be attributed to this. Not only is it common knowledge that wood-fuel and charcoal entrepreneurs add illegal wood fuel and charcoal to licensed output, but even a large proportion is said to be removed free of charge 'legally'.

This short discussion on lack of reliable data sources suggests that, on the one hand, the forestry authorities are handicapped in their planning exercises and, on the other, no accurate assessment of the impact of the removal and cutting of vegetation on the environment is possible. One thing which all concerned agree upon, however, is that excessive cutting of wood resources without replacement contributes to deforestation in the Eastern (the location of the refugee settlements) and Central Regions of the country. Given this dearth of data, the effort made in this research project to measure accurately fuel and timber consumption in several refugee and local Sudanese villages, in the area most affected by the charcoal and wood-fuel industry, may considerably increase our fund of knowledge in this regard.

What is disturbing from the point of view of environmental sustainability is that more than 80% of the wood fuel and charcoal is produced in the Central and Eastern Regions of the country, where the forest resource is less than 8 million hectares, located mainly in the low-rainfall belt of 400–600 mm per annum (Paddon, 1989b). The country's forest resources are destroyed at a rate of 1.4 million hectares per year and it is just a question of time before the sources of supply within reach of the main population centres are exhausted (Paddon, 1989). The Gedaref district, where the refugee settlements are located, is one of the areas most seriously affected by the removal and cutting of vegetation for the purposes of mechanized agriculture and wood-fuel and charcoal production. It is important therefore to consider the problem of deforestation and wood-fuel, charcoal and timber supply and consumption in the refugee settlements and in the surrounding villages in this context.

Consumption of wood fuel and construction materials on the scheme

The aim of this section is to look at the sources of energy, availability of energy and amounts of the different energy sources used by each income group. The purposes are to examine whether availability of biomass as a source of wood fuel, poles (timber) for building and furniture, grass for thatch, gum arabic, frankincense and herbs has declined over time. One of the major factors that causes deforestation is the clearing of vast areas of land of woody biomass and shrubs for agricultural production (Agabawi, 1968, 1969). Roche, for example, states that Sudan has bulldozed 7 million acres of natural *Acacia* forest and replaced it with mechanized sorghum monoculture (Roche, 1989: 19). He further states that the scheme was abandoned after 3 years because yields declined to uneconomic levels. The major cause of deforestation in the Third World is said to be wood-fuel gathering which exceeds the rate of regeneration (Eckholm, 1975b, 1982, Digernes, 1977, 1979; Openshaw, 1978, 1974; USAID, 1980; UNPF, 1988; Munslow et al., 1989). In many African countries, traditional sources of energy such as wood fuel, animal dung and crop residues provide over 90% of the total energy needs of the countries (Mnzava, 1981). Openshaw also states that about 80% of all households in developing countries use wood fuel as their primary source of energy and it is even used by industries (Openshaw, 1974). Munslow et al. (1989) claim that wood fuel represented about 80% of the total energy consumption in the Southern African Development Cooperation Conference (SADCC) countries in 1985. In addition, Eckholm states, '[T]he accelerating degradation of woodlands throughout Africa caused in part by fuel gathering lies at the heart of what will likely be the most profound ecological challenge of the late 20th century' (Eckholm, 1975b: 8).

On the Qala en Nahal scheme, land clearance for cultivation constitutes the major pressure on the environment. This is exacerbated by excessive cutting of forest resources, including live trees, for firewood and charcoal consumption in the urban centres such as Gedaref, Khartoum and Omdurman. Local consumption of wood fuel and of timber for house building, furniture and fencing also adds pressure to the limited tree resources. The drastic increase of small stock on and around the scheme also limits the regeneration capacity of the coppiced trees (see Plates 5.1 and 5.2, p. 110). The pressure placed on trees at the initial settlement process was tremendous because of the refugees' need for cultivable land and shelter. In the refugee and Sudanese villages, poles and hewn wood are used for making houses.

Houses are constructed using wooden uprights and rafters to support the conical thatched roof. Trees are also cut to make doors, window-frames, beds, stools and tables. The overall demand placed on the limited biomass resources may lead to a considerable degree of depletion of vegetation resources. If the rate of offtake exceeds the rate of natural regeneration or restoration resulting from tree planting and coppice regrowth, the consequence may be not only depletion of woody resources, but deterioration in the agricultural production and living conditions of the communities concerned.

Timber consumption for house construction

In order to estimate the amount of timber consumed in the construction of the various types of huts, thirteen upper-income, thirteen middle-income and thirteen low-income refugee families were systematically selected and the amount of *korki* (straight poles used for roofing), *degag* (forked poles, not necessarily straight, used for supporting the roof) and *felekab* (bundles of twenty to twenty-five pieces of bamboo stems or *negab*) were carefully counted and their sizes measured. The materials for tying the thatch grass to the poles (i.e. *felekab*) are imported from distant places because bamboo trees are no longer available locally. Thus, their use is not expected to strain the local environment and hence they are not included in the calculations. Ten families from each of the three income groups were also selected in the surrounding Sudanese villages and the number of poles used in their huts were counted and the heights and circumferences of the poles were measured carefully.

In the technical literature, forestry quantities are measured in volumes. Thus, in order to convert the quantity of the building materials used in construction of the different types of huts into volumes of solid wood in m^3, actual measurements of the heights and circumferences of the poles used for roofing (*korki*) and the forked poles (*degag*) used for supporting the roof were carefully taken in all the huts owned by the thirty-nine refugee and thirty Sudanese families. The reason for taking separate measurements for the refugees and for the Sudanese families was because of the expectation that we would find differences in the amounts of building materials consumed by the two communities. The reason for dividing the families into three income categories was also important, because the number and sizes of huts owned were influenced by the economic position of the families in question.

In the 1991 scheme population census (ACORD, 1991), all the families were classified into three income categories. One of the main purposes of the census was to identify the needy families for distribution of relief during that particular hungry season. In the census, the three categories were referred to as vulnerable, needy and well-off. In non-crisis years, the economic status of the various families in the three income categories can be referred to as high-income, middle-income and low-income groups, without losing sight of the fact that these terms are understood in the context of the locally existing constraints and opportunities. Thus, for our purposes, the latter categorization is used. According to the 1991 population census, there were 5,567 refugee families among which 1,955 were poor (low-income group), 3,331 were in the middle-income group and 281 were well-off (ACORD, 1991). The corresponding figures for the Sudanese population were 213 low-income, 903 middle-income and 45 well-off.

The sample households in the various income groups were selected on the basis of the data available in the 1991 population census. This was also corroborated by the information that was available to the village officers, who not only were members of the villages concerned, but also had experience of work on the scheme for many years. The upper-income families were selected from those who owned a herd or several herds of livestock, and/or shops, local oil-presses (*asara*), bakeries, tractors, several *hawashas* (holdings), etc. The families representing the middle-income group were selected from those who supplemented their farm income with diverse activities. They included night-watchmen, dressers, oil-press owners, etc. The families from the low-income groups were selected from the daily labourers, vulnerable groups, beggars and shepherds. The latter lacked livestock of their own.

The demand for construction materials is one of the causes of depletion of the woody biomass in the area. In the case of stable communities, the demand for construction materials is spread over a long period of time and hence the impact on the environment may be offset by natural regeneration. About 18,000 refugees were relocated to the scheme between 1969 and 1971. The population on the scheme area suddenly increased from 1,300 (NEDC and ILACO, N.V., 1966) persons to over 19,000. The refugees had to cut down trees to construct dwellings. No alternative supplies of construction materials were provided by the refugee support systems. The new settlers were instead provided with transport facilities and axes to fell trees indiscriminately, partly to clear the land for the establishment of villages and farms and partly to provide construction materials. At that time, trees were abundant and neither the refugees, the government officers nor the aid workers were concerned at all with the long-term consequences of tree felling. The impact of this on the environment, the elders say, was dramatic. The attack on the relatively undisturbed natural environment was described by the elders who witnessed the destruction as 'ruthless'. The actions of those who were responsible for the establishment of the scheme – including government representatives – were devoid of any environmental concern.

In 1991, the refugee families in the upper-income group had, on average, 2.3 large, 2.4 medium and 1.0 small huts. Most of the rich families lived in large compounds with their married sons and close relatives. The families in the middle-income groups had on average 1.2 large, 0.8 medium and 1.0 small huts. The corresponding figures for the poor were 0.15 large, 0.7 medium and 0.5 small huts (Table 5.1). The number of huts owned by the well-off refugee families was greater than that owned by their Sudanese counterparts. Among the latter, the well-off had, on average, 1.5 large, 1.3 medium and 0.8 small huts. The middle-income families had 0.9 large, 1.0 medium and 0.7 small huts. None of the poor Sudanese families had a large hut. On average, they had 0.7 medium and 0.7 small huts. The general impression one gets from the data in Table 5.1 is that the refugees in the three categories seem to be better housed in terms of quantity of houses than the Sudanese. The houses, especially among refugee families, were also inequitably distributed. Access was a function of economic status.

The difference observed between the Sudanese and refugee families is compensated for by the fact that houses belonging to Sudanese families were invariably larger than those belonging to the refugees (Table 5.2). The average number of poles (*korki* and *degag*) used in the construction of Sudanese houses was greater than in the houses of the refugee families in all the three categories, namely large, medium and small houses (Table 5.2). The large huts in the refugee villages were only as large as the medium-sized huts in the Sudanese villages. The medium-sized huts in the refugee villages were also only as big as the small huts in the Sudanese villages. This difference was not due to differential access to wood resources. It was probably because, among some of the refugee groups, the seclusion of women required the families to have more huts because women lived in separate ones.

Table 5.1 Average number of huts per family in the three income groups

	Refugees	Sudanese
Upper income		
Large huts	2.30	1.50
Medium huts	2.40	1.30
Small huts	1.00	0.80
Middle income		
Large huts	1.20	0.90
Medium huts	0.80	1.00
Small huts	1.00	0.70
Low income		
Large huts	0.15	0.00
Medium huts	0.70	0.70
Small huts	0.50	0.70

Table 5.2 Average number of construction poles (*korkis* and *degags*) required by the three types of houses on the scheme

	Refugees		Sudanese	
	Korki	Degag	Korki	Degag
Large hut	33	22	38	23
Medium hut	25	16	32	22
Small hut	22	12	27	12

The Sudanese on the scheme were from either West Africa or western Sudan. Their women were not secluded. The participated in all kinds of economic activities. They also lived in the same houses with men. In total, there were 4,928 large, 4,700 medium and 4,600 small houses in the five refugee villages. In the six Sudanese villages, there were a total of 880 large, 1,111 medium and 817 small houses. The houses were distributed among the three income groups in the following way. In the refugee villages, out of the large houses, 646 belonged to the well-off, 3,997 to the medium-income and 293 to the poor families. Out of the medium-sized houses, 674 belonged to the well-off, 2,664 to the middle-income and 1,368 to the poor families. Out of the small houses, 281 belonged to the well-off, 3,331 to the middle-income and 997 to the poor families. In the six Sudanese villages, of the total large houses, 67.2 belonged to the well-off, 812.7 to the middle-income and none to the poor families. Out of the medium-sized houses, 58.5 belonged to rich, 903 to the middle-income and 149.1 to the poor families. Out of the small houses, 36 belonged to the rich, 632.1 to the middle-income and 149.1 to the poor families.

These figures are used to assess the impact of tree cutting for house construction on the environment. It is important to point out, however, that, although these measurements are important and are the first of their kind ever to be undertaken in the area, this alone may not show the amount of pressure exerted on the environment, because the main cause of depletion of forest resources in the area is external pressure associated with the expansion of mechanized rain-fed farming and the charcoal industry which supplies the towns and cities of the country.

The average volume of poles (*korki* and *degag*) required for the construction of a large hut in the refugee villages is about 0.51 m³, while the corresponding figure is 0.56 m³ in Sudanese villages (Table 5.3).[1] The volume of poles required for medium and small huts in the refugee villages is 0.43 m³ and 0.31 m,³ respectively. The corresponding figures for the Sudanese villages are 0.47 m³ and 0.31 m,³ respectively.

In Sudan 1 solid m³ of dry solid wood is equivalent to 700 kg (A.R. Paddon, FAO-supported Forestry Project Adviser, Forestry Corporation, Khartoum, pers. comm. December 1991). In Table 5.4, the latter figure is used to calculate the amount of timber required per hut in tonnes. The data in Table 5.4 are cross-sectional and hence do not show the impact of the demand for construction timber on vegetation over time. The years of arrival of the refugee household heads are given in Table 5.5.[2] The majority (about 72%) were relocated to the scheme between 1969 and 1971.

Table 5.3   Average volume of poles (*korkis* and *degags*) required per hut in solid wood (in m³)

	Refugees	Sudanese
Large hut	0.51	0.56
Medium hut	0.43	0.47
Small hut	0.31	0.37

Table 5.4   Total volume of poles used for construction

Type	Refugees		Sudanese	
	m³	Tonnes	m³	Tonnes
Large	1,974.7	1,382.3	396.1	277.3
Medium	1,412.3	988.6	400.0	280.0
Small	1,198.5	839.0	1,024.9	717.4
Total	4,585.5	3,209.9	1,821.0	1,274.7

Table 5.5   Distribution of the sample families by year of arrival on the scheme area

Year	Refugees		Sudanese	
	No.	%	No.	%
1950–55	0	0	6	6.6
1956–61	0	0	9	9.9
1962–64	0	0	8	8.8
1965–68	0	0	8	8.8
1969–71	155	72.1	5	5.5
1972–75	13	6.0	21	23.1
1976–78	19	8.8	6	6.5
1979–81	10	4.7	6	6.5
1982–84	10	4.7	17	18.7
1985–87	6	2.8	3	3.4
1988–91	2	0.9	2	2.2
Total	215	100.0	91	100.0

The age of a hut in the area is dependent on the particular soil condition on which it is erected and on whether buildings are attacked by termites and other insects. In some villages the problem of termites was more severe than in others. The data elicited from both Sudanese and refugee elders show that huts had to be renewed at least once every 5 years. Huts erected on sites with rodent infestations were repaired every 3 years. Often these repairs involved a change of thatch grass only. The old *korkis* and *degags* were used again.

The repairs that were undertaken at the end of the fifth year, however, involved complete replacement of the old poles. There were a total of about 14,229 houses in the refugee villages, among which 34.6% (4,928) were large, 33.0% (4,700.3) medium and 32.3% (4,600.5) small (Table 5.6). The data in Table 5.5 show the year of arrival of the families on the scheme. Every family built its own house during the first year. The data in Table 5.6 show that about 10,264 houses were renewed four times, 855 about 3.6 times, 1,257 about three times, 662 about 2.4 times, 662 about 1.6 times and 397 houses once. The 131 houses that were built between 1988 and 1991 were not renewed at all.

The refugee villages have, since the establishment of the scheme, consumed about 25,933 m³ of poles for initial construction and for renewal. The average amounts of timber required for large, medium and small huts are 0.51 m³, 0.43 m³ and 0.31 m³, respectively (Table 5.3). If we multiply the data in Table 5.6 by these figures we get a total of 21,347.3 m³. This was the amount of timber consumed for renewals. If we add to this the data used for initial construction (Table 5.4) we get a total of 25,933 m³ or 18,153 tonnes of poles.

The same procedure is used to calculate the amount of timber consumed for house construction in the six Sudanese villages from the time of the first arrival of the families in the present-day scheme area. As shown in Table 5.5, the first Sudanese families began to settle in the present-day scheme area in 1950. Thus, some of the huts in the Sudanese villages have been renewed up to eight times. The total amount of construction material used for renewal in the six Sudanese villages was 5,072.8 m³ and, if we add to this the 1,821.0 m³ for initial construction, the total amount of solid wood consumed for house construction in the Sudanese villages was in the range of 6,894 m³ or 4,826 tonnes of solid wood.

Firewood and charcoal consumption in the refugee and Sudanese villages

In rural Sudan, as in any other rural area in the developing world, wood fuel is the dominant source of energy. In order to estimate the amount of firewood and

Table 5.6 Total number of houses and frequency of renewal by size in the refugee villages 1975–1991

Frequency of renewal	Large	Medium	Small	Total
4.0	3,555.2	3,390.8	3,318.9	10,264.9
3.6	296.2	282.5	276.5	855.2
3.0	435.4	415.2	406.4	1,257.0
2.4	229.1	218.7	214.0	661.8
1.6	229.1	218.7	214.0	661.8
1.0	137.4	131.0	128.2	396.6
0.0	45.5	43.4	42.5	131.4
Total	4,928.0	4,700.3	4,600.5	14,228.7

charcoal consumption in the refugee settlements and in the surrounding Sudanese villages, twenty-four families, twelve from the refugees and another twelve from the Sudanese peasants in the surrounding Sudanese villages, were selected systematically from the three different income strata, namely upper, middle and lower income. The rationale for the systematic selection of the families from the three income strata is that it was assumed that access to wood fuel is to a large extent determined by its economic cost (Dewees, 1989) and consequently changes in patterns of consumption occur as its cost increases. The communities on the scheme are differentiated economically and it is assumed that their responses to the increasing cost in terms of the amount of wood fuel or wood-fuel substitutes they consume is determined by their socio-economic status.

The families' daily consumption of wood fuel and charcoal was measured accurately for 10 consecutive days. Each family was asked to display firewood and/or charcoal equivalent to the amount actually used on the day before. If wood fuel was used, each piece was measured by length and circumference using a steel tape-measure. If charcoal was used, the displayed amount was weighed by a simple 20 kg spring balance. These data were used to calculate the per capita and total volume of wood fuel consumed on the scheme. In order to ascertain that the amount of wood displayed was equivalent to the amount of wood actually consumed, the person in charge of the measurements visited the sample families unannounced, sometimes twice a day at random, when they were about to begin cooking their meals.[3] He stayed until the cooking was over and weighed every piece that was used and compared the results with the amount displayed on the following day. On this basis, annual per capita wood-fuel and charcoal consumptions were estimated. An estimate of the amount of wood fuel tapped in the last two decades and an assessment of the impact of this on the forest resources on and around the scheme were also made.

Initially, our intention was to monitor actual consumption during summer and winter periods. However, the field research revealed that seasonality in terms of weather fluctuations did not influence the patterns of wood-fuel consumption. This was because of the warm and hot climate. Wood-fuel is rarely used to provide warmth for houses. It is important to point out, however, that seasonality is not totally irrelevant to the patterns of wood-fuel consumption, but this had little to do with the changing weather conditions. During the cultivation season, not only are there competing demands for labour in the families' *hawashas* (holdings), but also the demand for agricultural labour on the rain-fed mechanized farms is high. Wages for agricultural labour are also high. With the rising opportunity cost of labour, the cost of wood-fuel gathering increases and consequently the price. As a result, the wealthy spend more to purchase wood fuel from the local market and maintain the same levels of consumption while others adopt lower patterns of consumption during the cultivation season. There are also some families who hoard wood fuel for the cultivation season when labour is unemployed or underemployed during the trough seasons.

In the past, during the summer months, consumption varied slightly among a few families because they used smoke to repel flies from animals. This is no longer practised because, instead of smoke to repel flies, farmers keep their animals on the hills during the rainy season, where there are fewer or no flies because of the winds. Milk is ferried by containers from the jebels to the villages daily. This is an adaptive response to the increasing cost of wood-fuel gathering and to declining grazing resources in the immediate vicinity of the villages (see Table 6.3).

On the scheme, the major sources of energy were firewood and charcoal.

Electricity was produced by three generators belonging to ACORD, the Commissioner's Office for Refugees (COR) and the Sudan Council of Churches (SCC). The generators supply electricity to the workshop, clinics and mosque. In the evenings between 7 and 10 o'clock, the generators supply electricity to ACORD and COR staff houses. All the generators were in Umsagata. None of the other villages had an electricity supply. Diesel was used for tractors, trucks, sawmills and water-pumps. Families used paraffin for lighting, but supplies were unreliable and sometimes the prices were unaffordable. Thus, whenever paraffin was in short supply, families used firewood for lighting. As can be seen from Table 5.7, except for a few families, firewood represented a major source of energy. It is important to note, however, that the majority also used charcoal in combination with firewood. The two sources of energy were not used exclusively. Firewood was used for cooking *injera*, *kitcha*, and porridge. These constituted the staple diet of the families. Charcoal is used for making *sebhi* (sauce), coffee and tea and for boiling milk and water. Charcoal was also used for melting soap for washing clothes and for ironing. About 71% of the Sudanese farmers and about 53% of the refugee families used charcoal.

There are a large number of families who supplemented their firewood and charcoal consumption with crop residues. Among the refugee families, about 20% sometimes use crop residues to supplement their energy needs. Among the Sudanese, nearly 70% use crop residues. This undoubtedly has a detrimental effect on the environment, because a surface cover of crop residues reduces wind velocity at the soil surface and absorbs some of the wind's power to erode. Crop residues are also used as fodder for animals. Thus, using crop residues as energy deprives many families of a source of animal fodder and indirectly of essential products, such as milk and ghee. A survey conducted by the NEA in the Eastern Region in 1988 estimated that only 11% of agriculture residues and 8% of animal wastes were utilized for energy (NEA, 1988). On the scheme, the use of animal waste and crop residues is higher than the regional averages and the reasons for this are varied. The explanation that comes to mind immediately is physical scarcity of wood fuel. As we shall see later, however, physical scarcity of wood fuel, manifest in substitution of crop residues and animal dung for wood fuel, is only one of a host of possible explanations. Some families on the scheme use crop residues and animal dung as a substitute for wood fuel because of shortage of family labour, because of lack of capital to hire labour for wood-fuel collection or to purchase wood fuel from the local market or because of the high opportunity cost of family resources, including labour. Those families who substituted crop residues, animal dung and grasses for wood fuel were invariably from the poor strata.

One way in which we tried to quantify the exact amount of firewood and charcoal consumption was to take actual measurements in systematically selected families for 10 consecutive days (Table 5.8). Not only do the results show the

Table 5.7   Distribution of families by sources of energy used (%)

	Refugees	Sudanese
Firewood	98.1	96.7
Charcoal	53.0	70.7
Crop residues	20.5	69.2
Animal dung	7.9	2.3
Grass	3.7	1.1

Table 5.8   Charcoal and firewood consumption per family per day (in kg)

	Refugees		Sudanese	
	Charcoal (kg)	Firewood (kg)	Charcoal (kg)	Firewood (kg)
Rich families	2.10	5.79	1.75	6.23
Middle-income families	1.20	5.02	1.24	5.10
Poor families	0.00	3.22	0.85	4.55
Overall average	0.83	4.43	0.84	5.04

quantities consumed by the three different income groups, but we also found that there was a clear difference in the patterns of wood-fuel consumption among the different income groups. For example, the rich families in both groups consumed more charcoal than the others. Among the refugees, none of the poor families consumed charcoal, while the middle-income group consumed only half the amount consumed by the well-off families. Among the local population, there was a difference in charcoal consumption between the three income groups, but the extent of the differences was narrower than among the refugee families. This suggests that the amount of charcoal consumption, unless produced by the con- sumer families themselves, is a function of income, i.e. families with higher incomes have a propensity to consume more charcoal than others. This was not only because the price of charcoal was higher than the price of firewood, but also because the latter could be collected by the families themselves, while charcoal was purchased from the local market. As will be pointed out later, most of the Sudanese farmers on the scheme engage in charcoal production and, as expected, the proportion of the Sudanese families using charcoal was higher (Table 5.7). Most of them were dependent on their own production while all the refugees bought charcoal from the local souk (market). It is interesting to observe that, while the well-off families among the refugees consumed more charcoal than the well-off Sudanese families, there was a clear difference in the amount consumed between the middle-income and lower-income families in the two groups. On average, the results show that the amount of firewood and charcoal consumed was slightly higher among the Sudanese than among the refugees.

The difference in the extent of use of crop residues as fuel between the refugees and the local population is explained by the fact that many of the farmers in the Sudanese villages did not have livestock. Among the refugees, crop residues were mainly used as stock feed and the majority of those refugees who used crop residues were from the poor section of the community. Although the number of families who use crop residues as fuel is still not very high among the refugees, during field research in 1982 the author found that none of the refugee families used crop residues for fuel. These findings suggest that some changes in the patterns of fuel consumption have taken place in response to the increasing cost of wood fuel.

About 8% of the refugees and about 2% of the Sudanese families also used dung or dung cakes as fuel. The reason why there were more refugees using dung as fuel may be explained by the fact that there was more livestock in the refugee village than in the Sudanese villages. However, the fact that only less than 10% of the families used dung may indicate that the degree of scarcity of wood fuel, in spite of the bare physical appearance of the landscape (in the vicinity of the villages), is not as severe as is generally said to be the case. Animal dung is a 'free good' on the scheme because it is not used as a fertilizer, and, if there were a severe scarcity of wood fuel, there would be more families using it as fuel. There was no evidence which suggested the existence of stigma attached to animal dung use as fuel. Animal dung produces little flame, but plenty of smoke, which is bad for the eyes. It is these features which seem to discourage its utilization as fuel. In countries where there is an acute shortage of wood fuel, smoke has not deterred people from using it. There were also a few poor and female-headed families who supplemented their firewood supply by *kawal* (*Cassia tora*) and other weeds. *Kawal* is an unpalatable tall weed, with thick but light stems, which grows abundantly in the degraded lands surrounding the villages. *Kawal* was used only by the poorest families because it did not generate much energy and it was easily extinguishable. Women had to keep blowing on it, producing more smoke, which many women thought would cause eye diseases. None of the families was limited to only one source of energy. Most of them combined two or more types of energy sources, depending on the season and their income.

The data in Table 5.9 show that the patterns of wood-fuel consumption are clearly determined by the particular family's socio-economic status. The average charcoal consumption per capita per annum was 0.43 m^3 and 0.63 m^3 for the refugees and the Sudanese, respectively. The average firewood consumption per capita per annum was 0.46 m^3 for the refugees and 0.54 m^3 for the local population. These data are used to estimate the total amount of wood fuel consumed during the period the Sudanese villages and the scheme have been in existence. The amounts of wood and charcoal consumed as fuel by each family since their arrival at what is now known as the scheme area are calculated separately.

The Sudanese families in what is now the scheme began settling in the area in the 1950s, and new families continued arriving uninterruptedly throughout the 1970s and 1980s. The first settlers among the refugees were relocated in 1969.[4] Official relocations were discontinued after 1971, but the spontaneous arrival of families continued uninterruptedly throughout the 1970s and 1980s. In 1978 the government relocated between 250 and 300 families to the scheme following its decision to phase out the transit centre at Wad Hileu near the border area (Kibreab, 1990b). The total amount of charcoal consumed by the 215 refugee sample households between 1969 and 1991 was about 8,518 m^3 or 5,963 tonnes.[5] Thus, the average amount of charcoal consumed by each refugee family between 1969 and 1991 was 40 m^3. The 5,567 refugee families used a total amount of 220,552.5 m^3 of charcoal between 1969 and 1991. In rural Sudan the unit of measurement of charcoal is a sack. How much a sack of charcoal weighs is dependent on various factors. A random weighing on the scheme showed that the average weight of a

Table 5.9   Annual per capita wood-fuel consumption on the scheme (in m^3)

	Refugees		Sudanese	
	Charcoal (m^3)	Firewood (m^3)	Charcoal (m^3)	Firewood (m^3)
Higher income	1.08	0.60	0.91	0.67
Middle income	0.62	0.52	0.65	0.55
Lower income	0.00	0.33	0.44	0.49
Average	0.43	0.46	0.63	0.54

sack filled with charcoal was about 38 kg. Thus, the total amount of charcoal consumed by all the refugee families on the scheme between 1969 and 1991 was about 4,062,809.6 sacks. The total amount of firewood consumed by the sample families between 1969 and 1991 was 9,119 m^3 or 6,383 tonnes. The average amount of firewood consumed per family during the same period was 42 m^3. Thus, the total amount that was consumed during the last 22 years by all the refugee families was 236,119.3 m^3 or 165,283.5 tonnes of firewood.

The total amount of charcoal consumed by the sample households in the Sudanese villages between 1950 and 1991 was 5,252 m^3 or 3,676 tonnes. The average amount of charcoal consumed per family during the same period was 58 m^3. Thus, the total amount consumed by the 1,161 families during the same period was 67,007 m^3 or 1,234,344.6 sacks.[6] The total amount of firewood consumed by the sample families between 1950 and 1991 was 4,511 m^3.[7] The average amount consumed per family between 1950 and 1991 was 50 m^3.[8] Thus, the total amount of firewood consumed by the population in the six Sudanese villages was 57,553 m^3 or 40,287.4 tonnes.

Activities for which wood fuel is used on the scheme

All the families used wood fuel for cooking, but not all the families used wood fuel for boiling water and milk and for melting soap. The proportion of the families who used wood fuel for boiling was higher among the refugees (65%) than among the local population (41%). Among both groups there were many families who did not boil water or milk at all (Table 5.10). This may give cause for concern regarding the preponderance of water- or milk-related diseases.

Table 5.10   Activities for which wood fuel is used on the scheme

	Refugees	Sudanese
For cooking	100.0	100.0
For boiling	65.0	40.6
To give warmth	0.5	3.3
To provide light	1.4	24.2

As expected, only a few families used wood fuel to give warmth to their houses. The area is hot and there is seldom need for heating. The use of paraffin was more widespread among the refugees than among the Sudanese families. Among the Sudanese there were about 24% who used firewood to provide light at night.

The impact of the use of wood fuel and construction materials on deforestation

It is interesting to examine the impact of overexploitation of forest resources for construction, firewood and charcoal on deforestation. The total amount of solid wood used for construction in the six refugee and six Sudanese villages was 25,933 m^3 (18,153.1 tonnes) and 6,894 m^3 (4,825.8 tonnes), respectively. The total amount of charcoal consumed by the six refugee and six Sudanese villages was

220,552.52 m^3 (154,386.76 tonnes) and 67,007.276 m^3 (46,905.093 tonnes), respectively. The total amount of firewood consumed by the six refugee villages and six Sudanese villages was 236,119.28 m^3 (165,283.5 tonnes) and 57,553.368 m^3 (40,287.358 tonnes), respectively.

According to estimates of the Forestry Corporation in Khartoum, 1,000 kg (1 tonne) of dry-weight wood produces about 300 kg of charcoal (usable lumps). Using this conversion factor, the total amount of 287,559.8 m^3 charcoal consumed by the refugee and Sudanese villages is equivalent to 958,532.65 m^3 of solid-volume dry wood.[9] Thus, the total amount of biomass extracted for the purposes of construction of houses and firewood and charcoal consumption in the Qala en Nahal scheme is in the range of 1,285,032.3 m^3 solid-volume wood. The area is located in what is known as known as low-rainfall woodland savannah where the annual allowable cut in the 1980s was 0.26 m^3/ha (Whitney, 1991: 117). The term 'allowable cut' refers to the amount of wood that can be tapped on a sustained yield basis each year and is often matched to the net annual productivity of the forest resources. In the study area whether the amount of wood that is removed exceeds the annual productivity is not easy to determine with certainty. The regenerative capacity of the forest resources is limited by rainfall and by animals which feed on coppice regrowth and seedlings.

Using these data, it would have been possible to calculate the amount of deforestation attributable to the consumption of household wood fuel and construction materials, but household wood fuel and timber consumption at the local level are only two of many factors that have been contributing to the problem of deforestation. These include clearing of land by local and commercial farmers for cultivation and collection of firewood and commercial charcoal making to supply the urban areas such as Gedaref, Wad Madeni, Sennar and Khartoum. Since there are no records of the amount of firewood collected and charcoal produced by wholesalers on and around the scheme area, it is impossible to quantify how much of the deforestation on and off the scheme area is due to commercial production of wood fuel.

However, it is common knowledge that one of the major causes of depletion of the forest resources on and around the scheme area is commercial charcoal production. The charcoal wholesalers are issued licences by the forestry authorities for charcoal making. Subsequently, they hire labourers and, for months on end, tree felling continues. The charcoal produced on the settlement is then transported to the cities, where the demand is high. This has caused more destruction to the tree cover than any amount of trees removed by the refugees or the local Sudanese. In 1987 alone, ten trucks with trailers were seen in Umsagata loaded with charcoal on their way to Gedaref (Key informants, 1991). A truck and a trailer could carry up to 1,500 bags of charcoal at 38 kg per sack. The amount of trees cut to produce the charcoal equivalent to a truck load with a trailer is in the range of 5 *feddans*. Given the sparse population of trees and their small size on the scheme areas, the area affected by tree destruction to produce the same amount is far more than 5 *feddans*.

Calculations on the precise impact on deforestation of local-level wood-fuel and timber consumption are difficult to come by because the existing conversion factors are too general. They are aggregated at a regional level. The variation in plant density between the different areas in the region is so great that the existing conversion factors are of little value. According to an assessment made by the NEA, the average volume of forest resources in the Eastern Region was 3 m^3/ha or 1.5 m^3 per acre or *feddan* in 1983 (NEA, 1983). Since 1983, a considerable amount of

Plates 5.1 and 5.2   Trucks heading for Khartoum and Omdurman. The cities depend on charcoal and firewood to meet their energy needs. Ninety-eight per cent of all charcoal and 81 per cent of all firewood consumed by the major cities comes from the Central and Eastern regions where 95 per cent of the refugees live. (Photo: Gaim Kibreab)

forest resources have been depleted and the average forestry resource in the region in 1991 was far less than in 1983. Since most of the firewood used by the refugee families comprises of drywood, it does not make sense to extrapolate the total deforested area from the per capita consumption. The rate of regeneration of coppiced trees is also unknown at the micro-level.

However, available evidence suggests that the rate of regeneration of coppiced trees is far higher than uncoppiced trees. The results of our survey show that the areas on and around the scheme are heavily deforested. The most dominant tree species in the area are *Balanites aegyptiaca*, *Acacia seyal*, *Acacia senegal*, *Acacia mellifera*, *Zizyphus spina-christi* and *Combretum hartmannianum*. These trees are heavily exploited on and around the scheme area. Inside the scheme area, there are some trees, located mainly inside the individual farmers' plots. Between 1 and 2 km from the scheme, none of these trees except *C. hartmannianum* exists. The area is completely devoid of trees. As the distance from the scheme increases, the level of intensity of forest-resource use eases and, consequently, the vegetation density is considerably higher. However, as we saw in Chapter 3, the pressure on forest resources comes not only from the population on the scheme, but also from commercial farmers, charcoal wholesalers (who vertically integrate production, transportation and marketing) and outsiders, such as pastoralists, who use the area in their north-south movements at the beginning and end of the rainy seasons. In drought years, pastoralists from distant areas are pulled by the availability of perennial water supply on the scheme, and their livestock add pressure to the already stressed vegetation resources. Nevertheless, the level of intensity of economic activity reflected in deforestation is more conspicuous in the immediate neighbourhood of the scheme and on the scheme itself than in the rest of the district. The evidence that emerges from this study is that the annual offtake rate, in terms of land clearance, grazing and browsing, of wood-fuel and construction timber on and around the scheme seems to exceed the rate of natural regeneration.

Changes between 1982 and 1992 and consequences of biomass depletion

The depletion of common resources, especially woodland resources, was expected to have far-reaching consequences for the family budget, the level of wood-fuel consumption, the family division of labour and the burden on women and children. The following questions are addressed. How severe is the wood-fuel shortage faced by the households? Is this accompanied by a price rise? Does this impose strains on family budgets? Does wood-fuel scarcity have differential effects on wealthy and poor families? How far has the distance to wood-fuel resources increased and how large is the radius of the depleted vegetation from each village? Is the increased distance of wood-fuel resources placing a higher demand on women's labour time and how far does this compete with labour time required for agricultural production, child-rearing and domestic chores?

Although Table 5.11 shows that the availability of forest resources has declined since the establishment of the scheme in 1969, the severity of wood-fuel shortage experienced by the families is dependent upon their socio-economic status. The findings show that, in most cases, wood-fuel consumption is a function of capital or labour availability. Whenever either of these two resources was available, physical scarcity of wood fuel was not an issue. Wood-fuel shortage was most acute among

5.11   Change in availability of common resources from time of joining scheme

	Increased	Decreased	Unchanged
Wood fuel	+		
Poles	+		
Grass for thatch	+		
Gum arabic	+		
Frankincense	+		
Browse	+		
Medicinal herbs	+		

poor, female-headed, families without able-bodied (female or male) members. Poor families who allocated the labour time of their family members to wage employment or cattle/sheep herding (for remuneration) outside the scheme, especially during the hungry periods (rainy seasons), were also faced with wood-fuel shortages. The remaining family labour time was allocated for weeding the families' *hawashas*. For those families with low resource (labour and capital) endowments, both the opportunity cost of labour during periods of peak labour demand and the price of wood fuel are so high that their consumption of wood fuel declines considerably. This period usually coincides with the exhaustion of the poor families' food savings from the previous season's harvests and their scarce resources are used to obtain food instead of wood fuel.

One change observed between 1982 and 1993 is an increase in wood-fuel prices. In 1983 one sack of charcoal was about £S3.50. The price doubled between 1983 and 1987. In view of the high inflation rate that characterized the Sudanese national economy in the 1980s, the price increase cannot be regarded as substantial. After 1987, however, charcoal prices began rising astronomically, but so did the price of most commodities, including labour. Between 1986 and 1991, the price of charcoal increased by over 650%. After the second half of 1991, the price was changing every month. In about 6 months, charcoal prices increased by about 200% (Table 5.12). Part of the increase is due to seasonality. Wood-fuel gathering competes with agriculture for labour during the cultivation season and, as a result, wood-fuel prices tend to increase because of increased cost of gathering.

A most dramatic increase occurred between 1991 and 1993 when charcoal prices increased by nearly 470%. Are these dramatic price increases attributable to physical scarcity of wood fuel? The data in Table 5.12 are misleading if considered independent of changes of prices of other commodities, including wage labour, and the dramatic loss of value of the Sudanese currency. In the last few years, the Sudanese pound (£S) has been devalued drastically. In March 1993, about £S123 was equivalent to $US1. In April 1994, the corresponding value of $US1 was £S400. Sudan experienced progressive economic decline and soaring inflation throughout the 1980s. The socio-economic decay reached unprecedented levels during the first 4 years of the 1990s. Even though there are no reliable data on inflation, especially for the rural areas, available evidence suggests that in 1993 the rate of inflation was over 150% or more. The 1993 ACORD report, for example, states: '[T]he inflation rate continued high – some reports say 150% – and prices of most items rose steadily through the year. This included locally produced products such as meat, sugar; services such as labour, as well as imported items or services derived from them' (ACORD, 1993: 1). In view of this, it is difficult to attribute the drastic increase of prices solely to scarcity of wood fuel. If the prices of

Table 5.12 Prices of charcoal made from *Acacia seyal* in the settlement area 1986–1993 in £S

	Farm gate	Without sack in Umsagata	With sack in Umsagata
1983	n.a.	3.50	4.50
1986	3.00	4.00	5.00
1987	5.00	7.00	8.00
1988	10.00	12.00	15.00
1989	15.00	20.00	25.00
1990	25.00	30.00	35.00
1991			
1st 6 months	40.00	45.00	50–55
3rd quarter	60.00	65.00	70.00
4th quarter	80–120	130.00–140	160–170
1993	n.a.	800.00	n.a.

n.a., not available.
Sources: Collected from the records of the Umsagata wood-fuel market 1986–1991, and ACORD, 1993.

everything else, including labour, have increased drastically, the soaring wood-fuel prices are to a large extent due to inflation as well as the increased cost of gathering. If we remove the effect of devaluation of the Sudanese pound, the changes in wood-fuel prices are moderate. It cannot be denied, however, that the increased distance of wood-fuel sources and consequently the increased time and effort made to gather and transport wood fuel have some influence on wood-fuel prices, but this, as pointed out earlier, is determined by labour availability.

Whether the soaring wood-fuel prices impose a strain on the family budget is determined by each family's economic status. The differential impact of wood-fuel scarcity on the different income groups is clear from the data in Tables 5.8 and 5.9. The poor refugee families do not consume charcoal and the wealthy Sudanese families consume more than twice the amount of poor Sudanese families. The amount of firewood consumed by poor families is also far less than the amount consumed by well-off families. Compared with the past, the outlays of those who depend on the wood-fuel market have increased in relative terms. The results show that, for the families that were dependent on the market, outlays on wood fuel represented a considerable proportion of their budgets on energy. Among the higher-income and middle-income groups, the mean monthly outlays on wood fuel were £S109.3 and £S52.0, respectively. The poor made no outlays on wood fuel. In the Sudanese villages, the average monthly outlay on wood fuel was insignificant because most of the families depended on firewood and charcoal produced by themselves.

One important change observed in the last 10 years in the supply of energy on the scheme is that the radius of the land stripped of vegetation has increased considerably. It is interesting to observe that, except in some protected sites such as the few *hashab* (*A. senegal*) orchards and a few trees on individual *hawashas*, a concentric pattern of forest resource utilization has arisen on and around the scheme area. There is an economic principle underlying such a concentric pattern of resource use. This economic principle, based on spatial patterns of resource utilization, was first expounded by von Thünen in 1875 and Lösch in 1954, and refined by Dunn in 1954 (for discussion see Whitney, 1991: 117). The underlying principle of this conceptual construct is 'the type of intensity of economic activity is dependent on its location in respect to the market. As distance from a market centre

Plates 5.3 and 5.4
Supplying firewood and fences
to the refugee settlements.
Refugees cut trees for lack of
alternatives to build shelters
and collect wood to meet their
subsistence energy needs, but
isn't the amount they consume
insignificant to be the cause of
deforestation? Is the image of
refugees degrading the land to
a barren scene a misconception
or real in the Sudan? (Photo:
Gaim Kibreab)

increases, the profitability of producing that product declines until it reaches zero, and it is no longer produced' (Whitney, 1991: 117). In subsistence fuel gathering, this is expressed in terms of effort and time spent on collecting and ferrying the wood to the village either for personal consumption or for sale. The general trend on and around the scheme is that firewood gatherers overexploit the nearest locations to their villages before they move into the next location, which requires more time and effort for gathering and ferrying. Firewood gatherers, especially those who do not use animal carriers, seldom move to more distant locations before the exhaustion of all nearby plant species that can be used for firewood. This is clear from our findings, in which the areas located nearest the villages are left devoid of trees that can be used for firewood. What is interesting is that the level of intensity of forest-resource overexploitation or deforestation was far more severe in the areas located in the immediate neighbourhood of the scheme than in the areas within the scheme. This is mainly because some of the trees located inside the individual farms are protected against felling by outsiders. If we take as our point of departure the outer edges of the scheme, there is clear evidence to show that the level of intensity of forest-resource use (deforestation) is a decreasing function of distance from the scheme, where the intensity of human interference is highest. The sudden increase of population that took place following the establishment of the scheme in 1969 put heavy pressure on the vegetation resources. The data in Table 5.11 clearly show that the availability of vegetation products has decreased since the establishment of the villages in the area. In 1991 the bare ground surrounding the villages that was stripped of vegetation was much larger than it was in 1982.

One of the consequences of this has been that the distance to the source of firewood has increased. However, although the time spent on gathering wood fuel and travelling has increased in the last 10 years, the increase has not been as dramatic as one would expect. In 1982, on average, one trip of firewood collection (round-trip travelling and wood-fuel gathering) took about 1.7 hours, while in 1991 the corresponding mean was, for the refugee villages, 4.05 hours (SD 2.54) and, for the local population, 4.84 hours (SD 3.04). A family of an average size needs to make two trips a week if no other means of transport is used, one trip a week if a donkey is used and one trip a fortnight if a camel is used. Thus, the refugee families and the local population (only those who did not use other means of transport) spent a maximum of 8.10 and 9.7 hours a week, respectively, on firewood collection. Those who used donkeys and camels spent less time.

Does the activity of wood-fuel gathering consume a high proportion of the families' labour time? The answer depends on the demographic compositions of the families and the opportunity costs of family labour. For those families without able-bodied adults, 8 hours a week is too much, but not for those with a large number of able-bodied family members. During cultivation seasons, there are competing demands for family labour time and 8 hours may represent a drain on the family labour that could otherwise be allocated for farming activities. During the trough seasons, when labour is abundant, 8 hours a week is not much. In about 10 years, the amount of time spent on a single trip has increased by about 138%, but looking at the change alone does not give a correct picture, because the benchmark (1.7 hours) is low. In absolute terms, the time spent on gathering and travelling is by no means excessive. In 1982, no data were collected for the local population and hence it is not possible to say how great the change has been for the Sudanese villages.

Another change observed during the last 10 years on the scheme is commercialization of wood-fuel production. In 1982 fewer families met all their wood-fuel needs from the local market. In 1991, however, about 33% of the refugee families

Plate 5.5 People on the edge are forced to sacrifice the future in order to salvage the present. 'Do you expect the trees to stand green when the stomachs of my children burn?' – A local farmer cutting trees to produce charcoal for sale. (Photo: Gaim Kibreab)

met their full energy needs from the local market. The energy needs of the remaining 67% were met both through self-collection and from the market. It is important to note that even those families that collected their own firewood bought charcoal from the local market. Self-collection is no longer dominant. Only the destitute families were fully dependent on self-collected energy sources. The picture is different among the local population. Among the latter, self-collection is still dominant. In 1991, only 6% were not engaged in collection of wood fuel.

The important question that springs to mind is whether the emergence of wood-fuel markets in the refugee villages is the outcome of wood-fuel scarcity or of specialization and exchange. Even though the proportion of families now relying on the market has increased, it has to be pointed out that even in 1982 there were a considerable number of families who did not gather their own wood fuel but depended on the local market. These were people who were engaged in diverse income-generating activities, such as retail trade, wage employment and migration (of male household heads) in search of opportunities for income-generating activities. In the Qala en Nahal scheme, the wood-fuel market is nearly as old as the scheme itself. There was a wood-fuel market before wood fuel became scarce. Although it cannot be denied that the relative scarcity of wood fuel has, during the last decade, led to consolidation of the wood-fuel market, the emergence of the latter was independent of physical scarcity of wood fuel.

One of the central assumptions underlying the analysis of the so-called wood-fuel crisis in Third World rural areas is the heavy burden placed on women and children as the major collectors of wood fuel. This is because, as the distance of the sources of wood fuel increases, travelling, searching, gathering and ferrying become burdensome, making women's life unbearable.[10] One of the unexpected findings of this study is the converse of this conventional wisdom. On the scheme, as the distance of wood-fuel resources increased, firewood collection ceased being the domain of women. Not only has men's participation in firewood collection increased during the last decade, but the participation of women in the activity has declined drastically. The depletion of vegetation that can be used for wood fuel in the vicinity of the scheme area and the consequent increase of effort and time required for collection and transportation have induced changes in the gender-based division of family labour.

In 1982, the number of married women and unmarried females who were engaged in firewood collection was much more than in 1991. Among the refugees, only in 5.6% families were married women involved in firewood collection in 1991. The picture among the local Sudanese families is different, because 53% of the married women were involved in firewood collection. Among the refugees, unmarried adolescent females were also no longer dominant in the activity. Only in 7.8% of the families were unmarried females involved in firewood gathering.[11] The corresponding figure for the Sudanese villages was 67%. In the refugee villages, 47.4% of the men and 46.0% of the adolescent boys were involved in firewood collection. In the local Sudanese villages, the corresponding figures were 57.1% and 58.2%, respectively. One of the reasons for the downscaling of the involvement of women in firewood collection is the increase in distance, which has made the activity more toilsome and burdensome for females. About 82% and 57% of the refugee and Sudanese respondents, respectively, thought that the source of firewood was too far and the activity too toilsome for women and adolescent females to participate in as effectively as before.

The important explanation, however, is not the increased burden and toil involved in the activity as such, but rather the increased conflict arising from the demand for women's labour time. Women's work in subsistence economies has always been burdensome and toilsome and there have been few or no changes in history that have been induced by the need to make the tasks of women easier. The increased amount of time expended on firewood collection and transportation has meant increased conflicts with women's domestic chores. If women are absent for the best part of a day collecting wood fuel, most of the reproduction chores (child-rearing and domestic work) will be left unattended to. In these communities, men never participate in domestic chores. Thus, the downscaling of women's involvement in wood-fuel collection is an inevitable consequence, on the one hand, of the depletion of forest resources in the vicinity of the settlement centres and, on the other, of men's failure to participate in domestic chores. These results show that the depletion of biomass in the vicinity of the villages has led to a considerable change in the patterns of division of family labour, at least in the refugee villages.

It is important to point out, however, that the low level of women refugees' participation in firewood collection is not solely attributable to wood-fuel scarcity in the vicinity of the scheme. There are other factors which contribute to this. First, the majority of the refugees are Moslems and many women do not participate in work outside the family homes. These religious norms are much more strictly enforced in the 1990s than they were in the early 1980s. Islam is therefore one of the factors that limits the women refugees' participation in firewood collection. It has to be pointed out, however, that the rate of participation has declined even among non-Moslems or non-strict Moslems.

The third factor which contributes to the decline of women's participation in firewood collection is insecurity. Some village elders expressed concern about the security risks that could face women firewood collectors. The risk of robbery and sexual attack, they argue, increases with distance. Since the 1984–1985 famine, armed robbery of livestock has become a problem in the area and females no longer feel safe to travel far afield. Thus, scarcity, religion and insecurity have coalesced to reduce women's participation in firewood collection.

Other changes observed between 1982 and 1993 include a slight shift from charcoal to increased firewood consumption and partial substitution of wood fuel with other biomass such as crop residues and animal dung, albeit on a limited scale. In 1982, timber for construction was harvested from woodland resources outside the scheme. Gradually, construction timber became scarce on and around the scheme area. At the beginning of the 1990s, almost all villages bought construction timber (*dagag* and *korki*) from Gedaref and other distant places, because there were no longer *kitir* (*A. mellifera*) trees for providing the quantities demanded. In view of the distance of the timber markets, lorries have replaced donkeys and camels for ferrying timber. By 1993, timber collection had almost ceased as an economic activity, because nearly all the big trees had been removed during land clearance for cultivation or felled for charcoal production. Animal pressure means that there is little respite for coppice regrowth to reach maturity.

How do the farmers cope with the diminishing sources of wood fuel? The analysis has hitherto rested on the 'physical notion of natural resource deficiencies' (Stanley, 1968), based on objective assessment of the physical environment. Hitherto the subjective domain of the farmers' experiences has not been examined. This is vital because as Stanley states, 'scarcity touches on the problem of linkages between objective and subjective realms of experience' (Stanley, 1968: 856). If we disregard the subjective experiences of the farmers and their coping strategies, we may be misled into concluding, from the marked physical depletion of the forest resources, that the farmers are suffering severe wood-fuel shortages. Whether the farmers on the scheme suffer wood-fuel shortages cannot be ascertained solely from 'scientific-observer models'. It is important, therefore, to understand how the farmers view the impact of the diminishing wood-fuel resources on their patterns of consumption. In view of the changes in vegetation resources that have occurred on and around the scheme, one might plausibly assume that wood-fuel scarcity would rank among the most critical problems facing the farmers. Asked to state the most critical environmental problems that face the farmers on the scheme in order of priorities, none of the sample household heads mentioned wood fuel. The most critical constraints mentioned, in order of priorities, included land shortage, soil exhaustion, weed infestation, lack of adequate rainfall and labour and capital shortages. In view of the seasonal nature of agricultural production in the area, labour shortage was experienced during peak periods in the cycle of agricultural production.

These data do not suggest that there is no wood-fuel shortage on the scheme. The implication is that the farmers do not suffer passively the consequences of environmental changes, but they develop innovative strategies which enable them to cope with the changes effectively. In the following paragraphs, the coping strategies developed by the farmers to respond to wood-fuel scarcity, and the increased costs and physical burden of wood-fuel gathering/carrying will be discussed. The burden of carrying wood fuel has increased with the distance of wood-fuel sources. In response to this, more animals of burden (camels and donkeys) are used in the collection of firewood. In 1982, donkeys were used to collect firewood, but there were also large numbers of human carriers. By 1992, the number of human carriers had been reduced drastically. If this trend continues, human carriers of firewood may cease to exist and be replaced by donkeys and camels. This suggests that the depletion of forest resources around the scheme area has not led to increased human drudgery.

The farmers have reduced their patterns of wood-fuel consumption in response to the changes, without necessarily compromising their habitual food consumption. Patterns of wood-fuel consumption are dynamic and can be adjusted in response to changes in supply. According to a forestry study commissioned by ACORD (then Euro Action Acord), the per capita charcoal and firewood consumptions among the refugees on the scheme in 1983 were 1.151 m^3 and 0.395 m^3 per annum, respectively (Howard, 1983). In 1991, the annual average per capita consumption of charcoal and firewood of the three income groups was 0.43 m^3 and 0.46 m^3, respectively (Table 5.9). In nearly a decade, per capita charcoal consumption has decreased by about 168%, while per capita consumption of firewood has increased by 16% for the same period. The results show that, in view of the environmental changes that have taken place in terms of deforestation, the cost of obtaining wood fuel has increased substantially. Unlike at the beginning of the 1980s, charcoal is no longer produced in the vicinity of the villages. Not only has the distance increased, but the density of potential trees for charcoal production has been reduced and more time is required for collection. Most of the charcoal consumed on the scheme is obtained through the market-place where there is competition with the urban centres. Thus, the response of the farmers has been to cut down on charcoal consumption. What is interesting, however, is that, despite this large reduction in patterns of charcoal consumption, none of the respondents mentioned wood-fuel shortage as a major problem. This may suggest that in the early 1980s, when there was no serious problem of deforestation, the cost of obtaining wood fuel was low and patterns of consumption were high. As the cost of obtaining wood fuel increased, the levels of consumption lessened. The results of the survey show that about 75% of the refugee families cope with the problem of wood-fuel shortage and high prices by using less wood fuel. The patterns of consumption of 25% of the families (the well-off) were not affected by scarcity of wood fuel. This suggests that physical scarcity is a relative concept, even in societies where there is a limited degree of social and economic differentiation. For the well-off families, there was no scarcity.

In the literature on wood fuel, it is often assumed that, as the costs of obtaining wood fuel increase or supply decreases, there is a tendency to shift from firewood to charcoal consumption. The converse was found to be the case here. The obvious explanation for this is that the majority of the refugee farmers do not produce charcoal for their own consumption. Charcoal is obtained through the market-place while most firewood is collected by the farmers. Thus, when the price of charcoal increases because of high demand in the urban centres and diminishing supply, more farmers resort to self-collection of firewood to meet their energy needs. Also, the drastic cuts in charcoal consumption were not accompanied by changes in food consumption. If the change in patterns of wood fuel had precipitated changes in food consumption, the farmers would undoubtedly have perceived the scarcity as a problem. The reason why the farmers did not think the drastic changes in patterns of wood-fuel consumption constituted a problem was because the cuts were accompanied by some innovative changes which enabled them to maximize energy use from the available, but diminishing, sources.

The following are some of the innovative changes observed. The purpose of the changes was to minimize wood-fuel consumption and to maximize fire efficiency. In 1982, the dominant cooking method comprised three stones assembled in a kitchen (usually a shade – Arabic, *rakouba*) outside the main buildings. The three stones are used to provide support for a cooking pot for the traditional sorghum porridge, which is round in shape, and the square metal plate for baking *injera* or *kisra*. In 1991, there were many families who had substituted their three-stone stove with an improved mud stove, which is more energy-efficient. The square metal plate is supported on a clay wall with a hole in the front to insert the firewood and a hole at the back to allow the combustion gases to escape. A similar mud stove is constructed for the round pot to cook sorghum porridge. This mud stove is common in the refugees' country of origin, but it was only adopted in the refugee villages in response to dwindling wood-fuel supply. The advantage of the mud stove is that it is easy to construct, reduces heat loss, improves control of the burning rate of firewood and maximizes transfer of the available heat to the cooking pot or plate. Although no measurements were taken to estimate the amount of heat saved in comparison to the three-stone stove, the farmers say the innovation has enabled them to cut firewood consumption drastically.

The other benefit associated with the adoption of the mud-stove is that its embers produce substantial amounts of charcoal, which are extinguished for future use or are removed to a charcoal stove for the purposes of cooking sauces or boiling tea, coffee or milk. One way in which wood-fuel consumption is reduced is by efficient fire management. In 1982–1983, it was common to see women leaving fire burning after they finished cooking. Now, it is extinguished immediately. In the past families cooked three times a day. Now, the poor sections of the population consume less wood fuel by cooking once instead of the usual three times a day. Evening meals or lunches cooked in the morning or on previous evenings are consumed without being warmed. It is not clear how far this compromises their health and quality of life.

On the scheme, extended families share a compound and their food is cooked together. This collective cooking (though not by design) seems to reduce wood-fuel consumption. Many families also respond to wood-fuel scarcity by consuming their courtyard (zariba) fences. In 1982 most of the houses in the six refugee villages had zaribas surrounded by fences and nearly every compound also had a shade (rakouba). During that time, only a handful of houses were without fenced courtyards and shades. In 1991, the number of families that had fences around their houses and shades in their compounds was reduced substantially. Most of the families have either used their fences and shades as firewood or the cutting of trees in the vicinity of the villages has increased the cost of repair beyond the means of many of the families. Fenced zaribas and shades provide privacy and protection against the sun, respectively. However, some families make trade-offs between these facilities and increased outlays in terms of labour time and cash.

In the past, flies were repelled from animals during the rainy season by using smoke. Now, animals are moved to the hills instead. Many families now use unmelted soap to wash their clothes. There are some families who used alternative sources of energy, such as crop residues, dung cakes and grass (Table 5.7). There is also a noticeable shift from the customary practice of using dry wood and dead branches as firewood to the cutting of live trees for future use. In the early 1980s, it was unusual for the communities to cut live trees for firewood. It is now common in the villages to see a few people collecting and storing in their courtyards green branches and live trees for future use. Charcoal producers, both commercial and local, have always cut live and green branches, but even this is more accelerated at present than in the past.[12]

Wood-fuel consumers have also become less selective. This is reflected in the fact that less preferred plant species are used as wood fuel. In the past, when there was no shortage of trees, A. seyal (talih) was the most preferred species for charcoal production. Now even A. senegal is used for charcoal production. Charcoal producers use any available species, including Balanites, which in the past was considered taboo. *Balanites* was known as a devil's tree, whose smoke when used as firewood or charcoal was believed to cause tuberculosis. The superstition has vanished in the face of diminishing forest resources. All these changes have enabled the farmers to cut wood-fuel consumption, without a marked shift to consumption of foodstuffs that require less cooking time.

Conclusion

Provision of energy for refugees is seldom an issue among aid agencies. When a large-scale refugee influx occurs, the common practice is to use locally available vegetation resources for camp and settlement construction as well as for wood fuel. This is plainly stated by the United Nations High Commissioner for Refugees (UNHCR), '[A]s long as there were bushes within sight, no one ever asked where starving refugees would get the three tons of firewood needed to cook each ton of wheat and beans supplied by humanitarian agencies' (UNHCR, 1992b: 5). It is the failure to address this issue which is at the heart of the problem of vegetation-resource depletion in and around refugee camps, reception centres and settlements. It is only when refugee camps or reception centres are located in deserts that relief agencies provide tents for shelter and paraffin for fuel. In the areas where there are vegetation resources, no matter how meagre, no such items are provided. Nature is expected to supply these items indefinitely.

In Sudan no substitutes for wood-fuel energy are provided for refugees and no measures are taken to introduce energy-saving stoves. The Qala en Nahal scheme is among the oldest refugee settlements in Africa. Over time, wood-fuel and timber consumption by the refugees has exacerbated the problem of deforestation. The forces degrading vegetation resources are, however, in most cases independent of the refugees. The major causes of deforestation in the Gedaref district are expansion of mechanized rain-fed agriculture, production of charcoal to meet the demand in the urban centres, population increase, lack of local control of forest resources and inability of the government to enforce forestry laws and by-laws. The depletion of the vegetation resources on and around the scheme cannot be understood in isolation from the pressures exerted from outside the settler community. It is not local wood-fuel consumption which constitutes a major threat to the woodland resources on and around the scheme. Until the beginning of the 1980s, refugees mainly consumed dead wood and this did not have a negative impact on the stock or regenerative capability of the woodland resources. Live trees were cut for timber and the coppiced trees regenerated in the following seasons. This alone would not have caused deforestation because of the ability of the trees to regenerate and because of the limited local wood-fuel and timber requirements.

Since the mid-1980s, however, most of the adult Sudanese in the area and some refugees began to cut large amounts of trees to produce charcoal for sale to wholesalers, who come from distant areas. As farm incomes dwindled, resulting from a combination of shortage of rain, soil exhaustion and inadequate weeding, many families resorted to charcoal making to make ends meet. From the mid-1980s, people even began to cut live trees, not only for charcoal production, but also for firewood. This has affected the vegetation resources in a detrimental way.

The distance of wood-fuel resources has increased over time. Experiences elsewhere suggest that such changes place a heavy burden on women and children as collectors of wood fuel. On the scheme, however, the reverse is observed. Increased distance has resulted in lower demand on women's and female children's labour time. Firewood collection is no longer the domain of women.[13] Men's involvement in firewood collection has increased considerably. This is because, as the rate of tapping and distance increase, not only is more time spent on collection and travelling, but the activity also becomes more toilsome and burdensome for females. However, in societies where women are assigned a subservient position, changes are seldom effected in order to relieve women of travail. The most important explanation for this change is, rather, the conflict arising from the demand for women's labour time. If women spend most of their time travelling, collecting and carrying wood fuel, domestic work, which is the exclusive domain of women, may suffer, threatening the well-being of the families. Other changes observed include commercialization of wood-fuel production. For many families, wood fuel is no longer a 'free good'. It has become commoditized. For many families, self-collection is becoming less important. This has enabled many families to earn an income from the sale of firewood and charcoal within and outside the scheme. One way in which the poor families cope with the shortage of wood fuel is by cutting consumption. There were families who cooked only once a day.

There were two ways in which the detrimental impacts of the refugees on the vegetation resources could have been avoided. First, if the refugees had been provided with alternative construction materials and commercial fuels, as well as cooking devices, their impact on the vegetation resources would have been less damaging. Second, if the refugees and the local Sudanese communities had been given control over the local vegetation resources, they would have devised institutional arrangements and enforcement mechanisms to regulate access to and use of such resources. This would also have enabled them to deny access to outsiders. There is an evident link between land clearance for cultivation, felling of trees for wood-fuel and timber consumption and depletion of woody resources on and around the scheme, but this has not yet engendered a wood-fuel crisis at the local level.

Notes

1. One cubic metre (m^3) of solid dry wood weighs 700 kilograms (kg).
2. For the exact year of arrival at the scheme by every family, see footnote 4.
3. This was after each family agreed to be included in the sample.
4. Number of families by year of arrival (the sample families).

Year	No. of refugee families	No. of Sudanese families	Year	No. of refugee families	No. of Sudanese families
1950	–	2	1974	3	2
1951	–	2	1975	5	7
1955	–	2	1976	2	2
1956	–	4	1977	6	2
1960	–	2	1978	11	2
1961	–	3	1989	3	0
1962	–	1	1980	4	3
1963	–	3	1981	3	3
1964	–	4	1982	3	7
1965	–	3	1983	2	4
1966	–	2	1984	5	6
1967	–	2	1985	4	1
1968	–	1	1986	1	2
1969	2	2	1987	1	0
1970	135	2	1988	2	1
1971	18	1	1989	0	1
1972	5	7			
1973	–	5	Total	215	91

5. The average family size among the refugees was 5.02 persons.

6. All the figures are adjusted for the year of arrival of the individual families.

7. The average family size in the Sudanese villages was 4.84 and the number of families was 1161.

8. It has to be pointed out that this is an average figure and not necessarily true for every family. The time of arrival of the families was different and hence the amount they consumed was also different. The figure of 49.57 m^3 and all the other figures are averages.

9. One m^3=0.7 tonne: 1 tonne of dry-weight wood=0.3 tonne of charcoal. The total amount of charcoal consumed in the twelve villages between 1950 and 1991 was 287,559.8 m^3. This is equivalent to 201,291.86 tonnes (287,559.8 m^3×0.7). The latter is equivalent to 670,972.87 tonnes dry solid wood (201,291.86/0.3). The latter is again equivalent to 958,532.67 m^3 (670,972.87/0.7).

10. Charcoal production is monopolized by men. Women on the scheme do not participate in charcoal production.

11. This is excluding collection of supplementary fuels, such as crop residues, dry weeds and animal dung.

12. The extent of live tree-cutting is more common among commercial charcoal producers and local farmers than among the refugees. The presence of a forest guard in the refugee settlement seems to deter the refugees from cutting and ferrying live trees to their homes. Owing to political vulnerability, the degree of compliance with forestry regulations was evidently higher among refugees than among commercial charcoal producers and to some extent local farmers.

13. Among some of the refugee groups, firewood collection was never the exclusive domain of women because of religious and cultural norms which precluded women from participating in economic activities outside the home. But in recent years the number of women involved in firewood collection even among the other groups has declined drastically.

6

Overstocking and the Problem of Overgrazing of Range Resources

> Although overstocking, overgrazing and desertification may be occurring, too often these processes are simply invoked without evidence to back up their existence. (K. Homewood and W.A. Rodgers, 1987)

The question of range degradation as a consequence of overstocking in the arid and semiarid regions of Africa has been receiving substantial attention in the literature. Widespread academic interest notwithstanding, however, there is still lack of a detailed knowledge on the relationships between climate, primary productivity, secondary productivity, soil erosion and stocking rates. The mainstream view which attributed decline in primary productivity to high stocking rates and consequently considered control of 'excessive livestock numbers' as a panacea is no longer taken for granted. This position, which defines range-land degradation as being solely the consequence of overstocking, is set up as a target for criticism in the recent literature. Sandford, among others, argues that the causes of range-land degradation are so many and so variable that it is untenable to attribute it solely to overstocking (Sandford, 1982a). The concept of carrying capacity constituted the pillar on which the mainstream view rested. According to Dixon et al., 'overgrazing occurs when livestock population per capita area of the ecosystem exceeds the safe stocking rate at that time. It is usually associated with increased livestock population or decreasing areas of pasture' (Dixon et al., 1988: 29). It is important to state, however, that not only is there disagreement about the causes of range-resource decline in the arid and semiarid regions of Africa, but there is also no universally valid criterion by which to determine what constitutes a 'safe stocking rate'. Although the phrase 'safe stocking rate' is not defined by the authors, it is clear from the literature that its implication is the same as 'carrying capacity', which refers to stocking density per unit area of range-lands designed to enable range managers to balance grazing pressure against the natural regenerative capability of plants. A stocking density that exceeds this benchmark is said to upset the balance, resulting in range-land degradation. In the arid and semiarid regions, what constitutes a 'safe stocking rate' is a complex issue because it depends on so many factors, such as the specific management objective, climate, level of sensitivity and resilience of the land in question to grazing pressure and characteristics of the vegetation concerned.

This suggests that not only are the criteria of measuring degradation and the causes of animal forage fluctuation varied, but high stocking rates *per se* may not constitute overgrazing in all given circumstances. Without denying the inter-relationships of the different variables, the emphasis of explanations by different researchers is radically varied. Behnke and Scoones, for example, argue that there is no biologically optimal and universally valid carrying capacity which can be defined independently of the different management objectives associated with different forms of animal exploitation. In their model, carrying capacity is a function of economic objectives (Behnke and Scoones, 1993). Bartels et al. also argue that in spite of its semblance of objectivity, carrying capacity means different things to different people, depending on what they want to achieve. It may not even mean the same to livestock producers (Bartels *et al.*, 1993: 89): 'it may mean one thing to a commercial rancher in America and quite another to a subsistence pastoralist in sub-Saharan Africa'.[1] This is because different livestock managers have different definitions because the *raison d'être* of their economic activities may be different. A manager whose economic objectives is to maximize profit by slaughtering or selling fattened stocks cannot tolerate the same level of livestock forage depletion, as peasants would, if her/his aim is to stay in business. Thus, some estimates suggest that economic carrying capacity for commercial beef production is half or a third of estimated ecological carrying capacity (Bartels *et al.*, 1993: 89). In comparison with a commercial beef producer, a subsistence-orientated pastoralist may, at some cost in terms of output, health and higher natural mortality, be capable of maintaining high levels of total output at stocking densities approaching ecological carrying capacity (Bartels *et al.*, 1993: 89). Subsistence economies can continue to function even in the face of drastically declining marginal productivity levels. This is, among other things, due to the fact that, unlike commercial dairy farmers, subsistence-orientated pastoralists harvest animal output in the form of live products such as milk and power (for traction and transport) that do not require animal slaughter. This enables them to keep a larger number of animals per unit area of grazing.

Sandford argues that, in the arid and semiarid regions, availability of forage is a function of rainfall. He states that, in dry areas, interannual and seasonal differences in rainfall cause corresponding fluctuations in forage availabilities (Sandford, 1982b). The importance of rainfall in determining forage conditions is also underscored by Behnke and Scoones, who note that, in situations where physical factors such as rainfall and temperature fluctuate widely, 'these non-biological variables will have a greater impact on plant growth than marginal changes in grazing pressure caused by stocking densities' (Behnke and Scoones, 1993). The scarcity of fodder whenever it occurs is said to be due to too little rainfall rather than too many animals (Behnke and Scoones, 1993).

There are also those who attribute forage productivity decline not to stocking densities as such, but to the intrinsic attributes of the range lands in question. Different land-forms have different sensitivity and resilience levels and their exposure to similar grazing pressures does not necessarily result in the same degree of degradation (Walker, 1980). Yet others place greater emphasis on the characteristics of the vegetation resource itself. According to Walker *et al.*, (1981) since the vegetation in the arid and semiarid range lands is continuously disturbed, it has adapted to disturbance and possesses an enhanced capacity to recover from disturbance. Thus, the so-called density-induced degradation of range resources can no longer be taken for granted.

These disparate views suggest that there is need, on the one hand, to recognize the multi-causality of the problem of range-resource scarcity in the arid and semiarid regions of Africa and, on the other, to seek explanations for the problem of fluctuating vegetation resources beyond the catch-all problem of 'overstocking'. These views seem to challenge the central tenet of the mainstream literature, which holds 'overstocking' to be the major source of the problem of range-land degradation. Some of these views are still untested models, but nevertheless open new ground for empirical investigation.

There seems to be a consensus among many researchers that concentration of livestock near watering-points and settlements tends to lead to fluctuations in species composition, decline in plant biomass cover and soil degradation by trampling and eating (Digernes, 1977, 1979; Grainger, 1982: Ibrahim, 1984; Dixon et al., 1989). This environmental decline may in turn detrimentally affect livestock health, leading to a fall in production of milk, meat and power (for traction and transport) and to a higher rate of mortality (UNCOD, 1977). A decline in the welfare of herders is also predicted as a consequence. However, the consequences of forage-resource depletion near watering points and settlements for livestock productivity are dependent on the actual grazing systems and on the availability of grazing resources outside these sites. Furthermore, the consequences of livestock-productivity decline on herders' welfare is also dependent on whether there are opportunities for earning an income outside the livestock sector such as wage labour, petty trading, migration, etc.

In fact, there are some researchers who argue that, in fluctuating climates, rainfall, not forage availability, may ultimately be the variable which limits animal population growth (Behnke and Scoones, 1993). Our own findings also show that in grazing systems in which medium- and long-distance migrations are major components, animal population growth in a given area is not dependent on the conditions of forage resources in that particular area. Although the absolute limit of production from the animal system is dependent on the primary productivity of the grazing resource (Tapson, 1993), in situations such as Qala en Nahal, where the centre-piece of the grazing system is migration developed in response to temporal and spatial variations of rainfall and forage, the relationship between primary production (forage) and secondary production (livestock) may not always be clear at the micro level. In this study, the results of the vegetation survey show that there have been changes in species composition, resulting in the reduction of palatable and the increase of unpalatable vegetation as well as in the drastic increase of annuals at the expense of perennial grasses and forbs. There has also been a decline in plant biomass and cover (see Chapter 3) as well as loss of soil nutrients (see Chapter 2). For example, the drastic increase of Cassia tora (unpalatable annual) and the dissipation of the most preferred species for grazing such as Blepharis ciliaris and Farsetia longiseliqua, which before the increased intensity of encroachment of mechanized rain-fed farming were dominant as fodder plants (Harrison and Jackson, 1958) with an extremely high nutritive value, are an indication of the extent of the pressure exerted on the vegetation resources.

Two questions spring to mind. First, are these changes attributable to over-stocking? Second, have the loss of soil and soil nutrients and decline in forage resulted in a decline in livestock population?[2] Given the obvious dependence of livestock production on primary production, it was plausible to expect a decline in stock numbers accompanied by high mortality. The evidence, however, as we shall see later, points surprisingly in the opposite direction. There are also studies elsewhere in Sudan which show, despite widespread environmental stress, a considerable increase in livestock size, especially in goats, sheep and camels (Digernes, 1977). In the arid regions of India, the study by Shankarnarayan et al. (1985) also shows a considerable increase of ovines (sheep and goats) at the expense of bovines (cattle).

In some of the arid and semiarid regions, livestock build-up may not necessarily reflect availability of adequate or untapped range resources, but herders may build up their stock in response to increased food insecurity. However, this pursuit would be unachievable if the areas concerned are overgrazed or have experienced irreversible deterioration in productive capability. In grazing systems which exploit variations in the environment, the negative consequences of forage decline in one area may be overcome by transhumant patterns of cyclical herd movements.

Because of the arid and semi-arid nature of the environment they occupy, agropastoralists and pastoralists in the region have for generations developed viable management systems in response to changing conditions and needs. Thus, even though the grazing areas on the scheme and its environs are subjected to encroachment of agriculture and intensive harvesting of trees for commercial charcoal production, the farmers, as the principal agents in shaping their own destiny, have devised efficient range resource-management regimes that enable them to cope with the constraints they face in their environment. Although the non-cultivable sites were subjected to intensive grazing, the high growth rate of livestock population, including those types not involved in long-distance migration, is a sign of the farmers' sagacity in devising grazing and feeding systems that are tailored to suit their particular situation. As we shall see later, this innovative management is based on a combination of mobility designed to exploit variations in the environment and stall-feeding of milking cows and small stock during dry seasons.

The point of departure in this chapter is that, whenever there was degradation of grazing and browse resources on and around the scheme area, it was more often than not independent of the overstocking explanations common in much of the literature. The scarcity of fodder and browse, whenever it existed, was due to encroachment of agriculture in grazing areas and harvesting of trees, including live and young ones, rather than due to too many animals. This is exacerbated by fluctuating rainfall and high temperatures. The maintenance of livestock on the scheme is contingent upon migration and the ability to utilize effectively variations in rainfall and pasture. The empirical problem at issue in this regard is by no means peculiar to the scheme, but is general in the district.

Livestock population on the scheme

As the area under cultivation extended progressively on to increasingly marginal lands and woodlands (due to immigration, natural population growth and consequently rising subsistence demands), which were previously used as sources of fuel wood and range resources, wet-season grazing pressure increased on the ever-shrinking remaining land. This placed heavy pressure on the grassland during the wet growing season, when plant growth was most critical for survival and reproduction. The refugees that were relocated during the early period of the scheme's history brought hardly any stock with them. Some who managed to do so were those who used to cross borders as pastoralists between Eritrea and Sudan long before the emergence of the political crisis that created the refugee situation. Generally, reliable statistics on livestock population are difficult to collect among traditional herders because of their reluctance to reveal stock numbers to strangers and because of the complexity of ownership.[3] Among some of the herder communities, revealing stock numbers is considered to be a harbinger of bad luck (Kibreab, 1985). The situation is further exacerbated by the fact that dry cattle and sheep are kept outside the scheme during most of the year. Livestock numbers on the scheme sometimes swell and sometimes shrink in response to availability of water and pasture. In addition, livestock on the scheme are heavily taxed under the new government's laws and thus herders are reluctant to reveal the actual size of their ownership. In 1995 the following taxes were levied in Sudanese pounds per head: camel – £S1,000, cow – £S600, sheep – £S500, donkey – £S200 and goat – £S400; huts were taxed at £S200 per hut.

Table 6.1   Livestock population 1976–1991

	1976[a]	1980[b]	1984[c]	1988[d]	1991[e]
Cattle	2,233	3,079	16,620	27,590	66,095
Camels	n.a.	60	198	250	188
Sheep	n.a.	n.a.	5,400	b.n.a.	31,040
Goats	n.a.	n.a.	10,700	b.n.a.	31,320
Donkeys	n.a.	100	3,780	4,000	n.a.

n.a., not available; b.n.a., breakdown not available.
Sources:
a. Hunting Technical Service, 1976.
b. COR Administration Records, 1980, Umsagata.
c. ACORD, 1984
d. ACORD records based on extrapolation from the 1984 figures.
e. ACORD, 1991.

The data in Table 6.1 show that the number of livestock on the scheme rose greatly in the 1980s. Between 1976 and 1980, the cattle population increased by about 38%. The corresponding figures for the period 1980–1984, 1984–1988 and 1988–1991 were 504.7%, 66.0% and 139%, respectively. The number of camels fluctuated over the years, but did not show drastic changes. There was a slight increase between 1980 and 1984, but by 1991 the number of camels had declined to the 1980 level. Some of the refugees, especially among the Beni Amer, had camels among their livestock before they became refugees. The explanations why there is no build-up of camels include, first, that camels depend on tall grasses, trees and shrubs. These species are depleted on and around the scheme areas, mainly because of invasion of cultivation. Second, camels have a higher reproductive and maturity age (3 years) than goats (1 year), sheep (1 year) and cattle (2 years). Third, camels, compared with the other animals raised by the refugees, are selective grazers. With the increased depletion of the range resources, the preferred species have either disappeared or declined considerably. Fourth, camels are used as transport animals for both long and short distances. Lorries (long distance) and donkeys (short distance) have proved more cost-effective substitutes in this regard. Fifth, the demand for camel meat compared with beef and mutton is low.

The number of sheep increased very greatly. In just over a decade (1980–1991), the sheep population increased by about 475%. The corresponding figure for goats during the same period was about 193%. These data show that the 1980s witnessed a dramatic increase in livestock population. In 1991, the total number of livestock was equivalent to 82,542 livestock units (LLU).[4] (The major sources for the data were the vaccination, *hafir* (watering-point) and the Commissioner's Office for Refugees (COR) livestock records.[5] The refugee families were investing considerably in the purchase of livestock throughout the 1980s and early 1990s.[6]

Livestock population on and around the scheme varies with relative availability of water and grazing. Thus, although the figures were derived from the vaccination and water-charge records, the proportion of the animals kept on the scheme throughout the year was not possible to determine with certainty. As we shall see later, the supply of water for livestock had improved following the excavation of the *hafirs* by ACORD. Dry cattle and sheep are involved in long-distance seasonal movements. They spend only a few weeks on and around the scheme on their way to and from the Butana plains, Rahad and the Ethiopian border areas (see Table 6.3). Often it is

only milking cows, small stock and donkeys that are kept on the scheme throughout the year. The number and types of livestock owned by the families on the
scheme are given in Table 6.2. The data obviously include more animals than those
which were normally kept within the scheme area throughout the year.

The total livestock population that are kept within the scheme area may be
estimated on the basis of the results of the survey (Table 6.2). In 1991, there were
5,567 and 1,161 families in the refugee and surrounding Sudanese villages,
respectively. If we generalize the results of the findings of the survey to the total
population,[7] the total numbers of livestock kept on the scheme at the time of the
survey were 35,629 cattle, 278 camels, 15,810 goats, 15,588 sheep and 2,004
donkeys in the refugee villages. The corresponding figures in the Sudanese villages
were 627 cattle, 128 camels, 1,834 goats, 731 sheep and 441 donkeys.

The data were collected in November and December 1991. At that particular
time, about 54% of the cattle, 50% of the sheep and 51% of the goats were on the

Table 6.2   Livestock ownership per family in the three refugee villages (Salmin, Umsagata
and Umbrush) and the surrounding Sudanese villages

	Refugees (mean)	Sudanese (mean)
Cattle	6.40	0.54
Camel	0.05	0.11
Sheep	2.80	0.63
Goats	2.84	1.58
Donkeys	0.36	0.38

Table 6.3   Seasonal locations by type of livestock

	Wet season (June–Sept.)	Early dry season (Oct.–Dec.)	Mid-dry season (Jan.–Feb.)	Late dry season (March–May)
Cattle				
Milk herd	QEN (hill/a)	QEN (hill/a	QEN (farms)	QEN (farms)
Dry (large)	Butana plains	Rahad River	Rahad/QEN/ farms	Rahad/Ethiopia
Dry (small)	QEN (hill/a)	QEN (hill/a)	QEN/farms	QEN/farms
Sheep				
Large flock	Butana plains	Rahad River	Rahad/QEN/ farms	Rahad/QEN/ farms
Small flock	QEN (hill/a, v/a)	QEN (hill/a)	Rahad/QEN/ farms	QEN/farms
Goats	QEN (hill/a, v/a)	QEN (hill/a, v/a)	Rahad/ QEN/farms	QEN/farms
Donkeys	QEN (hill/a, v/a)	QEN (hill/a, v/a)	QEN/farms	QEN/farms

QEN, scheme area; hill/a, hill areas; v/a, village areas; farms, cultivated areas.
Source: Interview with herders at Umsagata, Umbrush and Salmin and with the former
ACORD Live Stock Officer (LSO) Saleh, A. (1991), Umsagata.

scheme. The remaining were in the Rahad area (Table 6.3). The proportion of livestock involved in transhumant patterns of cyclical movements cannot be extrapolated from these figures because, in November/December, there is more stock on the scheme than at any other time. During this period, livestock forage in the form of postharvest forage is relatively plentiful and some herders bring their stock to the scheme and its environs from the Butana plains to take advantage of postharvest grazing. In the dry and wet seasons, the number of animals kept on the scheme, especially cattle and sheep, is far lower. It is still interesting to note, however, that, even during November/December, when water and forage are relatively bountiful, nearly 50% of all the livestock were kept at some distance from the scheme. During most of the year, including the wet season, dry cattle, sheep and a considerable proportion of goats are involved in transhumant patterns of cyclical movements (Table 6.3). These grazing systems are developed in response to lack of adequate pasture and water. As we shall see later, this strategy is adopted to avoid density-induced scarcity of forage, which may affect primary and secondary productivities as well as herders' well-being. Mobility and the capacity to maximize appropriation of fodder in remote areas by taking advantage of variations in the environment also reduce the pressure on the grazing and browse resources. These are used by milking cows and small stock.

Livestock management

Pastoral and agropastoral societies in north-eastern Africa have, since the colonial period, often lived 'on the razor's edge of survival', due either to external demands or to ecological crises, which are common in the arid and semiarid environments they occupy. Their coping mechanisms and their psychological make-up are shaped by such a reality (Kibreab, 1994c). Their resource-management systems are also developed in response to the constraints and opportunities inherent in their environments. The grazing systems in the study area are, for example, the result of a dense social network, in which people have over time built up knowledge which enables them to understand intimately variations in the environment. The threat of forage scarcity engendered by an interplay between natural causes, such as rainfall fluctuations, and human interference, in the form of rapid expansion of mechanized rain-fed agriculture, is continuously present. Not only does rainfall fluctuate from season to season within the year, but the extent of temporal and spatial variations is wide and unpredictable. Thus, even though the transhumant patterns of the cyclical movements of their herds are based on roughly 'predictable' environmental fluctuations, the extent of environmental uncertainties manifest in temporal and spatial variations is so wide that accurate predictions of range conditions are not possible and the herders cannot rely on the assumption that forage yields will be the same as in the previous season. The quantity and quality of currently available forage cannot be predicted from past experience. This is not to suggest that past experience is not important, but, in view of the fast-changing conditions in the area, the timing and direction of the movements of the herds are reviewed every season. Herders do this on the basis of their accumulated knowledge and current information about forage conditions and movement of other herds in the areas of potential destination for every season. In light of the rapid invasion of mechanized rain-fed agriculture in grazing areas and stock routes, as well as competition among herders for scarce pasture and water, the fund of knowledge is updated continuously. Information is collected through social networks and reconnaissance excursions to the potential areas of migration. The collection of information prior to change of location is pivotal because livestock maintenance on the scheme is contingent upon their short-, medium- and long-distance migration. It is this careful information gathering and their expectation of range conditions based on their past experiences that enable them to plan the routes and the areas of destination.

This pattern of livestock-management system seems to be common among pastoral communities in the arid and semiarid regions in Africa. In a widely quoted chapter, Sandford identifies two dominant pastoral stocking strategies developed in response to environmental instabilities engendered by seasonal and interannual fluctuations of rainfall (Sandford, 1982b: 61). These two strategies are 'opportunistic' and 'conservative'. With the former, the number of livestock varies 'in accordance with the current availability of forage'. Stocks are increased in good years and reduced in bad years (Sandford, 1982b: 62). With an opportunistic stocking strategy, timeliness of the decision to destock in bad years is critical. If livestock numbers are 'reduced too little and too late . . . as a consequence ecological degradation may occur'. Sandford distinguishes an 'efficient opportunistic strategy' in which the decision to destock is taken at the right time. Conservative stocking strategy is defined as 'one which maintains a population of grazing animals at a relatively constant level, without overgrazing, through good and bad years alike' (Sandford, 1982b: 62). The adoption of this strategy entails cost because, in good years, livestock numbers are not allowed to grow to feed on the additional forage.

According to the plan of the government and the United Nations High Commissioner for Refugees (UNHCR), the economy of the Qala en Nahal refugee settlement scheme was designed to be agriculturally based, with tractors being used for cultivation. No animal power was required for traction. Because livestock production was not part of the initial plan, no grazing land was allocated to support animal production. Livestock production was introduced independently on the refugees' own initiative. In the early period, there was adequate fallow and residual land (uncultivated), where livestock grazed. There were also adequate browse resources on and around the scheme area. The number of livestock was also small and forage was not an issue.

Gradually, the population on the scheme increased substantially due to immigration and natural growth and consequently all the cultivable land was brought under the plough. The refugees could not bring land outside the designated area under cultivation in response to increased subsistence demand. This was forbidden by law. One of the consequences of this was that fallow periods were eliminated from the farming cycle and continuous monocropping led to crop yield decline (see Chapter 4).

One of the responses of the farmers to the declining productivity of arable land was to building up their livestock. Since this happened in the context of shortage of land, migratory patterns of forage exploitation were from the outset a cardinal feature of livestock production (Table 6.3). Owing to shortage of grazing and browse resources on and around the scheme, due to land shortage, expansion of arable agriculture and felling of trees for commercial charcoal production, the farmers have developed an innovative livestock-management system designed to exploit variations in the environment and to minimize pressure on the limited range resources.

The major factors that influence the management decisions of livestock owners on the scheme, especially with regard to location, are forage, water, security, nutritional status of family members and avoidance of diseases. The single major constraint faced by livestock owners on the scheme is lack of wet- and dry-season grazing. About 99% of livestock owners in the refugee villages stated that the grazing and browse areas have shrunk drastically over time. The corresponding figure for the Sudanese villages was 100%. The results of another study, which the author conducted in 1982 (Kibreab, 1987) showed that shortage of forage was most critical during dry seasons, but by 1991 the problem of wet-season grazing had become more critical. This is not necessarily only because of the increased number of livestock. The main cause of wet-season shortage of forage (grasses and browse) is a result of expansion of cultivation on to previous grazing lands. The severity of shortage of range resources during both the wet and the dry seasons, is a clear indication of the problem of shrinkage of grazing areas. In the respondents' view (both Sudanese and refugees), the major causes of shortage of forage were land shortage (within the scheme) and expansion of commercial mechanized rain-fed agriculture (in the immediate surroundings of the scheme). However, water still remained an important factor influencing stock owners' management decisions.[8]

With the crises of livelihoods in the area and in neighbouring countries and the increased availability of weapons, the frequency of criminal acts related to livestock theft has increased dramatically in recent years. Thus, security considerations have assumed increased importance in influencing livestock locations during the different seasons. The rate of livestock theft in the Butana plains has increased drastically since the 1984–1985 drought and some refugee farmers are becoming more vigilant in moving their dry cattle and sheep to the Butana. Livestock products constitute the major source of protein, especially for children and lactating mothers in the villages. Thus, the need to supply the families with milk and meat even during the dry season is also a factor that influences the location of milking cows during the different seasons.

The soils of the central clay plains, including the site where the scheme is located, are muddy and sticky during the rainy season. They are also heavily infested with biting flies during the same period. There are four discernible periods in which livestock change locations. These shifts in location are designed to maximize: (i) utilization of forage resources by exploiting variations in the environment in terms of time and space; (ii) access to water; (iii) livestock security (against theft); (iv) supply of animal products (milk and meat) to family members in the villages; and (v) livestock health.

In order to maximize the efficient use of range resources by taking advantage of variations in forage availabilities in space and time, owners divide their cattle into two distinct categories, namely milk cows plus calves and dry cattle (dry cows, weaned calves, heifers and bulls). The dry cattle constitute between 65 and 75% of the total herd (interview with herders and ACORD LSO, 1991). The dry cattle, as can be seen from Table 6.3, and some of the milk cows are kept outside the scheme throughout the year. The number of milking cows kept with the dry cattle varies with the herders' (those who migrate with the stock) need for milk (food) and with forage availability on and around the scheme. Milking cows (the balance) are kept on the scheme area as long as they remain lactating. However, it was not only the families' need for milk that determined the duration of stay of the milking cows on and around the scheme, but forage and water availability was also important. The number of milking cows on and around the scheme peaks in the immediate postharvest period (November–December), suggesting fodder availability is decisive in influencing owners' decisions. During the dry season, most of the milking cows are dependent on cut feed, mainly in the form of crop residues, including sesame cakes.

It is important to point out, however, that labour, not only in terms of availability, but also in terms of opportunity cost, was crucial in determining the individual families' response to forage scarcity. For example, those families that owned only a few head of cattle kept them on the scheme throughout the year, even when they were not lactating. In light of their small number, long-distance migration was not considered cost-effective in terms of family labour allocation. In the majority of cases, however, this was overcome by devising a system of collective grazing, in which owners hired a shepherd (refugee) paid by common contributions. Collective grazing opportunities may not be feasible in the future, because, with the shrinkage of grazing areas precipitated by rainfall fluctuations and expansion of mechanized rain-fed agriculture, it may no longer be possible to keep large numbers of animals together. One way in which herders in the area cope with shrinking grazing areas is by dividing their herds into smaller units in order to maximize appropriation of forage in different locations. This leads to higher labour input and consequently competes with other demands for family labour, especially during the cultivation season. However, with the decline of crop yields (see Chapter 4), animal production has become most favoured and a sizeable proportion of the families' labour is allocated to it. One way in which herders save labour during the cultivation season is by migrating to distant areas, such as northern Butana, where the invasion of commercial agriculture into grazing areas is limited because of low and highly variable rainfall. These areas are drier and primary productivity is low. This is compensated for by the vastness of the area.

As can be seen from the data in Table 6.3, the dry herds of cattle graze in the Butana plains during the wet season of June–September. Butana refers to the zone of grasslands bounded by the Blue Nile and the main Nile up to Atbara town, the River Atbara and the area bordering Ethiopia. The northern half of the Butana, where there are vast stretches of grasslands intermingled with *Acacia mellifera*, is not cultivable because of low and erratic rainfall and hence constitutes an important grazing resource for the pastoralists of the Eastern State and other visiting tribes (Suliman, 1986). The Butana is located in a transitional zone between the arid Sahara to the north and the humid savannah to the south, comprising open, flat grazing land with an annual rainfall of 100 mm in the north and 500 mm in the south, with an annual variability ranging from 20% in the south to over 45% in the north (Mohamed and Abu Sin, 1992). Although the Butana is the home of the Shukriya and other allied minor tribes, its southern part has always been used as wet-season grazing by the visiting southern tribes. The refugees have also adapted to this migratory pattern of forage exploitation.

During the early dry season (October–December), when the surface waters in the Butana dry up, cattle are moved southwards to the Rahad area, where there is a secure perennial supply of water. In recent years, owing to shrinkage of grazing areas in the Butana due to expansion of mechanized rain-fed agriculture (southern part) and increased pressure on range resources due to high animal population density in the remaining grazing areas, the southward movements have been taking place before the harvesting of the crops in southern Gedaref. That is why there has been a surge of conflicts between commercial farmers and herders. In recent years, animal trespass into cropped or near cropped areas has become the cause of frequent seizures and impoundment of animals by farmers. Often the seized animals are repossessed only after payment of heavy fines. Thus, one way in which herders avoid this cost is by moving their cattle to the northern Butana plains during the rainy season, when the risk of trespass into cropped areas is minimal.

In the postharvest season, beginning in mid-December, the dry herds return to the scheme to graze the crop residues in *meshruas* (fields). In the past, the herds grazed in the *meshruas* until February, but the period spent on the scheme is getting shorter and shorter as many farmers have in recent years begun to cut and collect sorghum stalks either for sale or for stall-feeding of their own animals. Even during this period, dry herds are watered in the Rahad every other day and that is why they graze only in the *meshruas* located in the southern part of the scheme.

In the 1970s, postharvest residues on the cropped area (*meshruas*) used to revert to common property, open to all, including non-scheme residents. Even today, postharvest crop-residue grazing is generally open to all, but often the fields are stripped of all crop residues and herbage before they are opened for common grazing. Owing to expansion of cultivation within the scheme area and the consequent shrinkage of the grazing areas, access to and quality of grazing resources have been deteriorating considerably. As a result, most milking cows and donkeys are provided with supplementary stall feeds during the dry season. In recent years, the demand for cut feed has increased dramatically. For example, during the harvest season in November and December 1991, the price of sesame cakes was £S7/lb. The price of a 2 kg bundle of sorghum stalks was £S5. In the past, before the shrinkage of the grazing areas and before the drastic increase in animal population, crop residues were free goods. Since the mid-1980s, crop residues and all herbage grown on the individual farms has become commoditized. Crop residues are now of high economic value and, at times, the revenue derived from the sale of such residues is higher than the value of the crop produced. In fact in the long term this may engender undesirable cultural practices, in which farmers with sufficient land may, instead of practising fallowing and crop rotation, resort to the practice of continuous monocropping of sorghum in order to sell the stalks. Sorghum being a soil-exhaustive crop, this may exacerbate the problem of depletion of soil nutrients. Families without livestock (the poor) welcome the commoditization of crop residues because they are then able to earn an income.

In March, dry herds are moved again towards the south-east along the Rahad River. In recent years, herders have been migrating as far as Begemedir in Ethiopia during the dry seasons. Before the political changes in Ethiopia (May 1991), the parts of Ethiopia where the refugee herders migrated were controlled by the Ethiopian People's Revolutionary Party (EPRP), which, according to the herders, charged heavy grazing fees. In view of the abundance of forage resources in those parts of Ethiopia, refugee herders were not discouraged by the payment of such fees.

At the beginning of the rainy season, usually in July, dry herds return to the scheme on their way again to the Butana plains. They make a pause for a few days to collect the cows that have dried up and to leave new milking cows. The pattern of movement is to a certain extent similar to that practised by Sudanese pastoralists, except that Sudanese herders rarely cross over the Ethiopian borders in search of pasture.

Milk herds are grazed in the vicinity of the villages, but during the rainy months, especially during July and August, the scarcity of forage, infestation of the clay plains by biting flies and muddy clays necessitate their removal to the jebels and pediments. Most of the milking cows return during the evening for milking, but some are taken too far away to allow return in the evenings. Milk in this case is brought to the villages by donkeys, camels or humans. During some seasons when there is low rainfall, shortage of water and forage compels owners to move their milking herds to the Rahad area and milk is ferried to the villages by lorries.

Generally, the large flocks of sheep follow the same pattern of movement, i.e.

they are moved to the Butana plains during the rainy season and to the Rahad River during the early period of the dry season and they return to the southern part of the scheme in the postharvest period. When the dry cattle herds move as far as Ethiopia, the sheep are left to graze in the Rahad area during most of the year. The small stock of sheep is kept in the vicinity of the scheme except in periods of water and forage scarcity. Most goats are kept throughout the year on and around the scheme, except in bad years when they are moved to the Rahad area in response to grazing, water and browse scarcity. Donkeys never leave the scheme except when they accompany dry herds to ferry salt for livestock consumption.

This management scheme, based on migratory patterns of range-land use, has enabled the owners to overcome the scarcity of forage resources, to preserve the limited available forage and water resources on the scheme for milking cattle and small stock, to avoid the muddy and sticky soils of the clay plains and hence improve animal health, to surmount the lash of biting flies during the wet season and to dodge conflicts with commercial and small farmers over animal trespass of cropped fields.

To what extent does this livestock-management system fit into the so-called 'opportunistic' pastoral strategy? It is opportunistic inasmuch as stocking rates on and around the scheme are adjusted in response to forage availability and migratory patterns of resource use are adopted to exploit variations in the environment. The management system developed by the refugee herders, however, differs from the 'opportunistic' strategy as outlined by Sandford (1982b), as well as by Westoby *et al.* (1989), where destocking in bad years and restocking in good years are key features of the model. In the refugees' livestock-management system, migratory patterns of forage exploitation and not destocking are the key element. Except in bad years, in which animal loss due to death is higher than in years of good rainfall, destocking as a means of stock control is an unfamiliar practice. Rainfall is extremely unpredictable in the area and, if destocking is to be used as a means of reducing stocking rates in bad years, herders should have a fair knowledge as to the cyclical occurrence of such spells. Sandford himself is aware of this weakness in the model, but suggests no escape. At present no such knowledge exists. The other problem associated with destocking and restocking is variable livestock prices. In bad years (drought) livestock prices drop and they rise during good years. If destocking and restocking are to be used as useful instruments for coping with environmental instability, livestock prices during both periods should be comparable, but in reality they are not.

Even though no voluntary destocking takes place, natural death during bad years, especially among calves, is high and this may put a limit to the rate of livestock growth. The management system developed by the refugee herders, irrespective of the method used to adjust livestock numbers to forage availability on and around the scheme, seems to have avoided irreversible damage to the limited amount of wet- and dry-season forage resources. Without fluctuating stocking rates due to migration, the extent of the damage that might have been caused to range resources would have been more serious. The most important achievement of the migratory patterns of range-land use developed by the refugee herders is that, in spite of the negative changes in vegetation resources observed in Chapter 3, livestock population has been increasing dramatically. The changes in vegetation resources observed in Chapter 3 have not resulted in a decline in livestock productivity (see Tables 6.1, 6.2 and 6.4). In view of the economic definition of degradation adopted in this study, the question that springs to mind is that if the refugee herders, by developing a dynamic livestock-management system, have averted the potential detrimental economic consequences (decline in livestock productivity) of the vegetation changes, can we speak of range-land degradation? If range degradation is defined in economic terms – for example, 'vegetation change is of no intrinsic interest unless it also provides reliable evidence of changes in livestock productivity' (Behnke and Scoones, 1993: 20) – this may essentially be the case in pastoral systems in which livestock raising is a dominant economic activity and vegetation resources are used mainly for livestock forage.

There are, however, some considerations that need to be taken into account in interpreting the effects of the vegetation changes on the livelihoods of the farmers on the scheme. First, although the data in Tables 6.1 and 6.2 show that the growth of livestock population is not affected by the changes in vegetation, we know little about the costs that are incurred by individual families in terms of diminished output of milk, meat and power (for transportation),[9] as well as animal health, due to forage scarcity. This, however, relates only to those animals which do not engage in migration, such as milking cows, donkeys and small stock. Second, on the scheme, livestock production is one of the diverse economic activities on which the livelihoods of the farmers depend. Some of these economic activities are likely to be affected by vegetation changes in a detrimental way.

Even though livestock production has been gaining prominence since the 1980s in the economic life of the scheme, crop production still represents the chief activity of the majority of the farmers. The reduction of perennial plant cover, especially on the jebels and pediments where there are shallow soils, has exacerbated the problem of soil erosion. The effect of soil erosion is clearer on slopes comprising red soils where grass and tree cover is reduced by grazing and tree felling for charcoal production. Although at the heart of these problems lies land shortage, within the existing constraints, some of these are attributable to intensive livestock grazing and browsing. For example, some of the milking cattle which are kept on the jebels during the day are brought to the villages at night. Their trekking up and down the hills often intensifies soil erosion, as gullies are formed along the tracks. The large increase of goats (browse stock) also seems to have prevented the regrowth of coppiced or establishment of woody vegetation.

Although the decline of crop yields experienced by the farmers is a result of multiple forces, and hence it is not easy to measure the role of specific factors in the process of change, it is generally agreed that vegetation, especially woody plants, facilitates replenishment of soil nutrients in semiarid savannahs (Coppock, 1993). For example, some calculations of nutrient budgets made by Billè and Cora in the semiarid region of southern Ethiopia showed 'leaf litter from at least 200 woody plants per hectare could provide roughly 57% and 21% of the annual turnover for nitrogen and phosphorus, respectively' (cited in Coppock, 1993). Hatton and Smart's findings also show that, following a 24-year exclusion of wild herbivores in the Ugandan savannah, an increase in *Acacia* occurred and, compared with unprotected sites, 'top soils of protected sites showed up to a five-fold increase in exchangeable actions, a 50% increase in nitrogen, and up to a 30% increase in organic matter' (cited in Coppock, 1993). Radwanski and Wickens' findings in Sudan also showed that *Acacia albida* improved the fertility of top soils (Radwanski and Wickens, 1967).

Coppock notes that whether interactions among woody and herbaceous plants are positive, neutral or negative depends on soil texture, soil fertility, harshness of climate, density and maturity of the woody layer and potential for species-specific composition based on the compatibility of the seeds, juveniles and mature forms of plants (Coppock, 1993). In the study area, where vertisol clay soils are dominant, soil fertility was found to be higher on the woody sites than on the continuously cultivated plots (see Table 2.1). Thus, the decline in soil fertility manifest in low crop yields (see Table 4.1) may be partially linked to the changes of vegetation resources.

Another major consequence of depletion of the vegetation resources is that, in comparison with the past, the cost of obtaining fuel wood in terms of labour time, drudgery and expenditure has increased drastically (Chapter 5). As a consequence, the poor are forced to consume less and lower-quality fuel wood. For those who depend on the wood-fuel market, their outlays have increased. In the past, fuel-wood sales represented an important source of income for the poor; however, with the increased distance of fuel-wood sources, the activity is now falling to those families who have camels, donkeys and larger family sizes. The poor are for the most part excluded. Big trees are almost non-existent except on individual *hawashas* and, as a result, most people now obtain construction timber through the market from as far as Gedaref town. The cost of obtaining thatch grass has also increased drastically with the depletion of grassland resources in the vicinity of the villages.

Crop residues are cut and collected for stall-feeding. This is a reflection of forage scarcity. If there were no scarcity of forage, crop residues would have been consumed *in situ* and consequently the amount of labour inputs required for cutting, collecting and transportation would have been saved for other income-generating activities. Sorghum stalks and other crop residues would have also been incorporated into the soil to improve soil nutrients and protect the top soils against wind erosion. Herding has also become a full-time activity in which one or more family members are allocated to the task. If there were adequate vegetation resources, herding would have been combined with other activities, enabling the families to save labour. If it were not for the scarcity of forage resulting from vegetation change, more milking cattle would have also been kept on the scheme and the supply of animal products (milk and meat) would have improved, at least during the wet season. The costs of weeding have also soared in terms of family and hired labour inputs, among other things, due to exhaustion of soil nutrients, which has resulted in a change in plant-species composition. Since the mid-1980s, previously rare plant species such as *Striga* have become major causes of crop failure or crop yield decline (see Chapter 4).

Thus, even though the vegetation change that occurred on the Qala en Nahal scheme and its environs does not provide reliable evidence of changes in livestock productivity, at least in terms of numbers, all the above-stated losses are directly or indirectly related to vegetation changes. The fact that the changes in vegetation have not affected the growth rate of animal population is not to suggest that there have been no economic losses suffered by the farmers.

Types of livestock

Cattle, goats, sheep, donkeys and a few camels are owned by both the Sudanese and refugee families on the scheme. The structure of livestock ownership has changed considerably in a matter of a few years. In 1988 cattle were owned by only 40% of the families (Flint, 1988). At the end of 1991 about 75% of the families in Umbrush, Salmin and Umsagata owned cattle. This represents a dramatic increase over a few years. Cattle are high-value animals not only because of the high market value they command, but also because families with cattle have a special status in the communities. This is because 'Eritrean stock-owners regard the number of cattle possessed by any individual as the index of his wealth and standing in the community' (War Office Working Party, 1947c: 19). The most important explanation, however, lies in the fact that more and more families have recently been investing in cattle in response to forage scarcity on and around the scheme area. Because cattle are involved in medium- and long-distance migration, their productivity and health is not markedly affected by the scarcity of forage on and around the scheme. There has also been a considerable increase in the number of families owning sheep. In 1988 only 20% of the families owned sheep (Flint, 1988). By 1991, the number of families owning sheep had increased to 36%. Sheep are kept outside the scheme throughout the year and are not subjected to the stress caused by scarcity of range resources on and around the scheme.

Most goats and donkeys are kept on the scheme throughout the year unless there is scarcity of forage and water. This often occurs in periods of low rainfall. The families' investment decisions are, therefore, influenced by the range conditions on and around the scheme. In 1988 goats were owned by about 67% of the families (Flint, 1988). By 1991 this had declined slightly, to 65%. In 1988 about 75% of the families owned donkeys. In 1991 almost the same proportion (74%) reported having donkeys. These data show that one way in which the farmers cope with the problem of forage scarcity is by changing their stocking composition or by allocating the greater part of their investment to the type of stock least dependent on range resources available on and around the scheme. In other words their investments are designed to fit into their systems of management, whose major feature is medium- and long-distance migration. Investment in cattle and sheep has increased drastically while investment in donkeys and goats has remained similar to 1984 levels.

A change in cattle species composition has also taken place, again in response to the need to adapt to the physical environment of the area. The cattle that were brought to the scheme in the 1970s included the short, compact and variously coloured Eritrean highland species known as *arado*, which is native to the Eritrean highlands, and the well-built, tall, black-and-white-coated lowland breed, Barka, found in the plains of the Western Province of Eritrea (War Office Working Party, 1947c: 19). The highland species was unsuitable for the new environment and the refugees have changed the composition of their cattle by buying Barka bulls and introducing them to the herds (a refugee cited in Fre, 1982). At present, the livestock owned by the refugees are predominantly of Sudanese origin or Begait, but a few of mixed breed are found. The goats owned by the refugees are also all of Sudanese origin because the Eritrean breeds would not survive in the Sudanese environment (Fre, 1982).

The general cattle ownership of the families in all the villages cannot be generalized from the above-given figures because cattle are unequally distributed between the six refugee villages (Table 6.4). In this study, the sample households were drawn from Salmin, Umsagata and Umbrush, where owners of the large herds of cattle live.[10] Not many of the Saho families in the villages of Adingrar, Umzurzur and Dehema own large numbers of cattle. Thus, if the sample had included families from these three villages, the mean figure for cattle ownership would have been less, but for goats it would have been slightly more. These differences notwithstanding, however, there has been a drastic increase in the number of families owning cattle, even in the poor villages of Dehema, Adingrar and Umzurzur. For example, in Adingrar, Umzurzur and Dehema, the number of cattle increased by 260%, 1,200% and 260%, respectively, between 1984 and 1991. These changes are from lower benchmarks and, in spite of the high rate of increases, per capita cattle ownership is

Table 6.4   Livestock population distribution in the villages 1984 and 1991

Village	1984					1991				
	Cattle	Sheep	Goats	Donkeys	Camels	Cattle	Sheep	Goats	Donkeys	Camels
Salmin	8,000	3,000	5,000	2,000	60	34,063	18,000	10,800	n.a.	50
Umsagata	5,020	1,000	1,200	1,000	68	18,072	3,600	4,320	n.a.	68
Adingrar	300	200	1,400	200	15	1,080	720	5,040	n.a.	15
Umbrush	3,000	700	1,300	250	36	10,800	2,520	4,680	n.a.	36
Umzurzur	100	300	1,500	100	10	1,360	5,480	5,400	n.a.	10
Dehema	200	200	300	230	9	720	720	1,080	n.a.	9
Total	16,620	5,400	10,700	3,900	198	66,095	31,040	31,320	n.a.	188

Sources: for 1984, Devitt and Tahir, 1984; for 1991, ACORD (1991) Livestock Survey, Umsagata.

still higher in the three villages included in the study than in Dehema, Umzurzur and Adingrar (Table 6.4).

Goats, donkeys and sheep are more evenly distributed between the six villages. In fact the number of families owning subsistence stock (goats and donkeys) are as high as in the rich villages. For example, in 1985, 75% of the families in Salmin, Umbrush and Dehema owned goats, while in Umzurzur about 80% of the families had goats. In Umsagata the corresponding figure was only 45% (Devitt and Tahir, 1984). In Salmin, Umsagata and Umbrush about 75% of the families owned donkeys in 1984. The corresponding figures for Dehema and Umzurzur were 55 and 65%, respectively (Devitt and Tahir, 1984).

Donkeys and camels are not bred on the settlement. They are used for transport, e.g. as pack-animals for water, firewood thatch grass, crop and human transport and sometimes the herders would use them for carrying salt for the herds, especially when they are setting off for the dry- or wet-season migration. Only cattle and goats are milked. Cattle milk is normally sold, while that of goats is consumed by children. There has been a tremendous increase of prices over the last few years. In 1982, 1 lb of milk was sold at £S0.15. In 1986, 1 lb of milk was sold at £S0.50. In 1991 the corresponding price was in the range of £S10. This drastic increase is not solely explained by demand-side factors. Owing to the expansion of cultivation within the scheme, the grazing areas have shrunk and consequently the cost of obtaining animal fodder has increased drastically, in terms of both labour inputs and cash outlays. During most of the dry season, milking cows are provided with cut feed. In recent years, the cost of cut feed has increased greatly and with that the cost of milk production. Part of the increase in milk prices is also attributable to inflation. It is not possible to state how much of this increase is attributable to inflation because of the absence of data on the consumer-price index for the rural areas.

Causes of decline of range resources

The major range resources on and around the scheme comprise non-crop herbage, browse vegetation and crop residues. These are located on and outside the cropped areas. Non-cropped grazing areas are located in the immediate vicinity of the villages, jebels, pediments and flooded areas. In 1983, the total area of uncultivated land was in the range of 25,885 *feddans* (Howard, 1983). The grazing area around the villages was estimated at 7,295 *feddans*. The rest of this was *Boswellia–Combretum* woodland on hills (6,271 *feddans*), *Combretum* shrub savannah on hills (1,723 *feddans*), *Combretum* tree savannah (4,094 *feddans*) and *Acacia* low woodland (6,502 *feddans*). The woodlands are depleted due to the combined effects of expansion of mechanized rain-fed agriculture, tree felling for charcoal, firewood and construction, browse pressures and trampling of regrowth of coppiced trees and seedlings. This has led to reduction of grazing and browse resources. The removal of vegetation in these sites has increased the risk of erosion, reflected in sheet erosion and gully formation, especially at higher elevations. The 7,295 *feddans* of grazing area around the villages was, by the end of 1991, for the most part covered with unpalatable species such as *C. tora*, where no grazing could take place. A further 7,271 *feddans* of *Boswellia-Combretum* on hills and pediments that was observed in 1983 is now so denuded that there is virtually no vegetation left for browse and grazing. The only grazing areas available are some patches of *Acacia* low woodland on the clay plains. These are also in the process of being invaded by annual grasses such as *C. tora* (*kawal*). This indicates the extent of the pressure imposed on the remaining range resources. It is the reason why the majority of the livestock are kept off the scheme. If all animals were kept on the scheme, there would have been density-dependent problems of overgrazing. However, the grazing-management system – long-distance migration of dry cattle and sheep – is devised, among other things, to avoid the problem of overstocking on the forage resources, which are already under heavy pressure, independent of the number of livestock.

The expansion of cultivation on to the former grazing areas has drastically reduced the availability of wet-season grazing. The consequence has been concentration of the non-migrating livestock on limited areas. This has inevitably resulted in overuse of the grassland, by both trampling and eating. This is exacerbated by the selective grazing habits of cattle, which lead to the dissipation of the most preferred species. Most of the wet-season grazing areas are in the jebels and pediments (see Table 6.3). The removal of vegetation from these sites has accelerated the process of soil loss through erosion, further reducing wet-season forage availability.

In semiarid regions such as the study area, where rainfall fluctuates widely not only between one year and another, but also between short distances, the job of establishing causation of change in forage availability is an onerous task. Generally, the decline of range-land resources is a result of multiple forces and consequently it is difficult to measure with an acceptable degree of certainty the role of the specific factors in the process of change, for example, in this case the role of rainfall, expansion of cultivation and stocking rates. In the study area, the vegetation indicators suggest that the forage resources on and around the scheme are diminishing. For example, the average yield in one quadrat was 307.6 g of biomass in 1987. By 1991 this had fallen sharply to only 137 g. The data in Chapter 3 not only show changes in plant biomass and cover, but also drastic increases in unpalatable annuals (see Table 3.6).

Two questions need to be asked. First, do changes in vegetation in terms of species composition, plant biomass and cover constitute degradation? Second, how far are the vegetation changes that have occurred in the study area attributable to human-induced 'degradation'? The first question is extremely controversial. There are those who argue that since tropical savannah is among the most variable terrestrial ecosystems (Walker and Noy-Meir, 1982), it is exceptionally difficult to distinguish between 'drought-induced fluctuations and permanent changes in vegetation states' (Grouzis cited in Behnke and Scoones, 1993: 21) caused by human interference.

Those who place emphasis on rainfall, as opposed to human-induced change, such as high stocking rates, argue that in tropical savannah rainfall fluctuates not only seasonally, but also interannually (Sandford, 1982b: 61). Rainfall fluctuation is said to cause fluctuation in forage availability (Sandford, 1982b: 61). In situations where rainfall and temperature are fluctuating, rainfall has a greater impact on plant growth than grazing pressure caused by high stocking rates (Behnke and Scoones, 1993: 8).

There are others who argue that fluctuation in species composition, plant biomass and cover are intrinsic features of arid and semiarid range lands, which are subjected to erratic rainfall (Walker *et al*, 1981). Vegetation in these areas is also said to possess 'enhanced capacity to recover from disturbance' because it has adjusted to the fluctuating environmental conditions. This suggests that vegetation changes in the form of species composition, plant biomass and cover are no indication of permanent 'degradation'. In Behnke and Scoones' view, in environments where there are wide rainfall fluctuations, 'degradation could be said to occur only when the vegetation had crossed, or was at risk of crossing, critical thresholds which prevent or severely inhibit its subsequent return to a more productive state' (Behnke and Scoones, 1993: 21).

These views no doubt raise some critical methodological and theoretical issues, which have a direct bearing on the effectiveness of reliance on vegetation indicators for the assessment of range degradation. The major problem associated with this method is that not only do the results say little about long-term degradation, but causation is not easy to establish. In the study area, no long-term measurement of the productivity of vegetation exists. Therefore, there is no evidence which suggests that the changes in vegetation that have occurred not only between 1987 and 1991 (see Chapter 3), but also between the different distance ranges, i.e. measured from the centre of highest intensity of human activities (see Fig. 3.1), are a reflection of 'temporary disturbance' or are the result of permanent human-induced degradation. The critical variable on which the above-discussed literature rests is rainfall fluctuation, which is said to cause changes in vegetation species composition, plant biomass and cover.

Can the changes in vegetation that have occurred between 1987 and 1991 in the study area be ascribed to rainfall fluctuations? Before 1984, there were no rainfall gauging stations on the scheme. The nearest station where rainfall data were recorded was at Qala en Nahal town about 30 km north of the scheme. Since 1984, however, rainfall is carefully gauged in six stations on the scheme itself. Since recording began, there have been two drought years – 1984 and 1990. The former was more severe than the latter (see Table 4.9). The average rainfall for the last 10 years was 610 mm. In 1987 and 1991, the total amounts of rainfall were 581 mm and 549 mm, respectively (see Table 4.9). The total amount of rainfall was slightly more (32 mm) in 1987 than in 1991. However, in such environments, plant growth is dependent not only on total annual rainfall, but also on distribution. As can be seen from Table 4.9, distribution was more even in 1987 than in 1991. This is evident from the data. In 1987, on average, there were 47 days with rain as opposed to 23 days in 1991. The average number of days with rain for the period between 1984 and 1993 was 38. The number of days with rain in 1991 when the vegetation survey was conducted was, therefore, exceptionally low, even though the variation of the annual average from the average of the 10-year period was not considerable (62 mm). In the study area, where rainfall is low, it is not clear whether a difference of 32 mm (between 1987 and 1991) would make any difference to plant growth. Since annuals are susceptible to slight fluctuations in rainfall (Coppock, 1993), a difference of 32 mm is likely to have an impact on plant growth.

The question is how much of the vegetation changes that occurred between 1987 and 1991 is attributable to the differences in the amount and distribution of rainfall between the two years. If this has an influence on plant growth, its impact is likely to be limited to the data on biomass production per unit area (see Table 3.11). The other changes observed, such as the invasion of the sites in the vicinity of villages, watering-points, animal and human tracks, hills and pediments by unpalatable plant species such as *C. tora*, the drastic reduction of perennial grasses or the stripping of large tracts of land of trees and shrubs, are difficult to attribute solely to such minor differences in amount and distribution of rainfall.

The results of the vegetation survey also show that the intensity of vegetation change was found to be an increasing function of proximity to the sites where the degree of human activities was highest. As one moves away from the scheme, the occurrence of palatable and nutritious plant species, perennial grasses and plant cover increases. At the heart of these changes is land shortage, but, within that given framework, the factors that seem to have contributed significantly to the changes observed are fluctuation in rainfall, expansion of cultivation from both within and without, tree felling for commercial charcoal production, timber for house construction, firewood for local consumption and grazing, browse and trampling pressures. No doubt, the changes have negative impacts on the capacity of the system to meet short-term needs, but there is nothing which suggests that under appropriate management these cannot be reversed.

The deforestation of the jebels and pediments, the depletion of the grass resources reflected in reduced amount of biomass and the invasion of the former grazing areas lying immediately around the villages by unpalatable vegetation species, the spreading of such species to the jebels, the pediments and the *hafirs*, and the general deterioration of vegetation cover are indications of the mounting pressure on the grazing and browse resources. These findings are also confirmed by information elicited from key informants who have experienced the changes that have taken place over time directly. The data elicited from the sample households (local population and the refugee) also show the same results. The refugee and Sudanese farmers attribute the causes of range-resource depletion, in order of priority, to reduction of grazing lands and browse resources due to expansion of mechanized rain-fed cultivation from within and without, tree felling for commercial charcoal production, increased encroachment on the forage and water resources by livestock belonging to Sudanese nomads who come from distant areas and livestock build-up within the scheme.

If it is true that there has been a problem of overgrazing, the consequence would have been a decline in livestock productivity in terms of numbers. What we see on the scheme, however, is not a decline in livestock population, but a dramatic increase. Perhaps the rapid livestock build-up that has been taking place on the scheme indicates that the condition of the range resources on and around the scheme is, after all, still good. A key factor that has enabled the scheme population to build up their stock is long- and medium-distance migration. The removal of the animals from the scheme during the wet season relieves the pressure of selective grazing of the preferred species. This relief from pressure gives the growing grasses temporary respite not only to grow, but also to propagate themselves.

If all livestock were kept on and around the scheme during the wet season, most of the palatable vegetation would probably have been hit hard and the level of change in plant-species composition and consequently the substitution of the palatable and nutritious plant species by unpalatable and less nutritious ones would have been more dramatic. It has to be admitted, however, that the increase in livestock numbers has not been taking place only outside the scheme, but also inside the scheme. In fact, after the excavation of the *hafirs* (see following section), the problem of water shortage was mitigated and the number of livestock kept on the scheme has increased considerably. This may suggest that water and not lack of grazing or feed was the major limiting factor on livestock production before the excavation of the *hafirs*. Even though after mid-December, cattle, sheep and donkeys that remain on the scheme are mostly dependent on stored crop residues, herbage in the fields or sesame cakes, it cannot be denied that this would have not been possible if there were severe range degradation. the expansion of cultivation has led to increased supply of dry-season animal feed. There is no doubt, however, that the shrinkage of grazing areas, deforestation, a change of species composition of grasses and increased livestock population have led to a considerable reduction of the available biomass for wet-season grazing. This is considered to be one of the most critical constraints on livestock production in the area. The difficult question is whether or not this constitutes range-resource degradation. If range degradation implies irreversibility of productive capability, there is little evidence to suggest that this is occurring.

The findings of the vegetation survey show a decline in range resources at a particular point, but since the period covered by the study was only 5 years and other time-series data on range productivity and plant-species composition are lacking, it cannot be concluded with confidence that the range resources on and around the scheme have been irreversibly degraded. In fact, on sites where livestock were excluded, shrubs and grasses exhibited remarkable ability and vigour of recovery. For example, one of the reasons why the ACORD tree-plantation plots were stripped of the fences, apparently by herders on the scheme, was to allow access for livestock to the vegetation, which had grown with remarkable vigour within the enclosed sites (see Chapter 9). This may suggest that, even though there have been unmistakable indications of range-resource depletion resulting from the combination of shrinkage of grazing areas due to expansion of cultivation on to previous grazing lands, deforestation of the jebel and pediment areas, a change in composition of plant species, i.e. the decrease of palatable and increase of non-palatable or less palatable vegetation, and increased animal population, it is difficult to state with certainty that the range resources are degraded. If that were the case, the population would have had no opportunity to increase their livestock size within the scheme, or the rate of loss of herds due to natural death would have been higher than is the case at present. Even during severe drought years such as 1990, the rate of stock loss reported was not large.

Whether the high pressure on range resources that exists in the settlement constitutes degradation depends on our definition. If by range degradation is meant reduction of capability to satisfy actual demands placed on the range resources (Blaikie and Brookfield, 1987) without implying irreversibility, there is no doubt that the sustainability of the resource in many sites is in danger. In the absence of restorative measures and/or considerable reduction of the levels of intensity of use, depletion of the range resources may be inevitable. The fact that there is decline in range productivity, as we saw earlier, is an indication of reduction of capacity of the range resources to satisfy actual demands.

If, however, degradation implies permanent loss of productivity of land without any opportunity for recovery 'except at prohibitive cost' (Sandford, 1982a: 45),[11] then the areas where such a level of degradation has occurred are extremely limited. These areas include the permanent livestock routes to and from the villages, the areas lying immediately around the villages which are invaded by annuals like *C. tora* and the sites lying immediately around the watering-points (*hafirs*). Even these may only indicate short-term changes rather than permanent deterioration in productive capability. If loss of range-resource capability includes temporary changes resulting from weather and grazing pressure fluctuations, then a larger area of the scheme may be considered as degraded. Abel and Blaikie define range degradation as 'an effectively permanent decline in the rate at which the land yields livestock products under a given system of management. "Effectively" means that natural processes will not rehabilitate the land within a timescale relevant to humans, and that capital or labour invested in rehabilitation are not justified' (Abel and Blaikie, 1989: 113). Degradation here refers to irreversible decline or to damage beyond repair. It is not possible to state with certainty how much of the vegetation decline that has occurred on and around the scheme is reversible and how much is irreversible because time-series data are lacking, but the fact that the denuded sites, when relieved from cultivation, grazing and browse pressure through enclosure, exhibited a feature of rapid recovery may suggest that, with improved management and investment, it may be possible to reverse the decline that has occurred over time. Besides, the fact that the number of livestock has increased in the last half decade suggests that the resource users have successfully devised a management system that adapts to the situation. The question is how long can they do this?

Behnke and Scoones (1993) argue that vegetation change does not necessarily indicate range degradation. Obviously, not all kinds of vegetation change necessarily indicate range degradation. This may depend on how 'degradation' is defined. If it is defined as an 'irreversible decline', then, before vegetation change can be taken as an indication of 'degradation', it has to be established that the observed changes are irreversible. If the present state of knowledge allows this to be established,[12] there is no reason why vegetation change cannot indicate range 'degradation'. However, assuming, first, that 'degradation' is defined as a reduction of 'productive capability' (Blaikie and Brookfield, 1987) without necessarily implying permanent changes, second, that the changes are not solely due to fluctuations in rainfall and, third, that it is established that the changes have resulted in losses of income by the people who use the resources,[13] it is not clear why this should not indicate range decline. In the study area, even though no relationship was observed between vegetation changes and growth of livestock numbers (the latter were kept outside the study area), there was considerable income forgone by the farmers due to the fact that their animals had to change location because of scarcity of forage resources in the vicinity of their settlements.

The vegetation survey has undoubtedly established a marked vegetation change, reflected in reduction of biomass availability and vegetation cover and a change in species composition with increases in unpalatable plant species and annuals at the cost of perennial and nutritious plant species. The data were not collected over an extended period of time and consequently one has to be cautious about concluding too much from the evidence by implying that this constitutes a 'permanent change in vegetation states'. The data do not in any way warrant drawing such a conclusion. However, in view of the fact that different areas have been affected differently depending on their location *vis-à-vis* the centre of population concentrations, the data suggest that the vegetation changes that have occurred cannot be solely due to fluctuations in rainfall. If rainfall is the only key explanatory variable, why is the invasion of unpalatable annuals such as *C. tora* more widespread on the sites where the impact of human interference in the form of grazing pressure and trampling has been most intensive? Why is the occurrence of sites stripped of vegetation more pronounced in the immediate surroundings of the villages and watering-points? Although none of these shows that the changes are solely human-induced or are permanent, there is no way one could exclude human interference (cultivation, grazing, browsing and tree felling) from the explanation, which seems to be the case in the literature discussed above. The latter represents a rethinking of range ecology and is developed as a critique and alternative to the explanation offered by the mainstream literature, which places undue emphasis on human interference to the neglect of drought-induced fluctuations in primary productivity. The findings of this study suggest that the changes that have occurred are due to a combination of natural factors and human interference. What needs to be emphasized here, however, is that, irrespective of the causes of the changes, there is no evidence to suggest that they are permanent.

It seems that, as Stoddart *et al.* state, a botanical approach to the assessment of range deterioration is valuable because often vegetation change precedes both reduced livestock production and increased levels of soil loss (Stoddart *et al.*, 1975: 267). In the study area, it has been established that loss of vegetation cover in the hills and pediments has been followed by increased levels of soil loss and V-shaped gully formations (see Chapter 2). There is, however, no evidence to suggest that loss of vegetation cover has led to reduced livestock production, at least in terms of numbers, except in drought years. It is important to point out, however, that this is not to suggest that the scarcity of forage resources on and around the scheme area has no impact on outputs of livestock products such as milk, meat and power. (There are no data on these.) Since migration is a key feature in the system of management in the study area, the build-up of livestock that occurred during the 1980s and early 1990s does not suggest that no deterioration of the range resources has occurred on and around the scheme area. Nor is it suggested that the botanical approach used in this study to assess the deterioration of the range resources on and around the scheme is not fruitful. This approach has been useful in the assessment of changes in forage resources that have occurred, albeit over a limited period, as a result of a combination of natural processes and human and animal interference.

It is, however, true that, given the erratic and low rainfall conditions in the arid and semiarid regions, where there are large fluctuations in species composition and plant biomass and cover, the long-term sustainability of the given range resources may not be easily indicated from the results of a non-longitudinal vegetation survey. The available rainfall data do not seem to have varied considerably during the last 40 years. A study commissioned by USAID in the Gedaref district shows that the climate in the district where the Qala en Nahal scheme is located 'remained fairly constant over the past forty years and does not account for environmental changes in the Gedaref district' (Gedaref District Study, 1985: 55). Although the reliability of the rainfall data in Sudan is questionable, the available evidence still suggests that human and livestock interference is an important factor contributing to deterioration of range resources.

Two other factors also seem to contribute to deterioration of range resources on the scheme. These are augmentation of dry-season water-supply, which induces some farmers to keep their livestock on the scheme throughout the year, and lack of tenurial rights, which prevents the scheme residents from denying access to those who encroach upon the range resources within the scheme. These factors are discussed later.

Impact of water resources on livestock production

Historically, the major constraint on livestock production in the area was lack of water during the dry season. The main sources of water-supply were shallow wells and surface water during the rainy season. Both sources dried up during the dry season and the few inhabitants of the area migrated to the Rahad River or Bazura. Between the establishment of the scheme and 1986, water-supply for both domestic and livestock uses was largely dependent upon a pipeline extending from the Rahad River to the different settlement sites. Supplies were extremely irregular. Breakdowns of pumps and pipes and shortages in fuel and lubricant supplies were very frequent (Kibreab, 1987). Both animals and humans competed for the limited supplies. The problem of water-supply during the dry seasons was often so severe that COR used to prohibit the families from keeping animals during the dry seasons. This prohibition was applied haphazardly depending on the severity of the water shortage.

ACORD excavated six rain-fed catchment *hafirs* (reservoirs) in 1986 with a total holding capacity of 200,000 m³ to enable the farmers to overcome the problem of water-supply for livestock during the dry seasons. This has improved the water-supply situation greatly, but it has also imposed further pressure on the resources as more and more animals are kept on the scheme. The improved supply of water to livestock has had both positive and negative impacts. On the one hand, water availability during the dry season has enabled those with a few cattle and sheep to keep their stock on the scheme during the dry season. This has improved the supply of milk to some families. Although most family labour is either underemployed or unemployed during the dry season, for families that own only a few head, keeping their livestock on the scheme is more cost-effective. Some families save labour and cash by keeping their livestock on the scheme. When livestock engage in long-distance migration, they are looked after by one or more members of the families or the latter have to contribute cash to meet the costs of hiring a collective herder. On the scheme, collective herding is widely practised. Costs are shared by many families who own one or more head of livestock, but not exceeding five.[14] This releases labour time for other income-generating activities, such as wage labour and fetching water, firewood and thatch grass for sale.

It is important to point out, however, that, if the improvement of water-supply encourages more families to keep their animals on and around the scheme area, density-induced degradation of the forage resources may take place, and more livestock may be lost as a result. The grazing strategy based on migratory patterns exploiting variations in the environment is mainly developed in response to forage scarcity. Therefore the number of families that are induced to keep their livestock on the scheme throughout the year because of improved water-supply is not likely to be great. No major changes in the 'opportunistic' system of grazing is expected to take place as a result of the *hafirs*.

Land degradation around watering-points is a common problem in the arid and semiarid regions. This is also true for the sites lying immediately around *hafirs* on the scheme. The results of the vegetation survey showed drastic biomass decline and a change in the species composition of the grasses and forbs around the *hafirs*. The positive thing about the *hafirs* constructed by ACORD was, however, their location. They are situated within cultivable *hawashas* so that livestock have no access to them for at least 5–6 months of the year, i.e. from the onset of rains (beginning of cultivation season) until after harvest. This seems to have mitigated the problem of overgrazing around the *hafirs*.

Range-resource usership rights

Although expansion of cultivation within and around the scheme has dramatically reduced wet-season grazing, postharvest grazing has increased substantially as a result. The common resources such as water (surface rainwater, streams, wells, etc.), grazing areas and woodlands on and around the scheme are owned by the government. This has in effect meant *de facto* conversion of such resources into open-access resources (see Chapter 8). The essential feature of an open-access resource is absence of private, communal or effective government ownership and hence lack of institutional rules governing allocation and use. As a result, the resource is open to all. The *de facto* open-access resources on and around the scheme are readily available for exploitation even by non-scheme residents and this has added pressure on the natural resources. The common resources on and around the scheme, including postharvest crop residues, are openly accessible, not only to the scheme residents, but even to pastoralists who come from distant areas. One way in which the farmers avoid their crop residues being exploited by outsiders is by removing them from the fields for sale or stall-feeding.

One of the negative consequences of lack of tenurial rights of the scheme residents is their inability to deny access to outsiders (see Chapter 8). For example, when the supply of water was augmented after the excavation of the rain-fed *hafirs* by ACORD, pastoralists from remote areas were pulled to the scheme in the immediate postharvest period. Not only does this cause additional pressure on grazing resources, but conflicts over water rights are increasingly becoming a problem. For example, during the 1990 drought, livestock from as far as El Fau and the Central State flooded into the scheme in search of water. The stocking rate

Plate 6.1   Crop residues are cut and collected for sale or stall-feeding instead of being incorporated into the soil to improve soil nutrients and to prevent or minimize wind erosion. (Photo: Gaim Kibreab)

increased over a short time. The visiting pastoralists practised excessive tree-lopping for their animals as the grass cover was dissipated.

Access rights to water and forage within the scheme were negotiated with COR without consultation with the communities, because, as mentioned earlier, formally the state is the sole owner of such resources. In 1990, one person was killed and another injured as a result of conflicts over water rights between the scheme residents and the outsiders who came to the scheme to water their livestock (ACORD, 1990). Among the scheme settlers, there seem to be tacit rules which require herders to remove their dry cattle beyond a certain number from the scheme during the dry season so that the available water, grazing and browse resources are made available only to milking cows and to small stock. In the past few years, however, these tacitly existing rules have been weakened, partly because of encroachment by herders who come from remote areas and who disregard the informally existing principles, norms and rules of range- and water-resource use. What incenses the scheme residents most is the attempt by visiting pastoralists to exploit the water and forage resources within the scheme that are reserved for milking cows and small stock.

Since the improvement of the water-supply for livestock, COR has relaxed its prohibition and there is no limit to the number of animals that may be kept on and around the scheme. This has led outsiders to use water, grazing and browse resources within the scheme carelessly. The consequence of this has been not only competition over resources, but that many refugees are beginning to keep their dry cattle on the scheme. They do this to discourage outsiders from coming to the scheme to graze their animals. This has further increased the pressure on grazing and browse resources. This may in the future weaken the carefully designed migratory patterns of forage exploitation. In the context of the mounting competition, devolution of control of the local resources to the scheme residents may be the only effective and viable option that could avert the threat of density-induced range-resource decline.

Why the livestock build-up?

It is clear from the data (see Tables 6.1, 6.2 and 6.4) that there has been a discernible trend in livestock build-up. The families are investing their scarce resources in livestock. What is interesting is the absence of any significant corresponding investment in crop production expressed in the purchase of farm equipment, fertilizers, insecticides, construction of degradation-countering structures, etc. The failure of the farmers to make investments in land is not only due to their financial inability, because some of them can afford to invest in such inputs. There are various institutional, motivational and disincentive structures that discourage the refugees from investing in crop production (see Chapter 8), but which encourage them to invest their scarce resources in building up their livestock ownership. The following are some of these factors.

Flexibility and insurance against crop failure
In arid and semiarid regions, livestock farming enjoys a comparative advantage over crop production. This is due to the agroclimatic and land-resource base of the arid and semiarid regions. The low and erratic rainfall make such regions more suitable to livestock raising than to arable farming. Livestock are mobile and are thus less affected by the effects of localized droughts than crops are. The flexible

Plate 6.2   With increasing risk of crop failure precipitated by lack of adequate rainfall and soil exhaustion, many refugee families have been building up their livestock. Livestock are mobile and are less affected by the effects of localized droughts. (Photo: Gaim Kibreab)

management system developed by the farmers on the scheme, based on transhumant cyclical patterns of herd movement which exploits variations in pasture and water availabilities (see Table 6.3), indicates that livestock production is better suited to the climatic instabilities prevailing in the area. Livestock production enhances the producers' ability to adapt to the environment. One of the greatest achievements of technological advancement in agriculture is the reversal in the order of sequence of the process of adaptation. In societies where no advanced technology constitutes an important component in the factors of production, to a greater extent it is man who adapts to the environment, while in societies where the productive forces are developed, man is able to manipulate the environment to optimize stability and homogeneity. The transformation of part of the Sinai desert to a green oasis after Israeli occupation is a case in point. The ability of the communities on the scheme to manipulate the environment is little or non-existent, but, within that given constraint, their livestock-management system based on herd mobility is designed to facilitate their adaptation to the environment, which is more often than not in a state of non-equilibrium.

Crop production is quite a risky enterprise. There have been recurrent crop failures due to inadequate rainfall or uneven distribution. Mobility also assumes a special importance among refugee populations because they are prohibited by law to bring new arable land outside the designated area under cultivation in response to increased subsistence demand. As livestock owners, refugees enjoy unrestricted access to temporally and spatially differentiated range resources. Crop yields have also been declining considerably since the mid-1980s, among other things due to depletion of soil nutrients resulting from continuous cropping without fallowing and manure/fertilizer application (see Chapter 4). It seems that many of the farmers have lost confidence in the ability of the land to produce enough to enable them to meet their costs of subsistence. Animals serve as insurance against crop failure because they represent the capital with which to buy food crops.

In the arid and semiarid areas, increased food insecurity leads to livestock build-up, which is the traditional response to such situations. The decrease of per capita share of cultivable land, accompanied by a decline in soil fertility caused by nutrient depletion resulting from continuous monocropping, is inducing the individual members of the community to seek alternative sources of survival. One of the important alternative economic activities is rebuilding of livestock. Livestock production provides a viable window of exit in an otherwise bleak situation.

Lack of tenurial security

Land on the scheme is owned and allocated by COR, as the government body responsible for refugee affairs (see Chapter 8). Formally land in the settlement is not a commodity which can be disposed of at will. The plots are allocated to the refugees by COR and the former have only the right of usufruct. When they leave the land for any reason, they lose their right of usufruct. The land in question reverts to COR. Legally, the right of usufruct cannot be transferred to other refugees in any form, not even through inheritance (Kibreab, 1987). The consequence of this is that the means of the rich members of the community to acquire additional land that would justify investment in tractors and other inputs is extremely limited. Even though many holdings have changed hands since the first allocations were made, the limited level of land concentration has only occurred within the confines of the scheme. The refugees are not allowed to extend their farming activities beyond the designated areas. As a result, the farmers do not consider it worthwhile to invest their limited resources in improvement of their *hawashas* because there is no incentive encouraging them to do so.

Asset transferability

Refugees' investment decisions are not always solely governed by considerations of opportunities for higher returns. The possibility to transfer the asset (object of investment) to their countries of origin during repatriation plays a central role in their investment decisions. Investment in livestock to the neglect of crop production is not only a result of environmental instability. There are rational calculations behind their investment decisions. The refugees perceive their presence in Sudan as transient. They have always hoped to return home one day. Thus, livestock have special attraction because they can be taken home during repatriation. This is reinforced by the fact that livestock, especially cattle and sheep, can be taken back to Eritrea even without the knowledge and consent of either government. As we saw earlier, it is common for herders from the scheme to migrate as far as Ethiopia in search of pasture during the dry seasons. This is done without the knowledge and consent of either government. Animals are in this case used as a store of assets, which is generally important among communities inhabiting unstable environ-ments. In such environments, livestock are a means of production and a store of value.

Labour-saving strategy

The cost of crop production has been drastically increasing because of weed infestation caused, *inter alia*, by continuous cropping and changes in plant-species composition. The infestation of the fields by noxious weeds such as *Striga* and *adar* (false sorghum) is closely associated with the problem of the age of the fields and consequently with depletion of soil nutrients. Historically, it was common practice in the area to cultivate a piece of land for about five seasons and then to abandon it when noxious weeds appeared. The refugees can no longer resort to such cultural practices because they are only allocated a single plot, which is 10 *feddans* or less. Many families crop their plots continuously, even when production falls, for lack of an alternative source of income. Consequently the amount of labour for weeding per unit area has increased drastically. Not many families can perform this task without resorting to hired labour. This, coupled with the high demand for agricultural labour in the rain-fed mechanized agriculture outside the scheme, has pushed wages up. Thus, it makes economic sense for many families to shift the emphasis from crop production to livestock raising. The latter is not often labour-intensive. In such communities livestock production does not consume large amounts of labour input because the majority of the animals, especially cattle and sheep, get the forage they need directly from grazing. Grazing saves labour because it is an activity 'in which appropriation and consumption are unified over space and time' (Damodaran, 1988: 2213). Unlike other subsistence activities in which appropriation is not separated from consumption in space and time, no mediation of the labour process is required to connect the two activities. With the shrinkage of the open-range resources, the animals kept on the scheme are stall-fed during most of the year and an increasing amount of labour is expended in cutting, collecting and transporting sorghum stalks and other kinds of fodder. However, since the majority of cattle and sheep are kept outside the scheme and goats feed on roughage without receiving any supplementary feed, compared with crop production livestock production is still a labour-saving activity.[15] A herd of cattle or sheep is looked after by one or two members of the family and the rest of the members are released for farm or non-farm income-generating activities. This has enabled many families to diversify their sources of income and to spread the risk of failure.

Increased supply of veterinary services

Like anywhere else in the Sudan, livestock contract a wide range of diseases, the most significant among which are rinderpest, anthrax, haemorrhagic septicaemia, contagious bovine/caprine pleuropneumonia, black quarter and trypanosomiasis. Among the most important parasites, ticks cause major losses. Apart from causing mastitis (by secondary infection of the wounds by microbes), ticks also act as host of the causative organism of heart water. Trypanosomiasis is mainly brought by animals crossing into Ethiopia (interview with A. Saleh, 1991). The quality of veterinary services has greatly improved, and heavy losses from infectious or contagious disease have been largely reduced. This is one of the factors that has contributed to the build-up of livestock population (interview with A. Saleh, 1991).

It is worthwhile stating, however, that, with the shrinkage of range resources on and around the scheme, nutritional disorders are gaining significance among the animals not involved in long-distance migration. Most important among these is vitamin A deficiency. At present up to 70% of the livestock population on the scheme are affected by deficiency in vitamin A towards the drier parts of the year (interview with A. Saleh, 1991). The main reason is a lack of any sources of the precursors of the vitamin commonly obtained from green fodder.

Other reasons which contribute to the farmers' decision to invest in livestock include, first, the refugees being former agropastoralists, milk still has a special importance in their diet and food habits. Second, the value of the Sudanese pound is deteriorating dramatically over time, but livestock prices have been increasing considerably. It makes economic sense to invest in livestock and buy food crops from the proceeds of livestock sales. Livestock can also be transacted in cross-border trade in currency that has a higher exchange value against the Sudanese pound, such as the Ethiopian birr. Third, a considerable proportion of the refugees came from agropastoral and pastoral backgrounds, where mixed herds were maintained. In Eritrea, it was even common for sedentary agricultural communities to maintain large numbers of livestock. Animals were sources of protein, income (exchange), draught energy (oxen and donkeys) and fertilizers (animal wastes). On the scheme, neither manure nor draught energy is used, but, since the refugees hope to return home, considerations of future needs influence their investment decisions. Fourth, deforestation has reduced the population of biting flies during the rainy season and the problem of animal disease is reduced. Fifth, ACORD's excavation of six *hafirs* with a capacity of 200,000 m³ has enabled the families to overcome the problem of dry-season water shortage.

Conclusion

The majority of the refugees on the scheme were of agropastoral and pastoral origin. Nevertheless, no provision was made for livestock production when the scheme was planned and implemented. Consequently, no land was allocated for livestock grazing. The areas that were unsuitable for crop production were used for grazing. When the scheme was established, only a few families brought livestock and there were enough forage resources on and around the scheme areas. Before the soil lost some of its fertility, many families produced surplus crops and the proceeds were invested in livestock. Those who did not produce surplus devised alternative means of building up their stock. It was common among members of poor families, for example, to migrate to distant places to work as shepherds with Sudanese nomadic and seminomadic groups, where payments were in kind (sheep). The common rate of payment was an expecting ewe per month per shepherd. Generally, the migrants worked for a year or two and returned home with 12 or 24 sheep and their offspring, respectively.

When the refugees made their own adjustment in terms of building up their stocks – large and small – they were faced with shortage of water and pasture. This was exacerbated by the fact that even the sites previously considered unsuitable for crop production were brought under cultivation. In order to offset pressure on the range resources on and around the scheme areas and to avoid loss of livestock productivity, the refugees devised migratory patterns of range-land exploitation by taking advantage of variations in the environment. This 'opportunistic' grazing strategy is observed by the majority of the herders.

Most of the refugees have invested in livestock in response to the diminishing returns of the arable land. Under the existing physical conditions and institutional restrictions, crop production has become a risky activity. One way in which the refugees spread risk is by diversifying their economic activities. In comparison with crop production, livestock can minimize the effect of drought by moving to less affected areas. The value of the Sudanese currency is depreciating with every passing week and it makes sense to store one's wealth in livestock. When inflation is increasing, investment in livestock makes economic sense because, in such a situation, livestock become a store of value in real terms. Given the socio-economic backgrounds of the refugees, milk is important in their diet. Livestock ownership is also a symbol of a higher social status. However, given the entrenchment of market forces in the area, it is unlikely that people invest in livestock to boost their social status any more. It is rational economic calculations that are decisive in their investment decisions. Livestock can also be easily transferred to Eritrea during repatriation. For those who want to return, it makes economic sense to invest in movable rather than in immovable property such as land.

Notes

1. Bartels *et al.* (1993) argue that the decisive thing is their interest, i.e. whether their primary interest is livestock production, resource conservation or wildlife management.
2. The choice of population and not productivity is deliberate. This is because there are no data on offtakes and milk and meat production.
3. In many cases livestock were owned collectively by members of a large family, even when each had their own families.
4. Livestock unit conversions: cattle=1.0; small stock=0.2; donkeys=0.6; camels=2.0
5. Livestock owners paid water charges to COR. The *hafirs* were only open to the members of the particular refugee villages. When they were made accessible at the end of the harvest period, every livestock owner registered the number of livestock s/he wished to water in the *hafirs*. These records were useful for estimating the total number of livestock available in the villages. There was also a regular annual vaccination campaign against rinderpest, organized by the Organization of African Unity (OAU) and the European Economic Community (EEC). All owners brought their livestock annually to the vaccination centres. The vaccination records are therefore useful data sources for the estimation of livestock population in the scheme.
6. This fact was established by the data obtained from the Bazura livestock market. By looking at the records at the Bazura livestock market it was possible to see the types and the numbers of livestock purchased by the families in the scheme. Livestock theft is rampant in the area. In order to discourage the selling of stolen livestock in the region, the authorities in the market keep records of livestock transactions, including the sellers' and the purchasers' names, their villages and their villages' sheikhs' names, and numbers. If these records are kept properly, they may be quite useful sources for future studies.
7. As will be discussed later, the villages are not equally endowed with the same number of livestock and the results cannot be generalized. This will only be done for analytical purposes.
8. All the respondents pointed out lack of water during the dry season as being a problem in the area.
9. Animal power is only used for transportation and not for traction. Tractors are used for cultivation.
10. Since one of the aims of the study was to look at the problem of overgrazing as one of the possible causes of inappropriate land-use practice that may cause unsustainable resource use, the villages where there were higher per capita livestock holdings were deliberately selected.
11. Sandford defines environmental degradation as 'an irreversible (except at prohibitive cost) decline in the productivity of land and water resources' (Sandford, 1982a: 45).
12. I am not sure whether this is possible. The available evidence suggests that it is not. Behnke and Scoones (1993), referring to Friedel (1991) and Laycock (1991), state that current knowledge of the dynamics of savannah ecosystems frequently does not allow a distinction to be made between drought-induced fluctuations and permanent changes in vegetation states.
13. This implies that the income losses suffered are due to decreases in perennial grasses, increases in undesired annuals, decreases in palatable and nutritious plant species and increases in unpalatable and non-nutritious ones.
14. If a family owns more than five head of livestock, especially cattle, they are herded separately.
15. The only exception is when livestock are watered from deep shallow wells. In that case, livestock production can be labour-intensive.

7 Institutions and Resource-management Systems in Eritrea, the Refugees' Country of Origin

> Institutions affect human choice by influencing the availability of information and resources, by shaping incentives, and by establishing the basic rules of social transactions. (N. Nicholson, 1988)

One of the central concerns of this study has been to understand the institutional and socio-economic situation which defines the context within which the farmers on the scheme earn their livelihoods. It is assumed that the way they relate to the natural environment within and outside the scheme at the present is to a considerable extent influenced not only by the parameters that define the space within which they currently operate, but also by their past experiences. Thus an attempt is made to present a brief history of the institutions that had evolved over time to govern the allocation and use of the natural resources in the parts of Eritrea where the refugees came from.[1] Institutions here refer to constraints devised by human beings to provide a framework within which human interaction takes place (North, 1993: 4). Institutions are formal and informal. The former refers to rules which are deliberately devised by people and the latter refers to conventions and codes of behaviour (North, 1993: 4). The formal rules discussed in this chapter are those stipulated in the Eritrean codes of customary laws. These laws are important from a resource-management point of view because they either prohibited individuals from doing certain acts or prescribed the conditions under which the said acts could be undertaken.

The land-tenure systems in Eritrea are not described in this chapter in detail nor are the changes that were effected by Italian, British and Ethiopian occupations. Most of the data in this chapter are about the traditional resource-management systems that existed in the pre-1960 period. The changes that have occurred since then are not taken into account. As in many other rural societies in Africa, the history of traditional resource management in these particular communities still remains unrecorded. In an attempt to compensate for the paucity of written historical data necessary in the task of recreating the past, an attempt has been made to capture the changes through building on information from scattered sources at village level. The information was gathered through in-depth interviews with community leaders, knowledgeable elderly and focus groups who have survived the changes both in their country of origin and in their present location. The in-depth interviews were conducted by the author with thirty-five refugees and eight Sudanese peasants, who were systematically selected. (For the list of the persons interviewed and for their ethnic and tribal affiliations see Table 7.1.) The selection of the interviewees was made in consultation with the village agricultural officers and in most cases they represented the most articulate and knowledgeable individuals available in the communities.

The persons included in these interviews represented all the ethnic groups living on the scheme, namely individuals from the Beni Amer, Saho, Maria, Nara,

Table 7.1 Interviewees by ethnicity, area of origin, occupation and year of arrival in Sudan and the scheme

Name	Age	Ethnicity	Area of origin	Former occupation	Present occupation	Arrival in Sudan	Arrival in Qala en Nahal
Refugee farmers							
Hirun	70	Saho	Serae	Agropast.	Farmer	1967	1971
Jaber	68	Saho	Serae	Farmer	Vet. as.	1967	1971
M. Osman	57	Tigre	Gash	Agropast.	Farmer	1967	1971
Habash	75	Tigre	Gash	Agropast	Farmer	1967	1970
Ahmed	61	Saho	A. Guzai	Agropast.	Farmer	1968	1972
Kisha	71	Tigre	Barka	Nomad	Farmer	1967	1971
Bekhit	72	Bilen	Senhit	Farmer	Farmer	1968	1970
Seiday	80	Tigre	Tessenei	Nomad	Merch.	1967	1970
Sh. Ali	78	Saho	A. Guzai	Agropast.	Farmer	1970	1972
M. Saleh	73	Saho	Gash	Agropast.	Farmer	1968	1971
H. Ali	87	Tigre	Gash	Farmer	Farmer	1967	1970
O. Adem	69	Nara	Gash	Farmer	Tailor	1967	1971
Hiyabu	69	Tigrinya	Senhit	Farmer	Farmer	1978	1979
Omran	78	Tigre	Senhit	Farmer	Farmer	1974	1978
Mentai	83	Tigre	Barka	Nomad	Farmer	1967	1970
Longi	70	Nara	Gash	Farmer	Farmer	1967	1971
M. Hamid	68	Tigre	Tessenei	Agropast.	Farmer	1974	1979
M. AlHaj	59	Saho	A. Guzai	Farmer	Farmer	1974	1978
Surur	68	Saho	Serae	Farmer	Merch.	1974	1978
Gebremedhin	45	Tigrinya	Serae	Farmer	Guard	1974	1979
Temno	58	Bilen	Senhit	Farmer	Farmer	1974	1978
J. Omer	82	Saho	Serae	Farmer	Farmer	1967	1970
Shiker	67	Bilen	Senhit	Farmer	Farmer	1967	1971
Dawud	69	Saho	A.Guzai	Agropast.	Farmer	1967	1970
N. Adem	73	Tigre	Sahel	Farmer	Farmer	1967	1972
Shabir	75	Nara	Gash	Farmer	Farmer	1967	1970
Kahel	69	Bilen	Senhit	Farmer	Farmer	1974	1978
A. Adem	72	Tigre	Tessenei	Nomad	Farmer	1977	1979
Ismail	78	Saho	A. Guzai	Agropast.	Farmer	1968	1972
I. Omer	64	Tigre	Gash	Farmer	Farmer	1967	1970
Talke	40	Saho	Gash	Farmer	Farmer	1967	1971
Husein	75	Tigre	Semhar	Nomad	Farmer	1967	1971
Ibrahim	79	Tigre	Barka	Agropast.	Farmer	1967	1970
Mahmoud	81	Tigre	Gash	Agropast.	Farmer	1974	1978
S. Osman	76	Tigre	Barka	Nomad	Farmer	1967	1970
Sudanese farmers							
Kassala	68	Sudan	Nigeria	Farmer	Farmer	1943	1952
Bekhit	47	Sudan	W. Sudan	Farmer	Farmer	Sudanese	1968
Kered	70	Sudan	Bolos	Farmer	Farmer	Sudanese	Born in area
M. Saleh	76	Sudan	Umsag	Farmer	Farmer	1946	1949
Ibrahim	71	Sudan	Umsag	Farmer	Farmer	1951	1950
Babikir	69	Sudan	Dehema	Farmer	Farmer	1961	1956
Husein	71	Sudan	Dehema	Farmer	Farmer	Sudanese	1960
Adem	68	Sudan	Umsag	Farmer	Farmer	1959	1980

A. Guzai, Akele-Guzai; Agropast., agropastoralist; Vet. as., veterinary assistant; Merch., merchant.

Tigrinya, Bilen, Mensà and Beit Juk. In view of the fact that Eritrea represents a 'mosaic of tribes, races, linguistic groups' as a result of being the scene of migrations into its territory and across it for many centuries (BMA, 1943), an attempt was made to get a representative picture. Younger persons were, however, deliberately excluded whenever a choice existed because they lacked direct experience in their country of origin. Whenever younger individuals were included, it was due to lack of choice. Among the Tigrinya, for example, there were no old people. The average age of all the interviewees was 70.3 years among the refugees. The corresponding figure for the Sudanese farmers was 67.5 years. Information elicited from each interviewee was carefully counter-checked by information elicited from others coming from the same area and with the same ethnic backgrounds.

Even though useful data were elicited from the interviewees, the task of recreating the past from fragmented historical sources, especially from oral sources, is a delicate and sometimes risky exercise. Although this is more true in societies where there is a dearth of written historical sources, all reconstructions of history are fraught with similar problems. Even written historical sources are seldom complete enough to enable the historian to recreate the past as it existed. One of the shortcomings of historical accounts derived from oral sources is the possibility of eliciting inaccurate information due to memory decay of the interviewees concerned. Precautionary measures were therefore taken to minimize this risk. Firstly, questions were deliberately kept at the general level requiring no memories of facts or dates, and, secondly, the issues discussed were deliberately limited to the informants' lifespan. The data elicited from the informants are considered to be reliable as there is a strong tradition of oral history or system of genealogical memory through which information from the past, including knowledge about environmental management, is transmitted from generation to generation.

This method of transmitting information is common among preliterate societies. For example, in 1947 representatives of one of the serf groups (tigre) stated that the deficiency in written sources in their communities was compensated for by 'the well known system of genealogical memory, both amongst the Christians and the Moslem populations of the place; genealogical memory, which places on record facts and events in support of which tradition supplies details, not only simple erroneous legends' (Letter of Tigre Representatives, 1947).

The major objective was to understand the traditional natural resource-management systems that existed in Eritrea and to find out whether the refugee communities at present use the same resource-management systems in the settlements. The questions put to the interviewees were open-ended and semi-structured. As far as possible, the same questions were put to each interviewee. Digressions were, however, common.

Socio-economic backgrounds of the refugees on the scheme

The Saho-speaking ethnic group is the largest among the refugees on the scheme (Table 7.2). Their traditional homeland is the area between the Red Sea coast and the mountains of eastern Akele-Guzai. Before their flight to Sudan, the Saho-speaking refugees derived their livelihood from livestock (cattle, sheep and goats) and rain-fed and irrigated cultivation (BMA, 1943: 57). At the beginning of the 1940s, a report by the British Military Administration (BMA) regarding one of the Saho tribes (Asaorta) stated: '[T]he trend from the nomadic herdsmen to sedentary

Table 7.2   Ethnic composition of the six refugee villages in the Qala en Nahal settlement

Ethnicity	Size (%)
Saho	34.7
Beni Amer	30.2
Maria	11.9
Nara	10.5
Bilen	3.0
Tigray	2.0
Beit Juk	1.8
Tigrinya	1.7
Others	4.0
Total	100.0

Source: ACORD, Population census, 1985.

cultivators, already marked in the recent past of the tribe, is clearly progressing, and will in the future create the difficult problem of a large hungry tribe pressing upon the landed people of the highlands' (BMA, 1943: 57). Most of the Saho on the scheme had adapted to sedentary agriculture before their flight to Sudan. The process of sedentarization, which had begun in the mid-nineteenth century, might not have been completed, but none of the Saho-speaking refugees interviewed viewed themselves and their compatriots as nomadic.

The Beni Amer are the second largest group among the refugees on the scheme (Table 7.2). The dominant source of livelihood of the Beni Amer was nomadic pastoralism and their wealth comprised camels, cattle, sheep and goats. Even though they were engaged in crop production, their main source of livelihood was livestock herding (BMA, 1943: 8). During the dry season, the Beni Amer migrated to distant places in search of water and pasture, as far as eastern Sudan and the valleys of Keren, Akele-Guzai and Serae (BMA, 1943: 8). During the rainy seasons, they returned to the Barka valley, where they had their permanent and semi-permanent villages.

The third largest group among the refugees on the scheme is the Maria. According to a report by the BMA, the Maria (Black and Red) were characterized as cultivators and livestock herders with the bulk of their incomes derived from the latter (BMA, 1943: 8). However, the data elicited from the Maria interviewees on the scheme suggest that, despite the livestock herders' involvement in seasonal migration to distant pastures during the dry seasons, they considered themselves as settled agriculturalists. The long-distance migrations were adopted in response to the impoverished environmental conditions of their areas of origin. In most nomadic societies, the basic natural resources are owned in common. In the Maria land, however, the land-tenure system was predominantly based on hereditary individual and family ownership (risti), derived from the principle of first occupation by a remote ancestor. According to the Maria's own account, before they migrated to the pasture-abundant area in the western lowlands, most of their subsistence was derived from dry-land cultivation and livestock herding. Later they were forced by the poor soils and mountainous terrain of the Maria lands to migrate to the Gash valley, where there were abundant grazing lands and many of them resorted to a seminomadic way of life. Before their flight to Sudan, the Maria lived in the Barka and Gash-Setit regions. The other groups among the refugees on the scheme, such as the Tigrinya, Bilen, Beit Juk, Mensà and Nara, were sedentary farmers in their respective regions (BMA, 1943). The Bilen, Nara, Tigrinya and Tigreans (from northern Ethiopia) were sedentary agriculturalists who derived their livelihoods from mixed husbandry (crop and livestock production).

The data elicited from the interviewees as well as from the available archival documents suggest that most of the ethnic groups on the scheme, except the Beni Amer, were sedentary cultivators who combined crop and livestock production. For some, the process of transformation from nomadic pastoralism to sedentarism was unfinished but had been telescoped by the social and economic uprooting experienced during flight and exile. The data elicited from the interviewees show that, before the disruption of the traditional resource-management systems by the forces of change, such as colonial alienation of land and population pressure (human and animal) on resources, access and usership rights of the natural resources were regulated by formal and informal institutional rules. The rules were enforced by elaborate mechanisms operating at local and district levels. The *raison d'être* of these resource-regulating institutions was to secure sources of livelihoods within a semiarid environmental context that was, more often than not, unstable and in a state of disequilibrium. The resource-management system was designed to meet human and livestock needs without damaging the capability of the environment to regenerate itself. The key factor which promoted the evolution and enforcement of the rules which fostered mutual restraint and individual/collective discipline for the common good of the communities as a whole was communal or individual tenurial security. Since the turn of the century, however, several interacting factors have contributed to the weakening of the traditional natural resource-management regimes in some parts of the country. Eritrea is not a land-abundant country and the available resources were also unevenly distributed between the different regions. Some parts were densely populated, barren, mountainous, dry and uncultivable, while others were fertile and well watered. The latter were suitable for cultivation and livestock production. In areas like the plateau (Hamasen, Akele-Guzai and Serae) and Senhit (Beit Juk, Halhal, Lower Anseba, Mensà, Maria and the rest of the areas inhabited by the Bilen), arable lands were owned either on an individual or family (ownership by the kindred, *enda*[2]) basis or collectively on the basis of the village or a group of villages. Pasture lands, water resources and woodlands that lay within the boundaries of the village/s were, however, invariably owned in common. No individual ownership rights could be established over these common resources. Although there is a dearth of data on the history of village formation in the country, oral history indicates that, at the initial stage, land belonged to a patriarchal family group living as a single household for several generations. The family group continued to occupy isolated areas and, over time and with natural population growth, the patriarchal family broke down, developed into an *enda* (kindred) and formed a village of its own. There are many villages throughout Eritrea where *enda* or *deki* (lit. sons) stand as a prefix to the family names of the founders of the villages concerned. The alternative was for the patriarchal family groups to cluster together with other neighbouring patriarchal groups and form a village based on residence and not kinship.

The central hypothesis underlying the analysis in this chapter is that, since institutional rules and arrangements for the management of scarce resources are developed in response to the need to regulate access to, control of and use of scarce resources, it is assumed that social institutions are more developed, more explicit and more formalized in the communities where there is collective, family or individual tenurial security and where the resources in question are more scarce. This will be illustrated by a discussion of two contrasting regions in Eritrea: on the one hand, the plateau and Senhit, where there was tenurial security and acute resource scarcity, and, on the other, the western lowlands, where the traditional resource users lacked tenurial security (because their lands were alienated by colonial decision) and where there was no scarcity of arable, grazing and woodlands.[3]

Scarcity, tenurial security and development of resource-regulating institutions: the example of the plateau

One of the dominant types of land-tenure systems on the Eritrean plateau was collective or village ownership, in which entitlement was based on residence and where neither hereditary rights nor individual exclusive rights could be recognized and established. The collectivity was constituted of a village or group of villages or a district. This type of land-ownership was known as *diesa*. It was universal in Hamasen and widespread in north and south Akele-Guzai, but was weakly represented in Serae and central Akel-Guzai (Nadel, 1946a). Arable land and common property resources (CPRs) were managed by the communities. Shares of arable land were redistributed periodically by the custodians, who ascended to such social position either hereditarily or through election. CPRs – water resources (streams), grazing areas, woodlands, wastes and human and animals routes – were managed and utilized in common. Only certified members of recognized groups had the right to use these resources. Individual plots between the redistribution periods were managed as private property, with strict limitations imposed on the right of disposal in any form. Users had only right of usufruct.

The second type of land tenure was private ownership, based either on family ownership (*risti*) or on hereditary individual ownership (*tselmi*). Family ownership of land was a paramount land title deeply rooted in the social structure of the society (BMA, 1943). *Risti* land-ownership rights were originally derived from the first occupation of land by a remote ancestor of an individual or a family. Over time, with the natural growth of the first occupants, the title to land changed to a collective title. The rules governing individual allocation and use within the *risti* lands varied from place to place. In certain places, the collective title was maintained and well defined. Mechanisms were also developed ensuring the usufructuary rights of the individual descendants of the first occupants. Each individual family within the *enda* (kindred) was allocated a number of plots scattered throughout the *enda*'s arable lands. The title to a share in the *risti* lands by descendants was absolute (Adkeme Melega, 1936: 8) but not the right to a given individual plot. The individual also had the right to dispose of his/her land, provided the *enda* members were in agreement. The offer had to be made first to the other *enda* members or, if they declined, to members of the village (*Fitih Mehari*, 1913: Art. 54 (2); Show-Ate Anseba, 1910: Art. 103; Adkeme Melega, 1936: 10; Lego Chewa, 1938: Art. 20; Saho Tribes, 1943: Art. 176). If both declined, the plot within the *risti* land could be offered to other buyers. Often the right of pre-emption did not apply to sharecropping arrangements. The owner or the possessor of land was free to enter into a sharecropping arrangement with anyone, except with the colonialists (Italians) (Lego Chewa, 1938: Art. 19). This pre-emptive right was evolved as an important mechanism to exclude outsiders from gaining entry into the exclusive *risti* and communally owned lands. In districts like Lego Chewa, permanent alienation of *risti* land in any form was prohibited because land was not viewed as a commodity to be sold or exchanged (Lego Chewa, 1938: Art. 20). Temporary disposal was, however, allowed. Land was perceived as serving as a lineage dating back many centuries which nurtured links with the past and the future. Persons without land were viewed as lacking roots, lineage or heritage. That was the rationale of prohibiting permanent alienation of land. The *risti* type of ownership was dominant in Senhit (the areas inhabited by Maria, Bilen, Beit Juk, Mensà and some of the Tigrinya in Lower Anseba) and parts of the plateau (e.g. *Fitih Mehari*, 1913: Art. 54 (1)) Among the Maria, Mensà, Beit Juk and Halhal, the right of pre-emption by relatives, members of kinship and fellow villagers was strictly observed.

In other parts, the collective owners of *risti* lands exercised strict control over the rights of the individual to the hereditary *risti* lands. Arable lands were periodically redistributed among individual family members by lot. Individuals with rights of usufruct could not dispose of land. This type of family ownership was not basically different from village ownership. In most cases in the three categories of land ownership, the heirs were sons in the patrilineal descent line. Men justified the exclusion of women by the need to keep land as an exclusive right. Women might be married outside the family or village; hence husbands and their descendants might claim their land rights, which might lead to loss of such rights to outsiders. A female without brothers had in many districts the right to inherit the lands of her parents as if she were a male, provided she resided in her parents' village permanently (e.g. Show-Ate Anseba, 1910: Art. 25; Lego Chewa, 1938: Art. 12). She was not, however, allowed to sell the land she inherited (Show-Ate Anseba, 1910: Art. 25). A woman with brothers was excluded from inheritance (Show-Ate Anseba, 1910: Art. 25). Women who passed the culturally defined 'marriageable' age were also entitled to a share.[4]

In the two varieties – hereditary individual (*tselmi*) and family (*risti*) owner-ship – land-ownership was considered absolute, but was still subject to certain attenuations prescribed by custom. That is, the family or the individual was free to exercise the right of ownership provided the land in question was utilized in a manner not objectionable to customary practice. The common feature of the three land-ownership systems that were dominant on the plateau was their exclusive nature. All the three forms of ownership were exclusive rights, in which entitle-ments were determined by either descent or residence. In the *diesa* system, land rights were acquired through residence. Every member of the village community with a *tisha* (habitation) in the given villages was entitled to a share in the village arable land and CPRs. It was difficult and often impossible for outsiders to acquire village membership unless they were able to trace the origin of a certain remote ancestor to the village in question (Adgna Tegeleba, 1938: Art. 134). The line of demarcation between the three categories of land-ownership was sometimes fluid. They often interfaced with each other in the transactions that occurred between the members of the families. In certain situations, *enda* ownership evolved into individual private property through inheritance and continuous redistribution among the family members. The three categories of ownership entailed 'permanent titles to land, that is, ownership in the strict sense of the word' (Nadel, 1946a: 6).

There were also other less important types of land tenure. Individual ownership of land through purchase of *risti* land in return for money was one. The land acquired through purchase was known as *grat worki*. There were elaborate substantive and procedural rules that regulated the sale and resale of *worki* lands. If an owner of *worki* land wanted to sell his land, the former *risti* owners had a pre-emptive right to repurchase the land in question before other buyers. Only when they declined the offer would land be sold to others. In Serae, *worki* landowners had no obligation to resell to the original *risti* owners. Other types included sharecropping arrangements, in which land was leased on a basis of annual rent or share of produce. This arrangement was also common between absentee landlords, especially urban dwellers, and their relatives in the villages or poor peasants. There were also immigrants who acquired land-ownership through uninterrupted squatting for 40 years or more.

The problem of land hunger was most severe, and consequently competition for land fiercest, on the plateau. However, it was there that the traditional resource-management systems were relatively most developed. The history of human settlement and agricultural production on the Eritrean plateau and in Tigray is among the oldest in Africa (see Butzer, 1981; Markakis, 1990). For example, Markakis, referring to the northern plateau[5] stated, '[T]he oldest and largest group with a continuous record of occupation and cultivation of this territory are the Abyssinians of the northern plateau. The use of the oxen-drawn plough was universal here in a relatively intensive system of cultivation with multiple cropping, crop rotation and fallowing' (Markakis, 1990: 8). The total area of the Eritrean plateau, comprising the three provinces of Hamasen, Serae and Akele-Guzai, in the 1940s was in the range of 5,500 square miles. Although there are no accurate recent population figures, the area was considered among the most densely populated places in the region. As early as the 1940s, the population density was 80 per square mile. However, since a good part of the plateau was uncultivable, the man-to-arable-land ratio was much higher than this (1947a). Another report indicated that there were over 170 persons per 100 acres of cultivated land (Four Power Commission, 1947: Appendix 34).

On the plateau, there was tenurial security for those who possessed land, but land was a scarce resource and competition for land among the user groups was severe. It was in response to this situation that elaborate resource-regulating institutions evolved to regulate access to and use of the scarce resources owned in common, individually or on a family basis. The scarcity of land and CPRs on the Eritrean plateau induced the evolution of intricate institutions and complex control mechanisms for regulating allocation, use and conservation of such scarce resources. There were, for example, eight comprehensive codes of customary laws on the plateau. The codes of customary laws covered a great variety of subjects including land tenure, management of CPRs, civil law, family law, penal law, etc. All disputes over land rights or utilization of natural resources were settled by the interpretation and application of these laws. What the users could do or could not do with the resources they owned individually or in common were spelled out in the various codes of customary laws in great detail. Non-compliance was strictly prohibited. These customary laws existed for many centuries in the precolonial period, but they were codified for the first time between 1910 and 1938.

The Eritrean customary laws were the foundation on which the stability of the cultural system rested and were also instrumental in maintaining the balance between the demand for natural resources and the ability of the environment to supply such resources. The central planks of the customary laws were arbitration and conciliation. Nadel, one of the few authorities on Eritrean land-tenure systems and customary laws stated,

> [E]ven the formal trial by customary law . . . contains a strong element of arbitration and conciliation. Indeed, it is one of its dominant characteristics that it relies as much on the voluntary actions and undertakings of the parties to the dispute as on the authority of the court. The whole customary law of Eritrea can only be understood as a law which evolved in a society with no special executive body to enforce judicial orders and decisions. The . . . society which created this law knew no police or prisons. Its law was a

body of abstract rules, accepted in principle by the people at large, but enforceable in a concrete case only through private action . . . *surely behind them are those ultimate, forceful sanctions – group morality and public opinion . . . The people of Eritrea are extremely proud of their customary law and consider it wellnigh infallible.* (Nadel, 1946b: 107 – emphasis added).

The effectiveness of the customary law as an instrument of resource regulation was derived not only from group morality and public opinion, but also from its enforceability at law. For example, parties to agreements, conciliations, judicial decisions, conventions, etc. took an oath – *fetsmi* – to bind themselves.

Even though the conciliations, agreements, conventions, etc. were entered into voluntarily, they had legal validity – a validity which was, in theory, timeless (Nadel, 1946b: 107). A conciliation or a mutually binding contractual agreement reached under oath could be dissolved only by mutual agreement or a convention by consensus. A one-sided breach or repudiation was treated as a 'serious offence, tantamount to perjury, and punishable like that crime . . . interdependence of voluntary undertakings and legal sanctions was typical of Eritrean customary law' (Nadel, 1946b; 107). The binding power of the oath was religious, and its primary sanction supernatural. In former days *fetsmi* had to be taken by a grave, in the presence of a priest and with all the solemnity of a ritual act (Nadel, 1946b: 107). The laws were passed by the representatives of the communities, who agreed to bind themselves by oath, and this discouraged people from going their own way and from disregarding, for example, the rules that regulated access to and use of resources.

The codes of customary laws contain an untapped mine of information which sheds light on the traditional resource-management systems and institutional arrangements which provided a favourable framework for the sustainable use of resources owned in common. The customary rules were based on traditions, customs, beliefs, moral values and taboos. The customary laws throughout Ethiopia were repealed following the promulgation of the Ethiopian Civil Code in 1960. Following the annexation of Eritrea by Ethiopia in 1962, the Eritrean customary laws were also repealed formally. However, the Ethiopian state had no control over most of the Eritrean rural areas and the promulgation of its Civil Code had little or no effect on the validity of the Eritrean customary laws.

The codes of the Eritrean customary laws are important to understand the land-tenure systems that existed on the plateau prior to and after the advent of colonialism. The customary laws were enforceable throughout the Italian colonial period (1890–1941). During the colonial periods, jurisdiction on land matters were in the first and second instances adjudicated by the traditional village or district chiefs where customary laws were applied. Only appeal cases were heard by the colonial authorities (Nadel, 1946b). The Italian government had made some attempts to modify the traditional practice in which jurisdiction in land disputes was vested in the chiefs of the community in whose territory the land was situated. The chiefs also exercised jurisdiction over litigation between members of the landlord community and the outsiders who held land by special arrangements, e.g. through lease, gift or sharecropping in the area concerned. The Italian colonial government introduced three grades of jurisdiction, corresponding to the different types of land litigation. Land disputes between individuals of the same village or district and of the same ethnic descent and religion came before the village chief or district chief in the first and second instance; appeal was to the Italian official (Nadel, 1946b). The pith of the Eritrean customary law was arbitration and reconciliation and often the chief appointed three elders (*shimagelle*) as arbitrators – one for each party and the third as an impartial member. Land disputes between individuals belonging to different districts, ethnic groups and religions were tried by the Italian officials. Disputes involving whole *endas*, tribes and villages were tried by the Governor of the colony (Nadel, 1946b). According to Nadel this hierarchical judicature '. . . remained largely theory; in reality, the Italian officials often let these inter-group disputes be examined and tried by chiefs or the *ad hoc* appointed tribunals of elders – the Governor or *Residente* restricting his intervention largely to the signing of their judgement' (Nadel, 1946b). The BMA (1941–1952) did not intervene with the jurisdiction of the village or district chiefs. Only collective disputes were tried by the Senior Civil Affairs Officer of the Administrative Division, in accordance with the powers delegated to him by the Chief Administrator of Eritrea (Nadel, 1946b).

Eritrea represents a mosaic of traditions and cultures stemming from the varied socio-economic and cultural backgrounds of its population. The diversity of the country and its people in terms of topography, ecology, livelihoods and traditions is so considerable that the differences defy any generalization regarding land-use practices, land-tenure systems and resource-management regimes that evolved over time in the different parts of the country. In spite of this diversity, however, the data gathered from the codes of the customary laws and from the interviewees show that, in their stable state, in the areas where there were secure collective or individual property rights and where there was scarcity of land and CPRs, explicit sets of resource-regulating institutional rules evolved that were elevated to the status of customary law. The resource-regulating institutional arrangements were passed through consensus in meetings attended by elected representatives of all the *endas* (kindred groups) residing in the districts concerned (Lego Chewa, 1938: Art. 67). According to the code of customary law of the Lego Chewa district, for example, a law was passed only by the assembly of representatives of all the *endas* residing in the district and every resident of the district had a duty to observe the laws strictly (Lego Chewa, 1938: Art. 67). Laws passed without the approval of the representatives of all the *endas* in the district were not enforceable or were null and void (Lego Chewa, 1938: Art. 67).

The districts where there were security of tenure and scarcity of resources, due to physical constraints or population pressure, had committees either elected by the members of the identifiable groups (Adgnate Geleba, 1938: Art. 31) or appointed by the *cheka* (chief), who enforced the resource-regulating institutional arrangements. These committees also operated as *aquaro* (custodians) of the natural resources within the district (Show Ate Anseba, 1910; Adkeme Melega, 1936). Most of the villages also had committees, entrusted with the responsibility of excluding outsiders, known as *gelafo* (screeners). The natural resources were only accessible to certified members of a recognized group. Outsiders were excluded. These institutional arrangements provided a favourable framework for relative stability of the traditional agrarian and pastoral economies. Whenever possible, this was achieved by limiting the level of capacity utilization in the different ecological zones to environmentally sustainable levels.

The traditional resource-management regimes were developed in response to the need to allocate, use and conserve the scarce resources that were at the disposal of the communities concerned. The data elicited from the codes of the customary laws of the various ethnic groups and from the individuals representing the various groups in the settlements clearly show that there was a correlation, on the one hand, between tenurial security and scarcity of resources caused by population pressure and/or by unfavourable physical conditions of the natural environment and, on the other, the presence of well-developed and elaborate methods of traditional resource-management regimes. However, this is not to suggest that the

communities that lacked tenurial security and faced no resource scarcity were
unable to evolve any form of resource-management systems. This is only said to
emphasize the fact that such resource management regimes were more explicit and
more formalized in the areas where people had permanent individual or collective
titles to resources and/or when people derived their livelihoods from fixed or
diminishing resources, such as on the Eritrean plateau, namely the provinces of
Akele-Guzai, Serae, Hamasen and Senhit (Lower Anseba, Medri Bilen, Beit Juk,
Halhal, Maria and Mensà).

Periodic redistribution and sustainability of land use

The key element in the communal land-tenure system was periodic redistribution
of land among certified members of a family, kindred, district or village. In Akele-
Guzai redistribution took place every seventh year (Adgnate Geleba, 1938: Art.
239) and in Lego Chewa every eighth year (Lego Chewa, 1938: Art. 14). The
principle underlying periodic redistribution was equity. As Nadel observed: '[T]o
ensure an almost mathematically exact division, the available village land is graded
according to its fertility. In the most common system of grading we meet with three
categories (though some communities have adopted more numerous grades). They
were known as walakha (most fertile land), dukha (land of medium fertility) and
gereb (poor land)' (Nadel, 1946a: 13).

Distribution to individual farmers was made by drawing of lots for their share from
each category of land. The individual usufruct was limited to the periods between
the redistributions, but the individual's right to arable land within the collectively
owned village land was inalienable. However, over time, as land became scarce and
with the increased integration of the rural economy into the wider national economy
(monetization), general rights began to be replaced by specific rights to particular
pieces, as a result of which indefinite postponement of the periodic redistribution of
the land led to a gradual institutionalization of de facto individual private property in
land. Generally, however, there were rules governing redistribution. When the
redistributed land required fallowing, individual families received three or more
fields. New demands were met from the communal land bank which was
periodically restocked by recovering land of extinct families and 50% of the land of
families whose male head died (Lego Chewa, 1938: Art. 14). These lands reverted to
the custodians of communal lands. There were also well-defined procedures
regulating the actual distribution (Lego Chewa, 1938: Art. 14). In order to ensure
equity and to stem any form of abuse, the drawing of lots was supervised by the
village chief, the village priest or sheikh and three elected elders known as shimagelle
(committee). The right of individuals to dispose of their individual usufruct was
forbidden in communal land (diesa) ownership. Absentees could not hold land rights
in diesa (Lego Chewa, 1938: Art. 12). Diesa or communal ownership ensured
equitable distribution of land in terms of both quantity and quality.

> The practical significance of this communal ownership 'by rotation' is evident (and is
> borne out by the explanation which the people themselves offer). It represents a system
> supremely adapted to a country where land is of very unequal value and where the
> pressure on the land is great. Through this system every family is given an equal share, or
> the chance of such a share, of good and bad land alike. (Nadel, 1946a: 14)

The questions that spring to mind are: (i) did warieda (periodic redistribution) of the
family and communally owned lands provide incentives to individual holders to use

the fields with restraint in the periods between redistributions; (ii) did the farmers make investments to improve the quality of the land; or (iii) did the periodic redistributions encourage overuse and underinvestment because of the possibility of transfer or externalizing the costs to the next allocatees? One of the arguments used by the British colonial officers was that holders of individual usufruct would have no incentive to improve the land where ownership changed hands every few years. It was argued that, if land was allocated on a rotational basis, there would be an incentive for the individual holder to work the land to depletion without caring about the state of the land when it was handed over to the next member of the village.

It was probably this rationale that motivated the Eritrean government to promulgate a land statute concerning *diesa* lands in which redistribution of arable land was to take place every 27 years instead of the customary 7 years (Beyene, 1990: 42). This was meant to provide an incentive to holders to make investments to improve the quality of the land. Frequent changing of hands was believed to discourage investment. This legislation was never implemented (Beyene, 1990: 42). The land policy of the nascent Eritrean state is also strongly permeated by such 'modernist' thinking, in which the communal and family land-tenure systems are considered as impediments to economic development (see, for example, Government of the State of Eritrea, 1994; Land Commissioner for Eritrea, 1994). Development is conceptualized as a modernizing process, which aims to transform traditional practices and institutions instead of building upon them.

Whether periodic redistribution (every 7 years) of communally owned lands discouraged long-term investment in land improvements is an empirical question, but, even at the theoretical level, if we assume the individual holders were rational decision-makers (which they were), the immediate question that they would ask themselves when considering working their lands to exhaustion would be: 'What if every one else did the same?' By asking themselves such a simple but fundamental question, each would realize that it would be in their own individual interests not to deplete but to improve the common resource. Since land was redistributed by rotation, each person's well-being depended upon what s/he did to his/her land and upon what others did to theirs. An individual's action was often a function of the expectation he had about the actions of the other fellow villagers. An assurance was provided via an institutional rule that each member of the user group would improve and use the land with restraint by following the tacitly prescribed rules of fallowing, manuring and cropping patterns.

One of the key roles institutional rules played in the *diesa* (communal) and *enda* ownership of land on the Eritrean plateau was to eliminate the element of uncertainty and to create uniformity in the way farmers used the common resource. The individual holder of the communal land had, therefore, a clear incentive, obligation and moral pressure to improve the land even when it was known to him that the particular piece of land he held would in the next *warieda* (redistribution) be reallocated to any other member of the village. The farmers' future well-being was tied together by their mutual dependence on each other's actions. Every individual had a choice either to work the land to exhaustion, which would have meant threatening the subsistence security of the present and the future generations, or to use it with restraint and to make investments in its improvement.

The available evidence suggests that the farmers often saw no dichotomy between their individual and communal interests. This was because the sustainability of the land-resource base was dependent on whether all individual users improved their holdings. If everyone invested to improve the quality of the land s/he possessed, all would be better off in the next redistribution. If everyone worked her/his land to exhaustion, all would be worse off. It was, therefore, in the interest of each holder to improve the land because it was the only way to get others to do likewise. Their individual and communal interests were inextricably tied together and it was this awareness that encouraged the villages in question to evolve institutional safeguards that discouraged individual excess.

What is interesting is that, even though arable land was redistributed every 7 or 8 years, there was tree tenure even when the trees were planted on land which during redistribution went to another person. Trees belonged to the person who planted them (Lego Chewa, 1938: Arts 14 and 31). Members of the recognized group of resource users were allowed to cut timber for construction, but not only were the amounts and the types of trees specified, but felling for this purpose could take place only during the rainy season, specifically between 16 of June and the end of August, when not only the capacity of coppiced trees to regenerate (because of the summer rains) is highest, but also the risk of destruction of the budding plants by browsing animals is minimum because of alternative forage availability. This was to allow regeneration (Lego Chewa, 1938: Art. 32). There were also certain types of trees which had religious significance and were thus protected, for example, *ahwi* in Lego Chewa (1938: Art. 32). The cutting of trees in places considered as holy was also strictly prohibited (Lego Chewa, 1938: Art. 32). These sites still constitute green oasis reserves in different parts of highland Eritrea. Useful plant species were also protected. For example, according to the Show–Ate Anseba customary law, it was prohibited to cut fruit-bearing trees such as *dairo, sagla, chekomte, humer, gaba, hamta,* etc. (Show–Ate Anseba, 1910: Art. 103). These trees were important sources of food, especially in times of crop failure or scarcity. These perennial trees, unlike annual crops, do not die when rains fail or when the rain is inadequate. Thus, they were important sources of food and were therefore protected everywhere (Lego Chewa, 1938: Art. 32).

The resource-regulating institutional arrangements were strictly observed, partly because of the moral pressure imposed on 'free-riders', but also because of the heavy fines imposed on rule breakers. For example, people who used a common threshing ground were required to contribute their labour to prepare the ground. Those who failed to do so were heavily fined (Lego Chewa, 1938: Art. 24). Any person who tried to have a free-ride by not contributing money or labour to the production of a common good, such as sinking of wells, construction and repair of roads, churches, etc., was heavily fined (Lego Chewa, 1938: Art. 26). According to the Show–Ate Anseba customary law, the charge for inadvertent violation of resource-regulating rules or any other violation was a fat cow. If, however, the offence against common resource-management rules was intentional, the penalty was four fat cows (Show–Ate Anseba, 1910: Art. 67). The cows were to be slaughtered at the venue (Awde Berhanu) where the customary laws were passed or amended. The code of customary law of Adkeme Melega (1936) also imposed heavy fines on those who failed to observe communal rules. However, it was not only fear of penalties that promoted individual or group compliance with communal resource-regulating institutional arrangements; the relationships resulting from the process of socialization also greatly contributed to corporate behaviour. Some communities who use non-market institutions have a means by which they socialize their offspring from early childhood to develop what is considered honourable and appropriate behaviour. Such a process of socialization is designed to imbue individuals with social values and norms that discourage the pursuit of self-interest at the cost of one's kith and kin. This system of socialization was widespread in rural Eritrea, especially in the areas where resources were owned collectively. In some parts of Eritrea, pursuit of self-interest to the detriment of one's fellow villagers' or kinship groups' interests was a taboo and most inappropriate behaviour. The social costs of such behaviour in terms of loss of reputation and respect often outweighed the expected economic gains to be had from free-riding or defecting (non-compliance). The tendency was therefore to conform to the norms and to the accepted standards rather than to defect. The cost of defecting in terms of working one's holding carelessly or to exhaustion was too high. Not only did this lead to loss of reputation, but it also involved the risk of exclusion. The villages had built-in safeguards against individual excesses or individual mismanagement of the collective property. For example, unlike in *risti* and individual ownerships, communal land ownership required every individual holder to work his land with utmost care so that it could be transmitted to the next generation undiminished. No absenteeism was allowed either (Lego Chewa, 1938: Art. 12). On the parts of the Eritrean plateau where land was owned communally, the general principle that guided individual action in the interest of the common good could be described by the maxim 'you must work your land, lest you forfeit it' (Nadel, 1946a: 14–15). In Nadel's view, communal ownership was more efficient than *risti* (individual or collective family ownership) because the latter 'involves absenteeism and various forms of tenancy, which can hardly be called a spur to improvement and interest' (Nadel, 1946a: 14–15).

On the Eritrean plateau, where land was redistributed periodically, most people lived within the margin of subsistence. In order to meet the annual subsistence need of the farm families, every farmer, driven by the need to make ends meet, worked his land with utmost care. Under the existing technology, increased labour input, terracing, ridging and manure application were the main inputs used to improve the structures, textures and fertility of soils. In light of the high population density, the subsistence security of the individual families could be threatened without such improvements. Thus, every farmer, in an attempt to meet her/his family's need, was forced to make improvements to his holdings so that yields per unit area cultivated could be increased. Thus, the changing of ownership of holdings every few years did not operate as a disincentive for the individual farmers. Each community member had a responsibility to leave the collectively owned property to the next generation as much as possible in undiminished form. In precapitalist rural Eritrea, land was viewed as a resource that had to be transmitted to the future generation. Every generation was viewed as a custodian of the resources for the future generation. This was confirmed by Nadel's findings.

> [T]he argument [against communal ownership and periodical redistribution] ignores an important fact – the spirit of communal responsibility in these communities, which makes the temporary landholder work in the interest of his successors as well, since they all belong to a closely knit social unit. The rules of fallow-lying and the building and upkeep of terraces, which outlive individual tenure, prove this communal spirit convincingly. (Nadel, 1946a: 14–15)

The village lands, both arable and grazing, were the property of the whole village and the former were periodically redistributed to the members of the user community. The members had a corporate interest in making sure that the resources were used in a manner that would maintain their long-term sustainability so that they could be transferred to the future generation in an undiminished state. There were therefore institutional rules which regulated cropping patterns, sequences of cultivation and fallow periods, and land redistribution followed the cycle of cultivation and fallow. The changing hands of the village fields was also designed to take place after the fallow period. Villages which cultivated their fields for 2 years and left them fallow for 1 year as a rule redistributed them every 3 years. Those which cultivated their fields for 3 years, with 2 years' fallow, redistributed such fields every 5 years. The maximum period was 7–8 years. The need for regularity and uniformity required strict compliance, with the cultivation and fallowing sequences prescribed institutionally. There was no room for defecting because this would upset the order and regularity required by the *warieda* institution (periodic redistribution of communally owned lands). Every time during the *warieda*, the village community reviewed the availability of the village CPRs. Collective decisions were taken either to make additional allocations to increase the available CPRs or to bring part of the latter under cultivation if this was demanded by human *vis-à-vis* livestock growth. Individual encroachment on CPRs was strictly forbidden and there were sets of rules which stipulated sanctions against offenders.

The data collected from the various codes of customary laws show that not only was it incumbent on every member of the user group to comply with the existing institutional rules, but everyone was also responsible for policing and monitoring the compliance of their fellow villagers and identifying trespassers from outside. Some villages even hired a special enforcer paid by the villagers (Karneshim, 1910: Art. 4; Lego Chewa, 1938: Art. 72). This measure was taken if defecting was considered a problem. This was often the case in reserved pastures (*hezati*) of a village, on which cultivation, grazing and physical access were forbidden during most of the year. Only plough oxen were allowed to graze in the *hezati* during a certain period of the year.

Tacit and explicit social controls were also developed to regulate resource use and to ensure that the common resources were managed sustainably. Rotational grazing was commonly practised to avoid the problem of overgrazing. During the dry season only milking cows, calves, goats, sheep, donkeys and draught animals were kept in and around the villages. Dry cows, heifers and bulls were moved to Bahri or to the western lowlands. This management system was designed to exploit variations in the environment.

Generally, no serious enforcement problems were faced because collective decisions were taken concerning allocation and use of the CPRs including the communally owned arable land. Every member of the user group therefore had an incentive to cooperate in enforcing the decision. Trespassers from outside the user community were easily identified because villagers knew and recognized each other. Free-riders and trespassers were therefore reported promptly to the *shimagelle* and the *cheka* (chief), who had a mandate from the village assemblies to enforce the rules (Lego Chewa, 1938: Art. 26). Major decisions regarding CPRs were taken in village assemblies. The assemblies were often held annually and were attended by all male adults or their representatives. In order to increase participation, the assemblies were held during the trough season when agricultural labour was unemployed or underemployed. On the Eritrean plateau and in the other areas where the *risti* and *diesa* types of land ownership were dominant, people lived concentrated in large villages.

The plateau has been subjected to heavy and intensive human and animal pressures over many centuries, so the fact that it has been able to sustain growing human and animal populations in the context of technological stagnation is surprising. This was probably possible due to the intricate and wide-ranging set of rules, enforcement mechanisms and conservation methods that have evolved over time in response to the need to derive sources of livelihood from fixed or diminishing resources in the context of an unstable environment.

Resource abundance, tenurial insecurity and development of resource-management systems: the example of the Beni Amer in the western lowlands

The situation of the Beni Amer in the western lowlands is in sharp contrast to that described above. The Beni Amer are the second largest group among the refugees in the Qala en Nahal scheme (see Table 7.2). Before their flight to Sudan, they derived their livelihood from mixed husbandry – livestock and cultivation. Livestock production was combined with dry-land cultivation and transhumance. Although the majority of the Beni Amer were nomadic herdsmen, in the last 100 years they have been progressively adapting to a semisettled way of agropastoral life (Nadel, 1945). In light of the external pressure manifested in the encroachment on their traditional grazing resources and recurrent droughts, many of them were unable to derive adequate sources of livelihood from livestock rearing. Thus, mixed husbandry was developed in response to the changing circumstances in which they found themselves. In fact, contrary to what is widely believed to be the case, there were some clans among the Beni Amer who, as far back as they could remember, had been sedentary cultivators. Among these were the Ad Towas, Ad Bekhit, Ad Taule and Ad Sala (BMA, 1943: 7). The majority of the Beni Amer were, however, nomadic herdsmen, whose wealth lay in camels, cattle, sheep and goats (BMA, 1943: 7).

The Beni Amer lived scattered over large tracts of land in the western lowlands, down to the Rivers Gash and Setit in the south, and in the east up to the mountains stretching north between the valleys of Barka and Anseba. Given the semiarid nature of parts of the territory they occupied, seasonal southward migration in search of water and pasture for humans and livestock was a necessity imposed by the varied and unstable nature of their environment. During the wet season between May and October, pasture was abundant in most of the areas they occupied. During the dry season, water and fodder were scarce in the east. The need to take advantage of the variation of water and pasture, therefore, necessitated migration to the banks of the Barka River and to the south to the Rivers Gash and Setit. Some groups also moved seasonally to the valleys of Keren, Akele-Guzai and Serae (BMA, 1943: 8). Even though families moved far afield with their livestock during the dry season wherever the grasses were greener, they always returned to their villages in the summer in the Barka valley. Usually, many family members, milking cows and small stock remained behind and only one or two members of the families moved with the livestock to the south. Only in drought years did all family members join their livestock in the seasonal movements, leaving their hamlets and villages on the Barka River temporarily empty.

The boundaries of the grazing areas belonging to the various sections of the Beni Amer tribe and the livestock routes for the seasonal movements were defined by habit and traditional tacit agreements only (Nadel, 1945: 52). The interesting question is whether the resources used by the various Beni Amer clans (as defined by custom and tradition) were exclusive rights solely open to the certified members of the section of the tribe in question. Or were the arable land, grazing, woodland and water sources open-access resources? The available evidence suggest that there were no rigid boundaries or exclusive grazing rights. Such boundaries were even absent *vis-à-vis* their alien neighbours, into whose territory the Beni Amer occasionally penetrated. This often led to quarrels and disputes between the different ethnic groups (Nadel, 1945: 52). Nadel sees the concept of fixed boundaries, as well as institutional accountability and amenability to political control, as incompatible with the nomadic lifestyle of the Beni Amer, who kept on moving over scattered territories in search of better grazing resources. 'Physical dispersion makes for looseness of organization . . . The clans are not amenable to unitary command' (Nadel, 1945: 60). The only time the Beni Amer tribesmen have contact with each other, Nadel argues, is in 'marriage and occasional feasts . . . but hardly any institution exists which would nurse and periodically reawaken this unity' (Nadel, 1945: 60). In his view, the drive of every herdsman to search for grazing impeded the emergence of a strong central leadership. He further states,

> [T]he economic habits foster a kindred outlook and mentality. The individual male is born into a scattered and broken up group . . . He knows intimately only his few neighbours on the pastures or in the nearest camp. His knowledge of the rest of the clan, of his chief and paramount chief is . . . indirect and of secondary interest . . . Thus everyday life breeds in the Beni Amer a narrow individualism. (Nadel, 1945: 60)

If this is true, the community would find it difficult or impossible to organize itself for collective action or to reach agreements in order to regulate access to and use of CPRs and to enforce such agreements. Among traditional communities, most collective actions and decisions are based on consensus. A community which lacks social cohesion and traditional institutions cannot work out binding rules to govern the behaviour of its members. The corollary of this is that the spirit of communal responsibility and corporate outlook is absent and without these neither reaching a collective decision nor enforcement of such decisions is possible. The precondition for collective and voluntary action is the spirit of communal responsibility. Thus, the possibility for such a community to develop institutions that would regulate use and access rights to scarce resources would be limited.

As opposed to the situation prevailing in the areas faced with scarcity of land resources where there were tacit and explicit institutional arrangements and rules governing resource allocation and use, in the Beni Amer areas no collective decisions or rules regarding allocation and utilization of the collective resources existed. This is clear from their customary laws, in which there were no rules designed to regulate access to and use of resources. The main concerns of their customary laws were family and criminal laws.

The central question that springs to mind is whether the non-existence of institutions concerned with the management of CPRs was due to the inability of the scattered nomadic way of life (which in Nadel's view was not amenable to unitary command) to evolve such institutions or whether their absence was a reflection of the fact that such institutions had no significant role to play because the resources from which the Beni Amer derived their livelihoods were not scarce and needed no regulation. Institutions emerge in response to a need to solve problems. Traditional resource management regimes are, therefore, developed in response to the need to regulate access to and use and control of scarce resources which would otherwise be depleted because of overuse and underinvestment. If competition for resources is fierce, the absence of regulation may also lead to bloodshed. Thus, the need for resource-regulating institutions becomes imperative.

There is ample evidence to show that nomadic lifestyle *per se* does not impede the evolution of traditional resource-management systems when there is a demand for such institutions. Although it may represent a slight digression, this can be demonstrated by the example of the former nomadic and seminomadic Saho groups. The Saho were until the mid-nineteenth century nomadic herdsmen who migrated seasonally over long distances in search of water sources and pastures. The traditional homelands of the Saho are the coastal depression between Massawa in the north, the Gulf of Zula in the east and the escarpment of Akele-Guzai in the west. According to the 1943 population census, out of the 41,000 Saho, about 31,000 lived in the escarpment of Akele-Guzai and 93% were categorized as 'nomadic' (Longrigg, 1945: Appendix C). Except for the few settled agriculturalists on the plateau, Trevaskis also referred to the Saho as nomadic and semi-nomadic (Trevaskis, 1960: 15). Whether up to 90% were nomadic as late as 1941 is a moot question. The movement of the Saho westward and the process of taking to a sedentary livelihood began as early as the mid-nineteenth century[6] and it sounds implausible to state that, 100 years after, only 7% had become sedentarized.

When their traditional grazing areas were reduced and their seasonal migration routes were disrupted due to drought, environmental degradation, population pressure, colonial land alienation and increased competition with the seasonally migrating sedentary farmers from the plateau, the need for institutional rules governing allocation and use of the diminishing scarce resources emerged. Gradually, institutional rules, enforcement mechanisms and political organizations almost identical to those on the plateau among the Christian population evolved. When they moved westwards to the areas inhabited by sedentary farmers, one way in which they gained access to arable and grazing lands was by entering into a social convention of friendship and mutual assistance with the original occupiers (Nadel, 1946a: 16). This gave rise to the need to develop a complex set of rules spelling out the obligations and benefits for both parties. Enforcement mechanisms were also developed to monitor compliance and to implement the agreements.

The institutional arrangement that developed to accommodate the need of the migrants for land was known as *sedbi* or family lease agreement.[7] Since the mid-nineteenth century, the Saho tribes, who used to live in the coastal plains and in the mountainous areas of Akele-Guzai, began to move westwards to areas which were already occupied by the sedentary farmers on the plateau. The process of sedenterization of the former nomadic groups led to greater competition for arable land in the areas formerly dominated by the sedentary groups. When unoccupied land was unavailable, the former nomads gained access to rights of usufruct through conventions, pacts and contractual agreements with the original occupiers. Thus, the institution of *sedbi* was developed to regulate the relationship between landowners and landless immigrants. The *sedbi* contractual agreement involved a quite complex set of rules governing the relationship between the villages.

> The sedbi pacts thus link group with group. Mostly they are many generations old. They are concluded for indefinite periods – 'for ever', as the people themselves say – and cannot be easily terminated. As a rule both parties must agree to the termination. A unilateral notice by the landlords can be given only for two reasons: their own need of the land, or a failure, on the part of the [*sedbi* holder], to fulfil the many social obligations entailed in the sedbi pact. (Nadel, 1946a: 16)

The institutional arrangements in the *sedbi* pact were designed to preclude disputes or abuse of the pact. Access rights secured through *sedbi* involved payment of rent to the original landowners. The payment was ceremonial and symbolic. It was a gesture of recognition of the ownership rights and a sign of respect for the original occupiers. The rules surrounding the *sedbi* agreements were designed to ensure the property rights of the landowners and to prevent claims by the immigrants.

> Thus the payment of the rent is surrounded with formalities. Annually . . . the tenant will visit his landlord, bringing with him small gifts as well as the rent. The landlord will regularly visit his tenant and inspect the land in order to ascertain, again in the presence

of witnesses, that the tenant has observed the terms of the lease and has not illicitly extended his cultivation. (Nadel, 1946a: 16)

This clearly shows that traditional resource users when confronted with resource scarcity were able to work out solutions to their common problems by pursuing cooperative strategies that promoted mutual beneficiary outcomes. Not only were they able to negotiate such institutional arrangements, but they have always been able to enforce such agreements without any interference from outside.

What is interesting is that despite their previous nomadic habits, the Saho not only demonstrated an impressive adaptive capacity to sedentary livelihood among the sedentary farmers on the plateau, but have also developed intricate substantive and procedural customary rules to govern the allocation and use of CPRs, including arable land, in less than 100 years. The code of customary law, which was consolidated in 1943 by the four paramount chiefs of the Saho tribes (Nazir Basha Abubeker of the Asaorta, Cavaliere Official Alibeke Mohamed, Nazir of the Minafere, Cavliere Ona Ali Bunshum Suleman, Nazir of Hazo, and Fitewrari Abdella Suleman, Nazir of the Debere Mella tribe) and their followers, was as comprehensive as the codes of customary laws of the regions on the plateau. Although the customary laws of the Saho-speaking groups were codified for the first time in 1943, they were in use since time immemorial (preamble of the Saho Tribes' Code of Customary law, 1943). As opposed to the customary law of the Beni Amer, the major preoccupation of the code of customary law of the Saho tribes was regulation of access to and use of arable land, pasture, water, animal routes, etc.

Most of the institutional rules, enforcement mechanisms, political organizations and methods of soil conservation and fertility maintenance were as advanced as among the sedentary plateau population, who had a much longer history of sedentarization. In the Saho homelands, both arable resources and CPRs were exclusively accessible to certified members of the user community. Outsiders were strictly excluded. For example, a person who grazed his animals on land for which he lacked entitlement through descent or residence was fined heavily (Saho Tribes, 1943: Art. 84 and 89). Outsiders could only gain access to the exclusive resources through explicit permission from the original occupiers (Art. 92).[8] There were also monitors who supervised compliance and who brought to communal justice those who disobeyed the community rules. The monitors were appointed by the chief (Art. 189). The charges paid by offenders were utilized for funding community projects such as mosques and schools (Art. 190). What is interesting is that when the Saho tribes took to a sedentary livelihood on the plateau, they immediately developed complex resource management systems and methods of conservation in order to manage the scarce resources. In the villages where there were acute land shortages, such as Irafele, Wangebo, Hadis, Bada (Akele-Guzai), etc., relatively sophisticated methods of traditional husbandry – cultivation and soil and water conservation – evolved to make the best out of the poor physical environment. Recession cultivation after the retreating of flood waters also became common in these villages. However, when the Saho tribes migrated to the western lowlands, where there was relatively abundant arable and cultivable land, they applied none of these agricultural techniques in their new place of residence. In fact, it is worth noting that, in their new place of residence, their intensive farming systems gave way to extensive practices of resource use, i.e. intensification gave way to disintensification. This suggests that resource-management systems are developed in response to the need to manage scarce resources. Among the subsistence producers, these institutional innovations were developed in response to the need to maintain subsistence activities at a level that was at least adequate for survival. It was the drive to avert the threat of subsistence insecurity in an environment endowed with unfavourable climatic and soil conditions that engendered adaptive change. In these subsistence economies, survival was the motive force that initiated cultural change. When resources were of relative abundance, even those with long-established traditions abandoned such systems. This was because the pressure on the cultural status quo ceased as the demand on the environment, induced by subsistence insecurity, diminished.

The fact that the Saho, despite their previous nomadic habits, were able to evolve complex formal and informal institutional rules governing access to and use of resources when they were confronted with the need to eke out a living from scarce and qualitatively diminishing natural resources and that they abandoned these innovations when they migrated to the Barka valley, where there were abundant pasture, arable and woodlands, suggests that the absence of such resource-regulating institutions among the Beni Amer cannot be explained by their nomadic habits and by what Nadel refers to as 'narrow individualism'. The Beni Amer lands represented a situation of relative resource abundance (BMA, 1943b) and the absence of formalized systems of resource management was a reflection of such abundance. If Nadel's characterization of the Beni Amer's narrow individualism was correct, the phenomenon itself was probably an adaptation to this relative resource abundance.

One of Nadel's contentions as to why the Beni Amer were not amenable to political control and unitary command was because of the nomadic habits of the tribe (Nadel, 1945: 61). Not only is this contention contradicted by the account which the people themselves offer, but there are other independent accounts which do not lend support to this claim. According to Paul, in the early eighteenth century the Beni Amer were probably '. . . the most powerful tribal confederation between the Gash valley and the sea. They had absorbed or conquered all the smaller peoples in their vicinity, and not even the Habab cared to indulge in open conflict with them' (Paul, 1950: 226). If the Beni Amer were not amenable to 'political control' and 'unitary command', how could they form a confederation and conquer other peoples? Their victory over other groups reflected their political cohesion. In fact, not only does Paul's account suggest that the Beni Amer's nomadic habits were amenable to political control, but he even states 'there was that in them that made them always remarkably amenable to constituted authority' (Paul, 1950: 226).

The account of the political history of the Beni Amer as told by their elders is inconsistent with Nadel's interpretation. The Ben Amer were unified by common descent, by allegiance to a traditional political leadership and by territorial rights. They had, as far back as they could remember,[9] a central leadership in the person of the *shum* (in recent years sometimes referred to as *nazir*), who was in the earlier periods known as the *diglal*. A report by the BMA at the beginning of the 1940s, for example, observed, '[T]he Beni Amer confederacy as a whole is under a paramount chief, who styles himself Diglal and comes . . . from the tribe Degga. The reigning Diglal is Geilani Hussein' (BMA, 1943: 7). The *diglal/shum* had various representatives (sheikhs) in every settlement or clan of the Beni Amer. The sheikhs were authorized to deal with all matters ranging from tribute collection, criminal offences and settlement of disputes that arose within the clans and with their neighbouring communities. The leadership structure comprised the *shum* and the sheikhs. Many of the clans came under the leadership of one *shum*. The *shum*'s decision regarding any matter within his jurisdiction was binding on every community member. Whenever there was a serious matter, the *shum* was required to seek advice from the clan council

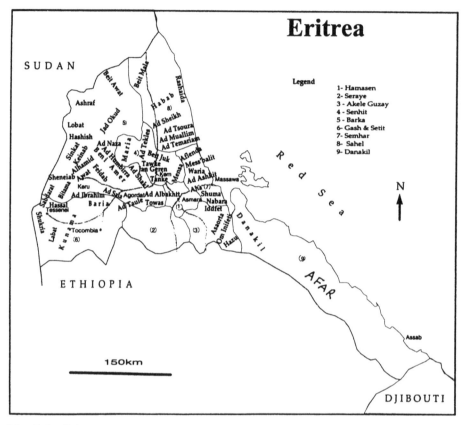

Map 7.1   Eritrea
Source: Public Record Office, London, FO/371/35658, 1940s. This map does not
show the international boundaries of Eritrea.

and the sheikhs. The *shum* and the sheikhs were revered by the members of the clans
or tribes. Their authority was derived from historically evolved tradition. The bond
of common descent was strong and social support networks were quite solid. The
political unity of the Beni Amer was also sustained by a common religion – Islam.
The majority acknowledged the spiritual leadership of the Morghani family, which
held the same ecclesiastical position in eastern Sudan (BMA, 1943: 8).

Thus, the absence of institutions concerned with allocation and use of resources
was not due to the fact that the Beni Amer way of life was not amenable to political
and institutional control, but it was mainly due to the fact that the abundance of the
land resource did not necessitate the evolution of institutions concerned with
allocation and use of natural resources. Whenever there was a need for regulation of
access to and use of a scarce common resource, social institutions evolved without
being impeded by the Beni Amer's nomadic habits. In the Beni Amer lands, water
was a scarce resource. During the dry season, water supply was limited to few
boreholes and wells. Some of the wells were owned privately and others by a group
of families within a village or even by the whole village. When water sources were
owned collectively, the user communities evolved intricate rules to regulate access
and use of such a scarce resource. The rules were quite similar to the rules that

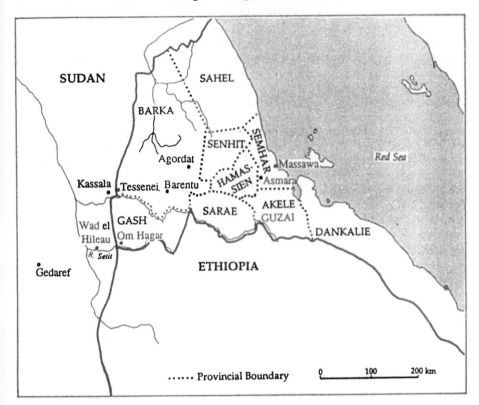

Map 7.2 Provincial boundaries and key cities in Western Eritrea
This map does not show the international boundaries of Eritrea.

existed elsewhere in the country where arable resources and other CPRs were owned and controlled collectively.

Every certified member of a user group was entitled to use the village or family water resource, but there were elaborate rules that regulated the timing and amount that could be appropriated by individual herdsmen. Livestock were also watered on different days. For example, camels were only watered once every 4–5 days, cattle every 2 days and sheep and goats every day. There were rules which spelled out the responsibilities of every user regarding the water resource and accessories. If livestock were watered from a common trough, every herdsman was required to leave the trough in the same state as he found it. They evolved mechanisms to enforce such collective rules. There were also other rules which were strictly observed by the Beni Amer. For example, if one's herds suffered from a contagious disease, there were collectively prescribed rules which the owner had to abide by to prevent the spreading of the disease.

The area inhabited by the Beni Amer, or the whole western lowlands including the Gash and Setit valleys, were state domain lands. The Beni Amer therefore had rights of usufruct only. The ownership of the resources was vested in the state. Although there is no doubt that lack of full ownership over the resources might somehow have contributed to the absence of resource-regulating institutions, it cannot be claimed that it was the only factor impeding the evolution of resource-management systems. This is because, although land was formally owned by the colonial state, in reality the latter did not exercise any meaningful control over access to most of the expropriated resources in the western lowlands. If there were demands for such institutions, their emergence would not have been hampered by formal state ownership of the natural resources in the area. Because neither the Beni Amer nor the state exercised control over the resources, de facto both the arable land and the rest of the CPRs were open-access and readily available for exploitation.

The relative abundance of resources in the Beni Amer lands did not in any way mean that the communities were devoid of any tacit or explicit rules governing grazing resources. It was, for example, common for the Beni Amer to remove their camels, dry cattle, bulls, heifers and sheep from the vicinity of settlements during the dry seasons, leaving behind only milking cows, calves, donkeys and goats. During the rainy season, all livestock returned to the settlements, to be moved again after 2–3 months. Generally, this pattern of rotational grazing was observed by all herdsmen, but, if one chose to leave his/her dry animals in the village, there was nothing the community could do to force him to practise rotational gazing. There were no explicit collective decisions or rules governing the range lands. Each livestock owner was free to decide whether to move his livestock or to leave them in the village throughout the year. Individual evaluation of the range productivity rather than collective decision was decisive in the individual Beni Amer herdsman's decision.

Since the Beni Amer were scattered over large tracts of land, there was no shortage of either arable or pasture lands. Thus, outsiders could gain access both to arable and pasture lands simply by asking the village leadership in whose territory the resource was located. Arable land could be cleared at will by members of the Beni Amer even without consultation with the sheikh or the community. There was no limit to the amount of land members of the community could clear for cultivation. However, since the major means of livelihood was livestock raising, only small plots were cultivated to produce the family's own needs. The data elicited from our informants suggest that the institution of private or even communal land ownership was alien to the Beni Amer culture. As one of the Beni Amer elders put it, 'land was a "God-given" open-access resource free to all those with good intentions' (interview with Beni Amer elder, 1991). He defined 'good intentions' as willingness and commitment not to cause harm to the grasses and the water resources and consequently to those whose well-being was dependent on such resources. He further stated that, when using these resources, 'individuals should take into account other herders' needs and the rights of the grasses and the water resources to make themselves available to future generations'. This may suggest the existence of informal norms influencing the decision of individuals when using a common resource.

The Beni Amer did not use any techniques of soil conservation except that shifting cultivation was used to counter soil-fertility decline. The community was not familiar with any other forms of conservation methods. Terracing was unknown to the Beni Amer. The practices of manuring or rotation of crops to maintain soil fertility were also unknown. Owing to the abundance of arable land, all could afford to abandon their plots after a few seasons' cultivation when crop yields showed a sign of decline. Sorghum and millet were sometimes rotated but it was not clear whether this was dictated by the dietary habits of the households or by the need to maintain soil fertility.

Arable and range lands were abundant. As a result, there was a clear tendency to use land extensively to produce just enough for subsistence without engaging in hard work. One factor which featured in all the interviews with the representatives of the Beni Amer was that, in the pre-flight period, labour productivity was high and the workload was relatively light. Since land was in abundant supply, bush fallowing was commonly used to replenish soil fertility. After three or four seasons of cultivation, most of the farmers abandoned their plots and opened up new fields where the return to labour was higher. It was common to return to the old plots after 6–8 years if they remained unoccupied. More often than not, most of them did not return to these plots.

In the following section, the coping strategies that were developed by the peasant, agropastoral and pastoral communities to counter resource depletion precipitated by natural processes and human interferences in a context of population pressure will be presented.

Coping strategies to counter land degradation

The refugee communities have diverse cultural backgrounds and the measures they take to counter soil exhaustion, erosion and fertility decline are influenced by this cultural and consequently experiential diversity. The environments where the refugees came from (before flight) and their origins varied widely in terms of climate, topography, farming systems, social structures, socio-economic backgrounds, ethnicity, etc. They included a diverse mixture of nomadic pastoralists, agropastoralists, agriculturalists, urban dwellers, skilled, semiskilled and unskilled labourers and landed and landless classes (Kibreab, 1987: Table 4.12). The majority of the refugees being of rural origin, there is a clear link or bifurcation between ethnic origin and former bases of livelihoods and experiences (socio-economic backgrounds). This is because rural communities are less occupationally differentiated than urban dwellers. Ethnic diversity is, therefore, a good measure of the level of cultural pluralism that exists among the refugee communities in terms of experiences and socio-economic backgrounds.

The socio-economic backgrounds of the population are as varied as their ethnicity and their traditional resource-management regimes, including management of arable land. In order to show whether their knowledge of conservation is influenced by their ethnicity and consequently by their experiential diversity, the respondents were asked to state the conservation methods their communities used to counter land degradation (soil erosion and fertility decline) in their country of origin before their displacement. The results show, as expected, a strong relationship between knowledge of conservation methods and cultural backgrounds, past experiences and socio-economic backgrounds.

A series of discussions with key informants from the various ethnic groups on the scheme revealed that the groups that came from the areas where there was a long history of sedentary farming and shortage of land supply due to high population density and steep slopes knew and used sophisticated methods of terracing, not only to prevent soil erosion, but to transform hills and mountainous areas into cultivable land. Without terracing, such areas would be washed away by rain erosion. The Saho who came from the eastern escarpment and the Tigrinya from the overpopulated highlands were able to cope with the pressure of population on the land partly by transforming entire hills and steep slopes into arable land and partly by pursuing farming systems based on crop rotation, intercropping, manure application, short fallows and the leaving of grass strips and uncleared standing trees on the boundaries of farms, etc. This is discernible from the data in Table 7.3, where the Tigrinya, Saho, Bilen, Beit Juk and the Maria, who were all settled agriculturalists, knew diverse methods of soil conservation and yield decline-countering methods, as opposed to the Beni Amer, who were mainly of agropastoral or nomadic backgrounds.

Table 7.3 shows the dominant methods of soil conservation used by the various ethnic groups. The farming systems of the Tigrinya and Bilen ethnic groups included diverse methods of soil-conservation methods such as stone-walled diversions, structures across slopes, ridging along the contour, barriers of brushwood or stones to accumulate debris in gullies and the planting of trees. The data suggest that whether the farmers developed conservation methods was determined mainly by whether the area they occupied was erosion-prone. People in flat plains are seldom faced with problems of soil erosion. As a result, their farming systems may not include erosion-countering measures, e.g. the Nara ethnic groups in the Gash Setit, in spite of their sedentary way of life, knew little about erosion-countering measures.

The Saho ethnic groups have diverse backgrounds. Some were settled agriculturalists who combined crop with livestock production, but with more emphasis on the former. Others were agropastoralists, who derived their sources of livelihood from both crop production and livestock herding, with more emphasis on the latter. Extensive interviews with various key informants clearly show that there were no pure nomadic pastoralists among them. This was true at least from the middle of the twentieth century (Nadel, 1946a). The Saho from eastern Akele-Guzai, for example, constructed, before the the the onset of the rains, earthen terraces on the boundaries of the holdings, which were designed to check run-off and conserve moisture. In an area where rainfall was inadequate and erratic, this was an indispensable method of water harvesting. Terraces were constructed in a manner that would not detrimentally affect accessibility to run-off by farmers downstream. Access to run-off was regulated by the same informal community rules and institutions that applied to the management of the CPRs.

Table 7.3 Common methods applied to counter soil erosion prior to displacement, by ethnicity (socio-economic backgrounds) (%)

Methods	II	III	IV	V	VI	VII	VIII	IX
Stone-walled terraces	++++	+++	−	++	+	++++	−	+++
Making of earth bunds	++++	++	−	+	+	+++	+	+++
Stone-walled diversion	++++	++	−	+	−	++++		−++
Structures across slope	++++	++	−	+	++	+++	−	+
Ridging along the contour	++++	+	−	−	−	++	−	+
Stands of trees	++++	+	−	+	++	+++	−	++
Barriers of brushwood or stones to accumulate debris in gullies	++++	++	−	+	+	+++	+	+
Don't know[a]	0	2	8	3	1	0	1	0

$\chi^2=264$, d.f.$=56$, $P<0.0001$.

II, Tigrinya: III; Saho; IV, Beni Amer; V, Maria; VI, Nara; VII, Bilen; VIII, Hedareb; IX, Beit Juk.

++++, The method was practised by or known to 100% of respondents; +++, the method was practised by or known to 75% of respondents; ++, the method was practised by or known to 50% of respondents; +, the method was practised by or known to 25% of respondents; −, the method was not known or was known to less than 25% of respondents.

[a]Those who did not know were those who came to Sudan too young or were born on the scheme.

Some of the Maria (Tigre-speaking) were also settled agropastoralists in their areas of origin. The majority of the Maria group who were included in the study or those who lived in Qala en Nahal did not come directly from northern Senhit to Sudan. The majority came from the Gash Setit valleys, where they had migrated in search of arable and grazing lands before and during the first three decades of this century. Their areas of origin were characterized by shortage of arable and grazing lands. In their areas of origin, not only was land in short supply, but the dominant form of property right of arable land was *resti*, which, with increasing population, led to overfragmentation of holdings, reducing many of them below economic levels.

In order to raise productivity per unit of crop land in the context of shortage of land supply and growing population, the Maria developed two adaptive responses. Firstly, they used diverse conservation works and agronomic methods in their areas of origin and, secondly, a considerable number migrated to the Gash and Setit areas, where there was an adequate supply of arable and grazing lands. What was striking among the Maria who had migrated to the Gash and Setit areas was that they did not introduce their conservation and agronomic skills into the new area. Their land-use practices therefore became extensive and, over time, exploitative.

There are three possible explanations for this. Firstly, the climate, topography, quality of the soils, etc. of the new area were different from their areas of origin. This rendered their traditional resource-management regime inoperative because their knowledge was location-specific. Secondly, unlike in their area of origin, where there was a shortage of land supply (arable and grazing), in the area of their destination land supply was in excess of demand. Thus, the need for austere land-use practice was not considered important, at least in the short term. Thirdly, the Maria, as a minority, were absorbed and instead adapted to the dominant extensive land-use practices of the new area. In their area of origin, they had established property rights over resources in a geographically defined territory, where they could make decisions with respect to land-use practices. They also had a leadership which monitored the behaviour of resource users with respect to implementation of the decisions regarding the use of commonly owned resources. The tribal leadership not only monitored compliance, but fined 'free-riders'. After migration, the conditions under which the community conducted its affairs changed and so did its traditional resource-management regime. It is not surprising, therefore, that the Maria, after migrating to the Gash Setit, abandoned their traditional resource-management regime and emulated the dominant land-use practice in the area of destination.

The same is also true of the Saho who had migrated to the Barka area (Quorequen) from Serae in the mid-1950s, following the withdrawal of the BMA from Eritrea. The aftermath of the withdrawal of the BMA was characterized by political instability, which led to internal displacement of some sections of the Eritrean population. One of Ethiopia's strategies for legitimizing its claim over Eritrea was by trying to sow discord and disharmony among the various peacefully coexisting ethnic and religious groups in the country. The Saho on the scheme were victims of the Ethiopian 'grand strategy' of 'divide and rule'. At that time, they were living in Serae province in harmony with their neighbours. In the mid-1950s, they were subjected to harassment by their neighbours and were consequently forced into internal displacement, mainly to the western lowlands in the environs of Agordat, where they were favourably received by the then governor of the Barka province, who was himself a Saho.[10] They were allocated state domain lands by the governor until they fled to Sudan in 1967 to escape the violence perpetrated by the Ethiopian forces of occupation.

This background information represents a necessary digression. What is interesting is that when the Saho lived in Serae, where there was higher population density and scarce supply of land resource, they used diverse methods of conservation to counter natural-resource degradation. However, when they migrated to the Barka area, where there was a relatively abundant supply of arable and grazing lands, they made no attempt to introduce their indigenous technical knowledge into their new place of residence.[11]

The refugee communities on the scheme had different indigenous technical knowledge about soil and water conservation. Each group's indigenous technical knowledge was developed to overcome a specific constraint and, as expected, natural-resource conservation methods were found to be more advanced among those who were faced with the problem of land shortage and who derived their livelihoods mainly from crop production. The Beni Amer derived their livelihood from both crop production and livestock herding. Although there was variation between the various clans, depending on the location of their former habitation and the level of integration into the national market economy, among the majority livestock herding seemed to be the dominant economic activity. Their crop-production activities did not therefore place pressure on the arable land resource. Their areas of origin were also in the majority of cases sparsely populated.

The topography of the Beni Amer's areas of origin consists of flat plains, such as the Upper and Lower Barka as well as the Gash Setit in the western lowlands. Since most of the techniques given in Table 7.3 refer to erosion-countering measures on slopes and mountainous topographies, it is understandable that the Beni Amer knew nothing about erosion-countering measures. Owing to the flat terrain of their areas of origin and their dominant sources of livelihood, soil erosion was never a serious constraint on agricultural production. Soil erosion was not one of the bottlenecks the community had to come to grips with, and understandably the majority had no idea about how to overcome or minimize the consequences of soil erosion.

Among the Beni Amer only shifting cultivation (bush fallow) was used to counter fertility decline while, for example, among the Tigrinya and others, organic manure, intercropping, crop rotation, etc. were used (Table 7.4). This is influenced by climate, quality of soil, basis of livelihood and topography. For example, in the past, in the Eritrean highlands, favourable climatic and ecological conditions (such as sufficient rainfall, moderate temperature and good-quality soils) supported the growth of diverse crops, which mitigated land degradation resulting from continuous cultivation. A considerable proportion of the Hedareb group also did not know about an effective way of countering soil erosion, and this was understandable for almost exactly the same reasons as those applicable to the Beni Amer. The Hedareb live in a similar ecological zone to the Beni Amer and their socio-economic backgrounds are similar. A few of the Hedareb, however, knew some erosion-countering measures. The data in Tables 7.3 and 7.4 clearly show that the former settled agriculturalists such as the Tigrinya, Bilen and Beit Juk had a well-developed knowledge about erosion- and fertility-countering measures.

Before the refugees fled their country, bush fallow was the major technique used by the agropastoral or pastoral people. These communities came from areas in Eritrea where there was no shortage of land. Among the refugees who came from the land-scarce areas, bush fallow was either not used or used only marginally. It was only among the Beni Amer, Maria[12] and Nara that it was widely practised. It is important to note, however, that the term bush fallow is misleading in this case. In African traditional agricultural systems, bush fallow generally suggests that land is

7.4: Traditional knowledge or techniques applied to counter fertility decline prior to displacement, by ethnicity

Methods	II	III	IV	V	VI	VII	VIII	IX
Forest fallow	−	−	−	−	−	−	−	−
Bush fallow	−	−	+++	++	++++	−	++++	−
Short fallow	+	++	++	++	++	+	++	+
Organic manure	++++	++	−	+	++	+++	+	+++
Fertilizer	−	−	−	+	−	−	−	−
Crop rotation	++++	++	−	−	−	+++	−	++
Intercropping	++++	+	−	−	−	+++	−	+
Vegetation burning	+	+	+	−	++	++	+	−
Don't know[a]	0	2	8	3	1	0	1	0

$\chi^2 = 200$, d.f. = 49, $P < 0.001$.
II, Tigrinya; III, Saho; IV, Beni Amer; V, Maria; VI, Nara; VII, Bilen; VIII, Hedareb; IX, Beit Juk.
++++, Practised by all or known to all; +++, practised by or known to 75% of respondents; ++, practised by or known to 50% of respondents; +, practised by or known to 25% of respondents; −, not practised by or known to any or known to less than 25% of respondents.
[a]Those who did not know were those who came as children or were born in Sudan.

left to remain fallow for 7–8 years' duration, sometimes even up to 10–15 years and in some cases even for 25 years (Nye and Greenland, 1960). Among the 120 respondents who used bush fallow to replenish soil fertility, the average duration of the fallow period was 3 years after 5–6 years of cropping. Among the Beni Amer, shifting cultivation often involved change of location of cropped area and people. This was due to the fact that most of them were engaged in seasonal migration in search of pasture and water. This notwithstanding, however, even most of the Beni Amer families had permanent arable gardens in the river basins, which were cropped without fallow periods because they were fertilized by soils carried by floods from upstream. The fact that the duration of the fallow periods was short is an indication of relative shortage of land supply. These data show that the way people respond to deterioration of their environment, reflected among other things in depletion of soil nutrients and soil erosion, is influenced not only by the level of natural-resource endowment but also by their cultural and socio-economic backgrounds. Often the two are inextricably linked. As depicted by the data in Tables 7.3 and 7.4, the Eritrean peasantry used a great variety of conservation and other methods to counter land degradation or to minimize its consequences. The most important methods are discussed below.

Diversification of crops

One of the methods by which farmers countered land degradation was by restructuring or by diversification of the types of crops planted. Various crops were planted to match the different climatic and soil conditions. These were, for example, drought-resistant, moisture-efficient, quick-maturing and nitrogen-fixing. Climatic and soil conditions allowing, farmers planted a great variety of crops. This was done in response to the dietary needs of their families, market values, the erratic rainfall conditions, terrains, soils and the need to conserve and improve soil fertility. The major crops grown included cereals, oil-seeds, legumes, tobacco, cotton, earth-nuts and vegetables. Cereals included teff (*Eragrostis abyssinica*), *dagussa* (*Eleusine coracana*), barley, wheat, maize, sorghum, *zangeda*, millet, etc. (War Office Working Party, 1947c: 16–17). A great variety of leguminous (nitrogen-fixing) crops were also grown, such as chickpeas, beans, lentils, green peppers, onions, linseed, etc. Various types of oil-seeds including sesame, groundnuts, etc. were also grown. Citrus fruit trees, coffee and a great variety of vegetables introduced by the colonialists were also grown (War Office Working Party, 1947c: 16–17). Leguminous or nitrogen-fixing crops played a key role in the maintenance of soil fertility and in countering land degradation. In some parts of the plateau, multicropping was also practised. Following the harvest of the summer crops, fast-maturing crops such as barley and peas were grown by taking advantage of the small rains that fell between March and April. Legumes were often intercropped with cereals such as maize, sorghum and millet. Mixed cropping was adopted partly to replenish soil fertility and partly to spread risk. High-yielding but slow-maturing crops were mixed with fast-maturing but low-yielding crops. If the rains were good, the high-yielding crop eclipsed the low-yielding crop, but, if the rains were poor, the low-yielding and fast-maturing crop met the subsistence need of farmers.

Manuring

The other common method by which farmers maintained soil fertility or averted severe depletion of the arable land was by intensive use of organic manure. 'The people are thus well aware of the value of manure' (BMA, 1944: 4). This was done either by ferrying refuse and dung from the villages to the farms or by keeping livestock on the farms in the postharvest periods. Work teams were often organized on a mutual-help basis to carry manure from villages to farms. When farms lay fallow, cattle were kept in makeshift pens in order to fertilize the different parts of a given farm. It was common among landowners who lacked livestock of their own to grant exclusive grazing rights to cattle owners when their farms lay fallow in return for keeping the cattle in makeshift pens on the fallow land.

Terracing and water harvesting

The other method used by farmers to maintain soil fertility, to increase moisture availability and to overcome the problem of soil erosion was the use of comprehensive terracing. In his visit to the Eritrean plateau in the 1890s, Wylde stated, '[N]o expensive European engineers are required for this work, as the natives . . . thoroughly understand terrace cultivation and irrigation, and hardly waste a drop of water' (Wylde, 1901: 125). In the mid-1940s, Nadel also stated, '[T]he Eritrean cultivator makes extensive use of terracing where his farms lie on sloping ground; the terraces are well built and are kept up with much care' (Nadel, 1946a: 4). In some parts of the plateau, highly sophisticated terracing techniques were used to convert high terrains into cultivable fields. It was common for farmers on the plateau to construct contour ridges on foothills in order to spread rainwater carried by small streams down the hills. My own father's land in Lower Anseba in a village called Habrom Habarm was carved from hills and deep gullies with admirable skill. After my father's investment of large amounts of labour time to construct terraces, contour ridges and stone walls, the farm became the largest and most fertile in all the surrounding villages. Without the sophisticated methods of soil conservation and my father's deftness, the site would have been not only wasted, but a cause of loss of soil through erosion in the surrounding area. After the construction of walls to fill the large V-shaped gullies, the whole area became stabilized. The farm has been under continuous cultivation since it was opened for the first time, in the

1930s, without any sign of fertility loss. In the area, continuous cropping is one of the causes of yield decline, but this example suggests that, under favourable climatic conditions and proper management, high productivity levels can be sustained and depletion of soil nutrients can be countered. This example is cited not as unique, but to show the level of knowledge that underpinned the farming systems on the Eritrean plateau.

On the plateau, relatively advanced water-harvesting techniques were also constructed by farmers, using simple hand tools. This was widespread even among the Saho farmers, who cultivated marginal arable lands in the mountainous areas around Amba Soira and on the eastern edge of the escarpment in Akele-Guzai. In order to demonstrate this, one of the interviewees drew a sophisticated sketch of the earthen structures they used to construct before the onset of the rains on the boundaries of their farms. The aim was to check run-off and to conserve moisture by saving the flow of rainwater coming down the hills. Terraces were constructed across the slope; they could be one-sided, two-sided or even four-sided depending on the strength of the structures and the intensity of the flow of the rainwater. Irrigation was also used to cultivate gardens located in water basins. Recession cultivation on retreated or seasonally dried-up flood waters was also widespread among the Saho farmers on the eastern escarpment of Akele-Guzai.

Short fallow periods

The other dominant method used by farmers to maintain soil fertility was the practice of short fallow periods. 'In most parts of Eritrea fields are cultivated for only three years in succession and left fallow for two. In more fertile areas the period of cultivation is extended to five years' (BMA, 1944: 4). In light of the land shortage in the area, forest fallow and bush fallow were out of the question. Under the then existing conditions of land scarcity, only short fallow periods were alternated with 3 years of continuous cropping. The frequency of fallowing as well as the duration of fallow periods was determined by the conditions of supply and demand for land. In the areas which were heavily populated, fallow periods were reduced to 1 year. *Gedena* farms, i.e. farms lying close to villages, were often cultivated continuously because they were effectively fertilized by refuse and animal dung (BMA, 1944: 4). It is interesting to observe that, despite the land shortage under which the farmers on the plateau were operating, short fallow periods as a method of countering soil-fertility decline were common. Short fallow periods were practised mainly to increase moisture availability rather than to replenish soil nutrients through regrowth of vegetation on the fallow areas. Fields were left uncropped for one or two seasons, during which time the soils were turned three or four times to conserve moisture. The decayed weeds also contributed to improvement of soil fertility. In view of the land shortage faced by the farmers, this method was effective in countering yield decline. Intercropping was also practised among the plateau farmers.

Seasonal and permanent migration

One of the factors that contributed to sustainable resource use in the regions of high population density was out-migration. Out-migration was either seasonal or permanent. People and animals migrated from the areas of high population concentration to the sparsely populated and relatively resource-abundant lowland areas in the eastern, western and southern plains of the country. For example, it was customary for the people of southern Akele-Guzai to move in the summer months to the Hazomo plains in search of arable land and pasture. In the winter months, the people of northern Akele-Guzai and eastern Hamasen moved to the eastern lowlands in the areas around Ailet and Ghinda. The people of north-eastern Hamasen also moved during the winter months to the foothills and to the lowlands of the crown lands in Bahri to cultivate and to graze their livestock. The people of western and southern Serae also moved seasonally to the areas around Agordat and Tekombia in search of arable land and pasture. A considerable proportion of the people of north-western and south-western Hamasen as well as southern Senhit (Lower Anseba) moved to eastern Barka, Gash, Setit and even as far as Tigray during the dry seasons. Before the advent of Italian colonialism (1890), one way in which the Habab from northern Eritrea responded to the problem of environmental stress resulting from overstocking and overcultivation was by migrating with their livestock to the western lowlands (Nadel, 1945). It was customary for the Maria to move their livestock to the Gash and Setit valleys in search of pasture lands (Nadel, 1945).

During the coastal rains, from November to February, the livestock herders of the Saho tribes lived in the plain west of the Bay of Zula; from May to July they moved up the foothills and western edge of the plateau, which at that time of the year were covered with rich vegetation, and then to the plateau (BMA, 1943: 56–57). The movement from the plateau to the coastal area and the eastern escarpment during the winter months was facilitated by the coexistence of double climes of the two zones. On the plateau, the rainy season is between May and October. The coastal areas and the eastern escarpment enjoy winter rains between November and February. Thus, the seasonal migrations were designed to take advantage of these two climatic variations. The rainy season in the western lowlands is the same as that on the plateau. Migration to these areas was therefore induced by abundance of pasture and arable land and shortage of the same resources in the areas of origin of the migrants. Not only did out-migration enable the migrants to earn incomes, but their departure eased the pressure on the resources in the sending areas and access to resources per capita among those who stayed put increased.

In the last three to five decades, most of the migrants have stopped their homeward movements in favour of permanent settlement in the Barka and Gash Setit valleys in the western lowlands. As the population increased in the sending areas, it was no longer possible to bring new areas under cultivation and the available methods of countering fertility decline were not enough to absorb the growing population. Gradually, what once used to be seasonal migrations turned into permanent settlements in the western lowlands, where there was a greater supply of range and arable lands. This started, as we saw earlier, as a seasonal migration, but over time many of the migrants from the highlands, including those from Habab and Maria Tselam, decided to bring their families and to settle there permanently. There are many villages in western and north-western Hamasen, Lower Anseba, Maria Tselam and Habab, which either have been completely abandoned or have drastically reduced populations because of permanent migrations to the western lowlands, where arable and pasture lands were relatively abundant. Some of these villages on the plateau were among the largest and oldest villages in the country. To mention but a few, these include Habela, Deda, Liban, Deki-Dashem, Deki-Shehai, Melezanai, Deke-Andu and many smaller villages. Some of these permanent migrations (e.g. Habab) took place as early as the time when the territory was under Egyptian rule (1870s). Other migrations have been taking place since the first and second decades of this century (e.g. Maria). Permanent migrations from the plateau began mainly between the 1960s and 1970s.

All land situated below 850 m above sea level was converted into crown land by the 1909 and 1926 colonial land statutes. Formally, that meant outright expropriation of 'native' land rights. The rights of the agropastoral communities in the western lowlands, especially in the Barka and Gash Setit valleys, were further undermined at the end of the 1960s and early 1970s, when the pressure on the land in the highlands became severe, threatening the survival of many of the farmers. This was partly due to overfragmentation of the holdings to uneconomic levels and partly due to loss of productivity resulting from overcultivation. Thus, as stated earlier, many of the people, especially those from western and north-western Hamasen and southern Senhit, saw an opportunity to migrate to the thinly populated fertile plains of the Barka and Gash Setit valleys to settle permanently. These areas were in the past used for seasonal livestock migration; thus the migrants were familiar with the areas. During the dry seasons most of the dry (non-milking) cattle were moved to these areas.

Not only did this period coincide with the beginning of the Eritrean struggle for national independence but the Barka valley was actually its birthplace. One of the instruments used by the Ethiopian state to weaken the nationalist movement was to encourage or even provide incentives to immigrants from the plateau, where there was land hunger, to migrate and to settle permanently in the western lowlands. This represented a serious encroachment on the traditional grazing rights of the pastoralists. This gradually led to the weakening of the customary rights of the local population. Ethiopia's aim was to nip the fledgling national liberation movement in the bud by facilitating migration of a large Christian population, which it wrongly assumed would weaken the liberation movement.

The fact that the highlanders for the first time considered permanent settlement in the hot and malaria-infested lowlands shows that the level of population pressure had increased considerably. This is because settlement in the lowlands had never been an option favoured by the highland populations. The highlanders were reluctant to abandon their villages, which have historically been the focus of social life, and they also detested the harsh climate and the malaria-infested areas. When population pressure on the plateau, exacerbated by the colonial alienation of land, led to fierce competition for arable and grazing lands between the 1930s and 1950s, the peasantry on the plateau was faced with two options, namely to '. . . expand or to starve; and in this plight, the spacious and thinly populated lands of the Moslem tribes beckoned invitingly. Any mass migration to these lowland prairies was precluded by the . . . [highland peasantry's] distaste for the intense summer heat and their fear for malaria' (Trevaski, 1960: 55). From the 1960s onwards, neither the distaste for the climate nor the fear for malaria stopped many peasants from migrating permanently to the lowland prairies in search of alternative arable and pasture lands.

The ownership rights of pastoral nomads and agropastoralists were abrogated when their traditional lands were converted into state property during the first decade of this century, but until the late 1950s and early 1960s this had not substantially affected their usership rights. Formally, the lands were turned into state property with the enactment of the land statute of 1909, as amended in 1926. In reality, however, the traditional user communities continued exercising de facto ownership rights as if the crown lands were their own. It was only with the influx of large numbers of immigrants and the expansion of cash-crop production (cotton and sesame) by commercial farmers that they lost control over some of the arable lands and the CPRs.

Since the 1950s, the traditional resource-management regimes among the

Eritrean traditional resource users have been undergoing fundamental changes due to political instability, population pressure, commercialization of agriculture and misguided government policies. The population pressure in some areas has led to breakdowns of traditional resource-management regimes with the consequence of resource overuse, manifested in overgrazing, overcultivation and excessive tree felling. The situation was exacerbated by political instability, which disrupted the traditional transhumant mobility developed in response to variation in the environment. When insecurity and deliberate government actions prevented seasonal mobility, people and livestock were forcibly kept in limited geographical areas, which induced inappropriate land-use practices with inevitable resource depletion.

There are no studies to show the environmental consequences of these migrations, either in the areas of origin or at the destination. Mass migration from the densely populated villages no doubt eased the pressure on the land, but the departure of the most productive members of the populations may also have led to the neglect of conservation works which may have accelerated the problem of land degradation in the sending areas. The influx of large numbers with different techniques of production and resource-management regimes, developed in response to highland environmental conditions, may also have had a detrimental effect on resource use in the lowlands. These issues are interesting, but cannot be determined a priori.

Conclusion

In Eritrea, although there were diverse types of land-ownership rights, all of them, except those in the state domain lands, entailed permanent titles to land. As we saw earlier, *risti*, *tselmi* and *diesa* ownership rights were widespread in many parts of Eritrea, such as Akele-Guzai, Serae, Hamasen, Halhal, Beit Juk, Medri-Bilen, Maria Tselam and Nara lands. In all these areas, CPRs such as water-holes, wells,[13] grazing lands, woodlands, livestock routes, etc. were owned and utilized collectively. They were also managed sustainably by the commoners. All these were exclusive property resources accessible only to certified members of the given community. Outsiders were only allowed temporary access and through prior agreements in which the conditions of entry and use were determined in advance. Every certified member of the collective user group also had a right to use the CPRs and an obligation to comply with the institutional rules governing access to and use of such resources. The communities had devised enforcement mechanisms to implement the said rules and to monitor the behaviour of their members. There were also different mechanisms which fostered collective discipline, designed to impose on members of the user groups some form of limitation on their activities in the presumed interest of the communities concerned as a whole. Most of these communities had a traditional and hereditary leadership, who commanded great respect because of their authority, which stemmed from remote ancestries. Given the scarcity of the natural-resource base in these areas, not only had the communities devised institutional decisions, enforcement mechanisms and collective discipline, but they also used different methods of conservation, partly to counter land degradation and partly to increase the productive capacity of their land resource. Whenever these proved inadequate, the pressure on the land was offset by temporary and permanent migration to areas of relative resource abundance.

In the majority of cases, the migrant communities rarely introduced their traditional resource-management systems to the new areas. The tendency was to adapt to production systems prevalent at the area of destination. The Saho that migrated from eastern Akele-Guzai to the western part of the province and Serae not only adapted to the sedentary lifestyle, but also lost no time in adapting to the resource-management regimes which existed in the areas. When they migrated again to the western lowlands in the 1950s, many of them reverted to a seminomadic way of life. When the Maria migrated to the western lowlands between the 1920s and 1940s, they also reverted to a seminomadic way of life. The migrants from the plateau to the Barka, Gash and Setit valleys also abandoned their long-established techniques of preventing soil erosion (terracing) and maintaining soil fertility such as the use of organic manure. This was partly because land was not in short supply and partly because some of the diverse indigenous technical knowledge was location-specific.

There were also temporary titles of lease and usufruct which did not give rise to ownership, but only to possessory (usufructuary) rights on property belonging to the state, individuals or village communities. In Bahri and the western lowlands, the traditional and immigrant resource users had only rights of use on government lands. In the state domain lands, especially in the western lowlands, the user communities did not, in the majority of cases, devise resource-regulating institutions. This was not because of the communities' inability to devise such systems, but because the natural resources from which they derived their livelihood were not scarce. The fact that the user communities lacked permanent titles to the resources they utilized might also have been a contributory factor to the failure to devise institutional rules governing the use of such resources. The implication of this is that it is only in situations where there is a permanent collective or individual ownership (security of tenure) that such institutions facilitate the emergence of regulatory systems that conserve and allocate resources efficiently. In situations where there is no individual or collective permanent title to resources, such resources are open-access or 'free-rider' resources. Thus, it becomes difficult or even impossible to devise regulatory systems for the conservation, regulation of use and efficient allocation of such resources.

The Eritrean experience shows that, if resources are abundant, the role of social institutions in the management of such resources is minimal. This is illustrated by looking at the various groups of the refugee communities in the period preceding their flight to Sudan when they occupied different ecological zones and natural-resource endowments and population densities varied considerably. It is striking to note that, among the communities where resource endowments in relation to population were scarce and where there were secure tenurial systems (communal, family or individual), elaborate institutional rules, enforcement mechanisms and advanced environmental conservation methods emerged to regulate access, control and use as well as to ensure long-term sustainability of the existing arable lands and CPRs. In these situations, the *raison d'être* of social institutions was to ensure subsistence security, equitable distribution of resources and sustainability of CPRs. This was done by striking a balance between the objectives of avoidance of overuse and achievement of optimal use. Except in famine years, whenever it was required by resource conservation, the former prevailed over the latter. In the areas where natural resources were abundant, institutions did not play important regulatory and allocative roles. Individuals were free to decide to use the abundant resources with minimal communal interference.

In the following chapter, the existing land-tenure system on the scheme is described. An attempt is also made to answer the following questions. Do the institutional decision systems and enforcement mechanisms that existed in many parts of Eritrea in the pre-flight period still exist on the scheme? If the institutional decision systems are absent, what were the factors that weakened or undermined their existence? Does the land-tenure system existing on the scheme facilitate devising a regulatory system that would help conserve and allocate the resources efficiently? Do the refugees apply the same or similar indigenous technical knowledge to that applied in their country of origin on the scheme? If not, why not?

Notes

1. The available fragmentary data at the Qala en Nahal scheme do not extend beyond the end of the 1960s. To unravel some of the factors that influence the way the refugee farmers use the resources on and around the scheme requires looking beyond the 1960s.
2. The *enda* is a basic kinship unit. It consists of the offspring of a common ancestor, many generations back, by whose name the *enda* is known.
3. This was at least true until the 1960s.
4. The so-called 'marriageable' age was defined by customary law.
5. The northern plateau in this case refers to the Ethiopian and Eritrean plateau.
6. Nadel, writing in the mid-1940s, stated that it was in the last 100 years that these people began to adapt to a sedentary way of life by migrating westward amidst the plateau population (Nadel, 1946a: 3).
7. According to the report prepared in the Native Affairs Section of the BMA in Eritrea, *sedbi* means 'alliance'. It was a means by which tribal or other groups enter into a pact of friendship and mutual assistance. The *sedbi* institution is believed to have emerged to govern the terms of the pact entered between the former nomadic group immigrants and the original occupiers of the land in the plateau. The institution of *sedbi* was more explicit and formalized in the Akele-Guzai province, where the former nomadic groups had penetrated in search of arable land (BMA, 1944: 16).
8. Art. 92, Saho Tribes' Code of Customary Law, 1943.
9. The Beni Amer have a strong oral tradition. Their history is transmitted from one generation to the other carefully.
10. The governor of the Barka province at that time was Ali Haseno. It is an interesting territory of future research to look at the role played by the governor in pulling the roughly estimated number of 5,000 Saho families from Tigray, Obel, Hazemo and elsewhere to Quorequen with their traditional chief, Saad Aghà anear Ogardet, where they received arable and grazing lands belonging to the state.
11. It is important to state, however, that they stayed in the Gash area for only 13 years (1954–1967) before they were forced to flee to Sudan. They did not stay long enough, as the Maria did in the western lowlands, to be able to introduce their previous techniques of degradation-countering measures. This is not to suggest, however, that they would have made use of their knowledge if they had stayed longer. Such speculation lacks an empirical basis.
12. This refers to the areas where the Maria lived before their flight to Sudan, not to their areas of origin.
13. Wells sunk by individuals were owned accordingly.

8

Institutions, Social Stability and Depletion of Common Resources on the Scheme

> Institutions include any form of constraint that human beings devise to shape human interaction . . . Institutional constraints include both what individuals are prohibited from doing and, sometimes, under what conditions some individuals are permitted to undertake certain activities. (D. North, 1993)

The preceding chapters measured and examined, among other things, the extent and the causes of land degradation (reduction in productive capability) in physical and social terms. After identifying to what extent and why land degradation has been taking place, the complex question remained: why do resource users make land-use decisions which deplete the scarce resources or use their resources in a manner which not only is unsustainable, but also threatens the future of their own children?[1] The chapter examines the factors that induce the resource users at the local level to resort to inappropriate land-use practices. It considers the effects of security of tenure and refugee status, mechanisms for control, land availability and the role of traditional leadership and moral authority in the regulation of use and access to resources. The role of environmental awareness in conservation will be discussed in the following chapter.

Tenurial security and conservation

One of the working hypotheses of this study has been that insecurity of tenure (individual, family or communal) not only discourages investing labour and capital in building conservation works, maintaining such works and undertaking other degradation-reducing measures, but can also potentially engender careless and voracious land-use practices which risk damaging the environment. So it is important to examine the tenurial status of refugees and local Sudanese and to see whether or not the existing arrangements constrain or promote an ecologically sustainable system of resource management. The land-tenure system in the refugee settlements is examined in the context of the general land laws of the country and the tenurial status of the Sudanese small farmers in the area.

Following the independence of Sudan in the mid-1950s, the demand for cultivable land increased in the central rain lands of the Gedaref district. The Ministry of Interior enacted the 'Scheme for the Disposal of Rainlands, 1959', which established a Land Allotment Board to lease land to private tractor owners. The right of ownership, however, was always retained by the government. Applicants had to be Sudanese, have access to the necessary agricultural machinery, have the necessary capital to meet the running costs and new investments and have agricultural knowledge, experience, managerial ability and time (Agabawi, 1968). The last four criteria indicate the government's determination to exclude absenteeism in mechanized rain-fed crop production. Despite these criteria, most mechanized rain-fed schemes are operated by *wakils* (representatives) while leaseholders are engaged in non-farm, commercial or other activities in the cities. In practice, then, the leaseholders' agricultural knowledge, experience, managerial skill and time mattered little to both the distribution and the operation of such schemes.

In Sudan, both small farmers and pastoralists lack formal secure and permanent title to land and to the other Common-property resources (CPRs) from which they derive their livelihoods. As Horowitz and Salem-Murdock point out, however, there are gross discrepancies between formal and effective land tenure systems in the rural areas of Sudan. 'In law, all unregistered land belongs to the state. In practice, however, access to most grazing land and rainfed agricultural land (other than mechanized schemes) is regulated by local principles of tenure' (Horowitz and Salem-Murdock, 1991). This view overlooks the tenurial insecurity the Unregistered Land Act (ULA) has caused for traditional resource users. In passing this Act, in 1970, the state vested in itself absolute power to expropriate any unregistered land at will. This enabled it to allocate land for development projects operated by both the public and the private sectors without being constrained by communal or tribal land rights. Section 4 (1) of the Act states:

> [N]otwithstanding anything contained in the Land Settlement and Registration Act, 1925 or any other law in force, *all land of any kind whether waste, forest, occupied or unoccupied, which is not registered before the commencement of this Act shall, on such commencement, be the property of the Government and shall be deemed to have been registered as such, as if the provisions of the Land Settlement and Registration Act, 1925, have been duly complied with.* (ULA, 1970 – emphasis added)

One of the cornerstones of the condominium government's land policies, as stipulated in the Land Settlement and Registration Ordinance of 1925, had been to register all land. Despite this intention, however, on the eve of independence in 1956, most arable, wood and grazing lands were owned and controlled by tribal communities and individuals. The 1970 legislation, unlike its predecessor, not only gave government presumptive ownership unless proved otherwise, but granted undisputed and full ownership over all unregistered lands. The only exception was when the President of the Republic exempted a certain piece of land on the grounds that it would be unjust to apply the provisions of the Act because it was used by private persons long before the commencement of the Act (ULA, 1970: section 3). No measures of redress were provided by the Act against presidential denial of exemption. The decision of the President was final and subject to no review. The Act also prohibited establishment of easements,[2] acquisition of rights on or titles to such land by prescription (ULA, 1970: section 5) unless the President of the Republic had ordered that the provisions of the Act should not apply.[3] The legislation further stated, '[I]f any person is in occupation of any land which is registered or deemed to be registered in the name of the Government, the Government may order his eviction from such land and may use reasonable force if necessary' (ULA, 1970: section 8). The impact of this legislation on the country's system of land tenure and on the environment was dramatic. Following the promulgation of the ULA (1970), about 90% of the Gedaref district's land, including all its forests, rangelands, water, and so on, came formally under government control (Abu Sin, 1989a). Even though the ULA was repealed by the Civil Transaction Act of 1984,[4] the latter also states that all unregistered land belongs to the government.

Below it will be argued that Sudan's environmental problems in general, and problems in the Gedaref region in particular, stem, *inter alia*, mainly from the nationalization of previously sustainably managed resources. Worse still, the drastic changes to ownership and control structures introduced by the Act were implemented in the complete absence of land-use policies. In 1960, the Soil Conservation, Land Use and Water Programming Administration presented a proposal on land-use policy, but the proposal was not approved. To date there is no land-use policy for the country as a whole. For example, in 1975 a reconnaissance team of the National Research Council and the Ministry of Agriculture, Food and Natural Resources stated:

> [I]t was evident to the reconnaissance teams, both from their own observations and from discussions with Provincial Governors and their staffs, that the most fundamental contributory factors in the current crisis are the lack of any natural resource and land use planning policies. From these basic deficiencies stem many other serious omissions: no natural resource legislation and no means of implementing (and enforcing) management policies; no range management procedures; no control of water resources; no control of stocking rates; no agricultural policy or management. It is not surprising, under the present conditions of increasing population pressure, that the land is incapable of withstanding the present levels of exploitation. (Lamprey, 1988: 4)

After 1970, the government could allocate any unregistered land to an alternative use by invoking section 8 of the Act. In this way, the state has justified expropriations of resources previously controlled by the small farmers and pastoralists in the central rain lands and elsewhere in the country; most of the mechanized rain-fed or irrigated schemes were established on 'unregistered' and yet traditionally used land. The problem stemmed not only from the fact that the state took upon itself the right to expropriate land for investment, but also from their failure to elaborate a system of codifying customary land rights.

Access to grazing land and rain-fed agricultural land is regulated by customary law only where land has not been targeted for development or until the government or one of its development agencies decides to exercise its right of ownership under the ULA (1970). This suggests that, in the long run, no occupier of unregistered land has secure tenurial status. In some areas, where traditional land-tenure systems are still intact, the coming into force of the ULA notwithstanding, local access to and use of resources are still regulated by customary laws. Thus, disregarding the lack of permanent titles and the risk of future loss of ownership to commercial farmers or the government, Sudanese farmers and pastoralists perceive their rights to grazing and cultivation of lands within the boundaries of their traditional communal or tribal territories as a 'God-given' and as an inherent attribute of belonging to a given tribe or community. As we shall see below, the refugees do not consider their right to grazing and arable land in Sudan as a 'God-given right'. They do not see their right to arable, grazing, woodlands and water resources entailing any more than the right of usufruct or temporary use of property belonging to the state (Table 8.1).

Refugees' tenurial rights are governed neither by customary principles nor by the general land laws of the country, but rather by the Regulation of Asylum Act (1974). A special institutional arrangement is made for the refugee settlements and their administration. The government, by virtue of its ownership right of unregistered land, designates land for the establishment of refugee settlements. One example of this is the setting aside of about 40,000 *feddans* of land by presidential decree near Jebel Meharigat in the area west of the Gedaref – Kashm el Girba road (Huntings Technical Services, 1976). The Asylum Act states explicitly that '*no*

Table 8.1   Distribution by perception of ownership of *hawashas*

	Refugees (n = 215)	Sudanese (n = 91)
The government	98.6	3.3
The village	1.4	2.2
The sheik	0.0	0.0
The farmer him/herself	0.0	94.5
Total	100.0	100.0

refugee shall own lands or immoveables in the Sudan' (Regulation of Asylum Act, 1974: section 9 – emphasis added). The policy governing the refugees' right to land is codified in the draft implementation of the Asylum Act, according to which:

> [T]he Minister shall allocate agricultural land within the settlement area for individual refugees during their stay in the country and according to the Government's investment system. *Such land may not be inherited, or prescribed but may be transferred to family members. The refugees should not dispose of land in the way of rent or in any other way for the benefit of another person except with the permission of the authorities.* (Cited in Kibreab, 1987 – emphasis added)

Arguably, the tenurial status of the refugees in the settlements is not markedly different from the general tenurial status of their Sudanese counterparts in the area on unregistered land. But, de facto, traditional forms of tenure still continue to exist in the areas where there has been no marked expansion of mechanized rain-fed farming. In fact, in the Qala en Nahal area, where the refugee settlements are located, the Sudanese farmers consider their holdings as their own private property which they can dispose of at will (Table 8.1). Where potentially cultivable land exists, it is allocated by the village sheikhs and the allocatees (holders) would subsequently consider the cleared land as their own to dispose of in any form.

One of the consequences of the acute shortage of arable land in the refugee settlement has been the emergence of a land market. Some refugees clandestinely enter into sharecropping arrangements, or sell, pledge, mortgage or give away part or all their *hawashas* (holdings) as if they were the rightful owners of such land. These transactions could at any time be declared null and void if brought to the attention of the settlement manager (*mudhir*). The degree of autonomy enjoyed by the Sudanese farmers, in spite of the absence of *de jure* land rights, was much greater than that of the refugee farmers in terms of the freedom to dispose of their land at will. The limitations or threats to local small farmers' rights of land-ownership (as they perceived it) were represented by the growth of *Acacia senegal* trees, which could result in repossession of the *hawashas* by the concession holders and by the expansion of commercial agriculture, which often encroached upon fallow areas and areas of potential expansion. This was as a consequence of the Unregistered Land Act (1970).

The data in Table 8.1 show that nearly 95% of the Sudanese cultivators in the area considered the land they were cultivating as their own private property while almost all refugees considered themselves as only having the right of use of government land. The 'ownership rights' of the peasants are not legally enforceable. However, it is not only the peasants in this area who consider the land under their possession as private holding. Studies elsewhere in Sudan draw the same conclusion.

For example, Halaand found the same perceptions in southern Darfur, where continuously cultivated land was considered by the farmers as their own private property (Halaand, 1980). Other studies show this to be true in north Kordofan (Reeves and Frankenberger, 1981) and in White Nile Province (Horowitz and Salem-Murdock, 1991).

In areas where there has been no marked expansion of mechanized rain-fed crop production, state ownership or arable land has been formal rather than real. Often there is no direct government interference in the manner land rights are enjoyed by the traditional users unless the areas concerned are targeted for development. This is not, however, achieved by design, but rather by government inefficiency. The government has been unable to enforce the new institutional arrangements. If it is true, therefore, that lack of security of individual or communal tenure (real and/or perceptual) has a bearing on the behaviour of resource users, it follows theoretically that the Sudanese sedentary farmers in the areas in which they perceive their tenurial status as 'secure' will be more concerned with the long-term sustainability of the environment than the refugees, who consider themselves as temporary resource users.

Of the sample refugee household heads, 49% thought that, since the ownership of the land belonged to the government of Sudan, so should the responsibility of undertaking and maintaining conservation work. Another 12% stated that it should be the responsibility of the United Nations High Commissioner for Refugees (UNHCR). Only 37% considered it their own responsibility to carry out conservation work on their holdings. The response of the Sudanese farmers was radically different: none expected others to undertake conservation work on their behalf. This does not imply, however, that the Sudanese farmers are actually undertaking conservation work. The data are about perceptions rather than about actual behaviour. The results, nevertheless, clearly show that lack of secure tenure is a relevant factor which can potentially influence the conservation investment decisions of resource users. This indicates that whether or not farmers will invest their scarce resources in measures that counter reduction of the productive capability of land (degradation) is, among other things, determined by tenurial security. However, whether small farmers invest their scarce resources in natural-resource conservation is not solely a function of tenurial security (labour availability is also important) although tenurial security may be the most decisive factor influencing investment decisions in conservation work. On the scheme, there is evidence to suggest that it is easier to implement natural-resource conservation or land degradation-countering programmes among the Sudanese farmers, who consider the land they are cultivating as their own individual private property, than among the refugees, who regard themselves as having no right other than usufruct. The actual difference may disappear when the government decides to exercise its right of ownership in the areas where only de facto traditional rights of ownership still exist.

Indigenous farming knowledge and conservation

Since the refugees are of diverse ethnic and socio-economic backgrounds, it is interesting to see if their perceptions about their responsibilities to undertake conservation work are influenced by their previous backgrounds.[5] The results show a statistically significant relationship between sense of dependence on outside intervention and the background characteristics of the respondents (Table 8.2).[6]

Table 8.2   Farmers' views concerning responsibility for undertaking conservation work (%)

Ethnicity	Government	Farmer himself	UNHCR	ACORD	Backgrounds
Tigrinya	25.0	75.0	0.0	0.0	Sedentary
Saho	56.4	33.3	10.2	0.0	Agropastoral
Beni Amer	67.4	20.0	10.5	2.1	Pastoral
Maria	22.6	48.4	25.8	3.2	Agropastoral
Nara	30.8	61.5	7.7	0.0	Sedentary
Bilen	40.0	20.0	40.0	0.0	Sedentary
Hedareb	33.3	66.7	0.0	0.0	Pastoral
Beit Juk	8.3	91.7	0.0	0.0	Sedentary

$\chi^2 = 70$, d.f.$= 7$, P<0.001.
UNHCR, United Nations High Commissioner for Refugees; ACORD.

With the exception of the Hedareb, the sense of dependence was much higher among the former pastoralists and agropastoralists, who had not previously had experience in this sort of conservation work, than among the former sedentary farmers. The farmers with sedentary backgrounds, such as the Tigrinya, Nara and Beit Juk, saw it as their own responsibility to carry out environmental conservation on their farms. Thus, even though lack of tenurial security is an important factor influencing farmers' potential investment decisions, among some of the refugee groups this is exacerbated by unreasonable dependence on outside assistance and unfamiliarity with local environmental conditions.

In practice, however, few refugees or, for that matter, Sudanese farmers engage in any visible conservation activities. Since there is an association between previous experiences in conservation work and willingness to undertake such work on the scheme, the lack of willingness expressed by the individuals who came from the areas where conservation know-how did not exist may be taken as a reflection of lack of knowledge rather than lack of willingness to undertake conservation work and to maintain such work.

Is there evidence to show that the refugees with their tenurial insecurity are using the natural environment carelessly? There is no conclusive evidence which lends support to this thesis. The difference in tenurial insecurity between the two communities is a matter of degree. Among the refugee respondents, only 18% think that they are careless resource users in comparison with the Sudanese farmers, whereas, among the Sudanese farmers, 44% think that some of the refugees use the natural resources in the area carelessly without being bothered about long-term sustainability. This alleged careless use of resources specifically refers to livestock trespass on cropped land. There are more refugee families who own livestock than among the local population (see Chapter 6). One of the problems mentioned by the local people in having refugees in the area, therefore, is animal trespass on cropped areas. Even though there is a statistically significant relationship between the respondents' nationality and their perception regarding the refugees' careless attitude in terms of resource use,[7] the majority do not consider refugees as careless users of natural resources. However, the fact that 18% of the refugee respondents look upon themselves as careless resource users may suggest that there is a relationship (albeit weak) between tenurial security and sustainable resource use or willingness to undertake conservation work.

On balance, the presence of the refugees in the area was deemed beneficial. This is because the local people see that their presence has brought them more benefits than harm in terms of water supply, health care, tractors, schools, markets, access roads, etc. The two communities live in relative peace and harmony. The major concern of the local population was about what would happen to their area when the refugees return to their country of origin. The major causes of environmental degradation in the area are attributed by the local population not to the refugees, but rather to expansion of commercial mechanized rain-fed agriculture and charcoal production by wholesalers who come from distant urban areas.

Farm size and conservation

The central question that we need to ask is whether there is a marked difference between the refugee and Sudanese farmers regarding investment in conservation work and/or in undertaking other degradation-countering measures. The practice of fallow periods as a technique of restoring and conserving soil fertility has almost disappeared (see Chapters 2 and 4). Some Sudanese farmers were still practising short fallow periods to conserve and restore soil fertility on their plots, albeit on a reduced scale.

The data in Table 8.3 show this to be a function of accessibility to adequate arable land. Among refugees, land shortage was the main reason for practising continuous cropping without any form of fallow. Most of the refugee farmers have been cultivating their *hawashas* continuously since the inception of the settlement. The mean land size of the Sudanese farmers is much bigger than that of the refugees and consequently the practice of fallow periods was more prevalent on the Sudanese farms. Among the Sudanese respondents, about 52% left part of their *hawashas* to rest. Of the 48% who did not practise fallowing, 70% were unable to do so because of land shortage. The difference in fallowing practice among the refugees and Sudanese is not the result of differential tenurial status but stems from differential access to arable land. The mean land size per family among the Sudanese was 25.36 *feddans* as opposed to 9.27 *feddans* per landowning family among the refugees. About 36% of the refugee families are landless and the mean farm size for all the refugee families is below 5 *feddans*.

Land shortage, however, cannot explain the refugee farmers' failure to undertake other agricultural techniques that would help them to restore and conserve soil fertility. Since lack of adequate land precluded them from leaving part or all their farms to lie fallow, this should have given them an impetus or a good reason to search for an alternative technique of restoring soil fertility or for countering the degrading effects of continuous cropping.

The literature on traditional agriculture abounds with postulates which suggest an inverse relationship between population pressure and shifts in land-use practices, namely a shift from extensive to intensive cultivation (see Chapter 1). Thus, as expected, the practice of fallow periods was more common among the Sudanese farmers, where the land/man ratio was relatively higher than among the refugees.

Table 8.3 Distribution of respondents by reasons that precluded practice of fallow periods (%)

	Refugee	Sudanese
Land shortage	97.0	70.0
Fear of losing land possession	3.0	30.0

$\chi^2 = 53$, d.f. $= 2$, P<0.001.

Among refugees, cultivation was more intensive. But intensification in this case does not imply application of innovative agricultural techniques, such as the use of manure or other fertilizers or the planting of leguminous crops, etc. Neither the refugee farmers nor the Sudanese in the area applied these agricultural practices. Intensification on the scheme refers to increased frequency with which the available land is cropped without fallow. The consequence of this intensification in the absence of agricultural techniques which offset its impact was overcultivation, manifested in depletion of soil nutrients necessary for crop plant growth. As expected, the problem of overcultivation was more severe among the refugee farmers than among the Sudanese and this difference is attributed to differential access to arable land.

Governance of the common resources on the scheme

Are the arable lands, pasture, water, livestock routes and woodlands on the scheme CPRs managed collectively by the community, or are they 'open-access' resources? Each regime has radically different management implications for the use of and access to such resources. The question of management of access to and use of 'common' property is still a subject of heated debate among social scientists. There are some who argue that 'common' property is by its very nature liable to induce unsustainable land-use practices which undermine the existence of the common property itself. One of the major exponents of this view is the biologist, Hardin, who, in a discussion of the world population problem, took the example of common pasture used by all members of a community to show what he called the 'tragedy of the commons', which obtained in the case of grazing too many individually owned cattle on a given area of common pasture. Hardin argued that, since the private benefit of grazing an additional head of cattle on a common pasture exceeds the private cost, because the latter is shared by all the members of the community or the cost is externalized, the rational herdsman will add another animal to his herd and the same decision will be reached by all members of the collectivity and the outcome is tragic, reflected in the complete dissipation of the resource owned in common (Hardin, 1968). Owing to the inability of the user community to make and enforce rules that discourage individual excess, resource overexploitation – destruction of the common pasture – is unavoidable: hence the famous phrase, the 'tragedy of the commons'. The solution suggested by the exponents of the 'tragedy of the commons' model is privatization or forcible imposition of rules from outside, i.e. heavy-handed state intervention (Hardin, 1978: 314).

Exponents of the property-rights paradigm also argue that, in the absence of a property right which embodies a cost-reward structure by internalizing costs and benefits, each user will be motivated to overuse the resource owned in common and to underinvest in the resource. The outcome is dissipation of the resource concerned (Cheung, 1970; Demsetz, 1972; Johnson, 1972). The solution they suggest is privatization, where costs and benefits would be internalized and consequently there would be an incentive for efficient allocation of the resource. Smith, for example, argues: '[T]he only way to avoid the tragedy of the commons in natural resources and wildlife is to end the common property system by creating a system of private property rights' (Smith, 1981: 467). In a similar fashion to that of Hardin, Picaredi and Seifert attribute the disaster that afflicted the Sahel to what they call the 'tragedy of the commons syndrome', resulting from exploitative traditional pastoral land-use practices, which they assume is inherent in the pastoralists' culture (Picaredi and Seifert, 1976).

Hardin's 'tragedy of the commons' and the arguments embodied in the property-right paradigm have been heavily criticized, both for lack of empirical evidence and for the failure to distinguish at conceptual level between CPRs, where there are a series of customary rules regulating individual rights of access, and 'open-access' resource, where the rules regulating individual rights of access are lacking (Circiacy-Wantrup and Bishop, 1975; Runge, 1983, 1984; Shepherd, 1989).

In the case of CPRs, there are tacit and explicit traditional sets of rules which regulate individual rights of access, and a situation of overexploitation does not occur for lack of resource-regulating rules and enforcement mechanisms (Runge, 1983, 1984). The social pressure on individual members to cooperate and to practise self-restraint with regard to use of CPRs is very strong, and 'free-riding' is not a common occurrence. Access is exclusively limited to members of the collectivity and outsiders are excluded, while with 'free access' entry is open to all, including outsiders. The problem of an 'open-access' resource lies in this unlimited right of entry (Runge, 1983). There is empirical evidence that disruption of traditional arrangements that protected and regulated the use of CPRs, either by land reform or by extension of state ownership over previous 'common' resources, has led to overexploitation of such resources because of their *de facto* conversion into 'open-access' resources (Jodha, 1980, 1985, 1987).

It is important then to determine whether the pasture, water, woodlands and animal routes on the scheme are CPRs, owned and controlled by the collectivity, or whether they are 'open-access' resources, in which there is unlimited entry and where there are no rules regulating access and use. The distinction is not only important regarding regulation of access by individual members in the collectivity, but whether or not the collectivity can deny access to outsiders is determined by such a distinction. If the resources within the scheme are 'open-access', not only are they expected to be depleted as a result of external pressure (such as tree-lopping for charcoal production, tapping of gum arabic from the *Acacia senegal* trees, exploitation of water resources by outsiders), but individual rights of access and use are not subject to customary regulation. Thus, resource overexploitation may be inevitable.

The grazing lands, livestock routes, woodlands and natural water resources on the scheme are not sustainably and equitably managed either by the members of the user community or by the government. Thus, they should be distinguished from CPRs. CPRs refer to the resources which are accessible to all members of a given identifiable community and to which no individual in that community or outside that community has exclusive property or access rights. In many Third World countries, CPRs play significant roles in the sustenance of the life of the rural poor. However, whether CPRs are used in a sustainable manner and constitute a source of sustenance to the rural poor depends, on the one hand, on the existing institutional arrangements which govern ownership and control rights and, on the other, on the way use and access to such resources are regulated. This is not to suggest, however, that all CPRs which are regulated by local resource users are always used sustainably. In most cases, this is an empirical question. However, in comparison with state-owned common resources, community-controlled CPRs tend to be more sustainable.

For example, in rural Sudan CPRs have traditionally included village arable lands, grazing lands, including permanent uncultivable pastures, fallow lands, postharvest cropped areas, woodlands, some river basins, stock migration routes and water sources, with the exception of wells, which can sometimes be owned by an individual or a group of families. With the exception of the riverine areas, where arable land was privately owned, each tribe had its own large tribal territory, known as *dar*. The resources within the *dars* were considered to be the property of a whole tribe (Awad, 1975; El Mahdi, 1976). The heads of tribes and their subordinates were the custodians of the tribes' territory, which they managed with the advice and assistance of a council of subchiefs. Arable land was allotted by the sheikh in council to the members of the tribe, which was divided into *omedias* (sections of the tribe) and further subdivided into *feriqs* (subsections). Every member was entitled to a plot of land to cultivate and to utilize any form of wildlife that existed upon it (Awad, 1975: 217). Individual families also had the right to a plot of land for hut/s and a compound. In the less densely populated areas, the same system is still in operation. Outside the land allotted to individual members, the remaining CPRs were owned communally in the form of a village, group of villages or subsections of a tribe (*feriq*). The institution of CPRs in the refugees' country of origin and in Sudan is an old one. In Sudan the institution of the CPRs was weakened and in some places eliminated after the promulgation and enforcement of the ULA (1970).

The distinguishing features of CPRs are, first, that ownership or usufructuary rights, including security against arbitrary eviction, are in the hands of the user community. Control of the resources is exercised by the same community, often with no significant outside interference. Second, collective and individual rights of access and use are regulated by a series of tacit and explicit institutional rules. The key role played by institutions in the management of CPRs is to reduce uncertainty among individual members of the user group, by defining and stabilizing their expectations (Bromley and Chapagain, 1984: 870: North, 1993: 6), and to 'organize, process and store the essential information required to coordinate human behaviour' (Runge, 1983). Third, at the local level, hereditary or elected leaderships or community officers supervise the application of regulations. In traditional societies where there is a certain degree of integration into a modern state structure, the effectiveness of traditional institutional arrangements and the authority of traditional rule-enforcers can be strengthened if such rules and the decisions of the traditional enforcers are enforceable at law. Such was the case, for example, in Eritrea (the refugees' country) prior to 1960 and in Sudan prior to 1970.

Although the power of traditional leaders was often limited to the enforcement of regulations and decisions agreed upon by corporate kin groups, village communities or tribes, their authority often included imposing sanctions on those who infringed communal rules and was facilitated by the respect and reverence traditional leaders enjoyed among their fellow villagers or tribesmen.[8] In many traditional rural African societies, the moral authority of elders and community leaders constitutes an important asset in the governance of local natural resources. This special status enabled the traditional institutions to bring social and moral pressures to bear on individuals to cooperate and to practise self-restraint in the use of resources owned in common. Fourth, unlike 'open-access' resources of 'free-rider' resources, where there is unrestricted entry and where there are no resource use-regulating institutions, CPRs are exclusive resources, accessible only to certified members of an identifiable user community, whether tribe, village or group of villages. Outsiders are excluded. Access by the latter is only possible through pacts and agreements, in which conditions of use are spelled out in detail.

For example, as we saw in Chapter 7, in the refugees' country of origin when the former nomads (the Saho/Asaorta groups) began moving westwards in the second half of the nineteenth century in search of arable land, water and pasture, one way in which they gained access to arable land and CPRs was be entering into mutually binding contractual agreements with the landowning villages at the places of destination. Their obligations included paying traditional dues to the landowners in recognition of the rights of the autochthons' resource ownership. In the tribal territories (*dars*) in Sudan, prior to the enactment of the ULA (1970), outsiders were allowed access to water resources and arable and grazing lands only after they had secured permission from the leaderships of the tribes and after payment of traditional dues. The agreements spelled out in detail the conditions for use and the outsiders concerned were required to follow strictly the terms of such agreements. In order to leave no room for claims of permanent title to land, such agreements were often renegotiated and renewed annually.[9] Throughout Sudan, each tribe had its own *dar* (homeland), where no other tribe could cultivate, graze or water themselves or their animals except by permission (El Mahdi, 1976: 95). All these measures were designed to halt resource depletion due to overuse and mismanagement.

The grazing lands, woodlands, livestock routes and water resources as well as the arable lands on the scheme are owned by the government. As in the rest of rural Sudan, the government has not been able to enforce its own laws, owing to under-developed administrative, physical, financial and logistical infrastructures as well as corruption. As a result, the resources on the scheme have, *de facto*, become open-access resources, readily available for exploitation by the scheme residents and outsiders.

Thus, it may be better conceptually and practically to refer to the resources on and around the scheme as 'open-access' or 'free-rider' resources, or simply as commons, which are completely different from CPRs. The latter are managed by the user community in question, which often has exclusive property rights, including the authority to devise and enforce resource-regulating institutional rules governing the behaviour of the members when they use the resources owned in common. In order to avoid the confusion which permeates the bulk of the mainstream literature and the debate on CPRs, it is important to bear in mind this important distinction. Commons are 'free-rider' resources, while CPRs are resources sustainably[10] and equitably managed by the commoners for the common well-being. This is not to suggest, however, that no degradation ever occurs in CPRs owned and controlled by local resource users. Degradation has multiple causes, and absence of institutional constraints is only one of the factors, albeit probably the most important one.

The tribal structures in Sudan were by no means democratic, nor were the resources equitably distributed. Even though every member had the right of access to property owned in common (pasture, forest and water resources), inasmuch as the members had differential access to labour and capital (e.g. livestock) appropri-ation was a function of economic status and family size. Those who had more livestock and more family members appropriated more from the property owned in common.

The results of this study show that, in a situation where communities lack ownership or usufructuary rights over common resources with a guarantee against future arbitrary eviction by decisions of governments or commercial interests, they are not able to work out effective regulation of resources use and access. In a situation like this, common resources can only be managed sustainably through externally imposed and enforced institutional arrangements. As we shall see below, the problem on the scheme emanates not only from government ownership of the common resources, but mainly from the government's inability to enforce its own institutional arrangements. The consequence of this is that, *de facto*, neither the behaviour of the user communities nor that of the outsiders who use the resources on the scheme is subject to any regulation. The behaviour of all the people who use the commons on the scheme area is, as a result, more or less chaotic, i.e. all act to promote their individual interest, disregarding communal responsibility.

It is quite interesting to observe that even the Sudanese farmers consider the common resources (save the arable plots) on the scheme as belonging to the government and not to themselves (Table 8.4). The arable land cultivated by the Sudanese farmers was not registered in 1970 when the ULA came into force, and hence it became government property. This fact of law notwithstanding, however, the Sudanese farmers consider their holdings as their own private property (see Table 8.1). Why is it, then, that the Sudanese farmers, by the same token, do not consider the common resources on the scheme as their own? It is because the common resources are open to all, including those without any traditional territorial claim.

In the case of arable land, however, especially when such land is cropped and not targeted for development either by the government or by one of the commercial farmers, there is little outside interference with the farmers' right of usufruct. Thus *de facto*, the farmers are free even to dispose of their right of usufruct in any form. This transaction, however, is not enforceable at law, but, this fact notwithstanding, disposal of arable land is common. This again is a consequence of weak government, which took upon itself responsibilities (nationalization of all unregistered land) for which it lacked administrative, financial and manpower capability to enforce. Thus, the farmers have a reason to consider their holdings as belonging to themselves in spite of the fact that the state can revoke such rights at any time by invoking section 8 of the ULA (1970). The greatest damage state ownership has caused in Sudan is that it has shifted the locus of decision-making and thus concern for sustainable use of the common resources from the communities to the seat of the regional or central governments. Centralization of political authority in Sudan has undermined people's sense of responsibility for common resources.

Before their flight, the refugee communities were in control of the CPRs. This was true even in those areas where arable, pasture and woodlands were owned by the government (see Chapter 7). According to the refugee respondents before they fled their country, use of and access to woodlands, natural water resources and grazing lands were regulated by the community (80.5%), by the government (13.0%) and by the government and community (7%) (Table 8.5). Generally, government ownership of a resource cannot be equated with a free-rider' situation, but, when weak governments are unable to enforce their own institutional decisions regarding access to and use of common resources, the resources in question become, de facto, 'open-access' resources. In Chapter 7, it was shown that in the pre-flight period, the groups that had tenurial security and problems of resource scarcity had their own institutional arrangements which regulated access to and use of the CPRs.

Here, as elsewhere in the country, the government has been unable to enforce its own institutional arrangements. Thus, *de facto*, the grazing and woodlands as well as

Table 8.4   Perception of ownership and control of the common resources (grazing, woodlands, water sources and stock routes) on the scheme (%)

	Refugees	Sudanese
The government of Sudan	97.6	100.0
The village	0.0	0.0
The Sudanese Arabs	1.9	0.0
The amir of Qala en Nahal	0.5	0.0
Total	100.0	100.0

Table 8.5 Perception of regulation of access to and use of common resources on the scheme (%)

	Refugees	Sudanese
Customary rules of refugees	2.3	0.0
Customary rules of the Sudanese	0.0	23.1
Statutory laws	82.4	70.3
No rules or laws	15.3	6.6
Total	100.0	100.0

the natural water resources on the scheme are 'open' or 'free-rider' resources, where there is unlimited entry not only by the members of the local population in the area, but also by commercial farmers and charcoal producers from distant places such as Sennar, Gedaref, Omdurman and Khartoum. As can be seen from Table 8.6, the scheme population is unable to exclude outsiders. This has led to external pressure such as encroachment on forest and grazing resources by commercial farmers, tree-lopping by herdsmen, excessive tree-felling for charcoal production by wholesalers, tapping of gum arabic from the *A. senegal* trees and exploitation of water resources. Depletion of the common resources is not only caused by outsiders, but also by the uncontrolled behaviour of the members of the user communities themselves, because *de facto* individual rights of access and use are not subject to any customary or statutory regulations.

The inability of the community to exclude others, in combination with population pressure, has led to overexploitation of the common resources. For example, about 93% of the refugees and 95.5% of the local Sudanese state that the major cause of depletion of the woodlands is commercial charcoal production by people who come from distant areas. However, the common resources within the scheme are not only depleted due to the non-exclusive nature of the resources and due to lack of regulation, but also because this has generated a more desperate survival strategy. There is a saying in Tigre, one of the languages spoken by the refugees on the scheme, which goes 'if you can't help it, join those who plunder your house'. Such an attitude is a reflection of powerlessness and can have negative environmental consequences.

The ferocious competition that characterizes common-resource utilization on the scheme can be illustrated by the following two examples. In one of the Sudanese villages, we came across a man who was cutting trees to make charcoal. He knew that tree cutting without permission from the Forestry Department in Qala en Nahal town or Hawata was illegal. He was also aware of the importance of trees for the purpose of environmental protection. In spite of this, however, the man did not restrain himself from committing a 'criminal' act and environmental damage. In his view, if he did not cut the trees, others (villagers and outsiders) would cut them.

Table 8.6 Are outsiders allowed to exploit the commons on the scheme?

	Refugees	Sudanese
Yes	97.7	90.1
No	2.3	9.9
Total	100.0	100.0

Thus, he saw no logic in self-restraint. He was involved in fierce competition for a 'free-rider' resource. He was trying to cut as many trees as possible before his fellow villagers, refugees or commercial charcoal producers came to do the same. In a situation where the local communities lacked collective or individual property rights to regulate access to and use of such resources and where the government concerned lacked the means or the will to enforce and monitor user compliance with existing laws and by-laws, the people see no purpose in self-restraint.

In another Sudanese village, we came across another man who had collected a large amount of trees for charcoal production. We asked him how it felt to cut the young live trees which were important for preservation of the fragile environment. He said, 'It feels terribly bad, but my feeling is irrelevant because, if I don't cut these trees today, they will not be there tomorrow. Others will come and cut them.' People were engaged in a destructive race where in the end every one involved, including the environment, would be left worse off. The motto seems to be 'Grab as many common resources as possible before they are grabbed by others.' Environmental concern seemed to be remote for those who lived not only on the edge of survival, but also in permanent fear of losing access to the available local resources. This behaviour was widespread throughout the villages in the area. State ownership of the common resources and the state's subsequent inability to enforce its own laws has set in motion unrestrained covetous acts by the members of the user communities. Outsiders were also behaving in the same or an even more rapacious way against the natural environment. This competition has resulted in severe depletion of the resources within and around the scheme. The situation can be described by a Turkish saying: 'One has to be a despicable fool not to help oneself to state property' (quoted in Berkes and Farvar, 1989). This is reminiscent of the 'tragedy of the commons' model, in which every member of the common resource-user groups fiercely pursued his self-interest to the detriment of the common good. Such an individual is, in Hardin's words, 'locked into a system that compels him' to deplete the common resource (Hardin, 1968: 1244). However, unlike both in the 'tragedy of the commons' model and in the property-rights paradigm, the source of the problem of the common-resource depletion on the scheme, as well as in many other parts of Sudan, does not emanate from the collective ownership of the resources in question, but rather from the lack of it.

Given the history of these communities, if the resource in question, in our example here the woodlands, were owned communally, it is plausible to imagine a situation in which the community would devise institutional constraints and enforcement mechanisms to regulate access to and use of the collective good. Such institutional rules would have provided assurance to the individual members of the user group regarding the actions of the other members. If, for example, the two farmers just mentioned had been assured via institutional rules that the resources in their village would only be accessible to members of the village and that their fellow villagers would use the resources with restraint in accordance with the existing tacit and explicit arrangements designed to halt depletion, it would have been in their own self-interest to comply with the same rules. There would have been no need for them to engage in thoughtless exploitation of the common resources. The problem of uncertainty about the actions of other users of a common resource is eliminated only by an assurance provided via social institutions. On the scheme, traditional social institutions have lost their traditional role because government ownership has effectively converted the former CPRs into 'free-rider' or 'open-access' resources, which require no regulatory rules. This has induced thoughtless competition between the refugees, local Sudanese, migrant Sudanese, commercial farmers and commercial charcoal producers. The outcome is inevitably tragic. The situation is, however, better described as the 'tragedy of government intervention' rather than the 'tragedy of the commons'.

The forestry officer in the Commissioner's Office for Refugees (COR) at Umsagata responsible for the enforcement of the government regulations regarding use of and access to the common resources does not have the necessary logistics to enforce such rules. He had only occasional access to a tractor to supervise the whole scheme area. Tractors are no match for the well-maintained trucks and lorries operated by charcoal wholesalers. As a result, he has been unable to supervise the application of the regulations. The officer in charge was aware of the sorry state of the surrounding environment and he fully recognized the cause of the depletion, but he lacked all the necessary resources to enforce the regulations (Nejmedin, COR forestry guard and agricultural officer, pers. comm., 1991, 1994). His attitude was one of despair. In his own words, 'I have lost the fight against the tree cutters. Soon there will be no need to fight because there will be no trees to protect.'

Charcoal production is one of the most important income-generating activities on the scheme. Among the Sudanese local farmers, there are only a few male adults who do not engage in charcoal making. According to the refugee respondents, about 99% of the able-bodied local Sudanese males engage in charcoal production during the dry season. The corresponding estimate of the Sudanese farmers themselves is 78%. The data, in spite of their considerable difference, show that charcoal production by the local Sudanese farmers is one of the major causes of deforestation on the scheme. Unlike firewood pickers, who rely on deadwood, charcoal producers cut live *Acacia* trees indiscriminately. There were also some refugees who were engaged in charcoal production, but contrary to our expectation they numbered only a few. Among the Sudanese respondents only 4% reported that refugees cut trees for charcoal production. The refugees' own corresponding estimate is less than 1%. The low-level participation of the refugees in charcoal production is partly explained by their vulnerable position and partly by lack of the skill and tools (e.g. axes and sacks) required for charcoal making. Because of their status, refugees are more inclined to comply with government regulations than non-displaced populations, fearing that lack of respect for government regulations may negatively affect the attitude of the authorities towards them. The refugees also understand that they are aliens and their welfare is dependent on the goodwill of the authorities. Thus, they are keen to maintain a good rapport with the representatives of the government on site. In the COR officer's view, it was easier to enforce woodland usership regulations among the refugees than among the local Sudanese. With the dramatic change of the ratio between population and exploitable resources, the extent of vegetation deletion is increasing at an alarming pace. According to Devitt and Tahir (1984) there were only about twenty charcoal makers on the scheme in 1984. The number of charcoal makers has now increased dramatically. This is a reflection of the worsening living conditions, caused, among other things, by reduction in the productive capability of the basic resource – land – resulting from overuse.

The user communities are fully aware of the causes of the depletion on the scheme. In discussions with community leaders and elders, it came out clearly that, in their view, it was lack of control by the local communities and their inability to exclude outsiders that lay at the heart of the problem. They argue that, if such powers had existed at the local level, everyone would have felt responsible for using the common resources in a sustainable way. The community would also have been able to control the behaviour of the members of the user community by working

Table 8.7   Farmers' views on who should control the common resources on and around the scheme from the point of view of sustainability

	Refugees	Sudanese
The government	7.0	2.2
The community	87.0	96.7
The individual users	3.3	1.1
The community and government	2.7	0.0
Total	100.0	100.0

out institutional arrangements and by imposing sanctions against rule-breakers. The solution suggested by the farmers was to devolve control over the common resources to the local community (Table 8.7). In view of the changes in social relations, status, values and roles that have taken place, resulting from flight and exile, this may not be easy. This is likely to be exacerbated by the diversity of the backgrounds of the refugee groups.

It is interesting to observe that privatization was not considered a preferable option by either the refugee or the Sudanese farmers. Devolution of control to individual users was only appealing to an insignificant minority (about 3% among refugees and 1% among the Sudanese). About 3% of the refugees considered joint control by the government and the community to be a viable solution. None of the Sudanese considered this to be a feasible solution. The reasons why these refugees thought joint control would be viable was because of awareness of their vulnerable position. They pointed out that, left on their own, they would not be able to keep outsiders out because no Sudanese would respect their decision. They said, 'No one listens to a *lagèe* [refugee].' They argued that, even with the authority to exclude outsiders, their vulnerable status would prevent them from enforcing such a regulation. This was also partly a reflection of an awareness on the part of the refugee farmers about the limitations and inadequacies of the existing traditional social institutions to exercise control over the behaviour of the individual members of the refugee farmers.

If the resources on the scheme were owned by their own communities, 83.3% of the refugees and 78% of the local Sudanese farmers said that they would have been more motivated to use the resources sustainably for the common well-being. This could be achieved, in their view, first, by excluding those without usership rights (outsiders) or, if they allowed outsiders to use the resources within the scheme temporarily, by imposing upon them special conditions of use; second, by imposing on the members of the user community norms and rules that would govern access and use; and, third, by undertaking restorative management of the resources. Only about 17% of the refugees and 22% of the local Sudanese farmers thought ownership rights would not significantly affect the behaviour of individual users. This was because, in their view, under the existing resource endowments and state of confinement under which the communities eke out a meagre living, there was no room for implementing a sound resource-management regime.

Impact of refugee status, lack of social stability and uncertainty on resource use

The way refugee communities relate to the natural environment may also be affected by their status. The existing literature abounds with a myriad of untested and impressionistic statements and assumptions, such as that refugees resort to destructive and exploitative land-use practices because of lack of commitment to the area of their temporary residence (Chapter 1). This may empirically be true or false, but to my knowledge there is a dearth of data to confirm or refute such assumptions. Here, not only is the question whether refugee status is a factor that influences decisions regarding use of local resources measured at a perceptual level, but an attempt is also made to measure this empirically by examining the differential responses of the local Sudanese and the refugee farmers to a tree-planting project which was designed to counter the problem of land degradation on the scheme.

Generally, refugee communities are not stable communities. They are displaced communities. Most refugee communities are gripped with the dream of returning home and thus hope that the factors that prompted them to flee will come to an end. They may therefore lack permanent commitment to their places of 'temporary' residence. Even though the root cause of environmental degradation in areas inhabited by refugee communities stems from lack of an adequate resource base, tenurial security and freedom of movement and residence, as well as from their inability to exclude outsiders from gaining access to the natural resources within the areas of their habitation, there is probably a limited relationship between refugee status and unsustainable resource use. If there is such a relationship, even under conditions in which the woodlands, grazing lands (permanent pastures, uncultivable and fallow lands), crop lands after harvest and livestock watering-points (*hafirs*) were not open-access, there would still be theoretically conceivable factors which may suggest that the individual members of the refugee communities would have less incentive to observe traditional customary rules of CPR use.

One of the reasons why traditional customary CPR management systems are effective is because the collectivity concerned can bring pressure to bear on rule-breakers. This is because there are a multitude of ties which bind them to the resource group they may offend. The close-knit institutional customary network that existed in parts of Eritrea where some of the refugees came from had built-in safety measures against possible 'free-riding' (see Chapter 7). The individual was dependent on the collectivity both economically and socially. The right of access to arable land was, for example, ensured through belonging to a certain clan, kinship or residential group. Hence, members of the community had an incentive to observe resource-use rules prescribed by the collectivity. On the scheme, arable land and grazing rights are not allocated to individual refugee households by the collectivity, but rather by a formal government authority (COR). Even if traditional regulations of resource use were to be applicable, the individual refugee would have no incentive to comply with such collective rules. The community is unable to enforce rules on its individual members when the economic tie which binds the member to the collectivity has been weakened or has disappeared completely. The individual refugee is dependent for his and his family's sustenance more on his own efforts, on COR and on the refugee support systems than on the collectivity.

Generally, it may be an oversimplification to reduce the motive for individual cooperation and collective action, reflected in compliance with customary common-property rules, to pure economic incentive. In some situations, non-economic incentives are as important in discouraging or precluding 'free-riding' and promoting self-restraint and cooperative behaviour. However, when mere survival becomes a priority and when local communities lose control over the allocation of the basis of survival, social institutions also lose their legitimacy. As a result, a breakdown of institutional rules and enforcement mechanisms of traditional resource-management systems ensues. The structure of such a situation allows the community neither to reward the cooperative, i.e. those who comply with its rules, nor to punish the recalcitrant, i.e. those who infringe its rules. There is little or nothing that motivates individuals to cooperate.

Refugee movements are generally involuntary and this is what distinguishes refugees from migrants (Kibreab, 1987). Despite long exile, most refugees long for their homeland and live in hope of returning to their country one day (Kibreab, 1995). Millions of African refugees have returned to their countries following the cessation of the reasons which prompted their flight (Betts, 1980, 1981; Adepeju, 1982; RPG, 1986; Kibreab, 1987, 1989, 1991). Not only do refugees return to their homelands following the elimination of the sources of the conflicts that force them to flee, but most refugees are also seized with the dream of returning to their homelands. They are uncertain as to how long they will stay in the country of asylum. The 1951 United Nations (UN) and the 1969 Organization of African Unity (OAU) Conventions specifically state that refugees lose their status following the resolution of the circumstances in connection with which they were recognized as refugees (UN, 1951: Art. IC(5); OAU, 1969: Art 1(4e)). After the cessation of the circumstances which prompted them to flee, they are required to return to their countries. It is not known when these changes may occur.

Generally, 'refugee' is a formal status which implies non-membership in the surrounding environment and society. Psychologically, refugees, especially those in camps, transit centres and settlements, tend to be predominantly backward-looking in the sense that their past is very much a focus of their present. This is exacerbated by the problem of uncertainty. The two characteristics combined together may discourage some refugees from developing roots in the host country for fear of being uprooted once more for a new start. It is worth noting, however, that self-settled refugees may not exhibit such characteristics. This suggests that this characteristic is not an intrinsic feature of being a refugee. It is rather a result of how refugees are received and how refugee aid is managed. Sometimes refugee status and uncertainty may, irrespective of the underlying cause, theoretically influence the resource use and management practices of involuntarily resettled refugee communities.

The governing principle in African traditional farming systems is risk minimization, in which strategies are developed not only to ensure short-term survival but also to maintain long-term productivity, in order to make such resources available for the coming generation. As long as refugees are uncertain about their future in the country of asylum, they may not be to a large extent concerned with long-term sustainability. Their major preoccupation may be to maximize short-term gains. African refugees are received as temporary guests and many of them are reluctant to assimilate into host societies (Armstrong, 1988; Kibreab, 1989) and this seems to have a bearing on how they use the environment. They are discouraged by the host governments' policies from integrating into the host countries because they are expected to return home when the problems that created the situation are eliminated. The policy of the government of Sudan is not any different. As we saw earlier, land is allocated to refugees 'during their stay in the country' and such land 'may not be inherited' (Regulation of Asylum Act, 1974). As long as they do not see any future for themselves and their children in their present area of residence, they may not use the resources with restraint and/or may not invest their scarce labour in soil conservation and maintenance activities.

Does uncertainty therefore discourage the refugees from making long-term investments to conserve the natural environment and to use the land with restraint?

About 75% of the refugees reported that they are discouraged from making long-term investments, partly by the way their presence is perceived by the host government and partly by the uncertainty regarding how long they would stay in the country of asylum and by the dream of returning home. Only 25% said they were not in any way discouraged from making long-term investments by their refugee status.

The Sudanese farmers were also constrained by uncertainty emanating from fear they may sometime in the future lose access to the local resources because of the expansion of rain-fed mechanized farming. However, the level of uncertainty was not comparable to that experienced by the refugee farmers.

Breakdown of traditional authority and its consequence for resource management

The traditional institutions which played an important role in devising and enforcing rules governing the use of and access to resources controlled in common are effectively weakened in exile. This is due to the experiences, deprivations and powerlessness associated with flight and exile, such as loss of possessions and control over resources, intermingling of previously autonomous villages or residentially defined kinship, lineage, tribal or ethnic groups, population pressure, insufficiency of resource base and external demands for resources within the scheme. Although all the above factors have directly and indirectly contributed to the weakening of traditional authorities and social institutions, the most critical factor seems to be loss of control over local resources. On the scheme, as pointed out earlier, these are owned by the government. In the pre-flight period, even though the right of access of individuals to arable land and to CPRs was determined by membership of a residentially defined village/s, kinship, lineage or tribe, the traditional leaders and elders played a central role in the administration of these rights and in the settlement of disputes over resources. On the scheme, community leadership functions are performed by COR officers. The traditional leaders have, therefore, been effectively stripped of the core of their powers, authority and prestige. This has rendered them redundant because they have no functions to fulfil.

In the past, although the supreme organ of decision-making was the assembly of senior males or of all adult males, community elders, tribal chiefs (nazirs or *shums*), *meslenes* (district chiefs), *chikas*, sheikhs and *shimagelles* played key roles not only as conveners of such assemblies, but through their opinions, which carried considerable weight and markedly influenced decisions by virtue of the moral authority they possessed. They also had a mandate to enforce the rules or decisions. In the past, their main roles included: allocation of arable land to fellow villagers; demarcation of arable and grazing lands; arbitration and reconciliation of disputes over resources and other issues; enforcement of institutional rules as prescribed in customary laws or decisions of kinship, clan or village/s assemblies; and negotiation with others for access to and use of scarce resources.

When flight alienated the traditional leaderships from their power base, namely arable land and CPRs, which were previously allocated and managed by them, people no longer felt obliged to respect them. Consequently, the traditional leaders and elders lost their political and moral authority. They were no longer respected and revered. As a result, collective discipline began to break down. What used to be tight-knit tribal, ethnic and village leaderships were replaced by many sheikhs elected in the reception centres or the settlements on the instruction of relief agencies and Sudan government settlement authorities. Refugee programmes also created new requirements which the old traditional leaderships could not fulfil, including literacy in order to keep records of relief distributions, ability to organize and distribute relief hand-outs, ability to interact and communicate with camp or settlement authorities and expatriate relief workers, etc. Not many of the former traditional leaders were able to meet these demands. Moral authority and descent were no longer relevant factors in the election of new sheikhs. The most important quality of a sheikh became the ability to negotiate more assistance from the refugee support systems. The traditional leaders were least equipped to undertake new leadership tasks and they gave way to more forceful, persistent, unrelenting and articulate individuals. Unlike the traditional tribal and clan leaders (nazirs, *meslenes*, *chikas*, sheikhs and village or clan councils), the new sheikhs lack authority over their 'followers'. The consent of their fellow tribes or villagers could no longer be taken for granted.

As a result of loss of family members and scattering of relatives associated with the war, most of the present sheikhdoms in the settlements constitute no more than a collection of distantly related nuclear families, often, but not always, from the same clan and area. In the pre-flight period as well as when the refugees first came to Sudan, most families, except the Tigrinya, came under a few powerful traditional leaders. The establishment of the scheme coincided with the enactment of the ULA (1970). Following the establishment of the settlement, the people's local government at Qala en Nahal town and COR wasted no time in replacing the weakened traditional leadership among the refugee communities. This was done by appointing a residents' three-person committee in every village, known as *legina*. In the majority of cases, the members of the *legina* had no links with the once respected and revered traditional leaders and hence they enjoyed no marked respect and reverence. The institution of the *legina* is considered by the villagers to be the extended arm of COR. People do not feel bound by its decisions.

Thus, the institution of the *legina* does not play a significant role in the formulation and enforcement of traditional resource-management systems. The refugee communities in Qala en Nahal are now fragmented into small vying groups, reflected in the amoebic multiplication of the sheikhdoms (Table 8.8). Overall there are 5,528 families and 221 sheikhs in the six refugee villages in Qala en Nahal. The average size of a sheikhdom among the refugee is 25.1 families. Among the Beni Amer there are seventy-three sheikhs and only 1,880 families.

In 1972 Salmin had only thirteen sheikhs, in 1988 this increased to fifty-six and in 1991 to sixty-two. In Umbrush there were thirteen sheikhs in 1972. In 1982 they had increased to nineteen and in 1984, during the drought period, the number of sheikhs reached forty-one as compared with thirty-nine in 1991. The reason why there were less sheikhs in 1991 than in 1984 was because some had returned to Eritrea. Such has been the case with every village in the settlement (Table 8.8). Even in the villages where there is no mixing of ethnic groups (like Adingrar and Umzurzur where only the Saho/Asaorta live), the level of fragmentation and breakdown of community cohesion is equally alarming.

In the pre-flight period, most of these communities were strongly unified by common descent, common territorial rights and allegiance to a single political leadership – *diglal*, nazir, *shum*, *meslene*, clan council, etc. For example, strictly speaking, the Beni Amer is not a tribe, but a loosely knit confederation of tribal units of different origins (Paul, 1950; Harrison, 1958). However, even though they were physically scattered over large tracts of land, they were unified by collective territorial rights and allegiance to a political leadership. Each kinship constituted a

Table 8.8   Number of sheikhs and families per sheikhdom on the scheme

Village	Ethnicity	Sheikhdoms	Families	Average size of sheikhdom
Refugees				
Umbrush	Beni Amer	22	356	16.1
Salmin		42	1,116	26.6
Umsagata		9	408	45.0
Umbrush	Saho	8	98	12.5
Salmin		1	7	7.0
Umsagata		15	367	24.5
Dehema		17	530	31.2
Adingrar		25	767	30.7
Umzurzur		28	638	22.8
Umbrush	Maria	1	26	26.0
Salmin		2	70	35.0
Umsagata		12	338	28.2
Umbrush	Nara	1	95	95.0
Salmin		13	212	16.3
Umsagata		4	124	31.0
Dehema		1	6	6.0
Umbrush	Tigrinya	3	41	13.7
Umsagata		2	20	10.0
Dehema		3	35	11.7
Salmin	Bilen	1	40	40.0
Umsagata		1	39	39.0
Umbrush	Beit Juk	4	94	23.5
Dehema		1	20	20.0
Umbrush	Ad Shuma	1	11	11.0
Dehema		1	23	23.0
Salmin	Algeden	2	37	18.5
Umsagata	Hedareb	1	10	10.0
Total		221	5,528	25.1
Sudanese villagers				
Umsagata	Sudanese	2	313	156.5
Shangya		1	68	68.0
Utash		1	126	126.0
Salmin Dajo		1	86	86.0
Dehema		2	414	207.0
Huweig		1	41	41.0
Total		8	1,048	131.0

political unit. Chieftainship among the Beni Amer was vested in the *nahtab* class and they acknowledged the supremacy of the *diglal*. Each clan had its own clan head or *omda* and each kinship group had its own headman or sheikh. At the top, the *diglal* or the nazir enjoyed overall supremacy. A monograph prepared by the Native Affairs section of the Secretariat of the British Military Administration (BMA) in Eritrea in 1943, for example, stated that the term 'tribe' as applied to the Beni Amer was:

a misnomer. For the Beni Amer are a conglomerate of tribes, often of diverse origin rather than a solid, single ethnic unit. Their union is largely political and in the nature of a loose confederation which pays allegiance to a common paramount chief, the Diglal, and acknowledges a common caste known as Nabtab . . . the Nabtab of the Beni Amer cuts across the existing tribal divisions, as well as probably the divisions of ethnic descent. (BMA, 1944: 6)

Succession to the offices was hereditary (Nadel, 1945: 61). The rules and procedures governing succession were complex. For example, when a clan head died, all the *nabtab* held a meeting in council to elect an executive committee with a mandate to take final decisions. The newly elected clan head had to be confirmed formally by the paramount chief, the *diglal*, before he could resume leadership (Nadel, 1945: 61).

It is important to note that, in the pre-flight period, it was not only the Beni Amer that were strongly unified by common descent, common territorial rights and allegiance to a single political leadership. Before 1940, the Maria (both Tselam and Keyah) had a single paramount chief known as *shum*. After 1940, the two sections each had their own *shum*, to whom all the Maria paid undisputed allegiance (BMA, 1944: 17). The Mensa, the Beit Juk and the Habab (Beit Asgede, Ad Tekles and Ad Temariam) each had their own paramount chief known as *kantibai* (BMA, 1944: 18–19). The tribal governments of the Saho subtribes were also in the hands of elected heads of the autonomous units, known as *shum*. The *shum* had under him the heads of kinship groups, called *nabara*. In 1933, the colonial government united the whole Asaorta tribe under a paramount chief, who was invested with rank first of bey and later pasha (BMA, 1944: 62). It was stated, '[T]hough this office is not traditional, the present chief, still the first paramount chief of the Asaorta, has some claim to the leadership of his tribe, for he comes from its senior section, and traces his descent in direct line to the tribal ancestor' (BMA, 1944: 62).

It is worthwhile to observe that the powers of the traditional leaders were to some extent weakened even in the pre-flight period, mainly because of the revolts of the serfs against the feudal lords from whom the chiefs and the hereditary heads of the tribes and clans came. For example, the above cited report stated,

[T]he economic and social relations between masters and serfs have undergone considerable changes in the past, and are even now moving towards a re-definition. Among the Belein, for examle, the serfs have bought land from their masters, a transaction which is forbidden by custom, and have thus become landlords in their own right; dues paid on the land are the last remnants of the old landlord-tenant relationship. Sometimes serfs have refused to continue the customary gifts and have obtained exemption from these obligations – *de facto*, no *de jure*, in the eyes of the rulers. Serfs have even declined to perform their duty *par excellence*, the milking of cows, much to the annoyance of their helpless masters. These changes have reached different stages in different tribes. The serf obligations have almost disappeared among the Belein; they are fast disappearing among the Mensa; the first signs of the coming change are visible among the Ad Tekles and Beit Juk; only among the Maria and Habab are the old customs still in force. (BMA, 1944: 15)

In spite of these changes, when the refugees fled their country beginning in the 1960s, most of them were united under either hereditary or elected paramount chiefs. For example, when over 5,000 Saho/Asaorta families migrated to the Barka valley (Koroken) from the Eritrean plateau (mainly from Obel and Hazemo) and from Tigray in the mid-1950s, they were unified by a collective allegiance to a single leaer, Saad Akha. In exile, the sheikhs lack the charisma, moral authority and influence of their predecessors. For example, most of the Saho in the Qala en Nahal villages are from the Barka valley (Koroken). They are also fragmented into ninety-four sheikhdoms. There is no paramount chief to whom the ninety-four sheikhs are accountable.

The structure of the Sudanese sheikhdoms is markedly different from that of the refugee communities. The average size of the sheikhdoms in the Sudanese villages is 131 families. In fact, in the villages where there are more than one sheikh, the number of families per sheikhdom is 181.7. The sheikhdoms in the Sudanese villages are seven times larger than in the refugee villages. This shows that among the Sudanese villages there is still a certain degree of community cohesion, which under favourable conditions could facilitate local management of resources.

The consequence of this fragmentation on collective action is considerable. One such effect is to limit the sense of community. The community leaders on the scheme complain about the lack of discipline and the breakdown of the social values and norms that once characterized their communities. Unlike in the past, elders state, it has become impossible to reach a collective agreement on issues of common interest; people no longer seem to have common interests. Instead, small groups are competing fiercely for whatever benefit they may gain without considering the consequences of their competition on the well-being of their fellow villagers. Traditional leaders have lost the respect and the reverence they once enjoyed among the communities. Life in the settlement is breeding narrow individualism.

The existence of a cohesive community is of paramount importance for community management of CPRs. With such fragmentation and proliferation, production and consumption decisions, including exploitation of common resources, are dictated or governed by individual strategies rather than by collective interests. As can be seen from the data in Table 8.8, some of the sheikhdoms have less than ten families. A breakdown of the size of the sheikhdoms in the table shows that about 16%, 33%, 19% 10% and 8% have less than ten, twenty, thirty, forty and fifty families respectively. Only 13% have more than fifty families. This is unprecedented in the history of stable communities in Eritrea or Sudan. In the past, the communities were organized on the basis of village/s or sections of tribes and were formed around clan and tribal leaders or *meslenes*. The function of such traditional institutions, as stated before, was, among other things, to enforce customary laws, but in the settlements the roles of the sheikhdoms are reduced to mere physical distribution of relief in accordance with the criteria set by the settlement administration (COR).

In the pre-flight period, one of the key factors that contributed to sustainable use of CPRs was the existence of collective discipline. This imposed some form of limitation upon the activities of every member of the user community in the presumed common interest. In the elders' view, imposition of collective discipline is no longer possible. In the past, the views of elders and community leaders represented a collective opinion and influenced community action decisively. In the settlement, as one old man put it, 'Now, everyone says "it is your personal opinion and I have mine". If 100 persons attend a meeting, there are 100 different opinions and not many are willing to compromise' (refugee elder, pers. comm., 1991). The implication of this on collective resource management is that it is difficult or impossible to reach an agreement and to enforce such an agreement, for example, regarding limitation of levels of use intensity of common resources.

In spite of the apparent lack of community cohesion, 87% of the respondents see devolving responsibility for the management of the common resources to their community as a panacea for the problem of degradation. Despite their experience, the communities still believe that, given the opportunity, they would be able to devise effective institutional decision-making systems that would allow sustainable use of the common resources on the scheme and to enforce such rules. This may sound contradictory to the preceding arguments. However, it will be argued here that there is no such contradiction. One of the major causes of the breakdown of community life or cohesion on the scheme was loss of control over the basic resources, namely arable land, grazing lands, woodlands and water resources. Thus, the most effective way to reconstruct the communities is to devolve control over the local resources to the user communities themselves. It is only then that the communities will be able to control their social world by imposing their own laws upon it. And it is only when the communities are able to exercise control over the basis of their subsistence that their social institutions can regain their legitimacy and become effective guides to collective action. It is only then that communities can devise and enforce rules that prevail over individual self-interest in the service of the common good. At present, the resources from which individuals earn their livelihood are not controlled by the communities. Thus, the communities cannot work out rules and regulations regarding access to and use of resources which they do not control. Consequently, there is little or no incentive for individuals to respect or revere the traditional social institutions. Devolution of control over resources to the communities will tie individuals to the resource group and the need to gain access to sources of livelihood will make it incumbent on individuals to comply with institutional rules devised by the communities collectively.

The following example, insignificant as it is, may show that devolution of control over the resources can effectively resuscitate the traditional resource-management capacity of the communities. Water shortage for livestock has been one of the major constraints facing herdsmen on the scheme. This was partially solved following ACORD's excavation of rain-fed *hafirs* within the scheme. The management of the *hafirs* is handed over to each village. The villages have subsequently devised rules governing water allocation and use from the *hafirs*. Access to water from the *hafirs* is only open to residents of one of the refugee or Sudanese villages within the scheme. Outsiders, including refugees who are non-residents of the villages concerned, are excluded. The villages have worked out timetables for watering the different types of livestock. Camels, for example, are watered every 3–4 days, cattle every other day and goats, sheep and donkeys every day. Each village has employed a guard who enforces the rules and keeps records for purposes of the water-charge collection. The rules are applied strictly. The animals of those who break the rules are seized and impounded by the guards and are only repossessed after payment of fines. Against outsiders, the community stands united. In light of the water shortage in the area, herdsmen from outside the settlement often try to water their livestock in the *hafirs*. The refugee communities have demonstrated a remarkable capacity to mobilize themselves for collective action by devising and enforcing rules that define and allocate water user rights.

This does not, however, automatically suggest that the communities will be able to do the same with management of the other resources if given the chance. Water resources are easier to manage collectively than other common resources. However, the fact that they have been able to act as a corporate body to devise mutually binding arrangements and to enforce such arrangements suggests that, if they had control over the local resources, they would probably be able to manage such resources sustainably.

Conclusion

The refugee communities, especially those whose areas of origin (in Eritrea) were characterized by natural-resource scarcities and tenurial security, had evolved intricate resource-regulating institutions designed, among other things, to enable them to live in equilibrium with their resources without a major threat of hunger and irreversible environmental decline. This is not to suggest that the communities did not suffer from occasional food shortages. Indeed, crop failures precipitated by cyclical droughts were common occurrences in the areas they occupied. However, in order to avoid recurrent hunger and ecological disasters, the communities often restricted their demands for resources (e.g. by out-migration) to a level which the environment could supply naturally or undertook restorative measures to repair and conserve the productive capability of the land-resource base. The stimulus came, first, from the limitations which the physical environment (land shortage) imposed on the farming systems and, second, from secure individual, family or communal property rights.

On the scheme, there are neither resource-regulating local institutional arrangements designed to limit the level of intensity of resource use to sustainable levels nor conservation measures devised to restore and conserve the productive capability of the means of production – land. This is even true among those groups who had a long-established history of relatively advanced traditional resource-management systems. The explanation of this is inextricably intertwined with the experiences of the refugees and with the deprivations and powerlessness that permeate refugee life in government settlements.

Some of the interacting factors that contribute to inappropriate land-use practices among the refugees are, first, wrong government policies, which impose limitations on freedom of movement and residence. This constitutes the single major cause of land degradation on the scheme. Second, the government of Sudan accepted the refugees with the hope that they would soon return to their country. Consequently, they allocated insufficient amounts of land, which have over time become overfragmented and overused. This has rendered the refugees' previous methods of countering soil-fertility decline inoperative. Third, one of the consequences of exile is loss of stability and community cohesion. Devising and enforcement of resource-regulating institutions requires a certain degree of communal stability and cohesion, which is lacking among the refugee communities. As a result, production and consumption decisions are based on the principle of individual gain maximization, often to the neglect of the common good. Fourth, one of the consequences of flight is loss of moral authority of traditional leaders and their replacement by individuals who lack traditional legitimacy and reverence, but are accepted for their ability to deal with aid agencies and government authorities. These leaders play no role in resource management. Aid agencies usually contribute to the breakdown of traditional organization and leadership structures. Fifth, the refugees lack secure claims over the lands they cultivate and the common resources (woodlands, natural water, animal routes) they use on and around the scheme. The resources on the scheme are formally state property, but they are *de facto* open-access resources. As a result, the refugees have been unable, on the one hand, to regulate the way their members use the common resources and, on the other, to exclude outsiders. The inability of the refugee communities to exclude outsiders is a key element in the depletion of the vegetation resources on and around the scheme. Sixth, most of the refugees' previous resource-management systems, such as short fallow periods or planting to different crops to aid soil fertility (such as legumes), which minimized the effects of drought, can no longer be applied because of land shortage and climatic and soil conditions. Most of the refugees' knowledge was location-specific. Historically, the refugee communities, even before the pre-flight period, seldom introduced their own traditional resource-management systems to the areas where they migrated. The overwhelming tendency was to adapt to production systems of the areas of destination. The behaviour of the refugees in this sense has been consistent with their past. In the Gedaref district, the only fertility-restoring method used by the commercial and small farmers is shifting cultivation. The refugees cannot take advantage of this method because of land shortage. No other techniques are used by the Sudanese in the area to maintain soil fertility or to restore depleted soil nutrients. The same is true for the refugees.

Notes

1. Sustainability here refers to meeting 'the needs of the present without compromising the ability of the future generations to meet their own needs'.
2. A right accessible to an owner of land over the adjoining land of another.
3. This shows that the Unregistered Land Act (1970) eliminated a fundamental principle which constituted a cornerstone of the body of land legislation enacted during the colonial period. The Title of Lands Ordinance (1899) provided that registration should not affect the right to acquire a title by prescription. The Deeds Registration Ordinance (1908) made similar provision. The Land Settlement and Registration Ordinance (1925) also stated that registration of title did not necessarily affect the right of another person to acquire title of the registered property by prescription. The Prescription and Limitation Ordinance (1928) expressly provided that 'ownership of land may be acquired by peaceable, public and uninterrupted possession thereof by a person not being an usufructuary of a period of ten years, provided that if ownership is claimed against the Government the period shall be twenty years instead of ten'.
4. According to Abu Sin (1989a), this legislation came as part of the disputed September Laws.
5. In rural Eritrea, there is an association between socio-economic background and ethnic bifurcation.
6. When tested by means of the chi-square test a figure of about 70 was obtained.
7. This was tested by means of the chi-square statistic and the following values were obtained:

	Refugees	Sudanese
Yes	18.1	44.0
No	81.9	56.0

$R^2 = 20$, 2 d.f., $P < 0.1$.
8. This may not be the case everywhere in Africa. In some parts of Africa, chiefs and village headmen are powerless and without authority. Sahlins, for example, argues 'the Chieftain is usually spokesman of his group and master of its ceremonies, with otherwise little influence, few functions, and no privileges. One word from him and everyone does as he please' (cited in Netting, 1972: 221). In north-eastern Africa chiefs and village headmen enjoy a great deal of respect, reverence and privileges. Their decisions are crucial in the allocation and use of resources.
9. For similar interethnic or intertribal agreements that were renegotiated annually in the refugees' country of origin, see Nadel (1946a).
10. The issue of sustainability cannot, however, be taken for granted.

9 Ecological Perception and Conservation

> Poor people often destroy their environment – not because they are ignorant, but to survive. They overexploit thin soils, over-graze fragile grasslands, and cut down dwindling forest stocks for firewood. In the context of the short-term needs of an individual, each decision is rational; in a long-term and wider context, the effects are disastrous ... Poverty is both a cause and an effect of environmental degradation. (Ramphal in A. B. Durning, 1989b)

Ecological perceptions constitute the central tenet of most indigenous resource-management systems. Thus, a study of the refugees' ecological perceptions is crucial not only to understanding and predicting their resource-management decisions, but also to designing and implementing projects. The refugee farmers and their Sudanese neighbours have a wealth of traditional ecological knowledge about the physical and the biological environment such as soils, water, vegetation, wildlife, climate, etc. In this chapter, only the way the communities perceive trees and how this perception influences their response behaviour with regard to a tree-planting project are examined.

In view of the fact that the mainstream literature often attributes the problem of vegetation-resource depletion to subsistence producers' ignorance or lack of ecological knowledge, an attempt is made here to examine whether this constitutes one of the relevant factors in the explanation of the problem of deforestation. Although the available empirical evidence suggests that such claims lack a factual basis, it is important to examine how much of the problem of inappropriate land-use practices, especially the widespread destruction of trees, is attributable to lack of understanding of the relationship between trees and environmental protection. The way individuals perceive the natural environment is influenced by their inherited cultural knowledge and by knowledge acquired through personal experiences. Local resource-management decisions are not, however, solely the function of ecological knowledge. Issues such as tenurial rights, labour availability and motivation are important factors which influence the decision of local resource users.

The farming systems in many parts of Eritrea, where the majority of the refugees came from, contained a wealth of ecological knowledge and conservation practices designed to improve or preserve the productivity of the land (see Chapter 7). Other things being equal, such knowledge is important in shaping not only the present environmental perception of the individuals, but also in guiding their actions to undertake conservation work and to maintain such work. It is important to point out, however, that, under some circumstances, even communities with previous adequate indigenous environmental knowledge can pursue unsustainable land-use practices when relocated to an unfamiliar environment. This is because traditional ecological knowledge is, more often than not, inextricably woven into the social context in which it is developed. Social relationships are the foundation on which many traditional indigenous resource-management practices rest. A change in the nature of the social relationships or an imbalance in the man/resource ratio may make such knowledge irrelevant. For example, if the available resource base is limited and the population density is high, the need to secure a minimum stable income as well as the specificity of the environment concerned may render the communities' previous resource-management practices or indigenous knowledge inapplicable. This is because the main preoccupation of a community that operates at the minimum level of subsistence is immediate survival.

In traditional agriculture, the main technique farmers use to improve or preserve productivity is by reducing their resource demand to sustainable levels. This is often achieved by reduction in activity levels in a given geographical area. However, where resources are inadequate to allow rotational use of the available resources or when incomes are low and there is no surplus to forgo, there may be no alternative to increasing activity levels regardless of the environmental risks involved. In such a situation, previous environmental knowledge notwithstanding, land-use practices may become exploitative of the natural resources. Unfortunately, in extreme situations, as Perring observes, '[T]he cost of increased intensity is not just diminishing returns, it is potentially the complete collapse of the economic system' (Perring, 1989: 2). This may happen even in a situation where the actors are fully aware of the consequences of their behaviour. Increased activity levels are not simply a result of subsistence insecurity;[1] among displaced communities, lack of commitment emanating from an uncertain future may theoretically contribute to decisions to use resources without restraint. However, sometimes what appears to be lack of commitment could be a result of lack of choice. Analysis of the farmers' response to the tree-planting project designed to minimize the risk of land degradation may shed some light on these issues.

Ecological perception of the farmers

One of the key variables that influences the communities' (refugees and Sudanese) responses to conservation measures, for example, tree planting, is their ecological knowledge, i.e. the environmental benefits to be derived from growing trees. If the communities possess appropriate ecological knowledge, the central issue to be addressed is to what extent their behaviour is guided by such knowledge.

In the following paragraphs, the level of ecological knowledge of the farmers, measured in terms of their understanding of the relationship between trees and the environment, will be examined. The results of a series of discussions with key informants and elders in the Sudanese and refugee villages on and around the scheme clearly show that the communities have a clear understanding of the relationship between conservation and vegetation or between land degradation and devegetation. For example, one of the elders in Umsagata described the relationship as follows: 'The ability of bare ground to soak up rainwater is as poor as the ability of a hairless scalp to soak up cream' (interview with refugee elder, 1991, Umsagata). Another said, 'Bare ground is like a naked human body' (interview with refugee elder, 1991, Dehema).

These two quotations may indicate the level of ecological knowledge of the communities with regard to the critical role vegetation plays in countering soil erosion, increasing moisture infiltration and site beautification. The results of the survey as well as the discussions with key informants show that the refugee farmers perceive trees not only as providing wood fuel, building materials, food and fodder (economic benefits), but also as an important means of environmental protection.

The farmers are also aware of the aesthetic value of trees. The interviewees were asked to state the environmental and economic benefits trees provide and the results are given in Table 9.1. This long list of economic and environmental uses or benefits of trees stated by the interviewees is witness to the comprehensive ethnobotanical knowledge embodied in their culture. No major difference was observed between the level of knowledge of the former sedentary farmers, agropastoralists and pastoralists. The corollary to this set of results is that, as the trees are depleted, all or part of these stated benefits would be lost. It is plausible, therefore, to expect that the communities would do what is within their means not to deplete the trees or, if they were depleted, would take a keen interest in a project whose purpose it was to grow trees and eventually provide some of the benefits stated in Table 9.1.

Therefore, other things being equal, ecological knowledge or lack of it (ignorance) may have a serious impact on how resource users exploit the natural resources on which they and the future generations' livelihood and welfare depend. Environmental ignorance here refers to a situation in which, on the one hand, land users adopt land-use practices which accelerate the degrading processes of nature without being aware that such practices cause degradation, or, on the other hand, land users may be aware of the degrading consequence of their practices, but they may not see the need to take measures to counter degradation and the need to enhance the natural processes of repair, or they may not have the necessary

Table 9.1   Ethnobotanical knowledge among the refugee farmers on the scheme

1	Trees provide shade against heat from the sun
2	Trees are a source of beauty/have aesthetic values
3	Trees increase moisture infiltration
4	Roots pump nutrients from the subsoil to replenish soil fertility
5	Trees provide favourable conditions for growth of herbaceous grasses, which reduce run-off
6	Tree leaves enrich soil fertility
7	Trees increase probability of rain at the local level through influencing microclimatic conditions
8	Trees provide soil protection against wind and rain erosion
9	Trees are an important source of fodder
10	Trees are an important source of wood fuel
11	Trees provide the raw material for agricultural equipment
12	Trees are a principal source of construction materials
13	Trees provide tool handles, used for weapons, etc.
14	Trees provide furniture
15	Trees are an important source of income
16	Trees provide fibres for making mats, ropes and baskets
17	Trees are an important source of food – fruits, roots, bark, nuts and vegetables
18	Trees provide containers for water and milk
19	Trees are used for musical instruments
20	Trees are used for glues
21	Tree products are used for poisons
22	Trees are used for ritual purposes
23	Trees are used for hanging beehives
24	Trees produce gum
25	Trees provide medicinal herbs
26	Trees provide live fencing
27	Tree extracts are used for steam baths (*tish*) by women

knowledge of local systems of sustainable resource management to undertake such measures. It is theoretically conceivable to envisage a situation in which resource users may fail to take measures to offset the degrading impacts of their activities on the environment in spite of their awareness, knowledge and experience because the ecological criterion is only one of the multiple criteria on which resource-management decisions are taken. Each of these scenarios implies a different approach of intervention. The reasons for the differing attitudes are varied, but may include lack of incentives, labour, capital and tenurial security and the existence of an unfavourable institutional climate.

The data in Table 9.1 show that the farmers have a remarkable general knowledge about the importance of trees. It is important to note, however, that, in spite of this knowledge, they may see other disadvantages that outweigh these benefits and consequently may be reluctant to participate in tree-planting projects or may cut down trees which grow on and around their holdings. Thus, it is not enough to document the general ethnobotanical knowledge of the farmers, but one has to go beyond this and measure their actual behaviour towards trees that grow naturally on their holdings.

It is therefore important to examine how the refugee and the Sudanese local farmers perceive trees and natural vegetation on and near their farms. Do they perceive trees as serving a useful role such as maintaining soil fertility and protecting soil against wind and rain erosion? Do they, on the other hand, view trees as competitors with crops for space, nutrients and water, as casting shade on the cropped ground, or as a sanctuary for destructive birds and insects? Depending on farmers' perceptions of the above, trees may be cleared, lopped, burned, conserved, planted, etc. Ibrahim, in his study in Darfur, Sudan, found that farmers saw trees as competing for water and space with crops and felt they had to be cut down (Ibrahim, 1984). Sometimes, the fear of farmers is not imaginary. Some trees actually harbour destructive birds and insects which attack plants and crops (Agabawi, 1968). In such a situation, farmers may, in spite of their knowledge about the beneficial contribution of trees, be forced to make a trade-off between short- and long-term gains. The farmers distinguish between trees that have negative and positive effects, depending on their root and crown morphologies. The farmers were asked to state whether they considered the statements in Table 9.2 to be true about trees on farms and grazing areas. Among the 215 (refugee) sample household heads, only about 6% saw trees as competing for moisture and space. The corresponding figure for the Sudanese (ninety-one sample households) was about 11%. Thus, the latter families would cut them in order to make more space and moisture available to crops, which, in their view, have a more immediate and important value. About 9% of both groups also saw trees as casting shade over crops. This problem could be overcome by cutting the twigs and foliage only. Around 9%

Table 9.2   The disadvantages of trees in farms and grazing areas as perceived by farmers (%)

	Refugees	Sudanese
Trees compete with crops for space and water	6.3	10.8
Trees cause shade cast on cropped ground	8.9	9.5
Trees harbour destructive birds	9.4	9.0
Trees are sanctuary to destructive insects	9.2	7.2
Their positive contributions outweigh the above	66.2	63.5
Total	100.0	100.0

of both groups also considered trees as harbouring destructive birds. Another 9% among the refugees and 7% among the Sudanese farmers also considered trees as providing sanctuary to destructive insects. It is interesting to see that 66% of the refugee farmers and 63% of the Sudanese farmers saw trees as useful assets on their farms and on grazing areas.

In view of the fact that insect-pest attacks on crops have become a major problem on the scheme since the last decade, the farmers do not attribute these plagues to the few remaining trees. In fact, there seems to be a correlation between deforestation and the outbreak of insect pests in the area. The disappearance of trees has led to a drastic decline in the insect-eating bird population. This has in return led to insect-pest build-up. The outbreaks of insect-pest attacks since the mid-1980s have become one of the major causes of loss of yields on and around the scheme area (see Chapter 4). For example, in the 1985 cultivation season, grasshoppers, locusts and caterpillars (bollworms) attacked sorghum and millet between flowering and the milk stage and as a result crop yields diminished drastically. The three insects combined to cause yield reductions, varying 'from a few per cent in Salmin lands to 85% in some of Adingrar and Umbrush lands. Millet seemed to have been affected worse than sorghum' (ACORD, 1985a: 15).

The destruction of vegetation has exacerbated the ecological disequilibrium which is a typical feature of the arid and semiarid regions in Africa (Behnke and Scoones, 1993; Ellis *et al.*, 1993). Other studies in the clay plains of Sudan also show similar results. Simpson and Khalifa's findings, for example, showed that the rapid expansion of mechanized rain-fed crop production had led to the outbreak of pests and diseases (Simpson and Khalifa, 1976a). Not only had the outbreak of insect pests, most probably due to the disappearance of trees, led to diminished yield levels, but the need to undertake control measures has proved to be an extremely strenuous and labour-intensive activity. In the nearby mechanized rain-fed commercial farms, aerial sprays of chemicals are used to combat insect-pest attacks. On the scheme, biological controls are unknown. Instead, farmers resort to traditional methods by scaring off the locusts and the grasshoppers. This method requires a great deal of family labour time and perseverance. Caterpillars are also shaken off the crop plants by hand. These methods of combating the attack of insects is ineffective because the scaring of grasshoppers and locusts requires the coordination and cooperation of the entire work force in the village. Shaking off caterpillars from the crop plants is also not very effective because some of the dislodged caterpillars are able to reinfest the crops by climbing the crop plants in the following days. In Eritrea, the refugees' country of origin, this method of combating insect plagues was relatively effective because farmers possessed several small plots in different sites. Because the risk for simultaneous attack of insect pests in the different locations was minimal, the available family labour was enough to scare and shake off insect pests in the small individual plots. On the scheme, farmers are allocated up to 10 *feddans* of land on the same site and the available family labour is seldom enough to combat the attack. The problem of insect-pest attack is probably one of the indirect consequences of the ecological imbalance, which might have been exacerbated by land degradation in terms of vegetation destruction.

The data in Table 9.2 show that only a minority saw some negative effects of trees on crop production. This is not to suggest however, that only this group engages in tree cutting. It cannot also be taken for granted that those who are positively predisposed to trees would respond positively to a tree-planting project. If such were the case, there would be no cause for concern. As we saw in the preceding chapters, the land resource on the scheme compared with the population which it supported was extremely scarce. Farm incomes were so low that not many of the farmers had any surplus they could afford to forgo by assuming a liberal stance with regard to trees that might potentially contribute directly (by competing for moisture, nutrients, space and energy/sunlight) or indirectly (by harbouring destructive birds and insects) to a reduction in incomes. Thus, even the farmers who were environmentally conscious were forced to engage in cutting trees that grew on and around their farms. They did not, however, cut trees indiscriminately. A few trees which, in the farmers' view, did not compete for moisture, nutrients, space and energy and which did not cast shade on cropped ground, such as a few of the *Balanites aegyptiaca* (*hijlij*), were left undisturbed. They cut down trees because not only were their holdings small, but their productive capability was reduced due to overcultivation. Consequently, the utility of the marginal income that might be forgone was quite high. Thus, they could not afford to forgo any income loss. It is worthwhile to note, however, that the major cause of vegetation destruction is not due to the number of trees cut to overcome this problem. This plays only a minor role in the problem of deforestation.

It is important, however, to guard against construing the cutting of trees by such farmers as emanating from environmental ignorance or lack of concern for the need of the future generation. Looked at in the context of the technological and economic opportunities and constraints within which the farmers struggled to make ends meet, such behaviour made sense. As the margin of subsistence decreased, the opportunity cost of labour that could be used to scare off the birds or insects harboured by trees on and around the farms increased compared with what that labour time could earn elsewhere. The need to ensure immediate subsistence to the farm family therefore induced even the most environmentally conscious farmers to cut down trees that harboured destructive birds (such as *Quelea quelea*) and insects, disregarding the risk of land degradation.

How do the farmers explain the outbreak of insect pests? The widespread outbreak of insect plagues in recent years is, in the farmers' view, caused by dissipation of soil nutrients due to continuous cropping without fallow periods, use of fertilizers, planting of leguminous crops, etc. Their explanation may be indirectly linked to destruction of vegetation on and around the scheme. As Coppock states, 'woody plants have been found to have a potentially significant role in nutrient turn-over and replenishment of soil fertility in semi-arid savannas' (Coppock, 1993: 57). The climax vegetation of the clay plains is *Acacia* trees, which are deep-rooted, perennial, deciduous, nitrogen-fixing trees, whose removal eliminates the agency by which the topsoil receives nitrogen and other minerals brought up from deeper layers in the soil contour. When non-leguminous annual crops are grown on the areas stripped of the *Acacia* trees, the topsoil gets impoverished, which, among other things, leads to loss of yields. This is referred to by the farmers as soil exhaustion. Not only has the removal of *Acacia* trees on and around the scheme resulted in an impoverishment of the topsoil, but is has in turn led to a drastic reduction in insect-eating birds. Thus, the impoverishment of the topsoil (soil exhaustion), the destruction of vegetation and the outbreak of insect pests are caused by an interplay between inextricably intertwined factors, which may be results of human interference.

This suggests that an explanation of small farmers' land-use practices are difficult to understand unless they are placed in the broader political, economic and social contexts. This approach enables the researcher concerned to see the structure of the opportunities and constraints into which resource users are locked. Excessive cultivation, grazing and tree cutting constitute ignorance only when they are pursued in the presence of choices. For the majority of the farmers on the scheme, there is often no alternative to increasing intensity of resource use even when the resource users concerned are aware of the medium- and long-term consequences of such heightened resource-use intensity. Under stressful conditions of scarcity, where there are few or no alternatives to exploitative resource use, environmental awareness or lack of it has no great influence on the behaviour of traditional resource users. The need to survive under adverse conditions dictates land-use practices which are inconsistent with one's experience and knowledge. The corollary of this is that the need to survive by eking out a living from meagre and degraded resources also induces farmers operating within the subsistence margin to respond sluggishly to an investment opportunity which may contribute to sustainable resource use, e.g. tree planting. In the following section, the response of the farmers to the project of tree planting initiated by ACORD will be discussed and the underlying factors (in addition to the ones discussed above) influencing their responses will be explored.

Farmer participation in tree planting

Given the wide variety of uses of trees and in light of the relatively extensive ethnobotanical knowledge that exists among the farmers on the scheme, it is plausible to expect that the farmers would embrace a tree-planting project, which is, amongst other things, designed to halt land degradation and to increase the supply of products (wood fuel) which contribute substantially to their welfare. As Roche notes, trees represent an ecological underpinning of traditional agriculture (Roche, 1989) and the data in Table 9.1 suggest that the farmers are aware of this fact. The data elicited from the interviewees show that trees, when they exist in abundance, provide important supplementary sources of livelihood.

One of the most critical constraints on agricultural production in the area is shortage of and fluctuation in rainfall. All the farmers interviewed saw a positive relationship between occurrence of rainfall and dense vegetation cover. Syd Abdulahi A. Abu Kered, a local Sudanese notable, was born in Bolos, on the outskirts of the Qala en Nahal scheme, in 1923 (interview with A. A. Abu Kered, 1991).[2] According to him, the area used to be covered with thick savannah woodland and rainfall was abundant. With the influx of large numbers of immigrants from Chad, Nigeria and western Sudan and the expansion of mechanized agricultural production, large tracts of land were cleared of trees for agricultural production. This was exacerbated by exploitative tree cutting by commercial charcoal wholesalers who came to the area with licences, lorries and labourers to make charcoal (interview with A. A. Abu Kered, 1991). In his view, charcoal production and the expansion in mechanized rain-fed agriculture constitute the two major causes of vegetation depletion in the area. The situation was aggravated by the sudden relocation of 20,000 Eritrean refugees, who had to clear land for agriculture and to cut trees to establish villages and construct houses. He stated, '[T]he destruction of vegetation is the major cause of the recurrent droughts in the area.' Syd Kered said that it was possible in the past to predict the occurrence of rains with reasonable accuracy. This is no longer possible due to the dramatic depletion of the vegetation resources that have taken place on and around the scheme (interview with A. A. Abu Kered, 1991). In the farmers' view, unless corrective measures are taken, the collapse of the scheme and its environs is inevitable. That is what most of the farmers in the area believe. There is no doubt in the minds of the farmers that a vital relationship exists between vegetation cover and rainfall. This suggests that, as long as they believe such a strong relationship exists and as long as their basis of subsistence remains dependent on natural rains, it is plausible to assume that there is a *prima facie* incentive for the farmers to grow trees. Other things being equal, they will respond to a tree-planting project favourably in order to improve the occurrence of rainfall, improve soil fertility, halt further land degradation, boost the supply of fodder, wood fuel and food and improve or preserve the productivity of the land.

The components of the tree-planting project included: (i) production of seedlings in a project nursery; (ii) establishment of four plantations, three on denuded catchment areas and one of a water-logged site; (iii) distribution of shade trees for compound planting; (iv) distribution of *Acacia mellifera* seedlings to contact farmers to be used as live fencing for their *hawashas*; and (v) distribution of *Acacia senegal* to farmers interested in agroforestry. In 1987, about 94,000 seedlings were distributed to the six refugee villages and one Sudanese village – Shangiya (ACORD, Forestry Records, 1987–1989). The number of seedlings distributed in just 1 year indicates that, if successful, the programme could replenish the depleted vegetation on the scheme. However, the project was from the outset faced with problems that slowed down its progress. Of the three wood lots, only one was successfully established but it suffered from an early end to the rains. The other wood lots 'suffered from mishandling of seedlings and failure to give the programme the right priority' (ACORD, 1987b). By September of the same year, it was stated that the amenity tree planting in public areas and the 7,000 seedlings distributed for compound fencing had been successful (ACORD, 1987b).

At that stage, some of the problems facing the forestry programme included fire outbreaks (for example, in Umbrush) destruction by livestock, cracks, termites and dry weather. During the 1987 seedling distributions, only one Sudanese village was included. A second round of distribution took place in July 1989, in which another four villages benefited from the distribution. In July 1989, about 92,600 seedlings were distributed (ACORD, Forestry Records, 1987–1989). As far as could be established from the available records, between 1987 and 1989, over 186,000 seedlings were planted on the scheme.

The aims of the project were: to preserve the environment by planting trees in the villages and around farms through halting the further loss of soil in the denuded areas such as the jebels and pediments; to overcome the problem of land degradation around animal watering-points (*hafirs*); to provide sources of income from gum collection in *hashab* (gum arabic) gardens; to provide shade from the summer heat for families in their compounds and livestock and their herders in *hafirs*; and to solve the problem of scarcity of wood fuel. In the process, it was hoped that farmers would learn how to grow trees. The trees in the four plantation plots – *hafirs* (around animal watering-points), the European Economic Community (EEC) project, jebel Khanam and the public places – were planted by ACORD themselves. The seedlings for shade trees in compounds, the *A. mellifera* for live fencing in farms and the *A. senegal* seedlings for agroforestry (the cultivation of trees as an integral part of crop production) were distributed to individual farmers. In a semiarid area like the Qala en Nahal, where one of the major problems facing farmers is supply of water, growing of seedlings in nursery gardens and their distribution to farmers only represents a minor fraction of the total amount of work and resources required for the upkeep of trees throughout the span of their maturity.

Although it is important to know the number of seedlings a project distributes and plants, the survival rate of the trees planted and the training component are equally, if not more, important than the number of seedlings distributed and planted. The important criterion for evaluating such projects is whether the planting of trees sows the seeds of participation in a learning process.

There are no records of the survival rate of the trees planted. It was not possible for us to count the number of trees that have survived. Visits to the plantation plots and walks through the *hawashas*, however, showed that few trees have survived. Shade trees in residential compounds were the most successful. Of all the trees planted outside the compounds, the survival rate of *mosquite* trees was highest. By 1991, there was general agreement among the farmers, ACORD and the Commissioner's Office for Refugees (COR) staff that the reforestation programme had failed. It has to be noted, however, that the number of nim trees (for shade) in the residential compounds and the few others outside the compounds show that a few trees have survived here and there. In situations where there had been thoughtless destruction of vegetation, even the survival of a single tree is a measure of achievement.

During fieldwork in 1982 and 1983, the proportion of bare ground witnessed was much smaller than in 1991–1994. However, the number of shade trees in the courtyards of the refugee families is much greater today than it was then. The survival rate of seedlings distributed to the farmers can be estimated from the number of farmers that possess trees (see Table 9.3). As can be seen from Table 9.3, only 45% of the refugee respondents own trees. The corresponding figure for the Sudanese is 93%. Not all these trees were planted as part of the tree-plantation scheme. Most of the trees grew naturally on the edges of the *hawashas*.

There is a statistically significant difference between the Sudanese and the refugees regarding tree ownership. This may clearly suggest that there is a significant difference between the response of the Sudanese and the refugees to tree planting and to subsequent caring for the planted trees, which is consistent with the information gathered from ACORD's reports. According to ACORD's field staff, there was no difference in the response of the Sudanese and the refugee farmers regarding planting of trees on farms. Both were reluctant to plant trees on their farms, mainly for the reasons we saw earlier, but the Sudanese were more responsive to planting of trees in compounds (ACORD, 1988a). The data in Table 9.3 clearly show that the Sudanese in the area are much more responsive to the tree-planting project than the refugees. It is important to note, however, that the overwhelming majority did not own more than one or a maximum of two trees and nearly all of the trees were planted in compounds.

It was argued earlier that, given the farmers' awareness regarding the wide uses of trees, there was a *prima facie* incentive for the farmers to embrace the programme.

Table 9.3   Distribution of respondents by tree ownership

	Refugees	Sudanese
Tree owning	45.1	93.4
No trees owned	54.9	6.6
Total	100.0	100.0

$\chi^2=59.8$, d.f.$=1$, $P<0.01$.
Ownership here refers to possession, not to legal proprietorship, because the question of refugee entitlement to trees and products of trees is not clear in Sudan.

By so doing they could improve the quality of the environment and consequently their own quality of life. Their environmental awareness notwithstanding, however, the refugee farmers were extremely reluctant to accept the tree-planting programme as a priority. ACORD, for example, attributes the failure to lack of interest and motivation of the refugee farmers. 'It is important to note that there is a very real lack of motivation amongst the refugees towards growing trees. They do not own the land and thus cannot own any trees they may plant. They also take the view that by the time the trees have reached maturity they will have returned to their homeland' (ACORD, 1990: 9).

Why the sluggish response?

The reasons for the sluggish response of the refugee farmers to the tree-planting project are many and varied. The following are but some of the most important reasons.

Lack of tree tenure and future rights of exploitation

First, as stated by ACORD, the refugee farmers were reluctant to plant trees on land for which they lacked tenurial security. The central question is whether it follows automatically that farmers who plant trees on land for which they lack tenurial security cannot own the trees they plant on such lands. The refugee farmers and ACORD believe this to be the case. Strictly legally speaking, this is not necessarily the case in Sudan. The situation has substantially changed since the Forest Act (1989) came into force. The Act defines the phrase 'other forests' as including:

(a) Private forests established in any agricultural land owned or leased to people or which they traditionally cultivate, or which is surrounding their houses.

(b) Communal forests established by the citizens in their farms and around the cities and villages. (Forest Act, 1989: section 3).

This includes trees planted on land which, according to the Unregistered Land Act (1970), the Civil Transaction Act (1984) or the Land Settlement and Registration Act (1985), belongs to the government. According to these acts, all unregistered land is deemed to be government property. As we saw in the preceding chapters, nearly all the land (outside the riverine areas) traditionally utilized by the sedentary farmers and pastoralists falls in the category. Thus, trees planted on such lands are deemed private forests. The implication of this is that the persons who plant such trees have full right of disposal of the trees and their products. The Forest Act (1989) states, 'individuals, groups, committees and institutions who plant trees in areas described in section 3 hereof shall be entitled to use and deal with such trees and the produce thereof for such purposes as they may deem fit without any interference on the part of the corporation or its representatives' (Forest Act, 1989: section 18(2)). The only limitation to this right is section 17 of the Act.[3] This clearly suggests that the right of tenure of trees exists independent of the land on which they are planted. Thus in Sudan the widely held view that land-tenure systems are the main cause of failure of tree-planting programmes is not tenable.

It cannot be argued with full certainty, however, that the enactment of the Forest Act (1989) has eliminated the sense of insecurity experienced by farmers who may intend to grow trees on land which is not registered in their names. Any land that was not registered at the commencement of the Unregistered Land Act (1970) was deemed government land. The implication of this is that the government can in principle still allocate such land to an alternative use any time it deems fit, even when it contains trees planted by individuals or communities. Thus, the insecurity is always there. As El Mahdi states, 'legally speaking . . . persons who still remain in possession of such lands are no longer secure; and their ownership is reduced to a mere licence or "tenancy" act at will which may be revoked at any time when the Government invokes Section 8 of the Act and evicts the occupant' (El Mahdi, 1979: 9). Although it can be argued that the right of the person to trees planted on his farm or on land surrounding his house exists separately from the right to the land on which they are planted, whether such rights can be enjoyed or not is dependent on the stage in the span of maturity of trees in question. If government intervention occurs when the trees in question are small, this may represent bad investment of scarce resources – labour and water – because the trees at that particular stage of maturity may serve no purpose to the persons who planted them.

The law governing tree ownership seems to be unknown to the Sudanese farmers, refugees, COR and ACORD field officers on the scheme. Thus, all concerned are operating on the assumption that such rights do not exist. A right whose existence is unknown is as good as no right. The central question that must be addressed here, however, is whether the above-stated rights also apply to refugee farmers who plant trees on their farms and in land surrounding their houses as stipulated in the Forest Act (1989). As we saw earlier, not only are the land rights of the refugees regulated by a special act (Regulation of Asylum Act, 1974), but it is also explicitly stated that 'no refugee shall own lands or immovables in the Sudan' (Regulation of Asylum Act, 1974: section 9). What is land? 'Land', El Mahdi writes, 'includes benefits to arise out of land and buildings and things permanently fixed to land' (El Mahdi, 1979: 8). Are trees permanently fixed to land? He does not address the issue of trees, but he argues that buildings are land because they are permanently fixed to land. If, by the same token, trees are land, refugees cannot own trees (Regulation of Asylum Act, 1974: section 9). Are trees immovables? If things attached to land permanently are considered to be immovables, trees are also immovables and therefore they cannot be owned by refugees.

If the refugees' rights were governed by the general land laws of the country, it would have been possible to argue that the right to dispose of trees planted on a farm or on land surrounding one's house, as stipulated in the Forest Act (1989), would have prevailed over the principles stipulated in the Regulation of Asylum Act (1974), by virtue of a recency effect. However, their reception, movement, residence, rights of access to land, employment, etc. are regulated by special institutional arrangements. In this sense, refugee law in Sudan represents an aberration. Thus, it is plausible to assume that the rights given by the Forest Act (1989) to individual and community tree growers do not benefit refugees.

Are refugee communities also excluded from communal forest ownership? Communal forests are defined by the Forest Act (1989) as 'forests established by citizens' (Forest Act, 1989: section 3). Refugees are not citizens. Thus, they are not entitled to own communal forests. If the government wants to make the refugees feel secure about their rights and consequently to provide them with an incentive structure so as to participate actively in conservation work and maintenance of such work, they should receive information about the extent and limitations of their rights in this regard. This is not being done at present and hence there is a legitimate reason for the refugees to feel insecure about their rights. The lack of motivation exhibited by the refugee farmers to grow trees is therefore rational and predictable. The existing formal institutions have failed to eliminate the uncertainties and to provide incentives for the refugees.

If, as pointed out earlier, rights given to individual and community tree growers are unknown to the Sudanese local farmers, why do they respond more favourably to tree planting than the refugee farmers? As we saw earlier, traditional farmers and pastoralists in Sudan consider the lands in their possession as their own. They also consider buildings and trees growing on these lands as belonging to them (El Mahdi, 1979: 8). As long as they believe this to be true, it follows logically that they will respond positively to a programme of tree planting. The refugees consider neither the lands they cultivate nor the trees growing on them as their own. As a consequence, they are less motivated to participate in an activity such as tree planting, where their rights to the trees and to the produce of the trees they plant are in doubt.

In such a situation, the best way to secure the support and enthusiasm of the refugee farmers to the tree-planting project would have been to enter into negotiation by involving the refugees themselves with the government in the determination of their rights to the trees they were expected to plant. Without providing this assurance, it was unreasonable for COR and ACORD to expect the refugees to embrace the project. Agrarian producers operating at the minimum level of subsistence and who eke out a living from meagre resources in an uncertain environment can ill afford to 'squander' scarce resources – labour, land and water – on tree planting when they are not sure that they will reap the fruits of their investment (for the importance of tree tenure, see Fortmann, 1985). This behaviour is predictable and the agency that initiated the programme should have addressed the problem of tree tenure prior to the planning and implementation of the programme.

Given the de facto open-access nature of the common resources within and around the scheme, what guarantees did the refugees have that the trees they planted would not be cut down by others, including outsiders, as was the case with the other trees growing naturally on their farms and on lands surrounding their farms? If the farmers have been unable to stop people from cutting trees growing on and around their farms, how could they stop the cutting of the trees they planted on their farms or elsewhere unless special institutional arrangements were made to give them an exclusive right to such trees and unless effective enforcement mechanisms were established to protect such rights?

The dream of returning home, and long-term investment

One of the factors that contributes to our understanding of why the refugees lack motivation to plant trees is because of the nature of the investment itself. The span of maturity of trees varies depending on the species of the trees in question. Some trees may have a span of maturity which exceeds a human lifetime. Most of the trees planted on the scheme may not include such species. However, the refugees still hoped that the factors that forced them to flee would cease in the future (Kibreab, 1996). Many of them were reluctant to develop roots in the country of asylum. For some, tree planting symbolized putting down roots in an alien territory and this was construed by some of them as compromising one's national identity. The majority probably did not share this feeling, but many of those interviewed expressed such worries. Asked why they do not plant trees, one sheikh at Umsagata said, 'We consider ourselves as guests and tree planting is a long-term investment. We cannot wait for the trees to mature'. In the past, it was common among many of these communities to act in the interest of future generations (Nadel, 1946a), but on the scheme they are unwilling to invest their scarce resources in an activity from which they may not derive any direct benefits because, by the time the trees mature, they might have returned home. If the refugee communities have a history of making investments in the interest of future generations, why is it that they are unwilling to do the same on the scheme? Is it because they have undergone an attitudinal change precipitated by their experience in exile? Can it be argued that, if they had not undergone such changes, they would have felt responsible for the future need of those who may come to live in the area after them, in spite of their dream of returning home? Although the refugees have become more individualistic in exile (see Chapter 8), this particular behaviour does not represent a break from their past. In their country of origin, the future generations would have been descendants, while, in the case of the scheme, the beneficiaries would have been people with no connection. Thus, there is no reason to believe that not wanting to act in the interests of those moving into the area in the future is a result of attitudinal change. In any case, a community that lives within the subsistence margin can seldom afford such generosity.

Fear of relocation to a new site

Some of the settlers were relocated forcibly to the scheme in 1978 from Wad Hilew near the Eritrean border. By the time the decision of relocation was taken, the refugees considered themselves as established and thus, they resisted the decision fiercely (Kibreab, 1990b). The government implemented its decision, disregarding the refugees' resistance and wish to remain in the area (Kibreab, 1990). It seems that this has left behind a lasting fear and uncertainty about what the government and aid agencies could do in the future. They argue that they had developed Wad Hilew, but they were not allowed to stay. Some of them still fear that history may repeat itself. Given the need for large investments to relocate the population on the scheme to a new site, there is no objective ground for their fear. What matters, however, is what they believe, because this is what guides their decisions and actions.

Tree planting conflicts with animal production

The impetus for the programme came entirely from ACORD. It was stated in 1985 that there was very little response to ACORD's suggestions regarding forestry and soil conservation except in Salmin, where the forestry response was very positive (ACORD, 1985a: 10). The idea of tree planting did not emanate from the community nor was the community's support enlisted before the project was launched. The reforestation project was conceived in 1983, following the recommendation of a forestry consultant, who was commissioned by ACORD. In his view the success of a reforestation project was dependent on the cooperation and understanding of the people, but he did not consider it realistic to expect the community to contribute its labour to such a project (Howard, 1983: 40). Thus, the consultant concluded,

> [I] believe it will be impossible to convince people that they should provide their labour on a self help basis to plant, weed and protect extensive firewood plantations from fire and livestock ... I think that it would be unrealistic to expect the refugees to participate in planting of unallocated land destined to remain as a woodfuel plantation ... I recommend that the plantations be established by paid labour. (Howard, 1983: 40)

The forestry project was initiated and controlled by ACORD and the scheme residents were invited to participate on the basis of modalities already defined by

ACORD. If the idea of tree planting had been initiated by the scheme residents and ACORD had been invited to participate in the process, the project would have taken into account the constraints and opportunities that influenced the decisions and actions of the community. Instead of adopting a participatory project-planning approach, the project was identified, planned and implemented by ACORD. Community involvement, especially at the initial stage, was virtually absent. There is no doubt that the idea of initiating a reforestation project was critically needed. The high level of vegetation depletion and, consequently, land degradation was reason for serious concern and it was in response to this that ACORD initiated the reforestation programme. For example, in 1989, ACORD stated, '[F]orestry will remain an important component of the project in view of concern over environmental degradation in and around the scheme' (ACORD, 1989a). The farmers were also equally aware of the level of land degradation, but the demand for a tree-planting programme did not come from them. Nor was the programme a result of dialogue and interaction.

When the reforestation programme was undertaken, most of the livestock owners saw this as a further reduction of the common grazing land, which had already shrunk to unacceptable levels due to the expansion of cropped areas. One way in which the farmers responded to the reduction of the capacity of arable land was by building up their animal stocks (see Chapter 6). The allocation of the grazing and browse areas to tree plantation was considered by livestock owners as a threat to the strategy of building up livestock herds. The expansion of the cropped area on to previous grazing areas leads to frequent trespass and crop damage. The consequence of this is that the animals that are involved in the trespass are seized and impounded and are repossessed by their owners only after payment of heavy fines imposed by arbitrators or the police. Many of the livestock owners, therefore, saw the enclosures of the tree-planted sites not only as a loss of important grazing areas, but as a potential source of problems that would lead to increased seizure, impounding of animals and payment of fines. It was alleged by ACORD and COR that some herders, under the cover of darkness, removed the fences to graze their livestock (ACORD and COR field staff, Umsagata, pers comm., 1991). The animals destroyed the shoots and the seedlings by either eating them or trampling upon them. The iron angles which supported the fences were also stolen from the plantation plots and people allegedly used them for making beds. ACORD was left with no choice but to collect the remaining fences.

This is a classic and lamentable example of an imposed, but nevertheless useful, programme that failed, among other things, because of structural, motivational and institutional factors and because its initiators were unable to enlist the support and participation of the very people they intended to help.

Competition for family labour time

Tree planting in the climatic and soil conditions in the area competes for family labour and other resources. Water is a scarce and expensive commodity on the scheme. It is supplied via an extensive pumping plant from the Rahad River about 30 km away from the scheme. Supply is dependent on availability of fuel, spare parts and maintenance. Under such unreliable conditions, the opportunity cost of water becomes high, and for many farmers, it does not make sense to grow trees by using scarce water resources. Many of them consider watering their goats or donkeys as a priority. Digging and breaking through a subsoil layer to allow the establishment of tree roots in the hard clay soil is also energy-draining, which discourages many farmers. The major threats to trees are marauding animals during

Table 9.4   ACORD's budget 1984–1991 (% sterling)

	Budget	Agri-culture	Horti-culture	Soil cons.	Forestry	Water cons.	Livestock
1984	799,837	34,065	0	0	12,022	0	10,244
1985	1,912,115	26,000	0	0	25,000	0	61,000
1986	1,381,573	29,000	0	12,410	30,000	103,000	17,000
1987	1,722,956	17,631	4,500	1,500	4,500	1,000	17,650
1988	1,359,237	4,265	909	504	6,909	200	6,237
1989	814,564	9,000	0	0	0	0	11,500
1990	575,074	9,000	0	0	58,967	0	0
1991	1,117,320	5,500	0	0	2,500	0	1,000

Source: ACORD Books of Accounting.
cons., conservation.

the dry season. Thus, protection of trees in the dry season is a difficult task. This is even admitted by ACORD. They stated in one of their reports that 'uncontrolled grazing makes reforestation difficult without fencing which is inordinately expensive and out of the question for any farmer wishing, for instance, to put down some of his land to gum arabic' (ACORD, 1986b). All this suggests that the activity competes with other tasks which are considered more important to the survival of the communities.

Improper choice of seedlings and budgetary constraints
One of the causes of failure of the reforestation programme was the wrong choice of seedlings. The seedlings were collected from irrigated areas and were prepared for irrigated conditions. The seedlings died when they were transplanted into rain-fed dry conditions (ACORD, 1988a). The species were not drought-resistant. This suggests that, despite the fact that the forestry project had been under consideration since 1983, no adequate preparation was made to circumvent such avoidable mistakes.

The other factor which contributed to the failure of the reforestation programme was lack of adequate funds. As can be seen from ACORD's annual budgets (Table 9.4) it is clear that the forestry project was not a priority in ACORD's overall programme. In 1986, when the project was initiated, the total amount earmarked was £30,000, but in the following two years the allocation plummeted to £4,500 and £6,909, respectively. In 1990, a larger allocation was made for community forestry. When the Norwegian Refugee Council withdrew its financial support for ACORD's programmes in Qala en Nahal at the end of the 1980s, the forestry project became one of the first casualties.

On top of these factors, under the given constraints and uncertainties, tree planting seems to rank least in the farmers' inventory of priorities. They are faced with more serious problems that require immediate solutions. There is ample evidence to show that the communities are cognizant of the level of depletion of the tree resources on and off the scheme area. Also, they are perfectly capable of recognizing not only the economic and aesthetic values of trees, but also the critical role trees play in environmental protection. Their failure to respond to the opportunity provided by the programme of tree planting is, therefore, due neither to ignorance nor lack of environmental concern. It is because they are constrained by a variety of factors and growing trees does not make sense when viewed against the circumstances in which they eke out a living.

Conclusion

The wealth of ethnobotanical knowledge embodied in the refugee communities' culture implies that it is not because they are ignorant that they engage in destruction of tree resources. It is rather the need to make ends meet that forces the refugees and their Sudanese neighbours to clear trees for cultivation and for charcoal production for sale. Herders also lop trees to provide fodder for their animals. All forest resources belong to the state, but *de facto* they are open access resources. This means that outsiders are 'free' to cut trees. This seems to incite voracious behaviour among the local resource users. It is common among the refugees and Sudanese in the area to cut trees for pre-emptive purposes. The only way this uncertainty could be brought to an end is through devolution of control over the local resources to the immediate users.

The findings here also show that whether refugees participate in projects designed to promote environmental protection such as tree planting is not only a function of the existence of a body of resource knowledge. Before support for a tree-planting project can be enlisted, there are some critical issues that need to be addressed. The most important one is the question of tree tenure. For example, the tree-planting project initiated by ACORD was implemented without addressing this critical issue. It was not made clear to the refugees whether they would be able to own the trees they planted, to bequeath them to their offspring, to use their products, to dispose of them and to exclude others from using them. ACORD themselves did not have a clear picture of the situation. The other important issue is the question of whether the trees refugees plant would mature before repatriation. Otherwise this would constitute bad investment. Refugees, being people on the edge of survival, are reluctant to invest their scarce resources – labour and capital – on activities that would not be certain to bring them benefits. As people caught in the downward spiral of poverty, they are risk-averse. One should also make sure that such trees are not planted on land used for grazing or other purposes. All these are obvious factors that determine project participants' responses. Only projects that are imposed from outside without consultation with and participation of the 'beneficiaries' are faced with such problems.

Notes

1. Production for the market can also lead to increased intensity of resource use and be a cause of land degradation.
2. Bolos is a Sudanese village just off the scheme area, inhabited by the original occupants of the area.
3. Section 17 of the Forest Act (1989) states:

> The Minister, whenever he deems it necessary for the protection of any particular species of trees or confining tree felling to reserved areas only or within areas where regeneration is assured for the protection of soil, water resources and pasture, and any other natural resources within a particular area; or for the protection of highways, bridges, river banks and any other lines of communication, may issue orders to be published locally with provisions which prohibit or regulate any of the following things.

10 Population Pressure and Resource Depletion

A single child brings you happiness;
But many children bring you wealth. (Tigrinya proverb)

Before the establishment of the scheme (1969), there was little human interference with the natural environment of the area. Barbour, writing as late as 1961, stated that the present scheme area was not even used by the nomadic groups. Even the 'Shukria tribesmen, in their seasonal search for pasture, tended to avoid this region and seldom crossed the railway' into what is now the scheme area (Barbour, 1961: 194). This was mainly because of the dense vegetation, which provided a favourable habitat for sandflies. The latter are hostile to animals. Even though this was mostly true, according to the original settlers in Balos (one of the villages on the outskirts of the scheme), until the 1940s, the area represented an underutilized virgin savannah woodland, which was sometimes used as dry-season grazing by nomadic pastoralists such as the Shukria, Lahawin and Kenana (interview with A. A. Abu Kared, 1991).

However, there is evidence to suggest that the Gedaref district (the Qala en Nahal, Mufaza, Gallabat and the Atbara valley) was inhabited before the decimation of the population by a combination of wars, disease, famine, drought, cattle plague and invasion of the grass plains by *Acacia* forest (Mackinnon, 1948; Barbour, 1953; Graham, 1969). Mackinnon, for example, stated, '[M]any elders testify to the former existence of a heavy population up to the time of the Mahdiya in the middle eighties of the last century' (Mackinnon, 1948: 729). A population estimate made by the Governor General of Sudan, Wingate, showed that the population of Kassala Province was reduced dramatically between 1882 and 1903 from 500,000 to 80,000 (Reports 2/2/6, 1903). The estimated losses due to disease and warfare were said to be 300,000 and 120,000, respectively. The overall population in the country was said to be reduced from 8,525,000 to 1,870,000 (Reports 2/2/6, 1903: 79). After the decimation of the population during the Mahdiya, limited settlement by Sudanese Arabs seems to have begun in the 1920s. For example, one of our informants, a 68-year-old, Syd Abdulahi Ali Abu Kared, was born in Balos in 1923. There is also other evidence which suggests that settlement by the Arabs began at the latest in the early 1920s. For example, the right of ownership of gum arabic trees or *Acacia senegal* (Arabic, *hashab*) gardens by some individual families dates back to 1924, when the condominium government allocated such rights to notables of surrounding villages. However, the settlers were not more than a few families.

Other groups that began settling in the area during the 1940s and 1950s were the non-Arab West African immigrants, mainly known as Fellata. The villages of the latter group are all located within the scheme area. These groups no longer refer to themselves as Fellata, but rather as Sudanese, and mainly claim origin from the western provinces of Darfur and Kordofan. The refugees also refer to them as Sudanese. The original Arab Sudanese settlers, however, still refer to them as 'Nigerians', 'Malians' or 'Chadians', who came to the area to earn money as farm labourers on their way to and from the Holy City of Mecca in Saudi Arabia (Barbour, 1953: 55; Graham, 1969: 412).

Before the refugees' arrival, there was a high prevalence of wet-season diseases, the land was infested with biting flies and the lack of water in the dry season discouraged settlement. The distribution of human and animal settlements and land-use practices were strongly influenced by water availability from precipitation, surface flow or groundwater supplies. The areas where there was lack of drinking-water for humans and animals were underutilized while the patches of land where there were adequate perennial water-supplies were overexploited. The only sources of water-supply were a few wells and rain-fed *hafirs*, which dried up during the dry season around January (Barbour, 1953: 55; Graham, 1969: 412). Subsequently, the families would migrate to the Rahad River or the Qala en Nahal village about 30 km north of the present scheme area. Qala en Nahal village (now a town) was among the oldest settled areas in the district because water was available due to its unique location at the foot of the Qala en Nahal hills.

> The Qala en Nahal Hills are formed of the oldest rocks in the area, those of pre-Cambrian Basement Complex. Most are granitic but there are two groups of serpentine outcrops, one in the south and one in the north. The weathered rock is very porous and percolation is accelerated along numerous shearlines and faults. Here ample well-water is available throughout the year but because the rocks are so permeable the wells are the deepest in the whole area, reaching on average a depth of 130 ft (40 metres). (Graham, 1969: 414).

Permanent settlement in the whole district of Gedaref was limited to along the course of the Rahad River, the Gedaref ridge and the Qala en Nahal hills, where drinking-water was available throughout the year (Graham, 1969). But water-supply was not the only factor determining permanent settlement in the southern part of the district (including the area where the refugee settlement scheme is located), where rainfall is higher and yet population still remained low. This area had more vegetation and was inhospitable and unpleasant during the rainy season (Graham, 1969: 417). It was avoided by the livestock owners, who preferred to settle in the northern part of the district, where there was less vegetation.

The refugees were the first permanent settlers on the scheme area. This was made possible by the heavy investment of international refugee aid and particularly the provision of pumped water from the Rahad River (about 35 km away from the scheme). The six refugee villages and the Sudanese in the surrounding areas were served by the same water-supply system. The unhealthiness of the area for human habitation can be testified to by the large number of refugees who died in the process of making the wild environment habitable. This was due to the heavy vegetation cover, which provided a suitable habitat for sandflies, mosquitoes, snakes, etc. (Mahmoud Sheikh, Umsagata, pers. comm., December 1991). A refugee elder reported, '[W]hen we were first brought here, there were no roads or tracts. It was all very thick vegetation. Many months were spent in clearing land for cultivation and opening up roads to join the villages. I spent three nights in the bush from Umsagata to Umzurzur [now only 9 km apart] to visit relatives there' (interview with refugee elder, 1991).

Although these statements relate to the environment as it existed only 20 years ago, in terms of the environmental changes, measured in deforestation, that have occurred in the area, it seems as if there are centuries separating the period when the first relocations took place (1969) and the present. In the following sections, the growth of population since the establishment of the scheme and the relationship between population densities and the environment will be discussed.

Population growth on the scheme 1970–1991

Accurate population figures are lacking for the early periods of the scheme. As a result, different sources give different population sizes depending on the purposes the figures are designed to serve. According to official statistics, there were 30,000 refugees who lived on the scheme in 1980 (COR Administration Records, 1971–1994). The reliability of these data is questionable. Spooner, at that time ACORD's consultant, for example, stated that these data should be rejected because they were 'inaccurate and misleading and were compiled . . . in a confused . . . manner' (Spooner, 1981: 4). A population survey conducted by ACORD during that period showed that there were only 18,050 refugees on the scheme in 1980 (ACORD, 1981a; Spooner, 1981: 4). The official figures were 66% higher than the actual figures. Another ACORD document for 1981 gives a refugee population of 28,000 for the same period (ACORD, 1981b). The latter document represented about 55% more than the 1980 survey results and it was not possible to establish its source. The 1982–1983 ACORD report does not give an exact population figure. The size of the population on the scheme was vaguely referred to as 'in excess of 25,000 refugees' and '5,000 Sudanese farming families' (ACORD, 1983a). The latter is obviously inaccurate because there were not 5,000 Sudanese families on the scheme during that time. Even the total Sudanese population was much less than 5,000. In 1985, the official estimate of the refugee population on the scheme was 30,000 and 5,000 Sudanese (ACORD, 1985b). This is also contradicted by the results of the population census conducted during the same year. The results of the 1985 population census conducted by ACORD show that there were only 23,114 refugees and 3,248 Sudanese living on the scheme (ACORD, 1985c). ACORD's 1989 annual report quotes a total population figure of 35,000 refugees and 5,000 Sudanese living in eleven villages within the scheme (ACORD, 1989b). According to government sources, the total refugee population on the scheme in 1988 was 28,626 (Kibreab, 1994b: Table 1).

All these figures, except those based on actual population censuses, are contradictory, misleading and inadequately sourced. Most of the population figures are exaggerated estimates and should not be considered seriously. It is worth while to note, however, that refugee statistics are often unreliable and Qala en Nahal is no exception (Kibreab, 1991). In this case, it is not only the refugee statistics that are disputable. The size of the local population in the surrounding villages is equally exaggerated. In all the documents, the number of people is given as 5,000 up till 1985. This is unreasonable because population rarely remains static over a period of a decade and a half.

In 1976 there was a drastic decrease in the population on the scheme (Table 10.1). The explanation for this is linked to the mechanization of cultivation. On the scheme agricultural production is based on partial mechanization, i.e. cultivation is tractorized. The project was funded by the United Nations High Commissioner for Refugees (UNHCR) until 1973, after which it was handed over to the government of Sudan (Kibreab, 1987: Chapter 7). The latter in turn handed over the scheme to the local people's government in Qala en Nahal town, which lacked financial resources, manpower and administrative capacity and neglected the project completely.

The scheme was immediately faced with serious financial problems, reflected in the collapse of the tractor hire service (THS) (Kibreab, 1987: Chapter 7). By 1976 it became clear that the existence of the scheme was threatened and UNHCR mounted several missions to identify areas of intervention. The following quotation may give an indication of the reasons underlying the drastic decline in population on the scheme during that time. One of the missions which visited the scheme in 1976 stated:

> [W]e visited the tractor station in Umsagata and found it in a deplorable state. The workshop was void of any equipment; it was a hut, insufficient of size, too small to do any work ... Outside we saw 30 tractors, none of them in a working condition, all in different stages of decay ... There were also 17 disc planters, all in the same sorry state as the tractors. (Tuttas and Gaymans, 1976: 9)

Another UNHCR consultant, who visited the settlement during the same month, also remarked that 'all the Byelerus tractors were out of order and only one of the other 12 tractors, all Massey Ferguson, was in full running order' (Huntings Technical Service, 1976: 17). One of the immediate consequences of the deterioration of the tractor service was a drastic decline in the amount of land cultivated. The total cultivated area in the 1973 season was 39,390 *feddans* (Kibreab, 1987: Table 7.1), but after the handover, this plummeted to 16,495 *feddans* in 1974, to 6,735 *feddans* in 1975 and to 7,000 *feddans* in 1976. The effect of the deterioration of the tractors on farm income was drastic (Kibreab, 1987: 190). There was a total crop failure in the 1975–1976 season and income from sorghum and sesame production was nil for many of the refugee families (Hunting cited in Kibreab, 1987: 190). Livelihood crises and malnutrition ensued as a result. Although no reliable data exist, those who survived the crisis speak of the many lives that were lost during those days due to lack of adequate food (interview with Village Committee, 1991). One immediate consequence of the drastic loss of income was that a considerable proportion of the population left the settlement in search of an alternative means of livelihood.[1]

The population on the scheme in 1976 was 38% less than in 1970, suggesting the population was fluctuating with the scheme's economic performance (Table 10.1).

Table 10.1 Population of Qala en Nahal refugee villages 1970–1991 and Sudanese population in surrounding villages 1985–1991

	Salmin	Umsagata	Dehema	Adingrar	Umbrush	Umzurzur	Total
Refugees							
1970[a]	4,091	3,629	1,213	2,513	2,832	4,000	18,278
1976[b]	3,471	3,276	1,270	2,087	1,745	1,438	13,287
1980[c]	4,400	4,606	3,222	3,696	3,780	2,696	22,156
1981[d]	4,610	3,910	1,750	2,940	2,840	2,000	18,050
1983[e]	6,367	4,526	3,276	3,217	4,136	2,918	24,440
1985[f]	5,961	5,872	2,513	3,009	3,337	2,382	23,114
1991[g]	7,449	7,932	2,682	3,411	3,562	2,944	27,980

	Salmin	Umsagata	Dehema	Umbrush	Utash	Huweig	Shangiya	Total
Sudanese								
1985[f]	265	893	1,304	412	374	n.a.	n.a.	3,248
1991[g]	332	1,217	2,578	666	472	361	205	5,831

Sources: (a and c) Commissioner's Office for Refugees, Scheme Administration Agricultural File M/A/L/I/A/1, 1970–1980; (b) Tuttas and Gaymans, 1976; Huntings Technical Service, 1976; (d) Euro Action Accord Survey, Qala en Nahal, 1981; (e) G. Kibreab, Questionnaire Survey, and Sudan Council of Churches – Eastern Sudan Relief Programme, Anti-Tuberculosis Campaign Records, Umsagata, 1983; (f) ACORD, 1985c; (g) ACORD, 1991. ACORD (1985c, 1991) censuses based on total enumeration.

During that critical period, the availability of food seemed to be a decisive factor in limiting the number of people who could live on the scheme. The figures for 1980 were obtained from official sources and their reliability is questionable, because, even though there was a minor financial intervention by the UNHCR in 1978 (Kibreab, 1987), the sorry state of the tractors and, consequently, the economic status of the remaining farmers had not changed sufficiently to entice back those families that had left the scheme due to economic hardship associated with the tractor failure. Thus, it is reasonable to assume that the refugee population on the scheme in 1980 was in the range of 18,000, as the findings of ACORD's survey showed during the following year.

The major change in population size occurred when ACORD took over the management and refurbished the tractor hire service on the scheme in 1981. The main objectives of ACORD's involvement were:

(i) to design a system of tractor and land management in Qala en Nahal which will serve to ensure a viable and efficient tractor service giving maximum potential benefit to all refugee farmers; and

(ii) to identify areas which will benefit from the assistance of ACORD, particularly in relation to long-term self-sufficiency possibilities for the settlement. (ACORD, 1981c)

Accordingly, ACORD refurbished the tractor hire service by establishing an efficient management system and a modern workshop, and by purchasing new tractors (Kibreab, 1987). Following ACORD's involvement, the area cultivated by the tractor hire service and by the scheme population increased considerably, from 13,900 *feddans* (Kibreab, 1987) in 1980 to over 35,000 *feddans* (ACORD, 1983a). The population rose from 18,050 in 1981 to 24,440 in 1983. The improvement of the tractor hire service and favourable rainfall encouraged people to return to the scheme and cultivate their farms, and there was an increase in population of about 35% in just 3 years.

According to the birth records at the mother and child health (MCH) clinics in the six villages, the population on the scheme is characterized by a high birth rate (Sudan Council of Churches (SCC) records). There are no records of deaths; hence it is not possible to state accurately the annual rate of growth of the population on the scheme. According to the settlers, although the initial settlement phase was accompanied by very high death rates, the provision of basic health services and clean water has over time resulted in low death rates, presumably in the context of the same level of fertility. Until the refurbishment and improvement of the tractor hire service by ACORD, the population on the scheme remained stable and without major fluctuations throughout the decade (except 1976). For example, there was no population change between 1970 and 1980. The stagnation was due to the crisis in the method of cultivation. Between 1970 and 1990, the annual population growth rate in the Gedaref district was in the range of 2.5–3% (Abu Sin, 1989b). Assuming the same annual population growth, the rate of emigration from the settlement must have been between 2.5–3% of the total population per annum. The high rate of deaths that characterized the same period may have also contributed to the stagnation of the population.

In the period following ACORD's involvement, not only did emigration slow down, but the Qala en Nahal scheme began to pull other refugees who had relatives on the scheme from the other land, wage-earning settlements or reception centres in the region. For example, in a series of meetings which were attended by a total number of 1,600 family heads between 11 and 17 November 1985, it was pointed out that natural population increase and immigration of relatives and

Sudanese have caused *hawashas* (holdings) to be subdivided, putting pressure on the land resource (cited in ACORD, 1985a). Between 1985 and 1991 the scheme population (Sudanese and refugees) increased by about 29.4%.[2] The major increase was attributable to the large influx into the area of Sudanese and West African migrants due to deteriorating living conditions in their areas of origin. Between 1985 and 1991, the rate of growth of the Sudanese population on the scheme was about 80%. The corresponding figure for the refugees was only 21%. This represents an annul growth rate of 4.2% for both communities. According to government sources, the total refugee population on the scheme in March 1993 was 35,286 (COR, 1993). This figure sounds grossly exaggerated because, according to the results of the 1991 population census, there were only 27,980 refugees. The 1993 figures suggest that the refugee population had increased by nearly 26% in 2 years. Since there were some families who returned to Eritrea following the political changes in the country, the reliability of the 1993 statistics is questionable.

In fact, it is worth noting that, since a considerable number of the families whose *hawashas'* productivity declined left the scheme in search of alternative sources of livelihood, part of the population increase that has occurred since 1985 is due to immigration of Sudanese and West Africans.[3] Between 1970 and 1991 the population on the scheme increased by about 71.5%.[4] This represents an annual growth rate of about 3.4% over a period of two decades. A sizeable proportion of this increase is, however, attributable to immigration. After 1985, the majority of the immigrants were non-refugee families, attracted partly by the land availability in the environs of the Sudanese villages and partly by the social and physical infrastructural services on the scheme. Without the provision of a perennial water-supply, the area would not have been attractive to the migrants.[5]

Population pressure on scheme resources

The settlement was established to support less than 20,000 persons. Despite the fact that the population on the scheme has increased considerably, no additional land has been allocated to meet their growing needs. Although the population has increased by 71.5% since the establishment of the scheme, the land base within the scheme has remained constant, and neither chemical fertilizers nor organic manure is used to conserve or restore soil fertility. In addition, no legumes are planted to improve soil nutrients. Tractors are used for cultivation, but all other agricultural operations are performed manually. Until the mid-1960s, just a few years before the establishment of the refugee settlement, the area was almost empty, with only a very few families who migrated habitually during the dry seasons to the Rahad River, where there was a perennial water-source. In 1966, the total population on and around the present scheme area was only 1,300 (Salmin 100, Umsagata 400, Utash 300 and Dehema 300) (NEDEC and ILACO, N.V., 1966: 110). In 1991 the total population in the area was 33,811 (Table 10.1). During the establishment period (1969–1971), the transfer of nearly 20,000 people caused a rapid increase in population/resource ratio.[6] In 1991, the total number of Sudanese had increased to 5,831 persons. This represents about a 629% increase in 25 years. The pattern of settlement in southern Gedaref was determined mainly by the possibility of water-supply. The area was surveyed in 1966 and it was reported that 'the survey areas suffer an acute shortage of domestic water but water can often be found at the foot of jebels in the surrounding' areas (NEDEC and ILACO, N.V., 1966).

Major impacts of the establishment of the scheme were not only the sudden increase in population resulting from the relocation of nearly 20,000 refugees from the border areas, but also the provision of piped water throughout the year, which enabled the local population to overcome the constraint of domestic water shortage during the dry seasons. The availability of water and social services have become pull factors to migrants from different parts of Sudan, especially from the western regions. The high population pressure on the resources on the scheme is, therefore, exacerbated by the drastic increase of Sudanese migrants into the scheme area. Between 1985 and 1991 the total number of Sudanese inhabitants on the scheme area increased from 3,248 to 5,831. In a matter of 5 years, the Sudanese population has increased by about 80%.

The annual population growth rate (3.4%) in relation to the limited land-resource base is very high. The major cause of the increase is not a high birth rate as such, but immigration. The immigration of the Sudanese into the area is an indication of the deteriorating living conditions in the western provinces of the country. The fact that people are coming to the Qala en Nahal area despite the economic difficulties facing the population there shows that things are much worse in the southern and western provinces of the country. Although the population growth rate on the scheme compared with the average for the whole district is high, the reason why this has become a contributory factor to resource depletion is due to the confined state within which the refugees eke out their living. Since the refugees cannot bring new areas under cultivation in response to the population increase, the high growth rate is becoming an exacerbating factor to already overstretched resources. Thus, it is important to guard against attributing the cause of land degradation on the scheme solely to high population growth, because at the heart of the problem of land shortage is not high population growth as such. This is not to imply, however, that there is no high population density in relation to the available resources. The cause of the pressure is not rapid population growth, but the resources accessible to the population are not commensurate with the number of mouths that need to be fed from such resources. In refugee situations in which restrictions on freedom of movement and residence are imposed by governments of the countries of asylum, it is important to distinguish between pressures on resources caused by rapid population growth and those caused by high population density. The latter is a result of government decision, which is outside the control of the populations concerned.

If we exclude the immigrants, the rate of population growth among the refugees has been moderate. The modest population growth among the refugees, especially since the beginning of the 1980s does not, however, reflect low birth and high death rates. There is no evidence to suggest that the situation of the refugee population in this respect varies from that of the local population. The explanation is the emigration of a considerable number of the refugee community as one of the various coping strategies developed to overcome the acute land shortage within the scheme. Emigration enables the community members partly to relieve the pressure on the land and consequently to avert the threat of hunger for the remaining population and partly to earn an income elsewhere. Emigration from the settlements has over time become a means by which to offset the pressure on resources. Over time, out-migration – oscillatory and permanent – has become an effective mechanism for controlling population pressure on scheme resources. Even though the communities have not succeeded in maintaining ecological equilibrium (the environment in the arid and semi-arid regions is always in a state of disequilibrium, see Chapter 6), they have been able to minimize the occurrence of an ecological disaster and to avert the imminent threat of hunger.

This suggests that the refugee communities have, within the existing physical and institutional constraints, made their own adaptive response to the extremely limited land supply by reducing their demand on the natural resources to a level that would, at least in the future, avoid irreversible ecological damage on a considerable proportion of the scheme area. The response adopted by the community is to relate population growth on the scheme to the ability of the land and other related resources to provide the minimum base for subsistence.

This is very interesting because, as we saw earlier, the Regulation of Asylum Act (1974) formally places restriction upon the movement and residence of the refugees in the country. For the refugee communities, the Qala en Nahal settlement is the place of residence specified for them and emigration is strictly forbidden. This restriction notwithstanding, however, there is a continuous movement in and out of the settlement. This experience shows that, when there is an imbalance between the demand for natural resources and the environment's ability to supply such resources (within the framework of the technology in use), formal restrictions placed upon resource users' movements and residence are reduced to inoperative legal niceties by the sheer necessity of survival. Despite the government's intention to enforce a restriction on the movement and residence of the refugees in the settlement, the refugees always find a means by which to avoid government control and to emigrate in search of pasture, employment, or any other income-generating activities outside the scheme.[7] It is important to observe, however, that the government has effectively enforced the prohibition of expansion of cultivation by refugees outside the boundaries of the scheme.

Thus, in the semiarid region of Sudan where the refugee settlements are located, it is important to guard against viewing the problem of land degradation solely as a consequence of growing population and rising demands for subsistence requirements. Population pressure has only become a problem in the context of the political, institutional and physical constraints operative in the system. It is undoubtedly true that population pressure and consequently the demand for subsistence within the confines of the scheme have exerted immense pressure on the resources of the scheme, but, if the farmers were not in a state of confinement in terms of not being able to bring additional land outside the scheme into the production process, the pressure would have been less severe.

In order to understand the degree of population pressure on the resources, the population and the land-resource data in Tables 10.1 and 10.2 require further

Table 10.2   Land use in the Qala en Nahal settlement 1980

Item	Land type	*Feddans*[a]	%	Hectares
Total area	All land within scheme	98,450	100	41,349
Uncultivable	Villages, hills and rocky	20,850	21	8,757
Potentially cultivable	Undeveloped, problem and marginal land	77,450	79	32,529
Flood-risk land	Includes some woodland	8,400		3,528
Other woodland	In 1980 used for timber, charcoal and grazing	18,600		7,812
Non-cultivated	In 1980 season includes fallow/grazing	24,650		10,353
Cultivated area	In 1980 season	25,850		10,857

Source: Based on ACORD's measurements; Spooner, 1981.
[a] 1 *feddan* = 1.38 acres = 0.42 ha.

analysis. The total area of the scheme is 480 km² (24 km × 20 km (see Map 1.3)) and the total population in 1991 was 33,721 (Table 10.1). Thus, the population density in 1991 was 70.2 per km². However, since a considerable proportion of the land has always been uncultivable and many farmers have abandoned their farms because of soil exhaustion and weed infestation, the population density per cultivable land in 1991 was 120.5 per km². These figures say little on their own because the productive capability or the absorption capacity of land is highly variable. For example, in northern Zambia, where *chitemene* shifting cultivation is practised and where the soil is infertile, leached and acid, 6.6 persons per km² is considered to constitute overpopulation (Chidimayo, 1987: 20), while in Nepal rural population density reaches over 1,500 per km² (Blaikie and Brookfield, 1987: 37). Thus, population densities *per se* do not say much unless they are related to a specific system of resource management and the productive capability of the land in question.

The capacity of absorption and productive capability of land also vary according to the history of land use of the particular area. In the scheme area, the productive capability of land that has been continuously cultivated for 20 years is lower than a piece of land that has been recently brought under cultivation (see Chapter 2). Thus, the fact that most of the arable land on the scheme has been continuously cropped for over two decades without fallow periods, without application of manure or fertilizers and without planting of nitrogen-fixing leguminous crops suggests that the present population density – 120.5 persons per km² – is too high. The rate of population growth might not have been a problem, had the total amount of land allocated not been too small or had there been corrective measures, such as allocation of additional land, lifting of the limitation on freedom of move-ment and residence or relocation of the surplus population to a new site. It is in these contexts that population pressure has become one of the factors that has exacerbated the problem of resource depletion on the scheme.

According to the scheme manager (*mudhir*), there is empty land available for allocation, but the refugee farmers did not come to ask for it and some of them were even unwilling to cultivate the available land (Scheme Manager, Umsagata, pers. comm., November 1991). According to the farmers, the land the *mudhir* wanted to redistribute was once abandoned by other refugee farmers because of soil exhaustion. Understandably they did not want plots whose productive capability had been exhausted 'completely'. In the farmers' view, it was not considered worthwhile to invest their scarce labour and capital in rehabilitating land whose fertility was devoured by overuse or which they considered 'completely' exhausted. Preparing of degraded land in the Gedaref district is extremely labour-intensive because one of the consequences of overcultivation is increased weed infestation. The fact that there was unpossessed land which no farmer wanted to have in a situation where 36% of the families were landless is an indication of the severity of the level of loss of capability suffered by the available land resource.

Is population pressure one of the causes of land degradation on the scheme? Within the given physical constraints (soil and climatic conditions) and the limited resource base from which the farmers eke out a living, there is little doubt that the high population density on the scheme is one of the proximate causes that con-tributes to the deterioration of the land resource. However, the conditions under which the communities are operating are to a considerable extent defined by forces that are outside their control. In the following sections, the non-demographic factors that have contributed to inappropriate land-use practices are discussed.

Non-demographic factors as causes of resource depletion

It has to be emphasized that the ultimate factors underlying improper land-use practices on the scheme are represented in non-demographic factors such as: (i) allocation of inadequate land by the government, which allows no fallow periods and consequently induces continuous cultivation of the available land, leading to loss of mineral crop-plant foods, deterioration of organic matter, breakdown of soil texture and structure, and devegetation; (ii) limitation on the freedom of movement and residence, which has meant the inability to bring new areas outside the scheme under cultivation in response to population growth; (iii) horizontal expansion of commercial agriculture, which puts heavy additional pressure on the resources on and off the scheme area; (iv) inequitable distribution of the available land, on the one hand, between commercial farmers and subsistence producers and, on the other, between refugees and Sudanese subsistence farmers; (v) breakdown of traditional resource-management systems; and (vi) poverty. In the following sections how each of these non-demographic factors contributes to resource depletion on and outside the scheme area will be discussed.

Allocation of inadequate land

One of the ultimate causes of natural resource depletion on the scheme is the inadequacy of the amount of land allocated to the farmers. The government allocated too little land, disregarding the future needs of the communities arising from the need to conserve and restore soil fertility, as well as from population growth resulting from natural population growth and immigration. As we saw earlier, the Qala en Nahal refugee settlement scheme was established in 1969 to accommodate refugees fleeing from Eritrea. Among the first settlers, each family was allocated a *hawasha* measuring 200 m × 200 m (4 ha or 9.52 *feddans*). Those who arrived at a later period (1978–1979) were allocated plots varying from 5 to 2.5 *feddans* (Kibreab, 1987).

The total scheme area according to government records in 1980 was 74,000 *feddans* (31,080 ha) (Spooner, 1981), while the 1980 ACORD measurements (Spooner, 1981) showed the total area of the scheme as being 98,450 *feddans* (37,569 ha). Another ACORD document estimates the total area of the scheme at 106,144 *feddans* (44,580 ha) (Howard, 1983). The 1990 land-use survey conducted by the Commissioner's Office for Refugees (COR) in Umsagata, however, showed a total area of 79,375 *feddans* (33,337 ha). In view of the acute land shortage facing the settlers on the scheme, the discrepancy existing in the various data sources is considerable. However, only two of these data sources were based on actual measurements, i.e. the 1980 ACORD (Table 10.2) and 1990 COR land-use surveys (Table 10.3). Even between these two sources, there is a difference of about 19,000 *feddans* (8,000 ha).

During the 1980 season, of the 25,850 *feddans* that were cultivated, 13,900 *feddans* (55%) were cultivated by refugees and 11,900 *feddans* (45%) by Sudanese farmers. As can be seen from Table 10.3, the total area cultivated in 1990 had risen to 46,290 *feddans* (19,442 ha). This represents an increase of about 80% between 1980 and 1990 for both the Sudanese and the refugee population. In the 1990 season, the total area increased to 35,565 *feddans*. This represents an increase in the cultivated area by 156% in just 10 years between 1980 and 1990. This is excluding the area planted by alternative methods of cultivation, such as by *seluka* (digging stick), or by hired private tractors.

As can be seen in Table 10.2, about 21% (20,850 *feddans*) of the scheme was

Table 10.3   Total land-resource base in the Qala en Nahal refugee settlement scheme 1990 (in *feddans*: 1 *feddan* = 1.038 acres)

Village	I	II	III	IV	V	VI	Total
Refugee villages							
Salmin	4,885	890	4,747	690	850	80	12,140
Umsagata	4,420	1,490	4,000	550	850	210	11,520
Umbrush	5,510	455	1,945	150	1,430	300	9,820
Adingrar	4,080	1,015	2,060	560	500	45	8,260
Umzurzur	5,230	480	2,055	75	650	110	8,600
Dehema	5,025	2,135	1,345	0	815	0	9,320
Sub-total	29,100	6,465	16,153	2,765	5,095	745	48,760
Sudanese villages							
Umsagata	2,570	1,080	1,065	1,550	1,000	0	7,265
Dehema and Utash	3,585	1,120	380	1,200	500	0	6,785
Salmin Dajo	800	0	0	400	200	0	1,400
Shangiya and Huweig	1,170	350	1,050	1,160	470	70	3,970
Sub-total	8,125	2,550	2,495	4,310	2,170	815	19,420
Grand total	37,275	9,015	18,645	6,365	7,265	815	79,375

I, Cultivated using government tractors supplied by ACORD; II, cultivated by hired private tractors and *seluka*; III, abandoned or uncultivated during the 1990 season; IV, uncultivable; V, village sites and boundaries; VI, *hafir* sites (rain-fed reservoir).
Source: Compiled from the files of the 1990 Land Use Survey, Commissioner's Office for Refugees, Qala en Nahal (translation from Arabic).

uncultivable, comprising village sites, jebels (hills), pediments and rocky land. In the 1980 season, only 33% of the potentially cultivable area was cropped. By 1990, out of the 77,450 *feddans* of potentially cultivable land – and this is including problem, marginal and flood-risk lands – 64,450 *feddans* were under cultivation, but not necessarily every plot was cropped during that particular season (Table 10.3). In the 1990 season, 46,290 *feddans* of the potentially cultivable land were cropped while 18,645 *feddans* were either abandoned or were not cultivated during that season. In 1980, of the potentially cultivable land on the scheme, 18,600 *feddans* were used as a source of timber, fuel wood, charcoal and grazing. Part of the flood-risk land (8,400 *feddans*) was also woodland.

By 1990 of the total potentially cultivable land only 12,515 *feddans* were uncultivated, out of which 8,400 *feddans* were located in the flood-risk area. The area which was used as a source of timber, fuel wood, charcoal and grazing in the 1970s is now cleared for cultivation.

Table 10.2 does not contain a breakdown of the figures into land owned by the refugees and the Sudanese and hence does not show the gravity of the land shortage faced by the refugee families, due to the refugee community having far less access to arable land than the Sudanese farmers on the scheme. The gross area available to the refugees in 1980 was 56,000 *feddans* (ACORD, 1981b). It is interesting to observe, however, that the latest land-use survey, which was conducted by COR, the body responsible for the administration of the settlement and for the allocation and management of the natural resources on the scheme, shows that the total amount of land allocated to the six refugee villages on the scheme was 48,760 *feddans* and not 56,590 *feddans* as suggested in earlier land-use surveys. Of the

48,760 *feddans* about 35,565 *feddans* were under cultivation and the remaining 13,195 *feddans* were uncultivated, abandoned, uncultivable, villages and *hafirs* (Table 10.3). Unlike the old documents, which showed a certain amount of land allocated to the refugees represented in reserve, grazing and forest resources, the findings of the 1990 land-use survey do not indicate any remaining reserve, grazing or forest areas. These data clearly show that land on the settlement scheme is under heavy internal pressure. Pressure on scheme resources is not only exerted from within, however, but also exogenously.

By 1990, out of the total land resources available, 51,718 *feddans* were allocated to the refugee community (Table 10.3). This represents 96% of the total potentially cultivable land. It is worth while to state, however, that a considerable proportion of the so-called potentially cultivable land includes flood-risk, marginal, woodland and grazing lands. All the land which in 1980 was used for timber, charcoal, grazing etc. has been brought under cultivation. These data clearly show that one way in which the refugee community has tried to overcome the acute land shortage has been through expansion of cultivation on to marginal, flood-risk and grazing areas.

One of the major reasons why the designated scheme area was small was due to the government's perception of the refugee problem as being transient. The factors that prompted their flight were expected to be eliminated after some years, thereby allowing the refugees to return home. Thus, the long-term resource needs of the refugees were not taken into account when the settlement was planned at the end of the 1960s. Contrary to the government's expectation, the refugees stayed for over three decades and no additional land was allocated to meet their expanding needs, nor was the surplus population relocated, as happened for example, in Ulyamkulu in Tanzania.[8] Not surprisingly, the result was inappropriate land-use practices reflected in overcultivation, overgrazing and deforestation.

Inequitable distribution of resources

Inequitable distribution of resources is one of the major factors that contributes to the problem of natural-resource depletion on the schemes. This problem also seems to be generally true in many sub-Saharan African countries (Bernard and Thom, 1981; Repetto and Holmes, 1984; Ibrahim, 1989; Mohamed, 1990; Vivian, 1991; Ghai, 1992). Inequitable distribution of land between commercial farmers and the small Sudanese farmers, where each commercial allotment is over 1,500 *feddans* as opposed to that of the small Sudanese farmers and refugees, where the mean land size is 25 *feddans* and under 10 *feddans*, respectively. Land is also inequitably distributed between the Sudanese and refugee farmers within the scheme (Table 10.4).

As can be seen from the data in Table 10.4, about 16% of the refugee families have 5 *feddans* or less among the Sudanese only 2% have 5 *feddans*. No Sudanese family has less than 5 *feddans*. Of the refugee families, 98% have either 10 or less than 10 *feddans* while 82% of the Sudanese families have over 15 *feddans*. However, the data in Table 10.4 do not reflect the true picture of land possession among the refugee families. The sample respondents were deliberately selected from families that had land possessions. Of the refugee families 36% were landless in 1991 (ACORD, 1991). These landless families were excluded from the sample frame. None of the Sudanese families were landless. Despite the fact that disposal of land by refugees in any form is legally prohibited, the findings of a previous study by the author showed that there was a limited degree of land concentration in the hands of a few refugee families to the detriment of the poor (Kibreab, 1987).

The consequence of inequitable distribution of natural resources, especially land, is the creation, on the one hand, of a few wealthy families with a high

Table 10.4   Distribution of the refugee and Sudanese farmers by farm size in *feddans* (%)

Land size	Refugees ($n = 215$)	Sudanese ($n = 91$)
1–5	16.2	2.2
6–10	81.8	15.4
11–15	0.5	7.7
16–20	0.5	34.1
21–25	0.5	6.6
26–30	0.5	16.5
31–35	0.0	3.3
36–40	0.0	2.2
41–50	0.0	6.6
51–60	0.0	3.3
>60	0.0	2.2
Total	100.0	100.0

concentration of land-ownership and, on the other, destitute people pushed to the edge of hunger and forced by the sheer necessity of survival to eke out a living by exploiting the ever-decreasing land and other natural-resource bases. Inequality of access to natural resources forces destitute people to use land and other natural resources in an unsustainable manner in order to gain shelter, earn incomes from clearing marginal lands or sell the products of common property resources (CPRs) such as firewood, charcoal, thatching grass, fodder, water, etc. The confinement of the poor to marginal and degradation-prone areas has a tendency to intensify human and animal population pressures on such sites and the consequence is inappropriate land use, reflected in overcultivation, overgrazing and deforestation.

Policy of confinement

The centre-piece of the settlement policy of the government of Sudan is that refugees should be placed in organized settlements or transit centres (NCAR, 1980). This is designed to discourage refugees from self-settling among the Sudanese in rural and urban areas (Kibreab, 1994b).[9] Once refugees are placed in designated areas, they are forbidden by law to leave. Section 10 (2) of the Regulation of Asylum Act (1974) for example, states, '[N]o refugee shall depart from any place of residence specified for him. The penalty for contravening this subsection, shall be imprisonment for not more than one year.' For refugees in organized settlements, the government allocates a certain amount of land from which they may derive their livelihood. When the government allocates land, it often assumes that the refugees will eventually return home and no consideration is taken of population increase due either to natural growth or to immigration. No matter how long the refugees stay or no matter how much the population in designated areas increases, they are not allowed to extend cultivation beyond the boundaries of the specified areas. The factors that prompted the refugees in the Qala en Nahal scheme to flee remained unchanged and they stayed longer than expected. Over time, the population increased and, in the absence of corrective measures, this caused disequilibrium between the demand for natural resources and the environment's ability to supply such resources. In this regard, the situation of the refugee population on the Qala en Nahal scheme is best described by the term confinement.

Confinement occurs when a land use has to become more intensive than it has been previously, but without the technical inputs (such as fertilizers) or changes in cropping techniques that would allow it to be sustainable at the new intensity. Confinement can result when a population grows within a limited area; or when an extensive land use, like nomadic grazing, becomes more intensive, because part of the area available to it is taken over for another land use. (Grainger, 1990: 124)

The most important limiting factor on the Qala en Nahal scheme is the prohibition by law of emigration outside the settlement in response to the diminishing land-resource base and productivity of the available land. One of the critical consequences of this is that no new land outside the scheme can be brought into the production process by the refugee farmers even when the land-resource base becomes diminished in relation to the community's growing needs.

In view of the state of confinement under which the refugee farmers eke out their living, the evidence shows that there is an upper limit beyond which resource depletion is inevitable, resulting from overuse. The Boserupian postulate of change in agricultural techniques resulting from population pressure on resources has not taken place. This suggests that, in an artificially imposed state of confinement, population pressure on resources is not necessarily met by an intensification which offsets the degenerative changes precipitated by resource overuse. On the scheme the consequence instead has been overcultivation, soil erosion and overgrazing on the pediments and *jebels*. The high population density in a confined context is exerting heavy pressure on the renewable resources. These constraints can only be overcome either by undertaking measures that restrict the demand for resources to a level which the environment can supply naturally or by introducing an efficient resource-management system which increases the capacity of the environment to produce the renewable resources artificially. Otherwise a shift to exploitative land-use practice is inevitable.

Historically, one important way in which cultivators in the area offset the impact of population pressure on resources was by extending cultivation on to previously untapped, potentially cultivable land. In her early works, Boserup (1965 and 1970) put this form of response down to population pressure by peasants in the contemporary period and consequently dismissed as a false dichotomy the distinction made by the classical economists between cultivated and uncultivated land, or between the 'extensive' and 'intensive' margin of cultivation. According to the classical economists, especially Ricardo's conceptualization, agricultural production was based on this principle. He assumed that agricultural technique was fixed and output could only be increased by bringing new land under cultivation and, in the process, inferior land would be brought into the production process and consequently the productivity of labour would be subject to diminishing returns. In light of the inelasticity of agricultural production compared with industry, he postulated that overall economic expansion would be brought to a halt.

For Boserup (1965 and 1970) the most important consequence of population pressure was not putting hitherto uncultivated land under the plough, but, as we saw in Chapter 1, the increased frequency with which available land is cropped in response to population pressure on resources. In her view, the need to support a growing population would lead to a shift to more intensive methods. In this study, since the most important way in which farmers in the arid and semiarid regions cope with population pressure on resources is by expanding on to uncultivated areas, one of the root causes of the problem of reduction in the capability of the land on the scheme is the confinement of the refugees, precluding them from resorting to their traditional coping strategy. Among non-displaced peasant communities, the expansion of cultivation often occurs onto new, uncultivated areas, provided such land is available as well as accessible. By prohibiting the refugee population from expanding onto uncultivated areas in response to population pressure and productivity decline, the government has deprived them of a tried and tested coping strategy.

The land-use data from 1990 show that all the potential cultivable land, including the marginal and flood-risk lands, are brought under cultivation (Table 10.3). The refugee farmers are, as pointed out earlier, prohibited by law from looking for additional land outside the scheme. The only alternative they have is to cultivate the available land within the scheme more intensively. Intensification in the context of the scheme has been mainly in terms of increasing the frequency with which the existing land is cropped, without a major shift occurring in the agricultural techniques. On the scheme, increased frequency of cropping has pushed most of the existing arable land to the upper limit, resulting in farm ageing or soil exhaustion. This is reflected in the increased number of farms abandoned because of loss of productive capability.

Generally, there is no universally valid upper limit of the absorptive capacity of land. The productive capacity of land can be raised substantially through improved land-use techniques and productivity-boosting inputs, but not all societies have these opportunities at their disposal nor are all natural environments equally responsive to change in land use and fertilization. Allan, for example, argues, '[I]t must be obvious that any area of land will support in perpetuity only a limited number of people. An absolute limit is imposed by soil and climatic factors in so far as these are beyond human control, and a practical limit is set by the way in which the land is used' (Allan, 1972: 303). Some physical environments are more responsive to changes than others. For example, in the clay plains of Sudan where the Qala en Nahal scheme is located, available evidence suggests that the vertisols are not responsive to fertilizer application. Both the Soil Science Department at the University of Khartoum and the Soil Survey Administration in Wad Medani reported that application of nitrogen fertilizer on vertisols in the country shows only little or no economic increase in yields (cited in Dickinson, 1983: 36). Thus, contrary to Boserup's (1965) postulate, which seems not to recognize the existence of an upper limit of a land resource's absorptive capacity, or what others refer to as 'carrying capacity', depending on the conditions of the physical environment and agricultural techniques in use or the system of land use, there is a population limit beyond which a cycle of degenerative changes is set in motion which must result in deterioration or destruction of the land in use. '[T]he carrying capacity of an area is an estimate of the number of people that area will support in perpetuity, under a given system of land usage, without deterioration of land resources' (Allan, 1972: 317). Allan recognizes that wide variations in land carrying capacities exist in Africa, depending on land use, soil and climatic conditions. In his view, the critical population-density limit cannot be exceeded without setting in motion the process of land degradation (Allan, 1972: 317). For Boserup (1965 and 1970) such a threshold level does not exist because this would induce intensification, which would constantly shift upwards the capacity of the land to absorb a growing population.[10]

Within the given technological horizon, the climatic and soil conditions limit the degree of change farmers on the scheme could introduce in terms of restructuring the crops grown. Thus, the level of soil fertility is to a large extent determined by the number of years a certain plot has been under cropping. Hence, carrying-capacity calculations in this case are meaningless unless they are updated from time to time, taking into account not only the reduction in value of the land in question, but also the level of mobility of humans and livestock outside the scheme areas, searching for pasture and alternative income-generating opportunities.

Even though emigration is prohibited by law, the refugees have been emigrating illegally from the scheme in search of employment or other income-generating activities, although they have been unable to extend cultivation outside the settlement because such an activity is easily amenable to monitoring by the authorities and the local Sudanese. Since extending cultivation by the refugee farmers outside the designated areas constitutes competition for scarce arable land with the local farmers, the latter in many cases serve as a watchdog for the local authorities. Thus, the only area in which the restriction on mobility (confinement) has been effective is in stopping the refugee farmers from extending cultivation outside the confines of the scheme.

Commercialization of agriculture and other economic activities

The fourth non-demographic factor which is a major cause of natural resource depletion on the scheme is the commercialization of economic activities, especially agricultural production for export and domestic markets (for expansion of mechanized agriculture in the central rain lands of Sudan, see Simpson and Khalifa, 1976a, b; Bryant, 1977; Affan, 1984; O'Brien, 1985; Rünger, 1987; Rees, 1990). The exploitative land-use practices by small subsistence farmers and pastoralists are the result of intensified commercial land use. With expansion of commercial agricultural production, the resources at the disposal of the small farmers and pastoralists shrank, inducing exploitative land-use practices in the remaining areas. At present, most of the land in the vicinity of the scheme is swallowed up by the expansion of mechanized commercial farming. The scheme area is surrounded by mechanized rain-fed agriculture. Until recently, vast areas around the scheme were accessible both to the refugees and to their livestock. The emergence of large mechanized schemes very close to the settlement has imposed extremely high pressure on the refugees and their animals. Some of these schemes are owned by the Arab Investment Company (15,000 *feddans*), about 2 km to the south-east of Umzurzur village. This mechanized farm is within the scheme area. Other mechanized farms belong to the Simsim state farm of about 10,000 *feddans* to the east of the scheme, the Al Zaki scheme near Salmin village on the border of the scheme, the African Company south-east of the scheme and Sheik Mustafa El Amin close to Simsim. On the northern part of the scheme there are jebels which make expansion impossible. Expansion was only possible to the south and south-east of the scheme, but these areas are already allocated to commercial farming. There are no grazing lands left. Even the neighbouring Sudanese and pastoralists from distant areas share the remaining resources.

The scheme is bounded in the north by a cluster of small jebels (hills) and by woodland, which is now completely depleted due to excessive removal of vegetation cover by commercial farms for mechanized agriculture, fuel wood and charcoal production. On all the other sides, the scheme is surrounded by small- or large-scale agricultural schemes. What used to be a forest reserve to the south-west of the scheme has been cleared for commercial farming, and land to the south was cleared by a commercial company for the first time in 1988. The result of all these developments is to exacerbate the degree of the confinement and to restrict the farmers' access to off-scheme natural resources. Horizontal expansion of mechanized rain-fed agriculture is exerting heavy pressure on the scheme. For example, the 1989 ACORD report states:

[I]ncreasingly the programme area is being encroached upon by large commercial farming interests. Several times during the last 6 months COR have gone to court to prevent areas on the scheme's boundary, which are presently forest reserves, from being cleared by these commercial farming interests. Besides obviously resulting in a decrease in agricultural land around the scheme, which may otherwise be available for use by the growing scheme population the net effect is to make access for refugee-owned cattle increasingly difficult. (ACORD, 1989b)

This has greatly limited the possibility for the farmers to make meaningful adjustments. If, for example, the pressure on resources in the vicinity of the scheme were not intense, the scheme population would have been able to use these resources to graze their animals, collect fodder for stall-feeding, fuel wood, timber, thatch grass, honey, gum arabic, frankincense, etc. Before the depletion of the commons and encroachment on the latter by commercial expansion of agriculture, i.e. during the early period of the scheme, over 50% of all the respondents and over 90% of the poor families gathered food, fuel, fodder, timber, gum arabic and frankincense from the uncultivated land around the scheme area. The depletion of these resources has worsened the living conditions of the poor families. If the areas in the vicinity of the scheme were not swallowed up by expansion of commercial agriculture and other external pressures, the pressure on the resources on and immediately surrounding the scheme area would have significantly been eased.

This problem is also felt throughout the Gedaref district. The major problem of natural-resource depletion in the Gedaref district is inextricably linked with the horizontal expansion of commercial agriculture and charcoal production (Simpson and Khalifa, 1976a, b; O'Brien, 1983; Affan, 1984; El-Moula, 1985; Abu Sin, 1989b,1992; Baasher, 1989; Mohamed, 1989). In a period of not more than three decades, in the clay plains alone, huge tracts of land have been bulldozed, disregarding requirements for environmental protection as stipulated by the existing forestry and land-use laws and by-laws.

The problem of pressure on resources precipitated by expansion of commercial agriculture is not limited to the clay plains of Sudan. For example, in the Sahel region, despite the growth of population, the major cause of pressure on land has not been due to increased demand for subsistence needs, but has been mainly due to the expansion of commercial agricultural production (Repetto and Holmes, 1983). The introduction of cash crops such as groundnuts and cotton, introduced by the colonial governments and later sustained by the independent African states in the Sahelian countries, has, for example, created heavy pressure 'on land resource independent of the size of human population to be fed' (Ware cited in Repetto and Holmes, 1983). In Madagascar, the problem of overstocking was a result of increased demand for meat and of improved veterinary services, which were both due to colonialism (Darkoh, 1987). There are also examples which show that commercialization of economic activities could deplete natural resources even in the context of drastic population decline.[11]

Breakdown of traditional resource-management regimes

The fifth major non-demographic factor which has contributed to natural-resource depletion on the scheme is the breakdown of traditional natural-resource management systems (see Chapter 8). The available evidence shows that the traditional resource-management regimes among these communities were effective and efficient instruments of natural-resource allocation and regulation until they broke down under the pressure of the factors discussed heretofore, including population pressure. One of the key factors that brought about the breakdown of the previously effective traditional resource-management systems is the misguided government policy. This is not unique to Sudan; the disruptive roles played by the government of Sudan is a common feature in many Third World countries. For example, in Rajasthan, India, Jodha's findings show how institutional changes in the form of land reform implemented by the government led to the breakdown of previously existing traditional feudal natural-resource arrangements. The consequence of this had been depletion of the CPRs (Jodha, 1985).

In many African countries, where large amounts of land were expropriated for the establishment of plantation companies, European settlements or cash-crop production, traditional natural-resource management regimes broke down due to land shortage in the traditional sector, with the consequent result of over-exploitation of natural resources. In the post-colonial period, the breakdown of the traditional natural-resource management systems in many African countries is closely related to the presence of weak and corrupt governments, who, by abolishing or weakening the traditional natural-resource-management regimes, have, *de facto*, converted the previously strictly regulated rights of use and access to the natural resources into open-access resources, where there is unlimited entry and where there are no rules regulating access to and use of the resources concerned.

Not only in Sudan but in many parts of Africa, communal ownership and control of natural resources were widespread, ever since recorded history began, and are still practised in some areas, where there is little or no state intervention and where there is no ethnic or tribal intermingling or heavy population pressure on resources. In a pioneering study, Kjekshus argues that in East Africa during the precolonial period, near settlements and trade routes, permanent agriculture was sustained through sophisticated methods of conservation, such as terracing, irrigation, crop rotation and fertilizing (Kjekshus, 1977). Repetto and Holmes also state: '[T]he human ecology of most societies occupying precarious or fragile ecosystems encompassed controls over demographic change as well as controls over use of resources. Balance was sustained in part by social regulation of fertility, mortality, migration and marriage; in part by regulation of resource exploitation' (Repetto and Holmes, 1983: 617).

The findings of this study clearly show that the weakening and breakdown of the traditional communal-resource-management regimes on the scheme was, *inter alia*, precipitated partly by the pressure of exogenous factors and by the refugee experience rather than by their inherent inefficiency. Contrary to the claims made by the exponents of the 'tragedy of the commons' model and of the property-rights paradigm, one of the factors that lies at the heart of the problem of resource depletion experienced by the farmers on and off the scheme is the weakening or elimination of the communal systems of natural-resource ownership and control.

Poverty
In the Qala en Nahal area, not only do misguided government policies in agricultural development represent 'soil' or 'strip' mining and cause massive destruction of vegetation, but such policies have also indirectly caused poverty by pushing the refugees, the Sudanese small farmers and pastoralists on to ever smaller and ecologically marginal areas. The number of families who eke out a living from the marginal and degradation-prone sites has increased drastically in the past few years and the need to survive has become a major preoccupation of these families. In order to make ends meet, these families use the resources without regard to environmental protection. Environmental protection, i.e. long-term sustainability, is sacrificed in favour of short-term protection of human lives. In subsistence

economies, where almost every income is directly derived from the environment, protection of human lives and the environment are inextricably intertwined. They are two sides of the same coin. The farmers are aware of this relationship, but, when their immediate survival is threatened, they see no alternative but to do what they would under normal circumstance abhor doing, i.e. sacrifice sustainability to avert the threat of hunger. Consequently, a destructive scenario has been unfolding in the marginal and degradation-prone areas. As the resources become more exploited, returns diminished and the need to survive forced the people in such areas to resort to more exploitative land-use practices. This set in motion both the forces of resource degradation and perpetual poverty. The two reinforce each other. Thus, poverty has become a cause and effect of environmental degradation. In this analytical framework, poverty is an effect of misguided government policies, but, once it is brought into being by forces beyond the control of the poor, its feature changes from being an effect into being a cause of resource depletion. This scenario is eloquently summarized by Durning:

> Most of the world's looming environmental threats, from ground water contamination to climate change, are by-products of affluence. But poverty can drive ecological deterioration when desperate people over-exploit their resource base, sacrificing the future to salvage the present. The cruel logic of crucial short-term needs forces landless families to put rain forest plots to the torch and mountain slopes to the plough. Environmental decline, in return, perpetuates poverty, as degraded ecosystems offer diminishing yields to their poor inhabitants. A self-feeding downward spiral of economic deprivation and ecological degradation takes hold. (Durning, 1989b: 40)

The farmers in this study are aware of the deleterious environmental consequences of their acts, but the level of deprivation in terms of sources of livelihoods leaves no room to consider environmental protection in their production decisions. As Sen in a different, but similar, context states, 'the compulsion to acquire enough food may force vulnerable people to do things which they resent doing' (Sen, 1989). And, as Durning perceptively observes the poor may knowingly cause harm to their environment, especially when they are pushed to the brink of starvation because of eviction from familiar lands, through being driven to the frontier by population growth or being deprived of alternative sources of livelihood by misguided laws (Durning, 1989b: 41). The misguided law that is engendering such a situation on the scheme is the limitation imposed by the Regulation of Asylum Act (1974), which prohibits the refugees from bringing new areas into the production process in response to diminished productive capability of the arable land within the designated areas and in response to high population density on the available resources. This, as we saw earlier, has brought about an unsustainable farming system, where the plots are continuously cropped without fallow periods until the available soil nutrients are reduced drastically.

The poor, unlike other classes or groups in society, are directly dependent on the untransformed products of the natural environment for their survival and reproduction. The postulate that the poor knowingly cause harm to their environment may, therefore, sound anomalous because by doing that they are threatening not only the future of the next generation, but even their own long-term basis for survival. No one is more aware of this truth than the poor themselves. It is the drive to survive which forces them to do things which they would abhor doing under stable circumstances.

> In the rural Third World, human reliance on ecosystems goes unmediated by the long chains of commerce, industry and civil infrastructure that shape life in the rich countries.

For the have-nots, food comes from the soil, water from the stream, fuel from the woods, traction from the ox, fodder from the pasture, reeds to make mats from the stream bank, fruit from the trees around the hut. Poor people know that to endanger any of these things is to imperil themselves, and the lives of their offspring. (Durning, 1989b: 40–41).

A community without secure access to basic human needs loses the freedom to live up to its own standards. For humans whose present is imminently threatened by starvation, the future does not seem to carry much weight. Living near the subsistence margin, subject to the vagaries of nature, pushed from fertile lands, either by population pressure or by the diminished productive capability of previously fertile lands, and deprived of off-farm alternative sources of livelihood, the poor on and off the scheme are left with little or no scope for preoccupation with the future. The evidence from this study suggests that, before people can be concerned about the future, they have to be sure about their present survival. This is true even when they conceive the present and the future as a continuum.

The following episode may throw light on the issues at hand. In November 1991, we set out for one of the Sudanese villages in the Qala en Nahal scheme. The purpose of this visit was to interview the village sheikh (chief), who was entrusted with the responsibility to enforce, among other things, government laws and regulations concerning environmental protection at the local level. He was not available at his home and we were told to look for him in one of his farms. When we drove towards his *hawasha*, we found him busy cutting young *Acacia* trees for charcoal making. This came as a surprise, because the very person who was supposed to monitor the villagers' compliance with forestry laws and by-laws was himself a culprit. We raised this irregularity. Pointing at his stomach, laughingly, he said, 'I have to fill this first before I can serve anybody. If I don't cut these trees, my family will starve. Do you expect me to leave the trees to stand green when the stomachs of my children burn?' I said I would do the same in his situation. He also added, 'A government which does not meet the basic needs of its poor citizens loses automatically its right of governance of both people and natural resources.'

From the discussion, it became clear that he undoubtedly understood the link between vegetation and environmental protection, but, his understanding notwithstanding, he cut the trees on which his and his children's future depended. Asked if he thought his act constituted a theft, his answer was unequivocal. He did not think cutting trees belonging to a government constituted theft. In his view, theft meant stealing goods which have an owner, in which ownership is recognized and sanctioned socially. He stated that local goods which are not owned and controlled by the local communities or individual members of such communities, if left unpoliced, represented free goods accessible to all. He even challenged the right of the government to own woodlands, which historically belonged to the local people.

It is important to state that the link between poverty and environmental degradation is as elusive as the relationship between population density and environment. Opinions about this are also equally divided. For example, Barraclough and Ghimire emphatically dismiss the claim that poverty causes environmental degradation as fundamentally wrong (Barraclough and Ghimire, 1990: 13). Myers also argues that to blame poor migrants for destroying the forest is like blaming poor conscripts for the ravages of war (cited in Barraclough and Ghimire, 1990: 13). Myers' metaphor sheds light on the causal relationship between poverty and environmental degradation, but it is also important to state that not all forcible conscripts behave in the same way towards civilian populations. Some forcibly conscripted soldiers may be ruthless in their treatment of the victims of war while others may be sensitive and empathetic to the feelings and needs of those who get caught in the crossfire. By the same token, not all people pushed to marginality behave in an identical way towards the natural environment. That is where the role of environmental consciousness and education of the poor may sometimes become important. For example, in some areas, environmental degradation at the local level is not associated with the growing numbers of people as such, but with the influx of certain types of people or ethnic groups who lack proper knowledge of using the local environment (de Waal, 1989).

On the scheme, poverty is, among other things, a result of a misguided government policy and it does not, therefore, constitute an ultimate cause of environmental degradation. It is important to analyse the problem at two levels. At the first level poverty is a consequence of more deeply entrenched factors such as those discussed earlier, but at the second level it becomes a proximate cause of land degradation. On the scheme, it is in conjunction with the above-stated factors that poverty contributes to natural-resource depletion resulting from inappropriate land-use practices – overcultivation, overgrazing and deforestation. The role of government is inextricably linked to each factor. In this study, the root causes of natural-resource depletion or the change in land-use practices at the local level are sought in the wider underlying, institutional, socio-economic and political factors. Inappropriate land-use practices are treated as symptoms rather than as root causes of resource depletion.

In the past, when the pressure of the non-demographic factors underlying the problem of resource depletion was not evidently present, the human ecology of the societies inhabiting these unstable ecosystems developed effective and efficient resource-management regimes, which functioned as allocative and regulatory mechanisms of scarce resources. Extension to erosion-prone slopes and other marginal slopes was forbidden by traditional rules, and such rules were strictly enforced by the traditional leaders. The various types of fallow as a technique of conserving soil fertility and the enforcement of institutional rules which restricted expansion of cultivation on to marginal lands and which limited intensity of resource use to sustainable levels have historically proved to be ecologically sound, stable and efficient resource-management systems. With increased outside pressure on the subsistence economy due to land shortage and high population density in a confined context, cultivation on steep and highly erodible sites by the disen-franchised refugee farmers has become the only source of livelihood for many families. This has caused resource depletion, reflected in changes in plant-species composition, changes in soil structure and texture and erosion, resulting from inappropriate land-use practices, namely overcultivation, deforestation and overgrazing.

This seems to have been generally the case in many sub-Saharan African countries even during the colonial period. Some of the colonial governments prohibited cultivation of degradation-prone sites by law. For example, the Southern Rhodesian (now Zimbabwean) government passed the Native Husbandry Act in 1952 to promote good husbandry in the 'native' areas. In Kenya between 1937 and 1944 soil-conservation programmes were initiated by the colonial government in the 'native' areas. The enforcement of these laws was bitterly resisted by the Africans and thus could not be effective. Cultivation of the marginal soils was not therefore stopped and soil erosion continued unabated (for colonial land-use policies that failed, see Bernard and Thom, 1981; Darkoh, 1987). One of the main reasons why these land-use policies failed was because the Africans saw government policies and practices as being responsible for their relegation to the marginal areas.

The Africans held colonial land policies responsible for the disruption of their otherwise flexible and sustainable traditional agriculture and animal husbandry and hence were not responsive to conservation measures initiated by the colonial governments. As Bernard and Thom (1981) state, colonial policy had produced devastating results. Even in the postcolonial period, the environmental problems faced by many African peasants and pastoralists still remain inextricably interwoven with government policies and practices.

Conclusion

It has been argued throughout this study that the non-demographic factors are the ultimate causes of the resource depletion on the scheme. One of the consequences of high population pressure in a context of confinement and rapid commercial encroachment on small farming and grazing areas is the breakdown of traditional resource-management systems. In the study area, these resource-management regimes have been rendered obsolete because forest fallow, bush fallow and short fallow periods as techniques of soil-fertility conservation and restoration are no longer practised to regenerate vegetation and help counter soil-nutrient depletion. No alternative agricultural techniques have been adopted to offset the impact of the loss of productivity precipitated by the complete elimination or drastic reduction in the length of fallow periods. The evidence that emerges from this study suggests that even a flexible and adaptive traditional resource-management system may break down if the pressures exerted from within and without are greater than the system can withstand. If the pressure creates an acute scarcity of land supply in relation to the needs of the society in question, a breakdown of the traditional resource-management regime, with the resulting increased environmental stress, is inevitable. This is because, when non-farm income-generating opportunities are lacking, the margin of subsistence decreases progressively and the pressure to maximize short-term production grows stronger, even at the risk of threatening long-term ecological stability. This is precisely what has happened on the scheme. The pressure to eke out a living has become overwhelming and has consequently constrained the ability of the community to make innovative coping adjustments. By limiting the economic space, expansion of commercial rain-fed agriculture in the area in alignment with the other non-demographic factors discussed in the preceding chapter has undermined the ability of the scheme settlers to respond to the pressure in a non-exploitative way.

This shows that a community that operates within a given technique of production and an extremely limited supply of land is usually faced with declining average agricultural output as its population grows. Over time, this induces inappropriate land-use practices, extending cultivation on to marginal areas and/or continuous cultivation of the available arable land, resulting in the depletion of soil nutrients and in the exposure of the soil to wind and rain erosion (Dixon *et al.*, 1988; Munslow *et al.*, 1989; Grainger, 1990).

If the possibility of earning an income from off-farm economic activities and/or expanding agricultural production on to new arable land is limited or non-existent, the standard of living of the community concerned declines below customary levels. The community therefore responds in one or more of the following ways. One alternative by which the community tries to maintain overall production is by shortening the fallow period. The second possible response is to extend cultivation onto marginal soils and erosion-prone sites, such as higher slopes. In the absence of such pressures, such sites would be used as sources of fuel wood and pasture with the consequence of easing the pressure on the remaining lands. The expansion of cultivation onto marginal or degradation-prone sites has a tendency to unfold a scenario which, if not countered with corrective measures, could unleash the forces of natural-resource degradation. These degrading forces may in extreme situations cause irreversible ecological damage. The need to make ends meet forces the poor in the marginal areas to exploit the natural environment in a non-sustainable way. Thus, poverty, demographic pressure and a fragile environment reinforce each other, triggering off the ultimate causes of land degradation. In such circumstances, proximate causes, such as poverty, population density and the unstable environment characterized by high sensitivity and low resilience, constitute the immediate causes of resource depletion at the local level. One should not, however, lose sight of the underlying (ultimate) causes which induce such exploitative land-use practices. Thus, just as it is untenable to blame land degradation on rapid population growth, it is equally untenable to deny the role of high population density in the process of land degradation. Under certain historical, political, socio-economic and institutional conditions like those pertaining on the scheme, population pressure is a contributing factor to depletion of natural resources.

Notes

1. When I conducted a study among the urban refugees in Khartoum in the second half of the 1980s, I met many of these families resettled spontaneously on the outskirts of Khartoum – El Kala-Kila.
2. It is interesting to observe that the number of families living in the scheme was reduced by about 2.4%. This is difficult to explain unless we assume that single individuals have immigrated into the settlement between 1985 and 1991, which sounds unlikely. One possible explanation of this unexpected result could be the fact that the families that were repatriated to Eritrea in 1990 had left behind their dependents with their relatives in the settlements until the root cause of the conflict which prompted their flight ceased to exist in their country of origin. The repatriation of the refugee families occurred following the liberation of their villages of origin before the complete defeat of Ethiopia. At that time the refugees might have considered it risky to take the whole family. Some of the children may have been left in the settlement with relatives.
3. In view of the fact that some refugees have left the settlement in search of alternative sources of livelihood, the immigration of the Sudanese and West Africans into the area may sound anomalous. This is explained by the fact that the scarcity of resources is much more severe in the refugee villages than in the Sudanese villages. The non-refugee migrants obtained land with relative ease from the village sheikhs.
4. It is not known how many Sudanese there were in the present scheme area in 1970. The only figures available were for 1966. In 1966, there were about 1,300 Sudanese in the area. Before the establishment of the refugee scheme, the area was highly inhospitable. As a result, the death rate must have been high. If we assume an annual growth rate of 2.5%, the total Sudanese population in the present scheme area was in the range of 1,435.
5. Prior to the establishment of the settlement, the Sudanese villagers migrated to the Rahad River during the dry season. After the provision of a water-supply, this permanent settlement became a possibility. One of the most dramatic impacts of the refugee settlement was the supply of perennial water. Since the mid-1980s, ACORD has also excavated a number of rain-fed reservoirs (*hafirs*) for livestock. Not only has the availability of a water-supply during the dry season encouraged many refugee families to keep their livestock on the scheme throughout the year, but *hafirs* have had adverse effects on the resources of the scheme area, because the number of Sudanese herders visiting the scheme during the dry season has increased drastically.
6. In 1970, the population in the scheme area was increased from 1,435 persons to 19,713. The population was increased by 1,274% overnight.
7. The only form of emigration allowed by the settlement authorities is in connection with animal herding. In fact, this form of emigration is encouraged to ease the pressure on water during the dry season.
8. When the settlement of Ulyamkulu became overcrowded, the surplus population was relocated in 1976 to a new site – Mishamo – and the pressure on the resources in Ulyamkulu was relieved.

9. For more detailed information see G. Kibreab (1994b), 'The refugee problem in the Sudan', in Adelman and Sorenson (eds), *African Refugees: Development Aid and Repatriation*. Boulder: Westview.

10. The concept of 'carrying capacity' is often used uncritically in the literature on African agricultural systems and it is not always a useful tool of analysis. For an elaborate critique of the concept of carrying capacity see Scoones and Zaba (1994). 'Is "carrying capacity" a useful concept to apply to human population?' in Zaba and Clarke (eds), *Environment and Population Change*, Liege: Edwina editions, IUSSP.

11. According to Repetto and Holmes (1983) the 'native' population of North America lived in harmony with the natural environment until this was disturbed by the establishment of European settlements. The arrival of the Europeans, for example, led to drastic population decline among the 'native' population, due to the unfamiliar contagious diseases that came with the European settlers. The decline was estimated at up to 90% in some areas. Despite the drastic decline in population, however, commercialization and the demand for animal hides led to such overexploitation of animals in some areas that they became extinct.

11 The Farmer's Response to Land Degradation

Everything flows and nothing abides; everything gives way and nothing stays fixed . . .
You cannot step twice into the same river, for other waters and yet others go ever flowing
on . . . It is in changing that things find repose. (Heraclitus, *Fragments*)

In the preceding chapters, we saw that, within the given physical conditions (climatic and soil), the most critical constraint on agricultural production on the scheme is land shortage, which has, over time, led to inappropriate land-use practices with the consequence of soil-nutrient depletion and weed infestation, resulting in yield decline. In this chapter, the way the farmers respond to the problem of land shortage, in the context of the existing physical restriction on freedom of movement and residence and population pressure, is discussed.

Peasant and pastoral societies' responses to diminishing land resources or population pressure on available resources are varied. Bilsborrow, for example, summarizes the three major theoretically conceivable responses to population pressure in rural areas in the Third World as (i) demographic; (ii) economic; and (iii) demographic–economic (Bilsborrow, 1987: 185). Demographic responses include late marriages and/or celibacy, lower fertility through use of contraceptives, abstinence, abortions, etc. 'Demographic–economic' refers to out-migration, the indirect consequence of which is, on the one hand, to offset the pressure of population on the available resources and, on the other, to reduce exposure to the risk of pregnancy. The latter presupposes that one of the spouses migrates alone, leaving the other in the village concerned and that the duration of absence is reasonably long.

Here only the economic responses to diminishing land resources, caused by decreasing productive capability of the scarce land resource in the context of high population density, are examined. This is not to imply that demographic responses are unimportant, but, in a context where no accurate birth and death records are available, it is difficult to measure their significance. On the scheme, out-migration represents one of the important responses to diminishing resource availability, and this has an indirect influence on the fertility rate among the population. However, its quantitative impact is difficult to establish.

The data suggest that the farmers cope with the problem of land shortage or population pressure on resources in different ways. These include extending cultivation on to marginal and less suitable areas, sharecropping with refugee and Sudanese families, and renting of land from families who either have a surplus land resource[1] or who are unable to cultivate their holdings, mainly due to lack of family labour and/or capital to pay for seasonal labourers (Table 11.1). In the following sections, the different coping strategies adopted to overcome the pressure on the available resources are presented.

Table 11.1   Distribution of the refugee and Sudanese farmers by means of coping with
land shortage (%)

	Refugees (n = 215)	Sudanese (n = 91)
Cultivating new area	1.0	22.0
Expansion of cultivation to less suitable areas	9.0	13.0
Sharecropping with refugee families[a]	10.0	0.0
Sharecropping with Sudanese families	15.0	9.0
Supplementary income from off-farm activities	57.0	54.0
Renting land	7.0	2.0
Total	100.0	100.0

$\chi^2 = 54$, d.f. = 6, $P < 0.001$.
[a]Even those families who received no land allocations of their own from the Commissioner's Office for Refugees (COR), but who were at the time cultivating part of their parents' holdings, considered themselves as sharecroppers. That is the reason why the number of sharecroppers is high. Not all necessarily shared the produce with their parents, but they usually contributed labour to weed or prepare their parents' plots not in return for land, but because of cultural obligation. In these communities, it is common for parents to benefit from their offspring's free labour contribution.

Bringing new land into the production process

Peasant societies usually respond to population pressure by increasing the land area under cultivation. This, however, presupposes that untapped, potentially cultivable land is available and accessible. One way in which the Sudanese farmers coped with the problem of land shortage was by bringing new areas under cultivation. This option did not exist for the refugee farmers because of the legal restrictions on freedom of movement and residence imposed by the Regulation of Asylum Act (1974). Only 1% of the refugee farmers responded to the diminishing land-resource base by bringing a new area under cultivation. The fact that the refugee farmers are prohibited by law from bringing new areas under cultivation in response to land shortage, caused by declining productive capability or high population density, is at the heart of the problem of inappropriate land use. If the refugee farmers had been able to expand cultivation beyond the confines of the designated areas in response to increased demands for land, they would have been able to practise their traditional methods of restoring or maintaining soil fertility by leaving part of their plots to rest under natural fallow. This presupposes that there should be at least two holdings available for each family so that soil-fertility decline and the build-up of the sorghum root parasite Striga can be reversed under natural fallow. One of the most incessant demands of the farmers has, since the early 1980s, been for more land. This demand was raised not only by the landless families, but also by those families whose lands' productive capability had been diminished because of depletion of soil nutrients.

In spite of the restrictions, a few refugee families responded to the problem of land shortage by bringing some arable land into the production process (Table 11.1). Wealth and chance factors were the two elements that determined the individual farmers' access to additional land within the scheme. Those who had capital were able to increase their land possessions by using different means, such as social contacts with Sudanese farmers and settlement administrators or by renting, sharecropping and purchasing of land. In 1982, about 15% of the families had more land than was originally allocated to them (Kibreab, 1987: Table 5.5). Some rich families had as much as 50 or more *feddans* (Kibreab, 1987: Table 5.9).

Some of the farmers whose holdings were located on the periphery were also unofficially able to bring new areas under cultivation (see Map 1.3). For example, even though each *meshrua* is only 100 holdings, in the 1983 season 160.25 and 148.5 holdings were cultivated in *meshruas* 47 and 48, respectively (ACORD, 1983b). In 1984 and 1985, over 143 and 211.75 holdings were cultivated, respectively, in *meshrua* 9 (ACORD THS Records, 1984–1985). This was true for all the *meshruas* not bounded by cultivated land. Between 1983 and 1985, over 7,402 *feddans* or 779 holdings were brought under cultivation by extending the boundaries of the *meshruas* that were located on the periphery of the scheme (ACORD THS Records, 1983–1985). In light of the extremely limited land-resource base within the scheme, the amount of land the majority of refugees could bring into cultivation was unduly limited and hence the farmers tried to make ends meet by resorting to continuous cultivation of the available land.

Extension of cultivation on to marginal areas

The second coping strategy adopted by the communities was extending cultivation on to marginal areas. About 9% of the refugee farmers increased their holdings by expanding on to less suitable areas within the confines of the scheme (Table 11.1). These areas were previously used as sources of wood fuel, construction timber and grazing. One of the major problems facing the farmers was shrinkage of grazing areas and livestock trek routes because of expansion of cultivation (see Chapter 6). Expansion of cultivation on to the marginal areas had led to increased pressure on wet-season grazing in the remaining pasture. High animal pressure during wet seasons is one of the factors that contributes to disappearance of palatable plant species. Land shortage has forced many farmers to bring unsuitable sites into the production process. This not only leads to lower yields, but also contributes to the problem of soil erosion and deforestation (see Chapters 2 and 3). The less suitable sites included the *azaza* (reddish, shallow and poor soil where the rate of moisture infiltration is limited), the upper slopes, with a high risk of erosion, and flood and waterlogged areas.

Sharecropping

With increased deterioration of the quality of the arable land and consequently increased risk of crop failure, there were families who rented out their holdings in return for advance cash payments. This was a strategy devised partly to make immediate ends meet and partly to gain a space for allocating their family labour to non-farm and less risky economic activities. In view of the recurrent crop failures that the farmers have been experiencing during the past decade, many did not seem to see a secure future for themselves and their children on the exhausted land. There was uncertainty regarding the ability of the land to generate an adequate income to enable them to meet the costs of their subsistence.

A considerable proportion of the refugee families were therefore producing crops on additional land rented on a sharecropping basis. The fact that about 15%

were sharecropping with Sudanese farmers may suggest that the level of land shortage in the Sudanese villages was less severe than in the refugee villages. A sharecropping arrangement was also common between vulnerable and better-off refugee families. The latter had larger family sizes (labour) or capital to hire labourers. The produce was shared on the basis of the terms of the individual agreements. However, the existence of such arrangements does not imply that surplus arable land was available.

Land renting

Some families also cope with the problem of land shortage by renting land from some refugee families. The refugees are prohibited by law to dispose of land in any form (Regulation of Asylum Act, 1974). In spite of this formal restriction, however, land has become a commodity subject to all forms of informal transactions. This has led to inequitable distribution of the available land. Some families have over time succeeded in accumulating a considerable amount of arable land (Kibreab, 1987). Some of the land rented by the landless or by families whose land possession is inadequate to enable them to meet their subsistence needs belongs to such groups. By mid-1985, over 33% of all plots had changed hands without the knowledge of the government authorities. To reverse this development and to avoid further concentration of land into a few hands, a revised land-holding register was jointly prepared by ACORD and the Commissioner's Office for Refugees (COR) in 1985, but no measures were taken to effect land redistribution.

Difference in coping strategies

There is a significant difference in the way the two groups, namely the refugee and the Sudanese farmers, respond to the problem of land shortage (Table 11.1). As opposed to the refugee farmers, a considerable proportion of the local population (22%) opened up new arable land. This is, more than anything else, due to the legal restriction under which the refugee farmers eke out their living. In view of the fact that land exhaustion constitutes one of the key restraints on agricultural production (see Chapter 4), it is interesting to examine the measures the refugees and the Sudanese farmers undertake to overcome the problem.

Measures against land degradation

In the following section, within the existing physical (climatic and soil conditions) and resource-availability constraints, the measures the farmers undertake to counter depletion of soil nutrients will be discussed. The acuteness of the land shortage facing the farmers in the context of high population density has, among other things, rendered some of the traditional soil-nutrient-replenishing methods, such as forest fallow and bush fallow, inoperative (see Table 2.1). These methods are practised in conditions of a plentiful supply of land.

The common methods used by the farmers to restore and conserve soil fertility include short fallow periods and crop rotation (Table 11.2). A considerable proportion of the farmers also do nothing to counter soil exhaustion. These are discussed below.

Table 11.2   Distribution of the refugee and Sudanese farmers by measures of countering soil exhaustion (%)

	Refugees ($n = 192$)	Sudanese ($n = 83$)
Do nothing	17.0	10.0
Leave the plot or part of it to rest	2.0	44.0
Crop rotation	81.0	46.0
Use of organic manure	0.0	0.0

$\chi^2 = 24.1$, d.f. $= 4$, $P < 0.05$.

Short fallow

About 44% of the Sudanese farmers used short fallow periods (1 year) to restore or conserve soil fertility. Only an insignificant proportion of the refugee farmers (2%) used this method as a means of replenishing depleted soil nutrients. From an agronomic point of view, it is not certain if such short fallow periods have a positive effect on the process of replenishment of depleted soils because the fallow period is not long enough to allow regrowth of vegetation. However, annual fallow is not designed to replenish depleted soil nutrients by regeneration of vegetation cover, but rather to increase moisture availability for the next season. Turning of the soil several times during the rainy months can increase the rate of water infiltration and thus make more moisture available for the next cropping season.[2] The decomposed vegetation may also improve soil fertility. It is not a common practice among the farmers on the scheme to turn the soil of the fallow during the rains and it is not clear how leaving a farm to rest for one season contributes to increased moisture availability or improvement of soil nutrients for the following cropping season. In fact, the available evidence suggests that, if a farm is left uncultivated for 1 year after many years of continuous cropping, weeds grow more densely, requiring higher labour inputs in the following season. This seems to discourage some families from practising short fallow periods (interview with ACORD's Senior Agriculturalist, 1991).

Only short fallow periods and not forest or bush fallow are used to restore or conserve soil fertility. There are two possible explanations for the shortening of the fallow periods among the Sudanese farmers. These are land shortage in relation to demand and lack of tenurial security. The Sudanese farmers on the scheme are latecomers to the area and this has a bearing on their tenurial rights to trees, namely *Acacia senegal*. Until the establishment of the scheme, arable land use was very limited. There was only some local farming. Tapping of gum from both *A. senegal* and *Acacia seyal* was one of the most important sources of cash in the area (NEDEC and ILACO, N.V., 1966: 111). The Qala en Nahal area has always been a major source of gum collection. For example, between 1934 and 1941, of the total gum arabic sales in the Gedaref and Qala en Nahal markets, nearly 60% were collected from the latter (Tables 11.3 and 11.4). This indicates that the Qala en Nahal area was a major producer of gum arabic and frankincense before the expansion of mechanized rain-fed agriculture. Expansion of rain-fed farming has led to the destruction of *A. senegal* and *A. seyal* trees. In fact, in 1937 and 1938, of the total gum arabic sales in Gedaref and Qala en Nahal, 71% and 78%, respectively, were collected from the latter (Table 11.3 and 11.4).

With the extensive clearance of land for mechanized rain-fed cultivation and excessive tree felling for charcoal and firewood production, the gum-producing tree

Table 11.3   Gum sales collected from the markets in Gedaref and Qala en Nahal
1930–1941 (in kantars)

Year	Gedaref	Qala en Nahal	Total
1930	b.n.a.	b.n.a.	30,700
1931	b.n.a.	b.n.a.	84,114
1934	6,604	10,330	16,934
1935	6,746	13,744	20,490
1936	13,352	22,544	35,896
1937	6,580	16,327	22,907
1938	11,091	38,500	49,591
1939	12,134	17,737	29,871
1940	20,548	43,273	63,821
1941	15,508	21,898	37,406

b.n.a., Breakdown not available.
Source: Kassala Province Annual Reports 1934–1941, Kassala 2/12/44, National Record
Office, Khartoum.

Table 11.4   *Telh* sales collected from the markets in Gedaref and Qala en Nahal
(1935–1941) (in kantars)

Year	Gedaref	Qala en Nahal	Total
1935	12,039	3,078	15,117
1936	7,144	2,170	9,314
1937	16,611	5,453	22,064
1938	19,426	3,436	22,862
1939	11,803	2,769	14,572
1940	10,521	2,480	13,001
1941	4,127	410	4,537

Source: Kassala Province Annual Reports 1934–1941, Kassala 2/12/44, National Record
Office, Khartoum.

population declined substantially. In recent years, however, the farmers state that
A. senegal is the most dominant tree species that grows on fallow lands. In their
view, there is a linkage effect between degradation of the land and the re-
emergence of denser *A. senegal* trees.[3] The farmers have right of usufruct of the
farms they cultivate, but they lack the right to tap gum arabic, even from trees that
grow on the farms where they have the right of usufruct. Those who have exclusive
rights to tap gum arabic from the *A. senegal* trees are the original settlers, whose
rights go back to the 1920s.

   If a farmer with a right of usufruct leaves a certain part or all of her/his farm to
lie fallow until trees grow on it and if the trees are *A. senegal*, s/he has to leave the
trees including the land on which the trees are grown to the person who has the
property rights to the trees. The problem of losing arable land on which *A. senegal*
trees grow has become more serious with the increasing prices of gum arabic in the
world market and with the apparent encroachment of acacias on the fallow fields.
Thus, in order to avoid loss of arable land, immigrant farmers are reluctant to leave
their holding to remain fallow long enough to allow regrowth of *A. senegal* trees.
This is having a detrimental effect on soil fertility and consequently on the income

of the farmers. *Acacia* trees are deep-rooted and nitrogen-fixing and, by not leaving the land to rest under natural fallow, fewer trees grow, depriving the soil of nitrogen and other minerals brought up from the deeper layers in the soil profile. The fear of loss of usufructuary rights is inducing farmers to crop their farms continuously without fallow periods. This problem was only reported by the Sudanese farmers because the refugee farmers do not normally leave their land to remain fallow due to acute land shortage. According to COR regulations, the refugee farmers are also required to crop their holdings continuously. Failure to do so leads to repossession. This rule was for the first time relaxed in 1993 (ACORD, 1993).

Crop rotation

Crop rotation constitutes one of the most important measures for countering soil-fertility decline precipitated by continuous cultivation. Traditionally, only two crops are grown in the area, sorghum and sesame. In recent years, some farmers have started growing millet on smaller areas. None of the crops are leguminous or nitrogen-fixing and continuous planting of land with these crops leads to progressive impoverishment of the top soil. Thus, the effect of rotation of the two crops (sorghum and sesame) on soil-nutrient replenishment should not be overstated. In the absence of other alternatives, however, the farmers in the area attach great importance to such a system of rotation. Among the refugees, over 80% practise crop rotation. In effect this means that the holdings are sown to sesame followed by sorghum or vice versa. The climatic and soil conditions in the area do not seem to allow the farmers to change the composition or increase the number of crops grown. This would have enabled them to grow leguminous crops and to take advantage of the short cultivation season by planting fast-maturing varieties.

In order to show the trend in cropping pattern in a historical perspective, data from various sources were pieced together covering the period the settlement has been in existence (Table 11.5). There are some gaps in the data, but it is still clear that the refugee farmers' major instrument of countering fertility decline and weed infestation has been through rotation of the two crops (sorghum and sesame). The data show drastic fluctuations between the seasons. This is due to variation in rainfall distribution. Sesame is sown earlier than sorghum, mainly in June or early July. If there are no early rains, little or no sesame is grown. There is a discernible relationship between the rains and a higher ratio of land allocated to sesame production (Table 11.5). For the years where there was an early onset of rains, the ratio of sesame to sorghum was higher, but, whenever the onset of rains was late, the area cropped with sesame shrank. The rigidity of the climatic condition in the area imposes a serious limitation on the ability of the farmers to make adjustments in response to resource constraints or population pressure on resources. Whether farmers respond to population pressure on resources and diminishing productive capability of land by changing the structure of crops grown is determined by the soils and climatic conditions.

In Eritrea, where the refugees come from, especially in the highlands, diverse crops, namely cereals, oil-seeds, legumes, tobacco, coffee, cotton, earth-nuts, citrus fruits and vegetables, are grown. A report by the British Military Administration during the 1940s counted over 20 types of crops grown by the Eritrean farmers (FO 1015/43, 1947: 16–18). The farming system was more flexible, allowing the farmers to restructure the crops grown to restore and conserve fertility, to spread risks and to respond effectively to fluctuating climatic and soil conditions. In spite of their past experience, the farmers plant no legumes on the scheme (Table 11.5). However, even though only two crops are grown, the level of crop rotation

Table 11.5   Cropping pattern in the Qala en Nahal refugee settlement scheme 1971–1991 (%)

Year	Sorghum	Sesame	Millet	Legume
1971	73.2	26.8	0.0	0.0
1972	46.0	54.0	0.0	0.0
1973	89.0	11.0	0.0	0.0
1974	50.0	50.0	0.0	0.0
1976	65.0	35.0	0.0	0.0
1977	65.0	35.0	0.0	0.0
1978	57.0	43.0	0.0	0.0
1979	50.0	50.0	0.0	0.0
1980	51.0	49.0	0.0	0.0
1982	80.0	20.0	0.0	0.0
1983	59.6	40.4	0.0	0.0
1984	62.2	37.8	0.0	0.0
1985	70.0	29.0	1.0	0.0
1986	64.6	35.4	0.0	0.0
1987	45.5	52.5	1.8	0.2
1988	71.0	29.0	0.0	0.0
1991	59.7	25.7	14.6	0.0

Sources: 1971–1980 compiled from the records of the Commissioner's Office for Refugees, Qala en Nahal; 1981–1988 and 1991 compiled from ACORD's records of the tractor hire service, Qala en Nahal.

practised by the refugee farmers is much higher than among the commercial and peasant farmers in the Gedaref district.

In the commercial farming areas, between 1970 and 1989, the land planted to sesame fluctuated between 25% and 6% of the total area cultivated (Table 11.6), while on the scheme in certain seasons the ratio of sesame to sorghum was up to 50% or more (Table 11.5). The data in Table 11.6 clearly show that the decision of the Land Allotment Board to introduce eight-course rotation has fallen on deaf ears.

It is common among the commercial farmers to exploit a certain area of arable land for 8–9 years and then shift to a new area where productivity is expected to be higher because of centuries' accumulated fertility (Simpson and Khalifa, 1976a). The constraint of land shortage is not as severe as it is among the refugee farmers. While the commercial farmers responded to soil exhaustion by abandoning their schemes, the refugees responded to the same problem by rotational cropping, which limited, but by no means effectively, weed infestation and, in their view, even mitigated the consequences of soil exhaustion. Without rotational cropping, the farmers argued that most of the holdings would have been abandoned because of yield decline precipitated by depletion of soil nutrients and infestation by *Striga hermontheca*.

Sesame is grown by the farmers on the scheme for its beneficial effect of rotation and because it is a high-value cash crop. The farmers see sesame growing as an effective means of minimizing weed infestation and maximizing return per cropped area. Whenever there were early and adequate rains in a given season, farmers tried to maximize their annual incomes by allocating a greater part of their holdings to the high value crop – sesame.[4] The advantage sesame has over other crops such as legumes is the opportunity it provides to farmers to earn higher incomes and its

Table 11.6   Cropping pattern in the mechanized commercial-farming areas in Gedaref
district 1970–1989 (%)

Year	Sorghum	Sesame
1970	86.0	14.0
1971	84.0	16.0
1972	75.0	25.0
1973	76.0	24.0
1974	83.0	17.0
1975	87.0	13.0
1976	83.0	17.0
1977	85.0	15.0
1978	86.0	14.0
1979	91.0	9.0
1980	83.0	17.0
1981	87.0	13.0
1982	92.0	8.0
1983	93.0	7.0
1984	87.0	13.0
1985	88.0	12.0
1986	89.0	11.0
1987	87.0	13.0
1988	91.0	9.0
1989	94.0	6.0

Sources: 1970–1977 Mechanized Farming Corporation (MFC) *Agricultural Statistics Bulletin 2*, 1979; 1978–1983 MFC *Agricultural Statistics Bulletin 3*, 1984; the data for 1984–1989 are compiled from the archives of the MFC in Khartoum and Gedaref.

contribution to weed control without the farmers forgoing any income. However, if sesame were not a high-value crop, probably fewer farmers would have grown it for its beneficial effect of rotation. The farmers knew how to combat weed infestation, but they were unable to use such methods because the resource base on which their farming system was based did not allow any flexibility or diversification. The following methods (in rank order) could, according to the farmers, eradicate or minimize the effects of *S. hermontheca* infestation on crops. The best way reported to combat *Striga* infestation is by long fallow periods. Not only is this true in folk agronomy, but there seems to be scientific evidence to show that long fallow periods are an effective means of weed control. In a report on a soil survey in a nearby scheme (Umm Simsim and Umm Seinat), it is stated that a fallow period is often useful in eradicating annual weeds by exhausting the weed seed population, provided that the period is of sufficient length and is applied over a sufficiently large area. Perennial weeds are also sufficiently controlled by a fallow period (NEDEC and ILACO, N.V., 1966: 120). The second best way to combat *S. hermontheca* infestation, according to the farmers, is by late planting of crops in order to give respite to the weeds to grow and then to clear them before planting the crops. The third best way of combating *S. hermontheca* attack is by crop rotation, especially by inclusion of legumes.

This does not mean, however, that the farmers used these methods to combat *S. hermontheca* attack on their crops. In light of land shortage, long fallow periods were out of the question. They knew this method would help, but the limited resource base constrained their capacity to make changes in their land-use practices.

Delaying of sowing was also impractical and a risky option because the planting season is extremely short and they could not afford the luxury of waiting to give the weeds a chance to grow. Many of the farmers (Sudanese and refugees) saw a relationship between soil exhaustion and *S. hermontheca* and infestations of other weeds. Those who previously used manure to replenish soil nutrients also stated that manure application would help eradicate or control weeds. However, none of the farmers used this method to combat weed infestation because of fear of infestation by another weed species, locally known as *adar* (*Sorghum sudanense*), which is spread by animal droppings.

The practice of rotation (sesame following sorghum or vice versa) was the only method used by the farmers to minimize the effect of weed infestation. The effects of this method were limited or unsatisfactory because the number of crops grown are few due to the climatic and soil conditions. This suggests that the major constraint on the ability of the farmers to respond effectively to weed attack and to other allied factors that negatively affect crop yields is shortage of the basic resource – land. If the pressure on the available land resource were not acute, the effect of weed infestation would have been minimized. The problem of shortage of land is also exacerbated by the soil and climatic conditions, which limit the ability of the farming system to respond to the changing conditions flexibly.

The cropping pattern prevailing in the commercial farming areas and on the scheme clearly indicates that the main reason why commercial farmers did not practise rotational cropping was because their access to new arable land was not as restricted as it was for the scheme's refugee population. This suggests the existence of a hierarchy in the farmers' responses. Before farmers resort to intensive measures such as crop rotation, the first thing they do, if the opportunity exists, is either increase the area under cultivation or abandon the overused land and move to a new site.

Despite the limited rotational cropping (alternating sorghum and sesame) practised on the scheme, farmers' complaints about soil exhaustion and weed infestation were universal. This may suggest that over time continuous monocropping (alternating of the two crops notwithstanding) leads inevitably to depletion of soil nutrients. If such is the case, it is expected that, in the context of a proper incentive structure, the farmers would respond positively to a system of rotation that includes leguminous or nitrogen-fixing crops or plants. This will be discussed in the next chapter.

Previous indigenous knowledge and the present practice of natural-resource conservation

A considerable proportion of both groups (refugees and Sudanese) take no measures to counter soil-nutrient depletion (Table 11.2). The proportion of those who take no measures to overcome soil-fertility exhaustion is higher among the refugees than among the Sudanese. This may be partly explained by the fact that, under the existing technique of production, accessibility to adequate arable land is a precondition for resorting to traditional soil-depletion-countering measures, such as leaving parts or all of the holdings to lie fallow. However, even though this is fundamentally true, the failure to take fertility-replenishing measures may to a certain extent be influenced by the cultural and socio-economic backgrounds of the communities concerned. It is assumed here that the way agrarian communities understand reduction of productive capability of land and the coping strategies they devise to deal with the change are influenced by their previous experiences and cultural backgrounds.

If this is true, given their diverse socio-economic and cultural backgrounds, there may be a difference in how farmers coming from different groups respond to the problem of land degradation. The groups which had a long history of sedentary agricultural production and who were faced with a shortage of arable land had more advanced knowledge about degradation-countering or land-conservation measures than those who derived the major part of their livelihoods from pastoral activities in areas where there was abundant supply of land (Chapter 7). This did not, however, imply that pastoral communities took no land-degradation-countering measures. The strategies they devised to offset grazing pressure were different from the strategies developed by farming communities to respond to environmental deterioration of arable lands. In this section only the latter are considered.

Even though land was abundant before the arrival of the refugees, the practice of forest and bush fallow was not common among the local Sudanese farmers in the Qala en Nahal area. The mean duration of fallow periods was only 3.2 years, but after only two or three seasons of cropping. A study conducted in the area before the establishment of the scheme showed that agricultural-land use in the area was very limited (NEDEC and ILACO, N.V., 1966). There was only 'some local farming in the North'. Nevertheless, 2 or 3 years of farming was alternated with a fallow period of about 4 years. The extent of expansion of mechanized farming during the 1960s and beginning of the 1970s was limited and population was very low. When the refugee settlement was established in 1969–1970, the population in the area was only 1,435 persons (see Chapter 10). With the relocation of the refugees to the scheme, the population increased by 1,174%. In 1991 the total population on and around the scheme was nearly 35,000. This represented about a 2,339% increase in a matter of a quarter of a century.

Despite the fact that reduction of the productive capability of land, reflected in yield decline and weed infestation, in the context of a high population density was identified by the farmers as constituting a major constraint on agricultural production, a considerable proportion of the farmers did either little or nothing to minimize the effects of these constraints. Prior to their flight, a considerable proportion of the refugee farmers used different techniques to minimize the effect of loss of soil fertility and to counter soil erosion (see Chapter 7). For those who inhabited densely populated areas, such as the Eritrean plateau, this indigenous technical knowledge was important in minimizing the effect of high population pressure on resources. What is striking, however, is that despite the fact that soil exhaustion and weed infestation were identified by the farmers as the major constraints on agricultural production, none of these techniques except crop rotation were applied to minimize the effect of land degradation on their welfare. For example, random walks through the scheme area showed that many slopes were cut into V-shaped gullies. Most of these were on uncultivable areas, mainly on hills, pediments and foothills. In many cases, however, the gullies cut through several holdings and no structures were constructed by either the refugee or the Sudanese farmers to stop further formation of gullies or to minimize the consequences of those already formed. For the refugee farmers whose holdings were located on the flood-risk areas, flooding and deposition of sedimentation from upstream constituted a major problem. The rains in 1993, for example, were very heavy and 'most of the farms were destroyed by floods and weeds' (El Hadi, 1994). The extent of the damage caused by flooding was exacerbated by removal of vegetation. The result of forest destruction is that rainfall is no longer intercepted by tree canopies. Instead, rainfall falls heavily on the ground, eroding the bare surface soil. On the scheme, neither the Sudanese nor the refugee farmers undertake erosion-countering measures to minimize the effect of flooding and soil erosion. The same applies to restoration and conservation of depleted soil nutrients. In light of their previous advanced indigenous technical knowledge (see Chapter 7), it is interesting to examine why the refugee farmers do not use such knowledge to counter land degradation.

There are many factors that have rendered the refugees' traditional knowledge on conservation inapplicable. First, the scheme area is dominated by flat clay plains with slopes of less than 1°. The low slope angles reduce the quantity of run-off that can be generated by this type of land-form. The major cause of erosion stems not from the clay plains themselves but from small flooding and run-off coming from outside the plains. There are isolated single or groups of hills separated from each other by wide low-angled tracts of clay plains. The slope angles of the hills are invariably over 5° and usually vary from 20° to 30°. The hills are sites of concentration of run-off and, with the removal of vegetation, a large amount of soil is washed down the slope, causing erosion and deposition of sedimentation on the cultivable land situated beneath the hills. Parts of the clay plains are also eroded by streams flowing from north to south, which create broad valleys across the cultivable areas. The farmers whose farms were affected by the run-off coming from the hills, pediments and streams stated that there was little they could do to minimize the effects of the problem of erosion because an effective measure to counter this, in their view, would require earth-moving machinery, equipment and trucks to ferry stones and shrubs from distant places. Thus, the ability of the farmers to undertake erosion-countering measures was diminished by lack of equipment. In the Eritrean highlands, it was common for farmers to construct stone bunds and stone terraces with simple equipment, either to divert small floods or to slow down their speed, partly to prevent erosion and partly to harvest water. In order to minimize the risk of the stone bunds being washed away by floods, some of the structures were made permeable. The refugees lacked not only modern but even the simple equipment they had possessed in the pre-flight period. Such simple equipment would, however, have been inadequate in view of the magnitude of the run-off from the hills, pediments and streams.

Second, in some parts of Eritrea, such as the highlands, conservation work on this scale was undertaken on the basis of the mutual help of villagers. These forms of mutual help of labour have disappeared in the settlement and individual farmers have found it difficult to combat the erosional processes that are operative on their farms.

Third, stones and vegetation played important roles in the refugees' previous erosion-countering measures. Among the factors which contributed to conservation measures was not only the existence of indigenous technical knowledge, but also an abundant supply of stones, even in situ, which facilitated the farmers' efforts to undertake erosion-countering measures. Construction of stone-walled terraces, stone-walled diversions and structures across slopes required availability of stones in situ. Other methods, such as stands of trees and the creation of barriers of brushwood to accumulate debris in gullies, required trees. The scheme is not endowed with stones and most of it is stripped clean of trees and bushes. Not only did the refugees lack equipment, but they also lacked the means (raw materials) to apply their previous knowledge of conservation.

Fourth, the Sudanese small farmers on and around the scheme and the commercial farmers in the district use no erosion-countering measures. The refugee farmers are influenced by this. This was pointed out by several refugees, even by those who came from the parts of Eritrea where diverse methods of conservation were used to combat soil erosion. This is particularly interesting because it is consistent with the refugees' previous experiences. In the pre-flight period, when ethnic groups migrated to a new area, instead of introducing their own land-use practices they adapted to the land-use practices that existed in the areas of destination. When the peasants and agropastoralists from the plateau (Tigrinya and Saho) and the Maria from northern Senhit migrated to the Barka and Gash Setit valleys, none of them introduced their previous farming systems to the area. When the Saho groups migrated to Serea from eastern Akele-Guzai and eastern Hamasen, they adopted the land-use practices existing in their new place of residence (see Chapter 7). Given these experiences, it is not surprising to see that the refugees' previous traditional knowledge on conservation and other resource-management systems became inoperative. There seems to be a tendency among migrants to adapt to land-use patterns prevalent in areas of destination. The explanation for this is that land-use practices are not random occurrences, but are purposefully developed in response to particular local conditions, and they are therefore often location-specific. The failure of the refugees to apply their previous knowledge, for example, to counter the erosionary processes on the scheme is consistent with the general trend. What is intriguing here, however, is that this is happening in a situation where there is no viable local substitute and where the need for erosion-countering measures is critical.

Fifth, under the particular physical conditions and the level of poverty facing many of the refugee farmers, the opportunity cost of resources, including labour, that could be allocated to conservation measures is prohibitively high. This is exacerbated by lack of tenurial security and of long-term commitment of the refugee farmers to the area. However, the influence of lack of commitment engendered by refugee status is minimal because even the permanent residents undertake no measures to counter or minimize the effects of soil erosion.

The refugee farmers' previous knowledge of replenishing depleted soil nutrients has also been rendered more or less inapplicable in the particular situation of the scheme, due to unfavourable climatic conditions and the inadequacy of the resource base from which they derive their livelihoods. The scheme area being semiarid, rainfall distribution is unimodal, with a maximum in July and August and the period between October and May having little or no rainfall (see Tables 4.9 and 4.10). This physical condition, *inter alia*, precludes diversification of crops, including growing of nitrogen-fixing types, intercropping and multiple cropping. Among agrarian communities, these cropping patterns are devised not only to spread risk and to maximize returns, but also to replenish soil fertility. Thus, the ability of the farmers to practise their previous techniques of combating productive-capability reduction is effectively diminished by the unfavourable physical environment.

Fallowing as a technique of soil-nutrient replenishment has also become inoperative. Availability of an adequate resource base – land – is a prerequisite for using fallow periods to restore soil fertility. The conditions under which the refugee farmers eke out their living leave no room, not only for forest and bush fallow but also for short fallow periods to be practised. Most of the refugee families are preoccupied with their immediate survival, and future soil fertility is sacrificed to meet immediate needs. One of the most important methods the farmers used to restore soil fertility in their country of origin was organic manure application (see Chapter 7). On the scheme, neither the Sudanese nor the refugee farmers apply manure on their farms for fear of spreading a weed – *S. sudanense* (Arabic *adar*) – which belongs to the same botanic species as sorghum. This type of weed is allegedly spread by animal droppings and it is usual to come across farmers sweeping their farms of animal droppings.

Conclusion

At the heart of the problem of inappropriate land-use practices on and around the scheme lies the shortage of arable land. This is exacerbated by competing demands on the available scarce resource base and by the legal restriction imposed on freedom of movement and residence imposed on the refugees. The refugees, unlike the local population, cannot respond to the high population density and reduction of productivity by bringing new arable land under cultivation. The common responses to the problem of land shortage include out-migration, extending cultivation on to degradation-prone sites, sharecropping and renting of land.

The problem of land shortage had rendered the long-standing tradition of countering soil-nutrient depletion, e.g. fallowing, inoperative. This method, however, is still used by the local population. The common method of countering soil exhaustion and weed infestation used by the refugees is crop rotation, namely sorghum following sesame and vice versa. Neither of these two crops being leguminous, the role of this type of crop rotation in replenishing depleted soil nutrients should not be overstated.

Even though soil erosion and depletion of soil nutrients are increasingly becoming a problem, neither the Sudanese nor the refugee farmers undertake adequate measures to minimize the consequences. This is in spite of the fact that some of the refugee communities had well-developed resource-management systems in their country of origin. Some of the reasons that have rendered the refugees' traditional knowledge on conservation inapplicable are the specificity of the physical environment, lack of equipment, lack of labour, lack of tradition of erosion-countering practices in the area of destination and unfavourable climate, which precludes growing of diverse types of crops, including legumes.

Notes

1. Those families who had surplus cultivable land were invariably Sudanese farmers.
2. For example, on the Eritrean plateau, it was common to leave fields to lie fallow for one cropping season, in which the soil was turned several times during the rainy months to increase the rate of water infiltration and thus make more moisture available for the next cropping season.
3. In similar conditions, this would be referred to as bush encroachment on savannah grassland. On the scheme area, the process of woody encroachment is interrupted by expansion of mechanized rain-fed agriculture and browsing animals such as goats.
4. This is a new phenomenon because, until the early 1980s, the primary preoccupation of the farmers was production of food crops. Only the remaining land was allocated to cash-crop production.

12

Environmental Degradation and Predisposition to Change

The twenty years in exile have opened our eyes and we have no intention of shutting them again. We shall only move forward and never backwards. (M.O. Kisha, a refugee elder and former nomad)

We speak of change, but we do not think about it. We say that change exists, that everything changes, that change is the very law of things; yes, we say it and we repeat it; but those are only words, and we reason and philosophise as though change did not exist. (H. Bergson, 1992)

The cardinal question which springs to mind from the findings of the preceding chapters is whether the inadequacy of the resource base, which constitutes the single major threat to the subsistence security of the refugee farmers and renders their traditional resource-management systems inoperative, engenders a predisposition to change in general and to technological innovation in agriculture in particular. This will be measured: (i) by examining the farmers' responses to cultivation technology (tractorization); (ii) by looking at the kinds of non-farm income-generating activities the families, whose agricultural incomes have been deteriorating, undertake to counter this loss of income precipitated by reduction of productive capability of their lands; and (iii) by examining their responses to ACORD's natural-resource rehabilitation programme, whose objective has been to promote sustainable agricultural development. The latter will be the subject-matter of Chapter 13.

Although these criteria may enable us to measure how the farmers respond to the reduction in productive capability of the land resource, their failure to respond positively to a particular project or innovation may not necessarily show that they are unwilling to accept technological or other changes. Sometimes farmers' failure to respond to changes or to adopt innovations may be explained by problems associated with the innovation itself. The usual explanations as to why people fail to accept changes or to adopt innovations often conform to a stereotype along the following lines. 'People reject innovations or changes because they are naturally conservative, resistant to change, uncooperative, lacking motivation and understanding of the benefits to be had from change.' This kind of explanation is convenient, but deficient. A person may, for example, reject an innovation because s/he may be convinced that no benefits are to be had from adopting such an innovation; s/he may think that the innovation is risky or provides no better advantage than the present practice. Alternatively, the procedures adopted to disseminate the innovation may be amiss.

My point of departure in this regard is that, since people make rational decisions whether or not to adopt an innovation or to respond positively to changes, the explanations of the refugee farmers' responses to the changes will not be solely sought in their attitudes (attitudes are mutable), but also in the nature or attributes of the innovations themselves. In fact, among agrarian communities, it is not only

Plate 12.1   Within the given technological and physical constraints, the refugees leave no stone unturned to make ends meet. (Photo: Andes Press Agency/Carlos Reyes)

the attributes of the product (innovation) itself which determine farmers' responses; the manner in which the package is designed and implemented is also equally vital in influencing responses.

In Chapter 1, the population-based Boserupian model of agricultural change was presented. Here an attempt is made to use the model to describe and explain the behaviour of the refugee farmers in response to the challenges posed by high population density in a confined context. In the Boserupian model of agricultural change, if population density and decline in land availability put downward pressure on the customary standard of living of a community, there is a tendency to move from extensive to more intensive production systems (see Chapter 1). This may mean the introduction of fertilizers, manure, leguminous crops, fodder plants, multi-cropping, intercropping, crop rotation, etc. However, in Boserup's (1965 and 1970) model, population growth is a necessary but not sufficient condition, since each community has an array of choice variables on which it can allocate its labour. It is only when population growth results in increasing hardship in maintaining the prevailing standard of living that agrarian communities opt for more intensive agriculture (Darity, 1980: 139–40). The approach is based on a number of social and political assumptions, e.g. that choice is politically possible and that new lands are not available through migration or conquest (Pryor and Maurer, 1982). As Richard argues, however, Boserup's theory is a '"model" and not a history based upon detailed evidence and may be misleading as a basis for formulating agricultural development policy' (cited in Munslow, 1989: 26).

Wilkinson also sees economic development and change as being a result of 'ecological disequilibrium' (Wilkinson, 1973), reflected in a society outgrowing its productive resource base and productive system. He argues that, when a society moves out of ecological equilibrium, subsistence becomes a problem, economic conditions worsen and the society finds itself facing a number of difficulties which, together, indicate a mounting crisis. The real threat is that to the standard of living, which forces people to explore alternative means of livelihood. The key concept in Wilkinson's analysis is 'ecological equilibrium', which refers to 'any combination of a method and a rate of resource use which the environment can sustain indefinitely' (Wilkinson, 1973: 21). It may refer to a situation in which people restrict their demand for resources to a level which the environment can supply naturally, or it may refer to a balance struck on the basis of particular cultural patterns of resource management by which the environment's production of particular renewable resources is artificially increased. Societies are assumed to move out of 'ecological equilibrium' when a disturbance occurs to some part of the cultural system which acts as a restraint on population growth. The breakdown of the cultural restraint causes breakdown of local self-sufficiency, which in turn induces change and promotes involvement in the wider national economies, reflected in production for the market.

Wilkinson gives several examples of case-studies of precapitalist societies where scarcity of land resource in the face of population growth induced shifting from the production of food crops to the production of cash crops, rural–urban migration for wage employment and intensification of agricultural production, reflected in the introduction of new techniques of production. The centre-piece of Wilkinson's theory is that need is the cause of economic development and change. 'Only when the available slack in the resources base has been taken up is the pressure to innovate maximized' (Wilkinson, 1973: 21).

This description fits the situation on the scheme well. Not only was the arable land within the scheme fully allocated, but the arable land was incapable of further expansion. The population had also increased by over 71% in about 20 years (see Chapter 10) and by about 2,339% in 25 years.[1] This is excluding those who emigrated in search of alternative sources of livelihood. The key question is whether the tension or imbalance between high population density and the shortage of the land-resource base, exacerbated by land degradation has created willingness and readiness among the farmers to innovate, to accept changes in agricultural technique and to seek alternative sources of livelihood. In the following sections, the predisposition of the farmers to change and their coping strategies with the loss of income (food-crop production) precipitated by land degradation will be discussed.

Openness to a new cultivation technology – tractors

Prior to their flight, the refugees used human or draught energy for cultivation. Cultivation was carried out by ox-drawn implements. Sometimes camels were used instead of oxen. Among very poor families, donkeys were also used as a source of draught energy. All other agricultural operations were executed manually. The refugees were unfamiliar with all forms of motor-power energy, including tractor cultivation. On the scheme, cultivation is tractorized.

The refugees have diverse cultural backgrounds. There are over eleven ethnic groups with different socio-economic backgrounds (see Chapter 7).[2] The majority were formerly agropastoralists who derived their livelihood from a combination of dry-land rain-fed cultivation and livestock production. The dominant economic activity among some of the groups was raising of cattle, small ruminants and camels.

Cultivation was a supplementary economic activity. All groups, however, were familiar with the use of draught energy for cultivation.

Prior to their flight, the degree of their integration into the national and international economies in terms of participation in the wider division of labour, such as production of specialized crops for the market, varied from one ethnic group to another. Among the majority, subsistence production constituted the dominant form of economic activity.

After their relocation to the scheme, the refugee communities were faced with unfamiliar problems, which required new and unknown solutions. The familiar source of energy for cultivation – animal power – could not be utilized in the new environment for various reasons. Firstly, the early settlers did not bring livestock with them when they were first relocated to the scheme. Thus, they had no access to draught animals. Secondly, the agricultural policy of the government of Sudan in the Gedaref district was based on mechanization of cultivation (Kibreab, 1987). Nowhere in the district are oxen, camels or donkeys used for cultivation. Thirdly, unlike the easily friable soils in the refugees' country of origin, the dark, heavy, clay soils of the district – the vertisols – are believed to be too hard to be ploughed by oxen. Tractors and wide-disc levels had been used in the district since the 1940s (for the history of the early mechanized crop-production schemes, see Clouston, 1948; Laing, 1953; Davies, 1964). The traditional *seluka* (plough stick) cultivation was also unknown in the refugees' country of origin.

The United Nations High Commissioner for Refugees (UNHCR) and the government of Sudan, instead of utilizing a technology which the settlers were familiar with, chose to introduce a new technology which was unfamiliar to the former pastoralists, agropastoralists and sedentary farmers. The literature on peasant responses to change abounds with arguments which suggest peasant conservatism or resistance to innovation or to the introduction of new agricultural techniques or economic activities which represent a break or discontinuity with familiar practices. This was not true among the refugees in the study area. The refugee communities, for example, embraced technological change (introduction of tractors for cultivation) without any hesitation. The major explanation may lie not in a change of attitude (attitudes seldom change overnight), but in the fact that the conditions under which they used to conduct their day-to-day affairs had changed dramatically. With flight, they lost most of their material possessions, such as land, farm equipment and livestock, and the security associated with familiar environment, traditional organizations, social networks, etc. These losses were important in two respects. On the one hand, the fact that they were socially uprooted meant vulnerability to the whims and decisions of others over whom they lacked control. Their ability to resist change was dramatically weakened or broken due to social uprootedness. Secondly, resistance to change presupposes the existence of an alternative means of livelihood, which they lacked. The loss of all possessions meant complete dependence on refugee aid for survival. Their situation was exacerbated by the unfamiliarity of the new environment, which was far away from the border areas so that social or economic networks based on previous contacts could no longer be utilized. Thus, whether the refugee farmers liked the tractors or not, there was little they could do but to accept them. Their ability to 'exit' was shattered by lack of choice and control over their situation.

There are no studies on the initial response of the refugee farmers to the introduction of tractors, but the author's findings from the early 1980s and the beginning of the 1990s clearly show that, in the farmers' view, tractors are the best thing that ever happened to them. It is quite interesting to understand the factors underlying the farmers' positive response to the introduction of tractors, but it has to be admitted that this is methodologically formidable to come to grips with. The central question is whether the change in the method of cultivation was accepted because the refugees thought there was no other way of averting the threat of hunger (to overcome the problem of subsistence) or whether the same innovation would have been adopted even in the presence of a less efficient or more labour-intensive alternative method of cultivation.

Wilkinson, for example, argues that it is the appearance of subsistence problems that makes people willing to accept changes which previously required too much work or involved other prohibitive disadvantages:

> Most ... changes are accepted because they represent increases in efficiency for subsistence, not because they represent increases in efficiency for societies with adequate subsistence. This point was made explicit in a study of peasants' motives for changing their methods of cultivation. Peasants accept change in methods of cultivation to increase production not because they are cheaper or easier, i.e. more efficient. (Wilkinson, 1973)

There was no doubt that the refugee farmers, due to lack of access to an adequate resource base, economic uprooting and relocation to an unfamiliar and remote environment, were faced with serious subsistence problems and their sympathetic embracing of the new technology might have been due to their desire to overcome these difficulties. However, even though there is a clear linkage between their enthusiastic response to the change of method of cultivation and the level of deprivation they suffered, it cannot be stated with the same degree of certainty that their response would have been radically different had they been in their familiar habitat facing no imminent threat of hunger. The evidence suggests that economic and social uprootedness seem to have telescoped the process of change. It is plausible to argue that the process of change and adoption of the new method of cultivation would probably have been longer if the refugee communities had had an alternative viable method of cultivation.

It is not clear whether this kind of response is inherent in all displaced popula-tions. I think the key is not displacement as such, but rather the level of vulner-ability and deprivation experienced in connection with internal displacement or exile (refugee status). For example, I do not think that a self-settled refugee community that settles among its own co-ethnics in border areas, where the problem of subsistence and powerlessness may not be as acute as among relocatees (owing to kin hospitality), responds enthusiastically to technological change just because of refugee status. The lesson to be learned from this experience is probably that subsistence producers respond to change positively when they are under pressure posed by a crisis of livelihood. The greater the intensity of the livelihood crisis, the higher the predisposition to change.

Although the refugee farmers accepted change in the method of cultivation in order to increase production, the fact that tractors reduced the drudgery of cultivation and weeding seems to have positively influenced their attitudes. In the study area, hand cultivation is a slow and burdensome task. Thus, although the major reason for embracing the tractors was to increase production by bringing larger areas into the production process, the fact that tractors have freed the farmers from performing the arduous task of hand cultivation is highly valued (interview with Village Committee, 1991). The impact of the principle of 'least effort' on the attitude of the farmers towards tractors cannot be discounted, but there is no evidence to suggest that it was decisive in determining their response. In an extensive discussion with some of the notables among the refugee farmers, it

Plate 12.2   Two former nomads threshing the harvest of the season in Umsagata refugee settlement. Displacement has telescoped the process of transformation from pastoralism to sedentarism. (Photo: UNHCR/14017/W. Wallace)

became clear that they perceive tractors as signifying modernization. Asked whether they would revert to animal traction when they return to Eritrea, a prominent Beni Amer clan head in Salmin said, 'The 20 years in exile have opened our eyes and we have no intention of closing them again. We shall only move forward and never backwards' (Osman Kisha, 1991).

Reverting to animal traction after having used tractors for two decades was considered as darkness or retrogression. This view is widely held by most of the refugee farmers. In their view, the only problem emanating from tractor use was loss of freedom of choice with regard to the date of sowing, which in the existing climatic and soil conditions of the area is critical. One of the key factors which influences yield is optimal timeliness of sowing (see Chapter 4). At present, the way the tractor hire service is organized makes sowing of the individual farmers' plots a random occurrence. Some farmers' plots are cultivated too early, before the germination of weeds, others are sown at the optimal time and there are others on whose farms the tractors arrive too late. To overcome this constraint, many refugee farmers resort to alternative cultivation methods, such as the *seluka* and hired private tractors, but all would prefer tractors if they arrived at their plots at the right time. This suggests that, even though the refugees initially accepted the tractors to overcome an immediate subsistence problem, they understand the advantages to be had and they intend to stick to them to maximize wealth even when there are no problems of subsistence. There were some families, however, who preferred hand planting to mechanized planting, in order to have control over the time of sowing. All farmers are fully aware of the relationship between yields and timely planting.[3] There were also some farmers who preferred hand planting because, they argued, mechanized cultivation with the discs causes run-off, resulting in waste of moisture and soil nutrients, which they considered important for plant growth. The majority, however, were in favour of tractor cultivation.

Production for the market

The refugee farmers' willingness to change is not limited to acceptance of change in the methods of cultivation. Their predisposition to change is also indicated by the drastic moves they have taken from food production to production for the market. The overwhelming majority of the refugees were formerly subsistence producers, whose involvement in the national and international economies was either limited or non-existent. The two major crops grown on the scheme are sorghum and sesame. Sorghum is a staple crop and sesame is a cash crop. In the pre-flight period, the dominant sources of livelihood were livestock and subsistence-crop production of sorghum and/or millet. Production of cash crops was small or non-existent. It was common, however, for the communities to buy from the market commodities which they did not produce themselves, either from the proceeds of livestock sales or from a limited participation in the agricultural labour market. This has changed drastically. The communities' economic and social uprooting has led to the breakdown of self-sufficiency. This has motivated them to participate in the wider division of labour, *inter alia*, by producing specialized crops for the market.

Land is a scarce commodity in the settlement. Nevertheless, a considerable proportion of the arable land was allocated to production for the market (see Table 11.5). In some seasons, and this invariably coincided with the early onset of rains, the area of arable land allocated to sesame was either in parity with sorghum or more. This suggests that, if it were not for the late onset of rains, more of the scarce resource, land, would be allocated to production for the market. Between 1971 and 1990, the average proportion of the arable land allocated to sesame production was in the range of 37% of the total area cultivated. These results were unexpected because, between 1970 and 1989, of the total area under commercial mechanized farming in the district of Gedaref, only 13% was allocated to sesame (see Table 11.6). Sesame operations, especially harvesting, are extremely labour-intensive because of the seed's dehiscent nature. This may explain partially why commercial farmers in the region are reluctant to grow sesame. For example, the attempt to produce sesame on a large scale in the Gedaref district during the Second World War, designed to overcome the shortage of oil in the world market, was abandoned because the amount of labour required over a short time for harvesting sesame was considered to be too high, due to the crop's dehiscent nature. In light of the shortage of agricultural labour and the shortage of water supply in the Gedaref district, growing sesame on a large scale was considered unrealistic (Davies, 1964). By the same token, the present commercial farmers are reluctant to increase the ratio of the land allocated to sesame because this would undermine their strategy of maximizing short-term gains, which is achieved, among other things, by keeping the cost of production to a minimum, even at the expense of long-term sustainability.

Sesame is a high-value crop. In light of the land shortage faced by the farmers on the scheme, production of a high-value crop is one way in which they try to overcome the constraint of land shortage. Sesame production enables them to earn a higher income per unit of land cultivated. Even though sesame yield per unit of land cultivated is lower than that of sorghum (see Table 4.1), this is more than compensated for by the high relative price sesame commands in the market. The second reason why the refugee farmers allocate a considerable proportion of their land resource to production for the market is to spread risk in an environment characterized by recurrent crop failures due to the erratic and low rainfall, diseases, insect attacks and weed infestation (see Chapter 4).

The third reason why sesame is grown is to minimize soil exhaustion. Neither of the two crops, namely sorghum and sesame, is leguminous or nitrogen-fixing, but alternating the two crops seems to improve soil resilience against depletion. The fourth reason for growing sesame is to fight weed infestation. Sorghum is drastically affected by *Striga hermontheca*, but not sesame. Even though alternating of the two crops mitigates the disastrous effect of *Striga* attack, the seed remains dormant until the following season when the *hawasha* is planted to sorghum. Sorghum is also affected by *Sorghum sudanense*, which is easily weeded in a *hawasha* planted to sesame.

Non-farm income-generating activities

Prior to their flight, the major association with the market economy was limited to the sale of a few products (livestock or food crops) in order to obtain goods from the market-place which they did not produce themselves. There was little or no division of labour based on specialization and exchange. Although displacement is, more often than not, accompanied by social change, on the scheme the process of change, reflected in deepening division of labour, specialization and exchange, has been accelerated by the diminishing capability of the basic resource – land.

The changes include wage labour, cash-crop production, livestock production, trade, shepherding, firewood collection (for sale), water fetching (for sale), charcoal making, thatch-grass collection, etc. Except for livestock production, these are discussed below. (Livestock production was presented in Chapter 6.) Although all the farmers on the scheme have experienced loss of agricultural productivity, the consequences of these losses are varied, depending on the economic status of the individual families. The findings of the study show that the consequences of land degradation on the economic situation of the farmers at a household level are mediated by economic status. In fact, land degradation has been a bane for many but a boon for a few. The impoverishment of some families has been a source of cheap labour and a dumping ground for credits (*shail*) at prohibitive interest rates during the hungry periods.

In 1993, forty families from four refugee villages (Salmin, Umsagata, Dehema and Umzurzur), whose holdings' productivity was reduced progressively over time because of continuous monocropping and weed infestation, were systematically identified for an in-depth study of their coping strategies. The families were identified after thorough discussions with ACORD's village officers, sheikhs, *leginas* and key informants selected from the poor farmers and extension officers (Table 12.1).

On average, the plots of these forty families have been under continuous cultivation for about 17 years (Table 12.1). Although none of the families had abandoned their plots, average yield per *feddan* in these plots was much lower than the overall average in the scheme. The overall average yield for sorghum in 1992 was 1.57 sacks per *feddan* (see Table 4.1) – the highest since 1987 – while in these holdings the average yield was 0.5 sack per *feddan* (Table 12.1). The average annual per capita grain requirement for the same year was 2.0 sacks and total production in the forty holdings represented only 32% of the total grain requirement of the families.

Table 12.1   Families experiencing land-productivity decline

No.	I	II	III	IV	V	VI	VII	VIII
1	Salmin	Bisha	8	10	20	15	3	12
2		B. Amer	9	10	20	20	4	16
3		Bilen	4	10	20	8	4	4
4		Algeden	5	10	19	15	5	10
5		Nara	9	10	20	22	8	14
6		B. Amer	6	10	20	14	1	13
7		Algeden	6	10	19	15	5	10
8		Saho	7	10	20	14	1	13
9		Nara	7	10	19	10	2.5	7.5
10		B. Amer	6	10	20	15	0.25	14.75
11	Umsagata	Nara	8	10	22	20	9	11
12		Maria	13	10	21	24	5	19
13		B. Amer	7	10	22	10	4	6
14		Saho	9	10	19	18	10	8
15		Saho	10	10	21	16	12	4
16		B. Amer	13	10	22	20	6	16
17		Bilen	13	10	14	29	9	20
18		Bilen	11	10	12	25	12	13
19		Nara	8	10	22	18	7	11
20		Maria	7	10	21	20	4	16
21	Dehema	Saho	3	5	13	12	3	9
22		Saho	7	10	19	19	5	14
23		Saho	8	10	16	10	2	8
24		Saho	7	10	20	8	3	5
25		Bilen	6	10	13	12	2	10
26		Saho	5	5	13	12	2	10
27		Bilen	5	10	13	17	2	15
28		Tigrinya	8	10	13	10	1.5	8.5
29		Bilen	7	10	13	12	2	11
30		Saho	2	10	12	3	1	2
31	Zurzur	Saho	6	10	12	12	8	4
31		B. Amer	12	10	11	24	7	17
33		Saho	8	10	12	15	7	8
34		Saho	7	10	12	13	8	5
35		B. Amer	3	10	15	7	6	1
36		Saho	7	10	18	18	2	16
37		Saho	8	10	22	12	3	9
38		B. Amer	8	5	15	14	0	14
39		Saho	4	10	8	9	3	6
40		Saho	11	10	10	22	12	10

I, village name; II, ethnicity; III, family size; IV, land size in *feddans*; V, number of years their plot has been under continuous cropping; VI, annual grain requirement; VII, amount of grain harvested in 1992 in sacks; VIII, grain deficit in 1992 in sacks; B. Amer, Beni Amer.

How do these families make ends meet or what do they do to overcome the problem of subsistence? When they can no longer earn sufficient income from crop production because of diminishing returns of the soils or weed infestation, they are left with no choice but to allocate their major resource – family labour – to diverse farm and off-farm income-generating activities.

The responses of individual farmers to progressive crop-yield decline are dependent on various factors, i.e. on the options open to each family. The options are, among other things, mediated by economic status, social and family networks and demographic composition (age and sex structures) of the individual families. The insights in the following discussion are gained from the diverse responses devised by these families (Table 12.1). Nevertheless, the discussions below do not exclusively apply to the forty families. The purpose is, on the one hand, to show how the farmers respond to diminishing returns of agricultural production and, on the other, to examine the extent of the division of labour, based on specialization and exchange, which has been taking place, among other things, in response to the reduction in the productive capability of the basic resource – land.

Labour-market participation

One measure of the refugee families' predisposition to change is indicated by the level of their participation in the wage-labour market. In 1980, Spooner's findings showed that 17% of the households in Qala en Nahal were landless (Spooner, 1981). The level of landlessness was increasing from year to year, reaching about 27% in 1983 (Kibreab, 1987), 32% in 1985 (ACORD, 1985c) and 36% in 1991. The major source of livelihood of the landless households was income earned from wage labour. For example, in 1983, about 75% of the landless households' annual income was derived from wage labour (Kibreab, 1987). The fact that many refugees migrated, disregarding their host's decision to prohibit emigration, is a manifestation of the severity of the problem of subsistence they have been faced with.

Among the total household heads in the six refugee villages in Qala en Nahal, 55% worked for wages in 1982–1983 (Kibreab, 1987). The existing production techniques and population density, the limited capacity of absorption of the land resource and the consequently deteriorating conditions of living have been pushing a considerable number of families to leave the scheme temporarily or permanently in search of an alternative means of survival elsewhere. Many of those who left the scheme have even joined the ranks of the urban poor. A considerable proportion of the Saho group living in El Kala-Kila, in the suburbs of Khartoum, are migrants from Adingrar in the Qala en Nahal refugee settlement.[4]

One of the findings of the 1982–1983 study (Kibreab, 1985; 1987) was that the high population density and state of confinement had led to the fragmentation of holdings into farm units too small to provide for the normal contingencies of an average family. The acute land shortage and/or the high population density led to a *de facto* change in the land-tenure system. In spite of the legal prohibition, arable land became a commodity subject to rent, sale, mortgage, gift and sharecropping as if the fields belonged to those who had rights of possession. This suggests that one of the consequences of population pressure on resources is a change in land-tenure systems, even when such changes are not envisioned or are even prohibited by law.

Many new families have emerged, but no land redistribution has taken place to meet the needs of these families. Most of the families that were established later were dependent on the male side's parents for land. Many parents were therefore forced to share their 10-*feddan* or less than 10-*feddan* holdings with their married sons. This led gradually to overfragmentation of holdings below economic levels. Since the amount of land required by a family is, among other things, dependent on its productive capability, during the early years, when crop yields per unit land cultivated were higher, even the fragmented farms produced enough to meet the subsistence needs of many of the families concerned. When the productive capability of the land was reduced, oscillatory migration to the rain-fed mechanized and irrigated agricultural schemes became a widespread response by those farmers who were faced with diminishing farm incomes. Most of the migrants were male adults, single or married. They left the rest of their families on the scheme to cultivate the fragmented units of the holdings. After the mid-1980s, however, part of the seasonal oscillatory migration changed its character. Seasonal migration gave way to permanent out-migration of whole families from the scheme. With the increased problems or reduction of productive capability, some of those families whose holdings were overfragmented below economic levels migrated permanently in search of sources of livelihood elsewhere. Often it was younger families, dependent on land donated by their parents, who migrated from the scheme. This seems to have slightly mitigated the acute pressure on land and consequently the amount of land available to the remaining population increased.

In 1982–1983, there were many families that allocated part of their holdings to their married but landless sons. In 1991–1992, a considerable proportion of the fragmented units were reconsolidated into contiguous units because the small units had reverted to the original possessors following the permanent out-migration of some of the families. The division of the holdings into fragmented units could no longer provide for the customary contingencies of the families' lifetime. Hence, both the parent families (who allocated part of their holdings to their married sons) and the newly established families were left worse off. In the summer of 1990, a considerable number of families returned to the areas in Eritrea controlled by the Eritrean People's Liberation Front (EPLF), although the factors that prompted their flight had not been completely removed. Their return was to a large extent induced by the deteriorating living conditions in exile, mainly resulting from shrinkage and loss of fertility of the available land resource.

Wage labour, then, is one of the most important coping strategies devised to overcome the consequences of deteriorating income levels from agriculture. In both communities (Sudanese and refugees), the majority responded to the problem of land shortage and diminished productivity by selling their labour power to others. The refugee respondents were selected from the land-owning families. Therefore the 57% who worked for wage labour in response to diminishing productive capability of the land resource did not include the landless (see Table 11.1).

Although off-farm income-generating activities are becoming increasingly important as a means of diversification of economic activities among rural societies in Sudan, the fact that the majority of the respondent families relied on off-farm income-generating activities (57% refugees and 54% Sudanese) suggests that agricultural production on the scheme has over time become less important. For the majority, it is no longer possible to derive adequate incomes from the land to meet the basic needs of the farming communities. This was consistent with our expectation, because one of the consequences of land shortage has been continuous cropping, with the consequence of depletion of soil nutrients and infestation of the old fields by noxious weeds, resulting in yield decline (see Chapter 4). The participation of a large number of the families in wage labour does not suggest that the opportunity to sell one's labour power is readily available. Not only did many of them work for a limited period of time because of lack of demand, but many of them had to travel long distances and stay away from their families for months in search of employment opportunities. The fact that 57% of the land-holding families were engaged in wage labour is an indication of the former subsistence producers' openness to change.

Trading activities

The farmers' level of integration into the national and international economy and participation in the wider division of labour can also be inferred from the considerable number of diverse trading activities in the six refugee villages. For example, in 1983 there were 32 camel-powered oil-presses (*asara*), 36 restaurants (cafés), 15 bakeries, 21 butcher shops and 34 vegetable stalls in the six refugee villages (Kibreab, 1987). These diverse income-generating activities in the informal sector were undertaken partly to accumulate wealth, but to a large extent in response to diminishing returns of agricultural productivity. The mushrooming trade activities are not solely triggered by land degradation. There are a number of families who have accumulated enough wealth from both farm and off-farm income-generating activities and are fully dependent on hired labour while they (including members of their families) are engaged in full-time trade activities.

Some of these trade activities, however, are initiated by farmers who supplement the ever-shrinking returns from their ageing holdings. These are families who could no longer derive sufficient income from crop production. Thus, deterioration of agricultural production and consequently the drive to make ends meet by searching for an alternative means of livelihood has been the vehicle for change, diversification and greater flexibility. There were a number of traders who engaged in cross-border trade operations between Sudan and Eritrea. This was true even during the war. At that time, there were acute shortages of basic commodities in Eritrea and many Eritrean refugees from Sudan, including from the Qala en Nahal scheme, were involved in smuggling goods across the border. For some, this represented a lucrative activity. There were also some families who invested their proceeds from sesame sales in lorries. The latter are very few, but this shows the extent of specialization and exchange that permeates economic life on the scheme.

Firewood and thatch-grass collection

One of the consequences of deforestation in and around the scheme is a drastic increase in the cost of firewood collection (see Chapter 5). The depletion of forest resources in the vicinity of the scheme led to the increased distance of the sources of wood fuel. During the 1970s and 1980s, wood-fuel collection was not an independent activity. It was combined with other activities. People collected and carried firewood on their way home after herding their livestock or after farm work. Then, most families consumed self-collected firewood, although they obtained charcoal from the market-place. Since the mid-1980s, firewood collection is no longer combined with other activities. This has therefore given rise to increased specialization and exchange. Fewer families are dependent on self-collection and many donkey- and camel-owning individuals are engaged in firewood collection for sale. This constitutes an important source of income for families that have access to labour and pack-animals. Those families who owned pack-animals, but either lacked male adult members or were engaged in more profitable activities, devised income-sharing schemes with families who contributed labour. The incomes from firewood proceeds were shared equally.

Before the clearance of large tracts of land for cultivation and denudation of the savannah grasses in the hills and pediments, most families collected their own thatch grass for construction of huts. Like firewood, thatch-grass collection was combined with other activities. The cost of thatch-grass collection rose drastically with denudation of grass resources in the vicinity of the scheme. The consequence of this has been commoditization of thatch grass. Since the mid-1980s, most families have been obtaining thatch grass through the market-place. Although this may have affected some families in a detrimental way, for others this constitutes a reliable source of income. The activity, however, is undertaken only during the dry season.

Charcoal production

Charcoal production constitutes one of the major dry-season income-generating activities in the Sudanese villages (see Chapter 5). The number of refugees engaged independently in charcoal making is very small. However, there were a considerable number of male adult refugees who were engaged in charcoal production as contract workers with Sudanese charcoal wholesalers. In Sudan, charcoal production and marketing are vertically integrated in a rather sophisticated way. The activity is monopolized by rich merchants, known as wholesalers. Small producers lack licences and the necessary infrastructure to market their produce directly. They sell whatever they produce to wholesalers. The latter also hire contract workers, who make charcoal in return for cash payment. In recent years, the participation of refugees in contract work has considerably increased as a result of the diminishing productive capability of their plots.

One of the major reasons why refugees work as contract workers instead of making charcoal independently has to do with their political vulnerability. Wholesalers grant them protection. Legally, no person is allowed to cut trees or even to use dead wood for charcoal making (Forest Act, 1989). The Sudanese on and outside the scheme are not constrained by this prohibition, but most of the refugees comply with this constraint because of their refugee status (political vulnerability). The refugees are expected by the authorities, including the courts, to observe forestry and other laws more carefully than the citizens. Non-compliance is dealt with more severely with refugees than with citizens. This attitude seems to be common among many countries of asylum. For example, in Sweden, an immigrant or a refugee who 'repeatedly' commits a crime (including petty crimes) punishable with imprisonment is deported after serving his/her sentence to his/her country of origin.

Water sale

There is only one watering-point in every village. Some of the residential areas are far from these watering-points. This has led to the use of water tanks and bags ferried by donkeys. There is also usually a long queue at the watering-points and those families who engage in more profitable economic activities or who lack access to family labour obtain water through the market-place. Water is ferried to the gates of the families concerned by water sellers. This represents a good source of income for a considerable number of young boys and girls. Contractual arrangements between those who have young children and those who own animals of burden are common; incomes from water proceeds are shared. This activity was common even in the early 1980s, but the number of people engaged in the activity is increasing in proportion to the decreasing returns from the holdings. To the delight of consumers, this has led to increased competition and price cuts. However, the fact that the number of people engaged in the activity is increasing suggests the water market is not yet satiated.

Shepherding

One of the most important coping strategies developed by the refugee farmers to counter loss of income from crop production is livestock build-up (see Chapter 6). The refugees are former pastoralists and agropastoralists and livestock played a key role in their previous economic life. Initially the scheme was based solely on crop production. No allowance was made for raising livestock. The government and UNHCR, instead of building on the existing capacities, ignored the wealth of indigenous knowledge possessed by the communities on livestock production. Even though the refugees seized every opportunity to rebuild their stock, the need for this was more intensely felt as crop yields began to decline progressively. At the beginning of the 1980s, some of the rich families began investing their incomes from sesame proceeds in livestock, but it seems that it was land degradation, manifested in weed infestation and crop-yield decline (after the mid-1980s), that functioned as an incentive for the determination of the farmers to build up their stocks.

There was a consensus among the refugee farmers that restocking represented a viable option under the deteriorating soil and fluctuating rainfall conditions. However, only the well-off could afford to make this kind of investment. It was in this context that a considerable number of the poor refugees innovated a mechanism for restocking. Some migrated seasonally to the rain-fed mechanized and irrigated schemes to work for wages. During the dry season many individuals migrated to the Rahad and New Halfa to pick cotton[5] and to the regional towns to work as manual labourers in the booming construction industry. A sizeable proportion of these incomes is usually invested in livestock.

There were also many poor young males who migrated to distant places to work as shepherds for Sudanese pastoralists. Each was paid twelve expecting ewes per annum. Most of them stayed for more than two years. Many families rebuild their stock in this way. Upon return, some of them sell the sheep and use the proceeds to purchase cattle. This represents an innovative response to diminishing returns from crop production. In their country of origin, this kind of arrangement was not known.

Sale of crop residues

Until the beginning of the 1980s, postharvest grazing (crop residues) was an open-access resource open to all livestock owners. The grazing areas have shrunk over time as a result of expansion of cultivation. This, in combination with animal build-up, has created increased pressure on grazing and browsing resources. Since the mid-1980s, crop residues have become commoditized and cut feed constitutes a major animal fodder during the dry seasons. After harvest, crop residues are cut and collected either for sale or for the families' stock. For the poor families, this represents a substantial amount of income. One of the major causes of crop failure in the study area is lack of rainfall towards the end of the season. Sorghum stalks whose growth is interrupted by shortage of rainfall are considered to be good fodder and fetch high prices. Even during the wet seasons, there are also people who earn incomes from the sale of green grasses and palatable weeds.

Conclusion

Most of the non-farm income-generating activities are induced by diminishing value of the arable, grazing and woodlands. Environmental degradation has made the scheme settlers more predisposed to change and to engage in unfamiliar economic activities. In light of the limited off-farm income-earning opportunities, many families continue growing crops on their impoverished and weed-infested holdings. However, over time, farming has become only one of the diverse economic activities the communities engage in to make ends meet. In the absence of the incomes earned from the non-farm activities, the consequences of land degradation on the living conditions of the communities would have been deleterious. The diverse off-farm income-generating activities that permeate life on the scheme have mitigated the detrimental consequences of reduction in productive capability of their holdings.

The positive responses of the refugee farmers to the introduction of an unfamiliar method of cultivation (tractors and the wide-level disc harrows) and their participation in cash-crop production and in the commodity and labour markets show that they are willing to embrace changes and innovations, provided that such changes and innovations raise their incomes and their freedom of choice.[6] The fact that the refugee farmers, in spite of their previous precapitalist socio-economic backgrounds (measured in terms of labour- and commodity-market interactions), engage in myriad income-generating activities suggests that land degradation functions as a catalyst for economic change, manifested in specialization, exchange and diversification.

Notes

1. Before the establishment of the refugee settlement, the total population in and around the present scheme was only 1,300 persons.
2. In addition to those shown in Chapter 7, other minority groups such as the Bisha, Adshuma, Algeden and others, live in the settlements.
3. In a semiarid area such as the Qala en Nahal scheme, where there is a maximum of only 6 weeks' cultivation and planting time for a good harvest, timeliness of planting is critical.
4. This came as a surprise because in 1982 it was widely believed, including by the *mudhir* (settlement manager) at Umsagata (Qala en Nahal), that they had returned to Eritrea spontaneously. Given the restriction on freedom of movement and residence imposed by the government, the refugees leave the settlements illegally in search of employment elsewhere. Such out-migrations were often wrongly understood as spontaneous returns to the refugees' country of origin, when in reality most of those who left the scheme in response to diminishing land-base resources settled elsewhere in Sudan, including in urban centres.
5. Until the early 1980s, when there was adequate income from crop production and the demand for labour was relatively high, the participation of the refugees, even those who were in the wage-earning settlements (see Kibreab, 1990b), was minimal. In recent years, however, participation of refugees in cotton picking has increased considerably.
6. The farmers cannot know whether an innovation will enable them to increase their farm income before they adopt such an innovation. The most important thing in this process is whether the farmers perceive the changes as useful. That is why communication between extension officers and farmers is critical in the process of transfer of a new technology.

13

Farmers' Responses to ACORD's Natural-resource Programmes

I have since, in a special sense, come to believe in development; *which means the unfolding of what is there.* (G. K. Chesterton, 1936)

Development brings freedom, provided it is development of people. But people cannot be developed; they can only develop themselves ... He [a person] develops himself by what he does; he develops himself by making his own decisions; by increasing his understanding of what he is doing; and why; by increasing his own knowledge and ability; and by his own full participation as an equal in the life of the community he lives in. (J. Nyerere, 1973)

In 1974, the United Nations High Commissioner for Refugees (UNHCR) phased out its financial involvement on the scheme. The project was handed over to the people's local government at Qala en Nahal town. One of the immediate consequences of this was the collapse of the tractor hire service (THS). Consequently, the amount of cultivated land declined drastically. By 1975 and 1976, the total area cultivated by the THS plummeted to less than 25% of the total area that was cultivated in 1972 (Table 13.1). In 1976, crop yields were almost zero because of lack of capital to replace the worn-out machinery, to hire qualified manpower and to purchase spare parts, fuel and lubricants (Kibreab, 1987). An imminent threat to hunger faced the communities and 38% of the total population fled the scheme in search of livelihoods elsewhere. The initial decision to mechanize cultivation was based on an insufficient knowledge of the refugees' traditional methods of cultivation, because mechanization of cultivation was incompatible with the financial, technical and management skills of the farmers. The problem faced by the refugee farmers was perceived by UNHCR, donors, non-government organizations (NGOs) and the government of Sudan as being a technical one requiring a technical solution. The British Overseas Development Administration (ODA), therefore, donated £750,000 sterling at the 1980 Khartoum Conference on Refugees for the refurbishment of the THS provided the project was implemented by a non-governmental organization and not by the Commissioner's Office for Refugees (COR), as was the case with all previous refugee projects in the east. The initial objectives of ACORD's involvement on the scheme were purely technical, i.e. to refurbish the THS by utilizing the funds donated by ODA. According to the Letter of Intent signed by COR and ACORD, the objectives were:

(a) to design a system of tractor and land management in Qala en Nahal which will serve to ensure a viable and efficient tractor service giving maximum potential benefit to all refugee farmers;
(b) to facilitate the procurement of the additional machinery requested by the Sudan Government utilising funds committed by the ODA at the June 1980 Conference in Khartoum, taking account of those tractors which are either non-functional or which are reaching the end of their working life. Ensure uniformity of equipment and to provide a generous reserve tractor capacity;

Table 13.1   Summary of total area cultivated by the government/ACORD tractor hire service in the Qala en Nahal Refugee settlement 1971–1991

Season	Total area cultivated (*feddans*)	Change (index) (1980 = 100)
1971	13,353	96
1972	28,723	206
1974	16,495	119
1975	6,735	48
1976	7,000	50
1977	16,325	117
1978	21,058	151
1979	19,212	138
1980	13,900	100
1981	35,160	252
1982	37,274	268
1983	38,667	278
1984	31,198	224
1985	32,262	232
1986	39,000	280
1987	48,910	351
1988	36,935	266
1989	42,248	304
1990	34,650	249
1991	30,587.5	220

Sources: 1971–1980 Records of the Commissioner's Office for Refugees, Umsagata. 1982–1991 ACORD Tractor Hire Service Files, Umsagata. The area cultivated for the years 1988–1991 refers only to the area cultivated by ACORD's tractors. The areas cultivated by privately hired tractors, hand hoe and *seluka* are not included.

(c)   to develop an effective agricultural management structure to implement objective (a);
(d)   to organise a tractor operational training programme for locally recruited agricultural staff;
(e)   to make appropriate arrangements to ensure the effective overhaul and routine maintenance of Qala en Nahal's tractor fleet during the ACORD project period; and
(f)   (i) to develop the present mechanical workshop to provide comprehensive engineering services to the area and (ii) to develop the workshop as a training institute subject to the approval of the Sudanese Government. (ACORD, 1981b)

After the signing of the Letter of Intent, ACORD took up £552,000 of the ODA funds to use for refurbishing the scheme's tractor and machinery maintenance services (ACORD, 1981a). Through purchase and overhaul, ACORD created a fleet of thirty-seven Massey Ferguson tractors[1] and twenty-seven Massey Ferguson 360 wide-level disc harrows (WLDH).[2] The workshop was also built to provide maintenance services for the tractors and other machinery. Their involvement was preceded by a comprehensive socio-economic study (Spooner, 1981). However, the study did not include an environmental-impact assessment of the refurbished THS. At that time, neither the government of Sudan nor ACORD was concerned with the long-term environmental consequences of the improved efficiency of the method of cultivation. The sole concern was to overcome the technical constraint of mechanization, and ACORD performed this task with utmost efficiency.

Initially, it was intended that Spooner's study would form the basis for ACORD's intervention (Spooner, 1981). One of the findings of the study was a widespread landlessness and inequitable distribution of land among the settlers (Spooner, 1981). As a result, Spooner (their consultant) warned that there would be many families that would not benefit from improvement of the THS and recommended a fundamental rethinking of the approach:

> [O]riginally it was believed that by introducing improvements in the machines, their management and maintenance benefits could reach the whole community; an objective which is fundamental to the funding philosophy of ACORD. The land analysis carried out by ACORD has revealed that there are refugee families at the Scheme who do not have access to land and others that are so restricted that they are unlikely to be affected by a programme that concentrates upon the Scheme's machinery services. The results point to a need to rethink the approach taken in the funding and management of projects if the whole community is to benefit. (Spooner, 1981: 114)

Neither ACORD's management nor COR took heed of this advice. They proceeded, instead, with full force to establish an efficient THS to enable the land-owning farmers to increase total production by bringing new areas into the production process, disregarding the plight of the landless and the detrimental environmental consequence of the extensive farming system involved. Before ACORD's involvement, farmers were only cultivating part of their holdings, leaving the rest to lie fallow. This was not a matter of choice. The THS was inefficiently managed and only a small proportion of the cultivable land was cropped. The remaining land was left to rest. From the point of view of environmental sustainability, this constituted a blessing in disguise, but the cost in terms of loss of production was considerable. Following the establishment of an efficient and heavily subsidized tractor service, most of the farmers began cropping all their holdings continuously. In the 1982/83 season, the tractor operating cost per *feddan* was £S5.4, while the tractor hire charge was only £S1.5 per *feddan* (Kibreab, 1987: 198). In 1993, the tractor charges were still heavily subsidized, representing only 33% of the commercial rates charged in the area (ACORD, 1993).

In the state of confinement in which the farmers operated, the refurbishment of the THS under the efficient management of ACORD was at the heart of the problem of land degradation resulting from overcultivation. This was because, after the improvement of the THS, the farmers resorted to extensive cultivation, leaving no part of their holdings to lay fallow. The heavy subsidy of the THS (67%) also encouraged the farmers to resort to extensive cultivation (Table 13.1). The question here is not whether it was improper to refurbish the THS. The critical issue is the failure to consider the environmental implications of the new level of intensity of agricultural activity and land-use practices heralded by ACORD's refurbishment of the THS and their management of it. This was realized only when serious environmental damage had already occurred.

Although the problem of overcultivation in the context of acute shortage of land supply is inextricably linked with the refurbishment of the THS, it is not argued here that ACORD should not have refurbished the service. The thrust of the argument is that the whole concept of sustainable agricultural production, based on environmentally sound development of the natural resources of soils, water, vegetation and animals, was completely absent from the original objectives. The *raison d'être* of ACORD's involvement was simply to enable the farmers to overcome the constraint of cultivation, and ACORD performed this task with spectacular 'success', if success is a function of total amount of land cultivated.

Plate 13.1   Not only does the use of the wide level disc and tractors require clearance and uprooting of all types of vegetation, it also creates hard pan at the depth of the plough layer reducing water infiltration and increasing run-off. (Photo: Gaim Kibreab)

However, it was this misguided criterion which progressively undermined the independence of the farmers and the long-term productive capability of the natural resources.

In view of the acute shortage of land faced by the refugee farmers on the scheme, an innovative intervention should have been one that aimed at increasing yield per unit area cropped, rather than at increasing total production by bringing more of the scarce land into the production process. For obvious reasons, the task of increasing total production through extensive land use was easier to accomplish than to invest in intensive land-use practices to promote long-term sustainable resource use.

The question of whether the farmers would ever be able to sustain the activity (the THS) following the future withdrawal of ACORD's involvement was also overlooked. The situation is similar to the common problem created by aid regimes, in which recipients of international assistance revert to hunger after the phasing out of emergency relief operations. This problem often stems from the fact that people are made dependent for their survival on hand-outs without being enabled to grow their own food. The THS will most probably collapse in the immediate period after ACORD's withdrawal.

The farmers, both the refugees and the Sudanese, on the scheme will be faced with a crisis in the method of cultivation and consequently with livelihood difficulties, as was the case in 1974 following UNHCR's withdrawal of financial assistance. ACORD are aware of this possibility and that is why their involvement, which was targeted to come to an end after 3 years (1980–1983), was extended to 1993 when they suddenly decided to phase out their involvement. Even after 13 years, there were no signs that the farmers would be able to operate the THS independently of outside financial intervention. In view of the institutional restrictions and the extremely limited land-resource base under which the refugee populations operated, the kind of innovation needed, as stated earlier, was land-saving technological change.[3]

There is no doubt that short-term overall crop production increased as a result of the improved efficiency of the THS, manifested in a larger amount of land cultivated in a shorter period, but there is no evidence to suggest that yield per unit of land increased as a result. The only intervention which had an influence on yield per unit of land cultivated was the improvement of timeliness of cultivation, contributing to better crop growth and control of weeds when rainfall was adequate. However, not all the farmers benefited from this. For some, the tractors came too late. Late arrival of tractors was given by the farmers as one of the most critical constraints on agricultural production. In recent years, in response to this constraint, many farmers have begun to use manual planting techniques when they were unable to plant their farms at the optimal time.

Given the limited land resource, it should have been clear from the outset that progress would reach a dead end when the limits of arable expansion were reached. In view of the restrictions imposed by government policy, it was easy enough to envisage when land shortage would put an end to further expansion of cultivation. Although the root cause of the problem of overcultivation is the inadequate amount of land allocated to the scheme, this was exacerbated by the provision of an efficient and heavily subsidized THS, which tried to improve the living conditions of the farmers by practising extensive rather than intensive cultivation, which eventually turned out to be self-defeating.

Promotion of hand cultivation and local capacity building

After several years, ACORD understood the untenability of their approach and tried to change course by introducing new incentive structures designed, on the one hand, to reduce farmers' dependence on imported technology and, on the other, to promote indigenous technical knowledge in harmony with the ecosystem. In 1984, they revised their original objectives and tried to diversify their activities. One of the new project objectives was to promote 'production methods with low import dependence and in particular to encourage the use of hand and animal cultivation methods as alternatives to tractors' (cited in Grimwood and Hoy, 1986: 3). The objective of lessening dependence on imported technology and of encouraging hand cultivation based on indigenous technical knowledge was implemented by the introduction of interest-free agricultural credit. The objectives of the credit scheme were: (i) to encourage hand cultivation by offering credit to farmers prepared to forgo the use of the THS; (ii) to make the option of cheaper credit specifically available to disadvantaged families whether they used hand cultivation or the THS; and (iii) to keep the amount of funds needed for credit limited by lending only to these categories of disadvantaged and hand cultivators rather than to any scheme settler (Heney, 1986: 2–3).

Since the increased intensity of resource use in the context of limited land availability had caused damage to the ecosystem (through destruction of vegetation, extensive cultivation, overcultivation without fallowing), ACORD's change of emphasis from tractors to alternative methods of cultivation was innovative but unfortunately came a bit too late. The loan was issued in two instalments (two-thirds followed by one-third) and was subject to a field check by ACORD's field officers, checkers and sheikhs on the area of germinated crop before first payment and a further check on the adequacy of weeding before second payment. This was done partly to ensure ability of repayment and partly to make sure that the loan, which was designed to promote agricultural production, would not be used in other unrelated activities. The administration of the credit was highly paternalistic. Paternalism notwithstanding, however, it was successful in realizing the goal of promoting the use of indigenous technical knowledge and in lessening farmer dependence on imported cultivation technology.

The response of the farmers to the new incentive was dramatic. In the first year of its introduction, 1984, about 40% or 3,016 of the total number of farmers received loans. It is not clear from the records how many of the loan recipients obtained the loan for forgoing the subsidized THS (Heney, 1986). In 1985, however, among the 4,848 loans received by heads of households, 3,613 were for those forgoing use of the THS. This constituted 74% of the total number of farmers who opted out of using the subsidized THS (Heney, 1986: 3). Since some of these farmers who opted out of using the THS had hired private tractors to cultivate their farms, it is interesting to know what percentage cultivated their farms by using locally available resources and indigenous technical knowledge. In 1985, about 50% of the farmers on the scheme used a *seluka* (plough stick) to plant their holdings (Kidane, 1990: 39). This clearly suggests that the real bottleneck that had to be addressed to enable the refugee farmers to achieve self-reliance was not transfer of cultivation technology, but provision of credit to encourage an alternative system of cultivation based on locally available resources and skills.

The introduction of the incentive was therefore very effective in promoting farmer initiative and in breaking farmer dependence on the subsidized and imported technology. Following the introduction of the new incentive in 1984, a total area of 20,940 *feddans* were cultivated by alternative methods. These included *seluka* (11,538 *feddans*), *shettet* (5,295 *feddans*), private tractor hire (3,479 *feddans*), ox (23 *feddans*), donkey (311 *feddans*) and camel (294 *feddans*) (ACORD, 1985a). In 1985, the corresponding figure was 32,317 *feddans* and the methods used were *seluka* (16,940 *feddans*), *shettet* (5,673 *feddans*), private tractor hire (8,454 *feddans*), donkey (539 *feddans*) and camel (711 *feddans*) (ACORD, 1985a).

The introduction of the new incentive structure contributed considerably to local capacity building by helping to release farmer energy, which had been dwarfed by poverty in the pre-ACORD years and by heavy subsidy during the first years of ACORD's management. In 1984 and 1985, the total area cultivated by traditional methods of cultivation, namely animal traction, *seluka* and *shettet*, constituted 36% and 43%, respectively, of the total area cultivated during those seasons.

From capacity building to dependence

When the credit scheme was about to achieve its targeted goal, ACORD suddenly changed the criteria for eligibility. Opting out of using the subsidized THS was no longer a requirement to qualify for a loan. When the economy of the settlement, following the phasing out of UNHCR's assistance in 1974, was on the verge of total collapse, only a few farmers (15%) resorted to alternative methods of cultivation. The large areas cultivated by hand in 1984 and 1985, therefore, show that the nutritional status of the families had improved enough to enable them to undertake the hard work of *seluka* cultivation. The key, however, was the provision of credit at the most critical period of the farming cycle. By July, most farmers exhaust their crop savings from the previous season's harvest (Kibreab, 1987: Chapter 6). The availability of credit enabled many farmers to work on their farms instead of working for others, to meet their families' immediate needs during hungry seasons.

The positive response by the farmers to alternative cultivation and ACORD's subsequent introduction of new criteria for eligibility throw light on some fundamental and critical issues in the scheme's economic history. During the season the credit scheme was introduced, 36% of the total area was cultivated by alternative methods. In the following season this was increased to 43%. This clearly demonstrated the ability of the farmers to cultivate their own farms without being dependent on outside assistance, provided they received help during the critical period to overcome the shortage of food supply. This demolishes the myth that the soils of the area are only amenable to tractor cultivation.

The fact that a considerable proportion of the farmers could cultivate their farms by making their own independent arrangements and by using locally available resources and skills when given loans demonstrates that lack of cultivation technology (tractors) was not the most critical constraint. In response to the credit scheme, many farmers began to utilize their stored traditional technical knowledge by using human and animal power as a source of energy. This implies that, if the refugee farmers had been given credit, they would have been able to rely on alternative and sustainable methods of cultivation which would be more compatible with their own technical skills and financial means and the fragile environment.

In March 1986, ACORD sent a consultant to Qala en Nahal to study the credit scheme.[4] The consultant did not have enough time to study the impact of the credit scheme on the income of the recipient families. In the consultant's own words, '[I]t was not possible during the short time spent at Qala en Nahal in March 1986 to assess the consequences of ACORD's credit operations in terms of the benefits to the individual loan recipients' (Heney, 1986: iv). Improvement of family income was expected to result from timely weeding, but the central objective of the credit scheme was to promote farmer autonomy and to reduce dependence on imported technology, which was undermining the principle of long-term self-reliance and environmental sustainability. This was of strategic significance. The consultant, instead of asking whether or not the credit scheme was serving the objective it was designed to serve, namely promotion of alternative methods of cultivation, chose to dwell on a false and irrelevant problem (impact on incomes), overlooking the central issue of promotion of indigenous technology of cultivation. Not only did the consultant ask irrelevant questions, but, in spite of the fact that she did not have enough time to study the impact of the credit scheme on family incomes, introduced new criteria for eligibility which automatically forfeited the objective the credit scheme was designed to serve. These new criteria for credit eligibility eliminated the most crucial objective of the credit scheme, namely encouragement and promotion of hand cultivation and lessening of dependence on the subsidized THS.

One of the arguments presented as justification for the change of eligibility criteria was that repayment following one season's successful harvest was unsatisfactory. According to the consultant, repayment of debts on 10 March 1986 was only 31% (Heney, 1986: 4). However, the ACORD records show that by 31 July 1986 of the total old credit of £S863,280 about 63% (£S545,968) had been repaid in cash and grain (ACORD, 1987d). This was obviously unsatisfactory, but could not be used as justification to forfeit the central objective of the credit scheme. The consultant stated, '[E]ligibility for the 1986 loan will depend on: (i) being a bona fide settler on the scheme area; (ii) having land for farm; and (iii) having cleared all the 1984 loan, the 1985 loan and service charge, if these were taken' (Heney, 1986: 16). It was further stated that the 'method of cultivation and planting will not be a criterion for eligibility'. Applications for 1986 credit were to be processed in May and the changes were to be introduced in April. To qualify for the 1986 loan, the farmers with outstanding loans had to make good the arrears within 1 month. For poor farmers who had suffered a complete crop failure during the previous drought season (1984), this amounted to open exclusion. The major objective of the credit scheme was forfeited by these changes. The decisive element in the new eligibility criteria was nothing more than the same criterion used in commercial credit institutions, i.e. the ability to pay or creditworthiness. This drastic change, without prior warning, had serious consequences for ACORD's credibility. No wonder the refugees refer to ACORD as a *sherika* (company). The change in eligibility structure not only contradicted the original objectives of the credit scheme, but also defeated one of the central objectives of ACORD's involvement on the Qala en Nahal scheme, i.e. the promotion of production methods with low import dependence and, in particular, encouragement of the use of hand and animal cultivation methods as alternatives to tractors.

This was forfeited by the introduction of these new changes, which eliminated the incentive to forgo the subsidized THS. No explanation was given to the farmers. The radical changes were introduced without consultation with them. This is a classic example of a non-participatory, top-down and hierarchical decision-making process. ACORD's motive for changing the eligibility criterion, at a time when its credit scheme was about to achieve its stated goal, is difficult to understand. When opting out of the use of the THS was no longer a criterion of eligibility, the credit scheme was only open to those who could afford to clear their arrears. They later failed to make good future loans, which eventually led to the demise of the credit scheme. In 1988, the Programme Coordinator (PC) at Umsagata decided to end the credit scheme.

When forgoing of the THS or encouragement of alternative methods of cultivation ceased to be the objective of the credit scheme, many farmers gave up hand cultivation and reverted to dependence on the THS. The total area cultivated by tractors increased from 32,262 *feddans* in 1985 to 39,000 *feddans* in 1986 and this increased further to nearly 50,000 *feddans* in 1987 (Table 13.1). Although no data were available on the amount of land cultivated by hand after the change of the eligibility criteria, according to ACORD's extension workers and field officers, this decreased drastically in 1986 and in the years thereafter.

Advantages of manual cultivation

Grimwood and Hoy, basing their conclusions on results of field experiments conducted on the scheme, stated '[M]anual animal traction cultivation . . . has the advantage of improved soil conservation and the growing of perennial crops' (Grimwood and Hoy, 1986: 8). Manual cultivation is appropriate not only in terms of improving soil conservation, but also in reducing farmer dependence on imported technology and in promoting farmer autonomy without any loss in income. Cultural-practice trials, which were conducted on the scheme in three consecutive seasons (1986–1988), comparing tractor and hand cultivation methods, showed that a considerable amount of tillage and weeding labour time could be saved by using tractors for cultivation compared with manual cultivation, namely *seluka* and *shettet* (Willcocks and Twomlow, 1990: 6). On the scheme, this is not important because there is no labour shortage during the planting season.[5] The most interesting result of the field experiments on the scheme was that no significant differences in yields were observed between *seluka*- and tractor-planted crops (see also Table 13.2). Regarding the comparative yield results, 'the seluka planted crop with one manual weeding gave very similar yields to the two tractor tillage systems at any level of weeding' (Willcocks and Twomlow, 1990: 6). Analysis of economic gross margins generated by the different systems also showed conclusively that 'only the manual no till systems consistently provided better returns to the farmer/country'. Basing their findings on the results of the cultural trials at the scheme, Willcocks and Twomlow stated: '[W]hat is apparent from the results is that the economics of tractor planting is much more sensitive to grain prices than the two manual systems' (Willcocks and Twomlow, 1990: 6). These findings were published paradoxically during the same year when the incentive given to promote manual cultivation was rescinded. The results of the field trials show that, from the point of view of increasing productivity, there is no justification for the use of tractors. On the contrary, the provision of a subsidized THS led to the expansion of cultivation and, when the limit was reached, continuous cropping resulted in the undermining of long-term productivity, due to soil exhaustion.

In terms of returns per unit area cultivated, there is evidence in the district which shows the superiority of *seluka* to tractor cultivation. For example, in 1950 owing to a delay in the delivery of seed drills, about 5,000 *feddans* of sorghum were sown by *seluka* at Um Leiyun in the Gedaref district. The yield in the hand-sown (*seluka*) area was higher than in the land sown by drill (Laing, 1953: 18). In his comparative study of drill and *seluka* cultivation in 1951, Mitwakil also concluded, '[I]rrespective of other factors, sorghum sown by "seluka" appears to yield higher than sorghum sown by drill, whether the latter is thinned to individual plants or clumps' (Mitwakil cited in Laing, 1953: 21). The other method of hand cultivation, *shettet*, is only used in sesame planting and, as expected, the experiments on the scheme showed lower sorghum yields. The results were an indication of why the *shettet* is not used to plant sorghum in the area (Willcocks and Twomlow, 1990: 10–11).

The only advantage shown by the findings on tractor cultivation was the saving of labour, which is, relatively, not a scarce commodity on the scheme. What appears as a problem of labour shortage is actually a problem of capital shortage, which prevents many families, on the one hand, from working on their own farms during

Table 13.2 Sorghum yield comparison of cultivation technologies in the Qala en Nahal settlement (bags per ha – 1 bag = 90 kg)

| Weeding treatments | Methods of cultivation | | |
	Tractor with seed box	Tractor without seed box	Seluka
Zero weeding	15.2	14.2	11.5
One weeding	16.1	17.2	17.4
Two or more weedings	17.5	18.7	20.5
Average	16.3	16.7	16.5

Source: Kidane, 1990.

the hungry season and, on the other, from hiring wage labourers to supplement their family labour in the peak seasons (Kibreab, 1987: Chapter 6).

The solution to this constraint had already been found by ACORD's innovative introduction of the credit scheme, which made participation conditional on forgoing access to the subsidized THS. This eligibility criterion, which could have been the key to the promotion of a sustainable method of cultivation without reliance on imported technology, was eliminated by the very agency that had brought it into being. There was no economic or ecological rationale for changing the eligibility criteria.

Subsistence security and inappropriate land-use practice

The change introduced by ACORD did not abolish the credit scheme. Only the eligibility criteria were changed. Credit continued to be given to those who were able to clear the outstanding loans for the previous two seasons. The farmers were free after 1986 to use the loan for any purpose of their own choice, without being told what to do. It may be argued, therefore, that since the farmers allocated their scarce resources, including the loans, efficiently and rationally, they could be expected to freely forgo the THS and use manual cultivation to plant their crops in order to limit land-use practices to sustainable levels. This argument may sound correct theoretically, but it is invalid when considered in the context of the constraints and opportunities in which the refugee farmers eke out a meagre living.

The farmers, operating very close to the subsistence margin and being subject to the vagaries of climate (reflected in low, erratic and variable rainfall) and institutional restrictions, seek to maximize short-term gains in order to secure a stable source of subsistence, even at the risk of environmental depletion. As subsistence-security maximizers operating in an extremely uncertain environment with an acute shortage of land-resource base, the behaviour of the refugee farmers in terms of not opting out of using the subsidized THS in the interest of long-term resource sustainability is rational and hence predictable. The amount of labour time saved by tractors compared with manual cultivation was considerable. The field-trial experiments conducted on the scheme, for example, show that 'the first weeding of the manually planted stands required between 30 to 80% more labour than the tractor cultivated plots. The additional labour requirements for weeding manually prepared plots was substantially greater in the late planted trials for all the three years' (Willcocks and Twomlow, 1990: 6). It is further stated, '[W]eed levels on the manual no-till systems were 5 to 20 fold greater than the tractor tilled systems at first weeding in both early and late planted trials.' By allocating the labour time of the family members to different economic activities, many families (those who could afford to clear the arrears) were able to spread the risk of failure. A considerable amount of cultivation labour time was also saved by the use of tractors,[6] but the time saved was not used productively because the opportunity cost of the farmers' labour in the early planting season was near zero. In June, there is practically no demand for agricultural labour. Kidane, a former ACORD agricultural extension officer (AEO) on the scheme, lamented,

> [I]n the scheme when tractors are hired to cultivate the land, the farmers sit by the edge of their farm watching the tractors doing the job for them. Others keep themselves busy cutting trees to make charcoal and firewood so that they can pay the THS charges. It is very regrettable when agencies that claim to be development agencies approaching development in such a manner. Development at the expense of the environment, undermines the sustainability of long-term development. (Kidane, 1990: 39)

Some of the labour time that would have been used for weeding was saved and reallocated to alternative income-generating activities within and outside the settlements.

The quotation above shows that some of the labour time saved by the use of tractors for cultivation was used to destroy vegetation for charcoal making. Different family members migrated to areas where there was demand for labour, mainly to the commercial mechanized rain-fed and irrigated schemes. With the increased environmental uncertainty and land shortage, many of the farmers were supplementing their incomes from off-farm income-generating activities, including livestock husbandry. The provision of an efficient and subsidized THS and interest-free credit scheme in the context of limited land supply was instrumental in the intensification of agricultural and other activities, which eventually led to land degradation and consequently to deepening poverty.

Access to the subsidized THS and to interest-free credit meant that the intensity of agricultural activity could be increased without affecting the conditions of supply of family labour, because it was in turn augmented by hired labour, made possible by the credit scheme. In view of the environmental risks resulting from erratic, low and variable rainfall and soil-fertility decline, agricultural production on the scheme is a risky activity. The farmers tried to minimize the risk by seizing every opportunity to increase or maintain overall production and by allocating their labour time to diverse economic activities. ACORD's THS was instrumental in this respect, because, by freeing a certain amount of family labour, it enabled the farming families to diversify their activities. The provision of an efficient and subsidized THS meant the farmers were able to continuously crop their holdings in an attempt to maintain or increase overall production within the defined land resource and technological horizon. With an increased level of exploitation, however, the farmers were faced not only with the problem of diminishing returns, but also with exhaustion of the arable land resource, which led to deepening poverty among many of them. If forgoing the THS had remained as a precondition for gaining access to credit, this would have functioned as a safety-valve against increased levels of intensity of resource use or overexploitation of the arable land.

Although it is difficult to test empirically, the fact that the population in question consists of refugees does not seem to be a relevant variable in the explanation of their short-term gain-maximizing behaviour. Their refugee status is only relevant in terms of the restrictions imposed on their freedom of movement, residence and resource availability and the consequences of this status on the environment. It is these factors which force them to exploit the scarce resources in a non-sustainable manner in order to eke out a living. The space for manoeuvre to cope with environmental uncertainty is wider among their Sudanese neighbours than among the refugees. Any community that operates within the margins of subsistence, environmental insecurity and a state of confinement would have no other alternative except to increase the level of intensity of resource exploitation, even at the cost of environmental degradation. People on the edge of survival have no scope for long-term environmental concern. Before people on the edge can be expected to be concerned with long-term ecological sustainability, they have first to overcome the problem of immediate survival. The farmers were increasing the level of intensity of arable land use in order to make ends meet within a given framework, which was not of their own making. Thus, it is not surprising that the farmers responded positively to a method of cultivation which was consistent with their interest in maintaining overall production, resulting from increased intensity of exploitation of the exhaustible resource, even though such a level of intensity of agricultural activity was not sustainable in the long term.

ACORD's natural-resource programme

By 1986, ACORD realized that the increased level of intensity of resource use within the given technological horizon and the limited land-resource base was leading to a decline in yield resulting from weed infestation and soil exhaustion. Since there was an incessant farmer complaint about reduction of productive capability of the land, ACORD field staff began to carry out an adaptive research programme (ARP), while engaging simultaneously in extensive discussions with farmers. The findings of the ARP, which was conducted for several consecutive seasons, verified the claims of the farmers. It was concluded from the results of the ARP that 'falls in crop production are attributable to declines in soil fertility and increased weed burden (ACORD, 1987c: 4).

After the realization of the untenability of the productive system under the THS, ACORD decided to diversify its involvement, from the pure transfer of cultivation technology to the launching of a multi-faceted natural-resource-management programme. The natural-resource-management programme had the following components: (i) an ARP, including crop rotation trials, legume variety trials, *Striga* control trials, sesame variety trials and sorghum variety trials; (ii) a forestry and soil conservation programme, including production of 160,000 seedlings in a project nursery, establishment of four plantations, three on denuded catchment areas and one on a waterlogged site, distribution of shade trees for compound planting, distribution of *Acacia mellifera* seedlings to 'contact' farmers[7] to be used as fencing for their holdings, distribution of *Acacia senegal* to farmers interested in pursuing agroforestry and, where appropriate, soil conservation measures, such as bunding, ridging or the construction of check sites; and (iii) assistance in the rehabilitation of the domestic water-supply, including construction of seven village watering points and water conservation, i.e. financing of the excavation of six rain-fed *hafirs* (reservoirs) to store 200,000 m^3 storage for run-off water (rain-fed water reservoir) for livestock use.

According to the preamble of the project document, the major problems faced by the communities in the scheme were: (i) decline in soil fertility; (ii) increased weed burden; (iii) low nutritive value of local pasture flora: (iv) invasion of grazing by unpalatable species; (v) reduced grazing area due to the expansion of agricultural land; (vi) the lack of vitamin A in dry-season fodder, which prevents cattle from grazing at night, due to night-blindness; and (vii) problems associated with tractor cultivation (the project aimed to encourage an alternative method of cultivation by an animal-drawn cultivator–jab planter in response to these). These constraints were expected to be overcome by developing and implementing a farming system based on the successful results of the ARP. The results of the ARP showed that decline in soil fertility could be reversed by moving from continuous sorghum/sesame production to a planned four-course rotation, such as sesame, sorghum, legumes and millet.

Diffusion of the results of the adaptive research programme

In 1989, ACORD began diffusing the results of the ARP. The aim was to develop and implement a sustainable farming system based on the results of the ARP.

Generally, four phases can be identified in the process of adoption of an agricultural innovation. These are, firstly, awareness, in which farmers come to know about the existence of an innovation (information), secondly, interest generation, in which farmers become curious and ask questions and request the new technique, thirdly, a trial period, in which farmers get the innovation and try it on small parts of their farms, and, fourthly, adoption, in which farmers either accept or reject the innovation.

ACORD used different channels to disseminate the results of the ARP. The first was through 'field days', in which farmers, numbering between six and ten, were collected from each of the six refugee and two Sudanese villages to visit the trial sites of the ARP. The farmers were shown both the control plots without improvement (treatment) in terms of inputs and cultivation methods and the plots where improved methods of farming were applied. The improved seed varieties included *Striga*-resistant, short-duration or quick-maturing, drought-resistant and high-yielding types. The farmers also visited plots planted by animal-drawn jab planters, where new cultural practices, such as row planting and inter-row weeding pulled by a donkey or camel were applied. To demonstrate the effect of timely sowing on plant growth, the farmers also saw plots that were planted early and late in the cultivation seasons. The participants in the 'field days' were selected by the *legina* and the number of participants was small because of transport problems. The farmers were expected to inform other farmers about what they saw in the trial plots.

After the field days, ACORD did not wait to be approached by farmers to proceed to the next stage. According to the AEO, very few or no farmers came back either to ask questions about the innovation or to receive the innovation after the field days (interview with El-Hadi, 1991). The approach adopted by ACORD was to disseminate the successful results of the ARP, partly through what they called contact farmers and partly through an extended farming system funded by the European Economic Community (EEC).

In 1989, ten 'progressive' farmers were selected from each village to function as contact farmers. Eligibility criteria included: (i) being an influential personality; (ii) being articulate; (iii) willingness to cooperate with extension workers and to follow instructions; and (iv) the farmer should have his plot along a main road so that others would easily see the results for emulation (interview with El-Hadi, 1991). In 1988 and 1989, members of the contact farmers were selected by the agricultural extension workers in consultation with the village officers. In 1989, there were seven contact farmers in Dehema (refugees), four in Utash (Sudanese) and another three in Dehema (Sudanese). The contact farmers were expected to function as a link between the ARP and the communities by planting their holdings with improved seed varieties and by using jab-planter cultivation instead of tractors. This programme was discontinued when the extension officer resigned and his replacement found no records on the contact farmers in the following season. When a new extension officer was employed, he created his own contact farmers, losing whatever experience had been gained in the previous season.[8] This was due to poor documentation, a poor filing system and high staff turnover.

The fact that the 1989 contact farmers did not by themselves contact ACORD in order to benefit from the innovation during the 1990 cultivation season shows that they were uncertain about the benefits they could derive from the trial exercise. In 1990, the contact farmers were elected in a general meeting held in the souk (market) in Umsagata, where ACORD staff explained the benefits that could be had from the innovation and from utilization of the agricultural extension service.

The farm of each contact farmer was divided into four strips, planted to legumes, millet, sesame and sorghum. In the following seasons, the crops were rotated. The completion of a rotation cycle and the enrichment of soil nutrients required 4 years and it was only at the completion of the rotation cycle that higher yields were expected. Higher yields could, however, also be achieved earlier because of improved seed varieties, timely planting and extension services. The contact farmers were given 13 kg of seeds and extension services in order to improve cultural practices, such as optimal time of planting, weeding, insect control, thinning, harvesting and selection of seeds for the next season. The response of the selected farmers was positive during the first year because of the seed incentive given (to be repaid after harvest) (interview with El-Hadi, 1991).

The purposes of the following sections are to present some of the important components of ACORD's natural-resource-management programme and to study the responses of the farmers to the introduction of the new techniques of intensive agricultural production. Specifically, the responses of the farmers to the *Striga*-resistant sorghum seed variety, improved sesame seed, four-course crop rotation and new cultivation technology, the animal-drawn jab planter, will be examined. The jab planter was only implemented (except among the contact farmers) through a special project funded by the EEC, referred to hereafter as the 'EEC project'. The factors underlying their positive or negative responses will also be discussed.

Point of departure

It is hypothesized here that when the limit of expansion is reached and the existing land-use practices lead to loss of productivity, sheer survival needs create a higher propensity to innovate or to respond positively to innovative changes. What this means is that, if given an opportunity, the farmers on the scheme would switch over to a new technique of production that can offer the possibility of maintaining or improving the quality of land to be cultivated, despite the general reduction in fallow time. This could mean introducing fertilizers or leguminous fodder plants on a crop-rotation scheme, new cultivation technology and *Striga*-resistant and other improved seed varieties (Darity, 1980: 138).

The purpose is to examine whether the problem of diminishing productivity, with the consequent subsistence problems, has made the farmers open to the acceptance of change in the technique of production. The response of the farmers in adopting or rejecting the results of ACORD's ARP will be used to see whether they have, under pressure, become predisposed to change. Data on trial results of the various crops are collected from the records of ACORD's natural-resources programme. These data are compared with the crop yields of plots that were sown with local variety crops without rotation. If there is a considerable difference in yield, are the farmers encouraged by these results to adopt the successful results of the ARP? Since the factors that determine farmer response to agricultural innovation could not fully be ascertained from the data available in the records of the natural-resources programme, in-depth interviews were conducted with systematically selected community leaders and other key informants, mainly drawn from farmers who had once been or still were members of the so-called contact farmers (progressive farmers) or who had access to information about the availability of the improved seed varieties and other improved cultural practices. Extensive interviews were also conducted with Mr Elhadi Abdalla Mohamed, AEO, Mr Asim El Haj, Senior Agriculturalist, Mr Nejmedin Abdelrazic, COR's

Agricultural Officer, eight former and present village officers from Umsagata, Dehema, Salmin, Adingrar, Umzurzur and Umbrush and one Community Development Adviser.[9] In these interviews, technical information about the innovations, diffusion procedures, factors underlying farmers' responses, etc. was elicited.

Four-crop rotation

The four-field crop-rotation system began in 1986, but until 1989 the activity was conducted purely as scientific research with no link to the community. This was done in order to establish a trend, which required some continuous years of trial, before an attempt at dissemination. Dissemination of the results of the ARP began in 1989, i.e. 20 years after the establishment of the scheme. The aim of the dissemination was to encourage farmers to use four-course rotation cropping (legumes, millet, sesame and sorghum) and to plant weed-resistant seed varieties. The results of the ARP had shown that rotational cropping could, for example, counter drastic drops in crop productivity.

In the first instance, the benefits of crop rotation were clearly demonstrated by striking differences in the vegetative growth between plots where crop rotation was being practised and plots where there was no crop rotation (sorghum following sorghum). Sorghum, either following sesame or legumes, sesame following legumes and cowpeas following sesame consistently yielded well above other plots (Table 13.3). Early planting yielded more than late planting and, in the late planting, the improved variety of sorghum seed *yanwasha* consistently out-yielded the local *feterita* (ACORD, 1987c). Despite being a drought year, some of the legume varieties grown consistently yielded well in all villages (ACORD, 1987c).[10]

The plots were sown in 1986 with *yanwasha* (improved sorghum seed variety), *feterita* (local sorghum variety), cowpea and sesame, respectively (Table 13.3). In 1987, the plots were planted to cowpea + durra (sorghum), cowpea, hybrid durra, various beans, sesame and sorghum. The results show that crop rotation is an important factor which influences yields. For example, the highest yield was obtained from *yanwasha* (improved seed variety), followed by various beans. *Yanwasha* followed by sesame also gave good results. As expected, sesame following sesame and sorghum following sorghum gave the worst results. The same was also true of cowpea following cowpea. The results of the experiments showed that like

Table 13.3   Crop-rotation trials – early planting (all villages)

| 1986 Treatments | 1987 Treatments | | | |
	Yanwasha (kg/fd)	Feterita (kg/fd)	Cowpea (kg/fd)	Sesame (kg/fd)
Cowpea + durra	421.5	575.5	286.2	131.4
Cowpea	554.4	641.9	268.1	190.7
Hybrid durra	504.6	533.4	258.6	162.3
Various beans	801.1	647.9	293.9	183.8
Sesame	684.3	719.4	344.3	129.9
Sorghum	434.7	512.0	281.9	135.5

Source: ACORD, 1988b.
fd, *feddan*.

following like generally performed worse than any other combination (ACORD, 1987c). This clearly shows that monocropping is one of the causes of yield decline. The same trend is discernible in the data given in Tables 13.4 and 13.5, where the yields of the plot planted to the same crop in two consecutive seasons were the lowest, even given early planting. The highest yields were harvested in plots where sorghum was followed by leguminous crops. The data in these tables clearly show that crop rotation is most effective in early planting. Its effect on yield in plots planted late was not as impressive as in early sowing.

The data in Table 13.5 are compared with control trial plots which in 1986 and 1987 were planted to sorghum consecutively. The data are expressed in percentage of yield in the plots that were planted to sorghum following sorghum. For example, the trial plot that was planted to cowpea + durra in 1986 was planted to *yanwasha* in 1987 (early + late) and the yield represented 95% and 88%, respectively, of the yield of the plot that had been planted to sorghum in 1986 and 1987. The plot that was planted to various legumes in 1986 and then to *yanwasha* early in 1987 yielded 184%, i.e. 84% more than sorghum following sorghum. *Yanwasha* followed by various legume crops and *yanwasha* followed by sesame gave the highest yields. A comparison of yields between the improved seed varieties and local sorghum, sesame and millet seeds invariably showed higher yields (ACORD, 1988b).

Table 13.4   Crop-rotation trials – late planting (all villages)

1986 Treatments	1987 Treatments			
	Yanwasha (kg/fd)	Feterita (kg/fd)	Cowpea (kg/fd)	Sesame (kg/fd)
Cowpea + durra	447.7	326.4	161.7	94.8
Cowpea	423.8	300.9	154.5	89.4
Hybrid durra	403.5	274.5	170.8	102.9
Various beans	536.3	316.9	172.4	68.3
Sesame	616.0	336.9	202.4	62.2
Durra	511.7	284.2	159.3	80.3

Source: ACORD, 1988b.

Table 13.5   Crop-rotation trials – yield as a percentage of sorghum following sorghum

1986 Crop	1987 Crop			
	Yanwasha		Feterita	
	Early	Late	Early	Late
Cowpea + durra	95	88	112	115
Cowpea	128	83	125	106
Hybrid durra	116	97	104	97
Various legumes	184	105	127	112
Sesame	157	120	141	119
Durra	100	100	100	100

Source: ACORD, 1988b.

Weed-control trials

Weed infestation is one of the major causes of crop-fertility decline on the scheme (ACORD, 1987c, 1988b). One of the key components of ACORD's natural-resource-management programme was, therefore, to reverse the trend. Since the results of the crop and weed-control trials in the ARP showed encouraging results, ACORD decided to disseminate a sorghum seed variety which was not susceptible to *Striga* attack. In both the '*Striga* 87' trials and the '*Striga*-resistant variety trial', the resistant varieties showed much promise. Are the farmers therefore planting the *Striga*-resistant SRN39 seed? If not, what are the reasons? Hand weeding and organic-manure application were also shown to have residual benefit in some villages.

Response to the *Striga*-resistant SRN39 sorghum seed variety
In this section, not only are the farmers' responses to the *Striga*-resistant sorghum seed variety discussed, but whether there are discernible variations in the responses of the refugees and the Sudanese farmers to the innovation (SRN39) is considered. The results clearly show that, among the Sudanese peasants, the process between awareness and adoption was shorter than among the refugees. For example, the Sudanese farmers in Shangiya knew about the availability of the *Striga*-resistant SRN39 sorghum seed in 1988 and they tried it in small parts of their own holdings in 1989. During that season, there was one farmer who planted a *hawasha* to SRN39 and the total yield was ten sacks. The farmers pressed the seed-bank committee in the village to buy the ten sacks and, by 1990, all the farmers in the village embraced the *Striga*-resistant SRN39. In 1990, all the other seed varieties failed on the scheme. The rate of failure of other crops was estimated at 80–90%. SRN39 out-yielded all the other sorghum varieties. The estimated yield per *feddan* was about three sacks (interview with El-Hadi, 1991). This suggests that *Striga* infestation is a major cause of crop-yield decline.

The refugee villages have seed-bank committees, but there was no request raised by the villagers to buy SRN39 nor did the seed-bank committee take the initiative to obtain the improved seed. In fact, SRN39 was supplied by the community development section on the scheme on credit. 'The refugees rejected the seed.' They preferred the two local varieties, despite the imminent threat of crop failure due to *Striga* attack. Some of the refugee farmers who accepted SRN39 did so for lack of choice, when the local varieties were no longer available in the souk. Many of the Sudanese farmers came with demands to ACORD to exchange local-variety seeds with SRN39. In the AEO's view, the general trend on the scheme was that the adoption of SRN39 was increasing among all farmers, but the rate of adoption was much higher among the Sudanese than among the refugees (interview with El-Hadi, 1991). The interviewed refugee farmers were, however, unsympathetic to SRN39.

An attempt was made to see if the response of the refugee farmers was influenced by their socio-economic backgrounds (ethnicity). The immediate results were contrary to general expectation, but a closer examination showed that the real results were consistent with expectation. From the records of the community development section, the majority of the farmers who received the SRN39 seed were from Salmin village, where the experience of sedentary farming was the least. A survey conducted subsequent to the distribution of the seed, however, showed that only two farms were planted to SRN39. The rest of the distributed seeds were consumed by the farmers. The reasons why the refugee farmers rejected SRN39

Plate 13.2   All is not doom and gloom on and around the Scheme. A newly opened hawasha in the neighbouring Sudanese village of Shangiya planted with the Striga-*resistant crop, SRN39. (Photo: Gaim Kibreab)*

will be discussed and these responses will be compared with their responses to improved sesame seed varieties.

Response to improved sesame seed

ACORD had tested, in collaboration with Abu Naama Research Station, ten sesame seed varieties, out of which two have proved to be suitable for the scheme, namely A/1/9 and 30/15. The refugee farmers have embraced these seeds and in 1991 over 75% planted them on their farms.

Varied responses to sorghum and sesame improved seed varieties

The variation in the responses of the refugee farmers to the two improved varieties of seeds (sorghum and sesame) raises questions. Why were the refugee farmers, in spite of their constant complaints about noxious weed infestation, reluctant to adopt the *Striga*-resistant seed variety? And why did they embrace the improved sesame seed variety? If the refugee farmers were resistant to change, they could be expected to respond to both seeds in the same way. The fact that they accepted the improved sesame seed variety while rejecting the improved sorghum seed variety, despite the fact that *Striga* infestation constituted one of the most critical causes of decline in crop yields on the scheme, suggests that there must be a rationale underlying their decision (to reject SRN39 and to embrace A/1/9 and 30/15). The explanation is found partly in the nature of the crop (SRN39) and partly in the uncertainty involved in the innovation itself.

Firstly, sorghum is a staple food while sesame is a cash crop. Farmers who operate within the margin of subsistence are more averse to taking risks with food crops than with cash crops. Secondly, in arid and semiarid regions, rainfall fluctuations make agriculture a high-risk activity. The climate in the area is characterized by a short unimodal rainy season between June and September. Thus, duration of a crop, i.e. whether the crop in question is quick-maturing or not, in such climatic conditions is the key factor in determining farmer response. SRN39 is a long-duration crop. It gives 50% flowering in 75 days and matures 4 months after sowing. The two local seed varieties preferred by the refugee farmers are *mugud* and *ajab-sedo*, which are both local varieties and fast-maturing. *Ajab-sedo* matures in about 75 days. *Mugud* can be harvested in about 90 days. *Ajab-sedo* has large heads while *mugud* is medium-sized. In the farmers' view, fast-maturing crops can escape *Striga* attack. These two crops were known to the refugees for many years. They were tried and tested and the fact that they were preferred was consistent with the conceptual framework of risk aversion which is characteristic of farmers who operate within or below subsistence levels.

Thirdly, SRN39 was characterized by the farmers as a thirsty crop. This feature, in an area where scarcity and uncertainty of moisture availability act as sources of constant threat of drought and crop failure, is decisive in influencing the farmers' decision. In combination with low soil fertility resulting from overcultivation, scarcity of moisture puts a serious limit on the farmers' adaptive capacity. The question of moisture availability or lack of it is the single most important variable which shapes the farming systems in the study area.

The question that springs to mind is why do the Sudanese peasants on the scheme behave differently? The explanation lies in their differential access to arable land resources. The mean arable land size of the land-owning refugee families was 9.2 *feddans*, while the corresponding figure for the Sudanese peasants was 25.4 *feddans*. The implication of larger access to arable land on potential response of farmers to an innovation is that the risk of crop failure resulting from the adoption of an untried crop does not threaten their survival because they can spread the risk by allocating their holdings to various crops, including the known and tried local varieties. The price of failure is much higher among the refugee farmers than it is among the Sudanese peasants. One factor which influences farmer response is also farm location. SRN39 being a thirsty and long-duration crop, it thrives in waterlogged sites. For example, the Sudanese village of Shangiya, where the farmers have embraced the new crop, is located in foothills where the holdings are flooded by water from the hills and pediments during the rains. There is clear and direct evidence to show the linkage effect of farmer response and farm location, but a random walk by the author in the Sudanese villages of Shangiya and Bolos invariably showed that vegetative growth of SRN39 heads was more vigorous in waterlogged sites than in other sites, and this was confirmed by one of the *omdas*, who was one of the richest farmers in Bolos (interview with Abu Kared, 1991).

Fourthly, the superior quality of the improved variety of the sesame seed is unmistakably and visibly clear when compared with the local varieties. It is superior to the local varieties in terms of vegetative growth and in the quantity of oil extracted in the sesame oil-presses (*asara*). Sesame is planted earlier than sorghum and the farmers have less freedom of choice regarding sesame seeds. Only the improved varieties are made available by ACORD. There is no local variety that competes with the improved varieties. Thus, the farmers, in order not to lose the optimal date of sowing, take the seed that is made available to them, while for SRN39 there is always a competitive supply of other seed varieties in the local markets. The superiority of SRN39 seeds, on the other hand, is not that clear compared with the other local varieties. Some of its features also seem to influence farmers' decisions. Its colour is yellow, which is not appreciated by the refugee families. Its taste is different from that of the local varieties. Its head is medium-sized and not large, which negatively affects yield. Owing to the land-resource constraint under which they operate, farmers are very sensitive to marginal differences in yields.

There is also a difference of perception between the AEOs and the farmers. Scientifically, *Striga* resistance means that the crop concerned is not affected by its presence, i.e. the weed may be physically present, but it does not parasitize the resistant seed variety. No loss of nutrients is suffered by the crop plants. For the farmers, however, the appearance of the noxious weed, *Striga*, in the farm planted to SRN39 suggests that there is nothing different about the crop, or they assume that it is equally susceptible to attack. There is thus a difference of interpretation between the technical experts and the farmers. The latter have a tendency to be more empirical. For the farmers, real resistance implies elimination of the noxious weed. For the scientists, the key is not whether the weed grows or not, but whether it has an impact on the crop in question. The fact that the differences in perception remain unbridged is attributable to lack of effective communication between the extension officers and the farmers. One of the key elements in the process of imparting knowledge to farmers is effective communication based on mutual respect and trust.

Response to four-course crop rotation

How do the farmers respond to the four-crop rotation? The farmers refused to include legume crops, which are the key to the process of soil-nutrient replenishment. In this case, there was no variation in behaviour between the refugees and the Sudanese farmers. Without legumes the objective of the whole exercise of rotation is futile. The reason why they refused to grow leguminous crops was because the crop was highly susceptible to insect attacks. Thus, the farmers were only willing to include legumes in the rotation if they were provided with insecticides. In the first season, ACORD supplied the farmers with insecticides. Other reasons for the reluctance of the farmers to grow legumes included the heavy work involved, land scarcity and unpalatability of the legume crop varieties (interview with ACORD's contact farmers, 1991).

Not only have adoption rates of the four-crop rotation been low or non-existent among the scheme farmers, but some of the participants in the contact farmers' trial programme have even withdrawn from involvement. Since the first season, there has been no regular supply of insecticides. Most of the farmers who tried to grow the crop without treatment have failed. This has created strong doubts among the farmers as to the value of adopting the four-crop rotation. Being aware of the problem, ACORD's field office sent an order for pesticides in October 1990 to its head office in London. The order had not been delivered by December 1991. This has seriously affected the farmers' confidence. The agency had invested scarce manpower and capital resources for several years testing the suitability of the various types of legumes and it is not clear why this happened. There were some farmers who had planted legumes hoping that the consignment of pesticides would arrive, but to their dismay the outcome has been total crop failure in the part planted to legumes. This has shattered the farmers' confidence in the crop and has no doubt undermined ACORD's dissemination efforts and credibility.

An exceptional farmer

Exceptional phenomena are seldom interesting in scientific studies. However, sometimes individual case histories may provide windows of opportunity for understanding wider issues. It is with this in mind that the story of this exceptional farmer is presented. Among the former contact farmers interviewed, there was one who was extremely favourable to legume crops, even in the absence of insecticides (interview with Mehari Kahel, 1991). In 1989 he planted legumes on one-quarter of a *feddan* and the yield was one sack (92 kg). Legumes being a high-value crop, after saving seeds for the next season, he sold the rest at £S30 per kg. Yield was very high during the 1989 season because of early planting and adequate rainfall. In 1990, the farmer, encouraged by the results of the previous season, planted legumes on a bigger area. The crop failed because of late planting, inadequate rainfall and insect attack. The total yield was only 24 kg, compared with 92 kg in the previous season. In the farmer's view, there was a linkage effect between late planting and susceptibility to insect attacks. This important knowledge was acquired by the farmer in the process of trial and error. It was unknown to the extension workers (interview with EEC project participants, 1991). Refusing to be discouraged by the 1990 season failure, this farmer decided to persevere and planted legumes on one-quarter of a *feddan* again in 1991. The result in terms of yield was again discouraging, but the loss was compensated for, in his view, by increased productivity of other crops in the plots previously planted to legumes. The total yield in 1991 was only 28 kg. The farmer still intended to plant the crop, irrespective of yields, because, he stated, 'the main benefit is its contribution to soil fertility because of its leguminous nature' (interview with Temnewo Kahel, 1991). He had even selected three types of legume seeds to take with him to Eritrea. In his view, the major features of the legume varieties available on the scheme – and these were decisive in influencing the farmers' responses – were: firstly, the crop needed lots of moisture; secondly, it had to be planted early; thirdly, it was susceptible to insect attack; and, fourthly, it was extremely labour-intensive. Its susceptibility to insect attack and the problem of labour intensity could have been overcome by a secure supply of insecticides and provision of a credit scheme. ACORD did neither of these. The credit scheme was abolished in 1988.

How do we explain the strong enthusiasm of this farmer? One important factor seems to be his background. He is a Bilen who came from a village (Bogu) in Senhit province, where not only had sedentary farming been practised for many centuries, but also legume crops, as nitrogen-fixing and supplementary vegetable crops had constituted an integral part of the farming system. Inclusion of legume crops in the rotation was not new to him, except for the varieties used. This openness or predisposition to change was not, however, shared by the other farmers who had the same background and experiences. The question of opportunity cost of land was decisive. For them a plant which produced no crops was no use, irrespective of its value in terms of replenishment of soil nutrients. This attitude was predictable, because a community faced with an acute land shortage could not be expected to allocate part of its scarce arable land to legume crops when it was known that yields could be zero – for example, because of late planting or insect attacks. For the extension workers, legumes, even when they yielded no crops, were useful because they replenished the soil. This did not make sense to the farmers who tilled the soil in order to secure the minimum required for subsistence in an environment where the vagaries of nature made agricultural production a risky enterprise.

The partial explanation should therefore be sought in the level of subsistence security of that particular farmer, because he had other sources of income, e.g. a remittance, which enabled him to allocate part of his *hawasha* to leguminous crops. In other words, crop failure did not threaten his family's subsistence security. The most important factor seems to have been his internalization of the benefits to be had from inclusion of legumes in the farming system.

EEC project: a tool for dissemination of agricultural innovation?

The second channel through which the results of the ARP are expected to be diffused is through the EEC project in Dehema. (The project received its name from the funding agency – the EEC.) This is a pilot project established in 1989, funded by the EEC and implemented by ACORD. The EEC project aims, first, to develop and implement a farming system based on the successful results of the ARP in order to facilitate the formulation of a suitable extension package for the scheme. Second, through extension and training, it aims to encourage adoption of the system by other farmers in the programme area. Third, it seeks to provide employment opportunities for landless members of the vulnerable groups, with phased community management of the project, leading to total community control and self-reliance. Fourth, it aims to introduce a new type of animal-drawn tillage, a jab planter. Instead of using the tractor or the *seluka* (plough stick) or *shettet*, sowing is done with a new implement – the jab planter – in a new row arrangement. Fifth, it is intended to introduce a four-course rotation, comprising four crops with different plant-husbandry techniques and labour requirements. Finally, it aims to introduce a new animal-drawn inter-row weeder (ACORD, EEC Project Records). The main emphasis of the farming system adopted in the EEC project is on crop rotation, row planting and inter-row weeding. About 410 *feddans* of newly opened land was distributed, 10 *feddans* each, to forty families in Dehema village.

The total project duration was planned to be 9 years. ACORD provided services to the participants in the first 3 years. In the following 6 years, the participants were expected to follow the farming system without ACORD's support. According to the project agreements, during the first 3 years, the services included provision of free seeds, hiring of donkeys for the sowing and weeding, free pesticide control, empty sacks and cash compensation of £S1,500 per season for the different agricultural operations, from land clearing to harvesting.

The project participants are poor farmers, identified through a survey in two Sudanese villages, Dehema and Utash, and in one refugee village, Dehema. The project has 40 (13 female and 27 male heads of households – 28 refugees and 12 Sudanese) participants. By 1991 the three refugee women had withdrawn from the project. The remaining 10 women were Sudanese. No records exist as to why all the women refugees withdrew. This may suggest that their withdrawal was taken lightly. The explanations given by ACORD field staff are tautological because they do not go beyond the mere statement of the condition that is being explained. Their explanation conforms to a familiar stereotype. They state, 'The women refugees withdrew because they are conservative or participation in production is incompatible with the existing socio-cultural norms' (interviews with ACORD extension officers, 1991, 1992, 1994). The question that springs to mind is: was the project designed without taking cognizance of the existing cultural values and norms? This is unsatisfactory because, first, no socio-cultural values are immutable. Existing sociocultural values and norms change in the process of participation in production. Second, one of the central aims of development projects in such communities should be to contribute to the process of change in gender-based values, norms and roles which perpetuate the subservient position of women in society. On the scheme, it is common to see poor women participating in many economic activities unfettered by so-called conservative sociocultural values. Existing values, attitudes and norms were observed only when the subsistence security of the families concerned was not threatened. Thus, either a mistake was made in selection or the approach and the conditions under which they were asked to participate were not tailored to suit their needs.

Incentives were given to participant farmers in the form of 10 *feddans* of arable land and a non-repayable sum of £S1,500 per season to each participant farmer for the first three consecutive seasons. The cash incentive was given to encourage participation by eliminating the threat of subsistence insecurity that might have resulted from crop failure due to the introduction of new production techniques in the farming system. It was anticipated that the element of risk of failure or fear for a livelihood crisis would result in reluctance to adopt the untried and presumably risky crop varieties and the new method of cultivation. In the project, each farmer's plot was divided into four parts and four crops, namely sorghum, sesame, millet and legumes, were grown simultaneously on a rotational basis.

Out of the 500 *feddans*, 100 *feddans* were allocated to fodder production on a permanent pasture. It is not clear why the production of the fodder crop was not incorporated into the system of rotation. Experiences elsewhere, for example, the European open-field system in the medieval and postmedieval periods, clearly showed that the inclusion of fodder crops in the system of rotation was important in the process of replenishment of soil nutrients. In the EEC project, fodder was produced on a site which was allocated solely for that purpose. It was not part of the rotation. In 1989 fodder production failed because of non-viable seeds. It is not clear how this could happen in view of the fact that over seven fodder crops had been tested since 1986 before they were introduced to the farmers.

The EEC project has been in operation since 1989 and responsibility was handed over to the farmers in 1992. The services provided by ACORD in the first 3 years have come to an end and the participants are now expected to manage without any financial support. Although five years is not long enough to assess the performance of the project, the available data may enable us to raise some questions. One way in which performance can be measured is by looking at the average yields in the project and comparing these with the averages for the whole scheme. The average yield for legume crops in the EEC project in 1989 was 2.9 sacks per *feddan*. Yield variation between the different plots was very high. Legume yields varied from 0.0 to 7.5 sacks per *feddan*. Since no legumes were grown outside the EEC project, the results cannot be compared with yields elsewhere.

The average yield for sesame during the same season was 1.10 sacks per *feddan*. The corresponding figure for sorghum was 1.14 sacks per *feddan* (Table 13.6). In 1990, the average yields per *feddan* for sesame, millet, legume and sorghum were 1.06, 1.07, 0.41 and 0.83 sacks per *feddan*, respectively. Examination of yield figures of the 41 plots in the EEC project show that sorghum and legume yields are not influenced by the seed varieties. No one type of seed out-yielded the others consistently. The local varieties, such as local cowpea and *karakora*, seemed to be equally competitive. As pointed out earlier, yield levels varied greatly in the 41 plots. Agricultural productivity is influenced by an interplay between diverse, complex and interacting factors; hence it cannot be stated with certainty why yield levels varied so drastically among the 41 farms in the EEC project. In the agriculturalist's view, labour input levels were crucial.

The average yields for the whole scheme in 1989 were 1.84 and 0.83 sacks per

Table 13.6 Comparative averages of crop yields on the whole scheme and on the EEC project (sacks per *feddan*)

	Qala en Nahal scheme			EEC project		
Year	Sesame	Millet	Sorghum	Sesame	Millet	Sorghum
1989	0.83	n.a.	1.84	1.10	–	1.14
1990	0.39	0.53	0.26	1.06	1.07	0.83
1991	0.55	1.25	1.35	1.51	1.21	1.72
1992	1.48	1.63	1.57	1.44	2.00	2.38

Source: Compiled from ACORD's files at Umsagata.
n.a., not available.

feddan for sorghum and sesame, respectively (Table 13.6). It is surprising that sorghum yield was higher on the scheme as a whole than in the EEC project, despite the fact that the EEC project benefited from centuries of accumulated soil fertility. Sesame yield was higher in the EEC project than on the scheme as a whole, but the difference was not as high as was expected in light of the fact that the EEC project was implemented on virgin land, with improved cultural practices, new methods of cultivation (the jab planter) and improved seed varieties. The average yields for the 1990, 1991 and 1992 seasons were better in the EEC project than in the whole scheme, except for sesame in 1992 (Table 13.6). Crop yields in the EEC project for the three consecutive seasons show better results. Thus, even though no definite conclusion can be drawn from these results regarding whether this was due to the introduction of the four-crop system of rotation or due to the opening up of virgin land, there is no doubt that they show the benefits to be had from improved cultural practices. It is important to interpret the results with caution because the effect of crop rotation on yields can only be seen after the completion of the cycle. At this stage, some of the better results are attributable to centuries of accumulated fertility, improved seed varieties and timely planting and not necessarily to the four-course rotation.

Most of the farms in the Qala en Nahal scheme would have been under continuous cropping for over two decades and the low yields reflect the extent of depletion of soil nutrients. In 1991 the impression I had was that most of the participant farmers in the EEC project were responding to the incentives of cash and land rather than to the benefits of the system of rotation. This was confirmed by the information elicited in a series of in-depth interviews and discussions with participant farmers. The implementation of the project is expected to last for nine years, after which time the impact of crop rotation will be evaluated, but the cash incentives ceased in 1992. Those who withdraw before the end of the nine years will be required to repay the cash incentive they have received.

Response to legume crops in the EEC project
The farmers on the EEC project were willing to grow legume crops under two conditions, namely, the opportunity for early planting (early rains) and/or secure access to insecticides. The optimal planting time for legume crops is June and flowering should start in August; otherwise the plants become easy prey to insect attack (interview with former ACORD contact farmer, 1991). The only way to overcome this constraint is through the use of insecticides. Legume crops planted in the absence of these two conditions were destined to fail, and the farmers were

justifiably reluctant to allocate their scarce land and labour resources to such a crop. Through trial and error, the farmers have learned that legume crops planted later than June are susceptible to insect attack. Despite this, however, ACORD staff insisted on inclusion of legume crops in the rotation even when the sowing started in late July or August and no insecticides were available. The farmers with a choice refused to take heed of the advice of the extension workers, but those in the EEC project were unable to reject the imposition because they lacked choice of action and control over the land resource. The farmers were not in principle negative to the inclusion of legume crops in the rotation. Their reaction to the growing of legumes was determined by lack of the necessary conditions that would make the crop worth growing.

Response to jab-planter cultivation in the EEC project

One of the causes of the inappropriate land-use practices under the specific conditions existing in the scheme is use of a wrong technology (tractors). Tractorization in the context of a limited land-resource base has led to a dead end. It was this realization which induced ACORD to develop and test an animal-drawn implement, the jab planter. It was designed for row planting and inter-row weeding. The advantages of this innovation are that it is simple to operate, cheap and low import-dependent and could be produced locally. The most important advantages of the jab planter, according to ACORD, are deeper cultivation – about 7–10 cm as opposed to 5 cm or less in wide-level disc cultivation – and timely planting (interview with ACORD's Senior Agriculturalist, 1991). The latter stems from dependence on the THS, which, depending on the farmers' luck, could mean planting too early, before the emergence of weeds, or too late, when weeds are so numerous. The latter reduce the effectiveness of the wide-level disc as a means of weed control (ACORD, 1989/90). The development of the animal-drawn jab planter was, therefore, designed to enable the farmers to plant their farms during the optimal weeks of planting (ACORD, 1989/90).

Under the existing physical constraints, the adoption of the jab planter may certainly increase the freedom of the farmers to choose when to plant their crops. On the scheme, the most critical cultural practice is a system that makes timely use of scarce water resource. Hence, the adoption of the jab planter, all other things being equal, may represent an opportunity to increase yield per unit of land cultivated, resulting from optimal time of sowing.

The participant farmers' attitude towards the jab planter was invariably negative. The differences in yield levels between the EEC project and the whole scheme were minimal (Table 13.6). Thus, the question is whether the small incentive represented in minimal crop-yield increase[11] and improved timeliness of planting would encourage the farmers to shift to the new method of cultivation (jab planter), which usually implies increase in labour input for cultivation and weeding operations. One of the factors which had discouraged the development of an alternative method of cultivation was the abolition of the eligibility criterion for access to credit, in which opting out of the subsidized THS was no longer necessary for receiving loans. The consequence of this change was that many of the farmers reverted to the THS, neglecting manual cultivation.

The jab planter is not diffused among the farmers outside the EEC project. Thus, in order to assess farmer response to jab-planter cultivation, a series of discussions were held with members of the old and the new contact farmers and with the participants in the EEC project in Dehema village. The participants in the EEC project were poor and landless families who were given land and cash incentives in return for adoption of rotation, jab-planter cultivation, improved seed varieties, row sowing, inter-row weeding, etc. All these decisions were taken on technical grounds, disregarding the farmers' experiences and understanding. The prerequisite for participation in the project was unquestioned acceptance of the whole package. It was a classic example of a top-down non-participatory model of development. One of the beneficiaries described the situation as follows. 'We are reduced to non-thinking entities. We should do as we are told to do. Non-compliance results in outright dismissal' (interview with EEC project participants, 1991).[12] If the consequence of refusal to adopt the innovation (the jab planter) were not outright dismissal, none of the project participants would use it. For sorghum, millet and legume planting, the farmers referred to the jab planter as 'useless'. The only use they saw in the jab planter was for sesame planting. The reasons why the farmers dislike the jab planter is that they claim that cultivation is not deep enough. Seeds are left on the surface unburied and, if planting is not followed by heavy rains, the seeds are consumed by birds or ants. If small rains fall, the seeds easily rot. The experience of the farmers contradicted ACORD's view on the jab planter. One of the advantages of the jab planter in comparison to tractors was, according to ACORD, deeper cultivation. The farmers' experience shows the reverse. The jab planter, unlike the tractor, did not kill weeds. This resulted in increased labour required for weeding (interview with EEC project participants, 1991).

These views were even shared by the Bilen contact farmer, who, as we saw earlier, was extremely enthusiastic about legume crops. His attitude towards the jab planter was negative. He compared it with a toy. He argued that the jab planter did not kill weeds and it did not turn the soil. The consequence was that the seeds remained on the surface unburied and were picked up by birds. It was also labour-intensive, needing two persons and a donkey to operate. The farmer also expressed a strong bias against the use of donkeys for cultivation. To him the jab planter represented retrogression rather than progress: 'No meaningful agricultural development can happen by using donkeys. We used oxen and tractors for cultivation. I would not take a jab planter if it was given to me gratis.' In Eritrea donkeys are used as pack and not as draught animals. Such a strong negative attitude by a farmer who, in spite of the obvious constraints involved, had adopted legume crops in order to ensure long-term sustainable agricultural production raises serious causes for concern about the suitability of the jab planter.

Another interviewee stated, 'The good thing about the jab planter was that it allowed timely sowing, but it required higher labour inputs for weeding and seed bed preparation' (interview with Talke Omer, 1991). Many of the farmers used oxen and camels to plough their farms in Eritrea. On the scheme, the refugees have become deskilled because of their heavy reliance on the efficient and subsidized THS. The idea of animal traction is now being reintroduced over 20 years after the refugees have left their country. A considerable proportion were also born in exile, where the use of animal traction is unknown. The process of resuscitating a skill that has fallen into disuse can sometimes be more protracted than the task of instilling a new skill. The use of animal traction requires tenacity and perseverance. If it is not learned from childhood and practised with relative continuity, the task of instilling it into adult farmers may not be easy. The fact that farmers repeatedly referred to the problem of labour intensity involved in the use of the jab planter suggests that the use of animal draught was considered too hard and unpleasant by those who lacked the skill and by those who had become deskilled over time.

Jab planters tie labour not only for cultivation, but also for weeding. Tractors are labour-saving. This has enabled many farmers to allocate their family labour to diverse income-generating activities. In light of the diminishing returns and land exhaustion facing the farmers in crop production, one of the key strategies adopted by many families is an efficient, flexible and diversified allocation of family labour. This was best served by the use of tractors, which reduced the labour input required for cultivation and weeding. The opportunity cost of donkeys' labour time was also very high because there were many families who derived their livelihood by using donkeys to fetch water, wood fuel and thatch grass for sale. Thus, the unpopularity of the jab planter may partially be explained by its competition for family and donkeys' labour time. The farmers, however, argued that, if there were clear advantages, they would not hesitate to adopt the jab planter. They stated, 'We have happily embraced the improved sesame seed varieties, the *seluka*, *shettet*, etc. and if the jab planter were to enable us to overcome a constraint, we would happily embrace it. It neither reduces labour requirements nor improves productivity' (interview with EEC project participants, 1991).

It is also important to state that, outside the EEC project, neither a carrot nor a stick was used by ACORD to facilitate the diffusion of the innovation (improved seed varieties, rotation, jab planter, etc.). The proper stick to use would have been either to abolish the subsidy on the THS or to scale down the availability of the service in order to make it less accessible. Alternatively, in order to make the jab planter competitive with the THS, at the initial phase a loan package should have been incorporated to offset the off-farm income forgone by farmers who used the jab planter and opted out of use of the subsidized tractors. None of this happened when the jab planter was introduced.

Compared with tractors, the jab planter is sustainable both financially and ecologically, but its comparative advantage over the traditional method of cultivation, the *seluka*, is not clear to the farmers. Some of the farmers saw potential in the development of the jab planter. In its present form of construction, it is only good for sesame, but not for sorghum, millet and legume planting, argue the farmers. In their view, before it can serve such a purpose, it has to be modified considerably. One of the participant farmers in the EEC project had designed a model for making the necessary changes in the construction of the jab planter. He submitted his model to ACORD. In the view of the farmer who designed the modification, seeds should be broadcast and the disc of the jab planter should be forked with an iron sheet attached at the back to bury the seeds. ACORD ignored the farmer's invention (interview with A. Surur, 1991).

What the farmers could not understand was that they were not allowed to use the *seluka* to cultivate their plots in the EEC project. If ACORD's intention were, as stated in their reviewed statement of objectives, to promote production methods with low import dependence and to encourage the use of hand cultivation as an alternative to tractors (for the objectives, see Grimwood and Hoy, 1986: 3), why did they place such a heavy emphasis on the jab planter to the neglect of the accepted and tried methods of hand cultivation with practically no imported components? If incentives were given to farmers who used alternative methods of cultivation, the available evidence suggests that the *seluka* would have been the obvious choice. The farmers saw no justification for pushing them to adopt the jab planter to the neglect of the tried and familiar cultivation method – the *seluka*.

'Freedom' without choice

Is it morally or ethically justifiable to diffuse a new and untried technology by offering cash and land incentives to vulnerable members of a disenfranchised community who are on the edge of survival and hence unable to exercise choice? The price of refusal to adopt the new cultivation technology (jab planter) was too high for those farmers who were trapped in the depths of poverty because of landlessness and lack of off-farm income-generating opportunities. If this criticism is valid can ACORD be blamed for having taken advantage of the vulnerability and powerlessness of the poor farmers to test their new cultivation technology?

Others may consider the approach as innovative and the criticism as academic. As long as the farmers participated voluntarily and as long as the innovation contributed to the improvement of their long- and/or short-term living conditions, these critics may see no moral or ethical issues involved. The question that follows from such an argument is, however, whether there can be real voluntary participation in the absence of any opportunity for choice.

ACORD's decision to include only the landless and the poorest of the poor in the EEC project is commendable and it is consistent with their overall objective of helping the poorest of the poor. There are, however, some general ethical questions that can be raised in such an approach. The innovations in the EEC project were imposed from above. There was no farmer/agency interaction. The farmers were expected to follow strictly the instructions of the extension officers, who not only assumed they knew better, but also genuinely believed that they knew what was best for the farmers. For example, in 1992 two participants were dismissed from the EEC project 'for behaving against the project agreement' (ACORD, EEC project records, 1993). The two farmers used tractors to cultivate part of their plots instead of the animal-drawn jab planter. The main reason why they used tractors was to reduce the weed burden. They were replaced immediately after this was revealed to ACORD.

What is interesting is that the two farmers who defied the terms of the agreement were educated and had full-time jobs with another NGO operating on the scheme. The vulnerable families could not afford to do this because dismissal would mean loss of the basis of sustenance. This may suggest that there was a more positive relationship between farmer acceptance of the new technology and poverty. The row weeder was considered so bad that not many farmers wanted even to discuss it. In spite of this, the participants had to weed their plots using the row-weeding method.

The participant farmers were the most vulnerable, with no power over choice of action, access or control over resources or institutional affiliation. The participants were not only people who, as a result of uprooting and subsequent deprivation, had lost control over choices and resources, but they were also the least capable of resisting or rejecting an imposition from above. The imposition of the new method of cultivation and cultural practices was experienced by the poor farmers as a form of deprivation in which the ability to withdraw or exit from what they considered an unfair arrangement was restricted by lack of alternative means of survival. Many of the farmers' only chance of gaining access to arable land was through participation in the project; thus participation was considered a trade-off between autonomy and poverty. In the presence of an imminent threat of hunger and famine, the farmers' decision to forgo their autonomy or independence in order to avert the threat of hunger was rational and indeed predictable.

This represented a classic example of a non-participatory and a top-down development approach, in which the project 'beneficiaries' were put at the receiving end of the pipeline, with no possibility of influencing the design, planning and implementation of the project which aimed to make them self-supporting.

Participation in development refers to 'the organized efforts to increase control over resources and regulative institutions in given social situations, on the part of groups and movements hitherto excluded from such control' (Wolfe, 1983: 2). Participation in development is a process of empowerment of disadvantaged or vulnerable groups. The EEC project aimed at providing poor farmers with arable land on condition they followed the instructions given by the extension workers. This did not increase their control over the resources nor did it contribute to their empowerment, because they had no influence on the essential cultural practices such as what type of crops to plant, when to plant, how to plant, how to weed, etc. These were all outside their control. All these decisions were taken by ACORD staff, headed and dominated by an expatriate at the top. The possibility of the agriculturalist and the extension officers influencing the decisions of the expatriate was either non-existent or minimal. The farmers who deviated from the arrangements devised by ACORD were dismissed automatically. The position of programme coordinator (PC) has always been filled by expatriates, who manage the scheme from the top down.

Conclusion

The conceptual framework which constituted the point of departure in this chapter was to see whether populations faced with the problem of subsistence are responsive to change and whether or not refugee status has an influence on the response to innovative changes. The farmers, irrespective of their status, were responsive to change provided the consequences of the change did not threaten their subsistence security and the return or benefit to be had from adopting the change in the technique of production was substantial. Benefit is not necessarily measured in terms of long-term sustainability, but mainly in terms of the immediate income forgone, measured in the opportunity cost of land and family labour. This does not emanate from lack of ability to understand the importance of sustainable farming systems, but rather from the need to plan meticulously and carefully the allocation of land and labour time of the families to the different income-generating opportunities that are potentially available on and off the scheme areas. For many of the families, a simple misallocation of their resources, land and family labour could mean loss of one season's crop or one year's income. For the farmers, adoption of a new technique of production which requires an additional input of land or labour is considered risky because of the uncertainty involved.

The other activities for which substitutes are sought in the form of new innovations are known to them and, thus, the level of risk can be assessed a priori and the degree of uncertainty can be minimized. Therefore, the tendency among farmers living within the margin of subsistence is to go for what is known to the neglect of the unknown, even when they are aware that this decision may lead to a possible loss of a higher return or higher environmental risks. The majority are preoccupied with securing minimum and stable incomes for themselves and their families. Under the existing constraints and opportunities, the majority try to achieve this by sticking to what is known and by avoiding the new and the unknown, unless they are convinced beyond any shadow of doubt that there are no risks or uncertainties involved and that the benefits to be had are higher. The minimum assurance poor farmers require to voluntarily substitute their familiar farming technologies by adopting new and untried farming methods is that they will not be worse off than before. It is not because small farmers are conservative, as many claim, that they do not readily respond enthusiastically to an introduction of change in the technique of production; it is rather because of lack of buffers against possible failures. Their income flows, consumption levels and stocks or assets are at such a low level that few of them can withstand the consequences of misallocation of their scarce resources – land and labour.

An important factor which negatively affected the response of the farmers to the natural-resources programme was ACORD's failure to understand and adequately appreciate the farmers' traditional knowledge. No attempts were made to incorporate into research and extension practices the farmers' knowledge. Change was expected to result from transmitting to the farmers the findings of the formal experiments. The farmers were relegated to the receiving end and were seen by the extension officers either as 'progressive' or 'backward', depending on whether they adopted or rejected the findings of the trial experiments.

Notes

1. Of the 38 tractors, 21 were 265 Massey Ferguson and 17 were 165/185 Massey Ferguson.
2. Of the WLDH, 20 were new and seven were old.
3. The refugee farmers, as we saw earlier, were prohibited by law to extend cultivation beyond the confines of the scheme.
4. Since the terms of reference of the consultant were not incorporated in the report, it is not clear from the report what exactly the purpose of the consultation was.
5. The planting season invariably coincides with the period in which there is least demand for labour throughout the Eastern State.
6. Comparison of labour input in man-hour equivalent per ha in cultivating and planting, Qala en Nahal

Method of cultivation	Trial 1	Trial 2
Seluka	46.6 man-hours	25.6 man-hours
Tractor + seed box	0.6 tractor man-hours	0.6 tractor man-hours

Source: Kidane, 1990: Table 5.4.

7. These are the so-called progressive farmers, who are selected on the basis of a vague criterion – predisposition to change.
8. The project, despite its modern management, was equally affected by the common problem of lack of proper documentation and a poor filing system.
9. These were Habte Kesete (Wedi Bashai), Mohamed Berhan Omer, Kidane Gebremedhin, Ramedan Osman, Mehari Awate and Omer Mensur.
10. The information in these two paragraphs draws on ACORD (1987c). Palatability and storability were also investigated. All the high-yielding varieties were found to compare favourably with the local variety for taste, and the two legume crops – green mung and tepary bean – appear to be weevil-resistant.
11. It is even doubtful whether the minimal increase in yields is due to the introduction of the jab planter.
12. Personal interview with one of the beneficiary farmers at Dehema. The farmer did not want to be identified by name. He wanted to remain anonymous. Another farmer described the situation by stating, 'We sit down when we are told to sit down and we get up when we are told to do so'.

14 Concluding Remarks

Every chapter has a conclusion and hence no summary is provided here. Instead a number of general features that contribute to inappropriate land-use practices in refugee settlements are identified. Although the findings are based on the experience of the Qala en Nahal refugee settlement scheme, most of the issues raised have a wider application.

First, until the beginning of the 1990s, host-government policies, international assistance packages and research on refugees have been to a large extent environment-blind. The environment into which people moved and subsequently settled was considered as an inexhaustible resource and the impact of economic activities by a large number of impoverished people on environmental processes was perceived to be of little or no long-term consequence. Usually, newly relocated refugees to new and unfamiliar environments are provided with axes as an important component of the aid package to 'tame' the environment. For example, in Qala en Nahal during the establishment period, refugees were provided with axes and transport facilities to cut trees for construction materials. When large tracts of land were cleared for cultivation, no green belts were left for the purposes of environmental protection, as required by Sudanese forestry legislation. This was in spite of the fact that the implementing partner of the United Nations High Commissioner for Refugees (UNHCR) was the government itself.

Second, the deprivations and powerlessness associated with refugee status manifest in lack of choices engender land-use practices which have a detrimental impact on the environment. The scant available literature on environmental impacts of refugees abounds with impressionistic assertions which suggest that land-use practices adopted by refugees tend to be rapacious and devoid of long-term environmental considerations. If there is a relationship between inappropriate land-use practices and refugee status, as is widely held, the principal scientific question is: what is it in refugee status which engenders unsustainable and ravenous land-use practices? The most important factor is said to be the tendency among refugees to discount long-term costs in favour of maximizing short-term gains because of lack of long-term commitment to the host country.

The findings of this study show that the Eritrean refugees on the Qala en Nahal scheme have no special attributes which predispose them to develop more ravenous land-use practices than their Sudanese counterparts. In comparison with their Sudanese counterparts, there was no evidence which suggested that the refugees exhibited a higher propensity to use the resources on and around the scheme in a non-sustainable way. Most of the differences observed between the two communities in terms of land-use practices and responses to environmental stresses were attributable to differential access to resources and to other fundamental rights, such as freedom of movement and residence. The restriction on freedom of movement and residence has prevented the refugees from bringing new arable land into the production process in response to diminishing returns of the available land or in response to escalating population density. The problem of overcultivation, manifested in continuous cropping without fallow periods and in cultivation of degradation-prone sites, is inextricably linked with the inability of the refugee farmers to expand cultivation beyond the designated areas.

In fact, the reason why there has been no severe overgrazing despite the drastic increase of animal population on the scheme is because no restriction is imposed on the movement of animals. It is because of the opportunity provided by short-, medium- and long-distance livestock migrations that the refugee farmers have been able, on the one hand, to diversify their economic activities by investing in livestock in response to the decline of crop productivity and, on the other, to avoid irreversible and rapid deterioration in productive capability of the grazing resources. If the refugee farmers were not prohibited by law to expand cultivation beyond the confines of the scheme, the pressure on the resources would have been offset by bringing new areas outside the scheme under cultivation. The Sudanese peasants in the area are not limited by this legal constraint. Even though the resources available to the local population have been diminishing continuously because of expansion of mechanized rain-fed commercial agriculture, there is still room for limited expansion.

The fact that the refugees were hoping to return to Eritrea following the cessation of the causes that prompted their flight may suggest that they lacked long-term commitment to the area. However, since the resource base from which they eked out their living was so restricted, their lack of long-term commitment, though relevant, was not decisive in shaping their behaviour towards the natural environment.

Third, the various state governments' perception of the presence of the refugees as temporary has affected the environment in a detrimental way. This was found to be more damaging to the environment than the refugees' lack of long-term commitment to the settlement area. This is not true only in Sudan, however. It is rather the consequence of the way the refugee problem was conceptualized worldwide from the outset. The existing international and regional instruments relating to the status of refugees conceptualize international protection (refugee status) as transient, i.e. until refugees are able to enjoy access to national protection, either through voluntary repatriation or through acquiring the citizenship of the country of asylum. Article I C(5) of the United Nations 1951 Convention and Article 4(e) of the Organization of African Unity (OAU) Convention provide: '[T]his Convention shall cease to apply to any person falling under the terms of section A[1] if: he can no longer, because the circumstances in connection with which he has been recognized as a refugee have ceased to exist . . . ' (UN, 1951; OAU, 1969) or '[h]e has acquired a new nationality and enjoys the protection of the country of his new nationality' (UN, 1951: Art. I C(3); OAU, 1969: Art. 4(c)). Refugee status ceases when the conditions that prompt flight disappear.[2] In all African countries (except Tanzania), once the factors that prompt flight and which prevent those in exile from returning are eliminated, refugees are required to reavail themselves of the protection of the country of their nationality. The African regional refugee regime does not provide the option for naturalization. The placement of African refugees in spatially segregated sites (camps, reception centres and settlements) is an expression of this conceptualization. In Africa, refugee settlements are devised to prolong refugee status rather than to facilitate their integration into host societies (Kibreab, 1989, 1993). The effect of the existing institutional arrangement, i.e. the conceptualization of the refugee problem as a transient phenomenon, on the environment is manifold.

1. The amount of natural resources which host governments allocate to refugee settlements is influenced by this institutional framework. When allocating resources to refugee settlements, host governments seldom take into account the future needs of refugee communities that arise from natural population growth and immigration. This is because their presence is perceived as temporary. For example, at the heart of the problem of resource depletion on the Qala en Nahal scheme is the severe shortage of land, which has precipitated inappropriate land-use practices, manifested in overcultivation, deforestation and heavy pressure on range resources. The scheme was first established to accommodate about 20,000 refugees. A quarter of a century later, the population has doubled and no additional land allocations have been made to accommodate the new demands. The consequence has been a heightened level of intensity of resource use, resulting in a reduction of the productive capability of the available resources. The need to make ends meet from fixed resources whose returns are diminishing in the context of rising numbers has led to a further increase in the level of intensity of use, with the consequence of further diminishing returns. As returns diminished, land-use practices became more exploitative of the environment. The result of this land-use practice has been that the arable land is subjected to continuous cropping without fallow periods.

In view of the limited off-farm income-generating opportunities, the desperate need to make ends meet forced many refugee families to adopt non-sustainable resource-use practices. Within the given technique of agricultural production, in which no chemical fertilizers or organic manures are used, this vicious circle could only be broken by making additional land available to the refugees or by relocating the surplus population to a new or existing settlement. This corrective measure never took place in the Qala en Nahal settlement. The problem of inadequate land allocation was not limited to Sudan. The refugees in Ulyamkulu settlement in Tanzania were faced with the same problem in the mid-1970s. When the Tanzanian government saw that the refugees were not returning in the foreseeable future, they addressed the problem of land shortage by relocating the surplus population to a new settlement – Mishamo – in 1976.

2. The quantity and quality of rights accorded to refugees by host countries are also influenced by the existing institutional framework which perceives the refugee problem as a transient phenomenon. Refugees lack tenurial rights over the resources they use to earn their living. Tenurial rights over such resources consist of a collection of rights over land, water, woodlands, wildlife, pasture, etc. and their produce. These rights include the right of ownership, inheritance, use and disposal and the right to exclude others from gaining access or using such resources. These resources are potentially renewable, i.e. they are capable of sustaining human life and of being sustained indefinitely, but whether or not such resources sustain human life and are used sustainably depends on the institutional arrangements which define the relationship between people who purport to have a legitimate or illegitimate claim on the available resources. If the existing institutional arrangements are such that refugees are vested neither with individual nor communal property rights, nor secure rights of usufruct, which entitle them to limit the ability of outsiders to enjoy the benefits to be secured from the use of the enjoyment of the resources located within the scheme and to devise and enforce their own independent institutional arrangements at the local level to regulate the manner in which their members use the resources, their resource-use patterns tend to become exploitative. This is by no means unique to a refugee situation. This seems to lie at the heart of most environmental problems in rural Africa and Asia.

The findings of this study show that, although at the heart of the problem of land degradation lies the inadequacy of the land-resource base, the situation is exacerbated by lack of tenurial security. The consequence of this is that the refugee communities have not been able to devise their own institutional arrangements, on the one hand, to define their members' relationships to the local resources and, on the other, to exclude outsiders from using the scheme resources, especially arable land, forest and pasture resources. An institutional arrangement is inconceivable in the absence of communal or individual property rights, unless such an arrangement is imposed from outside. The effect of this institutional vacuum has been that individuals (members of the communities and outsiders) are free to exploit the scheme resources without being fettered by any form of conventions or rules which limit the level of intensity of resource use to a sustainable level. The absence of resource-regulating institutions has meant that no social or other sanctions are applied against excesses.

One of the reasons why the rights enjoyed by the refugees are less than those accessible to their Sudanese counterparts in the area is because they are accepted as temporary guests. Refugeehood is perceived by the government of Sudan as a transient phenomenon, irrespective of its duration. This was succinctly put by a former Sudanese Commissioner for Refugees, in which he stated, if you talk of integration 'as a sort of naturalization this is completely rejected in the Sudan . . . Being a refugee in a country for 20, 30 or 100 years, I don't think will deprive you of your own nationality . . . ' (Attiya cited in *Refugees*, 1988). He further stated, 'refugees should be given a certain place to live in, to continue their own sort of relations with their own people, not to forget their country, because we are not interested that they will forget their countries; *they have to go. We don't want more population in this country: it is enough*' (emphasis added). Consequently, the rights granted to the refugees are much fewer not only than those accessible to the Sudanese citizens in the area, but even than those enjoyed by new migrants from West Africa. The area is continuously receiving migrants from West Africa, who join their relatives in the villages. They are allocated land by the chiefs/sheikhs of the villages concerned and they live as if they were Sudanese citizens, while the refugees, despite the fact that they have been living in the area for over 25 years, are still labelled as aliens and suffer the deprivations and powerlessness associated with such a status.

In a discussion as to whether it would be more sensible in terms of environmental protection to allow the refugees to exercise control over the local resources, a Sudanese official said,

> [N]o guest has the right to claim a share in his/her host's property. A guest who claims such a right is treated with contempt and is automatically denied hospitality. We have allowed the refugees in our country the privilege to use our land and other resources temporarily provided they observe the conditions as defined by us strictly. Those who abuse this arrangement should not benefit from the hospitality of our people and government. (interview with COR official, 1993)

This is the principle underlying the government's policy establishing the relationship between the refugees in settlements and 'others' who utilize the scarce renewable resources within the areas designated for such settlements. There can be no contention with regard to the right of the government to define how its resources are to be used by aliens accepted as guests. The central question is whether the government has the necessary administrative, manpower and financial capability to enforce its own decisions and regulations. The resources on the scheme belong to the government formally and they are under the responsibility of the Commissioner's Office for Refugees (COR). This formal secure governmental claim to the resources notwithstanding, however, the scheme resources have *de facto* become open-access resources, i.e. free for all. They are the property of no one. The areas on and around the scheme are stripped of vegetation, partly because charcoal wholesalers come from as far as Gedaref, Wad Madeni, Omdurman and Khartoum to cut trees for charcoal making. COR's attempt to stop this is in vain because they do not have the necessary resources and manpower to patrol the area. The refugees are not in a position to keep outsiders away because they have no legal rights to do so. If the refugees and the Sudanese peasants had control over the local resources, including the right of policing, outsiders would have easily been kept away cost-effectively. It is the indirect 'open-access' nature of the resources on the scheme which is one of the keys to the problem of resource depletion. Following the enactment of the Unregistered Land Act (1970), all unregistered land had become government property. However, in comparison with refugees, rural Sudanese communities still enjoy a certain degree of autonomy. Access and use rights to local resources, especially to arable land, are still regulated by customary institutional arrangements unless the resources in question are targeted for development by the private or public sectors. Refugees have no such rights.

This lack of rights is to a certain extent a continuation of the government's perception of refugeehood as a transient phenomenon. If the refugees had been received on a permanent basis, their placement in spatially segregated sites would have been unnecessary.[3] If the refugees were allowed to settle among the Sudanese peasants, they would have enjoyed the same rights, including the right to exclude outsiders. It has to be pointed out, however, that since 1970, the right of the Sudanese peasants and pastoralists to exclude others has been undermined, especially if the outsider in question is a commercial farmer or a state corporation. At the local level, however, relationships between different communities are to a large extent still regulated by customary rules and conventions. The rural communities recognize each other's territorial rights.

3. The way host governments treat refugees also has an influence on the land-use practices adopted by refugees. If refugees are treated as temporary guests, how can they be expected to have a long-term commitment to the area of their 'temporary' abode? In light of this, it is not surprising if refugees adopt land-use practices which maximize short-term gains, discounting long-term environmental sustainability. As long as they are received and treated as guests, irrespective of the length of their stay in the countries of asylum, why should they adopt resource-use practices which promote long-term sustainability? For example, although the findings of this study show that there is little inherent in being a refugee which engenders unsustainable resource use, some of the refugee families were reluctant to engage in projects designed to promote long-term environmental protection such as tree planting. Although the tree-planting project had its own problems, which precipitated negative responses, there were some families who did not want to participate because they were hoping to return home before the maturation of the trees. This unstable attitude is not altogether the result of government policy, because the refugees' desire to return home is not entirely a function of the kind of treatment they receive. However, the fact that they are treated consistently in a manner that reminds them of their refugee status seems to reinforce their determination not only to return, but to consider the scheme area as nothing but a place of temporary abode. In fact, the failure of the refugees to respond positively to the tree-planting

project has little to do with lack of long-term commitment, because refugees, being rational decision-makers, are reluctant to invest their scarce resources – labour and water – in an activity which may not produce any benefit before repatriation.

4. Most of the refugee communities, prior to their flight to Sudan, had tacit or explicit resource-regulating institutions for managing the local resources (arable land, water, trees, pasture) and enforcement mechanisms in the form of traditional leadership and councils of elders, whose moral authority was anchored in the social structure of the communities concerned. Although some aspects of these institutions had already been weakened before the refugees fled to Sudan, it was in exile that the authority of the leaders was undermined. The factors that contributed to the weakening of the traditional leaders, who were in the past responsible for resource-related decisions, are inextricably intertwined with the refugee communities' lack of ownership or control over the scheme resources. In the past, the authority of the elders and leaders emanated not only from the traditions of the communities, but also from the control the leaders exercised over local resources.

One of the consequences of formal government control of the scheme resources is that the loci of resource-related decision-making have shifted from the traditional leaders and elders to state-controlled organizations, such as COR and the local government in Qala en Nahal town. This has drastically undermined the authority of the traditional leaders and elders. Aid agencies have also contributed to the weakening of the traditional leadership. Instead of utilizing the existing traditional organizational structures among the refugee communities, aid agencies created parallel organizational structures for distribution of emergency relief and other forms of assistance. This was effected in the name of 'efficiency'. For example, when ACORD tried to refurbish and restructure the tractor hire service (THS) in 1981, some of the traditional leaders – the sheikhs – resisted the change. ACORD undermined their authority by mobilizing some sections of the communities against them. The traditional leaders were often a bastion of social and economic inequality, but nevertheless they played a key role in maintaining community cohesion. Devising and enforcement of traditional resource-management systems require a certain degree of communal stability and cohesion. One of the consequences of exile among the refugee communities has been loss of stability and cohesion. As a result, production and consumption decisions are based on the principle of individual benefit maximization, often to the neglect of the common good.

On the scheme the new positions of leadership are filled by more articulate, tenacious and aggressive individuals, who lack legitimacy because they have no link with the families that traditionally occupied such positions. Often the new leaders are able to negotiate effectively with agencies and government authorities, but they lack social and political clout, as well as moral authority, to influence the patterns of resource use among the refugees. The loss of community cohesion is reflected, *inter alia*, in the amoebic multiplication of sheikhs (leaders). This is conducive neither to devising nor to enforcing resource-regulating institutions.

5. The rapid increase of population due to the establishment of the scheme in the previously sparsely populated area has had a negative impact on the environment. Prior to the establishment of the Qala en Nahal refugee scheme, the area was inhabited by not more than 1,300 people. The relocation of nearly 20,000 people increased the demand for firewood and timber for construction of huts and fences. Large tracts of land were also cleared for cultivation. Before the arrival of the

refugees, there was very little human interference. Three factors limited the level of intensity of resource use by humans and their animals: (i) in the rainy season, the area was inhospitable for animals because the clay plains turned into a sticky quagmire; (ii) during the rains the area was heavily infested by biting flies; herders therefore avoided the area in the rainy season and preferred to graze their animals in the north of the district, where there was less rainfall and vegetation; (iii) there was no perennial water-supply in the area and, during the dry season, the local inhabitants migrated to the Rahad River, where there was a permanent water-supply. As a result, the impacts of human and livestock populations were minimal during the rainy and dry seasons.

The major environmental impact of the refugee settlement consists in the elimination of the physical constraints which previously discouraged permanent human settlement in the area. The establishment of the scheme eliminated or minimized two of the three physical constraints that kept the level of intensity of resource use to the minimum. First, the removal of vegetation has dramatically reduced the severity of biting-fly infestation and consequently the area is no longer inhospitable during the rainy seasons. There are still biting flies in the area, but, in comparison with the past, the problem is not considered severe by livestock owners. Second, the establishment of the refugee settlement scheme was accompanied by provision of a perennial water-supply. Aid agencies, including the UNHCR, have invested in the water-supply system heavily. After the provision of permanent water, it was no longer necessary for the local population to migrate to the Rahad River. Until the mid-1980s there was still a shortage of dry-season water-supply for animals and herders that moved their dry cattle to the Rahad. The shortage of water-supply to animals was, however, solved following the excavation of large rain-fed *hafirs* (reservoirs) by ACORD.

The provision of water and the reduction of sandflies were the two major factors that led to increased levels of intensity of resource use in the area. The area receives migrants from as far as western Sudan and West Africa. Following the establishment of the settlements, the number of migrants settling in the area has increased dramatically. Since the elimination of the physical constraints, even the nomads, who, prior to the establishment of the scheme, dreaded the area, come to take advantage of the water-supply during the dry season. Thus, not only has the establishment of the settlement brought a large number of impoverished refugees to the area, but the reduction of vegetation and consequently sandflies and the provision of water and other social services have made the area attractive to migrants.

Whether this is a positive or negative impact is a moot point. Prior to the relocation of the refugees to the area, the environment was hostile to human and livestock habitation. The area was infested by sandflies and snakes. The removal of vegetation has made the area suitable for human and livestock habitation. There is no doubt that that provision of water and the removal of the vegetation are in this sense a positive environmental impact. However, at the same time, the threat to environmental sustainability is represented in the excessive removal of the vegetation resources. However, this cannot be solely attributed to the presence of the refugees.

At present, the area is subject to the unauthorized expansion of mechanized rain-fed agriculture and excessive tree felling by commercial charcoal producers. Thus, even in the absence of the refugee settlements, the negative environmental impacts would by now have been equally severe. Most of the areas in the Gedaref district are affected by the expansion of mechanized rain-fed agriculture and the area where the scheme is situated would have been no exception.

6. One of the consequences of the establishment of the scheme is development of the physical infrastructure. Thus, the provision of access roads has led to intensive exploitation of the previously untapped environment especially by firewood and charcoal wholesalers.

7. The ability of the refugees to apply their previous resource-management systems was curtailed by the specificity of the physical environment of the scheme area, but was mainly due to land shortage.

8. One of the factors which contributed to land degradation on the scheme is tractor cultivation with wide discs, because this has caused increased run-off, resulting in reduced moisture penetration and less water available for plant growth. The availability of the subsidized cheap THS has also encouraged extensive cultivation to the neglect of sound agricultural practices.

The factors that have contributed to the negative environmental impacts in the area are associated with the deprivations that accompany refugee status. Any community operating under similar structural and institutional constraints would have been forced to adopt similar land-use practices, irrespective of their status. The results of this study show that the area has suffered negative environmental impacts, but the question is whether the extent of the damage is reversible. Under favourable weather and management conditions, the available evidence suggests that the extent of degradation suffered by most sites is reversible. Degraded sites (manifested in the absence of vegetation cover) when relieved of human and animal interference exhibit a remarkable ability of recovery. This is probably because the environment has adjusted to high-level intensity of exploitation or is intrinsically resilient. The only exception to this, perhaps, are the areas invaded by the unpalatable annual, *Cassia tora*. Even in this case, there is no conclusive evidence to suggest that the changes are irreversible. Ecological studies in the district are quite recent and time-series data which indicate any pattern are lacking.

The same seems to be true of the arable land, whose fertility is devoured by overcultivation. Although there was clear evidence which suggested that continuous cultivation led to loss of soil fertility, measured in yield decline, there was no clear evidence which conclusively showed that continuous cultivation alone could reduce productivity to zero. If such is the case, 25 years (the age of the Qala en Nahal scheme) are not long enough to verify this. Under favourable rainfall conditions, whenever crop productivity was zero, it was due to the combined effects of soil-fertility loss, weed infestation, late planting, lack of improved seed varieties, etc. Even though there was an evident positive relationship between farm age, loss of soil fertility and weed population, the fact that under favourable rainfall conditions the farmers who weeded their farms adequately were able to harvest some yields (albeit very low) even after 22 years of continuous cultivation, without fallow periods or fertilizer application, suggests that the soils, after considerable initial loss of soil fertility, seem to stabilize at lower levels, without necessarily hitting 'rock-bottom'.

It is also worth stating that, in spite of the physical and institutional constraints within which they operated, the Eritrean refugees have demonstrated remarkable resilience and an ability to eke out a living from resources whose productive capability has been progressively diminishing because of increasing and burdensome demands. Like other African populations living on the edge of survival, these people have found ways of leading a meaningful life. There is much that is written about the failures of Africans, and the sufferings of the people of north-east Africa have been widely publicized. Much is written on why people die in this region, but the most difficult and interesting question is to understand and explain why they do not die and how anybody can survive in those unfavourable circumstances. Hopefully, *People on the Edge* has provided some of the explanations of how this is possible.

Notes

1. This refers to the definition of the term refugee. A refugee is defined as a person who 'as a result of events occurring before 1 January 1951 and owing to well-founded fear of being persecuted for reasons of race, religion, nationality, membership of a particular social group or political opinion, is outside the country of his nationality and is unable or, owing to such fear, is unwilling to avail himself of the protection of that country; or who, not having a nationality and being outside the country of his former habitual residence as a result of such events, is unable or, owing to such fear, is unwilling to return to it.'

2. In the Western countries, refugees once recognized can in most cases acquire citizenship, but such is not the case in Africa. There are no countries in Africa (except Tanzania) which allow refugees to be naturalized.

3. This is not said to challenge the rights of states to determine the conditions under which they receive refugees, because the existing international instruments relating to refugees allow them to do so. However, the legal rights of states notwithstanding, one of the major causes of inappropriate land-use practices among refugees is the consequence of the perception of host governments of refugeehood as being a transient phenomenon. Among other things, it is because of this perception that African countries place refugees in spatially segregated sites with an inadequate resource base and with limitations on their freedom of movement and residence.

References

Government of Eritrea

BMA (British Military Administration) (1943) *Races and Tribes of Eritrea*. Asmara, January.
BMA (British Military Administration) (1944) *Land Tenure on the Eritrean Plateau*. Asmara: Native Affairs Section.
Report by the War Office Working Party on Eritrea, March 1947. London: Public Record Office, FO/1015/43.
An Inquiry into the method of ascertaining the wishes of the inhabitants of Eritrea regarding their future government and an estimate of the response, January 1947, London: Public Record Office, FO/371/63175.
Government of the State of Eritrea (1994) Land Legislation. Legislation No. 58/1994. Asmara, August.
Land Commissioner for Eritrea (1994) Interview in *Eritrea Profile*. 5 November.

Eritrean codes of customary laws

Adgna Tegeleba Code of Customary Law (1938) Asmara: Petros Silla Printing Press.
Adkeme Melega Code of Customary Law (1936) Asmara: Petros Silla Printing Press.
Karneshim Code of Customary Law (1910) Asmara: Catholic Printing Press.
Lego Chewa Code of Customary Law (1938) Asmara: Petros Silla Printing Press.
Saho Tribes' (Asaorta, Minafere, Hazo and Debre Mella) Code of Customary Law (1943) EPLF translation.
Show-Ate Anseba Code of Customary Law (1910) Asmara: Catholic Printing Press.

Government of Sudan

COR (1970–80) Agricultural files M/A/L/I/A/1, Umsagata.
COR (1990) Land Use Survey, Umsagata.
COR (1993) Statistical Report March 1993. Khartoum: Documentation Centre, Statistics Division.
COR Administration Records (1971–1994) Umsagata.
COR Files (1978–1979) Umsagata.
COR official (1993) Interview. Khartoum.
Forest Act (1989) Government of Sudan.
Government of Sudan (1944) Report of the Soil Conservation Committee, Reports 2/23. Khartoum: National Records Office.
Reports 2/2/5 (1902) Council General's Annual Report. Khartoum: National Record Office.
Reports 2/2/6 (1903) Khartoum: National Record Office.
Reports 2/4/12 (1909) Khartoum: National Records Office.
ULA (Unregistered Land Act) (1970) Government of Sudan.

United Nations

Four Power Commission of Investigation for the Former Italian Colonies (1947b) *Report on Eritrea*, 'Pressure of Population', Appendix 34.

Letter of Tigre Representatives to the Four Power Commission of Investigation for the Former Italian Colonies (1947d), Appendix 18, *Report on Eritrea*. Keren, 25 November.

UN (United Nations) (1951) Convention Relating to the Status of Refugees.

UN (United Nations) (1983) GA. A/AC. 96/635 Executive Committee of the High Commissioner's Programme, Thirty Fourth Session, December.

UN (United Nations) (1984a) GA. A/38/526, August.

UN (United Nations) (1984b) GA. A/Conf. 25/1, January.

Organization of African Unity

OAU (1969) Convention Governing Specific Aspects of the Problem of Refugees in Africa.

ACORD documents

ACORD (1981a) Qala en Nahal Progress Report. Umsagata, August.

ACORD (1981b) ACORD Programme for the Management of the Mechanized Refugee Farming System in the Qala en Nahal Resettlement Area. Umsagata.

ACORD (1981c) Qala en Nahal Resettlement Scheme Project Identification Mission. Board Paper and Policy Recommendations. Prepared by B.C. Spooner.

ACORD (1983a) Progress Report on EAA's Involvement in Qala en Nahal Refugee Settlement, 1982–1983. Compiled by D.P. James, May.

ACORD (1983b) Tractor Hire Service Records. Umsagata.

ACORD (1984) Livestock Survey. Umsagata.

ACORD (1985a) 1985 Report. Umsagata, December.

ACORD (1985b) Qala en Nahal Refugee Settlement SUD/14, Progress Report, September.

ACORD (1985c) 1985 Population Census. Umsagata.

ACORD (1985d) Qala en Nahal 1985 Report, December.

ACORD (1986a) Report Presented at the Field Day, October.

ACORD (1987a) A Report Based on a Four Month Study on Tractor Hire Service, Umsagata, 18 October.

ACORD (1987b) Minutes of Staff Meeting, 23 September, Umsagata.

ACORD (1987c) Adaptive Research Programme Trial Results 1987, SUD 14–8701. Umsagata.

ACORD (1987d) Narrative Report April 1986–March 1987, May.

ACORD (1988a) Annual Report January 1988–December 1988.

ACORD (1988b) Adaptive Research Programme Trial Results. Umsagata.

ACORD (1989a) Qala en Nahal Refugee Settlement Project Proposal 1989–93, SUD 14–8910.

ACORD (1989b) Draft of Part of the Annual Report, Population Profile and Situation Analysis. Umsagata.

ACORD (1989c) Six Months Report January 1988–June 1989.

ACORD (1989/90) Adaptive Research Programme for Sesame Yield Improvement 1989/90. Umsagata.

ACORD (1990) Annual Report 1990. Umsagata.

ACORD (1991) Livestock Survey, Umsagata.

ACORD (1991) 1991 Population Census, Umsagata.

ACORD (1993) Qala en Nahal Programme (SUD/14), Annual Report, 1993.

ACORD Books of Accounting. Umsagata.
ACORD Documents. Umsagata.
ACORD, EEC Project Records. Umsagata.
ACORD Forestry Records (1987–1989).
ACORD's Crop Yield Surveys 1982–1990, Umsagata.
ACORD THS (Tractor Hire Service) Records (1981–1993) Umsagata.
Euro-Action Acord (1981) Qala en Nahal.

Interviewees

Abu Kared, A.A. (1991) Bolos's *omda*.
ACORD's contact farmers (1991) Dehema, Umbrush, Salmin and Umsagata.
ACORD's Senior Agriculturalist (1991) Umsagata.
ACORD extension officers (1991, 1992, 1994) Umsagata, Umbrush, Salmin, Dehema, Adingrar and Umzurzur.
Ad Shuma elders (1991–1994) Umsagata and Umzurzur.
Asim El Haj (1991) ACORD's Senior Agriculturalist (up to 1991). Umsagata.
Beni Amer elders (1991) Umsagata, Salmin and Umbrush.
EEC project participants (1991) Dehema.
El-Hadi Abdella Mohamed (1991, 1994) ACORD's Agricultural Extension Officer (up to 1991) and until December 1994 Senior Agriculturalist. Umsagata.
Former ACORD contact farmers (1991) Dehema.
Herders and former ACORD livestock officer (LSO) (1991) Umsagata.
Key informants (1991, 1994). Refugee and Sudanese farmers.
M.O. Kisha (1991, 1994), Salmin.
Mehari Kahel (1991) Dehema, November.
Refugee elders (1991) Dehema, Umsagata, Umbrush and Salmin.
Refugee elders (1992) Salmin, January.
Saleh, A. (1991) Former ACORD Livestock Officer. Umsagata.
Surur, A. (1991) Dehema.
Talke Omer (1991) Dehema.
Temnewo Kahel (1991) Dehema, November.
Village Committee (1991) Umsagata, Dehema, Umbrush and Salmin.

Unpublished documents and reports

Abdalla, E.H. (1987) Charcoal and Fuelwood Production in Sudan 1979/80–1984/85. Statistics from Forest Administration Royalty and Revenue Returns.
Abu Sin, M.E. (1989a) 'Legislation and institutional systems'. In Kassala Province Environmental Collection of Papers. Prepared for publication by M.E. Abu Sin, Institute of Environmental Studies, University of Khartoum.
Abu Sin, M.E. (1989b) 'Population dynamics'. In Kassala Province Environmental Collection of Papers. Prepared for publication by M.E. Abu Sin, Institute of Environmental Studies, University of Khartoum.
Abu Sin, M.E. (1992) An Overview of the Problem of Pastoralist Land Tenure: the Case of Sudan. Department of Geography, University of Khartoum.
Baasher, M.M. (1989) 'Ecology and natural resource base'. In Kassala Province Environmental Collection of Papers. prepared for publication by M.E. Abu Sin, Institute of Environmental Studies, University of Khartoum.
Barbour, K.M. (1953) Peasant Agriculture in the Anglo Egyptian Sudan. University of Khartoum.
Betts, T.F. (1980) Spontaneous Settlement of Rural Refugees in Africa: Part I: Zambia and Zaire. London: ACORD.

Betts, T.F. (1981) Spontaneous Settlement of Rural Refugees in Africa: Part II: Tanzania. London: ACORD.

Beyene, Teame (1990) Development of Land Tenure in Eritrea During the Last 100 Years. Himbol, Sahel (Tigrinya).

Black, R. (1993) Refugees and Environmental Change: Global Issues. Report prepared for ODA Population and Environment Research Programme, University of Bradford.

Coughlan, K.J., McGarry, D. and Smith, G.D. (1987) The Physical and Mechanical Characterization of Vertisols. First Regional Seminar. Nairobi: IBSRAM.

Devitt, P. and Tahir, A. (1984) Qala en Nahal Refugee Settlement Scheme: Preliminary Report on Water, Natural Resources and Livestock Development. Prepared for ACORD.

Dickinson, J. (1983) Qala en Nahal Refugee Settlement Scheme: Soil-Erosion, Fertility and Structure. An assessment of the problem and programme for action. Prepared for ACORD, London.

Dickinson, J. and Howard, W.J. (1983) Qala en Nahal Refugee Settlement Scheme, Soil-Erosion, Fertility, Structure and Forestry. Prepared for ACORD, London.

Digernes, T.H. (1977) 'Wood for Fuel – Energy Crisis Implying Desertification: the Case of Bara, the Sudan'. Samfunnsvitenskapelig embetseksamen, Geografisk inst., Bergen.

Duffield, M. (1991) The Internationalization of Public Welfare: Conflict of the Donor/NGO Safety Net. Paper for the Workshop on the Prospects for Peace, Recovery and Development in the Horn of Africa. The Hague: Institute of Social Studies, February.

Earl, D.E. (1984) Charcoal Production. SREP Report No. 002/Energy Research Council, USAID, Sudan.

El-Ashry, M.T. (1987) Degradation of Natural Resources in the Horn of Africa: Causes, Effects and Prevention. Paper presented at the Conference on Crisis in the Horn of Africa: causes and prospects, Woodrow Wilson International Centre, Washington DC, 17–20 June.

El Din Hago, T. (1989) 'Agricultural processes and systems'. In Kassala Province Environmental Collection of Papers. Prepared for publication by M.E. Abu Sin, Institute of Environmental Studies, University of Khartoum.

El Hassan, A.M. (1981) The Environmental Consequences of Open Grazing in the Central Butana, Sudan. Environmental Monograph Series No. 1, Institute of Environmental Studies, University of Khartoum.

El Khalil, M.E. (1981) 'The Impact of Mechanized Farming on the Soil Water Balance of Samsam Project'. Dissertation, Institute of Environmental Studies, University of Khartoum.

El-Moula (1985) On the Problem of Resource Management in the Sudan. Environmental Monograph Series No. 4, Institute of Environmental Studies, UK.

Flint, M.E.S. (1988) Natural Resource Management and Farming Systems at Qala en Nahal Refugee Settlement, Sudan, prepared for ACORD, London.

Fre, Z. (1982) Qala en Nahal on the Move: Euro-Sudano-Eritrean Approach to Agricultural Development.

Galal El Din El Tayeb (ed.) (1985) Gedaref District Study Area, Khartoum: Institute of Environmental Studies, University of Khartoum.

Ghai, D. (1992) Conservation, Livelihood and Democracy: Social Dynamics of Environmental Changes in Africa. Discussion Paper No. 33, United Nations Research Institute for Social Development, Geneva.

Grimwood, B. and Hoy, J.L. (1986) Project Monitoring Report. Sudan: Qala en Nahal Refugee Agricultural Settlement Visit 26–28 November.

Halaand, H. (1980) Problems of Savanna Development: the Sudan Case. Occasional Paper No. 19, Department of Social Anthropology, University of Bergen.

Harrison, M.N. (1958) Report on a Grazing Survey of the Sudan with Recommendations for Development and Improvement, March 1955. Khartoum: Department of Animal Production, March.

Harrison, M.N. and Jackson, J.K. (1958) Ecological Classification of the Vegetation of the Sudan. Sudan Government monograph.

Hassan, E.E. and Osman, M.S. (1972) Mechanization and its Effect on Environment. Khartoum: ALESCO.

Helin, W.H. (1990) Refugees and Forestry. Paper Prepared for the Forestry Support Programme, USA (typescript).

Heney, J.A. (1986) The Credit Programme at Qala en Nahal Refugee Settlement Scheme East Sudan: a report prepared following a consultancy visit to Qala en Nahal in March 1986 to examine the Credit Programme. Prepared for ACORD, London.

Howard, W.J. (1983) Qala en Nahal Refugee Settlement Scheme Forestry Study. Prepared for ACORD.

Hunting Technical Service (1976) Refugee Resettlement Project in the East-Central Sudan, Pre-investment Study. Report sponsored by UNHCR.

Hurni, H. (1982) Soil Conservation Research Project: Second Progress Report for the Year 1982. Addis Ababa: Soil and Water Conservation Division/Berne: University of Berne.

Ibrahim, F.N. (1978) The Problem of Desertification in the Republic of the Sudan with Special Reference to Northern Darfur Province. Monograph Series No. 8, Development Studies and Research Centre, University of Khartoum.

Ibrahim, S.E. (1989) South Kassala Nomadic Survey Socio-economic Project of Nomadic Pastoralists in the Eastern Refugee Reforestation Project Area. Consultant Report to CARE, Sudan.

ICVA/UNHCR (1985) ICVA/UNHCR Workshop on Development Approaches to Refugee Situations. Puidoux, 1–4 December.

IFAD (1986) Soil and Water Conservation in Sub-Saharan Africa: Issues and Options. Prepared by CDCS, The Free University of Amsterdam.

Iiaco, B.V. (1981) Agricultural Compendium for Rural Development in the Tropics and Sub-tropics. Amsterdam: Elsevier.

Islam, M. (1991) Ecological Catastrophes and Refugees in Bangladesh. Paper prepared for presentation at the Conference on Worldwide Refugee Movements, Development, Politics and Human Rights, New York, 8–9 November.

Karadawi, A. (1977) Political Refugees: A Case Study from the Sudan. M.Phil. thesis, University of Reading.

Kibreab, G. (1982) Questionnaire Survey, Umsagata.

Kibreab, G. (1985) 'An Agricultural Study of Refugee Land Settlements in Eastern Sudan'. PhD Dissertation, Department of Economic History, Uppsala University.

Kibreab, G. (1990c) Host governments and refugee perspectives on settlement and repatriation. Paper for the Conference on Development Strategies on Forced Migration in the Third World: Institute of Social Studies, The Hague, 22–29 August.

Kibreab, G. (1993) 'Integration of African refugees in first countries of asylum: past experiences and prospects for the 1990s'. In Rogers, R. and Russell, S. (eds) *Toward a New Global Refugee System* (forthcoming).

Kibreab, G. (1996) Ready and Willing . . . but Still Waiting: Factors Influencing the Decision of Eritrean Refugees in the Sudan to Return Home. A study for the Institute of Life and Peace, Uppsala, Sweden.

Kidane, K.S. (1990) 'Examining the Issues Raised by the Displacement of Indigenous Cultivation Technologies by Imported Cultivation Technology: the Case of Qala en Nahal, Eastern Sudan'. MSc Dissertation, Agricultural Extension and Rural Development Department, Reading University.

Laing, R.L. (1953) Mechanization in Agriculture in the Rainlands of the Anglo-Egyptian Sudan, 1948–1951. Khartoum: Sudan Survey Department.

Lind, L. and Peniston, B.J. (1991) Forestry Projects for Refugees and Displaced Persons: Guidelines for Project Managers. Office of International Forestry, Forestry Support Programme, USDA Forest Service, USA.

Long, L., Cecsarini, L. and Martin, J. (1990) The Local Impacts of Mozambican Refugees in Malawi. Report to USAID and the US Embassy, Lilongwe, Malawi.

Mechanized Farming Corporation (1979) Agricultural Statistics, Bulletin No. 2, Khartoum.

Mechanized Farming Corporation (1984) Agricultural Statistics, Bulletin No. 3. Khartoum.

Mohamed, El Sir A. (1989) Animal production process. In Kassala Province Environmental Collection of Papers. Prepared for publication by M.E. Abu Sin, Institute of Environmental Studies, University of Khartoum.

Mohamed, Y.A. (1990) Local Initiatives in Resource Management: Case Study of Wadaa Village, North Darfur, Sudan. Institute of Environmental Studies, University of Khartoum.

Mohamed, Y.A. and Abu Sin, M.E. (1992) Hema as a Range Management Approach in the Sudan: Case Study of Three Villages in the Butana. Institute of Environmental Studies and Department of Geography, University of Khartoum.

NCAR (National Committee for Aid to Refugees) (1980) Documentation for the June 1980 Khartoum Conference, Vols. 1–III. Khartoum.

NEA (National Energy Administration) (1983). Forestry and Fuelwood Resource Assessment. Khartoum, September.

NEA (National Energy Administration) (1987) Sudan Energy Handbook. Khartoum.

NEA (National Energy Administration) (1988) Regional Planning Section Report: Eastern Region, Khartoum.

NEA (National Energy Administration) (1991) Sudan Energy Handbook.

NEDEC and ILACO, N.V. (1966) Southern Gedaref Soil Survey, Umm Simsim and Umm Seinait Soil Survey and Land Classification Report. Report prepared for Ministry of Agriculture, October.

Olsson, K. and Rapp, A. (1988) Environmental Stress and Land Degradation in Central Sudan – Causes, Consequences and Methods of Monitoring. Paper for the International Conference on Environmental Stress and Security. 13–15 December, Royal Swedish Academy of Sciences, Stockholm.

Paddon, A.R. (1989a) Wood Energy Research and Development in Sudan. Paper presented at the 4th Extension and Communication Workshop, 18–28 March.

Paddon, A.R. (1989b) A Review of the Available Data Concerning the Amount of Charcoal and Fuelwood Produced in Sudan. Fuelwood Development for Energy in Sudan, GCP/SUD/033/NET, October.

Regulation of Asylum Act (1974) Act No. 45, Sudan Gazette No. 11162 Legis. Supp. 183.

Report of Meeting of Experts on Refugee Aid and Development (1983) Monte Pelerin, Switzerland, 29–31 August.

Report on Land Tenure Survey of Eritrea Province (1969) Prepared by the Department of Land Tenure, Ministry of Land Reform, Addis Ababa.

RPG (Refugee Policy Group) (1986) Older Refugee Settlements in Africa. Washington, DC.

RPG (Refugee Policy Group) (1992) Migration and the Environment. Draft Briefing Paper prepared for Conference on Migration and Environment, Nyon, Switzerland, 19–22 January.

Simpson, M. and Khalifa, A.H. (1976b) A Study of Agricultural Development in the Central Rainlands of the Sudan: an Interim Report. Occasional Paper No. 5, Economic and Social Research Council, National Council for Research, Khartoum.

Soil Survey Administration (1973) Key for the Identification of Soils in East Sudan, Kassala Province, Wad Madani.

Spooner, B.C. (1981) The Qala en Nahal Resettlement Scheme, Project Identification Mission: Board Paper and Policy Recommendations. Khartoum: ACORD.

Sudan Council of Churches, Eastern Sudan Relief Programme, Anti-Tuberculosis Campaign Records, Umsagata, 1983.

Suhrke, A. (1991) Ecological Crisis and Population Displacement. Talk given at the Conference on Worldwide Refugee Movements, New School for Social Research, New York, 9 November.

Tuttas, C.H. and Gaymans, H. (1976) Report on Mission to Gedaref Region. Khartoum: UNHCR Branch Office.

UNHCR (1991) *Rapport* 4, No. 10. Geneva.

UNHCR (1992a) *Refugees*, No. 89, May.

UNHCR (1992b) 'Limiting the wastelands'. *Refugees*, No. 89, May.

USAID (1980) The Socio-economic Context of Fuelwood Use in Small Rural Communities. AID Evaluation Special Study No. 1.

Van Deweg, R.F. (1987) Vertisols in Eastern Africa. First Regional Seminar. IBSRAM, Nairobi.

von Buchwald, U. (1992) Migration and Environment – the Limits and Possibilities of Disaster Relief. Paper for the German Red Cross Seminar for Journalists on 'Man in Disaster – Causes, Assistance and Prevention', Bonn, 27–28 April.

Westing, A.H. (1992) Environmental Refugees: a Growing Category of Displaced Persons (typescript).

Wolfe, M. (1983) Participation: the View from Above. Geneva: UNRISD, March.

Younis, M.G.A. (1983) 'Minerological Studies on Soils Derived from Red Northern Drift in Northwest Wales'. PhD dissertation, University Wales, UK.

Books, articles and published reports

Abel, N.O.J. and Blaikie, P.M. (1989) 'Land degradation, stocking rates and conservation policies in the communal rangelands of Botswana and Zimbabwe.' *Land Degradation and Rehabilitation* 1: 101–123.

Adepeju, A. (1982) 'The dimension of the refugee problem in Africa.' *African Affairs* 81 (322): 21–35.

Affan, K. (1984) *Towards an Appraisal of Tractorization Experience in Rainlands of Sudan.* Development Studies and Research Centre Monograph Series No. 19, University of Khartoum.

Agabawi, K.A. (1968) 'Some developments in rain-fed agriculture in central Sudan'. *Sudan Notes and Records* 49: 71–82.

Agabawi, K.A. (1969) 'Some developments in rain-fed agriculture in central Sudan – II'. *Sudan Notes and Records* 50: 106–129.

Ahlcrona, E. (1988) *The Impact of Climate and Man on Land Transformation in Central Sudan: Applications of Remote Sensing.* Meddelande från Lunds Universitets Geografiska Institutioner, avhandlingar 103. Lund: Lund University Press.

Allan, N.J.J. (1987) 'Impact of Afghan refugees on the vegetation resources of Pakistan's Hindukush-Himalaya.' *Mountain Research and Development* 7 (3): 200–204.

Allan, W.A. (1972) 'How much land does a man require?' In Prothero, R.M. (ed.) *People and Land in Africa South of the Sahara.* New York: Oxford University Press, pp 302–320.

Anderson, J.U. (1963) 'An improved pre-treatment for mineralogical analysis of samples containing organic matter.' *Clays and Clay Minerals* 10: 180–188.

Armstrong, A. (1988) 'Aspects of refugee well-being in settlement schemes: an examination of the Tanzanian case'. *Journal of Refugee Studies* 1(1): 57–73.

Attiya, H. (1988) Interview in *Refugees*, No. 52, April.

Awad, M.H. (1975) 'The evolution of landownership in the Sudan.' *Middle East Journal* 25: 213–228.

Bajracharya, D. (1983) 'Deforestation in the food/fuel context: historical and political perspectives from Nepal.' *Mountain Research and Development* 3: 227–240.

Barbour, K.M. (1961) *Republic of the Sudan.* London: University of London Press.

Barraclough, S. and Ghimire, K. (1990) The Social Dynamics of Deforestation in Developing Countries: Principal Issues and Research Priorities. UNRISD Discussion Paper 16, Geneva.

Bartels, G.B., Norton, B.E. and Perrier, G.K. (1993) 'An examination of the carrying capacity concept'. In Behnke, R.H., Scoones, I. and Kerven, C. (eds) *Range Ecology at Disequilibrium: New Models of Natural Variability and Pastoral Adaptation in African Savannas.* London: ODI, IIED and Commonwealth Secretariat, pp. 89–103.

Bebawi, F.F., El-Hag, G.A. and Khogali, M.M. (1985) 'The production of dura (*Sorghum vulgare*) in Sudan and the parasite buda (*Striga hermontheca*)'. In Davies, H.R.J. (ed.) *Natural Resources and Rural Development in Arid Lands: Case Studies from Sudan.* Tokyo: United Nations University, pp. 1–15.

Bebawi, F.F. and Farah, A.F. (1981) 'Effects of parasitic and non-parasitic weeds on sorghum. *Experimental Agriculture* 17 (4): 415–418.

Behnke, R.H. and Scoones, I. (1993) 'Rethinking range ecology: implications for rangelands management in Africa'. In Behnke, R.H., Scoones, I. and Kerven, C. (eds) *Range Ecology at Disequilibrium: New Models of Natural Variability and Pastoral Adaptation in African Savannas.* London: ODI, IIED and Commonwealth Secretariat, pp. 1–30.

Benneh, G. (1972) 'Systems of agriculture in tropical Africa.' *Economic Geography* 42 (244): 245–257.

Bergson, H. (1992) *The Creative Mind: an Introduction to Metaphysics.* New York: Carol Publishing Group.

Berkes, F. and Farvar, M.T. (1989) 'Introduction and overview.' In Birkes, F. (ed.) *Common Property Resources Ecology and Community-based Sustainable Development.* London: Belhaven Press, pp. 1–16.

Bernard, F.E. and Thom, D.J. (1981) 'Population pressure and human carrying capacity in selected locations of Machakos and Kitui districts.' *Journal of Developing Areas* 15: 381–406.

Bilsborrow, R.E. (1987) 'Population pressures and agricultural development in developing countries: a conceptual framework and recent evidence.' *World Development* 15 (2): 183–204.

Black, C.A. (ed.) (1965) *Methods of Soil Analysis,* 2 vols, Parts I and II. Monograph No. 9, American Society of Agronomy, Madison, Wisconsin, 1572 pp.

Blaikie, P. and Brookfield, H. (1987) *Land Degradation and Society.* London and New York: Methuen.

Boserup, E. (1965) *The Conditions of Agricultural Growth: the Economics of Agrarian Change Under Population Pressure.* London: Allen and Unwin.

Boserup, E. (1970) 'Present and potential food production in developing countries.' In Zelinsky, W. and Prothero, L.A. (eds) *Geography and the Crowding World.* London: Oxford University Press.

Boserup, E. (1975) 'The impact of population growth on agricultural output.' *Quarterly Journal of Agricultural Economics* 89: 257–270.

Boserup, E. (1981) *Population and Technological Change.* Chicago: University of Chicago.

Brady, N.C. (1974) *The Nature and Properties of Soils,* 8th edn. New York: Macmillan.

Bromley, D.W. and Chapagain, D.P. (1984) 'The village against the centre: resource depletion in South Asia'. *American Journal of Agricultural Economics* 66: 869–873.

Brookfield, H.C. (1972) 'Intensification and disintensification in Pacific agriculture: a theoretical approach.' *Pacific Viewpoint* 13: 30–48.

Bruggers R.L. *et al.* (1984) 'Bird damage to agriculture and crop protection efforts in the Sudan.' *FAO Plant Protection Bulletin* 32: 2–16.

Bryant, M. (1977) 'Bread-basket or dust-bowl?' *Sudanow* 2 (10): 42–46.

Butzer, K.W. (1981) 'Rise and fall of Axum, Ethiopia: a geo-archaeological interpretation.' *American Antiquity* 36 (3) 471–495.

Caplan, L. (1970) *Land and Social Change in East Nepal.* London: Routledge and Kegan Paul.

Chambers, R. (1983) *Rural Development: Putting the Last First.* London: Longman.

Chapil, W.S. (1962) 'A compact rating sieve and importance of dry sieving in physical soil analysis.' *Soil Science* 26 (4–6).

Chesterton, G.K. (1936) *Autobiography.* London: Hutchinson.

Cheung, S.N.S. (1970) 'The structure of a contract and the theory of a non-exclusive resource'. *Journal of Law and Economics* 13 (1): 49–69.

Chidimayo, E.N. (1987) 'A shifting cultivation land use system under population pressure in Zambia'. *Agroforestry Systems* 5: 15–25.

Christiansson, C. (1981) *Soil Erosion and Sedimentation in Semi-Arid Tanzania: Studies of Environmental Change and Ecological Imbalance.* Uppsala: Scandinavian Institute of African Studies.

Circiacy-Wantrup, S.V. and Bishop, R.C. (1975) 'Common property as a concept in natural resource policy'. *Natural Resources Journal* 15: 713–727.

Clay, J. and Holcomb, B.K. (1985) *Politics and the Ethiopian Famine 1984–85*. Cultural Survival Special Reports 20. Cambridge, Massachusetts.: Cultural Survival Inc.

Clay, J., Steingraber, S. and Niggli, P. (1988) *The Spoils of Famine: Ethiopian Famine Policy and Peasant Agriculture*. Cambridge, Massachusetts: Cultural Survival Inc.

Clouston, T.W. (1948) *Mechanization in Agriculture in the Rainlands of the Anglo-Egyptian Sudan, 1943–48*. Khartoum: Ministry of Agriculture.

Coppock, D.L. (1993) 'Vegetation and pastoral dynamics in the southern Ethiopian rangelands: implications for theory and management'. In Behnke, R.H., Scoones, I. and Kerven, C. (eds) *Range Ecology at Disequilibrium: New Models of Natural Variability and Pastoral Adaptation in African Savannas*. London: ODI, IIED and Commonwealth Secretariat, pp. 42–61.

Curry-Lindahl, K. (1974) 'Conservation problems and progress in equatorial African countries. *Environmental Conservation* 1 (2): 111–122.

Damodaran, A. (1988) 'Morphology of grazing and its crisis in sedentary communities'. *Economic and Political Weekly* 23 (13): A-29–A-34.

Darity, W.A., Jr (1980) 'The Boserup theory of agricultural growth: a model for agricultural economics'. *Journal of Development Economics* 7: 137–157.

Darkoh, M.B.K. (1987) 'Socio-economic and institutional factors behind desertification in southern Africa'. *Area* 19 (1): 25–33.

Davies, H.R.J. (1964) 'An agricultural revolution in the African Tropics: the development of mechanized agriculture on clay plains of the Republic of Sudan'. *Tijdschrift voor Econ. en Soc. Geografie* (55) 110–118.

Day, P.R. (1965) 'Particle fractionation and particle-size analysis.' In Black, C.A. (ed.) *Methods of Soil Analysis*, 2 vols, Parts I and II. Monograph No. 9, American Society of Agronomy, Madison, Wisconsin, pp. 545–566.

Demsetz, H. (1972) 'Toward a theory of property right'. *American Economic Review* 57 (2): 346–357.

de Waal, A. (1989) *Famine that Kills: Darfur, Sudan 1984–5*. Oxford: Clarendon.

Dewees, P.A. (1989) 'The woodfuel reconsidered: observations on the dynamics of abundance and scarcity'. *World Development* 17 (8): 1159–1172.

Digernes, T.H. (1979) 'Fuelwood crisis causing unfortunate land use – and the other way round.' Norsk Geografisk Tidskrift 33: 23–30.

Dixon, J.A., James, D.E. and Sherman, P.B. (1989) *The Economics of Dryland Management*. London: Earthscan Publications.

Dreze, J. and Sen, A. (1989) *Hunger and Public Action*. Oxford: Clarendon Press.

Durning, A.B. (1989a) *Action at Grassroots: Fighting Poverty and Environmental Decline*. Worldwatch Paper 88. Washington, DC: Worldwatch Institute.

Durning, A.B. (1989b) *Poverty and the Environment: Reversing the Downward Spiral*. Worldwatch Paper 92. Washington, DC: Worldwatch Institute.

Eckholm, E.P. (1975a) 'The deterioration of mountain environment.' *Science* 189 (4205): 764–70.

Eckholm, E.P. (1975b) *The Other Energy Crisis*. Worldwatch Paper 2. Washington, DC: Worldwatch Institute.

Eckholm, E.P. (1976) *Losing Ground: Environmental Stress and World Food Prospects*. New York: Norton.

Eckholm, E.P. (1979) *Planting for the Future*. Worldwatch Paper 26. Washington, DC: Worldwatch Institute.

Eckholm, E.P. (1982) *Down to Earth: Environment and Human Needs*. London: Pluto Press.

El-Hinnawi, E. (1985) *Environmental Refugees*. Nairobi: UNEP.

Elliott, C.C.H. (1989) 'The pest status of the quelea.' In Bruggers, R.L. and Elliott, C.C.H. (eds) *Quelea quelea: Africa's Bird Pest*. Oxford: Oxford University Press, pp. 17–34.

Ellis, J.E. *et al.* (1993) 'Climate variability, ecosystem stability, and the implications for range and livestock development.' In Behnke, R.H., Scoones, I. and Kerven, C. (eds) *Range Ecology at Disequilibrium: New Models of Natural Variability and Pastoral Adaptation in African Savannas*. London: ODI, IIED and Commonwealth Secretariat, pp. 31–41.

El Mahdi, S.M.A. (1976) 'Some general principles of acquisition of ownership of and rights over land by customary prescription in the Sudan.' *Journal of African Law* 20 (2): 79–99.

El Mahdi, S.M.A. (1979) *Introduction to the Land Law of the Sudan, Silver Jubilee 1956–1981*. Khartoum: University of Khartoum.

Ferris, E. (1993) *Beyond Borders: Refugees, Migrants and Human Rights in the Post-Cold War Era*. Geneva: World Council of Churches.

Fikre Mariam, T. (1991) 'Refugees in Ethiopia: some reflections on the ecological impact. *IDOC Internazionale* 2 (91): pages unnumbered.

Fitih Mehari (Two Mensà) (1913) Asmara: Swedish Evangelical Mission.

Fortmann, L. (1985) 'The tree tenure factor in agroforestry with particular reference to Africa.' *Agroforestry Systems* 2: 229–252.

Geertz, C. (1963) *Agricultural Involution: the Process of Ecological Change in Indonesia*. Berkeley and Los Angeles: University of California Press.

Gleave, M.B. and White, H.P. (1969) 'Population density and agricultural systems in West Africa.' In Thomas, M.F. and Whittington, G.W. (eds) *Environment and Land Use in Africa*. London: Methuen, pp. 272–297.

Graham, G. (1962) 'Man–Water relations in the east central Sudan.' In Thomas, M.F. and Whittington G.W. (eds) *Environment and Land Use in Africa*. London: Methuen, pp. 409–443.

Grainger, A. (1982) *Desertification: How People Make Deserts, How People Can Stop and Why They Don't*. London: Earthscan Publications.

Grainger, A. (1990) *The Threatening Desert: Controlling Desertification*. London: Earthscan Publications.

Greig-Smith, P. (1961) 'Data on pattern within plant communities: the analysis of pattern.' *Journal of Ecology* 49: 695–702.

Greig-Smith, P. (1964) *Quantitative Plant Ecology*. London: Butterworth.

Grigg, D. (1979) Ester Boserup's theory of agrarian change: a critical review.' *Progress in Human Geography* 3 (1): 61–84.

Hardin, G. (1968) 'The tragedy of the commons'. *Science* 162 (3859): 1243–1248.

Hardin, G. (1978) 'Political requirements for the preservation of our common heritage. In Bakow, H.P. (ed.) *Wildlife and America*. Washington, DC: Council on Environmental Quality.

Harrison, P. (1990) 'Beyond the blame game.' *Populi* 17 (3): 14–21.

Helldèn, U. (1991) 'Desertification – time for an assessment?' *Ambio* 20 (8): 372–383.

Homer-Dixon, T.F. (1992) 'On the threshold: environmental changes as cause of acute conflict.' *International Security* 16 (2): 76–116.

Homewood, K. and Rodgers, W.A. (1987) 'Pastoralism, conservation and the overgrazing controversy.' In Henderson, D. and Grove, R. (eds) *Conservation in Africa: People, Policies and Practice*. Cambridge: Cambridge University Press, pp. 111–128.

Horowitz, M.M. and Salem-Murdock, M. (1991) 'The political economy of desertification in White Nile Province, Sudan.' In Little, P.D. and Horowitz, M.M. with Nyerges, A.E. (eds) *Lands at Risk in the Third World: Local-Level Perspectives*. Boulder and London: Westview Press, pp. 95–113.

Hunter, J.M. and Ntiri, G.K. (1978) 'Speculations on the future of shifting agriculture in Africa.' *Journal of Developing Areas* 12 (2): 183–208.

Hurni, H. (1988) 'Degradation and conservation of the resources in the Ethiopian highlands.' *Mountain Research and Development* 8 (2–3): 123–130.

Hurtado, M.E. (1991) 'Population, economic development and environmental degradation: a complex relationship.' *Lifestyle Overloaded? Population and Environment in the Balance*. London: Action Aid, pp. 18–22.

Ibrahim, F.N. (1984) *Ecological Imbalance in the Republic of the Sudan with Reference to Desertification in Darfur*. Bayreuther Geowissenschaftliche Arbeiten, Vol. 6. Bayreuth.

ILO (International Labour Office) (1976) *Growth, Employment and Equity*. Geneva: ILO.

Ivens, E.W. (1989) *East African Weeds and Their Control*, new edn. Nairobi: Oxford University Press.

Jacobson, J.L. (1988) *Environmental Refugees: a Yardstick to Habitability.* Worldwatch Paper 86. Washington, DC: Worldwatch Institute.

Jodha, N.S. (1980) 'The process of desertification and the choice of interventions.' *Economic and Political Weekly* 15 (32): 1351–1356.

Jodha, N.S. (1985) 'Population growth and the decline of common property resources in Rajasthan, India.' *Population and Development Review* 11 (2): 247–264.

Jodha, N.S. (1987) 'A case study of the degradation of common property resources in India. In Blaikie, P. and Brookfield, H. (eds) *Land Degradation and Society.* London: Methuen, pp. 196–207.

Johnson, O.E.G. (1972) 'Economic analysis, the legal framework and land tenure systems.' *Journal of Law and Economics* 15 (1): 259–276.

Juo, A.L.R. and Lal, R. (1977) 'The effect of fallow and continuous cultivation on the chemical and physical properties of an Alfisol in western Nigeria'. *Plant and Soil* 47: 567–584.

Kibreab, G. (1987) *Refugees and Development in Africa. The Case of Eritrea.* Trenton, NJ: The Red Sea Press.

Kibreab, G. (1989) 'Local settlements in Africa: a misconceived option?' *Journal of Refugee Studies* 2 (4): 469–490.

Kibreab, G. (1990a) *Refugees in Somalia: a Burden, an Opportunity and a Challenge.* Nairobi: IDRC.

Kibreab, G. (1990b) *From Subsistence to Wage Labour: Refugee Settlements in the Central and Eastern Regions of the Sudan.* Trenton, NJ: The Red Sea Press.

Kibreab, G. (1991) *The State of the Art Review of Refugee Studies in Africa.* Research Report No. 26, Uppsala Papers in Economic History. Uppsala: Uppsala University.

Kibreab, G. (1994a) 'Migration, environment and refugeehood.' In Zaba, B. and Clark, J. (eds) *Environment and Population Change.* International Union for the Scientific Study of Population. Liège: Ordina Editions, pp. 115–130.

Kibreab, G. (1994b) 'Refugees in the Sudan: unresolved issues.' In Adelman, H. and Sorenson, J. (eds) *African Refugees: Development Aid and Repatriation.* Boulder: Westview Press, pp. 43–68.

Kibreab, G. (1994c) 'The myth of dependency among camp refugees in Somalia 1979–1989.' *Journal of Refugee Studies* 6 (4): 321–349.

Kibreab, G. (1996) 'Left in limbo: prospects for repatriation of Eritrean refugees from the Sudan and the response of the international community'. In Allen, T. (ed.) *In Search of Cool Ground: Homecoming in Northeastern Africa.* London: James Currey.

Kjekshus, H. (1977) *Ecology Control and Economic Development in East African History.* London: Heinemann (1977); with New Introduction (1996) London: James Currey.

Knibbe, M. (1964) *Soil Survey Report of Proposed MCPS in Southern Gedaref District: A. Rawashda–Gaboub Extension.* Report No. 10/KA./2, Soil Survey Division, Gezira Research Division Station, Wad Medani.

Krishnaji, N. and Satya Sekhar, P. (1991) 'Population and agricultural growth: a study in inter-regional variations.' *Economic and Political Weekly* 26 (26): A-63–A-68.

Lal, R. (1985) 'Environmental impact of deforestation and arable land use.' In Vanore, R. (ed.) *Proceedings of the Panel on Environmental Degradation and Rural Development Strategies.* Rome: AISI.

Lamprey, H.F. (1988) 'Report on the desert encroachment reconnaissance in northern Sudan: 21 October to 10 November 1975'. *Desertification Control Bulletin (UNEP)* 17: 1–7.

Laykock, W.A. (1991) 'Stable states and thresholds of range condition on North-American rangelands: a viewpoint.' *Journal of Range Management* 44 (5): 427–473.

Lazarus, D.S. (1990) 'Environmental refugees: new strangers at the door'. *Our Planet* 2 (3): 12–14.

Lockwood, M. (1991) 'Population and environmental change – local level processes and implications for policy.' In *Lifestyle Overloaded? Population and Environment in the Balance.* London: Action Aid, pp. 23–27.

Longrigg, S. (1945) *A Short History of Eritrea.* Westport, Connecticut: Greenwood Press.

McGregor, J. (1993) 'Refugees and the environment'. In Black, R. and Robinson, V. (eds) *Geography and Refugees: Pattern and Processes of Change*. London: Belhaven.

Mackinnon, E. (1948) 'Agriculture in Kassala Province.' In Tothill, J.D. (ed.) *Agriculture in the Sudan*. London: Oxford University Press, pp. 698–733.

McNamara, R. (1990) 'Population and Africa's development crisis.' *Populi* 17 (4): 36–43.

Malthus, T. (1798) *An Essay on the Principle of Population*. Published in Penguin Classics edition, 1970.

Mann, R.D. (1987) 'Development and the Sahel disaster: the case of the Gambia'. *Ecologist* 17 (2–3): 84–90.

Mann, R.D. (1990) 'Time running out: the urgent need for tree planting in Africa.' *Ecologist* 20 (2) 48–53.

Markakis, J. (1990) *National and Class Conflict in the Horn of Africa*. London and New Jersey: Zed Books.

Meihe, S. (1989) '*Acacia albida* and other multipurpose trees on the fur farmlands in the Jebel Marra highlands, western Darfur, Sudan.' In Nair, P.K.R. (ed.) *Agroforestry Systems in the Tropics*. Dordrecht; Kluwer Academic Publishers and ICRAF.

Mitchell, A.J.B. (1987) *Management Problems of Cotton on Vertisols in the Lower Shire Valley of Malawi*. Lilongwe: IBSARM.

Mnzava, E.M. (1981) 'Fuelwood: the private energy crisis of the poor.' *Ceres: FAO Review on Agriculture and Development* 14 (4): 35–39.

Molvaer, R.K. (1991) 'Environmentally induced Conflicts? A discussion based on studies from the Horn of Africa.' *Bulletin of Peace Proposals* 22: 175–188.

Mortimore, M. (1989) *Adapting to Drought*. Cambridge: Cambridge University Press.

Munslow, B. *et al*. (1989) *The Fuelwood Trap: a Study of the SADCC Region*. London: Earthscan Publications.

Myers, N. (1986) 'The environmental dimension to security issues.' *Environmentalist* 6 (4): 251–257.

Myers, N. (1989) 'Population growth, environmental decline and security issues in sub-Saharan Africa.' In Hjort af Ornäs, A. and Mohammed Salih, M.A. (eds) *Ecology and Politics: Environmental Stress and Security in Africa*. Uppsala: SIAS.

Nadel, S.F. (1945) 'Notes on the Beni Amer society.' *Sudan Notes and Records* 26 (1): 51–94.

Nadel, S.F. (1946a) 'Land tenure on the Eritrean plateau.' *Africa* 16 (1): 1–22.

Nadel, S.F. (1946b) 'Land tenure on the Eritrean plateau: Part II.' *Africa* 16 (2): 99–109.

Netting, R.M.C. (1972) 'Sacred power and centralization: aspects of political adaptation in Africa. In Spooner, B. (ed.) *Population Growth: Anthropological Implications*. Cambridge: Massachusetts Institute of Technology.

Nicholson, N. (1988) 'The state of the art.' In Ostrom, V., Feeny, D. and Picht, H. (eds) *Rethinking Institutional Analysis and Development: Issues, Alternatives and Choices*. San Francisco: International Centre for Economic Growth.

North, D.C. (1993) *Institutions, Institutional Change and Economic Performance*. Cambridge: Cambridge University Press.

Nye, P.N. and Greenland, D.J. (1960) *Soil Under Shifting Cultivation*. Technical Bulletin No. 51. London: Commonwealth Bureaus.

Nyerere, J.K. (1973) *Freedom and Development*. London: Oxford University Press.

O'Brien, J. (1983) 'The political economy of capitalist agriculture in the central rainlands of the Sudan.' *Labour, Capital and Society* 16 (1): 9–32.

O'Brien, J. (1985) 'Sowing the seeds of famine.' *ROAPE* 33: 23–32.

Openshaw, K. (1974) 'Woodfuels in the developing countries.' *New Scientist* 61: 271–272.

Openshaw, K. (1978) 'Woodfuel – a time for re-assessment.' *Natural Resources Forum* 3: 35–51.

Parker, C. and Reid, D.C. (1979) 'Host specificity in *Striga* species: some preliminary observations'. In *Proceedings of the 2nd International Symposium on Parasitic Weeds*, pp. 79–90.

Paul, A. (1950) 'Notes on the Beni Amer.' *Sudan Notes and Records* 31: 223–245.

Pausewang, S. (1973) *Methods and Concepts in Social Research in Rural Developing Society: a Critical Appraisal Based on Experience in Ethiopia*. Munich: Meltforum Verlag.

Perring, C. (1989) 'An optimal path to extinction? Poverty and resource degradation in the open agrarian economy.' *Journal of Development Economics* 30 (1): 1–24.

Picaredi, A.C. and Seifert, W.W. (1976) 'A tragedy of the commons in the Sahel.' *Technology Review.* May: 42–51.

Prescot, J.R.V. (1961) 'Overpopulation and overstocking in the native areas of Matabeleland.' *Geographical Journal* 127: 212–225.

Prothero, R.M. (1972) *Man and Land in Africa South of the Sahara.* New York: Oxford University Press.

Pryor, F.L. and Maurer, S.B. (1982) 'On induced economic change in precapitalist societies.' *Journal of Development Economics* 10: 325–353.

Radwanski, S.A. and Wickens, G.E. (1967) 'The ecology of *Acacia albida* on mantle soils in Zalingei, Jebel Mara, Sudan.' *Journal of Applied Ecology* 4: 569–579.

Rees, W.E. (1990) 'The ecology of sustainable development.' *Ecologist* 20 (1): 18–23.

Reeves, E.B. and Frankenberger, T. (1981) *Socio-economic Constraints to the Production, Distribution and Consumption of Millet, Sorghum and Cash Crops in North Kordofan, Sudan.* College of Agriculture Report No. 1. Lexington: University of Kentucky.

Repetto, R. and Holmes, T. (1983) 'The role of population in resource depletion in developing countries.' *Population Development Review* 9 (4): 609–632.

Roche, L. (1989) 'Forestry and famine: arguments against growth without development.' *Ecologist* 19 (1): 16–21.

Rosswall, T. (1976) 'The internal nitrogen cycle between micro-organisms, vegetation and soil.' In Svensson, B.H. and Söderlund, R. (eds) *Ecological Bulletins* 22: 157–167.

Runge, C.F. (1983) 'Common property externalities – isolation, assurance, and resource depletion in a traditional grazing context.' *American Journal of Agricultural Economics* 63 (4): 595–606.

Runge, C.F. (1984) 'Institutions and the free rider: the assurance problem in collective action.' *Journal of Politics* 46: 155–181.

Rünger, M. (1987) *Land Law and Land Use Control in Western Sudan: the Case of Southern Darfur.* London and Atlantic Highlands: Ithaca Press.

Sandford, S. (1982a) *Livestock in the Communal Areas of Zimbabwe: a Report to the Ministry of Lands, Resettlement and Rural Development.* London: Overseas Development Institute.

Sandford, S. (1982b) 'Pastoral strategies and desertification: opportunism and conservatism in dry lands.' In Spooner, B. and Mann, H.S. (eds) *Desertification and Development: Dryland Ecology in Social Perspective.* London, New York: Academic Press, pp. 61–80.

Scoones, I. and Zaba, B. (1994) 'Is carrying capacity a useful concept to apply to human population?' In Zaba and Clarke (eds) *Environment and Population Change.* Liège: Edwina Editions, IUSSP.

Sen, A. (1981) *Poverty and Famine: an Essay on Entitlement and Deprivation.* Oxford: Clarendon Press.

Sen, A. (1989) 'Food and Freedom.' *World Development* 17 (6): 769–778.

Shankarnarayan, K.A., Bohra, H.C. and Ghosha, P.K. (1985) 'The goat, an appropriate animal for arid and semi-arid regions.' *Economic and Political Weekly* 20 (45–47): A29–A34.

Shaw, R.P. (1989) 'Rapid population growth and environmental degradation: ultimate versus proximate factors.' *Environmental Conservation* 16 (3): 199–208.

Shepherd, G. (1989) 'The reality of the commons: answering Hardin? From Somalia.' *Development Policy Review* 7 (1): 50–63.

Simpson, I.G. and Simpson, M. (1991) 'Systems of agricultural production in central Sudan and Khartoum Province.' In Graig, G.M. (ed.) *The Agriculture of the Sudan.* Oxford University Press, pp. 253–279.

Simpson, M. and Khalifa, A.H. (1976a) 'Some thoughts on agricultural development in the central rainlands of the Sudan.' *Sudan Notes and Records* 57: 99–106.

Sinclair, A.R.E. and Wells, M.P. (1989) 'Population growth and poverty cycle in Africa: colliding ecological and economic processes?' *Food and Natural Resources*: 442–483.

Smith, R.J. (1981) 'Resolving the tragedy of the commons by creating private property rights in wildlife.' *CATO Journal* 1 (2): 439–468.

Stanley, M. (1968) 'Nature, culture and scarcity: foreword to a theoretical synthesis.' *American Sociological Review* 33 (6): 855–869.

Stoddart, L.A., Smith, A. and Box, T. (1975) *Range Management.* New York: McGraw Hill.

Suliman, M.M. (1986) Grazing and Range Management in the Butana Area, with Special Reference to El Rawashda Forest. Field Document 12. Khartoum.

Suliman, M.M. (1988) 'Dynamics of range plants and desertification monitoring in the Sudan.' *Desertification Control Bulletin* 16: 27–31.

Tamondong-Helin, S. and Helin, W. (1990–1991) *Migration and the Environment: Interrelationships in Sub-Saharan Africa.* Field Staff Reports: Africa No. 22. Published cooperatively by Universities Fieldstaff International and the National Heritage Institute.

Tapson, D. (1993) 'Biological sustainability in pastoral systems: the Kwazulu case.' In Behnke, R.H., Scones, I. and Kerven, C. (eds) *Range Ecology at Disequilibrium: New Models of Natural Variability and Pastoral Adaptation in African Savannas.* London: ODI, IIED and Commonwealth Secretariat, pp.118–135.

Tawney, R.H. (1966) *Land and Labor in China.* Boston: Beacon Press.

Tiffen, M., Mortimore, M. and Gichuki, F. (eds) (1994) *More People, Less Erosion: Environmental Recovery in Kenya.* Chichester: John Wiley & Sons.

Timberlake, L. (1985) *Africa in Crisis: the Causes, the Cures of Environmental Bankruptcy.* London: Earthscan Publications.

Trevaskis, G.K.N. (1960) *Eritrea, a Colony in Transition: 1945–52.* Westport, Connecticut: Greenwood Press.

Tully, D. (1983) 'The decision to migrate in the Sudan.' *Cultural Survival* 7 (4): 17–18.

UNCOD (1977) *Desertification: Its Causes and Consequences.* Oxford: Pergamon Press.

UNPF (United Nations Population Fund) (1988) *The State of World Population 1988.* New York: UN Population Fund.

US Committee for Refugees (1994) *World Refugee Survey 1993.* Washington, DC: American Council for Nationalities Service.

Vivian, J.M. (1991) *Greening at the Grassroots: People's Participation in Sustainable Development.* Geneva: UNRISD.

Walker, B.H. (1980) 'Stable production versus resilience: a grazing management conflict.' *Proceedings of the Grassland Society of Southern Africa* 15: 79–83.

Walker, B.H. and Noy-Meir, I. (1982) 'Aspects of the stability and resilience of savanna eco-systems.' In Huntley, B.J. and Walker, B.H. (eds) *Ecology of Tropical Savannas.* Ecological Studies No. 42. Berlin: Springer-Verlag.

Walker, B.H., Ludwig, D., Holling, G.S. and Peterman, R.M. (1981) 'Stability of semi-arid savanna grazing systems. *Journal of Ecology* 69: 473–498.

Warren, A. and Agnew, C. (1988) *An Assessment of Desertification and Land Degradation in Arid and Semi-Arid Areas.* Paper No. 2. London: International Institute for Environment and Development.

Westoby, M., Walker, B.H. and Noy-Meir, I. (1989) 'Opportunistic management for rangelands not at equilibrium.' *Journal of Range Management* 42: 266–274.

WFP (World Food Programme) (1992) 'The environmental impact of refugees.' *Food Aid Review* Rome: 38–39.

Whitney, J.B.R. (1991) 'Impact of fuelwood use on environmental degradation in the Sudan. In Little, P.D. and Horowitz, M.M. with Nyerges, A.E. (eds) *Lands at Risk in the Third World: Local Level Perspectives.* Boulder and London: Westview Press, pp. 115–143.

Wilkinson, R. (1973) *Poverty and Progress: an Ecological Model to Economic Development.* London: Methuen.

Willcocks, T.J. and Twomlow, S.J. (1990) An Evaluation of Sustainable Cultural Practices for Rain-fed Sorghum Production on Vertisols in East Sudan'. Berlin: Institute of Engineering Research.

Wylde, A.B. (1901) *Modern Abyssinia.* London: Methuen.

Young, L. (1985) 'A general assessment of the environmental impact of refugees in Somalia with attention to the refugee agricultural programme.' *Disasters* 9 (2): 122–133.

Index

337